JAN

Rt 5 Box

Summerville GA 30747

404-857-1488

Entrepreneurship

Entrepreneurship: Starting a New Business

ROBERT L. ANDERSON
College of Charleston

JOHN S. DUNKELBERG
Wake Forest University

1817

HARPER & ROW, PUBLISHERS, New York
Grand Rapids, Philadelphia, St. Louis, San Francisco,
London, Singapore, Sydney, Tokyo

Sponsoring Editor: Debra Riegert
Project Editor: Paula Cousin
Art Direction: Teresa J. Delgado
Text Design: Kay Wanous
Cover Coordinator: Mary Archondes
Cover Design: Kay Wanous
Production: Paula Roppolo

ENTREPRENEURSHIP: STARTING A NEW BUSINESS

Library of Congress Cataloging-in-Publication Data

Anderson, Robert Lee, 1940–
Entrepreneurship: starting a new business / Robert L. Anderson, John S. Dunkelberg.
p. cm.
ISBN 0-06-040281-4
1. New business enterprises—Management. I. Dunkelberg, John S.
II. Title.
HD62.5.A53 1990
658.1'1—dc20 89-24583
CIP

89 90 91 92 9 8 7 6 5 4 3 2 1

Contents

Preface

Every year thousands of new businesses are created. Some of these businesses are created by people who have had no previous business experience or formal training, and their success is often attributed to "luck." Other entrepreneurs "study" the startup process, and their success is often attributed to "hard work."

This book is intended to help students "study" the startup process. It provides students with the knowledge and tools necessary to successfully plan, design, and start up a new business. In addition, this book will help students learn how entrepreneurs avoid most of the pitfalls of new ventures.

We also realize that many of today's college students will start their own businesses, some even before they finish college and others soon afterwards. Therefore, this book has been written for those students who may be considering self-employment and also for those who are already committed entrepreneurs. We assume that students have some basic understanding of business fundamentals; however, in order to benefit from this book, major preparation in such areas as accounting, finance, and statistics is not required.

PEDAGOGY

The content of this text was influenced by the authors' inability to find in any single text a combination of basic business fundamentals and clear examples to give college students a "feel" for the entrepreneurial process. For this reason, this text has been written with a strong application orientation, making frequent use of examples, vignettes, incidents, and actual cases to both illustrate the concepts and involve students in "real world" examples.

First, included in each chapter is a feature entitled ASSEMBLING THE PIECES, which documents the startup of an actual gourmet food business. Here, we explain how two women who started this business perform the tasks discussed in the chapter. What will be evident to the reader is the fact that although these entrepreneurs did not always do what was considered correct, they did capitalize on whatever resources they had available.

In addition, boxed features called "The Inside View," found throughout each chapter, give recent actual experiences of entrepreneurs in situations that relate to the chapter coverage.

Finally we have included five comprehensive cases that are placed throughout the text in order to involve the student in the application of the complete startup process. These cases depict five different business situations. One of the cases is set in England, so students can determine if startups in foreign countries are substantially different from those in the United States.

ORGANIZATION OF THE TEXT

This text covers basic items that must be considered by every entrepreneur at some point during the startup phase, beginning with a chapter about selecting a business and ending with a chapter about starting a business. The rest of the chapters discuss the development of a business plan, the legal aspects of business, choosing a location, determining financial needs, and locating financing sources.

The subject of ethics is discussed throughout the entire text. Good ethical standards and behavior are constantly required in doing business and, therefore, the subject should not be discussed in isolation.

Here is a brief overview of some of the major features that have been designed to enhance the understanding of the entrepreneurial process.

- Chapter 1 contains an entrepreneur's checklist to permit the student to make a comparison with successful entrepreneurs.
- Chapter 2 contains a self-test for any potential entrepreneur.
- Chapter 3 considers the question of either beginning a business from scratch or purchasing one. Included is a 77-item checklist to be considered in a franchise agreement.
- Chapter 5 covers the need for the development of a business plan.
- Chapter 7 delves into the selection of a business location and includes a site-selection checklist.
- Chapters 9 and 10 cover the all-important subject of determining the financial needs of the startup enterprise and then cover specific sources of financing.
- Chapter 12 discusses marketing, pricing, and advertising.
- Chapter 13 considers the purchase of supplies and inventory systems.
- Chapter 14 covers the usually burdensome topic of cost and management of working capital.
- Chapter 17 contains comprehensive coverage of taxes and includes the necessary tax forms needed by entrepreneurs.
- Chapter 19 deals with business startups in other countries and discusses ways for American entrepreneurs to become involved in foreign trade.
- Additional chapters discuss subjects as diverse as computers and insurance.

ANCILLARY MATERIALS

The Instructor's Manual/Test Bank was written by us with the needs of the instructor in mind. It includes 50 transparency masters that can be used to enhance classroom presentation. In addition to the normal chapter outline and test bank, we have included suggestions in each chapter to help the instructor stimulate interest in the subject. Supplementary exercises, suggestions on speakers, and the titles of several videos and computer management simulations are included that will greatly enhance the teaching of the entrepreneurship process.

ACKNOWLEDGMENTS

This book is not just our own product. We have had considerable help from many dedicated people to whom we wish to extend our heartfelt thanks. Our respective deans were extremely understanding and supportive, as were our schools' secretaries and work-study students. We wish to thank individuals and other publishers who allowed us to use their copyrighted material. We also owe a considerable debt of gratitude to the people who reviewed our manuscript. Their suggestions helped to keep us on target. These reviewers include:

D. Ray Bagby, University of Baltimore
James J. Carroll, William Paterson College
Marc Dollinger, University of Indiana
Phyllis G. Holland, Valdosta State College
R. Duane Ireland, Baylor University
Jim Kennedy, Angelina College
Michael Pitts, Virginia Commonwealth University
David G. Watkin, Pennsylvania State University
Harold Wilson, Southern Illinois University

We also wish to thank both of our editors from Harper & Row: Jayne Maerker, who helped get us started and offered encouragement throughout the preparation of the manuscript, and Debra Riegert, who helped push us through the final stages when we would have preferred not to do the necessary and very important finishing touches. In addition, Paula Cousin, our project editor, did an outstanding job of seeing that we kept to our production schedule.

Finally, this book would have remained unwritten if we had not received encouragement, support, assistance, prodding, and understanding from our wives. Keeping us focused and on target was no easy task. Kathi and Lu, we owe you everything and so we dedicate this book to you.

Robert Anderson

John Dunkelberg

About the Authors

Robert Anderson and John Dunkelberg have a combined 30 years of teaching experience, primarily in management, finance, small-business management, and business policy. They also have over 20 years of industry experience including working in countries outside of the United States. Both have been involved in small businesses as part owners, as well as having been case writers for more than a dozen cases. As case writers, they have studied small, startup businesses in the United States and other countries, and all of their cases are based on field research. From these experiences, they have encountered both the joy of success and the pain of seeing things not work out the way they were planned.

CHAPTER 1

Introduction

Learning Objectives

After you have read this chapter, you will be able to do the following:

- Define small businesses.
- Discuss the importance of small business.
- Learn why small businesses fail.
- Examine the characteristics of entrepreneurs.
- Understand startup ethics.

Each year, between 600,000 and 1.5 million men and women choose to become self-employed. They begin their ventures with considerable enthusiasm, dedication, and hope, but unfortunately nearly 50 percent of them will be unsuccessful in their first year of operation. More businesses will fail in the next two or three years, leaving a very small percentage of startups that reach maturity. This book is intended to increase the survival odds of new ventures. We will present planning and design techniques that should enable dedicated entrepreneurs to establish new ventures that can beat the failure odds.

It is difficult to devise a startup strategy that is appropriate for all businesses because each new venture is unique. Some businesses start with no employees; some may have ten, twenty, or more. Some companies are founded by one person, whereas others are started by husband and wife, partners, or a team of entrepreneurs. Some businesses are started with barely enough capital; others are quite well financed. These differences notwithstanding, we will develop and discuss startup strategies that can be used by most entrepreneurs to overcome many of the obstacles encountered in creating a new venture.

SMALL BUSINESSES

It would appear that defining and describing small businesses would be a relatively simple task, since all of us know and deal daily with those operating in our neighborhoods. However, it is virtually impossible to compile an accurate statistical profile of a small business, because there is no widely accepted standard definition of a small business, not all startups are officially documented, and facts and figures pertaining to small businesses are collected and stored by a wide variety of organizations and government agencies (see The Inside View 1-1).

Even though we are unable to provide accurate startup figures and a precise definition of a small business, we can present some generally accepted numbers and a sense of the importance of small business in the American economy. Like Jay Finegan, we have derived our figures from a variety of sources, some more reputable or formal than others. We believe that the best single source of small-business data is the National Federation of Independent Business, a Washington lobbying group, which represents the interests of approximately a half million companies.

Definition of a Small Business

Perhaps the best place to begin for a definition of a small business is the Small Business Administration (SBA), the federal agency charged with representing and assisting American small businesses. The SBA, like many federal agencies, hedges its bets and attempts to include every possible type of business in its fairly precise definition.

1-1 *The Inside View*

SMALL BUSINESS STATISTICS

The first assignment of Jay Finegan (*Inc.* magazine's new man in Washington) was to ". . . get a statistical handle on the much-ballyhood 'Age of the Entrepreneur'." He was supposed to describe and define small businesses. His first rather simple question was how many small businesses are there? He first consulted Dun & Bradstreet because of that firm's listing of new corporations. He was informed that "new incorps" is a bad number ". . . because a lot of people incorporate for future use or for tax or legal purposes and does not really measure business activity." Next, Finegan contacted the National Federation of Independent Business (NFIB), the Small Business Administration, the Internal Revenue Service, the Commerce Department, the Bureau of the Census, and the Bureau of Labor Statistics without any luck. Finally, Finegan noted: "After picking my way through the statistical skunkworks of Washington, Wall Street, and Cambridge, Mass., after days on the phone and countless interviews, I had emerged empty-handed." There were new jobs created, more corporations, more phone installations, more employers, and more tax returns. "But the exact number of new businesses created last year in the United States? Hang it up."[1]

Small Business Administration's Definition.

- Two hundred fifty employees or fewer in manufacturing
- Annual receipts of $9 million or less in wholesaling
- Annual receipts or sales of $2 million or less in retail trades and services
- Average annual receipts for the preceding three years of $9.5 million or less in construction

The SBA goes on to caution that "since size is a relative concept and what is large in one industry in terms of employees or sales dollars is small in another, SBA's criteria vary from industry to industry and program to program to more accurately reflect the characteristics of small business and the objectives of SBA programs."[2]

General Definition. We believe that the SBA definition of a small business is too cumbersome and unnecessarily rigid; therefore, we present and accept the following definition, which has been drawn from many different sources:

1. ***Method of financing and operation.*** Generally, any business initially financed with personal funds (from the owner, his or her family, and friends or acquaintances) and operated primarily by the owner is a small business. We hasten to add that the criteria we use to define a small business are not inflexible, because it is possible to find very large companies that are financed and controlled by one person or a family.

2. ***Scope of operation.*** The operations of most small businesses tend to be local in scope, usually confined to one city or county. For a business to develop the networks and infrastructure necessary to serve a large geographic area, it must possess resources unavailable to small firms.

3. ***Relative size within industry.*** If other criteria seem to be inappropriate, it is possible to simply compare a business to others in its industry. If a firm is considerably smaller than its competitors, it can be assumed to be a small business. Again, this measure can be misleading if it is used by itself. For example, using only this criterion, we could argue that Chrysler, with its small share of the automobile market, is a small business.

Regardless of the definition used, it is a fact that nearly all businesses in this country are small. There are approximately fourteen million businesses in the United States and only fifteen thousand, according to the National Federation of Independent Business, have revenues in excess of $25 million.

Importance of Small Business

We may not know how many small businesses there are, or even exactly what a small business is, but we do know how important they are to the economy. First, small businesses are the primary creators of new jobs and the employers of a majority of the work force. Approximately two of every three new jobs are created by small businesses, and nearly 60 percent of the work force is employed by small companies. Second, small companies are an indispensable source of supplies and services for larger firms. Many major corporations rely on small businesses for parts and services which could not be supplied economically by other large companies. Third, small businesses can be more innovative than their larger counterparts. Since they are not hampered by multiple management layers and inflexible rules and procedures, small companies tend to develop more new products and services than do larger businesses. Finally, small businesses are often the only source of some services and products in rural areas or small towns.

In order to firmly establish their importance and develop common objectives, owners of small businesses periodically meet in Washington to forge an agenda for the coming years. In 1980 and 1986 approximately 1,800 small-business representatives met in Washington for the White House Conference on Small Business to discuss everything from the budget deficit to the availability of affordable insurance. The issues deemed important (see Figure 1.1) will probably become the objectives for small business for several years.

SMALL-BUSINESS FAILURE

We know that most of the men and women who choose to start their own business are dedicated, enthusiastic, and hardworking, and we know that small businesses are a vital part of our national economy. Why then, do so many small businesses fail? We have purposely used the phrase "so many" because nobody knows exactly how many small businesses fail each year. Since we are unable to precisely define small business, determine how many new businesses start up each year, or how many small businesses

FIGURE 1.1 White House Conference on Small Business: Top Ten Recommendations

1. Make liability insurance for small business less expensive and more available.
2. Do not allow government-mandated employee benefits, such as employer-paid health benefits, parental leave, etc.
3. Keep nonprofit organizations and government agencies from competing unfairly with small businesses.
4. Reduce the deficit and balance the federal budget.
5. Create a cabinet-level department of international trade to coordinate and focus on existing activities of federal agencies.
6. Encourage the advancement of entrepreneurial education and the study of the free enterprise system in schools and colleges.
7. Repeal the Davis–Bacon Act and the Service Contract Act.
8. Reform the social security system.
9. Enact S. 2760 with the Kasten–Lugar–Kassebaum Amendment to provide uniform **fault defenses** (businesses can defend against law suits) and the Pressler Amendment to eliminate joint and several liability.
10. Make the IRS subject to the Equal Access to Justice and the Regulatory Flexibility acts.

exist, it is easy to understand why it is difficult to determine how many businesses fail each year. We accept the estimate that approximately 50 percent of all startups fail in the first year and that 75 to 80 percent fail within the first three to five years. An article in *The Wall Street Journal* indicated that 79 percent of the businesses that failed in 1986 were less than ten years old.[3]

Definition of Failure

One reason it is so difficult to count the number of small-business failures is the lack of a universally accepted definition of failure. For example, does a firm have to declare bankruptcy before it is considered a failure, or has a firm failed when its owner simply decides to close down his or her marginally successful business? If two companies merge, one no longer exists, but has it failed? If an owner chooses to liquidate a business to use the proceeds for another venture, has the liquidated firm failed?

It is obvious that we could go on and on asking hypothetical failure questions; however, that does not get us any closer to a working definition of small-business failure. We believe that a business has failed when its liabilities exceed its assets, its cash flow is insufficient for normal operations, and the owner decides the company should be closed, liquidated, or sold to another individual or company. Even if the business continues operating under new management or as part of a healthier company, the original firm has failed and should be included in the annual business-failure statistics.

Reasons for Failure

Determining the number of startups and small-business failures is more difficult than explaining why new businesses fail. There have been numerous studies designed to uncover the major causes of business failure. The following are the most frequently identified causes of small business failure:

1. ***Poor management.*** Too many people feel that they have been successful employees and, therefore, should be successful managers. They start a business only to learn that to successfully operate a company requires considerable management skills, skills which they may not have yet developed.

2. ***Undercapitalization.*** Since small-business owners tend to be incurable optimists, they tend to underestimate their expenses and overestimate their revenue. When this happens, they soon find themselves unable to pay their bills.

3. ***Underestimating the competition.*** Too many people starting their own business expect the established competition to "accept" them and "share" their market with the startup. Competitors will usually do anything necessary to squelch the growth dreams of startups.

4. ***Poor planning.*** Too many people open a business with no idea of where the company is going after opening day.

5. ***Legal problems.*** Some businesses fail because the owners neglect to retain an attorney, or they fail to select an appropriate lawyer.

6. ***Accounting problems.*** Any business that doesn't have an appropriate, not necessarily complicated, accounting system is a prime candidate for failure.

7. *Lack of frugality.* Too many owners of new businesses want to go "first class." They do not hunt for bargains; instead they buy all new equipment, computerize too soon, and always pay cash for everything.

8. *Location.* In most businesses, particularly retail, choosing the wrong location can be terminal.

9. *Incapable or dishonest employees.* Most small businesses are labor intensive; therefore, their success depends heavily on capable, reliable, honest employees.

10. *Economic conditions.* Companies that begin operations in recessionary times greatly increase their failure potential.

This list is by no means exhaustive, nor is it mutually exclusive. In fact, if more than one of the mentioned ingredients is present at the same time, the likelihood of failure increases significantly. For an example of how even enthusiastic and committed people can fail in their own business, see The Inside View 1-2.

Avoiding Failure

Business failure is expensive and ego bruising—and avoidable. A committed business owner with management skills, adequate capital, competent employees, a needed product or service, and the right location should enjoy many years of success and profitability. Chances of success can be increased by selecting a business that has histor-

1-2 *The Inside View*

SMALL-BUSINESS FAILURE

After five years of teaching high-school English in Port Hueneme, California, Marilyn Kyd decided to change jobs. She was hired by a personnel agency in Oxnard (Ventura County), California. A year later she and a partner decided to open their own personnel agency. Every decision following their initial one was wrong, and eventually the company failed. The first mistake was locating the business in Santa Monica rather than in Oxnard, where the partners were well known. In addition, the office was too big, job openings were limited, and they could not attract competent employees. Looking back, Marilyn noted: "Our mistakes were obvious. We should have established our business in Ventura County. . . . Our office should have been more modest and easily accessible to drop-in trade—and about forty miles closer to home. And we should have scouted the advertising situation more thoroughly. . . . Our miscalculations were the result of planning so poor, we might be tempted, were it not true, to call it unbelievable." That failure cost each partner about $7,000.[4]

ically low failure rates. An SBA analysis of 1983 failures indicated that the following businesses are *least* likely to fail: funeral homes, tobacco wholesalers, fuel oil dealers, laundries and dry cleaners, drugstores, hotels, manufacturers of wood products, providers of personal services, beer and wine wholesalers, and service stations. Those businesses most likely to fail were small retailers, such as hobby, book, gift, and sporting goods stores, and florists.[5]

Not everyone would be happy owning one of the ten most failure-proof businesses, but what can a person who chooses a riskier business do to increase the chances of success? The remaining chapters of this book explain how a person can be successful in almost any reasonable, needed business.

ENTREPRENEURS

Joseph Schumpeter, one of the early economists to study entrepreneurs, believed that innovation or creativeness distinguished entrepreneurs from other businesspeople. He explained that acceptable entrepreneurial activity included the following: developing new goods or services; introducing new methods of production; identifying new markets; finding new sources of supply; and developing new organizational forms.[6] Since Schumpeter, many researchers and teachers have been trying to define entrepreneurship, and they have been attempting to differentiate entrepreneurs from other small-business owners.

Professor William Baumol, for example, believes that entrepreneurial activities fall into two primary types, which he calls "initiating" and "imitating."[7] Initiating entrepreneurs introduce products, productive techniques, and other items and procedures not previously available. Imitating entrepreneurs, on the other hand, disseminate the innovations of the initiating entrepreneurs.

Other people have also tried to distinguish between entrepreneurs who invent and those who present or perfect what the former have invented. For example, Carland et al., after a fairly exhaustive search of the entrepreneurial literature, proposed the following definitions:

> *Entrepreneur:* An entrepreneur is an individual who establishes and manages a business for the principal purpose of profit and growth. The entrepreneur is characterized principally by innovative behavior and will employ strategic management practices in the business.
>
> *Small Business Owner:* A small business owner is an individual who establishes and manages a business for the principal purpose of furthering personal goals. The business must be the primary source of income and will consume the majority of one's time and resources. The owner perceives the business as an extension of his or her personality, intricately bound with family needs and desires.[8]

We believe that most researchers are really splitting hairs when they try to differentiate entrepreneurs from other small-business owners. Therefore, in this book, we treat anyone who is willing to risk his or her money, time, and prestige on a new venture as an entrepreneur. We do believe, however, that there are characteristics and traits that differentiate entrepreneurs from people not self-employed.

Characteristics and Traits of Entrepreneurs

It would be possible to create a list of entrepreneurial characteristics that would cover several pages; however, such an extensive list would be no more helpful than a shorter list that included the most often cited and most generally accepted characteristics. The following are some of the most prominent entrepreneurial characteristics and traits:

Innovative. We have already mentioned that entrepreneurs are more innovative and creative than the average person. They have the unique ability to "see" products, services, or new operating techniques that others miss.

Willing to Take Risks. According to Schumpeter, "Risk-taking is in no case an element of the entrepreneurial function."[9] Most researchers agree that entrepreneurs are not "bet-the-ranch"-type gamblers; however, entrepreneurs will take moderate risks, especially if they can influence the outcome of an event.

Aggressive. Most entrepreneurs are aggressive in their dealings with other people. They know what they want to accomplish, and they are able to overcome obstacles.

Self-confident. Most entrepreneurs believe in themselves. In fact, some entrepreneurs are so self-confident that they refuse to let their employees make any decisions on their own.

Willing to Work Long Hours. Entrepreneurs are not "nine-to-five" people. They devote countless hours to their business, often at the expense of their families and friends. Entrepreneurs are usually considered to be workaholics. (Do the following short self-assessment exercise to find out if you have workaholic tendencies.)

Highly Competitive. For the true entrepreneur, there is only first or last, because second, third, etc., do not count. Entrepreneurs believe in win–lose situations, and they expect to win. For people who open and manage their own business, money is a means of keeping score. Most entrepreneurs are not really motivated by money, but they view it as an outward display of success. As Aristotle Onassis stated, "After a certain point, money is meaningless. It ceases to be the goal. The game is what counts." Or, according to Nelson Bunker Hunt, "Money never meant anything to us. It was just sort of how we kept score."

Superior in Conceptual Ability. Entrepreneurs have the ability to "see the big picture" while at the same time be aware of details. They are able to see both the forest and the trees.

Educated. Perhaps it is because of the increasingly technical nature of business that more entrepreneurs are college graduates now than in the past. Joseph Mancuso has found that 82 percent of the entrepreneurs he studied have a college degree or beyond.[10]

Healthy. While there is no evidence that entrepreneurs are inherently healthier than the rest of the population, they are "sick" less often than others because they won't

SELF-ASSESSMENT EXERCISE

DIAGNOSING WORKAHOLISM

Scale: 5—Never 4—Seldom 3—Occasionally 2—Usually 1—Always (Circle one.)

1.	I take work home evenings and/or weekends.	5	4	3	2	1
2.	I feel uneasy or guilty if I'm not working.	5	4	3	2	1
3.	I work late more frequently than my co-workers.	5	4	3	2	1
4.	I play as hard as I work.	5	4	3	2	1
5.	I avoid delegating work to others because no one else can do it quite right.	5	4	3	2	1
6.	I become restless or uneasy on vacation.	5	4	3	2	1
7.	Most of my reading is work related.	5	4	3	2	1
8.	I expect others to put in as many hours as I do.	5	4	3	2	1
9.	I communicate better with my co-workers than with family or friends.	5	4	3	2	1
10.	I find it difficult to relax.	5	4	3	2	1
11.	I tend to schedule more and more activities into less and less time.	5	4	3	2	1
12.	I work under a great deal of tension.	5	4	3	2	1
13.	I equate success with hard work.	5	4	3	2	1
14.	I have difficulty becoming involved with activities other than my job.	5	4	3	2	1
15.	I would rather be at work than most other places.	5	4	3	2	1
16.	My family or friends comment or complain about how much I work.	5	4	3	2	1
17.	Those who know me well would say that I am a perfectionist.	5	4	3	2	1
18.	I work harder than most others in my organization or line of work.	5	4	3	2	1
19.	I find myself working when I could be relaxing.	5	4	3	2	1
20.	I take pleasure in telling others how hard or long I work.	5	4	3	2	1

Source: Douglas Stewart, *The Power of People Skills* (New York: John Wiley & Sons, 1986), pp. 227–228. Used by permission.

Note: Pay special attention to those items for which you have circled a 1 or 2, for these are most indicative of a tendency toward workaholism.

let themselves be sick. Entrepreneurs will continue to work with headaches or other ailments which might keep others at home and away from work.

Are Entrepreneurs Different?

No list of characteristics can explain if or why entrepreneurs are different from other workers. There is no one "type" of person who is more likely to be an entrepreneur than someone else. An examination of the chief executive officers of the 500 fastest growing firms in America[11] provides the following information:

Education. Only 12 percent had a high school degree or less. The remainder had two of more years of college.

Economic Background. The majority of the CEOs (62 percent) were from middle-class or affluent families. Only 6 percent were from poor families, with the remainder (32 percent) from working-class backgrounds.

Religion. Most of the CEOs (50 percent) were Protestant, while 25 percent were Catholic. Of the remainder, 14 percent were Jewish, and the others belonged to some other demonination or none at all.

Income. The CEOs' median salary was $93,226 per year.

Miscellaneous. Of the CEOs in this group, 85 percent are married (70 percent to their first spouse); they have 1.4 children; they vote Republican; only 4 percent are women; and 73 percent used mostly personal savings to finance their business.

The conclusion drawn from this and many other studies is that it is nearly impossible to create a profile of an entrepreneur that would easily differentiate her or him from the average person in the work force. There are several different written tests that purport to indicate whether or not a person has entrepreneurial tendencies. We are unable to document the validity of such tests; however, we have included at the end of the chapter a sample test that might give you an inkling of your "calling."

Who Are Entrepreneurs?

As we have already mentioned, anyone can be an entrepreneur if he or she is willing to risk his or her own capital, time, and prestige on a business of his or her own. The vast majority of entrepreneurs are white males. For example, the following names of earlier entrepreneurs should be familiar to everyone: Henry Ford; George Westinghouse; William Wrigley, Jr.; Charles Rolls and (Frederick) Henry Royce; Burton Baskin and Irvine Robbins; King Camp Gillette; John Deere; Dan Gerber; and Calvin Klein. These are familiar names because these men have created large companies that bear their names. There are, of course, thousands of entrepreneurs who are less famous because their products or companies do not bear their names.

Entrepreneurs like Xavier Roberts (Cabbage Patch Kids), Paul Fireman (Reebok shoes), Donald Kingsborough (Teddy Ruxpin and Lazer Tag), and Roy Speer and Lowell Paxson (Home Shopping Network) may be less well known than those mentioned above; however, their contribution to the American economy is just as significant.

White Male Entrepreneurs. Most entrepreneurs are white males primarily because they have more opportunity to start a business than do women and other minorities. Large corporations afford white males the opportunity to gain valuable experience, which they can use in their own business. White males have numerous "networks" that support their entrepreneurial efforts. Perhaps the most important reason so many entrepreneurs are white males is access to capital; banks and other lending sources are more likely to lend startup money to white males than to women and other minorities. The conditions that tend to favor white male entrepreneurs over others are changing. More women, blacks, and immigrants are now becoming successful entrepreneurs.

Entrepreneurial Women. Until the 1960s it was unusual for women to be employed outside of the home, and female entrepreneurs were almost nonexistent. However, by 1986, more than 50 percent of women eighteen or older were in the work force, and that figure is projected to be nearly 60 percent by 1995. Women are avoiding typically female occupations such as nursing, retail sales, and teaching, and are choosing instead to enter male-dominated occupations where they can acquire management experience needed for eventual business ownership. Women now own more than a quarter of the nation's sole proprietorships, and they are starting new enterprises at more than three times the rate of men.[12]

Women who create new companies often start from their home and gradually move into an office or store. The following enterprises are most often owned by women:

Nonstore retailing
Real estate
Beauty salons
Schools
Accountants and bookkeepers
Doctors and dentists
Restaurants and bars
Insurance
Building maintenance
Orchestras and entertainment
Clothing stores
Photographic studios
Antique and secondhand shops
Lawyers
Grocery stores[13]

Women are finding it easier to get financing for their businesses now than in the past. They are networking more, and they now have role models. Female entrepreneurs such as Mary Kay Ash, Lane Bryant, Joyce Hall (Hallmark Greeting Cards), Gabrielle (Coco) Chanel, Elizabeth Arden, Fannie Meritt Farmer, and Sara Lee Lubin are proof that women can be successful business owners. We expect the ranks of female entrepreneurs to swell in the future, and the time is not far off when women owning their own business will be so common that it will not be newsworthy.

Black Entrepreneurs. Black entrepreneurs are even scarcer than female entrepreneurs. A study of the *Inc.* 500 fastest growing firms in America revealed that only two CEOs were black, ten were Asian, and eleven were Hispanic. Of the 100 top-ranked black-owned companies in the United States, only 4 had 1985 sales above $100 million. In contrast, the top 15 Hispanic-owned companies had sales in excess of $100 million.[14] There are a number of plausible explanations for the dearth of black entrepreneurs. Bondie Gambrell, a black real estate investor believes, "They [blacks] haven't wanted to venture out on their own. They have relied on others to make opportunities. They don't realize it doesn't kill your soul to be a capitalist."[15] Other reasons include lack of capital, lack of experience, the absence of a black network, lack of community support, and what some consider the insensitivity of white businesspeople (see The Inside View 1-3). As networks are formed and startup capital becomes available, more blacks will take the plunge and start their own businesses.

In a recent article, Linda Watkins[16] noted that minorities were once concentrated in mom-and-pop businesses like groceries, barbershops, and cleaners; however, now they are moving into fields like electronics and health care, advertising and real estate development, insurance and computer software. Stronger educational credentials, greater access to financing, government assistance, and a growing support network among minority-owned businesses have fueled the change.

Immigrant Entrepreneurs. Nearly 5 percent of Asians and 2 percent of Hispanics in the United States are self-employed. The chief reasons for Hispanic and Asian business success appears to be networking and community support. The most visible example of immigrant entrepreneurial success is the Cuban community in Miami. The Cuban immigrants did not come to America with large amounts of money or influential local contacts, but they did come with a strong desire to share in the fruits of a capitalist system. They started their own businesses, helped each other overcome obstacles, and patronized each others' business. The immigrants are successful entrepreneurs (see The Inside View 1-4 for an example of successful immigrant entrepreneurs).

1-3 *The Inside View*

REVLON ANGERS BLACKS

On January 20, 1987, *Essence* announced that it would no longer accept advertising from Revlon Inc., an account worth $400,000 in revenues last year. The monthly for black women was responding to a remark made by a Revlon executive disparaging black-owned hair-care companies. In a *Newsweek* interview, Irving J. Bottner, president of Revlon's Professional Products Division, said: "The black-owned businesses will disappear. They'll all be sold to the white companies." He added: "We are accused of taking business away from the black companies, but black consumers buy quality products—too often, their black brothers didn't do them any good." Other magazines are considering dropping Revlon advertising, and Lafayette Jones, executive director of American Health & Beauty Aids Institute (AHBAI), a trade association of black-owned hair-care companies, is looking for ways to retaliate. Jones said: "We don't complain about the competition, we complain about the fact that the playing field is not level." The biggest hurdle for black-owned companies is getting their products distributed.[17]

1-4 *The Inside View*

IMMIGRANT ENTREPRENEURS

Rosie Ruíz, Irma Linda Díaz, and Kwok Ming Wong worked for Aluminum Forge for seventeen years. They learned all aspects of the business and were relatively satisfied with their jobs; however, they wanted to do something on their own. Wong stated: "Working for somebody else, you're never secure. You could be the best today, and tomorrow they decide to let you go. But if you own the business, what the heck. You might have to work twice as hard, maybe three times, but at least you're your own boss. Nobody can say we don't need you anymore." The three women started Independent Forge Co. in 1975. That year, the three partners earned nothing. By 1984, the company had thirty-nine employees and $3.5 million in sales. There were many problems and obstacles that had to be overcome to get to $3.5 million in sales, but the partners are satisfied with their progress and they encourage others to start their own businesses.[18]

Entrepreneurial Teams

Is it possible for a business to be founded by more than one entrepreneur? More and more businesses are being started and successfully managed by more than one person. For example, the experience and complementary talents of Bill Murto, Jim Harris, and Rod Canion account for the amazing success of Compaq Computer Company (which had sales of $111 million in its first year of operation).[19] Other companies formed and managed by teams include Linear Technology Corp., Quantum Corp., and AST Research Inc. There is also a growing number of husband-and-wife teams starting and operating businesses. Fred W. Wasserman and Pamela K. Anderson started and run Maxicare Health Plans Inc.; Liz Claiborne and her husband, Arthur Ortenburg, started the company that bears her name; Melvin J. and Ellen R. Gordon are chairman and president, respectively, of Tootsie Roll Inc.; and Fred and Gale Hayman built Giorgio Beverly Hills into a $100-million-a-year boutique and fragrance line.[20] Perhaps two, three, or more heads are better than one.

Choosing Self-Employment

We have discussed entrepreneurial characteristics and who is likely to be an entrepreneur. Now it is time to consider the reasons why people who have worked for another company make the decision to start their own business. Very few people start a business without ever having worked for someone else or without the support of family and friends. In a survey of its readers, *Venture*[21] asked why they had left their jobs to go on their own. Respondents could cite multiple reasons for leaving, but the most prevalent reason (listed by 55 percent of the respondents) was "their independence had been thwarted by a previous employer." The other top reasons were desire for a new challenge (50 percent), inadequate compensation (39 percent), and lack of employer appreciation (38 percent).

The following are sample statements made by those who left jobs to start their own business: "I left my job because I wanted the chance to do things the way I knew they should be done"; "Working for a corporate giant like Amoco, you feel really cut off from the direction of the company"; "At J&J, everything was structured. Your day, your week, your year, was planned for you. I knew what I'd be doing tomorrow and where I'd be in ten to twenty years. It was comforting, but not stimulating"; and another said that he had ". . . no dissatisfaction with my job as it was. I just decided that if I was going to work that hard, I wanted to write my own destiny."

Multiple Startups

Not every entrepreneur is successful with his or her first startup, and not every entrepreneur with a successful startup stays with that business for very long. Tom Duck, Sr. (see The Inside View 1-5), is a good example of a person who founded a really successful business on his thirteenth attempt. Others include Phil Romano, who struck it rich with his twelfth restaurant, Richard Tanenbaum, whose eighth restaurant concept was a winner, and Richard S. Thorp, who claims to have started twenty-four businesses.[22] Many entrepreneurs enjoy the excitement and challenge of starting a business, but once it is operating successfully, they leave it to begin the process all over again.

1-5 *The Inside View*

THIRTEEN STARTUPS

When he was twenty-six, Tom Duck, Sr., of Tuscon opened an appliance store in Indianapolis, down the street from his previous employer, Sears Roebuck & Co. "I was buying my stoves from the same place that Sears was—but I was giving better prices," remembers Duck. After that business, it was toys and garish paintings, several types of insurance, auto-seat repairs, and a family motor coach association—none of which were great successes. Now, at seventy-two and on his thirteenth company, Duck finally seems to have made a score—a chain of 500 low-cost car-rental franchises, run mostly out of used-car dealerships in 41 states and Canada.[23]

Go for It

What we have seen in the first part of this chapter is that anyone can open her or his own business. Whether or not the business will be successful depends to a great extent on how realistic and well prepared the owner is. The remainder of this book is designed to help any would-be business owner plan and prepare for the new venture in order to maximize the probability of success. We encourage anyone who feels the urge to be self-employed to "go for it," but remember that success comes to those who are prepared.

ENTREPRENEURS AND ETHICS

It may seem unnecessary to advise startup entrepreneurs to be ethical; however, the evidence that unethical business activity seems to be increasing prompted us to include a section on ethics in this introductory chapter. It is no longer possible to ignore the stories about insider stock trading, firms accepting bribes and kickbacks, business owners not reporting all their income, companies making false claims about their products, and so on. At first glance it may seem that unethical behavior is a corporate activity and should, therefore, be of little concern to startup entrepreneurs. Unfortunately, this is not the case, as one can see from some of the entrepreneurs (see The Inside View 1-6) who have been found to be unethical. (There is a difficult-to-

1-6 *The Inside View*

UNETHICAL BUSINESS ACTIVITY

Robert L. Miller and Paul V. Fenton were both product managers at C. R. Bard Inc., a leading medical device company in Murray Hill, New Jersey. Miller was in charge of developing and marketing an improved pump-driven system to deliver intravenous drugs to patients. As members of their division's management team, Miller and Fenton had access to top-secret technical documents and production-cost figures for Bard's pumps. In 1984, Miller and Fenton abruptly left Bard to start their own company, Strato Medical Corp., to manufacture a competing pump. Bard sued Strato, its officers, and its backers, aiming to permanently enjoin them from marketing the pump. The judge who heard the case issued a one-year injunction against Strato's sale of its pump. Strato could probably have avoided the suit if its founders had been forthright with Bard from the outset, had quit the company sooner, and had developed their pump without relying on feedback from Bard's market trials.[24]

discern distinction between unethical and illegal activities, and one often leads to, or causes, the other.)

Ivan Boesky, the arbitrage entrepreneur, was found guilty of insider trading and fined $100 million and sentenced to jail. Boyd Jefferies, the founder of a Los Angeles-based securities firm, was charged with colluding with Boesky. Three top officers of a film recovery laboratory were convicted of on-the-job homicide after an employee died while working with toxic materials. Barry Minkow (the founder of ZZZZ Best Company) was accused of laundering money. It would be reassuring to know that these were just isolated cases and that the majority of America's executives and entrepreneurs were ethical and moral. As we shall see, there is more unethical behavior in business than previously believed.

The Decline of Ethics

The press, both popular and academic, is investigating and reporting on the decline of morality and ethics in the business community. The coverage of the Wall Street insider-trading scandal has been extensive and exhaustive. What surprised most people about that incident was that a majority of those implicated were well-educated young men, mostly in their thirties, many of whom made million-dollar salaries, drove fancy cars, and dined in top-notch restaurants. There appears to be a growing consensus that younger people are less ethical than earlier generations because they were not "taught" values and morals in school. It is argued that in the past, families, churches, and schools encouraged young people to adopt socially acceptable values and ethics. Once the values had been accepted, individuals were likely to become ethical executives and managers.

The absence of strong moral and ethical codes to guide today's executives and entrepreneurs is blamed on almost all segments of society. Businesses blame colleges for not teaching ethics; colleges claim that the public schools should stress ethics; the public schools believe that churches and parents should teach children morals and values; and so it goes. The fact is that more educational institutions, at the college and precollege level, are including ethics in their instructional programs.

Ethics Education

Colleges and universities are being encouraged to add ethics courses to their business curriculum. John Shad, the ex-Chairman of the Securities and Exchange Commission, donated $30 million to the Harvard Business School to establish a program in business ethics. Other academic institutions are also including ethics courses in their curricula, even though they have not received such handsome financial contributions.

College administrators encounter some problems when they try to introduce business ethics courses. The first problem arises from the reluctance of some faculty members to accept the "need" for ethics courses at the college level. There are still those who believe that values are set by the time people enter college and that one or more ethics courses will not change those values. Second, there is disagreement on where ethics courses belong in the curriculum. Some faculty prefer to teach separate ethics courses, whereas others want the teaching of ethics included in other core courses. Third, there is a problem of deciding who should teach ethics. Should people with backgrounds in philosophy and theology teach ethics, or should business faculty "learn" enough about ethics to teach ethical business activity courses?

These types of problems do not appear to be so prevalent in secondary schools. Character-building courses are being taught in school systems throughout the country. A program now in effect in major school districts like Chicago, St. Louis, and Miami stresses honesty, kindness, courage, justice, tolerance, freedom, and sound use of talents. Proponents of this program claim that it is effective; however, critics believe that courses that stress character development and ethical principles cannot be taught separately from religion.

Ethical Problems

During the startup process, entrepreneurs are called upon to make hundreds of decisions. At times it might be expedient to ignore or "bend" ethics; however, in the long run, ethical decisions are the only ones that will benefit entrepreneurs. Many influences (see Figure 1.2), such as individual factors, opportunity, and "significant others" should be considered before a decision is made. For example, the values, attitudes, and intentions of entrepreneurs will influence important startup decisions. Startup

FIGURE 1.2
Contingency Model of Ethical Decision Making

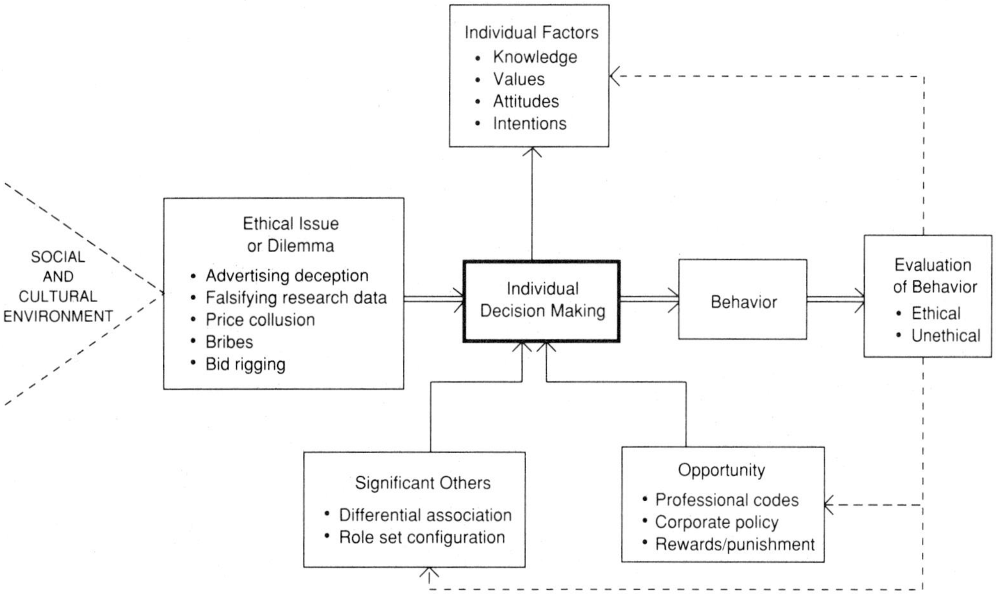

Source: O. C. Farrell and Larry Gresham, "A Contingency Framework for Understanding Ethical Decision Making in Marketing." Reprinted from *Journal of Marketing,* 49 (Summer 1985): 89. Published by the American Marketing Association. Used by permission.

entrepreneurs will need to rely on their ethical values when they develop advertising campaigns, recruit and select employees, enter into contracts with suppliers, calculate their tax obligations, price their products or services, and on numerous other occasions.

Most people would probably agree that there are many unethical business practices that should be eliminated. A study conducted by Vitell and Festervand[25] identified the following practices (in order of importance) as those which executives wanted to eliminate: price discrimination and unfair pricing; gifts, gratuities, and bribes; cheating of customers; unfair labor practices; dishonesty in making or keeping a contract; misleading advertising; unfair credit practices; and overselling. The list could be extended, but for our purpose it is sufficient to indicate that executives recognize that unethical practices do exist and they want to eliminate those practices.

Reasons for Unethical Practices

What causes basically honest people to engage in unethical practices? A number of reasons are offered to rationalize unethical behavior. First, if unethical acts benefit the company, the company will condone them and not punish the perpetrator. Managers seem to believe that any act or "deal" that improves the company's "bottom line" is acceptable even if it is unethical and has a negative impact on customers, competitors, etc. Second, activities are acceptable if "everyone" does them. Padding expense accounts, taking pencils home for the kids, or underreporting tips is OK because everyone else does it. Third, the activity is not truly unethical because, if it were, it would also be illegal. For some people, anything that is not specifically illegal cannot be unethical. Using a company car for personal use is not illegal; therefore, it cannot be wrong.

That unethical activities are acceptable as long as the perpetrator does not get caught is a fourth rationalization for engaging in them. If there are no checks and balances within an organization to detect unethical behavior, that behavior is likely to persist. If there is no way to know that company property is being misused, then what is the incentive to discontinue misusing it? Knowing that unethical practices might be detected and the guilty party exposed deters many employees from engaging in those practices. Finally, some people believe that unethical activities are acceptable as long as they do not harm any other person. It is the familiar concept of "victimless" crimes being less serious than other crimes; therefore, they should be unpunished.

Preventing Unethical Behavior

In a perfect world we would expect everyone to behave ethically, but this is not a perfect world. People need to have some set of guidelines or policies that indicate what is and what is not acceptable business behavior. To that extent, startup entrepreneurs should establish a code of ethics for their new businesses. Some people question the value of a code of ethics; however, Richard DeGeorge, a leading ethics scholar, defends them for the following reasons: The very exercise of developing a code of ethics is in itself worthwhile because it forces people to confront the problems, generates continuing discussion and possible modification of company rules and practices, encourages responsibility in new employees, provides employees with guidance if they are asked to do something they suspect might be unethical, and reassures both customers and the public of the fact that the firm adheres to moral principles.[26]

Ethical Codes. Developed before a business is even established, a code of ethics can serve the following purposes:

1. Eliminate undesirable practices, which could cause the company to lose customers.
2. Clarify company policy in areas of ethical uncertainty.
3. Help employees resolve ethical problems in the company's best interest.
4. Keep managers from treating employees unfairly.
5. Inform employees of what disciplinary action they can expect if they violate the code.
6. Inform customers and suppliers what the company accepts as ethical business behavior.
7. Advise competitors that the company will not engage in unethical competitive activities.

Items to Include in Ethical Codes. A code of ethics is a personalized statement of what behavior a company will accept; therefore, it is not possible to provide a standardized format. The following excerpts from Dow Chemical Company's policy statement will serve as an example of a large firm's ethical code:

> We are committed to exercising responsible care for our products both in manufacturing and distribution and later in their handling by distributors and use by our customers. This means assessing the environmental impact of the products and then taking appropriate steps to protect employee and public health, and the environment as a whole. In addition to safe production and distribution, as well as judicious customer use, it means we have a continuous concern for the ultimate disposal of our products in the environment. . . .

In many cases, professions develop ethical codes for their members. Accountants and lawyers, for example, have ethical codes that are intended to protect them, their clients, and their competitors. Many other professional associations have developed ethical codes to be observed by all members. Since we will be discussing franchising in Chapter 3, we have included the Code of Ethics for the International Franchise Association in this section (see Figure 1.3).

The Golden Rule. We conclude this section on ethics with a suggestion that startup entrepreneurs let their business activities be guided by the golden rule, that is, the traditional golden rule—Do unto others what you would have them do unto you—as opposed to the one accepted by some people—He who has the gold rules, or do unto others before they do it to you.

ASSEMBLING THE PIECES

We have presented our chapters as though creating a business were an orderly, sequential process; however, that is far from reality. The creation of a new venture is a chaotic process during which several simultaneous activities need to be completed before others can be undertaken. The process is like putting together a jigsaw puzzle: It is not over until all of the pieces have been assembled. To illustrate the startup

FIGURE 1.3 The International Franchise Association's Code of Ethics

1. In the advertisement and grant of franchises or dealerships, a member shall comply with all applicable laws and regulations, and the member's offering circulars shall be complete, accurate and not misleading with respect to the franchisee's or dealer's investment, the obligations of the member and the franchisee or dealer under the franchise or dealership, and all material facts relating to the franchise or dealership.

2. All matters material to the member's franchise or dealership shall be contained in one or more written agreements, which shall clearly set forth the terms of the relationships and the respective rights and obligations of the parties.

3. A member shall select and accept only those franchisees or dealers who, upon reasonable investigation, appear to possess the basic skills, education, experience, personal characteristics, and financial resources requisite to conduct the franchised business or dealership and meet the obligations of the franchisee or dealer under the franchise and other agreements. There shall be no discrimination in the granting of franchises based solely on race, color, religion, national origin, or sex. However, this in no way prohibits a franchisor from granting franchises to prospective franchisees as part of a program to make franchises available to persons lacking the capital, training, business experience, or other qualifications ordinarily required of franchisees or any other affirmative action program adopted by the franchisor.

4. A member shall provide reasonable guidance to its franchisees or dealers in a manner consistent with its franchise agreement.

5. Fairness shall characterize all dealings between a member and its franchisees or dealers. A member shall make every good faith effort to resolve complaints by and disputes with its franchisees or dealers through direct communication and negotiation. To the extent reasonably appropriate in the circumstances, a member shall give its franchisee or dealer notice of, and a reasonable opportunity to cure, a breach of their contractual relationship.

6. No member shall engage in the pyramid system of distribution. A pyramid is a system wherein a buyer's future compensation is expected to be based primarily upon recruitment of new participants, rather than upon the sales of products or services.

process, we will follow the planning and design activities that ultimately led to the creation of a new company. We could discuss the startup activities of Compaq Computer Corp. or one of the other nationally known fast-growth companies; however, we believe that these companies are so unique that they are not representative of most new ventures. We decided to examine the creation of a store that sells gourmet food, conducts cooking classes, and caters parties and other functions. This business is fairly typical of the hundreds of thousands of new ventures that are created each year.

In the remaining chapters we will include, under the heading "Assembling the Pieces," examples from the startup experiences of the owners of the gourmet food store. We begin in this chapter by presenting the résumés, which are similar to those of thousands of other entrepreneurs, of the two creators of the business.

Summary

Creating a new venture is exciting, challenging, frustrating, and rewarding. Approximately six hundred thousand new businesses are started annually, and about half will be out of existence within a year. Many owners of failed ventures will once again begin the process of creating a business while others will become disenchanted and elect to work for someone else. The businesses that succeed will make a significant contribution to the nation's economy. Small businesses employ more than half of the work force, and they create many more jobs than do large companies. Small businesses are an indispensable source of supplies and services for larger companies, and they are more innovative than bigger firms. Finally, small companies are often the only source of some services and products in rural areas or small towns.

Businesses that fail do so for any one or more of the following reasons: They were poorly managed; the owners did not have sufficient operating capital; the owners underestimated the strength of the competition; there was no realistic business plan; the company experienced legal or accounting problems; the owners chose to "go first class" and paid too much for their equipment, etc.; the business was located in the wrong place; the employees were incapable or dishonest; or economic conditions were unfavorable. Failed businesses could have been liquidated, sold to someone else, acquired by another company, or merged with a healthier firm, but they ceased to exist in their original form.

New ventures are created by entrepreneurs who have characteristics and traits that distinguish them from others. Most entrepreneurs are innovative, willing to take moderate risks, aggressive, self-confident, willing to work long hours, well educated, and quite healthy. They possess superior conceptual ability, and they have a strong need to succeed. Most entrepreneurs are white males; however, there are many more female and minority entrepreneurs now than there were a few years ago, and their numbers continue to increase.

Throughout the startup process, entrepreneurs make hundreds of decisions. They enter into contracts, select suppliers, hire employees, and make numerous other decisions. At times entrepreneurs might be tempted to overlook ethics in their dealings with others. Unethical activities may provide a short-term benefit; however, in the long run, ethical entreprenerus are the ones who will be successful. To provide ethical guidance for all employees, entrepreneurs should develop a code of ethics that eliminates undesirable practices, clarifies the company's ethics policy, helps employees resolve ethical problems, keeps managers from treating employees unfairly, and informs employees of disciplinary action resulting from unethical behavior. Startup entrepreneurs should adhere to the golden rule—do unto others as you would have them do unto you.

Assembling the Pieces

Résumé

Name:	Carol A. Tempel
Date of Birth:	June 28, 1941
Marital Status:	Husband: Dr. George E. Tempel Professor of Physiology Medical University of South Carolina
	Children: Michael, 10 Aaron, 6
Education:	Augustana College Rock Island, IL Majors: Biology and Secondary Education Minors: Chemistry and German Dates: September 1959 to June 1963 B.A. 1963
	California State University Los Angeles, CA
Experience:	Taught in schools in California, Illinois, Indiana, Missouri, and South Carolina from September 1963 until June 1980.
Business and Mgt. Experience:	Created the Charleston Spice Rack in Charleston, South Carolina, in 1979. Chair of several committees. Supervised and evaluated student teachers for three years.
References:	Provided on request.

Résumé

Name:	Jacqueline A. B. Boyd
Date of Birth:	October 15, 1950
Marital Status:	Married
Education:	B.S. cum laude, Business Administration College of Charleston (SC) 1981 Armstrong State College (GA) 1969–77, part time University of Georgia (Athens, GA) 1972 American Institute of Banking courses, Principles of Bank Operations, Law and Banking, and Accounting
Experience:	Partner, the Charleston Spice Rack First Federal Savings and Loan of Savannah, GA 1977 First Atlanta, GA 1972–76 First Bank of Savannah, GA 1970–72
References:	On file with Career Development, College of Charleston ■

entrepreneur's checklist

ENTREPRENEUR'S QUIZ

1. Was your father mostly present or absent during your early life at home?
_____ Present _____ Absent

2. Was your mother the dominant influence in your home?
_____ Yes _____ No

3. Was your home life difficult or easy?
_____ Difficult _____ Easy

4. Did you like school?
_____ Yes _____ No

5. Were you a top scholar?
_____ Yes _____ No

6. Did you have odd jobs and lots of duties at home at or before ten years of age?
_____ Yes _____ No

7. Were you the first-born child?
_____ Yes _____ No

8. Did you run with a group in school?
_____ Yes _____ No

9. Were you popular at school?
_____ Yes _____ No

10. Did you participate in school activities or sports?
_____ Yes _____ No

11. If so, did you tend to manage or assume the role of telling others what to do?
_____ Yes _____ No

12. Do you mostly read fiction or nonfiction?
_____ Fiction _____ Nonfiction

13. Do you like details?
_____ Yes _____ No

14. If you had to choose one, would you prefer that people like or respect you?
_____ Like _____ Respect

15. Are you impatient?
_____ Yes _____ No

16. Are you persistent?
_____ Yes _____ No

17. Did anyone ever tell you that you think differently from everyone else?
_____ Yes _____ No

18. If so, did it bother you?
_____ Yes _____ No

19. Do you ever hear ''inner voices'' telling you what to do?
_____ Yes _____ No

20. Do you like to take risks just for the thrill of it?
_____ Yes _____ No

21. Did anyone ever say you were stubborn?
_____ Yes _____ No

22. Do you enjoy being alone?
_____ Yes _____ No
23. Do you sleep as little as possible?
_____ Yes _____ No
24. Do you like to work in the garden or yard at home?
_____ Yes _____ No
25. Do you drink hard liquor at all?
_____ Yes _____ No
26. Do you find it easy to think in abstract terms unaided?
_____ Yes _____ No
27. Do you get sick often?
_____ Yes _____ No
28. Are you highly competitive?
_____ Yes _____ No
29. Are you aggressive?
_____ Yes _____ No
30. Are you decisive?
_____ Yes _____ No
31. Do you like action?
_____ Yes _____ No
32. Do you get bored easily?
_____ Yes _____ No
33. Does being around ''problem people'' disturb you?
_____ Yes _____ No
34. Are you authoritarian?
_____ Yes _____ No
35. Are you self-confident (even arrogant) at times?
_____ Yes _____ No
36. Can you work with someone you don't like?
_____ Yes _____ No
37. Can you concentrate for extended periods of time on one subject?
_____ Yes _____ No
38. Do you need occasional pep talks from others to keep you going?
_____ Yes _____ No
39. Do you like to tell your troubles to others?
_____ Yes _____ No
40. Do you repeat your mistakes?
_____ Yes _____ No
41. Are you energetic?
_____ Yes _____ No
42. Does money in itself motivate you?
_____ Yes _____ No
43. Do you have a career plan?
_____ Yes _____ No
44. Do you prefer to talk about the future or the past?
_____ Future _____ Past
45. Can you easily convince others to do it your way?
_____ Yes _____ No

46. Do you like to talk to people?
_____ Yes _____ No

47. Do most of your conversations discuss people or events and ideas?
_____ People _____ Events and Ideas

48. Under pressure, do you get better or worse?
_____ Better _____ Worse

49. Do you really like and respect yourself?
_____ Yes _____ No

50. Have you a hero or heroine as a secret role model?
_____ Yes _____ No

51. Do you harbor any inner feelings of guilt?
_____ Yes _____ No

52. Will you deliberately seek a direct confrontation to get what you are after?
_____ Yes _____ No

53. Do you believe there is any real security in anything?
_____ Yes _____ No

54. Do you often lose track of time?
_____ Yes _____ No

55. Do you socialize regularly?
_____ Yes _____ No

56. Do you like to go to parties?
_____ Yes _____ No

57. Do you read many books?
_____ Yes _____ No

58. Have you ever deliberately exceeded your authority at work?
_____ Yes _____ No

59. Are you optimistic?
_____ Yes _____ No

60. Do you worry about what others think about you?
_____ Yes _____ No

Scoring

Assign one point for each correct answer.

Now, before you add up your score, please remember this is not an infallible test. It reveals only if your basic character is similar to other successful entrepreneurs. What you choose to do about it is strictly up to you, as it should be.

ANSWERS

Question	Answer	Question	Answer	Question	Answer
1	Absent	8	No	15	Yes
2	Yes	9	No	16	Yes
3	Difficult	10	Yes	17	Yes
4	Yes	11	Yes	18	No
5	No	12	Nonfiction	19	Yes
6	Yes	13	No	20	Yes
7	Yes	14	Respect	21	Yes

Question	Answer	Question	Answer	Question	Answer
22	Yes	35	Yes	48	Better
23	Yes	36	Yes	49	Yes
24	No	37	Yes	50	Yes
25	No	38	No	51	Yes
26	Yes	39	No	52	Yes
27	No	40	No	53	No
28	Yes	41	Yes	54	Yes
29	Yes	42	No	55	No
30	Yes	43	Yes	56	No
31	Yes	44	Future	57	No
32	Yes	45	Yes	58	Yes
33	No	46	Yes	59	Yes
34	Yes	47	Events	60	No

Score	*Comments*
55–60	You are an entrepreneur and always have been! You will never be happy working for anyone but yourself, so get going! Do it now! You have been thinking and talking about it for years, right? You won't be content until you try, so give it a go! You have a good chance to do it.
45–54	You have entrepreneurial tendencies. If you don't have too much to lose, give it a shot. You are in the 50/50 range.
Under 45 29	Stay on someone else's payroll. As an entrepreneur, you enter a world with attitudes and behavior patterns too different from your own. Even if you survive, you won't like the game. It will upset you too much. Life's too short.

Source: Wilfred Tetreault and Robert Clements, *Starting Right in Your New Business*, © 1982, Addison-Wesley Publishing Co., Inc., Reading, MA, pps 229–235. Reprinted with Permission.

Questions for Review and Discussion

1. What is a small business?
2. Why is it so difficult to compile accurate statistics for small businesses?
3. How do small businesses contribute to the American economy?
4. What causes new businesses to fail?
5. Do you think entrepreneurs are different from other business owners?
6. What are the primary traits of entrepreneurs?
7. Why are so many entrepreneurs white males?
8. Why do you think so many women are now starting businesses?
9. Why do people choose to become self-employed?
10. Why do some entrepreneurs start a business, successfully operate it for a few years, sell it, and start all over again?

Notes

1. Jay Finegan, "The Entrepreneurial Numbers Game," *Inc.*, May 1986, pp. 31–36.
2. *SBA: A Manual for Student Counselors of the Small Business Institute,* p. 6.
3. ————, "Out of Business," *The Wall Street Journal,* 2 April, 1987, p. 31.
4. Marilyn Kyd, "The Little Business that Failed," *Venture,* December 1986, p. 112.
5. Sanford Jacobs, "The Most Likely to Survive—A Funeral Home or a Florist?" *The Wall Street Journal,* 16 September, 1985, p. 27.
6. Joseph Schumpeter, *The Theory of Economic Development* (Cambridge, MA: Harvard University Press, 1934).
7. William Baumol, "Entrepreneurship and a Century of Growth," *Journal of Business Venturing* (Spring 1986):141–145.
8. J. W. Carland, F. Hoy, W. R. Boulton, and J. C. Carland, "Differentiating Entrepreneurs from Small Business Owners: A Conceptualization," *Academy of Management Review* 9, no. 2 (1984):354–359.
9. Schumpeter, *The Theory of Economic Development,* p. 148.
10. Joseph Mancuso, "What Drives the Entrepreneur?" *Across the Board,* July–August 1984, 43–47.
11. Curtis Hartman, "Main Street Inc.," *Inc.*, June 1986, pp. 49–58.
12. Ellen Wojahn, "Why There Aren't More Women in This Magazine," *Inc.,* July 1986, pp. 45–48.
13. ————, "Women-owned Companies," *Inc.,* January 1987, p. 11.
14. Joel Kotkin, "The Reluctant Entrepreneurs," *Inc.,* September 1986, pp. 81–86.
15. Ibid, p. 82.
16. Linda Watkins, "Minority Entrepreneurs Venturing into Broader Range of Businesses," *The Wall Street Journal,* 25 March, 1987, p. 33.
17. Christine Dugas and Kenneth Dreyfack, "A Gaffe at Revlon Has the Black Community Seething," *Business Week,* 9 February, 1987, pp. 36–37.
18. ————, "The Spirit," *Inc.,* July 1985, 90–91.
19. Joel Kotkin, "The Hottest Entrepreneur in America Is . . . the 'Smart Team' at Compaq Computer," *Inc.,* February 1986, pp. 48–56.
20. Teresa Carson, Debra Michals, and Laurie Baum, "Honey, What Do You Say We Start Our Own Company?" *Business Week,* September 15, 1986, pp. 115–118.
21. Nancy Madlin, "The Venture Survey," *Venture,* October 1985, p. 24.
22. Curtis Hartman, "Main Street Inc.," *Inc.*, June 1986, pp. 49–58.
23. Ibid., p. 54.
24. Sallie Hofmeister and Jeff Shear, "The Trade Secrets Trap," *Venture,* June 1987, pp. 53–55.
25. Scott Vitell and Troy Festervand, "Business Ethics: Conflicts, Practices and Beliefs of Industrial Executives," *Journal of Business Ethics,* 6 (1987):111–122.
26. Richard DeGeorge, *Business Ethics* (New York: Macmillan, 1986).

CHAPTER 2

Selecting the Business

Learning Objectives

After you have read this chapter, you will be able to do the following:

- Examine the background of people who choose to become self-employed.
- Study the self-employment decision-making process.
- Learn how people choose the right business.
- Learn how markets can be analyzed to determine the need for new products and businesses.
- Learn how to identify trends that signal demand for new products or services.

"Cutting loose," "taking the plunge," "going for it," "breaking away," are all phrases used to describe someone who has decided to leave a company and start his or her own business. In the last chapter we concluded that anyone could make this decision and start a business but that half to three-quarters of these entrepreneurs would ultimately be unsuccessful. In this chapter we will examine the process of deciding to become self-employed, and we will discuss some of the characteristics of those who have made the decision.

Once people decide to become self-employed, they must choose the right business for them and then determine if there is a genuine need for that business. Too many fledgling entrepreneurs bypass the crucial market analysis process in their haste to open their business. They believe that "if I like handmade chocolates, or imported wines, or designer clothes, or personalized stationery, then so does everyone else, and my business will be a success." Unfortunately, that kind of thinking is flawed, and the only way to find out if others like the same products you do is to thoroughly analyze the market. In this chapter we will discuss the methods most commonly used to determine if there *really* is demand for a particular product or service.

Finally, we will look at some businesses that are currently popular and try to predict what new businesses are likely to become popular in the next decade. It is, after all, those entrepreneurs who anticipate new trends and are prepared to cater to new whims and demands who become rich and famous. There is also the possibility of misinterpreting trends and developing a new concept, product, or service that is not needed or accepted. If that happens, the entrepreneur fails and must begin all over again.

BECOMING SELF-EMPLOYED

If there are approximately 1.5 million startups each year, then at least that number of new business owners had to be created. Where did they come from, and how are they different from those who chose to remain in the employment of someone else? It is far easier to ask than to answer those questions. In fact, it is almost impossible to develop an accurate profile of the man or woman who decides to open a new business. In Chapter 1 we discussed some of the characteristics (education, gender, health, etc.) of entrepreneurs; therefore, we will not dwell on them again in this chapter. However, it is important to examine the age requirement or restrictions encountered by entrepreneurs.

How Old Are New-Venture Creators?

There are no age requirements for entrepreneurs; however, some research indicates that most people begin their own business between the ages of twenty-five and forty-five (see Figure 2.1). By the time a person is twenty-five, he or she should have acquired the experience necessary to operate a business, and when a person passes forty-five he or she has so many responsibilities and commitments that it is difficult to leave the security of a company to start a new business. As with so many rules, there are numerous exceptions to this one.

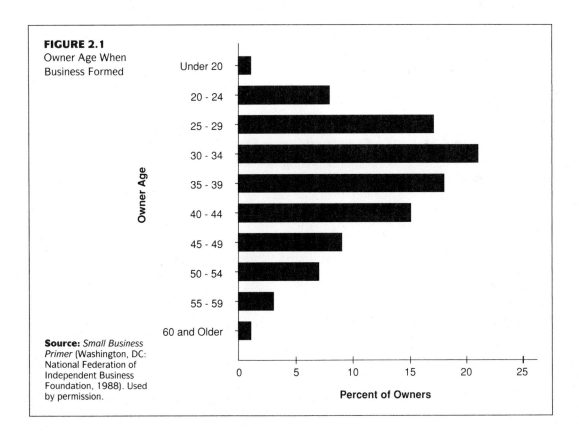

FIGURE 2.1
Owner Age When Business Formed

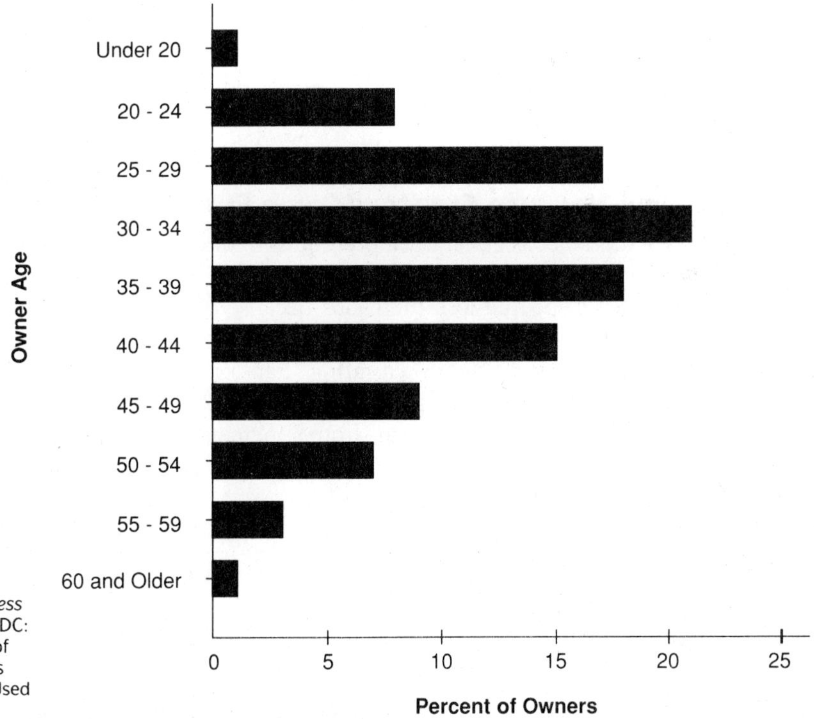

Source: *Small Business Primer* (Washington, DC: National Federation of Independent Business Foundation, 1988). Used by permission.

2-1 *The Inside View*

OLDER ENTREPRENEURS

Jacob E. Goldman, now sixty-five years old, retired from Ford Motor Co. and decided that he was not ready for a life of travel and leisure. He used business contacts to launch Cauzin Systems Inc., which was incorporated in 1984. The Waterbury, Connecticut, company makes a device that encodes data on strips of paper and an optical scanner that reads and enters the data into a personal computer. Goldman, who has a 10 percent share of Cauzin, claims it took him only two weeks to raise $750,000. "I called up people who knew me and who thought I would never back something I didn't believe in." Goldman avoided venture capitalists because he claims that "they just couldn't see a revolutionary idea."[1]

Thousands of people younger than twenty-five and older than forty-five have created successful new ventures. Many people who have worked for years with one or more companies retire and find that they are bored. They miss the excitement and activity of the business world, so they decide to start their own business (see The Inside View 2-1).

Where Do New-Venture Creators Come From?

Since experience is generally a prerequisite for opening a business, very few new venture creators start their own business without first having worked for someone else. Thousands of people lose their jobs because of layoffs, terminations, or forced early retirement as a result of corporate restructuring and mergers. Many of these people opt for a business of their own rather than for another job with a different company. James Challenger, a Chicago placement specialist, says 16 percent of fired executives are now starting businesses, up from 7 percent in 1987. Many managers are unsuccessful business owners because they do not anticipate the hours, stress, and funding demands of a new venture.[2]

Why Do Entrepreneurs Leave Their Employers?

We know that most people who start their own business have previously worked for another company. There are many reasons for a person to finally make the decision to break away and start his or her own business. Interviews with seventy-seven entrepreneurs whose businesses provided personal annual incomes in excess of $90,000 revealed that quite a few of them had quit their jobs to go into business for themselves because:

- They felt victimized by their employers.
- They did not want to have to justify their ideas to superiors.
- They did not fear failure but used it as a source of motivation.
- They were very self-confident and competitive.
- They enjoyed their businesses, so that work and pleasure blended together.
- They were individuals who thrived on risk and would begin new businesses when the old ones were profitable but thrill-free.
- They were open to all kinds of new ideas.
- They were reluctant to seek outside help, mainly because they truly enjoyed solving business problems themselves.
- They were convinced that most people didn't know what the hell they were doing.
- They believed their businesses were unique and that no one else truly understood them.[3]

When asked why they left their employers to start their own businesses, most entrepreneurs almost always cited independence and excitement as primary reasons. However, there are other valid reasons for starting a business; among them are the following:

1. ***A new invention.*** Frequently, a person invents or discovers a new product, service, or process that can best be exploited by starting a business to produce or sell it.

2. ***Ability to do it better than the boss.*** Many employees realize that their bosses are not the most capable people in the world. They reason that if the boss can make money with his or her limited ability, then "I can make more because I have more ability, drive, etc."

3. ***Challenge.*** Many people have the uncontrollable urge to prove to themselves and others that they can create something and operate it profitably.

4. ***Financial reward.*** Although most entrepreneurs do not consider cash accumulation to be terribly important, they do acknowledge that the prospect of earning a sizable income is appealing.

5. ***Social responsibility.*** Some entrepreneurs are genuinely socially responsible. They want to start a business that will create jobs and allow them to contribute to the welfare of their community.

6. ***Desire to build a legacy.*** Some entrepreneurs need to leave something "great" to their heirs.

SHOULD YOU START A BUSINESS?

We have provided a sample entrepreneurial test (see Chapter 1) and some generalizations about the people who start new businesses and why. In this section we will provide some other variables that should be evaluated by anyone seriously considering the creation of a new business. Since some of these variables are treated in more detail in subsequent chapters, we will simply introduce them and briefly discuss them in this chapter.

What Skills Do You Have?

Most of us mistakenly believe that we can do almost anything we truly want to do. Each person has strengths and limitations that need to be cataloged in order to determine if self-employment is appropriate. (An Entrepreneur's Checklist has been included at the end of this chapter to help you decide if self-employment is appropriate).

How Much Money Can You Invest?

It is virtually impossible to start a new business without committing personal funds to the venture. Friends, relatives, and certainly profit-making lending sources expect

FIGURE 2.2
Personal Financial Statement

______________________, 19____

Assets		
Cash		$__________
Savings accounts		__________
Stocks, bonds, other securities		__________
Accounts/Notes receivable		__________
Life insurance cash value		__________
Rebates/Refunds		__________
Autos/Other vehicles		__________
Real estate		__________
Vested pension plan/Retirement accounts		__________
Other assets		__________
	TOTAL ASSETS	$__________
Liabilities		
Accounts payable		$__________
Contracts payable		__________
Notes payable		__________
Taxes		__________
Real estate loans		__________
Other liabilities		__________
	TOTAL LIABILITIES	$__________
Total Assets	$__________	
Less Total Liabilities	−$__________	
	NET WORTH	$__________

you to commit all available funds to a project before they will lend any money to the business. Before even considering self-employment, you need to know how much you are worth. (See Figure 2.2 for a sample personal financial statement.)

Computing personal net worth gives you an idea of the total money available if you chose to liquidate all your assets. Since few people are willing to sell their house, boat, car, etc., to finance a new business, the net worth figure is somewhat misleading. Cash flow, income minus expenses, is actually more important than net worth.

What Is Your Cash Flow?

Unfortunately, too many entrepreneurs, eager to start and run their own business, forget that it will be several years before the company is profitable. They think that their new business will generate enough income to cover their monthly expenses. Taking a salary of a "draw" from a new business to cover living costs can doom the company to an early demise. To avoid bankrupting a new company, you should calculate your known income and expenses (see Figure 2.3). You may have income from your spouse, social security, or investments that will be needed to cover your basic expenses. Once you know how much money you have (net worth) and how much money you will need to live on (cash flow), you can decide if a startup is feasible.

FIGURE 2.3
Income and Living Expenses (Monthly)

Known Monthly Income			
1. Spouse's salary	_____	18. Life insurance	_____
2. Investment income	_____	19. Homeowner's insurance	_____
3. Social security	_____	20. Auto insurance	_____
4. Retirement income	_____	21. Medical insurance	_____
5. Other income	_____	22. Car payments	_____
6. Total Income	_____	23. Other debt	_____
Known Monthly Expenses		*Discretionary Expenses*	
7. Mortgage/rent	_____	24. Vacation	_____
8. Utilities	_____	25. Gifts	_____
9. Home repairs	_____	26. Charitable contributions	_____
10. Food and meals	_____	27. Professional fees	_____
11. Telephone	_____	28. Other	_____
12. School expenses	_____	29. Total Expenses	_____
13. Transportation	_____	(Subtract line 29 from 6.)	
14. Child care	_____		
15. Medical expenses	_____	30. First-Year Deficit or Surplus	_____
16. Clothing	_____	(Multiply line 29 by 12.)	
17. Personal	_____		

SELECTING THE RIGHT BUSINESS

For most people, selecting the business that best suits them is not a very difficult task. They simply decide to start a business with which they are familiar and in which they have worked for someone else. As we mentioned earlier, people often leave their employer because they feel that they can operate a similar business more profitably. For those entrepreneurs, the selection of their new business is a foregone conclusion. However, there are other entrepreneurs who know that they want to be self-employed but are not sure what kind of business to start. In this section we will examine some of the factors that should be considered by entrepreneurs trying to decide what business "fits" them best.

Business Growth

When selecting a new business, it is often easier to eliminate those that are inappropriate than it is to finally zero in on the correct choice. A good way to begin the elimination process is to check the past growth patterns of different businesses and, more important, to predict future growth. The following are the businesses most likely to grow significantly through the year 2000:

Commercial savings banks
Electronic component manufacturers
Paperboard container manufacturers
Computer and office machine manufacturers
Miscellaneous paper product manufacturers
Miscellaneous plastic product manufacturers
Basic steel manufacturers
Pharmaceutical manufacturers
Communication equipment manufacturers
Partition and fixture manufacturers[4]

While industry growth may provide some guidance as to what type of business to start, it is not an infallible indicator. For example, beauty shops, which grew by 153 percent from 1979 to 1984, have a notoriously high mortality rate. Growth rate is one helpful indicator, but it should be used in conjunction with other indicators.

Barriers to Entry

Another variable to consider is how difficult it is to enter a particular industry or occupation. Successful companies tend to erect barriers that block entry into their industry by other new companies. Sometimes these barriers can virtually block entry by any new firms, whereas in other instances, they may simply make entry more difficult. Harvard professor Michael Porter has identified the following six major barriers to entry:

Economies of Scale. Since economies of scale allow firms to reduce their unit costs, new entrants must have large facilities to be able to compete with entrenched companies. Established companies can reduce their prices to a point where new firms simply cannot match them.

Product Differentiation. Advertising, customer service, and exposure enable established companies to gain so much product recognition that it becomes difficult for new firms to compete with them with lesser-known products or brand names. Differentiation bars entry by forcing new companies to spend heavily to gain enough name recognition for them to take customers from the competition.

Capital Requirements. Some industries cannot be entered because the capital requirements are excessive. New firms would have difficulty raising sufficient capital to be competitive.

Switching Costs. "Switching costs" is the term applied to the one-time expense incurred by customers when they change from one supplier to another. If these costs are high, they constitute an effective barrier to entry for new firms.

Access to Distribution Channels. In some industries, established companies can so monopolize or dominate desirable distribution channels that new entrants cannot effectively distribute their products.

Cost Disadvantages Independent of Scale. Established companies enjoy cost advantages not related to scale, among them:

- Proprietary product knowledge (patents, copyrights, etc.)
- Favorable access to raw materials
- Favorable locations
- Government subsidies
- Learning or experience curve[5]

These barriers are not completely impenetrable; however, anyone planning to enter an industry with strong barriers would need much capital, an experienced management team, and many influential connections. For the average entrepreneur, industries with few or no barriers would be more appealing. The following are some businesses that can be started by someone with a little capital and some talent:

Lawn care	Baby-sitting
Bartending	Piano instruction
Equipment rental	Consulting
Appliance repair	Home painting
Flower decorating	Newsletters

While these businesses are easy to start, they have very little growth potential. To start a business that will grow and be profitable, entrepreneurs should select one that requires more startup capital and entails more risk. It would also be wise to choose a business that has high survivability potential. The following businesses are most likely to survive:

Veterinary services	Campgrounds and trailer parks
Funeral services	Medical practices
Dental practices	Barbershops
Commercial savings banks	Bowling and billiards establishments
Hotels and motels	Cash grain crops[6]

Selection Information

For the entrepreneur looking for the right kind of business, there are numerous sources of information on the advantages of different businesses. One of the most complete, and least expensive, sources is the Small Business Administration. For a nominal cost, the SBA will provide anyone with literally hundreds of pamphlets covering virtually all aspects of choosing, starting, and managing a small business. The following is a brief list of some available pamphlets which describe specific businesses:

0101 Building Service Contracting
0104 Radio–Television Repair Shop
0105 Retail Florists
0107 Hardware Store or Home Centers
0111 Sporting Goods Store
0112 Dry Cleaning
0114 Cosmetology
0115 Pest Control
0130 Fish Farming
0138 Home Furnishings
0142 Ice Cream
0150 Solar Energy

Initiating Entrepreneurs

In the preceding chapter, we briefly discussed the difference between initiating and imitating entrepreneurs. In this section, we will see how each decides which business is right for her or him. For the initiating entrepreneur, the right business is one developed around a new product, service, or process created through his or her innovative efforts. Not all entrepreneurs are innovators, and not all innovators are entrepreneurs; however, many innovative people do start and manage companies that market their own creations. Innovators have characteristics that differentiate them from other people. The following are skills usually possessed by innovators:

1. ***Innovators are opportunity oriented.*** Innovators are quick to take advantage of all opportunities. They search for unsolved problems, market inefficiencies, and unsatisfied needs of present and potential customer groups.

2. ***Innovators are strategists.*** Innovators have well-defined goals and objectives which are modified when necessary. They also have well-developed but flexible plans to achieve their goals and objectives.

3. ***Innovators "unhook" their prejudices.*** Innovators tend not to be myopic or "rule-bound" in their search for new products or services. They are willing to try new tactics and approaches to problem solving and opportunity creation.

4. ***Innovators are trend spotters.*** Innovators constantly monitor change in order to spot opportunities before anyone else does. They have the uncanny ability to decipher information and predict where events are headed.

5. ***Innovators are idea-oriented.*** Innovators are constantly generating new ideas or looking for other peoples' ideas to "borrow" and apply in new ways.

6. ***Innovators rely on intuition.*** Innovators use their intuition as sort of a sixth sense to assess risks, spot emerging patterns of change, and make complex decisions.

7. ***Innovators are very persistent.*** Innovators do not know when to give up or abandon a project. They are willing to work diligently until their project is successful or they are totally convinced that it is likely to end in failure.

8. ***Innovators are resourceful.*** Innovators can "come up" with whatever they need to accomplish their goals. They are consummate "scroungers."

9. ***Innovators are feedback oriented.*** Innovators need to have friends, colleagues, customers, etc., tell them how they are doing. Feedback guides their decisions and allows them to avoid prejudices and blind spots.

10. ***Innovators are team builders.*** Realizing that they cannot succeed alone, innovators build teams or networks to accomplish their goals.[7]

Imitating Entrepreneurs

Initiating entrepreneurs may be the heroes of entrepreneurial folklore; however, it is imitating entrepreneurs who are the vast majority of new venture creators. These are the people who, rather than create new products or services, start familiar businesses to meet a perceived market need. Imitating entrepreneurs create new restaurants, clothing stores, personnel agencies, appliance stores, etc., because there is a need for such establishments in their market area. In some instances, imitating entrepreneurs find new products (ones they have not invented) to manufacture and/or market. The following list of the ten most frequently started businesses demonstrates that most new ventures are created by imitating entrepreneurs:

Miscellaneous business services
Eating and drinking establishments
Miscellaneous shopping goods
Automotive repair shops
Residential construction
Machinery and equipment wholesalers
Real-estate operators
Miscellaneous retail stores
Furniture and furnishings retailers
Computer and data-processing services[8]

MARKET ANALYSIS

Once the "right" business has been selected, the next step in the startup process is to determine if there is any need for the product or service being offered. Unfortunately, too many eager entrepreneurs skip this step because they "know" that there is a need for the product. We often hear would-be entrepreneurs justify the need for their business with the following types of statements: "Since I like (product), everyone else will too"; "if (person) can make money selling (product), I know I can too"; "since there is no store selling (product) in my town, there must be a real need for one"; or "my (product) will be much better than anyone else's, so customers will abandon the competition and buy from me." The new business failure rate would be reduced significantly if more market analysis were done and if entrepreneurs would not ignore the results of the analysis.

When evaluating the market, the following questions suggested by William Osgood need to be answered:

1. Who exactly is your market?
2. What is the present size of the market?
3. What share of the market can you expect to have?
4. Does the market have growth potential?
5. Will your share of the market grow proportionally with overall market growth?
6. How will you satisfy your market?
7. How will you attract and keep this market?

8. How much will your product or service cost?
9. Will your price be competitive?
10. Why will customers pay your price?
11. What special advantages will you offer that could justify a higher price?[9]

Determining the existence of a need for a particular product or service in a specific market can be a time-consuming and costly process, but it is worth the time and the expense if it keeps unneeded businesses from being started. The market analysis depicted in Figure 2.4 should be conducted by all entrepreneurs considering a business startup. Entrepreneurs who have neither the time nor the ability to conduct such an analysis should pay someone else to do it for them (see The Inside View 2-2).

Objective of the Study

Is there "room" in the existing market for another business? This is the essential question that needs to be answered before an entrepreneur decides to start a new business. For the initiating entrepreneur, this question is more difficult to answer because he or she needs to do more research than the imitating entrepreneur needs to do. The initiating entrepreneur needs to do a product feasibility study as well as an analysis of potential demand for the product. Potential customers are shown a prototype or mock-up of the new product and are asked if they "might" buy it at a given price. A complete product feasibility study is quite complicated and beyond the scope of this book. We will concentrate on the market study needed by anyone who wants to start an "imitative" business.

FIGURE 2.4
Market Analysis

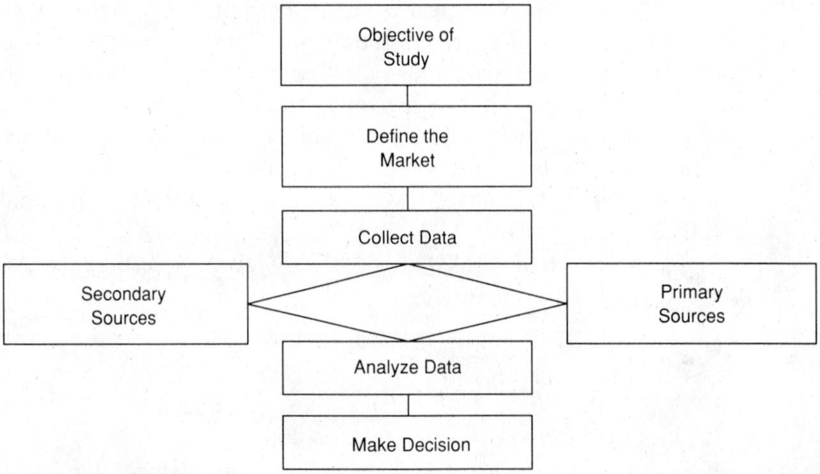

2-2 *The Inside View*

MARKET ANALYSIS COMPANIES

Market research has always been an industry in which connections and credibility have counted more for an entrepreneur than startup capital. But not anymore. "In the past this was not a capital-intensive industry," says Judy Corson, the partner and co-founder of Custom Research Inc., a firm that does market research for other companies. Because of the growing demand for market research, entrepreneurial firms continue to exploit the market even without expensive technology. The number of firms worldwide reached 1,160 in 1985, compared to 840 in 1980.[10]

Market Definition

The first step in the market analysis for a new business deals with market definition. Basically, the entrepreneur should identify both the geographic market and the customers he or she wishes to attract. For most startups, a city or portions of a city will be the intended geographic market; however, some startups may expect to cater to customers in larger areas, such as counties, states, or even several states. One mistake made by many people starting a business is to define too large a geographic market. It is wiser and safer to start small and then expand. A person planning to open a retail business, for example, should make sure that he or she can satisfy the needs of customers within a few blocks of the establishment before contemplating franchising agreements.

Once the geographic market has been defined, the next step is to identify the target customers. Eager entrepreneurs often claim that "everyone is my customer." This approach to the market is dangerous and often leads to business failure.

Consumers can be segmented in the following ways:

By Geography. We have already mentioned the desirability of defining a market geographically. For a local business, that task is rather simple, but what about the person who wants to start a mail-order business? Mail-order businesses may attract customers from throughout the country; therefore, an owner of such a business would need to be aware of regional preferences and peculiarities of potential customers.

By Demographics. The demographics (age, income, sex, etc.) of the target customers should be compiled and used as a basis for determining what particular customers need or want. Following is some demographic information that could prove helpful to anyone considering a startup:

Age	Purchasing habits
Income	Special interests
Education	Homeowner or renter
Sex	Eating preferences
Race	Leisure-time activities
Religion	Vacation preferences
Hobbies	Make of car owned
Marital status	Number and kinds of pets
Number of children	Occupation

By Psychographics. A relatively new market segmentation technique, psychographics groups people according to attitudes, life-styles, interests, or other personality characteristics. This approach to market segmentation is most useful when used in conjunction with the more traditional demographic approach.

By Benefit. Categorizing people by the benefits they expect to receive from a product is another way of effectively segmenting the market. For example, some people buy automobiles to "impress" others, some buy them to "get from one point to another," while others may buy a car for the thrill they get from driving. Knowing what people want from particular products makes it easier to better define the most appropriate target market.

Data Collection

Once the market has been defined geographically and by customer, it is time to begin the data-collection process. People considering a startup should be primarily concerned with needs, buying habits, etc., of the customers in their defined market; however, national and regional data can also be quite helpful. National and specific market information comes mainly from two sources, primary and secondary. Secondary sources are those containing information that has been already recorded (books, magazines, government documents, special reports, etc.). Primary information is gathered specifically for a person or group of people who need it to facilitate decision making.

Secondary Sources of Information. As soon as the market has been identified, entrepreneurs should go straight to their local libraries and plan to spend many days examining its contents. There are numerous books about all kinds of products and businesses as well as books that contain invaluable reams of statistical and demographic data. There are also many helpful business periodicals, among the more useful of which are: *Forbes, Inc., Business Week, The Harvard Business Review, Venture, Journal of Business Venturing,* and *Entrepreneur.* There are also numerous other periodicals that provide information about specific businesses or products.

There are other secondary sources of information that should be utilized. We present only a few such sources in this section because there are bibliographies that catalog all, or nearly all, available secondary sources. The following are some of the better known sources of secondary information:

1. ***Small Business Administration.*** As we mentioned earlier, the SBA is the principal government repository of small business information. It has numerous books, pamphlets, and other publications, which are either free or available for a nominal fee.

2. ***Robert Morris Associates (RMA).*** RMA publishes the Annual Statement Series, which is updated each year to provide accurate financial information. The Annual Statement Series contains financial information such as income statements, balance sheets, and key financial ratios on approximately a thousand industries.

3. ***Dun & Bradstreet.*** This organization publishes several guides and studies that provide key financial information about industries and individual companies.

4. ***Encyclopedia of Associations.*** This book lists associations, their addresses, and descriptions of their scope, activities, and publications.

5. ***Census of Population.*** This document, published by the Department of Commerce, contains demographic data for the entire nation.

6. ***Survey of Buying Power.*** This source contains information on population, households, income, retail sales, and merchandise line sales for the nation, states, and smaller geographic areas.

7. ***Statistical Abstract of the United States.*** This document contains data on population, vital statistics, labor force, income, prices, power, mining, and many other subjects.

8. ***The Small Business Reporter.*** This series, published by Bank of America, provides information on such topics as buying and selling businesses, acquiring financing, etc.

9. ***National Federation of Independent Business (NFIB).*** This association of approximately 500,000 businesspeople can provide a wealth of information about starting a business.

10. ***The Chamber of Commerce.*** Local chambers can supply data on consumer buying preferences, sales figures, population, income, and general business conditions.

11. ***City Hall.*** This is the place to go for traffic studies, new business startups, license requirements, and other important local information.

Primary Sources of Information. Primary information comes from the potential customer, other businesses, the competition, and personal observation. Basically, the entrepreneur asks questions that are designed to provide enough information to determine whether the business should be started or abandoned. (In some instances, it might be advisable to hire a professional to design and administer the questionnaire, and to organize and interpret the data.) Designing a questionnaire that will provide the needed information is the first step in collecting primary information. The following are some suggestions for developing an effective questionnaire:

1. Questions should be short and easily understandable. Respondents tend to ignore long questions or those that are ambiguous.
2. Questions should be easy to answer. Research indicates that yes/no questions are

most often answered by respondents; however, if this type of question doesn't provide enough information, then more involved questions may be appropriate.

3. Questions should be understandable to a variety of people.
4. Questions should not be offensive or insulting. People tend to stop answering questions as soon as they encounter an offensive or insulting question.
5. Be honest with the intent of the questionnaire. People should clearly understand the purpose of the questionnaire and how the results will be used.
6. Questions should not give the respondent an idea of the expected or preferred answer.
7. Questionnaires should be brief. Few people are willing to spend the time answering more than two or three pages of questions.

Once the questionnaire has been designed, the entrepreneur needs to decide how it should be administered. The most common methods of questioning people are: in person, by telephone, or by mail. Each of these methods is used, with varying degrees of success, by people considering a startup. Sometimes the most useful information can be gathered by using a combination of survey techniques. Before deciding which technique to use, an entrepreneur should examine the advantages and disadvantages of each (see Table 2.1).

Data Analysis

After information has been collected from both primary and secondary sources, it needs to be analyzed. Entrepreneurs who do their own data collection often accumulate more data than they need. They also collect some data that can be misleading or confusing. In the analysis process, it is necessary to identify inapplicable and misleading information. For example, incomplete questionnaires, outdated survey reports, and demographic data for other markets should be discarded. The data that are determined to be germane should be carefully studied and evaluated by the entrepreneur who must decide what the information is "telling" her or him.

The Decision

All of the preceding activities lead to the fateful moment when the "go/no go" decision must be made. At this point the entrepreneur must decide if all the analyzed data suggest starting the new business or abandoning the idea and going back to the drawing board. We do not mean to make it sound as though this is a simple decision, because it is not. Often the information collected is confusing, inconclusive, or even intentionally misleading (see The Inside View 2-3) forcing the entrepreneur to make a decision based on "gut feel."

We also know many people who ignored very conclusive market data and proceeded with their business because they "know the information is wrong," and anyway, "this is the business I always wanted to operate." There are also entrepreneurs who will repeat the analysis, looking for "new" evidence that will justify their decision to start their own business. Finally, it is possible to get misleading results because the people questioned did not know how to use the product or service being tested (see The Inside View 2-4).

2-3

The Inside View

MISLEADING MARKET ANALYSIS

In 1967, Wilson Harrell learned that Proctor & Gamble intended to enter a potentially lucrative niche in spray cleaners, which it previously considered to be too small to bother about. Harrell controlled most of the spray-cleaner market with his product Formula 409, which was produced by a struggling company he had purchased four years earlier for $30,000. Determined not to give up without a fight, Harrell learned that P&G's first assault would be a market test in Denver. Orders for Formula 409 were not refilled; the product was quietly withdrawn from the Denver market; and support advertising was discontinued. P&G failed to detect Harrell's ploy and sank millions of dollars into a national launch based on the fantastic results of its market test. Just before the launch started, Harrell overstocked store shelves with a discount offer customers couldn't refuse. Customers quickly bought enough Formula 409 to last them for six months. When P&G's product reached the stores, customers were not in the market for spray cleaners. Confused by the contradictory results of the market test and the launch, P&G withdrew from the market, losing about $25 million. In 1971, Harrell sold Formula 409 to P&G rival Clorox for $7.5 million and moved on to other ventures.[11]

2-4

The Inside View

PRODUCT MISUSE

Senator Phil Gramm (R, Texas) was called to the White House, where President Reagan showed him a new postage stamp honoring him and senators Rudman and Hollings for their budget-deficit-reducing Gramm–Rudman–Hollings Bill. The President informed Senator Gramm that the law required the stamp to be field tested before it could be issued. Washington, DC, was selected as the test market, and a number of stamps were issued to area residents and workers. The new stamp failed its field test because it would not stick to envelopes. Senator Gramm learned that the stamp would not stick because local bureaucrats were spitting on the wrong side.[12]

Table 2.1 Some Pros and Cons of Data-Collection Methods

	Personal		Telephone		Mail	
	Pros	*Cons*	*Pros*	*Cons*	*Pros*	*Cons*
Sampling accuracy	Easiest to develop representative samples. Best for completion rates.	Usually necessary to cluster interviews for cost efficiency. Intercept studies subject to bias in respondent selection.	Cost efficient not to cluster interviews by area.	Limited to telephone owner households.	Cost efficient not to cluster interviews by area. Easy to obtain sample dispersion.	Nonpanel surveys result in greater nonresponse. If panel, limited to those who agree to panel membership. Information may come from other household members.
Information requirements	Best for obtaining large amounts of information if done in respondent's home.	Intercept interviews may be hurried and dilute information quality.	Intermediate amount of information when calls are made at convenient times.	More difficult to obtain unstructured information. Limited use for collecting complex data.	Interview not rushed and can reflect thoughtful report.	Variable amount of information, depending on topic and the amount of respondent effort required. Limited use for collection of complex data. Not appropriate for questions that need spontaneous response.

Administration of instrument	Can present visual materials. Good for presentation of experimental tasks.	Interviewer-cheating problems.	Central location validation highly accurate through monitoring. Better controls over interviewer performance.	Visual materials cannot be presented.	No briefing of interviewers required.	Lack of control over who actually answers questionnaire.
Quality of response	Better response available because of exposure to higher-quality stimuli.	Strong potential for bias because of interviewer.	Best for obtaining reliable, spontaneous responses to standardized questions and phrasing.	Moderate potential for bias because of interviewer effect.	Anonymity helps to assure accuracy for sensitive topics.	Potential for error because of respondent confusion.
Timing	Relatively fast way to collect data.	Weather conditions can cause difficulty and delay.	Fastest way to collect data.	Capacity overload problems can cause delays.	Relative timing improves when mail is used for samples difficult to access.	Slowest way to collect data.

SOURCE: Melvin Prince, *Consumer Research for Management Decisions* (New York: John Wiley & Sons, 1982), pp. 13–14. Used by permission.

Business success is more likely if the startup decision is based on sound, objective, and reliable market research rather than solely on "gut-feel" or emotionalism.

BUSINESS TRENDS

Entrepreneurs who are likely to be most successful are those who can "spot" trends and start new businesses related to those trends. The person who markets a new product or service first is able to earn substantial profits while the competition catches up. Spotting or predicting trends is a risky proposition, and not very many people are successful at it; however, the following steps should improve an entrepreneur's trend-spotting ability:

1. Audit your information intake: Cut down on mental "junk food."
2. Rekindle your sense of awe: Don't be jaded or blasé.
3. Be constantly observant and inquisitive.
4. Ask questions.
5. Adopt the methods of full-time, professional trend-watchers.
6. Make your reading time count: Read on airplanes, in the doctor's office, etc.
7. Develop a system to organize information: Establish an easy-to-use file system, etc.
8. Monitor other information-rich media such as TV and radio.[13]

Innovative Businesses

Unfortunately, we have limited trend-spotting ability; therefore, we present in this section the following examples of recently opened "innovative" businesses that may be trendsetters (as reported in issues of *Inc.*, *Venture*, or *Business Week*):

- Tracy Brash and Michael Beyries founded Enfant Riant (French for "laughing child") to grow, process, and sell snails (escargot). The snails are sold in 7.5-ounce cans for $7 to $9 in 400 retail outlets in 44 states.
- Matthew Toia, D.V.M., has distinguished his animal hospital, the South Weymouth Animal Care Center, South Weymouth, Massachusetts, from other pet clinics by implementing a sort of animal insurance system—a health maintenance organization (HMO) for pets.
- Sharlyne Powell and Sharon McConnell started Women at Large to operate and franchise fitness programs for "large and extra-large" women.
- C. J. Rapp founded Jolt Co. to produce and bottle Jolt cola, a drink with "all the sugar and twice the caffeine."
- The Golf Center, a 23,000-square-foot indoor golf range started by Stephen Campbell, allows members to practice their drives, sharpen their putts, and chip their way out of sand traps without worrying about the weather.
- Elliot Clarke, a former senior vice president of Morgan Guaranty Trust Co., is now a deer farmer in Millbrook, New York. His neighbors are losing money on sheep and cattle, but he claims that raising deer is the only profitable form of farming he knows.

Miscellaneous Businesses. The following is an abbreviated list of entrepreneurial businesses and their associated startup costs[14] (see the *Venture* article for all 100 startups):

Business	*Cost*
Video Postcard	$1,650,000
Used Computers	345,000
Two-way Envelopes	2,000,000
Sugarless Popcorn	100,000
Picture Phones	2,000,000
His and Her Lingerie	50,000
Magazine on a Disk	49,000
Laser Encyclopedia	750,000
Airborne Limos	260,000
Bingo Newsletter	5,000
Bedside Computers	3,000,000
Medical Imaging	800,000
Foiling Video Pirates	350,000
Soccer Scores	250,000
On-line Yellow Pages	110,000
Mini Medical Labs	197,000
No-Drill Dentistry	8,500,000
Cash for Trash	133
Trade Shows Ahoy	100,000
Health Spa for Dogs	20,000

Summary

New-venture creators cannot be stereotyped. They are male or female, young or old, minority or white, educated or uneducated, urban or rural, and experienced or inexperienced. Many people arrive at the decision to start a business because they are dissatisfied with their jobs. They believe that they, not their employer, should benefit from their hard work and sacrifice. The following are other valid reasons for starting a business: a new invention; ability to do it better than the boss; challenge; social responsibility; and the need to build a legacy.

After deciding to become self-employed, the entrepreneur should select the "right" business to start. The entrepreneur should review published failure and success statistics, study the barriers to entry in different industries, and try to decide what kind of business he or she would find the most appealing. Perhaps the most reliable way to choose the best business would be to answer the question "What kind of work affords me the most fun and satisfaction?" After all, work should be enjoyable as well as financially rewarding.

Entrepreneurs should select enjoyable and rewarding businesses; however, they must also make sure that there is a real need for the business they select. Market analysis can indicate if a genuine need for the proposed product or service exists. Answers to the following questions can indicate whether the business should be started or abandoned: Who exactly is your market? What share of the market can you expect to have? Will the market continue to grow? How will you attract and keep this market? How much will your product or service cost? Will your price be competitive?

Information for the market analysis comes from both secondary and primary sources. Some secondary sources include the following: the Small Business Administration, Robert Morris Associates, Dun & Bradstreet, Statistical Abstract of the United States, the Chamber of Commerce, and City Hall. Primary information is collected from those people who are likely to be the firm's suppliers, competitors, and customers. This information can be collected by using well-developed questionnaires in personal, telephone, or mail interviews. Once the data have been analyzed, the entrepreneur can decide whether there really is a need for the product or whether a new business should be selected.

Assembling the Pieces

Choosing the Business and Analyzing the Market

Carol and Jacki wanted a full-time occupation, but they knew that they did not want to work for someone else. They owned and operated a very small company, the Charleston Spice Rack, which sold herbs and spices two days a week in the Charleston Market. Their customers were tourists, locals, and area restaurants. The company was successful; however, both Jacki and Carol wanted something bigger that would let them work all week rather than just on weekends.

To select the "best" business for them, Carol and Jacki had to determine what they liked to do. They knew that they wanted a food-related business because they were very interested in food and its preparation, and they already knew many people involved in other food-related businesses. Next, they studied the local market to find a neglected food-related niche. There were grocery stores, plenty of restaurants, two wine and cheese shops, restaurant supply stores, and shops that sold cooking utensils. However, there was no shop that specialized in a wide variety of gourmet foods such as coffee beans, imported wines and cheeses, specialty cooking utensils, imported olive oil, etc. Jacki and Carol had found their niche.

Once they decided on the kind of business that would be "best" for them, they began to test the market to determine if a genuine need for this type of shop existed. They talked to owners of similar shops in other cities to learn how they planned, promoted, and operated their businesses, and they gathered information on the kind of people who patronized gourmet shops. Having identified their target customers, Carol and Jacki began informally polling their friends and acquaintances to determine if a gourmet shop would succeed in the Charleston area. They also collected secondary information from the local chamber of commerce, city hall, and the library.

The final phase of market analysis involved the

creation of a focus group comprised of friends and food "experts." Group members discussed the pros and cons of the proposed business and made numerous suggestions and recommendations to Jacki and Carol. Finally, the group members completed a questionnaire developed by Carol and Jacki. All of the data collected and analyzed by Carol and Jacki convinced them that they had a viable business idea. They decided to proceed with the planning and designing of their gourmet food shop. ■

---

entrepreneur's checklist

SHOULD YOU START A BUSINESS?

Under each question, check the answer that says what you feel or comes closest to it. Be honest with yourself.

1. Are you a self-starter?
_____ I do things on my own. Nobody has to tell me to get going.
_____ If someone gets me started, I keep going all right.
_____ Easy does it. I don't put myself out until I have to.

2. How do you feel about other people?
_____ I like people. I can get along with just about anybody.
_____ I have plenty of friends—I don't need anyone else.
_____ Most people irritate me.

3. Can you lead others?
_____ I can get most people to go along when I start something.
_____ I can give the orders if someone tells me what we should do.
_____ I let someone else get things moving. Then I go along if I like it.

4. Can you take responsibility?
_____ I like to take charge of things and see them through.
_____ I'll take over if I have to, but I'd rather let someone else be responsible.
_____ There's always some eager beaver around wanting to show how smart he is. I say let him.

5. How good an organizer are you?
_____ I like to have a plan before I start. I'm usually the one to get things lined up when the group wants to do something.
_____ I do all right unless things get too confused. Then I quit.
_____ You get all set, and then something comes along and presents too many problems. So I just take things as they come.

6. How good a worker are you?
_____ I can keep going as long as I need to. I don't mind working hard for something I want.

_____ I'll work hard for a while, but when I've had enough, that's it.
_____ I can't see that hard work gets you anywhere.

7. Can you make decisions?
_____ I can make up my mind in a hurry if I have to. It usually turns out OK, too.
_____ I can if I have plenty of time. If I have to make up my mind fast, I think later I should have decided the other way.
_____ I don't like to be the one who has to decide things.

8. Can people trust what you say?
_____ You bet they can. I don't say things I don't mean.
_____ I try to be on the level most of the time, but sometimes I just say what's easiest.
_____ Why bother if the other fellow doesn't know the difference?

9. Can you stick with it?
_____ If I make up my mind to do something, I don't let anything stop me.
_____ I usually finish what I start—if it goes well.
_____ If it doesn't go OK right away, I quit. Why beat your brains out?

10. How good is your health?
_____ I never run down.
_____ I have enough energy for most things I want to do.
_____ I run out of energy sooner than most of my friends seem to.

Now count the checks you made.

How many checks are there beside the first answer to each question? _____
How many checks are there beside the second answer to each question? _____
How many checks are there beside the third answer to each question? _____

If most of your checks are beside the first answers, you probably have what it takes to run a business. If not, you're likely to have more trouble than you can handle by yourself. Better find a partner who is strong on the points you're weak on. If many checks are beside the third answer, not even a good partner will be able to shore you up.

Source: Checklist for Going into Business (Washington, DC: U.S. Small Business Administration, 1981).

Questions for Review and Discussion

1. What are some of the reasons for choosing to become self-employed?
2. Why do entrepreneurs leave their employers?
3. How can entrepreneurs select the "right" business?
4. What are the barriers that block entry to some industries?
5. What are the characteristics of innovators?
6. What are the sources of new products that can be manufactured and marketed by imitating entrepreneurs?
7. What is the purpose of market analysis?

8. What are some sources of secondary data?
9. What are the qualities of an effective questionnaire?
10. What can an entrepreneur do to become a better trend spotter?

Notes

1. Shelley Aspaklaria, "Startups After Sixty," *Venture* (September 1986), pp. 30–34.
2. ————, "Labor Letter," *The Wall Street Journal,* 24 May 1988, p. 1.
3. Carter Henderson, *Winners* (New York: Holt, Rinehart and Winston, 1985), pp. 13–14.
4. David Birch, "The Truth About Start-ups," *Inc.,* January 1988, pp. 14–15.
5. Michael Porter, *Competitive Strategy* (New York: The Free Press, 1980), pp. 7–12.
6. David Birch, "The Truth About Start-ups," pp. 14–15.
7. Dennis E. Waitley and Robert B. Tucker, *Winning the Innovation Game* (Old Tappan, NJ: Fleming H. Revell Co., 1986), pp. 40–41.
8. David Birch, "The Truth About Start-ups," pp. 14–15.
9. William Osgood, *Planning and Financing Your Business* (New York: Van Nostrand Reinhold, 1983), pp. 52–53.
10. Amy Saltzman, "Vision vs. Reality," *Venture,* October 1985, pp. 40–44.
11. Steven Solomon, *Small Business USA* (New York: Crown Publishers, Inc., 1986), pp. 15–16.
12. Senator Gramm, Speech to the Association for Private Enterprise Education, Atlanta, April 26, 1987.
13. Waitley and Tucker, *Winning the Innovation Game,* pp. 69–84.
14. Stephen Robinett, "Starting with an Idea," *Venture,* November 1985, pp. 38–80.

CHAPTER 3

Starting or Buying a Business

Learning Objectives

After you have read this chapter, you will be able to do the following:

- Consider the advantages and disadvantages of buying an established business.
- Examine methods of locating and evaluating prospective businesses to buy.
- Learn how to structure the purchase of a business.
- Consider the advantages and disadvantages of purchasing a franchise.
- Examine some available franchises.
- Consider the advantages and disadvantages of starting a business from scratch.

Making the decision to become self-employed marks the beginning of a long, complex process involving even more decisions, planning, and risk taking. Once entrepreneurs decide to "cut loose" and become their own boss, they need to select the type of business that is right for them. Having made these decisions, entrepreneurs then must decide whether they want to start a new business or buy an existing company that meets their needs. For the initiating entrepreneur, the decision will be to start a new business; however, imitating entrepreneurs may prefer to buy an operating business that has a "track record" of success and profitability.

Entrepreneurs have a third option, which minimizes the risk of failure even more. They can buy a franchise, which gives them the right to operate a Burger King, Midas Muffler, etc., in a specific territory. This option is probably not very attractive to the "die-hard" entrepreneur because there are usually too many "strings" attached to the franchise. The major decisions are made by the franchisor, with the franchisee acting primarily as the company's local representative. However, operating a franchise is more like being self-employed than working for someone else.

In this chapter we will examine the pros and cons of buying an established business, purchasing a franchise, and starting a business from scratch. We realize that every entrepreneur will choose the option that is right for him or her; however, since this book deals with the startup process, we will emphasize the "start-from-scratch" approach.

BUYING AN ESTABLISHED BUSINESS

For some entrepreneurs, the difficulties of starting a business from scratch are not worth the time and effort, and they are not willing to take the risk of failing in their new venture. These people might satisfy their need to be self-employed by buying someone else's business. While this method of becoming self-employed might be less risky than starting from scratch, it is by no means completely without risk. We will discuss some of the advantages and disadvantages of buying a business.

Advantages of Buying a Business

Perhaps the major advantage of buying an established business is that someone else has done all the hard work needed to get started: The market analysis has been done; licenses have been secured; the best site has been selected; etc. The new owner can just walk into the business and continue operations with no noticeable interruption. Other advantages include the following:

Time. Entrepreneurs are often in a hurry to achieve their goals and objectives. If they want to become self-employed in a hurry, they can buy a business and begin operations immediately.

Cost. Depending on the seller's motivations, it may be less expensive to get into the business by buying an established company than it would be to start from scratch. One caution to the buyer: If the deal appears to be too good to be true, it probably is. Do not buy a business just because it is inexpensive, but by the same token, do not pass up an opportunity to purchase at "below cost." It is possible to find some real bargains (see The Inside View 3-1).

3-1 *The Inside View*

BUYING UNDERPRICED BUSINESSES

Ronald C. Yanke's friends call him "Mr. Lucky" because, as one of his managers says, "Ron can fall in a barrel of manure and come up smelling like a rose." This is in reference to Mr. Yanke's apparent luck in purchasing underpriced businesses. Mr. Yanke relies on more than dumb luck when buying businesses, which he then turns over to others to manage on a day-to-day basis. The centerpiece of his expanding empire is a white-fir mill in Dinuba, California, which was losing money until he bought it in 1984 from then-bankrupt Wickes Co. Yanke has since acquired five other mills, also at fire-sale prices. After just two years, Yanke's consolidated companies, Sequoia Forest Industries, are "showing a good profit" on expected sales of $100 million.[1]

Initial Capital. In most cases, buying a business may not be significantly less expensive than starting from scratch; however, the amount of capital needed to become self-employed will be known. The buyer will not have to estimate or "guesstimate" the amount of initial capital needed.

Location. Established firms often have the best site because their founders had a wider choice of locations than that now available. There is a prime site in Charleston, South Carolina, which was a roast beef restaurant, then a barbecue restaurant, and now a Burger King. Each purchase demolished or significantly altered the existing building. The site, not the building, was valuable, especially to Burger King, which is now located across the street from McDonald's.

Inventory. The buyer of an established business does not have to order inventory or forecast what customers will buy and at what price. The previous owner should have gone through the trial-and-error phase of determining what will sell and what will not.

Personnel. As with inventory, the new buyer will not have to recruit, select, and train people to operate the business. The seller should have staffed the business with the best available employees.

Contracts and Licenses. An established business already has all the licenses required to operate legally, and contracts with landlords, suppliers, etc., should already be consummated and in effect.

Customers. Established businesses have already acquired a loyal customer base. The buyer does not have to do the marketing and promotion necessary to attract customers to a new business. The firm's mailing list and customer records can be a valuable asset to the new owner.

Image. A successful business can take several years to develop the positive image needed to perpetuate success and profitability. This image, sometimes referred to as goodwill or "going-concern" value, increases the new owner's chances of success.

Control Systems. The owner of an established business already has developed and installed accounting, financial, and record-keeping systems needed to ensure smooth business operations. The buyer, therefore, should need to do nothing more than "fine tune" the established systems.

Market Share. It might be possible to buy an established business that has a major share of its market. The buyer would not be overly concerned about other competitors "ruining" his or her new company. The buyer would also have fewer pricing and advertising concerns than he or she would have with a startup.

Credit. Owners of established businesses have already developed credit agreements with their financial sources, customers, and suppliers. Assuming that these agreements are satisfactory, a new buyer would merely have to reaffirm them.

Disadvantages of Buying a Business

What appear to be advantages can also be disadvantages. For example, the location may not be the best; the inventory may be outdated; the personnel could be inefficient; the lease and other contracts may not be favorable; etc. Other disadvantages include the following:

Lack of Challenge. Buying an established business does not afford entrepreneurs the challenge and excitement of starting a business that is exactly what they want. There is no ego gratification in owning a business that someone else created.

Misrepresentation. What you see is not always what you get. We don't mean to imply that sellers are dishonest, although there are those who are; however, few sellers will volunteer unfavorable information. Their position is that uncovering unfavorable information is the buyer's responsibility. Why should the seller point out the leaks in the roof, the questionable value of the accounts receivable, or the imminent departure of some key personnel? When it comes to purchasing an established business, caveat emptor (buyer beware) is still good advice.

Changing Conditions. Changing conditions, of which even the seller is unaware, could have an adverse effect on the business. For example, the area may be rezoned; there may be subtle population shifts; traffic patterns may be changed; or a major competitor might be entering the market. Any of these changes could have a devastating impact on even a successful business.

Prospective buyers should try to identify all of the possible advantages and disadvantages of a particular type of business. If, after careful evaluation, the advantages outweigh the disadvantages, the established business should be purchased. The next task is locating a suitable business that is for sale, or can be purchased (there is a difference).

Finding a Business to Buy

Having made the decision to buy a certain type of business, entrepreneurs need to find a suitable business to purchase. Locating a business that is for sale is not difficult, but all sources should be explored so that the "best" business can be identified. The following are some sources of information on businesses for sale:

Personal referrals
Landlords
Attorneys
Accountants
Bankers
SBA
Management consultants
Seller advertisements
Former employers
Shopping centers
Venture capitalists
Trade journals
Newspapers
Exchange meetings
Business counselors
Suppliers
Chamber of commerce
Acquaintances
Stockholders
Current employer
Bankruptcies
Brokers

While it is possible to find a suitable business from these sources, some experts suggest that it is better to buy a business that is not being offered for sale. To buy a not-for-sale business, entrepreneurs must locate a business that meets their needs, determine the "right" price, and then make the owner an offer. The owner may refuse to sell; however, if the price is attractive enough, he or she might decide the time is right to sell the business.

Business Brokers

Since many business purchases are now being handled by business brokers, it is important to know something about this relatively new occupation. Business brokers, who sell everything from the $50,000 liquor store to the $10-million computer firm, have doubled in number from 2,500 several years ago to about 5,000 today. Of the 500,000 businesses that were sold in 1986, 90 percent cost less than $5 million, and at least 25 percent of the transactions were handled by brokers. "The troubling point: Most of the broker-arranged deals were mishandled" maintains the Institute for Certified Business Counselors, a business broker trade group.[2]

Business brokerages are fairly unregulated, according to Raymond Thill, president of the International Business Brokers Association. He explains that anybody can hang out a shingle to buy and sell businesses. In some states, a real-estate license is required; however, even that is not a satisfactory means of validating brokers. Thill says there are several reasons why, as the number of business brokers goes up, membership in his association goes down. One reason is that "associations tend to compile statistics, to ask questions about sales volumes, commissions, and so forth."[3] For one man's search for a qualified broker see The Inside View 3-2.

Selecting the right broker requires patience and some skill. The following are some steps to take when selecting the "best" broker: Ask all the pertinent questions; find out how many sales he or she has made in the past; examine educational qualifi-

3-2 *The Inside View*

SEARCHING FOR A BROKER

Matt O'Connor, a 32-year-old former Big Eight CPA, started looking in 1982 for a small manufacturing company to buy. Over the next year, he spent countless hours talking to more than fifty brokers. O'Connor wanted to buy a company with sales under $5 million that would generate sufficient income to finance loans to cover the purchase price. When he called on several large business brokers, they told him his proposed deal fell below their minimum limit. Many of the smaller brokers he approached seemed baffled by his idea. In 1984 O'Connor did arrange to buy the twenty-employee Jebco Screw & Rivet Manufacturing Co. in Chicago—without a broker. Now he observes dryly, "There are a lot of brokers, and there are a few excellent ones."[4]

cations; ask for references; ask bankers about the broker's reputation; and, ask previous buyers and sellers about the broker. Investigation is necessary; however, entrepreneurs have the final responsibility for selecting the broker who will best represent their interest. Entrepreneurs should always be mindful of the fact that brokers' commissions are based on the selling price of the business; therefore, the higher the price, the larger the commission.

Reasons for Selling a Business

Regardless of who handles the purchase of the selected business or how it was located, prospective buyers need to determine why the firm is for sale. Uncovering the seller's motivation to sell his or her business will help determine the price that should be paid for the company. The greater the pressure on the seller to sell, the lower the price that should have to be paid for the business. John Stefanelli[5] suggests the following acceptable reasons for selling a business:

Tired of feeding the operation
Evaporation of tax shelter
Insufficient profits
Partnership dispute
Marital dispute
Death of working partner
Death of working spouse
Disinterested heirs
Illness
Other incapacity
Burnout
Retirement and desire for installment payments
Geographic relocation
Business expansion
Business consolidation
Demands of other business ventures
Fear of losing personal assets if the business is just beginning to lose money
Estate tax liability
Forced liquidation
Fear of impending competition
Lack of desire to do necessary remodeling
Fear of impending economic obsolescence
Shareholder dispute

What Is the Business Worth?

If the business that has been selected appears to be the right one and the seller's motives for selling are reasonable and legitimate, it is time to decide what the company is worth. The three basic ways to determine the value of a company are the comparison approach, cost approach, and discounted future-cash-flow approach.

Comparison Approach. This valuation method is perhaps the simplest to use and perhaps the least accurate. The business is compared to other similar businesses that have recently been sold to determine what the selling price should be. For example, if an entrepreneur were interested in purchasing a restaurant, he or she or his or her representative would look at the price recently paid for a similar restaurant and use that to establish the price of the restaurant considered.

Cost Approach. Using this method (also known as the "adjusted balance-sheet" approach), buyers or their representative would determine the present value of the assets, tangible and intangible, of the business and offer that amount to the owner for the purchase of the business. Some of the tangible assets that should be priced include the following:

Real estate (if not leased)
Lease agreements
Leasehold interests
Furniture, fixtures, and equipment
Accounts receivable (discounted for questionable accounts)
Prepaid expenses
Assumable licenses
Customer lists or records
Space available for sublease
Favorable supplier contracts
Seller training or assistance
Tax credits

There are also intangible assets, usually referred to as goodwill (discussed in the next section), which are included in the price of a business.

Discounted Future-Cash-Flow Approach. The price of a business is calculated from the present worth of future earnings. Earnings are projected over a period of five to ten years, at which time the business will still have value. Both the earnings and the value of the business after five or ten years are discounted to the present value, using a discount rate competitive with other capital investments of similar risk. The advantage of this approach is that the company's future, rather than its past is used to determine its value. The disadvantage, of course, is that no one can know what will happen in five or ten years.

Intangible Assets

There are intangible assets, such as patents, trademarks, goodwill, etc., that add to the cost of the business; however, goodwill is often the most difficult intangible asset to value. Goodwill, which is established over time, exists only in businesses that have earnings capacity in excess of the fair earning capacity of those businesses. Figure 3.1 is a sample form that can be used to calculate the selling price of a business.

Business Appraisers

If a buyer of a business is unsure of the true value of the company, he or she can hire an appraiser to determine the value. Business appraisers, like business brokers, run the gamut from excellent to totally incompetent. The number of appraisers has increased from a few hundred in 1980 to about 25,000 now, and there are few formally recognized qualifications for appraisers. The American Society of Appraisers (ASA) is an organization that invites qualified appraisers to become members if they meet the organization's requirements. ASA membership may be a signal of ability; however, only about 400 appraisers are members.[6] Business buyers should ask about an appraiser's background, qualifications, and past experience before making a final selection. John Bakken, the owner of a business valuation firm, says, "Anyone who isn't a CPA or an MBA and hasn't been out on the street for 20 years or so is going to have a hard time telling what a company's really worth."[7]

FIGURE 3.1 Estimated "True Selling Price"

Name____________ Address____________ Phone____________

ALL ASSETS (Excluding good will)

Accounts Receivable	$__________
Inventory (at current wholesale cost)	$__________
Work in progress	$__________
Furniture, fixtures and equipment (market value installed)	$__________
Leasehold improvements (minus used up life)	$__________
Franchise, trademarks and trade names	$__________
License(s) (ABC)	$__________
Lease value (residual and improvements, adjusted to market value)	$__________
Real Property__________	$__________
Customer(s) list(s)	$__________
Customer(s) contract(s)	$__________
Other assets (specify)__________	$__________
Other assets (specify)__________	$__________
Total asset value "A"	$__________

GOOD WILL:

Annual "true net profit"	$__________	
Deduct 10% annual interest on total asset value "A"	$__________	
Subtotal	$__________	
Risk factor ________(times subtotal) = good will		$__________
"True selling price" (asset plus good will)*		$__________

*Note: The total selling price of the business is less any outstanding liabilities such as, liens, encumbrances (notes), etc. The above information has been supplied by the seller from his books and financial records. The broker, or its agent, has reviewed these books and financial records. Broker, or its agent, does not warrant the accuracy of the information contained herein.

Source: Wilfred Tetreault, *Buying and Selling Opportunities* (Reading, MA: Addison-Wesley, 1981). Used by permission.

Arriving at the "Right" Price

We have discussed some of the special methods of valuing a business and the elements, such as tangible and intangible assets, that must be appraised. We have also indicated that buyers might want the opinion of an appraiser before arriving at the price. In the final analysis, however, the "right" price is the figure that both seller and buyer agree on. In most cases, the "right" price will probably favor either buyer or seller, depending on the circumstances surrounding the sale.

The Purchase Offer

Now that the value of the business being bought has been established, the buyer and his or her representative should develop a purchase offer that includes the necessary items and covenants. The following are some of the more important elements to be addressed in a purchase offer:

Price. It is important that the price the buyer is willing to pay be stipulated in the offer.

Method of Payment. If the seller is willing to finance the purchase of his or her business, conditions such as down payment and number of payments should be stipulated.

Lease and Leasehold Agreements. The buyer should indicate that he or she expects to assume the current lease and any existing leasehold improvements.

Contracts. The buyer should state whether he or she is willing to honor contracts with suppliers, unions, etc., which the seller has entered into.

Seller Assistance. It is common for a seller to train and assist the buyer for a few weeks to ensure a smooth business transition.

Personnel. The buyer should state whether or not he or she intends to retain the company's employees. If employees are retained, their accrued benefits, such as pensions and profit sharing, become the buyer's responsibility.

Operating Documents. The buyer should indicate that operating documents such as mailing lists, licenses, trade-secret agreements, and operating manuals are to remain with the business.

Intangible Assets. Buyer and seller should agree that the purchase will include customer lists, important telephone number lists, trade names, and all other intangible assets.

Assumption of Liabilities. If the buyer is willing to assume the seller's liabilities, this willingness should be stated in the offer.

Covenant Not to Compete. This stipulation may be the most important element to include in an offer of purchase because most businesses would fail if their previous owners started a similar business in the same market area. This covenant (see Figure 3.2) is an agreement that the seller will not compete with the buyer for a period of years within a certain geographic area.

Negotiating the Purchase

Once the purchase offer has been drawn up, it must be presented to the seller. It is unlikely that the seller will accept the offer without negotiating the price or some of the terms and conditions. There could be several negotiating sessions, depending primarily on the complexity of the purchase offer.

FIGURE 3.2
Covenant Not to Compete

Name of Business ____________________
Address ____________________
____
____

Phone Number ____________

Seller does covenant to the Buyer, his successor, and assigns, that he will not engage, directly or indirectly, in any business similar to or in competition with the business hereby being sold within a radius of __________ miles from the premises at (address) ______ for __________ years from the date of Buyer's possession thereof, either as a principal, agent, manager, employee, owner, partner, stockholder, director or officer of a corporation, trustee or consultant, or otherwise in any other capacity or be connected therewith in any other manner.

The value placed on this covenant is the sum of $__________.

Executed on __________, 19____ at (address) ______________

X ____________________ Dated ______________, 19___
Sellers

____
Print name(s) and title(s)

X ____________________ Dated ______________, 19___
Buyer(s)

____
Print name(s) and title(s)

Nonverbal Communication. During negotiating sessions, the astute buyer will be aware of the seller's nonverbal communications. What the seller does with his or her hands, legs, eyes, etc., can indicate how the offer has been received and whether it is likely to be accepted or rejected. There are many positive and negative signals that can indicate the outcome of the negotiations.[8] Any one of the following can signal "yes" or "maybe":

Positive Signals

- Straightening up his or her desk upon your entrance
- Firm, warm handshake not terminated abruptly
- Attentive posture (sits up in his or her seat and leans slightly toward you)
- Uncrossed arms, "open," sometimes on desk
- Relaxed hands (more open, less fistlike, not flat on desk)
- Little movement while seated (swiveling only to face or follow you)
- Relaxed facial muscles (especially the jaw)
- Crossed legs, casually open, or scissored apart at the knee
- Crossed legs, with ankle resting on opposite knee and the nearest hand resting on raised ankle
- Any casual personal action (e.g., tying a shoe, loosening a belt, or preening)
- Normal breathing
- Smiles or laughter prompted by something funny
- Stroking of chin (a fairly common "maybe")
- Reluctance to take a call
- Assumption of a more casual position
- Pacing while thinking

Any one or a combination of the following can signal "no":

Negative Signals

- Dead-center seated position, close behind desk
- Relaxed posture (leans way back, clasps hands, or crosses arms)
- Defensive movement (swivels away from you in chair)
- Avoidance of eye contact
- Closing of eyes in long, frequent blinks as you talk
- Pointing of pen or fingers at you
- Closed hands (almost in fists)
- Turned-up forearms (as a shield or obstacle between you)
- Feet flat on the floor, legs together, not crossed
- Forehead furrows; knit eyebrows
- Lips and mouth tight, set, and dry
- Formal gestures (e.g., puts on jacket, tightens tie, buttons jacket, rearranges scarf or jewelry)
- Cool response (doesn't return your smile)
- Head supported by hands
- Distracting movements (keeps plucking imaginary lint off clothes)
- Hands behind head (like a pillow)
- Lip biting
- Much nose rubbing (but doesn't have a cold)

Persuasion. Throughout the buy–sell negotiation process, each party will try to persuade the other than his or her offer or counteroffer is the most reasonable. If the buyer is able to purchase the business at the desired price, he or she must be more persuasive than the seller. If the buyer is not confident that his or her persuasive skills are equal to or better than the seller's, then a broker or agent should handle most of the bargaining. Persuasion will be used by entrepreneurs in all phases of a business startup: Bankers need to be persuaded to lend money to the business, landlords need to be persuaded to rent at favorable rates, suppliers may need to be persuaded to offer better credit terms, etc. Since persuasion is so important, we have included an Entrepreneur's Checklist (Nineteen Keys to Persuasion) at the end of this chapter. Anyone who finds that his or her persuasive skills are minimal should consider using third parties in key negotiations.

Closure

Negotiations can end in one of two ways: either both parties agree on price and terms, and the deal is consummated; or both parties cannot reach agreement, and the deal falls through. Assuming the former, the buyer and seller should formalize their agreement as soon as possible. Once agreement is reached and all documents have been signed and filed, the new owner is ready to start operating the business as soon as financing is arranged. In a few weeks or months the new owner will find out whether self-employment is preferable to working for someone else.

FRANCHISING

Another way to become self-employed is by buying a franchise. This is actually the easiest and least risky path to self-employment; however, there are those who would argue that franchises do not afford "true" self-employment because owners must abide by the rules and decisions of the franchisor. For example, anyone who buys a McDonald's franchise must adhere to the operating procedures explained in detail in a 700-plus-page manual. Very little is left to the discretion of the franchisee since the smallest procedure or detail is covered in the operating manual.

What Is a Franchise?

The first franchise (a French term that means "free from servitude") was started around 1863 by the Singer Sewing Machine Company, and the practice of franchising has flourished ever since. The following is a generally accepted definition for the term "franchise":

> A long-term, continuing business relationship wherein for a consideration, the franchisor grants to the franchisee a licensed right, subject to agreed-upon requirements and restrictions, to conduct business utilizing the trade and/or service marks of the franchisor and also provides to the franchisee advice and assistance in organizing, merchandising, and managing the business conducted pursuant to the licensee.[9]

Franchising's Contribution to the Economy

Every franchisee is an owner of a small business which contributes to the economy and provides jobs for local citizens. In 1985, sales by franchised outlets were over $500 billion, or 20 percent of the gross national product. More than 5.5 million people earn a living from a franchised business; nine out of ten people over age twelve eat in a fast-food restaurant regularly; more than 300,000 of us stay in Holiday Inns each night; one-third of every retail dollar is spent in a franchised business; and by the year 2000, one-half of every retail dollar spent will buy a franchised product or service.[10]

John Naisbitt, head of the Naisbitt group, was recently asked which types of franchised businesses would experience the most rapid growth in the future and why. His projections for the year 1990 are shown in the accompanying table. The following trends will contribute to the increase in franchised business sales:

	(Sales in Millions)		
Business Category	*1985*	*1990*	*Annual Growth (%)*
Restaurants (all types)	$48,926	$86,109	12.0
Retailing (nonfood)	18,790	33,560	12.3
Hotels, Motels, Campgrounds	14,631	22,511	9.0
Convenience Stores	12,309	19,377	9.5
Business Services	12,076	21,282	12.0
Automotive Products & Services	10,604	15,944	8.5
Food Retailing (other than convenience stores)	10,370	14,544	7.0
Rental Services (auto-truck)	5,282	8,900	11.0
Construction and Home Services	3,720	9,255	20.0
Recreation/Entertainment/Travel	1,840	6,573	29.0

1. The change from a manufacturing-based to a service-based economy. More service than product-providing businesses will be franchised.
2. Consumer preference for convenience and consistent quality—major strengths of franchising.
3. An increase in consumer demand for specialty items.
4. The increasing number of women and minorities in franchises. Women and minorities can find it easier to enter the labor force as franchisees rather than as employees working for someone else.
5. The numerous opportunities for the exportation of franchises to other countries.[11]

Growth and Cost of Franchised Businesses

We have discussed the past and projected growth of franchising; however, entrepreneurs are also interested in which particular franchises have grown the fastest and in how much franchises cost. In this section we present some material from the *Venture*

100[12] list of the fastest-growing franchises to illustrate growth and cost. The following were the ten fastest-growing franchises in 1986:

Franchise	*Percent Growth*
T. J. Cinnamons Bakeries	3,700
Novus Windshield Repair	2,400
The Box Shoppe	375
American Mobile Power Wash	347
Penguin's Place Frozen Yogurt	269
Hampton Inn	210
Dial-a-Gift	167
Stork News	152
Zack's	145
Chem-Dry	92

The cost of a franchise varies considerably and depends primarily on the services provided and the demand for the franchise. The following were the ten most expensive franchises in 1985:

Franchise	*Lowest Franchise Fee ($)*	*Lowest Startup Cost ($)*
Hampton Inn	$35,000	$2,309,000
Quality Inns Int'l.	25,000	1,883,000
Econo Lodge	20,000	1,800,000
Hardee's	15,000	418,000
Roy Rogers	25,000	371,000
McDonald's	22,500	340,500
Ponderosa	25,000	317,000
Jack-in-the-Box	25,000	306,300
Round Table Pizza	25,000	296,500
Super 9 Motels	20,000	300,000

The ten most expensive franchises might deter many would-be business owners; however, not all franchises have six- or seven-figure price tags. In fact, it is possible to become a franchisee for less than $1,000. The following are the ten least expensive franchises in America:

Franchise	*Lowest Franchise Fee ($)*	*Lowest Startup Cost ($)*
Packy the Shipper	$995	0
Novus Windshield Repair	600	$1,400
Sunshine Polishing Systems	975	1,700
Coverall	3,800	400
Stork News	5,000	0
Chem-Dry	4,600	4,400
Coustic-Glo	9,750	1,500
Jani-King	9,500	4,000
Duraclean	7,800	9,000
Video Data Services	13,950	3,000

Who Buys Franchises?

Anyone with $5,000 or more and a desire to be self-employed is a candidate for franchisee. We noted earlier, however, that initiating entrepreneurs would probably shun franchising because it did not allow them to express their creativity. Imitating entrepreneurs, on the other hand, might find franchising more to their liking. Franchising appears to be popular with women and minorities who may not have the same access to startup capital as do white males. People who are approaching retirement are also likely to buy a franchise to keep them busy in their "golden" years. Finally, people who change careers at a relatively young age (athletes, military personnel, etc.) may also choose a franchise as an additional source of income and employment (see The Inside View 3-3).

Franchising a Business

The process of franchising a business is relatively simple; however, no one should attempt franchising without the assistance of a capable, experienced attorney. The franchising process has several stages or phases. First, an entrepreneur (initiating or imitating) opens and operates a business. Second, if the business proves to be successful, the entrepreneur might decide that growth can best be achieved by selling the business concept to other people. Third, the entrepreneur and his or her attorney

3-3 *The Inside View*

ERVING TEAMS UP WITH THE REAL THING

Anticipating his retirement from the Philadelphia '76ers, Julius Erving decided to buy a franchise and remain in the City of Brotherly Love. In December 1985, Erving and entrepreneur J. Bruce Llewellyn bought the Philadelphia Coca-Cola Bottling Co. from Coca-Cola Bottling Co. of New York for more than $70 million. Llewellyn commented, "Julius is wrapped up ten months of the year with basketball. But he's a great personality in Philadelphia. When he's ready, we will be using his talents much more."

Llewellyn has been chairman of the Philadelphia company since he approached Coca-Cola USA about buying it in 1983. Coca-Cola wanted Llewellyn to get some experience first, so they worked out a plan for New York to buy the franchise, with the understanding that Llewellyn would buy it later. Llewellyn then bought stock in the New York Coca-Cola company and encouraged Erving to do the same. The stock they owned was then used to purchase the Philadelphia franchise from Coca-Cola Bottling Co. of New York.[13]

draw up the agreement, legal forms, etc., that protect both franchisor and franchisee. Next, the franchisor finds franchisees who are willing to run the franchise in accordance with the rules established by the franchisor. Finally, the new franchise begins operations with the assistance and guidance of the franchisor. There is no limit to the number of franchisees that can be added provided that the business continues to be profitable.

Anyone considering the creation of a new franchise should include the following items in the franchise prospectus:

1. Determine the capital limitations.
2. Identify the target market.
3. Determine the method of establishing the number of company-owned as well as franchised units.
4. Provide services that are really valuable to the franchisee.
5. Realistically evaluate present corporate abilities.
6. Design profit structures for present and future franchise owners and the franchising company.
7. Establish quality-control policies.
8. Set reasonable goals in all areas.
9. Develop an effective training program.
10. Design all sales, marketing, operational, etc., tools.[14]

For some entrepreneurs, the standard method of franchising a business is too slow and cumbersome. They choose another process known as conversion franchising. Rather than selling a few new franchises each year, conversion franchisors convince established, independent businesses to become their franchisees (see The Inside View 3-4). This method of franchising enables the franchisor to create many franchisees in a short time. The following are some fast-growing franchises that have used conversion franchising, along with the nature of the conversions: Novus Windshield Repair (former dealers); Friendship Inns (hotels formerly in membership organization); Express Services (acquired a competing employment agency); Service America (independent contractors); and Park Inns International (existing hotels).[15] One caveat is that an unsuccessful, independent businessperson could also be an unsuccessful franchisee.

Selecting the Right Franchise

If it is possible to buy a franchise in a business that sells almost any product or service to the public, how can an entrepreneur select the right franchise to purchase? We have already dealt with some of the selection criteria, namely growth and cost. The next most important criterion is probably the services or assistance provided by the franchisor. It is advisable to avoid franchises that take a large fee from the franchisee, provide minimal training, and give little ongoing guidance and support. At a minimum, the franchisor should provide the following assistance and information:

- *Location selection.* Franchisors should employ people who are aware of the qualities of successful locations.

3-4 The Inside View

CONVERSION FRANCHISING

In 1981, Dahlberg Inc. had sales of $12.1 million, up from $9.3 million the year before; however, the $760,000 net profit from 1980 had been replaced by a $644,000 deficit. The company, which manufactures hearing aids, suffered from inadequate distribution of its product. At the time, the company's products were carried by only 2,000 of the nation's 7,000 hearing-aid dealers. More distributors were needed. Now, most of the sales reps are gone, and there are fewer independent dealers carrying Dahlberg products than ever. Instead, the company sells most of its hearing aids through 242 franchised Miracle-Ear Centers—stores owned and operated by erstwhile independent dealers who have taken down their own signs to become Dahlberg franchisees. Earnings, meanwhile, have soared to $906,000 on sales of $31.1 million in 1985. These conversion-franchise operations are companies that have been built, in effect, around existing channels of distribution.[16]

- *Purchase or lease assistance.* Details of leasing or buying land or a building should be handled by the franchisor's representative.
- *Facility design and layout.* A new franchisee will need help designing, constructing, and laying out the new facility, so the franchisor should be willing to provide assistance in these areas.
- *Training.* Since all franchisees are expected to operate their businesses in the same manner, it is essential that the franchisor provide adequate initial and ongoing training.
- *Marketing.* The franchisor should pay part of the marketing costs incurred by the franchisee. It is also helpful if the franchisor regularly provides other marketing and promotion assistance.
- *Centralized buying.* It is less expensive and easier for the franchisee if the purchasing of supplies is handled by the franchisor.
- *Financial help.* The franchisor should help establish sound credit and bookkeeping systems for franchisees. Franchisors should also provide cash-flow and cash-management assistance.
- *Advertising.* Franchisors must be willing to advertise their product nationally in order to help their franchisees maintain profitability.
- *Standardized operating procedures.* There should be a manual detailing all operations so that franchises are the same wherever they may be located.
- *Fees.* It is important to know the amount of the initial franchise fee and what portion of profits the franchisee is required to remit to the franchisor.

- *Territory*. A potential franchisee should know whether he or she will have exclusive territorial rights for the franchise being purchased.
- *References*. It is extremely important to find out from other franchisees how their franchises have fared.
- *Renewal or termination*. Potential franchisees should determine the requirements for either terminating or renewing their franchise when it expires.

For a more extensive list of information to include, see "Seventy-seven Items to Consider in Your Franchise Agreement," at the end of this chapter.

The Franchise Agreement

After carefully studying the franchise offering, the potential franchisee should scrutinize the formal agreement, which must be signed to consummate the purchase of the franchise. In the past, franchising was an unregulated industry; however, now the Federal Trade Commission (FTC) regulates franchising with the Uniform Franchise Offering Circular (UFOC). Franchisors are now required by law to disclose the following information concerning:

- Directors and executive officers
- Litigation and bankruptcy histories
- The specific franchise offered
- Initial fees
- Future royalties/fees
- Purchasing requirements
- Required personal participation
- Past cancellation statistics
- Past renewal statistics
- Past termination statistics
- Type of training offered
- Assistance in site selection
- Financial statistics
- Description of the franchise
- Business experience of the franchisor
- Sales restrictions[17]

Failing to disclose this information can cost the franchisor up to $10,000 per violation per day. Therefore, it is important that the franchisor be as honest and forthright as possible and that the franchisee be fully aware of all of the stipulations in the agreement.

Financing Franchises

After the franchise has been selected and the offering and agreement scrutinized, entrepreneurs must obtain sufficient funds to cover the franchise fee and any necessary construction costs. Since some lending institutions are reluctant to lend money for the purchase of a franchise, particularly a relatively new one, franchisors are helping franchisees acquire the needed capital (see The Inside View 3-5). Even though

3-5 The Inside View

FRANCHISE FINANCING

When Stephen Lewis began looking for funds to finance a Numero Uno Pizza, Pasta & More franchise, he ran into a brick wall. Lewis had several years of fast-food experience; however, he did not have all the capital needed to purchase the franchise. Lewis was able to use his profit sharing and personal savings to pay the $25,000 franchise fee, and he intended to borrow the $75,000 he needed for real estate, equipment, and working capital from the SBA or local banks. Banks were willing to lend the money if Lewis would use his home as collateral. This proposition was unacceptable, so Lewis looked elsewhere. After exhausting the other options, Lewis asked Numero Uno for help. The company linked him with Great Western Leasing Corp., a subsidiary of Great Western Financial Corp. Great Western, which had worked on other Numero Uno deals, quickly agreed to finance the real estate and equipment package for the restaurant.[18]

franchisors will help with the financing of a franchise, they expect franchisees to first exhaust other funding sources.

While some franchisors will participate directly in the financing of a franchise, they are still in the minority. Entrepreneurs should expect to finance their franchise with funds acquired from other sources. The following are the primary sources of franchise financing:

- Personal savings
- Loans from family and friends
- Commercial banks and savings and loans
- Finance companies
- Equipment manufacturers
- Leasing companies
- Landlord improvements
- Limited partnerships
- Mortgage bankers
- Private placement
- Refinancing
- Small Business Administration[19]

Franchising Failure

While franchising is supposed to be one of the "safest" ways to become self-employed, there are some franchises that fail. Franchises that are unsuccessful usually fail for the same reasons other small businesses fail (see Chapter 1). As soon as a franchise is successful, it tends to attract many "copycat" franchisors who want to cash in on the boom. A good example of copycat franchising can be found in the fast-food industry. Following the example of McDonald's and Burger King, entrepreneurs began selling similar franchises for restaurants such as Flakey Jake's, D'Lites, the Fresh Cooker, and 1 Potato 2 Inc. During 1985 and 1986 these restaurants ended up in Chapter 11 bank-

3-6 The Inside View

FRANCHISE FAILURE

In 1980 Agostine Malerba of Philadelphia owned twelve Arthur Treacher's Fish & Chips franchises, with sales of almost $9 million. By 1984, he had closed them all and lost $2.5 million. Malerba's problems began when the original franchisor was bought out by Mrs. Paul's Kitchens, Inc. Franchisees were told that the only products they could use would be those manufactured or marketed by Mrs. Paul's. "We told them their product might be okay to sell in supermarkets, but people will not buy that quality of product at a restaurant," recalls Malerba. The company responded, "Either do it our way or get out." Malerba chose to get out. All told, more than fifty Arthur Treacher's franchises went bankrupt.[20]

ruptcy. Even successful franchises can become unsuccessful when larger corporations buy out the franchisor (see The Inside View 3-6). Entrepreneurs should investigate a franchise offering as carefully and thoroughly as they would investigate the purchase of any other business.

STARTING FROM SCRATCH

We have discussed two methods of becoming self-employed—buying an existing business and purchasing a franchise. We will now look briefly (briefly, because the remainder of the book is devoted to it) at the third option—starting a brand-new business. If established companies or franchises that manufacture or market a particular product do not exist, it is necessary to start a new company. Starting from scratch is the option preferred by those who are willing to accept the risk of failure. For them, the risk of failure is overshadowed by the challenge of creating something grand and lasting. Before choosing to start a new business, entrepreneurs must evaluate the advantages and disadvantages of startups, and, if the former do not eclipse the latter, they should probably buy a business or franchise.

Startup Advantages

The advantages of starting a new business are somewhat personal and depend on the personality, drive, education, etc., of the individual entrepreneur. However, there are some startup advantages on which most entrepreneurs will agree, such as the following:

1. ***Ego gratification.*** This is probably the foremost reason for starting a company from scratch. The founding entrepreneur is able to bask in the praise and admiration of friends, associates, and the media when (and if) the business he or she created becomes successful. The business has been personalized, and it often reflects the personality and value set of its creator.

2. ***Challenge.*** Creating a new business is considerably more challenging than buying a business or a franchise. Startup entrepreneurs can take pride in their ability to create a business from the ground up. They usually need the assistance of many other people; however, if the business is successful, its creator tends to claim the lion's share of the credit.

3. ***No preexisting mistakes.*** Startup entrepreneurs don't have to live with someone else's mistakes; they have ample opportunity to create their own. New-venture creators do not have to live with existing "wrong" decisions such as location, suppliers, personnel, etc. They are also not burdened with the responsibility of correcting past mistakes.

4. ***New plant and materials.*** Starting from scratch allows the entrepreneur to buy new equipment, supplies, inventory, etc. It is quite likely that a purchased business or franchise would have some obsolete equipment or inventory, which could be difficult to sell. In some cases, this desire to buy everything new can cause a business to fail. For example, creators of new restaurants usually want brand-new equipment when there is an ample supply of perfectly serviceable used equipment available (sold by restaurants that failed because their owners insisted on buying new equipment).

5. ***Job creation.*** When entrepreneurs create new ventures, they are adding new jobs to the economy. Since most new companies cannot offer salaries that compete with those of established firms, they often hire less experienced, younger people. For those people, finding a job in more mature firms could be difficult; therefore, new-venture jobs give the less employable an opportunity to become gainfully employed.

6. ***Social responsibility.*** Some people start new businesses because they want to give something back to the community. Providing jobs is only one aspect of social responsibility. Other aspects include providing services not available in the area, donating to charitable organizations, etc.

7. ***Creating a legacy.*** For some startup entrepreneurs, the long-term objective of starting a new company is to develop a thriving business that can be passed on to their heirs. In some ways this is an extension of ego gratification since the founder knows that the business, often named after him or her, could exist for several generations.

Startup Disadvantages

1. ***Failure.*** Buying an established business or a franchise is less risky than starting from scratch. For the startup entrepreneur, there are so many decisions to be made and so many opportunities to make mistakes that the likelihood of success is not great. As we noted in Chapter 1, failure can take the form of bankruptcy, liquidation, acquisition, merger, or simply closing the firm's doors.

2. ***Competition.*** Established businesses and franchises usually have captured a share of the market and are able to compete with similar businesses. Startups, however, must fight competitors for a share of the market if they are to survive. Established firms can be very vicious in their attempts to deny market share to startups.

3. ***Fatigue.*** Starting a business is hard work. Anyone not willing to devote sixteen to twenty hours a day, seven days a week to a startup should plan to buy a franchise or an existing business.

4. ***Frustration.*** Startup entrepreneurs invariably become frustrated when they are required to deal with the "system." Licenses and permits are granted by bureaucrats to whom time is not important; construction is always delayed; bankers take forever to decide on loan applications; new employees find better jobs; and so it goes. New-venture creators need to be physically and mentally fit in order to cope with these "minor" irritants.

Taking the Plunge

Once entrepreneurs have evaluated all of their options, they must choose to buy an established business, purchase a franchise, or start from scratch. We know that approximately 600,000 people choose the latter option. We also know that half to three-quarters of them will not be successful. The remaining chapters of this book are designed to improve those odds.

Summary

Anyone who decides to become self-employed can choose from three different options: buying an existing business, purchasing a franchise, or starting from scratch. There are advantages and disadvantages associated with each of these options, and only the entrepreneur can determine which option is best for her or him.

The advantages of buying a business include the following: it takes less time than starting from scratch; it may be a relatively inexpensive way of becoming self-employed; decisions concerning location, suppliers, inventory, personnel, etc., have already been made; the business has developed an image and a customer base; necessary control and credit systems are in place; and the business has captured a share of the market.

Buying an established business does not provide the challenge or sense of satisfaction that comes with starting from scratch. The new owner has to live with the mistakes and errors of the previous owner. Finally, changing economic or demographic factors can cause a once-successful business to fail. If an entrepreneur chooses to buy an existing business, he or she should use competent consultants, brokers, attorneys, etc., to determine the right price and ensure that the purchase is concluded correctly.

Entrepreneurs who feel that they need help running their own business should consider purchasing a franchise. Franchise owners receive training, marketing support, and guidance from the franchisor; however, there are franchises that do fail. In the long run, franchisees may find that they have traded their corporate employer for another employer—the franchisor. Anyone choosing a franchise should carefully study the franchise offering and agreement before signing any contracts.

The really adventurous entrepreneurs are most likely to choose to start a business from scratch. This is the most challenging way to become self-employed and also the most risky. Entrepreneurs who fail can go on to something else, but those who succeed can take great pride in their creations. The success rate can be increased by careful planning and study.

Assembling the Pieces

Jacki and Carol spent countless hours deciding what business they wanted to start. They polled friends, acquaintances, colleagues, and local restaurant owners to determine what gourmet food items were needed in the Charleston area. After much discussion they knew what their inventory would be, what services they should offer, and what type of image they wanted the business to project. The first order of business for Carol and Jacki was to search their market for an appropriate business that was for sale. There was no suitable gourmet food store.

Next, Jacki and Carol investigated franchising. There were franchises such as Hickory Farms (now out of business in Charleston), which sold cheeses and other food items; however, there were none that offered a combination of gourmet food, imported and domestic cheeses, and wines. Thus Carol and Jacki were left with only one option: Start their business from scratch. Once the startup decision was made, Carol and Jacki began the planning process in earnest. ■

entrepreneur's checklist

NINETEEN KEYS TO PERSUASION

In order to get people to do what you want them to do, you might consider the following nineteen keys and rate yourself on each on a scale of 1 to 5.

1. Persuade yourself: Do you have confidence in your case and have you a high enough expectation level? ____

2. How highly do your track record, reputation, and credentials rate with the other side? ____

3. Have you chosen an appropriate time and location and prepared the meeting place carefully to help your case? ____

4. Do you have an attention-getting lead into the situation, such as an opening offer that will be attractive to the other side? ____

5. Can you start with areas in which agreement can be reached most easily? ____

6. Do you know what will arouse wants and needs in the other side? ____

7. Do you try to stress the desirability of agreement and determine what will create interest in producing a change in the other side? ____

8. Do you know how to listen fully before making judgments and rebuttals? _____
9. How will you handle objections? Are you prepared to meet them before they arise? _____
10. Can you restate the other side's position as clearly as they could state it? _____
11. Are you ready with a specific proposal: What, where, when, how, and why? _____
12. What time limits should you set and upon what items? _____
13. Can you find common ground and see similarities between your position and theirs? _____
14. Do you have a system for tracking your progress toward your goals? _____
15. Are you using the power of repetition and persistence, turning the other person's arguments into an occasion for restating common goals and your own position? _____
16. Are you avoiding placing the other side on the defensive, thus arousing emotional responses, which will block progress? _____
17. Do you have an explicit conclusion in mind, and are you ready to settle quickly when you reach it? _____
18. Do you concentrate upon the features and benefits of your case first, leaving money, price, and terms of payment to the end? _____
19. Are you willing to be fooled just a little bit and to avoid overkilling the other side to produce mutual gain? _____

Total Points _____

95 points: A perfect score. If you rate 90 or over, you are probably going to do a great job of persuasion.

80 points: You have a superior chance.

70 points: You should restudy your strategy, tactics, and information to heighten your chances of producing change.

Under 60 points: Postpone the meeting and do some more homework.

Source: Earl Brooks and George Odiorne, *Managing by Negotiations* (New York: Van Nostrand Reinhold Co., Inc., 1984), pp. 86–88. Used by permission.

Seventy-seven Items to Consider in Your Franchise Agreement

1. What business are you in?
2. What business are you licensing?
3. Is there a territory involved?
4. Are there exclusive rights?
5. Is there new construction involved or conversion of existing structures?
6. What is the initial license fee?
7. What is the royalty fee?
8. What is the product sold or service performed?
9. Who is your franchisee contact person or key person?
10. What are the standards and specifications for controls?

11. Is there pro forma assistance for loan applications?
12. Will you assist in preparing a loan package?
13. Do you make loans or participate in loans?
14. Is there franchise-owner orientation training?
15. Is there manager–operator training?
16. Is there on-going training?
17. What manuals are furnished?
18. Is there grand-opening training?
19. What are your practices with regard to sale of supplies, furniture, and equipment?
20. Inspection criteria
21. Advertising requirements and participation
22. In-house publications for franchisee's edification
23. Bookkeeping and accounting assistance
24. Chart of accounts to be furnished
25. Consulting assistance
26. Recommendations and assistance in regard to franchisee associations or advisory councils
27. Complete outline of system standards
28. Licensing of what trademarks and trade names
29. Assistance regarding construction, conversion, etc.
30. Furnishing of plans and specifications
31. Number and type of inspections
32. Explanation of various technical terms
33. Accounting and reporting methods
34. Forms to be used
35. Time periods to be used for accounting
36. Payment requirements
37. Penalties for delinquencies
38. Record-retention requirements
39. Discounts for multiple-unit owners
40. Reduced royalties for distressed situations
41. System advertising and charges
42. Authorization for dissemination of confidential information
43. Insurance and indemnity requirements
44. Condemnation, destruction, and reconstruction requirements
45. Conditions governing desired sale of franchised business
46. First rights of refusal
47. Types of ownership permitted
48. Arbitration
49. Transfer of license fees
50. Conditions of termination
51. Responsibilities after termination
52. Transfer upon death
53. Options in event of default
54. Method of giving notices
55. Severability

56. Relationship of the parties
57. Disclaimer statements
58. Rights of inheritance
59. Renewal options
60. Liquidating damages
61. Maintenance requirements
62. Renovation requirements
63. Standards for supplies
64. Operating hours
65. Marketing assistance
66. Inspection of franchise records
67. Notification of other business activities
68. Right of assignment by franchisor
69. Terms of leases
70. Minimum volume required
71. Display requirements in unit
72. Display requirements in local market area
73. Service facility requirements
74. Credit relations
75. Inventory requirements
76. Decor requirements
77. Future name changes

Source: Lloyd Tarbutton, *Franchising: The How-To Book* (Englewood Cliffs, NJ: Prentice-Hall, Inc., 1986), pp. 84–87. Used by permission.

Questions for Review and Discussion

1. What are the advantages of buying an existing business?
2. What are the disadvantages of buying an existing business?
3. How can the worth of a business be determined?
4. Do you think business brokers and appraisers are helpful?
5. What elements should be addressed in a purchase offer?
6. Briefly explain the franchising concept.
7. Explain the franchising process.
8. What is conversion franchising?
9. What information are franchisors required to include in franchise agreements?
10. What are the advantages and disadvantages of starting a business from scratch?

Notes

1. Jonathan Levine, "Ron Yanke is Standing Tall in the Lumber Business," *Business Week,* 15 September 1986, pp. 126–128.
2. Constance Mitchell, "Buyer Beware," *The Wall Street Journal,* 24 March 1987, p. 1.
3. Susan Buchsbaum, "Cashing Out," *Inc.,* April 1986, p. 107.

4. Joe Rosenbloom, III, "Brokers for Hire," *Inc.*, March 1987, pp. 105–111.
5. John Stefanelli, *The Sale and Purchase of Restaurants* (New York: John Wiley & Sons, 1985), p. 158.
6. Stuart Weiss, "Business Appraising: Beware of Amateur Hour," *Business Week*, 9 February 1987, p. 74.
7. Nell Margolis, "Something of Value," *Inc.*, January 1986, pp. 103–104.
8. Ken Delmar, *Winning Moves* (New York: Warner Brooks, Inc., 1984), pp. 281–285.
9. Lloyd Tarbutton, *Franchising: The How-To Book* (Englewood Cliffs, NJ: Prentice-Hall, Inc., 1986), p. 2.
10. Meg Whitemore, "Small Business Enterprises That Add Up to Big Business Dollars," *Forbes*, 25 August 1986 (Special Advertising Section, pp. 2–6).
11. Meg Whitemore, "Franchising's Future," *Nation's Business*, February 1986, pp. 47–53.
12. ———, "On the Road to Ubiquity," *Venture*, November 1986, pp. 48–52.
13. ———, "Erving Teams Up with the Real Thing," *Venture*, March 1986, p. 18.
14. Lloyd Tarbutton, *Franchising: The How-To Book*, p. 18.
15. David Roth, "The Franchisor 50," *Venture*, February 1987, pp. 38–51.
16. Richard Kreisman, "Born-Again Dealers," *Inc.*, June 1986, pp. 123–126.
17. Lloyd Tarbutton, *Franchising: The How-To Book*, pp. 67–68.
18. ———, "Financing a Franchise," *Inc.*, April 1987, pp. 89–95.
19. Ibid., pp. 89–95.
20. Ellen Paris, "Franchising—Hope or Hype?" *Forbes*, 15 December 1986, pp. 42–43.

CHAPTER 4

Identifying Sources of Assistance

Learning Objectives

After you have read this chapter, you will be able to do the following:

- Identify sources of assistance for startup entrepreneurs.
- Present some of the strengths and weaknesses of each source.

Before starting a new business, most entrepreneurs know at least one aspect of their potential business very well. The person planning to open a Mexican restaurant may be a very good cook, having catered Mexican meals for large parties for several years. Another person may have collected, studied, and enjoyed antique furniture and furniture refinishing as a hobby for a number of years. Others may have noticed a need for a particular service through their own experiences. For example, a person may have had a very difficult time locating a hospital bed and other medical equipment needed to keep a parent at home rather than in a nursing home. In one case, such an experience revealed the need for medical equipment rentals, and after recognizing that need, a corporate sales manager became the owner of a new, fast-growing, and very profitable business.

Other individuals do not have any particular expertise, but they do have a burning desire to quit working for someone else and to start working for themselves. These individuals generally are enthusiastic and willing to work hard. There are, of course, many other scenarios about individuals who start a new business, but all possess some skills and lack others.

The objective of this chapter is to save the startup entrepreneur time in finding information that could be the key to a successful business. A recent study showed that the typical small-business owner/manager spends more than two hours per day seeking information.[1] This figure compares unfavorably to a reported average of only one hour and thirty minutes that managers in large corporations spend seeking information. What accounts for such a significant difference? Basically the difference exists because the small-business owner/manager is more concerned about the marketplace and growth potential. This fact is supported by the amount of time that entrepreneurs spend looking for market-based information, such as, sales data, competing product comparisons, and customer problems.

Small businesses are regular consumers of information, and studies have shown that they are able to read clues in the business environment and turn these clues into business opportunities.[2] In fact, small-business owners have been called gifted "readers" of the business environment. To help startup entrepreneurs become even better readers of clues, this chapter presents several sources of information and assistance.

The sources of assistance available to entrepreneurs will range from his or her friends to local and national government sources. This chapter will discuss the following sources of assistance:

Networking	City hall
Partnerships	Chambers of commerce
Franchisor assistance	Government assistance
Consultants	Libraries
Venture capitalists	College courses
Trade associations	

Although this is not an exhaustive list, the areas covered will give startup entrepreneurs an idea of just how much information is available to help them start their business with a good foundation.

NETWORKING

Networking in its simplest form is nothing more than seeking advice and assistance from friends or from friends of friends. Networking is asking people who are in the same business you are where they buy their insurance, what type of insurance coverage they have, who their accountant is, etc. Networking is basically free advice from people in whom you have some degree of confidence and who will generally give you a fair and honest answer.

Networks are built up through the entrepreneur's effort to expand his or her circle of friends and acquaintances. Obviously some people are more extroverted than others, but almost everyone knows people with whom he or she feels comfortable. A classic example of this can be seen by observing a group of distance runners. Studies have shown that distance runners tend to be introverted, but listening to a group of them together would belie that fact. All over the United States distance-running clubs have been formed, and over 70 percent of the membership are men and women between the ages of thirty and fifty. Besides the common bond of running, the members share information concerning their businesses, including job availability, good candidates for employment, sources of supplies, etc.

Networking Organizations

Other strong networking groups include the various civic organizations (Rotary, Lions, Jaycees), religious organizations (Christian Businessmen's Fellowship or local church membership), and social organizations (YMCA, local country club, Masonic Lodge, Urban League, Women's Network). In all these organizations, the entrepreneur can contribute something to his or her community as well as be part of a fairly extensive network.

At one time, networking was considered a "good-ole-boys" club, but networking in its truest form is a source of information and advice, not just a form of doing business with individuals known to the entrepreneur. Networks, therefore, can be a valuable source of assistance for the startup businessperson, but, as is true with all forms of advice and assistance, an entrepreneur should try a little of the advice before accepting a large quantity.

Board of Directors

Another way to build a network is to appoint "outside" members to the board of directors of the new firm. Most entrepreneurs want a board of directors with members who are comfortable to work with and who will not ask too many questions. Although outside board members may not be needed when the firm first organizes, the faster the firm is expected to grow and the more technical the area of business, the more an outside director, or directors, may be able to help.

The people who should be considered for outside directors are those from outside both the entrepreneur's family and business who can look the entrepreneur in the eye and tell him or her the truth as they see it, even if it is diametrically opposed to the entrepreneur's view. Outside directors must be knowledgeable about the business or the industry and must be able to persuade and encourage the owner/manager to do the necessary planning. These people are in short supply, but utilizing such a person could increase the firm's chances of success.

PARTNERSHIPS

Partnerships are a little like a marriage. The entrepreneur who joins a partner in a business venture, is going to have someone to share the business with, but that does not mean that both partners will have the same ideas about how that work should be done. Occasionally entrepreneurs are going to disagree with their partners (sometimes violently), but the partner is part of the business, and if the partnership is to survive, entrepreneurs must learn to listen to each other.

What is the value of a partnership? The value derives from the additional skills and capital brought to the partnership, the opportunity to have greater input in making critical business decisions, the ability to discuss different strategies with another person having a stake in the outcome, or the relief of having others with whom to share the work responsibility. Partnerships are best when the partners complement each other. The typical example is the partnership in which one partner is in charge of production while the other is in charge of marketing and sales, and the two talk to each other enough to know what the other is doing.

FRANCHISOR ASSISTANCE

Once a would-be entrepreneur starts looking for a business, the possibilities of going with a national, or even regional, franchisor must be considered (see Chapter 3). Why? Franchises did $591 billion in business in 1987, and employment in franchising is more than 7 million, or 6.3 percent of the U.S. work force.[3] The sheer size, the higher probability of success, the instant product or service recognition, and the training are factors in attracting people to a franchised business. The typical person starting a small business may be an excellent cook, barber, or real-estate sales person, but he or she usually does not know how to choose a location, buy supplies, hire and train employees, keep business records, calculate taxes, or set up an employee benefit plan. Most franchisors supply this expertise and, in so doing, greatly increase the probability of success for the entrepreneur.

Management Training

Besides just being their own bosses, entrepreneurs want to be successful. A report by Dun & Bradstreet estimates that 90 percent of all business failures can be attributed to poor management. Franchise operators receive training in management and business operation before they open for business. For example, McDonald's Hamburger U. is a school-like setting in which new franchisees receive a ten-day indoctrination into every aspect of the business. The company actually has an operating manual of over 700 pages that describes everything from how to sear a hamburger to how to maintain clean restrooms. The manual is designed to cover all the operations of the restaurant in order to ensure that the product sold in every franchisee's restaurant will be up to the uniform quality that customers expect when they walk into a McDonald's restaurant.

Other franchisors offer similar training. Shakey's Pizza Parlors offers its dealers and parlor managers both classroom and in-parlor instruction at Shakey University in St. Louis. Topics covered include the Shakey's philosophy, parlor management skills, and hands-on experience in an operating parlor environment. I Can't Believe It's Yogurt has set up Yogurt University at the company's headquarters in Dallas, Texas. The school gives new franchisees a ten-day immersion course in all aspects of operating a franchise. Topics covered vary from how to choose a good location for a store to how to make yogurt the company way.

Franchisee Support

The scope of assistance given the franchisee by different franchisors varies from a brief ten-page general outline to thick manuals on almost every phase of the business operation. Most of the best franchisors provide all the management and personnel training necessary to be successful. In addition to giving the new franchisee management training needed to start a business, training is continued after the franchisee begins operations.

Kentucky Fried Chicken, for example, provides additional training in maintaining excellent customer service, quality control, and even accounting methods. What the franchisor is attempting to accomplish with all this training is very simple. The franchisor makes money only if the franchisees are profitable. If the franchisees are profitable, then more budding entrepreneurs will want to join the venture. The more franchisees that join and become successful, the more profitable the franchise becomes. McDonald's is the quintessential model of how a franchise can be operated to the benefit of all concerned.

What the franchisor offers in assistance to the entrepreneur is a proven formula for business success. The formula spells out, sometimes in minute detail, everything from store location to advertising and from personnel training to pension planning. In essence, the franchisor offers an established brand name or service that is recognized by the public. In addition, the franchisor offers national and local advertising to help promote the product or service. In some cases, the franchisor also offers monetary assistance to help the franchisee through the startup phase.

Obviously the assistance and training pays off. The International Franchise Association's statistics show that over 90 percent of franchised businesses succeed whereas only about 13 percent of all new businesses succeed. Such a record explains why franchised operations account for about one-third of all retail dollars spent in the United States.

CONSULTANTS

As entrepreneurs start a new business, they encounter more and more problems and, at times, they seem to be spending the majority of their time "fighting fires" and less time in the overall startup of their enterprise. A typical example would be the startup entrepreneur opening a retail store and realizing that he or she does not have a system for inventory control and purchasing. Entrepreneurs have a choice: Stop what they are doing and develop a system; decide to develop a system later; or hire a consultant to develop a system for their business.

The resolution to these choices is fairly simple. If the entrepreneur has the time and the expertise to develop a good workable system, then he or she should do so. If, however, time is limited and expertise lacking, then he or she should consider obtaining outside assistance. One form of outside assistance is the consultant. Consultants can best serve the startup entrepreneur when they are employed to solve a particular problem. In fact, an increasing number of entrepreneurs are realizing that they can obtain needed part-time assistance from consultants, particularly those consultants who tailor their work to startup businesses.

Problems with Consultants

There are two major problems in working with consultants. First, the consultant may not really know how to solve a particular problem, and second, the entrepreneur may find the consultant's recommendations useless or implement only some of them. To avoid the first problem, entrepreneurs should not hire a consultant unless he or she has a good reputation for solving the particular problem the startup enterprise is facing. The entrepreneur can learn about the reputation of consultants from the experience of others (common use of the networking system described earlier). Entrepreneurs, in general, are quite open about their business problems and about their experiences with customers, suppliers, and consultants. One entrepreneur will almost always give another entrepreneur very honest and straightforward opinions.

The second problem is normally more serious. If entrepreneurs hire consultants, then why do they not, in general, follow the advice they pay for? The reasons given by entrepreneurs (with probable explanations in parentheses) include the following: (1) The consultant did not understand the business. (Did the entrepreneur take the time to explain the problem or did he or she not take the time to hire an expert?) (2) The recommendations were too complex. (Does this mean that the entrepreneur did not take the time to understand them or that he or she did not make the consultant explain them in sufficient detail?) (3) The recommendations would not work in this business. (How does the entrepreneur know they will not work if they haven't been tried before?) The list could go on, but the main point is that if the entrepreneur checks the credentials of the consultant before contracting for his or her services, then the entrepreneur should give serious consideration to the advice given.

A fiberglass boat manufacturer who thought that his main problem was the inability to obtain capital necessary to produce more boats hired a consultant. After a thorough review of the entire business, the consultant concluded that the owner was selling each boat for about 20 percent less than the cost of production. The owner insisted that he was making 20 percent profit on each boat and believed that he had employed the consultant only to produce the financial report required by the bank before it would grant a loan.

When the consultant produced pro forma statements indicating that the firm could be profitable and pay off a loan only by raising prices, the owner refused to consider the option. Actually, the boats were selling well because their quality was excellent and the price was about 30 percent below that of others of similar design and quality. Unfortunately, the owner was not able to obtain the needed capital to finance the production of more boats, and a producer of excellent boats went out of business six months later.

What Consultants Do

The work of the consultant consists of two major tasks: the determination of the cause of a problem or weakness and a recommendation for improvement. (Notice how the preceding example followed this pattern: The problem was too low a selling price, and the solution was to raise the price.) To be effective, entrepreneurs must cooperate with the consultant during the investigative stage (by providing access to financial and sales records and explaining the functioning of different departments or systems) and must realize that the recommendations are of little value unless they are followed.

The advantage of employing consultants is that they can be brought in to help solve particular problems, and then they are gone. (There are even consultants to

4-1 *The Inside View*

FRANCHISE CONSULTING[4]

Both franchisors and consultants can provide assistance to the startup entrepreneur, but who helps the entrepreneur who wishes to start a franchise? In this very tiny niche, the franchise consultant is available to offer advice.

Patrick Boroian is president of Francorp Inc., a franchise consulting firm that last year had revenues of about $5 million. Over 7,000 people call Francorp every year, each convinced that he or she has a great franchising concept. About 1,500 of those callers will attend a one-day seminar on franchising, and almost one-third will follow through with a visit to Francorp headquarters in Olympia Fields, a suburb of Chicago. Of the original 7,000 callers, only 80 or so will become franchisors.

Mr. Boroian's job often entails bringing dreamy people back down to earth. A major hurdle for the would-be franchisor is to have an operational prototype that has proven to be profitable. Mr. Boroian says, "We hear all the excuses about why it's not making money now but will in six months. Our philosophy is: Prove it."

Francorp helps would-be franchisors determine whether or not a business can, in fact, be replicated. They help prepare franchise circulars and other legal documents, write operational manuals, and help map marketing plans. For this, Francorp charges from $50,000 to $150,000 and has attracted major corporate clients, including ITT Corp., Deere & Co., and Hershey Foods Corp.

advise entrepreneurs on setting up franchises. See The Inside View 4-1.) The disadvantage is that the entrepreneur must live with the recommendations that are implemented on a day-to-day basis, but the consultant does not.

VENTURE CAPITALISTS

Venture capitalists can bring a lot more than just capital to a startup firm. Many venture capitalists are, or were, entrepreneurs who have capital to invest and, because of their own experiences, would rather invest in startup and small-growth firms than in larger corporations in which they would have very little influence. By investing in startup firms, they believe they are helping others who are attempting to achieve the same goal they did years before, and they believe they can help the new firm succeed. The experience that venture capitalists bring to the startup firm can be invaluable.

Due to their past experiences, either as entrepreneurs themselves or as financiers of others, venture capitalists have a wealth of information that can be of benefit to the startup operation. Often venture capitalists will request membership on the board of directors of the firms in which they invest. The value of board membership is that the startup entrepreneur has an interested, committed, and experienced outside board member who can provide an objective opinion on the many decisions that all startup firms must make.

Venture capitalists also can assist the company in locating management personnel, technical talent, marketing distributors, and other sources of professional help. Finally, the venture capitalist is already part of a network and, therefore, can bring the resources of that network to the startup entrepreneur.

TRADE ASSOCIATIONS

Trade associations are formal organizations of individuals and/or businesses in the same industry or profession. They range from the well-known National Restaurant Association to the less-well-known American Mushroom Institute. The membership of each individual trade association is united for the basic purpose of promoting a product or service. The promotion includes educating both the public and the association members. The services provided by associations include the following: (1) conducting seminars and conventions for members, (2) producing and distributing magazines and newsletters, (3) serving as a liaison between federal and local governments and the membership, (4) providing publicity and public relations programs for the industry, (5) researching, collecting data on and analyzing subjects of concern to the industry, and (6) maintaining membership directories. All of the foregoing can provide the startup entrepreneur with information and assistance.

Since a trade association is a great source of information and provides an instant network for the startup entrepreneur, how does he or she find out if the industry has a trade association? Most large public libraries have a copy of the *National Trade & Professional Associations of the United States and Canada*. This publication lists all known trade associations from the A/C Pipe Producers Association, an organization of nineteen asbestos and cement pipe companies, to the Zinc Institute, Inc., with a membership of over a hundred companies. The publication lists associations alphabetically, by a key word, and by geographic areas. For startup entrepreneurs, few sources of assistance will be as valuable as membership in a trade organization, and they should make every effort to determine if there is one serving their particular industry.

Conventions and Seminars

Attendance at trade association conventions and seminars has many advantages for the startup entrepreneur. First, he or she will meet others in the same field and will have the opportunity to begin building a network. Second, most conventions feature talks and exhibits that focus on the particular industry. These include information on what is working now and what the experts expect to see in the future. Third, many conventions offer sessions designed to help owners and managers with common business problems. These problems may be as simple as setting up record keeping or inventory control systems or as complex as how to use the futures market to hedge a bond issue or a foreign purchase.

Finally, most conventions will have a section where suppliers can exhibit and demonstrate their products. Just by walking around the exhibit area, the startup entrepreneur can view the various products and services available to his or her industry and can talk with other entrepreneurs about which products or services they have found to work best. This is an ideal place to compare the differences among competing products, to talk with suppliers, and even to purchase products or services.

Trade Publications

Trade publications are also a rich source of information, by virtue of both the articles written about the industry and the advertisements. The articles are generally written by editors or experts in a particular industry who address specific industry problems or solutions to problems. Articles that are accepted for publication are those that will have wide appeal to the general readership or, in other words, those that address important issues. A typical publication may have articles on record keeping, marketing, bringing new products to market, planning store or plant layouts, advertising, or tax planning. In addition, the advertisements in the publications may be of benefit to the entrepreneur who can learn what is available and then compare the various products or services.

Other Services of Trade Associations

Trade associations perform many other services for their membership. From an educational standpoint, trade associations sponsor short courses, clinics, seminars, and workshops for their members. They provide tests and manuals for employee training as well as films and cassettes for training purposes. Since all of these are directed at a specific industry, they are, therefore, very valuable to startup entrepreneurs who need assistance not only for themselves but for their employees. Some trade associations provide more specific assistance, such as producing accounting manuals and forms for use by their members, or they may have staff consultants who help in installing and maintaining accounting systems.

Trade associations may also offer marketing assistance by providing members with advertising materials such as point-of-purchase materials. In addition, the association may conduct surveys to determine future demands and trends, or secure advertising for the industry. General management assistance may also be given. For example, the association may sponsor seminars on employer/employee relations as well as workshops on job evaluation plans, motivation of employees, or employee fringe benefit programs.

Trade associations may do all of the above and provide assistance in many other areas, such as government relations, consumerism, ecology and environmental problems, publicity and public relations, and even research and development. The trade association can be an excellent source of assistance to startup entrepreneurs who should avail themselves of the extensive services provided.

CITY HALL

Many city governments are concerned only with the administrative and maintenance functions of the city; however, some cities maintain development offices whose primary function is to assist new businesses. If a city does have a development office, it can be a great source of assistance and information. Information with which development offices can provide the startup entrepreneur includes the following: (1) zoning regulations; (2) water and sewer availability, connection fees, and schedules; (3) local health and environmental regulations; (4) possible labor recruitment and training; (5) street pavement and maintenance; (6) information concerning business licenses; (7) local sales, income, and property tax regulations; and (8) availability of garbage collection.

The development office offers the startup entrepreneur the advantage of consulting only one source for information concerning the city, its laws, regulations, and services. In addition, while the startup entrepreneur is searching for answers to the thousands of questions that must be answered before opening his or her particular business, the development office may have gone through this exercise with hundreds of other startup businesses. The knowledge gained from this range of experience can be invaluable to startup entrepreneurs if they will avail themselves of the opportunity. (For an example of what one city is doing, see The Inside View 4-2.)

4-2 *The Inside View*

SMALL-BUSINESS CONSORTIUMS CAN HELP

More and more communities are beginning to realize that the economic lifeblood of a community is small business and dependence on a few large corporations can cause serious economic disruptions. In a span of two years, Winston-Salem, North Carolina, lost the corporate headquarters of a multibillion dollar corporation (R. J. Reynolds) to Atlanta, Georgia, had a large trucking firm declare bankruptcy, and then saw locally headquartered Piedmont Airlines purchased by U.S. Air. The economic and job loss to the community was huge. Winston-Salem, however, was already aware of the role played by small businesses in its economy (small businesses accounted for 97.5 percent of the 6,100 firms in the county) and had started the Consortium for Small Business Development in 1984. The consortium is composed of seven organizations:

1. Small-Business Group. The Small-Business Group, within the chamber of commerce, provides its members with counseling for startup or business problems, seminars, and workshops. Networking is encouraged through a social group (called "Business After Hours") that meets six times per year.

2. Retired Executives Volunteer Services (REVS). REVS consists of a group of retired business executives who offer free counseling to startup and small-business owners. REVS is also part of the chamber of commerce.

3. Small Business Center. The Small Business Center is located in the county's technical college. The center sponsors pre-business workshops, seminars, and courses on business subjects.

4. Business and Technology Center. In a modern building, over eighty firms, from gourmet caterers to word-processing services, share a sense of community and excitement about small business. The center offers several services that are shared by the owners, including reception services, word-processing and copying services, accounting, shipping and receiving, and temporary personnel services. The center, like many incubator centers throughout the United States, is affiliated with Control Data Corporation, which provides its considerable resources and support services at a local level in a cost-effective manner.

5. Small Business and Technology Development Center. Under the auspices of the SBA and the local state university, the center provides assistance in preparing business plans, workshops, and counseling. The center thus provides SBA services to the local business community.

6. Triad Minority Business Development Center. The center is part of the Chamber of Commerce and provides minority businesses with free referrals, loan development, consulting, and assistance in development of business plans.

7. City Development Office. The office has money available for new small businesses that will locate in the downtown area of the city. Services also include counseling and referrals.

Many cities will not have development offices, so getting through the bureaucratic maze for simple information may be frustrating. Thus, when you encounter helpful individuals, gain as much information as possible from them and then do not forget to thank them for their time.

THE CHAMBER OF COMMERCE

What the city government may not do in the way of business development the local chamber of commerce normally will. This organization is made up of and supported by local businesses. Its primary job is to promote business and the local community. It is usually very active in recruiting new businesses to a community.

For the startup entrepreneur, the chamber of commerce may have a small-business development center whose primary function is to assist the new or small business. This assistance consists of information concerning the overall business climate; labor availability and skills; demographics; and availability of buildings for offices, plants, warehouses, or retail and wholesale businesses. In addition, the small-business development center may conduct seminars and workshops, many times as co-sponsor with the local technical school or college. The topics of these workshops will vary from attributes of successful entrepreneurs to profit planning. Most of these workshops require a very minimal fee (such as $15 for a four-hour seminar) and tend to be conducted by knowledgeable instructors.

GOVERNMENT ASSISTANCE

An excellent source of assistance, the federal government provides help through the Department of Commerce, National Technical Information Service (NTIS), the Bureau of the Census, and the Small Business Administration (SBA). The Department of Commerce publishes two pamphlets, which are available in most public libraries: the *U.S. Industrial Outlook* and the *U.S. Statistical Abstract*. The *U.S. Industrial Outlook* traces the growth of over two hundred industries in the United States and provides five-year forecasts for each industry. These forecasts are helpful in the determination of trends.

For example, the growth in sales of desktop computers for the office may indicate an increased need for computer maintenance. In turn, this need could spur the development of a hot, new field of small businesses that maintain and service desktop computers. Thus, the enterprising entrepreneur could start a business promising 24-hour service on certain computer models and have a "loaner" computer available if repairs cannot be made within a 24-hour period. Obviously additional information is needed before a business of this type is started, but the initial idea can come from studying trends.

The *U.S. Statistical Abstract*, published annually, can be found in most public libraries. This book contains tables, charts, and graphs that present statistics on almost every aspect of the U.S. economy. The information ranges from Bureau of Census data on demographic data such as income, number of homes with television, and percent of income spent on food, to sales data on the number of videocassette recorders sold in each of the last five years.

There is a chart on the number of personal computers purchased by businesses, by the government, by educational institutions, by individuals for personal use in the home. Should an entrepreneur be thinking of starting a business in the leisure-time industry, there is a section on the increase in leisure-time activity by Americans. This book contains over eight hundred charts and graphs, and seemingly more data and even more trivia than the *Guiness Book of Records*.

The information, however, can be invaluable in helping entrepreneurs spot trends in their respective industries. For example, does the trend in VCR ownership indicate that the rentals of video tapes will increase, or that in the near future more VCR owners will want to start producing their own tapes from cam recorders? The entrepreneur could conclude that supplying the equipment necessary for budding movie producers may develop into a new industry.

National Technical Information

Technical information is available through the federally sponsored National Technical Information Service (NTIS). NTIS maintains abstracts and data bases in 28 different technical areas, such as engineering and energy. For entrepreneurs in technical industries, a little bit of information can often provide the solution needed for a tough production problem or indicate a particular area to be explored further. At least, the information can save the entrepreneur time looking for solutions to problems that have already been resolved.

Brochures on the information that is available may be obtained by writing the organization listed below:

National Technical Information Service
Department of Commerce
5285 Port Royal Road
Springfield, VA 22161

The Bureau of the Census collects and publishes data that can be invaluable to the startup entrepreneur. Although the Bureau of the Census is best known for the population reports gathered from its decennial data collecting, the bureau also takes a census of businesses on the second and seventh years of each decade. The information, similar to that found in the *Statistical Abstracts*, can reveal business trends that may indicate which industries are growing and which are maturing. A list of the bureau's publications may be obtained by writing the office listed below:

Public Information Office
Bureau of the Census
Department of Commerce
Washington, DC 20233

In addition, many other major publications produced by the federal government are on sale through the U.S. Government Printing Office. A free catalogue can be obtained by writing to the following organization:

Superintendent of Documents
U.S. Government Printing Office
Washington, DC 20401

The information available is voluminous, inexpensive, and frequently quite helpful. In solving the many problems encountered in the startup enterprise, entrepreneurs too often try to "reinvent the wheel" when the design for the wheel is already available in a government publication.

Small Business Administration

Government assistance is also available from the Small Business Administration (SBA). The SBA was established as an agency of the Department of Commerce in 1953 to help promote small business. The SBA provides assistance in the form of management assistance, management training, and publications.

Management Assistance. The SBA provides management assistance in the form of SBA field representatives, grants to consultants, and the Active Corps of Executives (ACE) and Service Corps of Retired Executives (SCORE) programs. The SBA has over eighty field offices in the United States staffed by field representatives whose primary duty is to assist small businesses. (The appendix to this chapter contains a partial list of SBA offices throughout the United States.)

Although these offices are generally understaffed, their strength comes from their ability to quickly locate information needed by the entrepreneur. In addition, the field representatives will offer some on-site consultations on basic business problems, or they will call on some local consultants to provide help for more specialized solutions. Many times the consulting comes from teams of college students working through the Small Business Institute. (For example, see The Inside View 4-3.)

The SBA also provides management consulting to small businesses through the ACE and SCORE programs. For the ACE program, the SBA recruits executives who

4-3 *The Inside View*

THE SBI CAN HELP[5]

The Small Business Administration, in conjunction with 530 colleges and universities in the United States, has established the Small Business Institute (SBI) to help new and small businesses. The SBI, usually located on the campus of a participating school, accepts those inquiries on which it feels qualified to work. Typically a team of students visits the business that is seeking help and tries to find a solution.

For example, when Harold Hull needed marketing advice for his small, family-owned company, Country Craft Braided Rugs, he found exactly what he needed from the SBI at the University of Connecticut. The student team conducted a marketing survey that led Hull to redirect his advertising from small local papers to statewide periodicals. Sales dramatically increased, rising almost 40 percent, with no decrease in profit margins. The cost of the survey was nothing. Hull's experience is far from unique.

Steven Permut of Yale's school of management has sent his marketing students to work with over 150 companies in the last ten years. Student teams from other schools have prepared marketing surveys, developed bookkeeping systems, helped write business plans, and performed other similar tasks—all at no cost to the business. Best of all, the recipients of SBI assistance give high marks to the quality of the students' work. Excellent advice for free is hard to beat!

are actively engaged in business. These volunteers provide free consulting to small business firms. The SCORE program is somewhat different, in that the SBA forms SCORE chapters, which consist of retired business people or retired professionals who are willing to help new, small businesses. Again the consultations are free.

The SBA also provides consulting advice through the Small Business Institute (SBI). SBI's are located on college campuses across the United States and provide a unique opportunity for college business majors and small businesses. Small businesses often need additional market information, better record-keeping systems, or other assistance. Presented with a given problem, the college students bring "book knowledge" and enthusiasm together to arrive at a solution for the business. The results often bring praise from entrepreneurs.

The SBA also provides management training for the startup entrepreneur in the form of pre-business workshops. The subjects covered in the workshops are designed to acquaint prospective owners with the financial and managerial requirements of the successful business startup. Topics include areas such as how to determine the personal characteristics of successful entrepreneurs, how to organize a business, how to sell a product or service, how to select and train staff, and how to determine what records are necessary both for financial accounting and for tax accounting. Most of these pre-business workshops are factual and include sobering statistics on the survival rate of new businesses.

Publications. Finally, the SBA provides assistance through its excellent publications. These publications may be divided into three groups: management aids, small-business bibliographies, and starting-out series. There are over eighty management-aid publications ranging from *The ABC's of Borrowing* to *Women's Handbook*. The small-business bibliographies contain more than twenty-four publications on subjects such as home businesses and personnel management. The final group of publications is aimed specifically at the startup business and contains over thirty booklets on specific types of businesses. For example, there is a booklet on retail florists and another on the ice cream business.

How good a job does the SBA do in filling the information needs of the startup and small businesses? A survey of readers of SBA publications indicated that 92 percent believed the publications were up to date, and virtually all respondents (93 percent) found the publications useful and practical. Interestingly, at the time of the survey (1984), most of the publications were free, but the respondents stated that they would have been willing to pay for them.[6]

LIBRARIES

The public library is a storehouse of information waiting to be tapped by the startup entrepreneur. The quality of the information is superb, and the cost is usually no more than the entrepreneurs' time. For the person thinking of starting his or her own business, the library is an excellent place to begin. If, for example, the would-be entrepreneur is thinking of opening a retail wine store, one of the first questions should concern the per capita income of those who live in the area where the store is to be located. A second question might involve the amount of that income likely to be spent on wines and liquors.

To locate this and other vital information, the interested researcher should go to the public library and ask for the research librarian of the business department. The researcher should tell the research librarian what he or she wishes to find, and in most cases, the librarian will either show the researcher where the information is or indicate how to find the information quickly. Why? Most libraries are woefully underused, and the librarians, who are usually well-trained, are very happy to apply their skills and to demonstrate the usefulness of the library. Unfortunately, most people think of the public library as a place to read articles in magazines or out-of-town newspapers or to check out a novel.

The typical approach to finding information in the library is to try to find it without asking for help. Most individuals are intimidated by their lack of research skills, and their ego prevents them from accepting their limitations. Therefore, some people spend considerable time looking through the stacks in the reference section of the library but find little information of value.

What help is available in the public library? The information available in the public library may be divided into the following broad categories: (1) the reference section, (2) the business periodical indexes, and (3) the book section.

Reference Section

Most of the books mentioned so far in this chapter are located in the reference section of the library. The reference section contains basic reference books such as *National Trade & Professional Associations of the United States and Canada, U.S. Industrial Outlook*, and *U.S. Statistical Abstract*. The reference section can best be described as the area of the library housing the books and catalogs that contain basic information. These books may yield financial data on certain types of firms (e.g., transportation, financial, or industrial firms) or a list of venture capital firms with the characteristics of the firms in which they will invest. Other reference books may contain the names and addresses of suppliers, advertisers, or consultants. The reference section also contains the periodical indexes.

Periodical Indexes

Periodical indexes contain indexes to articles in particular types of magazines, newspapers, or journals. For example, the *Business Periodicals Index* lists the latest articles in selected topic areas from such nationally known journals as *Business Week, Forbes, Fortune, Nation's Business, The Harvard Business Review, Inc.*, and dozens of others. If the topic is the marketing potential of laser discs, a late 1987 issue of the *Business Periodicals Index* listed three citations. Interested in wine coolers? The same issue had four subheadings under wine coolers including articles on the marketing, advertising, growth, and market-share potential of wine coolers.

The citation given in the *Business Periodicals Index* will list the title of the article, the author, the name of the periodical, the date, and the page numbers on which the article appears. Since most libraries keep recent editions of magazines and journals on the shelf, the researcher can go directly to the magazine section to read an article of interest. Older editions of magazines and journals are usually bound and put into the stacks like any other book. Since these bound editions are labeled by dates, finding an article is easy. The value of this type of research is difficult to overemphasize, for often the answer to a business problem has already been provided by someone else and published in a magazine or journal.

Book Section

The book section of the library is by far the biggest section but is of limited value to the startup entrepreneur. The biggest problem with books, as compared to periodicals, is the timeliness of the information presented. Periodicals can publish within a day or two of information receipt, but books require months. This fact differentiates the two sources of information. Periodicals have up-to-date information focused on a relatively narrow area, whereas books have more dated material but with a broader scope.

The following example illustrates how valuable books can be to the startup entrepreneur. Let us suppose that the entrepreneur wants information on personnel hiring policies. Articles in periodicals often focus only on a single aspect of the hiring process, for example, the interview or the legality of employment tests. A book on personnel practices may cover the entire hiring process from advertising the position or positions to the training program the employee will participate in before starting work. Books can point out the legal restrictions on what an employer can or cannot require as a condition of employment, what questions can be asked in the interview, or what may be promised in relation to prospects for long-term employment. The answers to these kinds of questions do not change rapidly from year to year.

Locating a book containing the information desired is easy. The interested entrepreneur should go to the card catalog, which in some libraries is on a computer data base, and look under the subject title (e.g., small-business personnel). If books on the subject are available in the library, they will be listed by title, author, and reference number along with brief descriptions of the books' contents. With this information, the librarian can quickly locate the book.

The library is an excellent source of information for entrepreneurs. From the information available, entrepreneurs can find help in deciding whether or not to start a business, what sort of business to start, and where the business should be located. A little time spent in the library can be worth thousands of dollars to the entrepreneur who takes the time to learn how to find information in this storehouse of knowledge.

COLLEGE COURSES

A final source of assistance that should not be overlooked may be a nearby technical school, college, or university. Schools of business have finally realized that the majority of their students are not going to work for large corporations but will more likely work for small businesses most of their working lives. During the last decade there has been an explosion on many college campuses of small-business and/or entrepreneurial courses. Nationally, more than 10,000 students are enrolled in entrepreneurial courses at over 350 colleges and universities. Universities such as the University of Pennsylvania's well-known Wharton School of Business have even established entrepreneurial centers.[7]

Many of these courses are being taught by entrepreneurs who still run their own firms. The experience they bring to the classroom is invaluable. Entrepreneurial courses offer students a chance to learn about the many pitfalls of starting and running a firm before they have to learn all their lessons firsthand. In addition, courses help the budding entrepreneur develop research and planning skills before the demands of day-to-day decision making push planning into the background.

Basically, college-level courses help by having would-be entrepreneurs go through the kind of planning sequence that they should go through before starting a real business but too often skip in their drive to get their business started. Finally, taking a college-level course gives the entrepreneur time to fully reflect on the risks inherent in starting and operating his or her own business. Most courses stress both the excitement and feeling of accomplishment derived from owning a business as well as the disappointment that results from failures. Through discussing ideas with other classmates who share the same dream of success, the would-be entrepreneur, hopefully, will acquire the knowledge and background necessary to succeed in starting his or her own business.

Summary

Knowledge is a key ingredient in the success of a startup enterprise. A great deal of valuable information is available at a very low cost to entrepreneurs who take the time to familiarize themselves with the various sources of assistance. In the startup of a business, the entrepreneur will spend more than two hours per day seeking information. Successful entrepreneurs are considered gifted readers of information who tend to react quickly to market information.

Several sources of assistance are available to the startup entrepreneur. Networking is the use of friends, associates, businesspeople, and acquaintances from civic or social clubs as sources of assistance or information. The entrepreneur can enlarge his or her network by appointing outside members to the board of directors of the new firm. Similarly, a partnership can increase the business knowledge available to the firm.

Franchisors also provide excellent assistance in the form of management training and business operation. The 90-percent success rate of franchised businesses attests to the quality and thoroughness of their programs. While franchisors furnish overall assistance, consultants can be utilized to solve specific problems. Within their area of expertise, consultants may be able to quickly pinpoint potential problems or provide solutions to existing ones.

Trade associations are potentially rich sources of assistance to startup firms. Services provided by trade associations include seminars and conventions, newsletters, government liaison, publicity, research, and membership directories. While trade associations limit their assistance to a specific industry, entrepreneurs also need local assistance from the municipality in which they will be doing business. City government offices can provide information concerning everything from zoning regulations to garbage collection. Some cities also offer assistance to startup businesses through development centers. Many times the city and the chamber of commerce work together to provide assistance to startup entrepreneurs.

The federal government provides the startup entrepreneur with several sources of information, including the Department of Commerce, National Technical Information Services, the Bureau of the Census, and the Small Business Administration. The SBA provides management assistance and training through its field offices and publishes numerous pamphlets on startup and small business management.

The final source of assistance presented in this chapter is also the most voluminous. The public library contains a huge amount of information that is free for the asking. Information in the library may be found in the reference section, the business periodical indexes, or in the book section.

All of the sources of assistance presented in this chapter are available to the startup entrepreneur. Most are excellent but inexpensive sources that the entrepreneur should explore. In today's highly competitive business environment, the startup business can literally "win with information" or lose without it.

Assembling the Pieces

Carol and Jacki utilized three excellent sources of assistance to help them in their successful startup. First, they acquired their knowledge of business through starting and operating a part-time business, and their knowledge of gourmet foods and wines through extensive reading. Second, they built a huge network. Together they belonged to over two dozen organizations. Finally, they used consultants in areas where they felt they needed assistance.

As they explored the possibilities of opening a gourmet food store, Carol and Jacki subscribed to and read twelve different magazines including the following: (1) *Entrée,* (2) *Fancy Food,* (3) *Gourmet Retailer,* (4) *Wine Advocate,* (5) *The Wine Spectator,* and (6) *Gourmet Food and Wine.*

Carol and Jacki built an extensive network of friends and associates through membership in over two dozen organizations. These organizations included the Charleston Women's Network, National Organization of Women, Chamber of Commerce, American Wine Society, Gourmet Club, League of Women Voters, Symphony Guild, PTA, Catering Association, and the local school board.

In their planning before startup, they sought the advice of an attorney, an accountant, and consultants from both the Small Business Administration and the Service Corps of Retired Executives. ■

Questions for Review and Discussion

1. How can entrepreneurs build a "network"?
2. Why are franchises so successful?

3. When should a consultant be utilized?
4. What assets does a venture capitalist bring to a startup firm?
5. Why should an entrepreneur attend a trade association convention?
6. What forms of local government assistance are available in your area?
7. How can the chamber of commerce help a new business?
8. For a library project, determine the demographic characteristics of your local area.
9. Visit a business incubator if one is located close to you.
10. As a project, choose a business that you think you would like to start. Using the sources available, show that the business has a high probability of success.

Notes

1. Lynn Johnson and Ralph Kuehn, "The Small Business Owner/Manager's Search for External Information," *Journal of Small Business Management* (July 1987):53–60.
2. J. F. White, "A Small Business Is Not a Little Big Business," *Harvard Business Review* (July/August 1981):18–23.
3. Janice Castro, "Franchising Fever," *Time,* 31 August 1987, pp. 36–38.
4. Steven Glante, "Consultants Cash In on Quest to Create Next McDonalds," *The Wall Street Journal,* 1 June 1987, p. 27.
5. William Logan, "Studies for Nothing, Advice for Free," *Venture,* November 1986, p. 106.
6. George Solomon, "Does the SBA Satisfy the Informational Needs of Small Business?" *Journal of Small Business Management* (October 1985):67–70.
7. Steven Galante, "Hot Classes on Campus Teach Students How to Be Owners," *The Wall Street Journal,* 12 October 1987, p. 25.

Appendix

SMALL BUSINESS ADMINISTRATION FIELD OFFICES

State	*Address*	*Telephone*
Alabama	908 S. 20th Street Birmingham, AL 35256	205-254-1341
Alaska	8th and C Streets Anchorage, AK 99501	907-271-4022
Arizona	3030 N. Central Avenue Phoenix, AZ 85012	602-241-2206
Arkansas	320 W. Capitol Street Little Rock, AR 72201	501-378-5277
California	211 Main Street San Francisco, CA 94105	415-974-0642
Colorado	721 19th Street Denver, CO 80202	303-844-2607

State	Address	Telephone
Connecticut	1 Hartford Square West Hartford, CT 06106	203-722-2511
Delaware	844 King Street Wilmington, DE 19801	302-573-6294
Florida	400 West Bay Street Jacksonville, FL 32202	904-791-3103
Georgia	52 North Main Street Statesboro, GA 30458	912-489-8719
Hawaii	300 Ala Moana Honolulu, HI 96850	808-546-8950
Idaho	1020 Main Street Boise, ID 83702	208-334-1696
Illinois	4 N. Old State Capitol Springfield, IL 62701	217-492-4416
Indiana	575 N. Pennsylvania St. Indianapolis, IN 46204	315-269-7272
Iowa	210 Walnut Street Des Moines, IA 50309	515-284-4567
Kansas	110 E. Waterman Street Wichita, KS 67202	316-269-6566
Kentucky	600 Federal Place Louisville, KY 40202	502-582-5971
Louisiana	500 Fannia Street Shreveport, LA 71101	318-226-5196
Maine	40 Western Avenue Augusta, ME 04330	207-622-8378
Maryland	8600 LaSalle Road Towson, MD 21204	301-962-2054
Massachusetts	150 Causeway Street Boston, MA 02114	617-223-4074
Michigan	477 Michigan Avenue Detroit, MI 48226	313-226-6075
Minnesota	100 N. 6th Street Minneapolis, MN 55403	612-349-3530
Mississippi	100 W. Capitol Street Jackson, MS 39269	601-960-4363
Missouri	815 Olive Street St. Louis, MO 63101	314-425-6600

State	Address	Telephone
Montana	301 South Park Helena, MT 59626	406-449-5381
Nebraska	19th and Farman Streets Omaha, NE 68102	402-221-3620
Nevada	301 E. Stewart Las Vegas, NV 89101	702-385-6611
New Hampshire	55 Pleasant Street Concord, NH 03301	603-224-4724
New Jersey	1800 E. Davis Street Camden, NJ 08104	609-757-5183
New Mexico	5000 Marble Avenue, N.E. Albuquerque, NM 87110	505-766-3430
New York	26 Federal Plaza New York, NY 10278	212-264-1318
North Carolina	230 S. Tryon Street Charlotte, NC 28202	704-371-6561
North Dakota	657 2nd Avenue, N. Fargo, ND 58102	701-237-5771
Ohio	1240 E. 9th Street Cleveland, OH 44199	216-522-4182
Oklahoma	200 N.W. 5th Street Oklahoma City, OK 73102	405-231-5237
Oregon	1220 S.W. 3rd Avenue Portland, OR 97204	503-294-5221
Pennsylvania	960 Penn Avenue Pittsburgh, PA	412-722-4306
Rhode Island	380 Westminster Mall Providence, RI 02903	401-528-4580
South Carolina	1835 Assembly Street Columbia, SC 29201	803-765-5373
South Dakota	101 S. Main Avenue Sioux Falls, SD 57102	605-336-2980
Tennessee	404 James Robertson Pkwy. Nashville, TN 37219	615-251-5850
Texas	1100 Commerce Street Dallas, TX 75242	214-767-0600
Utah	125 S. State Street Salt Lake City, UT 84138	801-524-5804

State	*Address*	*Telephone*
Vermont	87 State Street Montpelier, VT 05602	802-832-4422
Virginia	400 N. 8th Street Richmond, VA 23240	804-771-2741
Washington	915 2nd Avenue Seattle, WA 98174	206-442-5534
West Virginia	Charleston National Plaza Charleston, WV 25301	304-347-5220
Wisconsin	212 E. Washington Ave. Madison, WI 53703	608-264-5205
Wyoming	100 East B Street Casper, WY 82602	307-261-5761

Source: *The United States Government Manual 1985–86* (Washington, DC: U.S. Government Printing Office, 1985), pp. 625–26.

CHAPTER 5

Developing a Business Plan

Learning Objectives

After you have read this chapter, you will be able to do the following:

- Understand the need for a business plan.
- Avoid making planning mistakes.
- Determine what constitutes a good business plan.
- Prepare and package a plan.
- Choose the most appropriate plan-presentation techniques.

An astute observer once said, "When you are up to your waist in alligators, it is difficult to remember that you came to drain the swamp." The same can be said about starting a new venture without a workable business plan. The startup process is chaotic enough, but without a plan to follow, it becomes nearly impossible. There are those who believe that a business plan is unnecessary and that those who develop and follow one are too cautious and timid. Fortunately, the advocates of the ready, fire, aim method of venture creation are in the minority.

To develop or not to develop a plan is not a choice that most startup entrepreneurs have the luxury of making because most of them will be required to have one. Anyone who seeks assistance from the Small Business Administration (SBA), the Service Corps of Retired Executives (SCORE), or other similar groups will be required to develop a business plan. Similarly, any startup entrepreneur who requires external financing must develop a rather detailed business plan that answers the questions most often asked by lenders. Finally, anyone who needs to explain his or her new business to potential partners, employees, or suppliers can simplify the task by relying on a good business plan.

In this chapter, we will illustrate why a well-developed, reliable business plan is so important by presenting a case both for and against it. We will discuss the positive and negative aspects of constructing, packaging, and presenting a business plan, and then conclude with "Assembling the Pieces," which contains the complete business plan created by Jacki and Carol for their firm, In Good Taste.

This chapter appears in the first half of the text to let readers know that the development of a business plan is a key element of the startup process. However, the business plan cannot be completed until the information we discuss in following chapters has been collected and analyzed. For example, marketing and financial plans and forecasts, discussed later, are vital elements of the business plan.

TO PLAN OR NOT TO PLAN?

Very few people would undertake a transcontinental journey without first planning their route, methods of transport, etc; however, many people believe that they can create a new business without formally planning the venture. Once these entrepreneurs decide to become self-employed, they immediately begin looking for the right product, searching for the best location, lining up suppliers, and selecting the right employees. Much of this effort is wasted or misdirected because the entrepreneur is not following a logical sequence of events. A business plan is the best tool for efficiently sequencing startup activities. That fact notwithstanding, many entrepreneurs refuse to plan.

Not to Plan

It would be satisfying to be able to say that companies created without a business plan fail soon after startup. Then all startup entrepreneurs would work diligently on their personalized plans. The truth is that many successful companies such as Federal Express, Nike, and Hewlett-Packard Co. did little or no formal prestartup planning. The founders of these companies may not have felt the need for planning, or they may have had the plan "in their head." There are, however, some entrepreneurs who are adamantly opposed to any form of planning (see The Inside View 5-1).

Paul Newman avoids planning because it takes the fun of discovery out of doing business. Other antiplanning entrepreneurs have different reasons for not developing business plans. The following are some of the most frequently stated reasons for not planning:

1. Planning takes too much time.
2. Planning is too inaccurate.
3. Planning is too difficult.
4. Sticking to a business plan is too difficult.
5. Sticking to a business plan would inhibit innovation and growth.
6. Doing is more important than planning.

Some of these reasons are valid. For example, Mitchell Kapor, the founder of Lotus Development Corp., projected first-year sales of \$6 million. Sales for the first year were \$53 million. Similarly, Compaq Computer Corp. sold 50,000 machines its first year—double the number projected. However, for most entrepreneurs, inaccurate plans are better than no plans at all.

5-1 *The Inside View*

ANTIPLANNERS

One of the most devoutly antiplan companies is Newman's Own, the company founded and controlled by actor Paul Newman. The company, which makes salad dressing, popcorn, and spaghetti sauce, did not have a plan when it was founded in 1982 and still doesn't, even though its 1985 sales were $24 million. Newman and author A. E. Hotchner started the company with Newman's salad dressing. A marketing expert warned them that it would cost about $200,000 to test and introduce their products and that the venture could lose a million dollars the first year. Against their consultant's advice they proceeded, and with only $40,000 of their own money.

Newman and Hotchner have a more casual outlook than most entrepreneurs can afford: "We don't care whether the market growth is 25 percent or 12 percent, as long as we stay on the black side of the ledger," says Hotchner. Newman's antiplanning attitude is best summed up by the following quote on a sign at his company's Westport, Connecticut, headquarters: "'If we ever have a plan, we're screwed'—Paul Newman to himself at the Stork Club urinal, 1983."[1]

To Plan

We believe that all entrepreneurs should create a business plan before they create a business. We know that plans can be inaccurate and that it is impossible to anticipate all contingencies; however, the process of planning is as important to startup entrepreneurs as the plan itself. The exercise of sitting down and thinking through a business startup can be invaluable. Knowing what is to be done, why it's done, when it's done, how it will be done, and who will do it is a necessary precursor. Faith in a business plan and willingness to stick to it can increase an entrepreneur's chances for success and profitability (see The Inside View 5-2).

Planning is not a static activity. Once a plan has been developed, it is not cast in bronze and never changed. Any business plan should be modified as circumstances dictate or when a company has outgrown its original plan. A good business plan gives a company direction and helps management make the right decisions at the right times. Many entrepreneurs look back at their original plan and find nothing but inaccuracies but they also realize that they may never have gotten started without that first plan.

5-2 *The Inside View*

FOLLOWING THE PLAN

William Foster, the founder of Stratus Computer, Inc., developed his business plan carefully. He modeled it closely on the growth rates and balance sheets of five other big-league computer companies. In his plan, Foster projected that Stratus would sell $75 million of its computers by the fifth year. Stratus hit the projected total almost exactly. "That plan was something we took very seriously," says Foster, "Our first year of sales, in '82, we were behind plan, and we were really concerned; we really pushed hard. I'm convinced that if the original plan had had a lower goal, we would have achieved less."[2]

PLANNING MISTAKES

It would be difficult for startup entrepreneurs unaware of some of the more common planning mistakes to create an effective business plan. It is impossible to identify all of the problems associated with business plans; however, following are some of the most common mistakes to avoid:

1. The plan is not well conceived and vague.
2. The plan is meaningful only to its creator.
3. There is no flexibility built into the plan.
4. The plan is more wishful than realistic.
5. The plan is too product and manufacturing oriented.
6. Key pieces of information are missing.
7. There is no real evidence that a market for the product or service exists.
8. Financial projections are unrealistic.
9. There is no indication of when investors can expect to be repaid.
10. There is insufficient owner investment in the company.

BUSINESS-PLAN RECIPIENTS

Before startup entrepreneurs can determine what should be included in a business plan, they need to know who is going to read the plan. Different audiences need to be identified because each has different reasons for reading the plan, so information that is vital to one group may not be very important to another. It may even be necessary to create different versions of the business plan if it is likely that several diverse groups will be reviewing it. This does not mean that the information should be inconsistent but that the emphasis may vary from one plan to the other. The following are some of the potential recipients of a new venture's business plan:

- Lending institutions
- Potential lenders (friends, relatives, etc.)
- Suppliers
- Potential customers
- Employees
- Venture capitalists
- Small Business Administration
- Small Business Investment Companies
- Potential partners or managers

Lending Institutions

Very few entrepreneurs are able to completely finance their new businesses by themselves. They need external funding, which comes from lending institutions such as banks, savings and loan associations, and credit unions. Formal lenders, unlike family and friends, cannot lend money on faith. An entrepreneur's personal assurance that he or she will repay a loan does not satisfy lender requirements. Banks and other lenders are regulated and scrutinized by state and federal agencies, and they must prove that they grant only those loans that have a high probability of being repaid. If a loan is not repaid, lenders do not want to be left with nothing; therefore, they almost always insist on collateralizing a loan with tangible assets. If the new business is a failure, the bank wants to have something that can be repossessed and sold for a price high enough to cover the loan.

Potential Lenders

Many startups are partially funded by the friends and relatives of the owner. These people often lend money on nothing more tangible than faith in the entrepreneur; however, a business plan would help them feel more secure about making such a loan.

Suppliers

Established suppliers who have developed a loyal customer base may not be willing to add a relatively risky startup to their list of clients. Suppliers who examine the business plan of a startup want to see evidence of potential longevity and the ability to pay for supplies purchased. Many entrepreneurs want their suppliers to extend favorable credit terms to them in order to help ensure the success of the startup. Favorable credit terms will be granted only by suppliers who are convinced that the business will have sufficient cash flow to pay its bills in a timely manner.

Potential Customers

Most startup entrepreneurs would probably not think of showing their business plan to potential customers. However, those entrepreneurs whose business relies on several major customers should provide those customers with copies of their plans. For example, a new computer software business should show its business plan to some computer manufacturers. If the manufacturers believe in the startup business, they might agree to sell the firm's software with their computers. The startup has already increased its chances of survival by attracting some significant customers.

Potential customers who believe the startup will be successful may also be interested in investing in it. In the case of the software startup example, it is conceivable that a computer manufacturer who would buy software from the startup company would also agree to invest in it. Customers who might also be investors would certainly want to see a well-developed business plan that explains when they could expect to recoup their original investment.

Employees

Many startup entrepreneurs have difficulty explaining their new ventures to prospective employees and convincing them of the company's desirability as a workplace. A business plan, perhaps in a shortened form, could be used to explain the business, its objectives, and the owner's philosophy to new employees. In addition, employees who are familiar with a startup's business plan will be able to serve customers more efficiently and courteously because they will know what is expected of them. Employees are also potential investors. Those who own a part of the business in which they are employed are motivated to ensure its long-term success.

Venture Capitalists

Venture capitalists, either wealthy individuals or investing companies, are the most demanding business-plan recipients. They are primarily interested in the future profitability and value of a startup; therefore, they must be convinced that they will earn a substantial return on their investment within a few years. Unlike most bankers and other lenders, venture capitalists take an equity position in companies that accept money from them. Different venture capitalists have different ways of evaluating a business plan; therefore, entrepreneurs should know the biases of those who will read their plan. New York University's Center for Entrepreneurial Studies[3] examined the issues that venture capitalists believe can make or break a deal. The results of their survey showed the following:

Criterion	*Percent Who Think It Absolutely Essential*
Capability for sustained effort	64%
Degree of familiarity with market	62
Potential for at least ten times return in five to ten years	50
Demonstration of past leadership	50
Accurate evaluation of and appropriate reaction to risk	48
Liquidity of investment	44
Significant market growth	43
Relevant track record	37
Clear and thorough description of venture	31
Proprietary protection	29

Venture capitalists are not willing to spend a great deal of time on individual business plans because they receive many solicited and unsolicited plans from startup entrepreneurs. During a period of several months, one venture capital firm received 1,200 plans, 600 of which were read, 45 researched, and 14 actually funded. To be one of the few startups funded, new companies need precise, well-developed business plans. Brevity being a virtue, a basic rule of thumb is that a business plan should not exceed forty pages.

Small Business Administration (SBA)

As we mentioned in the previous chapter, the SBA is a good source of assistance for anyone interested in starting a business. While SBA employees will assist anyone with an idea for a business, they expect those they help to write a comprehensive business plan. SBA staffers will assist with the preparation of a plan; however, they will not write it for the startup entrepreneur. The SBA does have business-plan preparation guidelines to follow, and it has computer programs which can be used to project future income. All entrepreneurs contemplating the creation of a new business should avail themselves of the free assistance offered by the Small Business Administration.

Small Business Investment Corporations (SBICs)

Small Business Investment Corporations are investor organizations licensed by the SBA to invest in new and small businesses. SBICs are quasi-independent organizations that can lend to any new business or only to those in a specific industry. Entrepreneurs who solicit funds from SBICs should know that these organizations are quite similar to venture-capital firms. Like venture-capital firms, SBICs require a detailed business plan establishing the likelihood of the company's success and its ability to repay the investment. SBICs usually take an equity position in client companies and often provide management assistance to businesses that accept their money.

Potential Partners or Managers

If a new business requires more capital or skills than the startup entrepreneur possesses, he or she might choose to acquire one or more partners. Anyone who is considering partnership in a new venture would certainly want to read a well-developed business plan before making a final decision. Potential partners would want to know about the product, the market, channels of distribution, pricing, projected cash flow, and other key business elements. This information could be conveyed verbally to potential partners; however, it is easier to convey detailed information in written form. Like partners, key managers will want a considerable amount of information about any potential employer. Many talented managers have left major corporations to work for startups; however, they would not have made that transition without the detailed information provided by the startup company's business plan. For a summary of the characteristics and motivations of these and other business-plan recipients, see Table 5.1.

WHAT THE BUSINESS PLAN CONTAINS

There is no "standard format" for business plans. The contents of a business plan are often determined by the audience, the product, the market, etc. Before examining the construction of a business plan, we will present the plan elements considered impor-

Table 5.1 Motives and Information Needs of Business-Plan Recipients

Recipient	*Motives*	*What It Wants from the Deal*	*What Information It Needs*
Venture-capital firm, SBIC, individual investor	Profitable investment	Return on investment	Standard plan
Referral sources: accounting firms, law firms, financial planners	Aid their clients and associates	Fees, additional work	Standard plan
Funded companies	Help others	Satisfaction, credibility	Standard plan
Limited partnerships	Invest, acquire tax advantages	Return on investment, lower taxes	Standard plan, with emphasis on tax and revenue potential
Current employer	Improve sales, market share, company value	Improved sales, market share, firm value, image	Standard plan, with less emphasis on founders and more on product and market
Current or potential customers	Purchase a good product that meets their needs	Lower price, prestige, impact on final product	Information on product, funding needs, founders
Companies with compatible products, distributors, suppliers	Complement their products, cut R & D costs	Increased sales, lower costs, better image	Information on product, market, founders, funding, or other needs

SOURCE: Reprinted by permission of the publisher from Julie Brooks and Barry Stevens, *How to Write a Successful Business Plan* (New York: AMACOM, Division of American Management Association, 1987), p. 161. © 1987 Beta Enterprises, Inc. All rights reserved.

tant by Stanley Rich and David Gumpert, the directors of the MIT Enterprise Forum, a national clinic for providing assistance to emerging growth companies. Based on their experience with the MIT Enterprise Forum, they believe the following to be the key requirements of a plan that will win funding:

- It must be arranged appropriately, with an executive summary, a table of contents, and its chapters in the right order.

- It must be the right length and have the right appearance—not too long and not too short, not too fancy and not too plain.
- It must provide a clear picture of what the founders and the company expect to accomplish three to seven years into the future.
- It must explain in quantitative and qualitative terms the benefit to the user of the company's products or services.
- It must present hard evidence of the marketability of the products or services.
- It must justify financially the means chosen to sell the products or services.
- It must explain and justify the existing level of product development and describe in appropriate detail the manufacturing process and associated costs.
- It must portray the partners as a team of experienced managers with complementary business skills.
- It must suggest a high degree of product development and team sophistication.
- It must contain believable financial projections, with the explanations and documentation of key data.
- It must show how investors can cash out with appropriate capital appreciation in three to seven years.
- It must be presented to the most potentially receptive financiers possible to avoid wasting precious time as company funds dwindle.
- It must be easily and concisely explainable in a well-orchestrated oral presentation.[4]

While some of the advice given by Rich and Gumpert applies primarily to growing firms, most of it also applies to startups. Entrepreneurs should realize that their startup business plan will probably be modified for use after the company is operating. Preparing an accurate initial plan saves entrepreneurs considerable rewriting time and effort after their businesses become operational.

Business-Plan Outline

As we stated previously, there is no universally accepted format for business plans. However, investors, entrepreneurs, and others do generally agree on most of the important elements that should be included in a business plan. The following outline of a business plan should be acceptable to most interested parties:

Name of company	Marketing program
Table of contents	Management
Executive summary	Manufacturing
Company description	Financial information
Market and competition	Investment
Products	Appendices

Company Name

We will discuss the selection of appropriate company names in the next chapter; therefore, at this time, it will suffice to say that entrepreneurs have to choose between two options. They can give their own name to the business, or they can choose a name that might be more appropriate. Names that are descriptive, easy to remember, and easy to pronounce are best. Once entrepreneurs select a name for their business, they should check with state and federal authorities to be sure that another business has not already used it.

Table of Contents

A good table of contents is absolutely essential. Those who read business plans are often concerned with particular parts of the plan and want to be able to find them easily. For example, investors are primarily concerned with the financial information contained in a business plan. They want to be able to turn to the financial section without having to wade through the whole plan; therefore, it is essential that a table of contents identify all sections and list the correct page numbers.

Executive Summary

The executive summary—a brief outline of the "guts" of the business plan—is probably the most critical portion of the plan. Plan recipients usually read this section to find out what the proposed company will produce and sell, who will own and manage the company, and how much money is needed. If the summary is not interesting and informative, they will not read the remainder of the plan.

The executive summary should be no more than two or three pages and should answer the following questions:

Who will manage the company?
What are the managers' qualifications?
What is the product or service?
Is there a need for the product or service?
What other companies sell similar products or services?
How much capital will be needed?
How much money are the owners contributing?
When can investors expect to be repaid?

Company Description

This section can be used to "flesh out" the executive summary. Entrepreneurs can discuss, in detail, what they expect from their company, why they believe their company will be successful, and what they expect the business to be like in five to seven years. The following information should be included in this section of the plan:

- Location and facility
  - Description of the site
  - Description of the building or buildings
  - Ownership of the facilities (will they be purchased or leased?)
  - Layout of the facilities
- Form of ownership
  - Sole proprietorship
  - Partnership
  - Corporation

Goals and objectives
- Expected market share
- Anticipated growth
- Anticipated diversification

Market and Competition

It is vital to convince plan recipients that there is a genuine need for the proposed product or service. No supplier, investor, etc., will be likely to associate with a company that proposes to provide unwanted or unneeded products or services.

This section of the plan should provide answers to the following questions:

How large (geographically) is the market?
How large (number of consumers) is the market?
Who are the customers?
Why will customers choose this product or service?
Will this product be superior to competing products?
Will this product be less expensive than competing products?
What incentive will customers have to try this product?
Will customers become repeat buyers?
How will customer loyalty be established?
Who are the competitors?
Is the market dominated by one or two competitors?
Why will the competition "tolerate" a new entrant?

Products

A complete description of the product or products to be manufactured or marketed is essential. This description should be written without using jargon and technical terms so that laypeople can understand it.

A reader of the business plan is likely to want answers to the following product-related questions:

What is the purpose of the product? or what needs does the service meet? / " problems does it solve?
What does it cost to make the product?
What price will customers pay for the product?
How is this product different from competing products?
How complex is the product?
How long will the product last?
Is the product dangerous to use?
Will the product be guaranteed? warranties
Will instructions on the use of the product be complicated?
What is the likelihood of misuse?
Are there any government regulations affecting the product?
Can competitors easily produce a less-expensive product?
Can the product be patented?

Product liability

Marketing Program

Products do not sell themselves; therefore, anyone interested in a new company must be convinced that a marketing program that will maximize sales has been devised. This is usually the longest section of a business plan because it covers so many aspects of a new company. It should include the following items:

Channels of Distribution. It is necessary to explain how the product will reach the customers. Does the company plan to use wholesalers, or will it sell directly to retailers? Will the company bypass wholesalers and retailers and sell directly to customers? Will the company have factory outlets, or will it sell through catalogs? Readers will want answers to these questions.

Packaging. Attractive packaging and labeling can increase sales. This section of the plan should explain what packaging materials will be used, how the product will be packaged, and what graphics and slogans will be used to identify the product and differentiate it from its competition.

Advertising and Promotion. Effective advertising campaigns and special promotions are an integral part of selling a product. Customers who like a company's advertising are likely to try the company's product. The reverse is also true: Customers who are offended by a company's advertising are not likely to buy its product.

Service. After purchasing a product, most consumers want to know what kind of service they can expect to receive. People want to be sure that the company from which they buy will stand behind its products and service them when necessary. The business plan should explain how a company intends to service its products.

Pricing. The business plan should explain how the price or price range for a product was derived. There should also be justification of prices that might be higher than those charged by competitors.

Management

Most investors are more concerned about a new company's management than they are about the product or marketing programs. Investors want to know who the key managers are, what they have done in the past, and what they can be expected to do in the future. Entrepreneurs should convince plan recipients that they will not be running a one-person company. Investors need to know that there will be capable people assisting the entrepreneur in his or her new venture. The following information on key people should be included in the business plan:

Individual's name and age
Position in the company
Previous work experience
Educational background
Financial investment in the company, if any
Ability to grow with the company
Compensation plan

Manufacturing

Investors and other plan recipients are more interested in marketing the product than in manufacturing it; however, this section of the plan should not be neglected. This section should explain how the product will be made, what equipment and machinery will be used, how quality will be controlled, and how manufacturing costs will be minimized. Entrepreneurs should show that their manufacturing system is modern and efficient without being extravagant.

Financial Information

This is the most important section of a business plan, and it is the most difficult to prepare. Very few companies actually meet their financial projections. In some cases entrepreneurs are too conservative with their projections, but more often, they are overly optimistic. The two most frequently miscalculated dollar figures are revenue and total costs. Entrepreneurs tend to overestimate the former and underestimate the latter. The amount of information provided in this section depends on the entrepreneur's financial acumen; however, at a very minimum, a pro forma financial statement (Figure 5.1), a pro forma balance sheet (Figure 5.2), and a cash-flow forecast (Figure

FIGURE 5.1
Projected Profit and Loss Statement

Projected Profit and Loss Statement

	Month 1	Month 2	Month 3	Month 4	Month 5	Month 6	Month 7	Month 8	Month 9	Month 10	Month 11	Month 12
Total Net Sales												
Cost of Sales												
GROSS PROFIT												
Controllable Expenses Salaries												
Payroll taxes												
Security												
Advertising												
Automobile												
Dues and subscriptions												
Legal and accounting												
Office Supplies												
Telephone												
Utilities												
Miscellaneous												
Total Controllable Expenses												
Fixed Expenses Depreciation												
Insurance												
Rent												
Taxes and licences												
Loan payments												
Total Fixed Expenses												
TOTAL EXPENSES												
NET PROFIT (LOSS) (before taxes)												

FIGURE 5.2
Balance Sheet

____________________, 19_____

	Year I	*Year II*
Current Assets		
Cash	$__________	$__________
Accounts receivable	__________	__________
Inventory	__________	__________
Fixed Assets		
Real estate	__________	__________
Fixtures and equipment	__________	__________
Vehicles	__________	__________
Other Assets		
License	__________	__________
Goodwill	__________	__________
Total Assets	$__________	$__________
Current Liabilities		
Notes payable (due within 1 year)	$__________	$__________
Accounts payable	__________	__________
Accrued expenses	__________	__________
Taxes owed	__________	__________
Long-Term Liabilities		
Notes payable (due after 1 year)	__________	__________
Other	__________	__________
TOTAL LIABILITIES	$__________	$__________
NET WORTH (ASSETS minus LIABILITIES)	$__________	$__________

TOTAL LIABILITIES plus NET WORTH should equal ASSETS

5.3) should be included. Most investors want revenue and expense forecasts for three to five years.

Each new business is unique, but financial information should not be presented in a unique fashion. The examples of financial statements included here are fairly standard and should meet the requirements of most startups. Once the statements have been completed, they should be reviewed by knowledgeable, disinterested people such as bankers or SBA consultants. We have said that accuracy is difficult to achieve; however, reality is not. Any business plan that contains totally unrealistic revenue or cost projections will certainly be ignored.

Investment

Very few businesses are 100 percent leveraged. Lenders and investors expect startup entrepreneurs to put their own money into a business they want to start. In this sec-

FIGURE 5.3
Cash Flow Projections

Cash Flow Projections	Start-up or prior to loan	Month 1	Month 2	Month 3	Month 4	Month 5	Month 6	Month 7	Month 8	Month 9	Month 10	Month 11	Month 12	TOTAL
Cash (beginning of month) Cash on hand														
Cash in bank														
Cash in investments														
Total Cash														
Income (during month) Cash sales														
Credit sales payments														
Investment income														
Loans														
Other cash income														
Total Income														
TOTAL CASH AND INCOME														
Expenses (during month) Inventory or new material														
Wages (including owner's)														
Taxes														
Equipment expense														
Overhead														
Selling expense														
Transportation														
Loan repayment														
Other cash expenses														
Total Expenses														
CASH FLOW EXCESS (end of month)														
CASH FLOW CUMULATIVE (monthly)														

tion of the plan, entrepreneurs should explain how much money they are investing in the business, how much is being contributed by family and friends, and how much is needed from other external sources. Because bankers are so conservative, they expect entrepreneurs to contribute one dollar for each dollar loaned by the bank. Other investors are sometimes willing to take a greater risk and will contribute more money than the owner invests. However, these investors usually take an equity position in the new business which can easily amount to more than half of the company. Investors and lenders want to know how much money they are being asked to contribute, and they want to know when they can expect to recoup their investment.

Appendices

This section is where all of the lengthy descriptions of products, markets, and people should be included. Detailed descriptions of the product and schematics, along with the results of exhaustive market tests and studies, should be included this section. If the résumés of the key managers are fairly long, they, too, should be included in this section. Any documents that are not vital parts of the business plan but provide support for claims or projections should be included in this section.

PLAN PREPARATION

After entrepreneurs have decided what to include in their business plan, they need to think about preparing or packaging it. A poorly prepared plan will not be well received by any audience, but a "slick" or too professional-looking plan that tries to hide content weaknesses will also be rejected. Therefore, it is necessary to first collect all the pertinent information and then to package it in an appropriate form. Some entrepreneurs use consultants to actually write the business plan for their proposed startup. Most lenders, investors, etc., prefer to have entrepreneurs write their own plans because the completed plan then reflects the thoughts, philosophy, and goals of the entrepreneur.

Creating a Business Plan

Action-oriented entrepreneurs naturally prefer collecting data and planning to sitting down and writing their plans. Creating a business plan is difficult, time-consuming work, but it must be done if a business idea is to become a business reality. The following are some preparation suggestions:[5]

Personal Computers. The availability and low cost of personal computers and word-processing software make it possible for any entrepreneur to write his or her business plan on a computer. To incorporate constructive suggestions, it is much easier to alter a plan that is stored on a computer disk than one that has been prepared on a standard typewriter.

Printer. Once a plan has been created, it is stored on a disk and printed in "hard-copy" form so others can read the final document. It is better to use a good letter-quality printer rather than a dot-matrix printer (see Chapter 16).

Company Name. It is important to have the company name and the founders' names and addresses clearly displayed on the front page of the plan.

Summary and Table of Contents. In order to avoid discrepancies, the executive summary and table of contents should be written after the main body of the plan has been completed.

Table of Contents. Entrepreneurs need to be sure that every major topic, every figure or chart, and every appendix is correctly listed in the table of contents.

Graphic Format. Graphic formats for market and financial data should be used whenever possible, and pictures of the product should also be included. A visual business plan is more interesting to most readers than one devoid of pictures and graphs.

Check for Spelling. All business plans should be carefully checked to make sure that there are no misspelled words or grammar and math errors. Readers encountering numerous errors in the business plan will not be readers for long.

Paragraphs and Sentences. Each paragraph in the business plan should focus on one concept or fact and should not be too long. Sentence length should vary. Too many consecutive long sentences make a plan difficult to read. Variety in sentence length increases reader interest.

Packaging a Business Plan

How well a business plan is written is very important, but how the plan is packaged or put together is just as important. People who read business plans regularly are critical of plans that are sloppy or too "professional." A business plan should not necessarily be professionally printed on expensive paper and bound in leather. This gives the impression that the entrepreneur has spent too much money on the preparation of the document and that the fancy packaging might be masking a weak business concept.

Once a business plan has been prepared, it should be photocopied on standard paper and enclosed in simple covers. Each copy should be numbered, but the number of copies should be kept to a minimum. Readers who receive plan number 86 might wonder who received the other 85 copies. The plan should also be marked "CONFIDENTIAL." The information in the plan might be of value to competing businesses or other entrepreneurs; therefore, readers should know that the plan is for their consumption only.

PRESENTING BUSINESS PLANS

Entrepreneurs spend months collecting data, analyzing markets, soliciting advice, seeking funds, and writing and packaging a business plan. All of that time could be wasted if the plan is not presented effectively to its target audiences. Entrepreneurs should take the necessary steps to ensure that their plan gets to the right people and is not ignored. Presentation of business plans can be either oral or written. Either manner of presentation requires that the right people receive the plan.

Locating the Right Recipient

A business plan that winds up in the hands of an uninterested recipient might just as well have been thrown in the trash can. For example, most venture capitalists specialize in different industries or in businesses at different stages in their life cycle. Therefore, it would make no sense to send a plan for a business startup to a venture capitalist specializing in established growth companies. To avoid this problem, entrepreneurs should make some preliminary inquiries at banks, the SBA, offices of suppliers, etc., to determine who should receive the plan and who has the authority to make a decision about the business proposal. Once the right recipient has been identified, the method of plan presentation must be determined.

Written Presentation

In many cases the identified plan recipient will ask to have a copy of the business plan sent to him or her. Entrepreneurs should comply with such requests but should try to avoid submitting a written plan without some assurance that a personal meeting will also be arranged. The person receiving the business plan will initially scan it or spend a few minutes reading vital sections.

Once the plan has been submitted, the entrepreneur can no longer influence the reader by explaining or amplifying parts of the plan. If the plan recipient does not read it, just skims through it, or does not understand it, the plan will be rejected, and the entrepreneur will have to find an alternate recipient. Plans presented in person are more likely to be accepted than those that are simply submitted.

Oral Presentation

Many entrepreneurs dread making oral presentations, but they are the most effective means of convincing others to do something. Since most oral presentations will be made before an audience of investors, it is advisable to know what these people expect of a presentation. Investors and lenders usually employ the following criteria:

- Has the entrepreneur fully prepared himself or herself to make an oral presentation of the plan?
- How well does the entrepreneur explain the company's product and market?
- How well does the entrepreneur sell the company and its concept?
- Is the entrepreneur really market oriented, or is he or she too product oriented?
- Does the entrepreneur have the necessary experience and expertise to run a company?
- Does the entrepreneur respond intelligently to questions from the audience?
- Is the entrepreneur physically presentable?
- Can the entrepreneur accept constructive criticism?
- What is the interpersonal "chemistry" between the entrepreneur and the investors?[6]

Knowing what an audience expects makes it easier to prepare a successful oral presentation. To present their business plan effectively, entrepreneurs should be properly attired and totally familiar with the contents of the plan. Furthermore, they should speak plainly and clearly and not overreact to criticism. Likewise, they should not take up too much of the audience's time. Finally, they should be willing to answer all questions and be positive. The hope is that a well-crafted business plan combined with a good oral presentation will be well received by the audience.

Summary

There are entrepreneurs who have started businesses without a written plan and have been successful. There are more entrepreneurs, however, who have not been successful. Whether their failures were directly caused by their lack of a business plan is difficult to say. To maximize the chances for success, prudent entrepreneurs should have a well-developed, realistic business plan before they start a business. Business plans are complex and somewhat difficult to develop; however, the process itself should help startup entrepreneurs to clarify and solidify their own business concepts.

Entrepreneurs who need external financing, partners, suppliers, etc., do not have the luxury of choosing whether or not they will write a plan. They will be required to develop a reasonable, realistic business plan. Those entrepreneurs who write plans should be sure that their plans are not vague, meaningless, rigid, unrealistic, too product oriented, or incomplete. These are the types of mistakes that can lead to rejection of the plan and, ultimately, to the failure of the new venture.

Business plans can be "tailored" for different audiences. The information in each version of a plan should be the same; however, different parts should be emphasized. For example, financial data and projections should be highlighted for investors, while growth prospects should be emphasized for partners or key employees. Entrepreneurs should keep in mind that their business plans are likely to be read by lenders, investors, suppliers, employees, and other interested parties who can influence a new venture's success.

Regardless of who reads a business plan, its construction is fairly standard. Business plans usually consist of the following sections: company name, table of contents, executive summary, company description, market and competition, product description, marketing program, management, manufacturing, financial information, investment required, and appendices. Once conceptualized, a business plan should be well written (grammatically correct and free of spelling errors) and properly packaged. A business plan should be written on a personal computer and printed out by a good-quality printer.

The final step is to present the business plan to the appropriate audience—the person or persons who can make the decisions that will make the plan a reality. It is important for startup entrepreneurs to determine who should receive their business plans and, even more important, who should attend their presentation. Oral presentations are more effective than written presentations because they facilitate personal relationships and afford the presenter an opportunity to clarify any misunderstandings.

It is important for entrepreneurs to remember that their business plan should be the culmination of their investigatory and exploratory efforts. It is the physical representation of their business concept, and how well it is thought out can determine whether or not the business goes from concept to reality. However, entrepreneurs who become too enamored of the planning process should heed the words of Thomas Jones: "Believe me, if you are more intimately familiar with the ins and outs of your business plan than the psychology, needs and wants and potential 'future' needs and wants of your customers, you're starting your business with a blindfold."[7]

Assembling the Pieces

Jacki and Carol spent months analyzing their market, finding a location, determining their inventory needs, locating suppliers, and identifying financing sources before they opened In Good Taste. Their findings and expectations were incorporated in the business plan they developed and presented to several lenders, suppliers, friends, etc. The business plan that follows is not their original plan but one that was altered to incorporate the suggestions of interested parties whom Jacki and Carol invited to read it.

In Good Taste—Final Business Plan

The Charleston Spice Rack has been in operation for 5 years, offering gourmet herbs, spices, teas, nuts, essential oils, potpourri, product-related cookware, and gifts to retail customers on Saturdays in the historic city market. In addition, it has operated at specialty fairs, including the Porter-Gaude Christmas Art Show, the South Carolina Shrimp Festival, Womensfest, and the League of Women Voters' Kitchen Tour. It also wholesales herbs and spices to restaurants, specialty food stores, and other retailers. The sale of freshly cut, home grown herbs to restaurants and retailers is another product line introduced by The Charleston Spice Rack. The Charleston Spice Rack operates in partnership with Boyd and Tempel Enterprises in a mail-order enterprise and Fridays at the city market.

In May 1981, two Citadel Business majors conducted a feasibility study, The Charleston Spice Rack Expansion, to explore further avenues to increase income. At that time, they recommended the increase of restaurant trade and mail-order sales. Following their suggestions, The Charleston Spice Rack showed a 122% increase in gross sales in 1981, a 26% increase in 1982, and an anticipated 25% increase in 1983.

In October 1982, the owner of The Charleston Spice Rack, Carol A. Tempel, formed a partnership with Jacqueline A. Boyd, known as Boyd and Tempel Enterprises, to further develop and expand the mail-order trade. Since the formation of Boyd and Tempel Enterprises, the business has doubled its exposure time at the market and has acquired access to a Hewlett-Packard 86 with 128 K of RAM computer, which maintains, categorizes, and processes a mailing list of 1,200 names, thereby maximizing sales. For example, analysis showed that 28% of customers were ordering within 7 to 10 days after they received a catalog. In addition, the computer facilitated providing customers with up-dated catalogues, the announcement of another retail day at the city market, distribution and analysis of a customer survey, and determining and maintaining a timely analysis of cost and profits.

The 1981 feasibility study also explored the possibility of a shop. At the time, such expansion seemed too risky because:

1. The downtown-area merchants, such as Gita's Gourmet, Lid 'n' Ladle, and the Stockpot, provided too much competition and limited the development of other product lines compatible with the existing line of The Charleston Spice Rack.
2. Other shopping areas would lose the tourist trade, were far removed from home, had limited walk-in trade, and no compatible businesses nearby to justify the high initial investment and low probability of increasing sales.
3. A shop would demand too much of the owners' time.
4. The areas identified for expansion, i.e., restaurant and mail-order trade, did not require additional space away from home or justify the additional time and expense required to operate a shop.

Boyd and Tempel Enterprises has reinvestigated the feasbility of expanding to a shop in the Orange Grove shopping center in the West Ashley area of Charleston, South Carolina, at the intersection of Orange Grove and Sam Rittenberg blvds. and of joining both The Charleston Spice Rack and Boyd and Tempel Enterprises in a more efficient operation.

Our business plan includes the following:

I. Objectives

A. Remain in the Charleston Historic City Market on Saturdays to maintain income from tourism, downtown customers, and local people who frequent the market. This location will also help in compiling a list of names of people who are highly interested in our mail-order products and in providing the means to advertise and promote the location and products of the new shop.

B. Maintain wholesale restaurant trade in the downtown location and increase the opportunities for restaurant sales in the West Ashley and North Charleston areas. The shop will serve as a central workplace for this function.

C. Maintain and expand the mail-order division using the shop as the place for assembling and mailing orders. An increase in our product will also offer mail-order shoppers more items to purchase.

D. Develop a permanent retail shop to accommodate product expansion which meets the qualifications of our target market in a location which allows us to compete and increase our income. A shop will also facilitate more effective use of our time as well as employee time by attracting retail walk-in sales while mail-orders and restaurant orders are being prepared.

II. Scope of Proposed Shop

The proposed gourmet/specialty food shop, known as The Charleston Spice Rack and more . . . will be a friendly, innovative shop that will educate customers about their purchases. Customers will not have to be gourmet cooks to enjoy this shop, but if they are, they will appreciate it. It will be a place where people can make quick purchases of food or browse for gifts and planned purchases. It will occupy 1,200 square feet in the Orange Grove Shopping Center.

The store will feature products such as wine, cheese, herbs, spices, tea and coffee as well as gourmet and ethnic food specialties and condiments associated with the major products. There will be opportunities for customers to sample the coffees, teas, and cheeses. Party trays and gourmet picnic-type baskets for take-out will be available, too. The shop will also feature cookware related to the preparation and serving of these foods, i.e., coffee pots, peppermills, gadgets, etc., as well as a catalog or sample of larger pieces of cookware that can be special ordered and made available on a cost-plus basis. Permanent display areas will feature gift combinations that we have developed for individuals and business. Our close association with craftspeople in Charleston County will allow us to bring together locally made products that relate to foods, i.e., pottery, baskets, linens, and fresh produce. Freshly cut herbs and plants will be available on a seasonal basis. From time to time, we will offer cooking classes to further our customers' appreciation of our products. Again, we can use our own talents and those of individuals we know in the community.

In addition to the retail operation, a backroom workshop will enable us to prepare items for mail order and to fill restaurant orders.

The design for this store is being done by R. Gary Boyd, architect, and an interior designer will be consulted.

III. Potential Market for the Shop in Orange Grove Shopping Center

This shop location was chosen to develop a retail specialty food store because:

A. The proposed shop is within a shopping center that now has a mix of business such as The Upper Crust, The Ice Cream Machine, Harbortowne Records, Bessinger's Barbeque, Business Machines, a computer store, and The Catch, which already attract customers who so clearly mirror the image of our target market. The proposed business hours of 10 AM to 7 PM would accommodate desired walk-in trade.

B. The proposed shop is located in an attractive, well-designed center where customers in other stores can clearly see the shop. It is in a high-traffic area with easy access into and out of the center and ample parking. The location will allow customers traveling to or from work to pick up needed items quickly.

C. The shopping center is in an area whose demographics show the following: (1) this is an area of great growth; (2) 55,000 cars pass this area daily, and proposed interstates will not noticeably change the established traffic flow; (3) 45,000 families reside within a 5-mile radius of the shopping center as opposed to 4,000 families in the downtown Charleston area; and (4) residents have a high income level, live in West Ashley's more affluent subdivisions, and are members of ethnic groups who will appreciate the services as well as the high-quality gourmet and ethnic foods offered.

D. The location of the shop would be easily accessible to our present customers in North Charleston, Mt. Pleasant, and Summerville because of its central location and close proximity to Interstate 26 (1 mile) via Sam Rittenberg Blvd.

E. The shop location provides the opportunity to expand and compete because there are no specialty food shops serving this outlaying area. The closest shops, which are in downtown Charleston, all have parking problems; one cheese, wine, and coffee shop in South Windermere has the same parking problems; a coffee and tea shop in Citadel Mall has limited choices, untrained personnel, and a location not conducive to picking up items quickly; and the Piggly Wiggly provides cheeses and condiments but has untrained personnel, no easy access to quick service, and no quality wines. Also, no other shopping center possesses businesses that are compatible with our products or attract the same target market.

F. The shop location also allows for expanding an additional 600 square feet by adding a loft within the present 1,200 square feet.

G. While other less expensive locations have been explored, the lower cost cannot justify the location of the shop in an area that does not meet our customer profile.

H. The leasor of the shopping center also has given us permission to grow herbs on the landscaped islands within the parking lot and surrounding green areas.

IV. Plan for Reaching the Market

The Charleston Spice Rack and more . . . has many advertising advantages over a brand-new business. Our name is already recognized and associated with quality in the community; we can advertise our business through the popular Historic Charleston City Market; and we can send announcements to Charleston customers as well as our mail-order customers. The partners of this business are also active in 14 community organizations, which will provide initial avenues to publicize the new business.

Other means of advertising include:

(a) fliers in nearby subdivisions and office buildings

(b) announcements on radio, in newspapers, and billboards

(c) grand opening party for friends and business associates

(d) announcements at the Southern Living Cooking schools in Charleston and Columbia

(e) a human interest story in the business review section of the *News and Courier*

(f) ads in gourmet magazines—*Cuisine, Bon Appetit,* and *Food and Wine*

(g) signs on the outside of the store and in the window to introduce the shop to present customers in the shopping center

V. Methods for Operating this Business
- **A.** It will be a reorganization of the Boyd and Tempel Enterprises to cover ordering, sales, accounting, advertising, inventory, and employee hiring and training.
- **B.** Hours of operation will be Monday through Saturday, 10 AM to 7 PM.
- **C.** Two well-trained individuals who can speak knowledgeably and establish a rapport with our customers will be hired.
- **D.** Our plans to educate ourselves about the new product lines include:
  1. attending the gourmet food show in Washington, D.C., in June 1983 to meet suppliers of cheese and gourmet foods and attend the specialty-food-shop seminars
  2. visiting the Silver Palate and the Dean and Deluca shops in New York City as well as gourmet food shops in the Georgetown area of Washington, D.C.
  3. reading the *Gourmet Retailer, Specialty Food Merchandising Magazine, Food and Wine, Business of Herbs Trade Magazine,* the *New York Times,* the *Wall Street Journal,* and various other relevant publications
  4. computerizing our inventory, general ledger, accounts payable and receivable, and payroll with the assistance and review of an accountant
  5. training by the manager of Pearlsteine's Wine Division
  6. consulting C. & J. Jennings in Charleston about gourmet food

VI. Future Plans for Growth
- **A.** Expand gift ideas and produce a catalog for business.
- **B.** Expand product offerings for restaurants to include herbs, spices, nuts, extracts, coffee, and cheese.
- **C.** National advertising in gourmet magazines.

VII. Financial Information
- **A.** Boyd & Tempel
- **B.** Startup costs for In Good Taste ■

Boyd and Tempel
Capital Statement
May 31, 1983

JACQUELINE A. BOYD	
Balance forward	$ 560.83
Additional invest.	915.59
Subtotal	1,446.42
Share Income (loss)	(449.16)
New Balance	$1,027.26

	Spice Acct.	Investment	Total
CAROL A. TEMPEL			
Balance forward	$ 813.63	$169.03	982.66
Additional invest.	235.33	153.83	
Subtotal	1,048.96	322.86	$1,371.82
Share Income (loss)			(449.16)
New Balance			$ 922.66
Total Capital as of May 31, 1983			$1,949.92
Net Income (loss) to May 31, 1983			($898.32)

Boyd and Tempel
Income Statement
For Month Ended May 31, 1983

Sales	$2,815.04	
− Cost of Goods Sold	−1,107.00	
Gross Sales		$1,708.04
Operating Expenses:		
Accounting	$ 7.23	
Advertising	736.22	
Bank Charges	27.70	
Education	142.00	
Licenses	10.00	
Office	53.80	
Parking	2.80	
Postage	430.56	
Rent	312.00	
Subscriptions	39.00	
Returns	39.52	
Sales Tax	77.48	
Supplies	67.77	
Telephone	4.67	
Car Expense	655.61	
Total Expenses		$2,606.36
NET INCOME		($898.32)

Boyd and Tempel
Balance Sheet
May 31, 1983

Current Assets:		
Cash	$1,315.08	
Inventory	585.66	
Income from Sales Tax	1.73	
Interest	7.28	
Mail List	60.00	
Total Assets		$1,969.75
Liabilities:		
Sales Tax Payable	$19.83	
Total Liabilities		19.83
Capital Account:		
Jacqueline Boyd	$1,027.26	
Carol Tempel	922.66	
Total Capital		$1,949.92
TOTAL LIABILITIES & CAPITAL		$1,969.75

In Good Taste

STARTUP COST ESTIMATE (Based upon sales of $155,000/year)

	Monthly	Reserve
Salary of owner–managers	$1,700	$ 3,400
All other salary & wages	700	2,100
Rent	850	2,550
Advertising	500	1,500
Delivery expenses (restaurants)	40	120
Supplies		
General	200	600
Direct Charge	400	1,200
Telephone	60	120
Utilities	120	360
Insurance		
Life on Partners	40	200
Business	100	600
Loan repayment	1,000	3,000
Maintenance	200	600
Accountant		150
Miscellaneous	1,000	1,000
Subtotal	6,910	17,500
STARTUP COST PAY ONLY ONCE		
Fixtures and equipment		6,315
Decorating and remodeling		10,000
Installation of fixtures and equipment		2,400
Starting inventory		13,385
Deposits for public utilities		525
Legal & professional fees		650
Licenses and permits		480
Opening promotion		1,000
Cash		10,000
TOTAL ESTIMATED CASH NEEDED FOR STARTUP		$62,255

Shop in Orange Grove Plaza

SIZE: 1,200 Square feet (20′ × 60′) RENT: $8.50 sq. ft. plus 7% gross

Monthly:		
Rent	$ 850	
Telephone	60	
Utilities	120	
Insurance	100	
Advertising	500	
Payroll (2 @15 hrs/wk)	700	
Loan repayment	1,000	
	$ 3,330	
Break Even Sales:	$ 5,550/month	
	$222/day	
		51,000 Set-up cost
INITIAL INVESTMENT:	$61,000	10,000 Working Capital
For a 12% Return on Investment:	$12,870/month	
	514.80/day	

Charleston Spice Rack Customer Profile

Retail Market Customer

1. Role: They are the decision makers, users, and purchasers.
2. Income: Middle to high level
   Education Level: Majority have either post-secondary education or are college graduates.
3. Life-style: Single, independent, post college age
   Married, no children
   Parents with children 7 years and older
   Empty nesters, couples, age 45 to 65 (pre-retirement)
4. Personality Characteristics:
   Inquisitive, friendly, outgoing, trustful, high self-esteem, NOT snobbish.
   Interested in new and different things.
   Like to poke around through displays.
   Many grow herbs.
   Like the display—its uniqueness.
   Like to chat.
   Bring their friends to see us.
   Like the idea that we blend our own seasonings and grow some of our herbs.
   Test our information and ask questions.
   Appreciate quality, creativity, uniqueness.
   Creative in their cooking—willing to try new things.
   New to salt-free diets or are friends of others who are new to this diet.
   High percentage of Charleston residents.
   Receptive to add-on sales.

Male customers: Middle-aged, like to cook, interested in odd spices and blends, will urge wives to buy, often have a specialty they cook, more impulsive in their buying habits, repeat purchasers.

Female customers: Some are gourmet cooks, knowledgeable about the use of seasonings, buy several items, buy what they need, will buy blends if they are unique.

Restaurant-Wholesale Market

1. Role: Decision maker, user or seller, and/or purchaser.
2. Restaurant Ownership: Independently owned
   Shop Ownership: Independently owned
3. Characteristics of Restaurants:

Most are small, and two are expanding to new locations with different menus.

Specialize in gourmet cooking, preparing daily specialties.

Some restaurants are new in the area; others are Charleston traditions.

Some are chef–owner (easiest to deal with); others are group or partnerships.

All serve very good meals and search for the best quality and flexibility in ordering quantities that meet their needs.

Characteristics of Shops:

Specialty shops—a seafood store, a Charleston gift-oriented store, a South Carolina gift-oriented shop.

Most are new businesses looking for a new product to make their shops interesting.

4. Characteristics of Chefs (who become the purchasers or influence the decision of the purchaser)

Like to know the owner of the business.

Receptive to suggestions on use of seasonings.

Knowledgeable, creative, and friendly.

Appreciate fine herbs and spices.

Prepare specialties, such as wine vinegars, sausages, herb blends for resale.

Interested in freshly grown herbs.

Do not offer unsolicited feedback.

Some order when they need things; others want to be called periodically.

Some have standard menu items; some prepare what is available in season.

Chefs who influence purchasing need periodic personal contact.

Characteristics of Shop Purchasers:

Think herbs and spices are neat.

Are knowledgeable.

Choose items that apply to their specialty.

Look for items that make their shops more interesting.

Questions for Review and Discussion

1. Why should entrepreneurs have business plans?
2. What are the reasons given for not planning?
3. What are the common planning mistakes?
4. How would you tailor a business plan for different recipients?
5. What characteristics make a business plan attractive to venture capitalists?
6. Briefly explain the major components of a business plan.
7. What areas should the marketing program of a business plan cover?
8. Briefly outline the qualities of a good business plan.
9. How should an effective plan be prepared and presented?

Notes

1. Erik Larson, "The Best-Laid Plans," *Inc.*, February 1987, pp. 60–64.
2. Ibid.
3. Virginia Postrel, "What Investors Look For," *Inc.*, November 1986, p. 18.
4. Stanley Rich and David Gumpert, *Business Plans That Win $$$* (New York: Harper & Row, 1985), pp. 2–3.
5. Julie Brooks and Barry Stevens, *How to Write a Successful Business Plan* (New York: AMACOM, 1987), pp. 164–165.
6. Ibid. pp. 194–195.
7. Thomas Jones with T. P. Elsaesser, *Entrepreneurism* (New York: Donald I. Fine, Inc., 1987), p. 98.

DOORSTEP VIDEO, INC.

BACKGROUND

The growth of the video and electronic industry has always interested Clay Lindsay. Clay, a twenty-one-year-old college junior, planned to start and run his own business after graduation. He constantly thought about different business ventures that he felt could be profitable. He also wanted to start a business that was totally unique. While on Christmas break, Clay came up with an idea for what he thought could be a very successful business venture—a video rental store that delivers movies, similar to the established pizza delivery service.

Clay discussed his idea with his parents and close friends, who criticized the concept and doubted that such a business could be profitable. Clay's father, who had owned and operated a drugstore in downtown Salisbury, North Carolina, for over thirty years, was one of those who doubted its profitability; he thought that Clay should finish his education before becoming involved in a new, time-consuming business venture. Clay, however, did find support from a couple of friends. One, Brent Snipes, whom Clay had known for about eight years, was very interested and recommended that they pursue the idea as partners. Brent would graduate from college that May, although Clay would not finish for another year.

Brent and Clay planned to start the business in June, with Brent controlling the everyday operations, so that Clay could go home when necessary.

Name and Logo

The two budding entrepreneurs immediately began to brainstorm for ideas on what to name the business, and Clay came up with the name Doorstep Video. After discussing other possibilities, they adopted Doorstep Video because it was easy to remember and conveyed the concept of the business.

The next step, the design of a logo, took the two planners a little longer. They wanted a logo that would leave a lasting impression on customers and one that they would be proud to display. They decided that red and white would be the store colors because of their dominance. The design they finally adopted is shown below. Brent and Clay felt that such

DOORSTEP VIDEO inc. ®

"FROM OUR STORE TO YOUR DOOR"

This case was prepared by John Dunkelberg, Wake Forest University, and Robert Anderson, College of Charleston. Used by permission.

details were necessary to project a professional image. In particular, Clay wanted this business to be an independent one that operated as much like a major chain as possible.

Location

The next order of business was to determine the location. Brent and Clay had lived in Salisbury, North Carolina, all of their lives and felt that the contacts they had established in the area would be a major factor in the success of their planned business. Clay's father owned the building that housed his drugstore in the downtown shopping district, and Clay knew that there was vacant space in the building. Clay was able to convince his father to rent them a small space in the back of the store that was completely separate from the drugstore.

Brent and Clay knew that they had to establish a basic plan of operation including name, location, and a realistic plan in order to gain the support of their parents. This would be a key factor in their success. After learning about the preliminary steps the two had taken, Clay's parents seemed a little more receptive to the idea than they had been at first. Brent's parents, however, remained very skeptical, and Brent decided not to pursue the business venture.

Clay, who strongly believed in the idea, continued to develop a business plan by learning more about the video industry. He conducted an extensive search of the existing literature using a computer data-based search program at the college library. Although the number of existing articles on the videotape rental industry were few in number, Clay found several articles that gave him some ideas about the industry, the competition, and what the future might be like. A capsule summary and his findings indicated that the industry was passing from the pioneering stage into the fast-growth stage and that the future seemed to belong to the large, well-funded chain stores, which would contain thousands of titles. In addition, he spent many hours visiting existing video stores to see which of their features he liked.

About two months later, during his spring semester, Clay mentioned his idea to a fraternity brother, Garret Barnes, whom he had known for about two years. Garret thought the idea was worthwhile and was interested in becoming involved in it. Like Brent, Garret would graduate in May and would be able to begin work on a full-time basis. Clay had already developed a preliminary business plan that included an estimate of the startup costs. These figures indicated that an investment of approximately $14,000 was required to open the doors. After talking with their parents, Garret and Clay decided to explore the business venture further.

The Entrepreneurs

Clay Lindsay is from Salisbury, North Carolina, and is a business major at a nearby private university. He is active in his fraternity and has always been interested in assuming leadership positions. His goal is to be the proprietor of a business that offers a better product and/or service than its competitors. He also wants to establish a business in which he is interested and which has the potential for rapid growth. Clay's business experience includes working at his father's retail drugstore and gift shop, where he began working as a janitor when he was twelve. Later he was handling everyday functions such as personnel management, special promotions, the purchase of imported goods, and advertising. While in high school and college, Clay managed a gift shop for his father during the Christmas season.

Garret Barnes, a twenty-two-year-old native of Florida, is active in the student legislature and intramurals, and has served in leadership positions within his fraternity. Garret's interests include competitive sports and other extracurricular activities. His goal is to start a company that with his nurturing will later yield healthy returns for his future.

Prior to his involvement with Clay, Garret had no business experience; however, he was completing his Bachelor of Science degree in business. Garret thought this opportunity suited his needs perfectly and that it had the potential for a good career. Garret makes friends easily and works hard to make a good first impression on the people he meets. In his fraternity, Garret is known as a hard worker and one who handles public relations very well.

Video Industry

During the latter part of the 1970s, videocassette recorders

(VCRs) became popular. By the end of 1980, approximately 2 million homes had VCRs. At that time, the national sales rate of videocassette recorders was only 17,000 units per month, but by 1981, VCR sales had risen to over 140,000 units per month. In 1984, nearly 7.5 million VCRs were sold, and by the end of that year, VCRs were in 20 percent of the homes in America. By the end of 1987, 52 percent of American homes had at least one VCR.[1]

The rise in VCR sales was enhanced by an increase in the availability of prerecorded cassettes. In the late 1970s, the thought of selling prerecorded cassettes to consumers frightened the major movie and television studios in the United States. Many were afraid revenues from both television and movie theaters would be greatly decreased as viewers turned from movies and television to cassette tapes. However, a small number of studios decided to gamble on the idea of selling prerecorded cassettes to the home viewer. In the spring of 1978, there were only about a hundred prerecorded cassettes available through studio distributors.

After some thorough market research, several other studios decided to enter the market. The market research indicated that consumers preferred renting prerecorded cassette tapes to buying them by a margin of seven to one. At that time, cassette tapes sold for about $50 and rented for about $5 per day. Since then, the cost of renting videotapes has dropped from $5 per day to as low as $1 per day. This, of course, was caused by the increased competition within the industry. On the other hand, the price of prerecorded cassettes has risen to as much as $70 and sometimes even higher for the biggest hits.

The home video market changed rapidly. Rental and sales outlets seemed to pop up in every shopping area. The industry enjoyed incredible growth over the next five years, but with growth came change. When home video first started, there were two formats available, beta and VHS. Because they are not interchangeable, beta and VHS competed with each other in software and hardware: Those who own a beta VCR can show only beta tapes and vice versa. However, over the past several years the VHS format has become the dominant choice of consumers, with beta now accounting for only a small percentage of the market. At first, many video stores handled both VHS and beta software; however, today it is almost impossible to find a beta rental store.

In 1983, 11 million prerecorded videocassettes were sold to retailers. By 1984 that number had risen 100 percent to 22 million cassette tapes. As a result, rental stores can now offer a large selection of titles. The smaller stores carry as few as 500 titles, while the superstores may have 10,000 or more titles for the consumer to select from. Today, the average video specialty store carries about 2,600 different titles.[2]

The prerecorded cassettes are divided into two categories, A and B titles. The A titles are the "hit" videos and the most costly to produce. The "B" titles are those that are lesser known and are considered "low-budget" films. Examples of A titles would be *Top Gun* or *Fatal Attraction*; B titles would include *Creepozoids* or *The Curse*. Since the B titles are less expensive than the A titles, video rental stores do not have to rent them as often as the A titles to earn a profit. In the United States, the average number of rentals (per tape) for an A title is 108 and for B titles, 62.

The videotape rental industry is one of the nation's fastest growing and one of the most fragmented. Nationwide there are over 25,000 video rental stores, mostly small entrepreneurial-type operations. In addition, there are about 32,000 rental outlets, such as convenience stores, that rent videotapes as a sideline to their major business. These rental outlets usually carry only the newer movies, which they receive three to four weeks after the release date, and stock less than two hundred and fifty titles.

As often happens in fast-growth industries, a shakeout seems inevitable. Chain stores are starting to exert pressure on the smaller, undercapitalized stores, and the growth of the superstore chains, carrying more than six thousand five hundred titles, seems to be just around the corner.[3]

BUSINESS PLAN

Garret and Clay planned to operate their business in the back of a building owned by Clay's father. Since they plan only to take telephone orders for rental tape deliveries, they require only enough space to accommodate the storage of tapes, the order taker, and the driver. The existing space would require the construction of some walls to create a separate area for Doorstep Video's operations. (For store layout, see Exhibit 1.)

The rental business would operate much like a pizza delivery service, with customers calling and placing orders for videotapes which would be delivered in thirty minutes or less. Drivers would collect cash payment from customers. The planned hours of operation were Monday through Friday, from 4 PM to 12 AM, and Saturday and Sunday, from 12 PM to 12 AM.

Garret and Clay also planned to deliver popcorn and soft drinks along with the videos to create for their customers as much of the effect of a movie theater as possible without their leaving home.

EXHIBIT 1
DOORSTEP VIDEO FLOOR PLAN

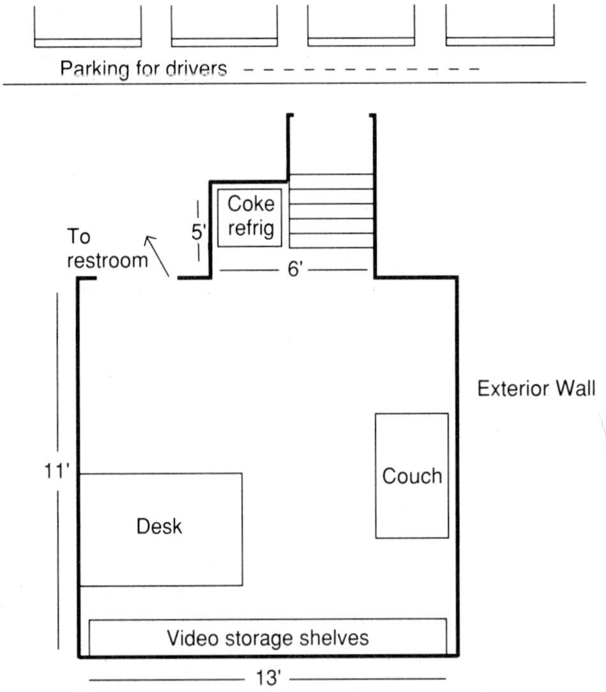

Note: All interior walls will be added by Clay and Garret to minimize cost. Total cost of the project will be $400.00.

Videos would be returned by the customer to one of four return boxes positioned strategically throughout the town. The videos would be delivered by part-time drivers, who could make approximately seven deliveries per hour. Drivers would be paid the minimum wage of $3.35 per hour plus an incentive rate of $.40 per delivery. Garret and Clay thought that by delivering the videos, the possibility for theft should decrease since they would actually know a customer's correct address.

Garret and Clay saw the potential for rapid growth in rental videotape delivery. Their goal was to test the concept in Salisbury and, if successful, to expand to locations in other relatively small citics. The reason for operating in small cities is that major chains only locate in larger cities, thereby allowing Doorstep Video to gain strength in the video industry through growth in the smaller markets.

Salisbury's Video Market

Salisbury, a small city in the center of North Carolina, has a population of about 25,000. Doorstep Video's delivery area would include the city and a few areas outside the city, with a total market of about 28,000 people. The per capita income in this area is approximately $10,000, while the average total household income is $28,000. Currently there are 14 video rental stores in Salisbury and an additional 14 convenience stores and other outlets that rent a small selection of videos.

Purchasing

A major consideration in any business is where to obtain merchandise. Since he was interested in buying used as well as new videocassettes, Clay contacted several such sources across the country. One source, International Movie Merchants (IMM), a used video distributor in Dallas, Oregon, agreed to supply Doorstep Video. IMM sent Clay a list of 500 used videos that would fill the needs of Doorstep Video. IMM quoted a price of $13,000 for the 500 videos, for an average cost of $26. After several changes, the list was approved, but because Clay believes that a buyer should never pay what the seller is asking, the price had to be negotiated. After a short time, the cost was finally set at $20.30 per video.

Doorstep Video also needed a source of new releases, which turned out to be Baker and Taylor Video, a major nationwide distributor. Baker and Taylor provided weekly catalogs listing all the new releases scheduled for the next several weeks. The average cost of a new release was $65.00 plus shipping, which usually added another $3.00. Garret later found another source, Schwartz Brothers, which offered savings of $1 to $2 per video, but shipping costs remained approximately $3.00. Schwartz Brothers also offered weekly catalogs listing all new releases as well as some special deals.

A key to buying new releases is knowing how many of each title to purchase. Garret took on this task, which included a lot of guesswork, basing his decisions on how similar titles had sold in the past and on how popular the title had been in the theater. Interestingly, Garret's research indicated that movies popular at the theater were not always popular as rentals. Conversely, some titles that were sleepers at the theater were in high demand in the rental stores. Because there was no obvious formula to use for deciding which new releases to buy, gut feeling played an important role in the selection process. Doorstep Video set its new-release budget at $1,500 per month. Since opened merchandise cannot be returned, Doorstep Video would be penalized for buying too many copies of a new release by having to sell its overstock to a used-video distributor like IMM. Unfortunately, these distributors purchase a video for about one-third of its original cost.

Doorstep Video also needed a source for the purchase of VCRs suitable for renting and the plastic carrying cases needed to protect the videos. Commtron, a major distributor in Atlanta, offered to sell Doorstep Videos the rental-type VCRs for $239 each. The cases ranged in price from $0.49 to $0.55, depending on the quantity ordered.

Inventory System

The inventory system used by Doorstep Video would be an index-card system. Each video would have a card which would be placed in the "out" file when the movie was rented. The customer's number as well as the date rented would be written on the card. This was not the most advanced or efficient system; however, given the company's limited funds, a computer system was out of the question.

As in other new technology-based industries, several very complete inventory systems were available for video rental stores. Interestingly, one of the best in the nation was produced and sold by a firm located in Salisbury. These systems are capable of handling up to 40,000 members and 100,000 videos. All transactions are recorded by a bar-code reader, which makes the system efficient and accurate. The systems provide important business information such as the names of customers with debit balances; the number of rentals per day, month, and year; rentals by customer; rentals per title; and are capable of performing other tasks helpful to management. The cost of such a system, including the computer and printer, is about $5,500.

Financing and Legal and Insurance Expenses

The total startup cost for Doorstep Video was estimated to be about $15,500 (see Exhibit 2). Based on an estimate of daily rentals, Clay and Garret projected weekly rentals of 513 titles, over the first three months (see Exhibit 3). The rental fee was $2.99 for one title and $2.50 each for two or more titles. Based on what they had observed in other stores and from what they had read in *Video Store*, a trade magazine, Clay estimated that the revenue from the average

EXHIBIT 2
Startup Costs—Doorstep Video

Inventory:	
500 Used Videos	$10,150
New Videos	$ 1,500
Rental VCR's 2@ $239	$ 478
Opening Advertising:	
Flyer Insert	$ 450
Printing	$ 416
Newspaper ads	$ 198
Furniture & Equipment	$ 900
Leasehold improvements	$ 400
Return Boxes 4 @ $50	$ 200
Insurance	$ 300
Shirts for employees	$ 170
Telephone installation	$ 95
Office Supplies	$ 60
Plastic cases for video tapes	$ 73
Licenses	$ 60
Legal & Professional	$ 49
Total Startup Costs	$15,499

rental would be $2.63. Monthly expenses were estimated to be $3,635 (see Exhibit 4). During the first year of operation, Garret, who would be managing the store, would receive $700 a month salary, and Clay, who would be only working part time, would not receive any compensation. Any profits would be used to purchase additional inventory. To finance the startup and leave funds available to cover any possible cash-flow problems over the startup period, Garret and Clay each agreed to put up $10,400 from their personal savings.

Because of potential liability problems, Clay and Garret decided to organize Doorstep Video as an S corporation, a form of business that allows small businesses to enjoy the limited liability benefits of the corporate form of organization

(*continued on page 136*)

EXHIBIT 3
Average Projected Video Rentals Per Day

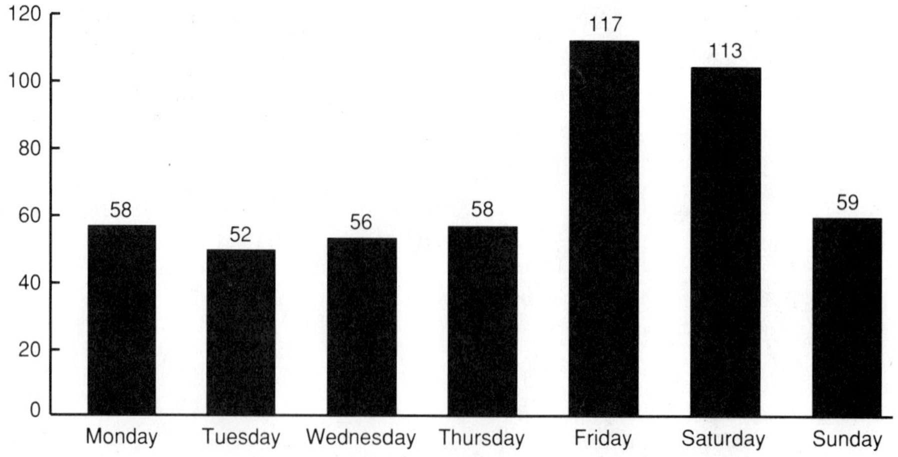
120
100
80
60
40
20
0
58
52
56
58
117
113
59
Monday
Tuesday
Wednesday
Thursday
Friday
Saturday
Sunday

EXHIBIT 4
Projected Monthly Expenses

Videos	$1,500
Gross Payroll	$1,100
Advertising	$ 300
Taxes	$ 370
Telephone	$ 115
Rent & Utilities	$ 100
Misc. Expenses	$ 120
Insurance	$ 30
Total Projected Monthly Expenses	$3,635

EXHIBIT 5
Membership Application

MEMBER #________

LAST NAME __________ FIRST NAME __________ NCDL # __________

ADDRESS __________ CITY __________

HOME PHONE __________ RELATIVE PHONE __________ RELATIVE NAME __________

EMPLOYER __________ DEPT. __________

WORK PHONE __________ SS# __________

REMARKS: __________

I, THE UNDERSIGNED, DO HEREBY ACCEPT THE VIDEOTAPE(S) AND/OR EQUIPMENT FOR THE PURPOSE OF PREVIEWING SAME IN MY HOME, AN ACKNOWLEDGE THAT THEY ARE IN GOOD WORKING CONDITION, AND AGREE TO PAY A STIPULATED HANDLING CHARGE THEREFORE, AND TO TAKE CARE OF ALL SAID TAPES AND/OR EQUIPMENT AND TO USE THEM IN A PROPER MANNER AND AGREE THAT IN THE EVENT ANY OF THE TAPES AND/OR EQUIPMENT ARE LOST, DESTROYED, OR STOLEN BEFORE THEY ARE RETURNED, TO PROMPTLY PAY THE FULL CASH VALUE OF SUCH VALUE, IN CASH AND IF DAMAGED OR INJURED IN ANY WAY TO PAY AN AMOUNT EQUAL TO THE REASONABLE COST OF REPAIRING THE SAME, AND FURTHER DO HEREBY EXONERATE, INDEMNIFY, AND SAVE HARMLESS THE COMPANY FROM ALL CLAIMS OR LIABILITIES TO ALL PARTIES FOR DAMAGE OR LOSS TO ANY PERSON, PERSONS, OR PROPERTY IN ANY WAY ARISING OUT OF OR DURING THE USE OF SAID VIDEOTAPE(S) AND/OR EQUIPMENT. I, THE UNDERSIGNED, FURTHER UNDERSTAND THAT THIS AGREEMENT IS BINDING FOR ALL VIDEOTAPE(S) AND/OR EQUIPMENT RENTED DURING THE DURATION OF MY MEMBERSHIP.

IT IS UNDERSTOOD THAT *FEDERAL LAW PROHIBITS THE REPRODUCTION OF ALL COPYRIGHTED VIDEOTAPES.*

SIGNED __________ DATE __________

as well as the benefits of being taxed as a partnership. They talked to an attorney, who agreed to handle the necessary incorporation paperwork for only $49. In addition, they had a membership application form designed to provide a measure of protection for Doorstep Video and also to serve as a contract between Doorstep and its customers (see Exhibit 5).

Clay talked to a local insurance agent about the coverage that Doorstep Video would need. The agent recommended a comprehensive policy that would cover the contents of the store up to $30,000 in case of fire or water damage. Theft insurance was not included. In addition, the drivers were covered by a rider that provided Doorstep Video with liability insurance for any claim that was in excess of the liability coverage from the driver's own insurance—since the drivers would be using their own cars for deliveries.

DECISION TIME

During the last week in April, with the spring semester almost complete, Garret and Clay need to make a decision on whether to go ahead with the startup of Doorstep Video or abandon their plans. They have contacted students at a local college and found several willing to work on a part-time basis. In addition, the local telephone company agreed to give them a local number that helped describe the purpose of their business—636-FAST.

They both feel that the idea of home delivery of rental videos is one they can build into a profitable business. Clay, however, does have one more year of college before he can devote full time to the business. To further complicate the decision, Garret has received a job offer in sales with a nationally known firm. They agree that they must make a decision no later than the first week in May.

REFERENCES

1. Subrata Chakravarty, "Give 'em Variety," *Forbes*, 2 May 1988, pp. 54–57.
2. "Video Marketing," published by *Video Store*, Hollywood, CA, 1987.
3. Ron Stodghill, "Will Video Chains Push Small Stores Out of the Picture?" *The Charlotte Observer*, 15 February 1988, pp. 1 and 13C.

QUESTIONS

1. Is home delivery a potentially profitable niche in the rental video tape industry?
2. What potential problem do you foresee in the home delivery of rental video tapes?
3. What would you do to make this startup have a better chance of being successful?
4. What is the future of the rental video tape industry? How will it evolve?
5. Would you give up a good paying job with managerial potential to start a business in a relatively small town?
6. Would you proceed with the startup of Doorstep Video? Why or why not?

CHAPTER 6

The Legal Aspects of Business

Learning Objectives

After you have read this chapter, you will be able to do the following:

- Determine why startup entrepreneurs need attorneys.
- Select and use lawyers.
- Describe the different forms of ownership.
- Identify various types of contracts that apply to startups.
- Understand patents, copyrights, and trademarks.

We know that businesses fail for many different reasons. Some causes, such as ineffective management and poor location, are difficult to foresee and to correct. However, a business should not fail because its owner ran afoul of the law. There are so many laws on the books that no entrepreneur could be expected to be familiar with more than a fraction of them, but the old cliché "what you don't know can hurt you" applies to all business owners. Since entrepreneurs are not expected to be legal experts, they will need someone who is an expert to advise them in legal matters. Entrepreneurs should select a competent attorney before they get very far into their startup planning.

There are approximately seven hundred thousand attorneys in the United States, more per capita than in any other country. In some instances, attorneys, have to create work to keep themselves fully employed. Ewell E. Murphy, Jr., a Houston attorney states that " . . . lawyers in the United States do things which need doing, but in other countries those things are done mostly by nonlawyers—by accountants, executives, bureaucrats, commissars, Zen abbots, witch doctors, Mafia capos, fakirs, and other assorted movers and shakers."[1] It is sometimes difficult to know when a lawyer is needed and what he or she can do for the startup company.

In this chapter we will examine the role of attorneys, how to select the right attorney, how to evaluate attorneys, etc. We will also discuss the most appropriate form of ownership for startups. We will present information about contracts and show how a business owner can protect products and property with patents, copyrights, and trademarks. Finally, we will briefly discuss bankruptcy, the penalty for committing too many mistakes.

USING LAWYERS

Only foolhardy entrepreneurs would consider starting a business or buying a business or franchise without the advice and counsel of a competent attorney. Once the self-employment decision has been made, the business creator should retain both an attorney and an accountant to guide him or her through the morass of legal and fiscal requirements. These two professionals will prove invaluable to the new business owner even though they will sometimes have conflicting opinions on important matters.

The Need for Lawyers

Only the simplest business can be started without the assistance of a lawyer. Someone who is thinking about turning a hobby into a business may not need a lawyer; however, any business that will have employees, a product, a shop or office, suppliers, creditors, distributors, and customers needs an attorney. In fact, anyone who is planning to start a business should retain an experienced attorney and use him or her whenever necessary. Lawyers would not be as necessary if we were not living in such a litigious society, but we are, and people seem to be willing to sue "at the drop of a hat."

The following are some examples of liability cases that businesses have lost:

1. Liability based on fingernail polish that caught fire when a cigarette ignited the fumes.
2. Liability based on a lawn mower that injured a person who was using the product to trim hedges.
3. Liability based on an oven door that collapsed, injuring a woman who was standing on it to clean the kitchen.
4. Liability based on a tire rated for 85 miles per hour that was involved in a crash by a drunk driver who was doing 100 miles per hour.[2]

Avoiding litigation is not the only reason to retain a lawyer. An attorney will be needed when leases and contracts are signed, key employees are hired, partnerships or corporations are formed, employees are terminated, and at other times. Poorly written leases and contracts can cause a company owner trouble, but the damage can usually be repaired before it causes significant problems for the business. Not so with punitive damages. Punitive damages, the money juries award people wronged by a company or its product, are so large that they can totally destroy a young business. An attorney can help a new business avoid incurring the punitive damages that juries seem more willing to award to plaintiffs (see The Inside View 6-1).

6-1 *The Inside View*

PUNITIVE DAMAGES

Punitive damages are frequently awarded by juries in product-liability lawsuits, and the consequences are severe: The awards, which often are six figures or more, may not be covered by liability insurance. Concealing information usually causes juries to rule against a company. Other factors that have led juries to award punitive damages include evidence that the company has knowingly violated a safety standard, used misleading advertising about the product's safety, ignored technical reports claiming an unreasonable hazard, demoted or fired a whistle-blower who voices safety concerns, poorly handled consumer safety complaints, or failed to conduct sufficient safety research.[3]

Selecting Lawyers

Having decided that there is a real need for an attorney, the next item on the entrepreneur's agenda should be the selection of the best one for the startup company. One of the first considerations is the size of the law firm. The following are some advantages of using a large firm:

1. The prestige of a large firm often intimidates opponents.
2. Through its association with a large law firm, it is easier for an unknown company to schedule appointments with banks, underwriters, etc.
3. A large firm has lawyers with a broad range of expertise.
4. A large law firm is more likely to have had exposure to a broad range of business problems.
5. Some larger firms charge new companies lower fees.

There are also reasons why a new business might be better represented by a smaller law firm. The following are some of the disadvantages of large law firms:

1. Most attorneys in large firms are not especially creative because creative people do not fit in well in large organizations.
2. A large firm is not likely to refer a client to an expert outside the firm.
3. Occasionally it might be necessary to use outside lawyers because the company's regular law firm has a conflict of interest in a particular case.
4. Larger firms try to maximize billable hours (the time a client is receiving advice or assistance).[4]

Locating Lawyers. In the past, finding lawyers was a rather difficult task. Lawyers did not advertise; therefore, entrepreneurs had to rely on referrals or the recommendations of acquaintances, other businesspeople, banks, etc. However, for the past ten years, lawyers have been allowed to advertise their services. Most lawyers rely on the Yellow Pages for their advertising, but some also use the media, brochures, seminars, and newsletters. While advertising legal services attracts new clients, some of the advertising is of questionable taste (see The Inside View 6-2).

Advertising and referrals may not be the best way to locate a lawyer for a business startup. There is an objective rating of lawyers in the *Martindale-Hubbell Law Directory*, the only comprehensive directory of lawyers. Not all attorneys listed in this directory are rated; however, it is good place to start the search for a reputable lawyer.

Selection Criteria. We know that one of the primary concerns of startup entrepreneurs is the size of the law firm to retain. Once the firm has been selected, it is then necessary to choose the individual lawyer within the firm who will represent the business. There are several criteria that can be used to select the right lawyer. The following are some of the more common:

1. *Other clients.* It would be inappropriate to select a lawyer who represents the competition. While it may be beneficial to use an attorney who specializes in a particular field, it will not help the startup business to have an attorney who is privy to sensitive material which might inadvertently be passed to competitors.
2. *Networks.* Even the best lawyers need to turn to other experts in certain situations; therefore, it is important to know whom the prospective lawyer consults when he or she needs advice.
3. *Values.* It is important to evaluate an attorney's value set or ethics before engaging her or him. Lawyers with questionble ethics may save the startup business money in the short run; however, he or she may cost the company more than it can afford in the long run.

6-2 The Inside View

ADVERTISING LEGAL SERVICES

In an effort to become known, the law firm of Vetter & White decided to use a promotional brochure. The firm's brochure features the usual photos of stern partners whose achievements are extolled. The brochure also contains this eyecatcher: a photo of two voluptuous nude women lounging in a bathtub. How is this relevant to the legal profession? "Like a bathtub," the caption reads, "trial lawyers have to fill up on the facts and the law of the case."[5]

4. ***Ability to assist.*** A lawyer should be able to devote the necessary time to the affairs of a startup. Often lawyers selected on the basis of their reputation do not have the time to assist new businesses.

5. ***Style.*** Paternalistic, highly opinionated, and excessively glib attorneys should be avoided.

6. ***Fees.*** Lawyers are free to choose how much they will charge for their services, so it is a good idea to do some comparison shopping based on cost. However, the lawyer with the lowest per hour cost is not necessarily the least expensive.

7. ***Small-business expertise.*** Some attorneys and law firms specialize in providing assistance to small businesses. Startup entrepreneurs should look for lawyers who normally represent new and small firms.

Legal Fees. Since legal fees are often the major source of friction between lawyer and client, it is advisable to know what the costs are and how to minimize them. Law firms, which bill by the hour, do not have much incentive to work quickly and efficiently. Marisa Manley, a New York attorney, suggests the following ways to control costs: find out who will be doing the work—senior partners, junior partners, associates, or paralegals; find out exactly what the hourly rates cover; probe those little costs like duplicating and telephone calls; set limits—stipulate that only requested services will be paid for; monitor the work; and review the bills.[6]

Lawyer–Client Relationship. Once a lawyer has been selected, startup entrepreneurs should take advantage of their rights as clients. Marc Lane has drafted the following client's "Bill of Rights":

1. ***Confidentiality.*** Client secrets and confidences should be preserved at all times.

2. ***Full disclosure of information.*** Clients have the right to be kept informed of everything concerning any pending legal matter and in a manner that is clear and precise.

3. ***Ultimate authority.*** The client, not the lawyer, makes final decisions about matters concerning her or him. The lawyer advises but does not decide.

4. ***Reasonable fees.*** There should be no "hidden" costs or charges for unnecessary or unauthorized services.

5. ***Competence.*** Clients have a right to loyal, skillful, and energetic representation by a lawyer who treats them courteously and considerately.

6. ***Termination.*** If all does not go well, clients have the right to call it quits upon payment of fair compensation for legal services properly performed.[7]

Legal Services

Once a lawyer has been selected, the next important step is to use his or her services effectively. The size of legal fees alone should be enough to discourage frivolous use of the company's lawyer. However, it is equally unwise to avoid using an attorney simply to save money. The following are some of the services entrepreneurs can reasonably expect from their attorneys:

Organization. An attorney should advise the startup entrepreneur on which form of business would be the best for his or her company—sole proprietorship, partnership, or corporation—and should also handle the legal requirements involved in its establishment.

Buying, Selling, Contracting, and Leasing. Starting a business usually involves negotiating with others to buy, contract, lease, or sell something. The entrepreneur who tries to save money by negotiating without the assistance of an attorney is not using good judgment. After all, lawyers are trained to negotiate the best deal for their clients.

Local Zoning, License, and Permit Requirements. It is virtually impossible to start a business without one or more permits or licenses. Attorneys should know what licenses and permits the startup business needs and how to acquire them. Even before a location is selected, the attorney should investigate zoning regulations, which are not always clear to laypeople.

Loans. Unless entrepreneurs have enough personal funds to finance a startup, they will have to rely on other individuals and institutions to provide the necessary startup capital. Lawyers should read all documents required by banks, investors, or other lending sources to identify any unacceptable terms or requirements.

Taxes. Tax evasion is illegal; tax avoidance is not. A good attorney, working with a competent accountant, can help minimize the amount of money a startup business pays for local, state, and federal taxes.

Abiding by the Law. There are thousands of local, state, and federal laws that apply to businesses. Many of these laws have been on the books for years and are no longer enforced; however, they could be used if it were to suit someone's purpose. Most lawyers are not familiar with all of the laws that apply to businesses, but they certainly know more about the laws and regulations than do most entrepreneurs and businesspeople.

Litigation. We have already discussed the devastation that punitive damages resulting from litigation can cause. Startup companies need to rely on their attorneys to help them avoid litigation. It is much less costly to buy legal advice that prevents litigious situations or events than it is to pay for court proceedings which could result in punitive damages.

Guidance on Future Plans. Attorneys can help startup entrepreneurs develop future plans. They can even advise on the practicality of starting a new venture. Wise entrepreneurs use their attorneys to full advantage when contemplating any future moves.

Lawyers can assist startup companies in many different ways; however, they are most effective if they are very familiar with the business. The following dos and don'ts about dealing with attorneys, suggested by Howard Stern,[8] will enable startup businesses to reap the most benefit from using attorneys:

- The lawyer should be part of the management team; let him or her participate in business decisions.
- Ask questions. Have the lawyer show you the law if you have any doubts.

- Differentiate between what you are entitled to legally and what you can negotiate.
- Give your attorney firm dates for responses and hold her or him accountable.
- Do not allow your attorney to reopen a deal that has already been closed.
- Do not let your attorney check things out in advance with government agencies unless you are prepared to accept a no or a maybe.
- Do not let your attorney engage in illegal work.
- Do not let nonattorneys in the company deal with outside attorneys by themselves.
- If your attorney tells you, "You hired me for my advice, and if you do not follow my advice you should get another attorney," get another attorney. Whether or not you follow advice is your decision.

Evaluating Lawyers

Whenever we pay for any services, we want to be sure that the person providing them is competent. Evaluating an attorney's performance is not particularly easy because he or she provides so many different services that it is difficult to compare his or her performance with that of other attorneys. Lawyers often claim that only they can evaluate the performance of other lawyers. Unfortunately, most entrepreneurs need to determine the value of their attorneys without the aid of other lawyers. Answers to the following questions will indicate how well an attorney is performing:

1. ***Does the lawyer respond in a timely fashion?*** Even the best advice is useless if it is given too late. Lawyers who take on too many clients tend to miss deadlines. An efficient lawyer should be able to say when he or she will complete an assignment and should meet that deadline most of the time. The mark of a good attorney is not necessarily fast work but rather a reasonable estimate of the time required for a response and a sincere commitment to fulfill that promise.

2. ***Does the lawyer speak your language?*** Any competent attorney should be able to prepare documents that are meaningful to a layperson. Lawyers do not impress their clients by littering their work with legal jargon. One of the primary responsibilities of an attorney is to make things clear and to avoid misunderstanding.

3. ***Does the lawyer make an occasional suggestion?*** Attorneys who speak only when spoken to do their clients a disservice. Competent lawyers will occasionally make suggestions to benefit their client's business.

4. ***Does the lawyer know your business?*** Competent attorneys familiarize themselves with their client's business. They visit the business, talk to employees, learn about the company's products or services, evaluate the competition, and talk to customers. Only then can a lawyer provide individualized assistance to a new business.

5. ***Does the law firm have a Washington office or a firm in Washington with which it has a close relationship?*** The government is so heavily involved in business regulations today that many problems simply cannot be solved without going to Washington. Also, advance information on key developments is usually easier to obtain in Washington than elsewhere. Attorneys can serve their clients more efficiently if they have a Washington connection; however, lack of a Washington connection does not necessarily preclude first-rate service.

6. ***Does the law firm send out client bulletins on recent developments?*** Many small law firms periodically send out bulletins about matters they know to be of interest to their clients. The bulletins are not expensive or personalized, but they do indicate that the firm is thinking about its clients.

7. ***Does the lawyer have a philosophy similar to yours?*** Lawyers are generally either conservative or aggressive in their approach to law and business. It is advisable to use an attorney whose philosophy is similar to yours. Entrepreneurs are entitled to know if they are getting conservative or aggressive advice and to participate in deciding how much risk they are willing to assume.

8. ***Does the lawyer keep current?*** Laws can change rapidly, so lawyers who do not participate in seminars, take short courses, attend professional meetings, or otherwise stay abreast of developments soon become obsolete. It is not a good idea to start a new venture with an obsolete lawyer.[9]

FORMS OF OWNERSHIP

One of the first decisions that startup entrepreneurs and their attorneys should make concerns the legal structure of the business. As we have mentioned, a company can be a sole proprietorship, a partnership, or a corporation. Each of these forms has advantages and disadvantages (see Table 6.1) to consider before selecting the most appropriate one. The form selected is not immutable. It is possible, for example, to start as a sole proprietorship, change into a partnership, and then become a corporation. It is also possible to reverse that process and change from corporate status to a partnership or proprietorship.

Sole Proprietorship

Because it is the simplest form of ownership, the *sole proprietorship* is the most prevalent. There are more proprietorships than partnerships and corporations combined. This form is usually chosen by people starting a new business because it doesn't require legal assistance or large sums of money. To establish a proprietorship, entrepreneurs need only to obtain the required licenses and permits, and begin operations. This form of ownership has advantages and disadvantages that should be evaluated.

Advantages. The following are some of the major advantages of sole proprietorships:

1. ***Simplicity.*** This is the easiest type of business to establish and operate. Lawyers are not needed to establish the business, and there are very few government requirements that apply to proprietorships.

2. ***Unilateral decision making.*** The owner makes all the decisions related to the business. He or she does not have to consult with co-owners or employees when a decision has to be made.

3. ***Unshared profits.*** All of the profits generated by the business revert to the owner. The owner may choose to share profits with employees, but he or she is not required or obligated to do so.

4. ***Flexibility.*** The freedom to plan and make decisions without consultation enables the proprietor to rapidly react to change and opportunities.

5. ***Tax benefits.*** Business losses can be deducted from the owner's personal income tax.

(*Text continues on page 152*)

Table 6.1 Comparison of the Corporation, S Corporation, Partnership, and Sole Proprietorship

Factor	*Corporation (Regular Corporation)*	*S Corporation (Small-Business Corporation)*	*Partnership*	*Sole Proprietorship*
Life	Unlimited or perpetual, unless limited by state law or terms of its charter.	Same as regular corporation. S corporation election may be revoked or terminated without affecting continuity of life.	Generally set up for a specific, agreed term; usually will be terminated by death, withdrawal, insolvency or legal disability of a general partner.	At death, business assets pass with proprietor's estate.
Entity	Completely separate from owners and recognized as such.	Same as regular corporation.	Generally recognized as separate by the business community, but not for all purposes.	Same as partnership.
Liability of owners	Limited. Shareholders are generally sheltered from any liabilities of the corporation.	Same as regular corporation.	Each general partner is fully liable as an individual for all debts. A limited partner's liability is usually limited to the amount of his or her capital contribution.	Owner has unlimited risk. Creditors can attach all personal assets for business debts.
Ease and effect of transfer of ownership interest	Generally, stock is easily and readily transferable, and transfer has no effect on the corporate entity.	Same as regular corporation. Consideration must be given to the effect of the transfer on the election to be sure it does not result in an unintended termination of S corporation status.	Transfer may require approval of all other partners and may cause termination of the old partnership and creation of a new one.	Transfer terminates entity and creates new firm.

Table 6.1 continued

Factor	*Corporation (Regular Corporation)*	*S Corporation (Small-Business Corporation)*	*Partnership*	*Sole Proprietorship*
Availability of public equity capital or debt financing	May sell stock or bonds to the public.	Limited in that there can be only one class of stock outstanding; however, different voting rights are allowable. The corporation can have "straight debt," which will not be treated as a second class of stock.	Limited to borrowing from partners or outsiders or to admitting new partners who contribute additional capital. Certain publicly traded partnerships (PTPs) can sell interests to the public.	Limited to owner's personal assets and outside credit.
Management of business operation	Much flexibility. Control can be exercised by a small number of officers without having to consult owners, regardless of the total number of shareholders.	About the same as a regular corporation, except that more active participation by all owners can usually be expected since the total number of shareholders cannot exceed 35.	Usually, all general partners will be active participants in management. However, other partners may grant management control to one or more partners by agreement.	Owner has complete control.
Who is the taxpayer?	The corporation is taxed on its taxable income, whether or not it is distributed to the shareholders. Dividend distributions are taxed again in the hands of the individual shareholders (the "double-taxation" effect).**	The shareholders are generally taxed on the taxable income of the corporation, whether or not it is distributed to them. The various attributes of the income or loss flow through to the shareholder.	The partners are taxed on the taxable income of the partnership, whether or not it is distributed to them. The various attributes of the income or loss flow through to the partners.	The owner is taxed on the taxable income, whether or not it is withdrawn by the owner.

Distribution of earnings	Taxable to shareholders as ordinary dividends to the extent of "earnings and profits."	No tax effect to shareholders, unless the distribution exceeds shareholder's tax basis in the corporation. Excess taxed as capital gain to shareholder until basis is reestablished.*	No tax effect on partners, unless distribution exceeds partner's tax basis. Excess taxed as capital gain to partner.*	No tax effect to proprietor.
Net operating loss	Deductible only by the corporation within prescribed carryback and carryover period. Additionally, may be limited by at-risk rules and passive-activity rules if closely held.	Deductible by shareholders, subject to adequate tax basis to cover losses and at-risk limitations. Also may be limited in deducting losses and credits due to lack of participation in affairs of entity (passive-activity loss rules).	Deductible by partners, subject to adequate tax basis to cover losses and at-risk limitations. Also may be limited in deducting losses and credits due to lack of participation in affairs of entity (passive-activity loss rules). Limited partners are presumed nonactive.	Deductible by owner, subject to adequate income to cover losses and at-risk rules.
Salaries paid to owners	When owners are employees, salaries are taxable to them and deductible by the corporation. Salaries must be reasonable in amount in relation to services rendered.	Same as regular corporation. The question of unreasonably large salaries is not as important unless salaries are used as a device for shifting income among shareholders within a family group.	Generally, amounts paid are considered partial distributions of income. If the distribution is a guaranteed payment of salary, it will be deductible by the partnership and ordinary income to the partner.	Sole proprietor is not an employee. Amount paid is considered a distribution of income.

Table 6.1 continued

Factor	*Corporation (Regular Corporation)*	*S Corporation (Small-Business Corporation)*	*Partnership*	*Sole Proprietorship*
Liquidation of the business	Generally results in taxable gain at the corporate level *and* the shareholder level. The corporation recognizes gain on the sale of any assets in liquidation (and/or the distribution of assets in liquidation) to the extent the selling price (fair market value) exceeds the corporation's tax basis in assets. The shareholder reports amounts received in excess of basis in stock as capital gain (ordinary income if the corporation is "collapsible").*	Same as regular corporation except no double taxation on gain at corporate level since it flows through to the shareholders and increases their tax basis in stock.	Normally, no tax unless cash or equivalent exceeds basis in partnership interest. Excess is taxed as a capital gain (ordinary income if the partnerhsip is "collapsible").*	No gain or loss until business or assets are sold to a third party.
Pension or profit-sharing plan	Owners who are employees can be included in a regular qualified plan; if a qualified plan is maintained, deductibility of IRA contributions by participating employees may be limited depending upon their income levels.	Generally, same as regular corporation with some additional restrictions imposed on owners.	Generally, same as regular corporation with some additional restrictions imposed on partners. Keogh Plan also available.	Generally, same as regular corporation with some additional restrictions imposed on owner. Keogh Plan also available.

Capital gains and losses	Taxed to the corporation at the same rate as ordinary income.*	Taxed to the shareholders as such.*	Taxed to the partners as such.*	Taxed to the owner as such.*
Tax on transfer of assets to business	Generally, none if the transferor(s) retains control of at least 80% of the corporation after the transfer (unless liabilities assumed by the corporation exceed transferor's tax basis).	Same as regular corporation.	None, unless liabilities assumed reduce transfer's tax basis in the partnership below zero.	None.
Allocation of net income or loss or different types of income and deductions among owners by agreement	Not possible.	Not possible.	Can be done as long as there is substantial economic effect to the agreement.	Not applicable.
Effect of death or sale of interest by owner on tax basis of assets in business	None.	None.	Election may be filed to adjust basis of partnership assets applicable to transferor partner's interest.	Upon death, basis adjusts to fair market value for heirs. Upon sale, basis adjustment not applicable.
Earnings accumulation	May be subject to penalty tax if accumulation is unreasonable.	No limit since all income is taxed to the shareholders whether distributed or not.	No limit since all income is taxed to partners whether distributed or not.	Same as partnership.

Table 6.1 continued

Factor	*Corporation (Regular Corporation)*	*S Corporation (Small-Business Corporation)*	*Partnership*	*Sole Proprietorship*
Passive investment income	May create a personal holding company taxed at penalty rates.	Generally no effect.	No effect.	No effect.
Selection of tax year	No restriction except for Personal Service Corporations (PSCs), which generally must use calendar year.	Calendar year, unless consent of the commissioner is obtained; generally, election allowed only if the tax year results in a deferral period not longer than three months.	Same as S corporation.	Same as that of the owner.
Sale of ownership interest	All capital gain unless corporation is "collapsible," then ordinary income.*	Same as regular corporation.	May be part capital gain and part ordinary income.*	Same as partnership.

Charitable contributions	Deductible by the corporation, limited to 10% of taxable income. Excess may be carried over.	Not deductible by the corporation on its return but may be deducted by the shareholders on their individual returns subject to the limitations applicable to individuals.	Not deductible by the partnership on its return but may be deducted by the partners on their individual returns subject to the limitations applicable to individuals.	Not deductible by the proprietorship but may be deducted by the owner on the individual return subject to the limitations applicable to individuals.
Alternative minimum tax (AMT)	Tax preference and adjustment items are subject to AMT at the corporate level. A corporation must pay the higher of the regular tax or the AMT.	Tax preference and adjustment items pass through to the shareholders.	Tax preference and adjustment items pass through to the partners.	Same as partnership.
	The corporate minimum tax has been vastly expanded by the Tax Reform Act of 1986 and affects a much greater number of taxpayers after 1986.			

*The Tax Reform Act of 1986 repealed the preferential capital gains rate; there is no rate differential between ordinary income and capital gains after 1987.
**PSCs are denied the benefit of the graduated corporate rates for tax years beginning after 1987.
SOURCE: Reprinted with permission from *An Entrepreneur's Guide to Starting a Business*, copyright 1988 by Arthur Andersen & Co.

6. *Minimal red tape.* There are very few reports or forms required by state or federal agencies.

Disadvantages. Sole proprietorships have several undeniable advantages over other forms of ownership; however, there are also some drawbacks associated with this form of ownership. The following are some of the disadvantages associated with sole proprietorships:

1. *Unlimited liability.* The sole proprietor is responsible for all of the company's debts. This liability extends to all the proprietor's assets, such as house, car, savings, and all other property. Some hazards may be insured against, but some risks are uninsurable, and liability for debts is boundless.

2. *Limited lifespan.* The business and the proprietor are essentially one and the same; therefore, if the owner quits the business or dies, the business ceases to exist.

3. *Limited expertise.* One person usually does not possess all the skills necessary to successfully operate a business. An entrepreneur may be a skilled salesperson but be totally devoid of manufacturing skills.

4. *Limited access to capital.* Banks and other lenders are reluctant to make loans that cannot be secured by assets. Proprietors often must pay very high interest rates for funds because of the risk involved in lending to them.

5. *Limited benefit deductibility.* Proprietors cannot take advantage of many of the deductible "fringes" enjoyed by corporate shareholder-employees, including sick pay; medical, dental, and hospitalization plans; group term life insurance; and more.

Partnership

Entrepreneurs who believe that the disadvantages of sole proprietorships outweigh the advantages may choose to form *partnerships* to minimize some of the proprietorship drawbacks. Partnerships can be as informal and as easy to form as proprietorships and can also offer entrepreneurs some advantages that proprietorships do not.

Advantages. In addition to ease of formation and relative simplicity, a partnership offers the following advantages:

1. *Complementary expertise.* Partners should have skills that are complementary. One partner might have enviable financial skills while another might be skilled in production.

2. *Joint decision making.* Since more than one person has a vested interest in the business, it is likely that decisions will be arrived at jointly and all partners will be committed to the decisions.

3. *Tax benefits.* The partnership is a tax reporter but not a taxpayer. Individual partners pay taxes on business profits or deduct losses from their individual tax returns.

4. *Greater access to capital.* Since partners can pool their personal assets, they should not need as much external financing as proprietorships do. It is also easier to borrow from lending sources when more than one person is obligated to repay the loan.

5. *Minimal red tape.* There are no state incorporation fees and few reports required by state and federal governments.

Disadvantages. While partnerships have advantages that proprietorships do not, they also have some drawbacks. The following are the major disadvantages of partnerships:

1. ***Unlimited liability.*** Each partner is liable for all of the partnership's debts, even those incurred by one partner without the knowledge or authorization of other partners.

2. ***Limited life.*** By definition, a partnership is technically dissolved at the death or withdrawal of any partner. However, it is possible for surviving partners to purchase the interests of the deceased person should there be a prior agreement to that effect.

3. ***Responsibility for each partner's actions.*** Partners are responsible for each other's actions and they cannot purchase bonding protection against the actions of other partners.

4. ***Shared profits.*** Profits must be shared among all partners; therefore, it is advisable to stipulate in the partnership agreement what percentage of the profits each partner is entitled to receive.

5. ***Conflict.*** Partnerships are often dissolved because the partners cannot get along. There may be personality conflicts or partners may have divergent goals for the company.

Kinds of Partnerships. The two most prevalent kinds of partnerships are *general* and *limited.* In a general partnership, each partner is responsible for the decisions and actions of all partners, and all partners are involved in the normal operations of the company. A limited partnership is composed of one or more general partners and one or more limited partners whose liability is limited to the amount of capital they invested in the company. Limited partners are not involved in the day-to-day operations of the company and are, therefore, often referred to as "silent partners."

Forming Partnerships. Because of the risk they are assuming, partners should seek legal advice from competent attorneys before entering into any partnership agreement. There is no "standard" partnership agreement, but the following are articles usually found in partnership agreements:

Name and purpose of the partnership
Duration of the agreement
Nature of partners (general or limited, active or silent)
Capital contributed by each partner
Responsibility and authority of each partner
How business expenses will be handled
Books, records, and accounting methods
Division of profits and losses
Withdrawals and salaries of partners
Death of a partner
Admission of new partners
Release of debts
Sale of partnership interests
Settlement of disputes (arbitration, etc.)
Required and prohibited acts

Distribution of assets in the event of dissolution
Additions or alterations of the partnership agreement

It is advisable to have an attorney draw up a partnership agreement because in the absence of such a document, the terms of the Uniform Partnership Act will prevail. This act contains the following key rules:

1. Any partner can bind other partners to business debts.
2. Partners are "individually and personally" liable for partnership debts if those debts exceed the assets of the partnership.
3. Any partner can terminate the partnership at any time for any reason.
4. The death of any partner automatically terminates the partnership.
5. The liability of a partner for partnership debts is "joint and several." (This means that each partner is liable for all the partnership debts.)
6. The basic rules of liability contained in this contract cannot be changed.
7. A partnership interest is subject to the normal rules of family law. (In divorce cases, this interest is treated like all other assets.)

Corporations

The third form of ownership available to entrepreneurs is *incorporation*. This is the most formal and costly form of ownership, but it has several advantages which should be considered. In this section we will discuss two kinds of corporations—the traditional *C corporation* and the newer *S corporation*.

Advantages. The following are some of the advantages of the corporate form of ownership:

1. ***Limited liability.*** The liability of stockholders, or owners, is limited to their investment. That means that owners cannot have their personal assets taken to satisfy corporate debt.

2. ***Separate entity.*** Corporations are legal entities separate and distinct from individuals.

3. ***Longevity.*** Corporations continue to exist even when owners die or withdraw from the company.

4. ***Professional management.*** It is possible to hire professional managers to operate the company.

5. ***Ability to attract funds.*** It is easier for corporations to acquire necessary capital than it is for proprietorships or partnerships.

Disadvantages. While incorporating facilitates professional management and growth, there are drawbacks that alienate entrepreneurs. The following are some of the major disadvantages of the corporate form:

1. ***Formality.*** It is a formal, structured way of doing business. The formation of corporations depends on the satisfaction of specific legal requirements.

2. ***Double taxation.*** Corporate income is taxed, and stockholders also pay taxes on the dividends they receive from the company; hence *double taxation*. (For more about taxes, see Chapter 17.)

3. ***Shared ownership.*** It may be necessary to grant professional managers partial ownership of the company to encourage their commitment to the firm's survival and growth.

4. ***Paperwork and red tape.*** Corporations are required to submit many more reports to federal agencies than are either proprietorships or partnerships.

5. ***Limited scope.*** Corporations can engage only in those activities covered by their charters.

Incorporating. The process of incorporating is relatively simple and straightforward, and can be done without attorneys in most states; however, this is one instance when it is advisable to use the services of a knowledgeable lawyer. The basic steps in the incorporation process are as follows:

Choose a company name.
Decide on the location.
Apply for an IRS identification number.
State the company's purpose.
Determine the duration of the corporation.
Name the original incorporators.
Decide how much stock to authorize.
Select officers and directors.
Draft corporate bylaws.

Name. A company's name, which can very well become one of its most valuable assets, should be carefully selected and protected (more about protection in the next section). People identify the company's products, image, and reputation with its name (see if you can match the companies listed on page 157 to the kind of business described); therefore, no entrepreneur should select a name for his or her company without care and deliberation. The first impulse of many an entrepreneur is to give his or her own name to the company. This is usually not a particularly good idea because it does not convey the purpose of the company to consumers. It is more appropriate to select a corporate name that is:

Easy to spell, recognize, and remember
Easy to pronounce (see The Inside View 6-3)
Adaptable to packaging and labeling needs
Unique
Informative
Not offensive
Short
Related to the product or service

Location. A company does not have to incorporate in the state in which it does business. Many companies choose to incorporate in Delaware because that state caters to corporations by providing the following advantages:

1. There is no corporate income tax on nonresident corporations, no tax on shares owned by nonresidents, and no inheritance tax for nonresident stockholders.
2. Stockholders and directors can meet outside of Delaware.

3. Only one incorporator is needed.
4. There are no minimal capital requirements.
5. Directors can change the bylaws by unanimous written consent rather than by vote at a formal meeting.
6. A Delaware corporation can own the stock of other corporations and all other kinds of property.
7. Any different kinds of business can be conducted in combination.
8. Dividends can be paid out of either profits or surplus.

These advantages do not mean that all new businesses should automatically choose to incorporate in Delaware. There are other criteria that should be evaluated. The following checklist could be used to select the most appropriate state in which to incorporate:

1. Compare the states' laws for their requirements for capitalization, directors' powers, and operational flexibility.
2. Compare incorporation fees and related taxes.
3. Consider the cost of qualifying a foreign (out-of-state) corporation in states in which the corporation will be doing business.
4. Examine statutes relating to tender offers.
5. Check on annual fees and taxes in each state.[11]

Identification number. Unlike consumers, the Internal Revenue Service does not care about a company's name; it identifies corporations only by number. Therefore, it is necessary to apply to the IRS for a number for a new corporation. IRS Form SS-4, Application for Employer Identification Number (see Figure 6.1), should be used to apply for the company's ID number.

6-3 *The Inside View*

PRONOUNCEABLE COMPANY NAMES

How is Precis, the name of Mitsubishi's car, pronounced? The company had three options to consider: The name could be PRAY-see, PREE-sus, or PRAY-sus. Marketing executives decided to find out what the different pronunciations meant to consumers. When consumers said "PRAY-sus," they thought of a family car. "PRAY-see" led them to expect a luxury or sports model. Only "PREE-sus" recalled the correct image of an economy car. The company settled on "PREE-sus," but it will have to educate the public before consumers learn to pronounce the name correctly.[10]

Try to match these businesses with the corresponding catchy name:

Business	*Name*
1. Pet suppliers and groomers	A. Sweet Nothings
2. Fine jewelers	B. Pic-a-Flick
3. Gifts and collectibles	C. Straightlace
4. Mini-storage	D. In Good Taste
5. Party and paper supply	E. Wedgies
6. Computer service center	F. A Pack Rat
7. Children's clothing	G. Murder by Design
8. Craft shop	H. Paper Chase
9. Dancing instruction	I. Beep One
10. Opticians	J. Dazzles
11. Day care	K. Electricities
12. Catering	L. Animal House
13. Car phones	M. My Favorite Things
14. Take-out food	N. Fete Accompli
15. China and glassware	O. If It's Paper
16. Consignment shop	P. Up-N-Running
17. Dry cleaners	Q. Repeat Boutique
18. Furniture repair	R. Outer Vision
19. Video rentals	S. Strip-Ease
20. Cocktail lounge	T. Idle Knot
21. Seafood restaurant	U. Happy Feet
22. Lingerie	V. Out to Lunch
23. Theatrical production company	W. Gingerbread House
24. Gourmet shop	X. Crystal Clear
25. Pizza parlor	Y. Pressing Club
26. Rare bookstore	Z. Castaways

Answers: 1.L., 2.J., 3.M., 4.F., 5.O., 6.P., 7.C., 8.T., 9.U., 10.R., 11.W., 12.N., 13.I., 14.V., 15.X., 16.Q., 17.Y., 18.S., 19.B., 20.K., 21.Z., 22.A., 23.G., 24.D., 25.E., 26.H.

Purpose. When a business is incorporated, the incorporators must explain what the company will be doing. The founders should state, in specific terms, what products or services the company will sell and should specify what other activities the company will engage in. Most companies include a general or catchall clause at the end of their purpose statement which says the company reserves the right to undertake any other activities in the future.

Duration. Most entrepreneurs expect their companies to last forever. In formal terms, the company is expected to exist "in perpetuity." However, some corporations are established for a specific period of time to accomplish stipulated goals. For these companies, the duration is specified, and the company ceases to exist at the end of that time.

FIGURE 6.1
IRS Form SS-4

Form **SS-4**
(Rev. November 1985)
Department of the Treasury
Internal Revenue Service

Application for Employer Identification Number
(For use by employers and others. Please read the separate instructions before completing this form.)
For Paperwork Reduction Act Notice, see separate instructions.

OMB No. 1545-0003
Expires 8-31-88

1 Name (True name. See instructions.)	2 Social security no., if sole proprietor	3 Ending month of accounting year
4 Trade name of business if different from item 1	5 General partner's name, if partnership; principal officer's name, if corporation; or grantor's name, if trust	
6 Address of principal place of business (Number and street)	7 Mailing address, if different	
8 City, state, and ZIP code	9 City, state, and ZIP code	

10 Type of organization ☐ Governmental ☐ Individual ☐ Nonprofit organization ☐ Trust ☐ Partnership ☐ Corporation ☐ Plan administrator ☐ Other (specify)

11 County of principal business location

12 Reason for applying ☐ Started new business ☐ Purchased going business ☐ Other (specify)

13 Acquisition or starting date (Mo., day, year). See instructions.

14 Nature of principal activity (See instructions.)

15 First date wages or annuities were paid or will be paid (Mo., day, year).

16 Peak number of employees expected in the next 12 months (If none, enter "0") ▶ Nonagricultural | Agricultural | Household

17 Does the applicant operate more than one place of business? ☐ Yes ☐ No

18 Most of the products or services are sold to whom? ☐ Business establishments (wholesale) ☐ General public (retail) ☐ Other (specify) ☐ N/A

19 If nature of business is manufacturing, state principal product and raw material used.

20 Has the applicant ever applied for an identification number for this or any other business? ☐ Yes ☐ No
If "Yes," enter name and trade name. Also enter approx. date, city, and state where the application was filed and previous number if known. ▶

Under penalties of perjury, I declare that I have examined this application, and to the best of my knowledge and belief it is true, correct, and complete.

Telephone number (include area code)

Signature and Title ▶ Date ▶

Please leave blank ▶	Geo.	Ind.	Class	Size	Reas. for appl.	**Part I**

Incorporators. Each original incorporator should be identified, and his or her legal address noted. Some states require that at least one of the original incorporators be a resident of the state in which the company is incorporated.

Stock. Companies are required to state how many and what type of stock they will authorize. It is normal to authorize a number of shares far greater than that intended to be issued because the company cannot issue more stock than it has authorized.

Officers and directors. The name and legal addresses of all original officers and directors should be registered.

Bylaws. Bylaws of the corporation usually include the following items: location of the company's primary office, time and place of required stockholder meetings, compensation and selection criteria of directors, method of selecting officers, declaration of dividends, the company's fiscal year; and any other items of importance.

The incorporation process is not particularly cumbersome or costly. Entrepreneurs can choose to incorporate their companies with or without the assistance of an attorney. For example, most states will provide entrepreneurs with an "incorporating kit" which includes samples of necessary forms and instructions. Whatever their choice, entrepreneurs will have an easier time incorporating if they follow some simple procedures (see the Entrepreneur's Checklist at the end of this chapter) designed to assist them or their lawyers.

S Corporations. The information presented up to this point applies to standard or C corporations. For some businesses, particularly for small ones, the standard form is not suitable. However, owners of smaller companies do have an alternative: They can elect to have S corporations. S corporations have the same advantages—such as continuity, limited liability, etc.—as C corporations have as well as others not associated with C corporations. The primary advantage of S corporations is that they are not subject to double taxation. Income is taxed the same way as in a partnership; that is, each owner reports profits or losses on his or her individual income tax return. Also, income can be deferred to different tax years.

Not every company can become an S corporation. The following are the eligibility requirements for S status:

1. The company must be domestic.
2. The company cannot be an ineligible corporation. An ineligible corporation is defined as a corporation which is:
   a. A member of an affiliated group.
   b. A financial institution.
   c. An insurance company subject to tax under Subchapter L.
3. The corporation cannot have more than thirty-five shareholders. Husband and wife and their estates are treated as one shareholder.
4. The stock must be owned by individuals or an estate.
5. The corporation cannot have nonresident alien shareholders.
6. The corporation cannot have more than one class of stock. Only issued-and-outstanding stock is to be counted.
7. The corporation must be primarily an active company and not merely a passive investor.

The election to become an S corporation is made by filing Form 2553 (see Figure 6.2) with the Internal Revenue Service center where the tax return will be filed. The consent to the election by *all* the shareholders of the corporation is required. The election must be made on or before the fifteenth day of the third month of the election year (the year in which stockholders agree to form an S corporation). The period for a new corporation does not begin until the corporation has shareholders, acquires assets, or begins doing business, whichever occurs first. If an S corporation terminates its election, it cannot become an S corporation again for five years.

1244 Stock. Pursuant to Section 1244 of the Internal Revenue Code, corporations can issue 1244 stock, which allows investors to write off losses. Ordinary losses are limited to $50,000 for single taxpayers and $100,000 for married taxpayers filing a joint return. To issue 1244 stock, corporations must meet the following requirements:

1. The company has received 50 percent of its gross receipts from operations (not passive interest) for as long as it has been in business over the past five years.
2. The stock is to be issued for cash or property, not stock or securities.

FIGURE 6.2
IRS Form 2553

Form **2553**
(Rev. February 1986)
Department of the Treasury
Internal Revenue Service

Election by a Small Business Corporation
(Under section 1362 of the Internal Revenue Code)
▶ For Paperwork Reduction Act Notice, see page 1 of instructions.
▶ See separate instructions.

OMB No. 1545-0146
Expires 1-31-89

Note: *This election, to be treated as an "S corporation," can be approved only if all the tests in Instruction B are met.*

Part I Election Information

Name of corporation (see instructions)	**Employer identification number** (see instructions)	Principal business activity and principal product or service (see instructions)
Number and street		Election is to be effective for tax year beginning (month, day, year)
City or town, state and ZIP code		Number of shares issued and outstanding (see instructions)
Is the corporation the outgrowth or continuation of any form of predecessor? . . . . ☐ Yes ☐ No If "Yes," state name of predecessor, type of organization, and period of its existence ▶		Date and place of incorporation

A If this election takes effect for the first tax year the corporation exists, enter the earliest of the following: (1) date the corporation first had shareholders, (2) date the corporation first had assets, or (3) date the corporation began doing business. ▶

B Selected tax year: Annual return will be filed for tax year ending (month and day) ▶ ....
See instructions before entering your tax year. If the tax year ends any date other than December 31, you must complete Part II or Part IV on back. You may want to complete Part III to make a back-up request.

C Name of each shareholder, person having a community property interest in the corporation's stock, and each tenant in common, joint tenant, and tenant by the entirety. (A husband and wife (and their estates) are counted as one shareholder in determining the number of shareholders without regard to the manner in which the stock is owned.)	D Shareholders' Consent Statement. We, the undersigned shareholders, consent to the corporation's election to be treated as an "S corporation" under section 1362(a). (Shareholders sign and date below.)*	E Stock owned		F Social security number (employer identification number for estates or trust)	G Tax year ends (month and day)
		Number of shares	Dates acquired		

*For this election to be valid, the consent of each shareholder, person having a community property interest in the corporation's stock, and each tenant in common, joint tenant, and tenant by the entirety must either appear above or be attached to this form. (See instructions for Column D, if continuation sheet or a separate consent statement is needed.)

Under penalties of perjury, I declare that I have examined this election, including accompanying schedules, and statements, and to the best of my knowledge and belief, it is true, correct, and complete.

Signature and Title of Officer ▶ **Date ▶**

See Parts II, III, and IV on back. Form **2553** (Rev. 2-86)

Part II Selection of Tax Year Under Revenue Procedure 83-25

H Check the applicable box below to indicate whether the corporation is:

☐ Adopting the tax year entered in item B, Part I.

☐ Retaining the tax year entered in item B, Part I.

☐ Changing to the tax year entered in item B, Part I.

I Check the applicable box below to indicate the representation statement the corporation is making as required under section 7.01 (item 4) of Revenue Procedure 83-25, 1983-1 C.B. 689.

☐ Under penalties of perjury, I represent that shareholders holding more than half of the shares of the stock (as of the first day of the tax year to which the request relates) of the corporation have the same tax year or are concurrently changing to the tax year that the corporation adopts, retains, or changes to per item B, Part I.

☐ Under penalties of perjury, I represent that shareholders holding more than half of the shares of the stock (as of the first day of the tax year to which the request relates) of the corporation have a tax year or are concurrently changing to a tax year that, although different from the tax year the corporation is adopting, retaining, or changing to per item B, Part I, results in a deferment of income to each of these shareholders of three months or less.

☐ Under penalties of perjury, I represent that the corporation is adopting, retaining, or changing to a tax year that coincides with its natural business year as verified by its satisfaction of the requirements of section 4.042(a), (b), (c), and (d) of Revenue Procedure 83-25.

J Check here ☐ if the tax year entered in item B, Part I, is requested under the provisions of section 8 of Revenue Procedure 83-25. Attach to Form 2553 a statement and other necessary information pursuant to the ruling request requirements of Revenue Procedure 85-1. The statement must include the business purpose for the desired tax year. See instructions.

Part III Back-Up Request by Certain Corporations Initially Selecting a Fiscal Year (See Instructions.)

Check here ☐ if the corporation agrees to adopt or to change to a tax year ending December 31 if necessary for IRS to accept this election for S corporation status (temporary regulations section 18.1378-1(b)(2)(ii)(A)). This back-up request does not apply if the fiscal tax year request is approved by IRS or if the election to be an S corporation is not accepted.

Part IV Request by Corporation for Tax Year Determination by IRS (See Instructions.)

Check here ☐ if the corporation requests the IRS to determine the permitted tax year for the corporation based on information submitted in Part I (and attached schedules). This request is made under provisions of temporary regulations section 18.1378-1(d).

★ U.S.G.P.O.: 1986-491-473/20122

3. The company has received $1 million or less for its stock, including the 1244 stock it is planning to sell.
4. The stock is newly issued.

Choosing the Best Form of Ownership

It is very difficult to say precisely which form of ownership is most appropriate for a given company. Entrepreneurs should evalute their individual needs and aspirations before choosing the form of ownership. It is somewhat comforting to know that this decision is not irrevocable. If the form selected proves to be inappropriate, another form can be selected. (An Ownership Checklist to aid in the selection of the most appropriate business form is presented at the end of this chapter.)

LEGAL DOCUMENTS

During the process of planning new businesses, entrepreneurs will sign many documents which can determine how successful their new ventures will be. The documents that we will discuss in this section include contracts, leases, and warranties. Startup entrepreneurs can find themselves in trouble before they even begin their new businesses if they do not execute legally correct documents. It is possible, but not advisable, to negotiate leases, contracts, etc., without the assistance of an attorney.

Contracts

Before a new business begins operating, its creator will have entered into contracts with several other individuals and companies. He or she will have signed contracts with suppliers, distributors, attorneys, insurance companies, the utility company, and a variety of other parties. Contracts can be complex or relatively simple, but to be valid, they must meet a few standard requirements.

Contract requirements. People planning to open a new business should be sure that all contracts they sign are valid. To be valid, a contract must satisfy the following major requirements:

1. The offer and the acceptance must be in identical terms. A supplier cannot be offering to deliver four cases of Robert Mondavi red table wine while the buyer is accepting four cases of Robert Mondavi white table wine.
2. The contract must impose an obligation on both parties. Typically, one party agrees to provide goods or services at a specified price by a given date, and the other party agrees to pay the specified price for those goods or services.
3. A contract cannot be in conflict with existing federal, state, or local laws. A drug smuggler can execute a written contract with his local dealer to deliver one kilo of cocaine at a particular price on a certain date, but the contract would be invalid because it violates the law.
4. There must be no perpetration of fraud by either party in arriving at the agreement. Fraud is any act, deed, or statement made by either party that is likely to deceive the other party.
5. All parties must be legally eligible to sign contracts. Minors, drunks, and the insane are not legally eligible to sign contracts.

6-4 *The Inside View*

LONG-TERM ORAL CONTRACTS

Robert Montgomery, a producer of videotapes used to train salespeople, agreed to produce twenty-five tapes for Futuristic Foods Inc., a New York company. Montgomery made the company promise it would use the tapes only for training its own people and would never sell the tapes to others. The tapes were produced in the allotted time, and Montgomery was paid the specified price of $1,600. A couple of months later, Futuristic formed Mind Trek Inc. to market Montgomery's tapes. Montgomery sued to stop Futuristic but lost. The judge explained that courts won't enforce an oral agreement that covers more than one year. Therefore, the proviso that Futuristic could never sell the tapes was invalid.[12]

Written Contracts. Contracts can be either written or oral. Both are usually valid, but in the case of oral contracts, entrepreneurs would do well to heed the remark made by W. C. Fields that "... oral contracts are not worth the paper they are written on." Under certain conditions, oral contracts are not valid or enforceable. For example, an oral contract that extends beyond one year is not valid (see The Inside View 6-4).

Even some written contracts are not enforceable, but they are more binding than oral contracts. Written contracts do not have to be long and complex to be valid, nor do they have to be written by an attorney. A receipt or a note scribbled on the back of an envelope could be acceptable if it contains the following four essential items:

1. Names all of the people involved in the transaction and the roles that they play.
2. Describes the transaction in complete detail. Both parties should state specifically what property, goods, etc., are being offered and accepted and for what consideration.
3. Specifies the value of the deal. Both sides must agree on the cost of the property, goods, etc., and the form of payment.
4. All parties to the contract must sign the document and must use their legal signatures.[13]

Enforcing contracts. Unfortunately, in many instances it becomes necessary to take action against someone who has not complied with the terms of a valid contract. If the content or interpretation of a contract is disputed, involved parties have two options—legal action or arbitration. In the first instance, either party would have his or her lawyer sue the other party for breach of contract. However, if both parties consent, their disagreement can be submitted to an arbitrator for settlement. The arbitrator, who might not be a lawyer, hears both sides of the dispute before deciding in favor of one party or the other. In some instances, the arbitrator might suggest a compromise that minimizes the costs to both parties.

Leases

Almost all startup entrepreneurs will be involved with leases of some sort. They will probably lease the company's premises, and they might also lease warehouse space, vehicles, machinery, equipment, and even employees (temporary help). Improperly executed leases can doom a company before it even opens its doors; therefore, it is highly advisable to have all leases checked by an attorney.

Building Lease. Since most new businesses will start out in leased premises, we will examine the items that should be included in an ideal lease. Inclusion of the following items in a lease should protect both the landlord and the tenant:

1. A description of the facilities to be leased and the condition of the premises.
2. A listing of common spaces, such as parking, loading docks, etc., used by all tenants.
3. Amount of rent and terms of payment.
4. Amount of security deposit required and the conditions for its return.
5. The length of the lease and any renewal options.
6. Permissible alterations and who pays for them.
7. Identification of who pays for maintenance, repairs, utilities, taxes, and insurance.
8. Conditions for subletting space and assigning the lease to another party.
9. Determination if competitors will be leased adjoining space.
10. A contingency clause allowing for termination of the lease if the building is damaged or destroyed.

There are numerous other clauses that attorneys might include in leases to protect their clients. Clauses pertaining to specific buildings, locations, etc., should be tailored by a lawyer to the needs of his or her client.

Other Leases. In addition to a building lease, it is quite likely that owners of new businesses will also enter into leases for other items. Many startup entrepreneurs will elect to lease some of their equipment, such as cash registers, computers, communication systems, etc. The terms and language of these leases will be similar to those of a building lease but will probably be shorter and less complex. Leases for automobiles and delivery vehicles, which are also quite common, are generally short, simple, and straightforward. Finally, owners of new businesses might choose to lease some of their employees. When employees are supplied by temporary employment agencies such as Manpower Inc., the business owner is in effect leasing those people.

Warranties

Anyone contemplating the establishment of a business that produces or sells goods over $5 or that provides services needs to be familiar with warranties and guarantees. We have already discussed some of the cases of consumers who have brought suit against companies that have resulted in punitive-damage awards. Now we will examine methods of protecting companies from legal action by consumers.

The Uniform Commercial Code (UCC) and the Magnuson–Moss Warranty Act deal with warranties and consumer protection. Companies can give customers full warranties, limited warranties, or no warranties at all.

Full Warranty. The following terms and conditions apply to both full and limited warranties:

1. Identify the person who can enforce the warranty (manufacturer, retailer, etc.) and state whether the warranty can be transferred to subsequent buyers.
2. Describe the products, parts, components, and characteristics covered as well as those excluded from the warranty.
3. State what the manufacturer will do and what items or services will be paid for by the seller and the buyer.
4. Stipulate the starting date of the warranty and its duration.
5. Explain how consumers can obtain warranty service and how disputes will be resolved.
6. State limitations on the duration of implied warranties and any exclusions or limitations on relief (such as consequential or incidental damages).
7. Explain consumers' legal rights under the warranty.[14]

In addition to the above terms and conditions, a full warranty includes the following:

1. The warrantor will repair or replace any defective part.
2. There is no time limit under the warranty.
3. There is no exclusion of payment for consequential or incidental damages unless clearly noted.
4. Products that cannot be repaired will be replaced.
5. Only reasonable, clearly stated duties can be imposed on the consumer.
6. Damage caused by negligent or unreasonable use is not covered by the warranty.

Limited Warranties. Some companies may choose not to provide all of the coverage a consumer receives from a full warranty. Instead, they may choose to offer consumers limited coverage. A limited warranty might cover labor; it may require the purchaser to return the product to the seller; it may offer only product replacement instead of a cash refund; or it may require consumers to pay for postage and handling when returning the product.

Implied Warranties. Warranties do not have to be written to exist. In several cases, courts have decided that consumers are protected by implied or unwritten warranties. An implied warranty is a provision that is recognized by law without regard for what the parties themselves might have intended or agreed to. It is not written anywhere and was probably not even discussed by buyer and seller. It is a binding contract between sellers and consumers.

Disclaimers. Companies that choose to limit their warranty liability must make a clear, intelligible statement disclaiming liability. The following is a typical disclaimer:

> There are no other warranties, promises, representations, or affirmations respecting the product or service to be supplied aside from those set forth herein. Any prior or subsequent

> written or oral warranties, promises, representations, or affirmations are specifically revoked and disclaimed and are agreed not to be a part of any agreement between the parties unless included in a written agreement signed by all parties.

In this age of consumerism, even this type of disclaimer does not always protect manufacturers and sellers. The company's lawyer should always be consulted about warranties and liability.

PATENTS, COPYRIGHTS, AND TRADEMARKS

Entrepreneurs who create new businesses often have something to protect from competitors. They may have new products, services, jingles, or logos which could make their new business unique and profitable. To protect products, ideas, and names, entrepreneurs can acquire patents, copyrights, or trademarks. These protective devices may not be foolproof, but without them, entrepreneurs can make no claims against other people who use their products or ideas.

Patents

If a person invents a product that is new or substantially improves an existing product, he or she may apply to the Patent and Trademark Office for a patent. If issued, the patent protects the product for seventeen years, and no other individual or company is allowed to make, use, or sell the product without the permission of the patent holder. The inventor of a new or improved product can submit to the Patent Office an application which includes the following: a written description of the item or process to be patented; a drawing of the item or process, if applicable; and the filing fee. While the patent application is being processed, the applicant may use the words "patent pending" to protect the item from other manufacturers.

Once a patent has been issued, the patent holder cannot assume that he or she will never have to challenge other manufacturers who infringe on the patent. The traditional method of dealing with infringers was to sue them. Until recently, patent appeals were handled by eleven circuit courts of appeal, but in 1982 the U.S. Court of Appeals for the Federal Circuit was formed in Washington, DC, and all appeals are now directed to it.

Legal action is expensive and not always successful, so people with patent complaints are using other means of settling patent disputes (see The Inside View 6-5). Those cases that do result in legal action are usually settled out of court. Defending patents in court is costly and extremely time consuming, and the outcome is unpredictable. However, in the final analysis, it is better to have a patent than to be sorry when someone imitates an unpatented product.

Copyrights

The device that protects items that cannot be patented is known as a *copyright*. The following items can be copyrighted: literary, musical, and dramatic works; pictorial, graphic, and sculptural works; motion pictures and other audiovisual works; and sound

6-5

The Inside View

SETTLING PATENT INFRINGEMENT CASES

Kroy Inc. sued Varitronic Systems Inc. (VSI) for patent infringement in July 1985. Using a new U.S. Patent and Trademark Office procedure that allows businesses to challenge each other's patents without litigation, VSI asked the office to reexamine Kroy's original patent. The fee for requesting the reexamination is $1,500. "We can do this for one-half the time and one-tenth the cost it would take to fight in court," says Michael Lasky, VSI's patent attorney. Once VSI had initiated the procedure, the patent office issued a preliminary report admitting that VSI had raised "substantial new questions of patentability." While the reexamination is underway, VSI doesn't have to worry about legal fees. Jerry Cohen, a Boston patent attorney, believes: "It [reexamination] pulls the situation down to a realm where the small company can be equal to a large one."[15]

recordings. The courts have also recently ruled that computer software can be copyrighted.

Only the author or creator of a work may apply for a copyright. Prior to the change in copyright laws in 1978, a copyright was secured by publication with the copyright notice or registration in the copyright office. Under the new law, no publication or registration is needed. Copyright is automatically awarded when the work is created; however, it is still advisable to formally register a work with the U.S. Copyright Office. Copyrights, whether registered or not, are usually valid for the life of the copyright holder plus fifty years beyond the holder's death.

Trademarks

One of the most important assets of a startup company is its name. We have discussed how important it is to select the most appropriate name for a new business. Having made the selection, entrepreneurs should make sure that no other business can use the same or similar name. This protection can be secured by registering the company's name with the state's attorney general or with the U.S. Commissioner of Patents. An application to register a trademark must be made in the name of the owner of the trademark. The application includes the following parts: a written application; a drawing of the trademark; five specimens or facsimiles; and the filing fee of $35. Trademarks are valid for twenty years and may be renewed for additional twenty-year periods unless previously canceled or surrendered.

6-6 *The Inside View*

TRADEMARK INFRINGEMENT

Susan Schultz, the owner of Blue Mountain Arts Inc., filed a $50 million suit against Hallmark Cards Inc. for copying her company's greeting-card concept. A federal judge slapped an injunction on Hallmark, ordering it to stop selling eighty-three cards pending resolution of the case. In finding that Blue Mountain likely could prove that Hallmark violated unfair-competition laws, the judge relied heavily on evidence that Hallmark deliberately copied the smaller company's cards and in so doing, violated Blue Mountain's "look" or "trade dress"—a legal concept that covers such things as packaging and design.[16]

Federal registration gives the owner of the trademark certain procedural rights should the owner decide to sue another company for infringing that trademark or trade name. Registration also protects a company's "look" or "trade dress" (see The Inside View 6-6). However, simply registering a trademark does not ensure an owner's substantive rights. Substantive rights are obtained by using the mark. Therefore, it is the use of the mark, not the registration of it, which gives a company most of its rights.

BANKRUPTCY

Why would anyone think about bankruptcy during the pre-startup planning process? Because poor legal advice, among other mistakes, can cause the untimely demise of many a fledgling business. Some new companies end up bankrupt because they selected the wrong lawyer, did not consult their lawyer on important issues, were given bad legal advice, or ignored good legal advice. We do not intend to belabor the bankruptcy issue; however, we believe that all entrepreneurs should know what the consequences of bad judgment or poor planning could be.

The Bankruptcy Act of 1978 superseded the Bankruptcy Act of 1898, which had been modified many times. The new code has the following eight odd-numbered substantive chapters:

Chapter 1 contains general definitions and rules.
Chapter 3 deals with case administration.
Chapter 5 concerns such issues as creditors' claims, debtors' duties and advantages, exemptions, and trustees' powers.
Chapter 7 explains liquidation procedures.
Chapter 9 concerns municipal debts.

Chapter 11 deals with business reorganizations.
Chapter 13 deals with debts of people with regular incomes.
Chapter 15 contains the provisions necessary to set up a new U.S. Trustee Pilot Program.

Bankruptcy filing under any of these chapters automatically nullifies all lawsuits against a company. Chapter 11 is used by companies that need time to reorganize and submit a plan for paying off their creditors. If the owners of a company cannot find a way to start business after a bankruptcy filing, they can liquidate. We expect all entrepreneurs who carefully study this textbook to have no need for bankrupty protection.

Summary

Startup entrepreneurs need good legal advice. Once they have made the self-employment decision, they should begin the attorney selection process. Before making the final selection, entrepreneurs should ask about an attorney's other clients, networks, values, willingness to assist, style, philosophy, and fees. Once the selection has been made, attorneys should be retained (not hired full time) and their services prudently used. Have lawyers to help select the best form of ownership, write contracts and leases, study zoning restrictions and license requirements, and to keep the company law abiding.

One of the first legal decisions confronting startup entrepreneurs is what form of ownership is most appropriate for the new business. Proprietorships are easy to form, simple to operate, flexible, and allow the owner to keep all the profits. On the negative side, proprietorships have unlimited liability, limited life, limited benefit deductibility, and limited access to capital. Partnerships have fewer of the disadvantages proprietorships have, plus the following advantages: complementary expertise, joint decision making, tax benefits, limited red tape, and easier access to capital. The disadvantages of partnerships include unlimited liability, limited life, shared responsibility for the actions and decisions of all partners, and shared profits. To avoid the disadvantages of proprietorships and partnerships, entrepreneurs can choose to incorporate.

Corporations eliminate some of the disadvantages of partnerships and proprietorships, such as unlimited liability, limited life, limited expertise, and limited access to capital. The primary drawback of corporations is double taxation. Corporate income is taxed, and then individual stockholders pay taxes on their corporate dividends. Other drawbacks include formality and rigidity, widely dispersed ownership, and excessive paperwork and red tape. It is possible to overcome some of the corporate drawbacks by selecting a special corporate form. In the case of the S corporation, double taxation is eliminated because the company is taxed like a partnership.

Once the form has been chosen, entrepreneurs should use their lawyers to draw up or evaluate all legal documents. Contracts and leases are very important documents not to be signed without the advice of an attorney. To provide startup businesses with maximum protection, contracts should be in writing. Contracts should also name all of the people involved in a transaction, describe the transaction in detail, specify the value of the deal, and contain the signatures of all parties to the contract. Like contracts, leases should be drawn up by an attorney. New businesses are likely to have a building lease, equipment leases, vehicle leases, and even employee leases.

Entrepreneurs who are starting a business with a unique product, service, or idea will need patents, copyrights, or trademarks for protection. Patents, which protect products, are effective for seventeen years. Literary works, sound recordings, computer software, etc., are protected by copyrights, which are valid for the life of the copyright holder plus fifty years beyond the holder's death. New businesses should protect their names from competitors by registering the name with the U.S. Commissioner of Patents or with the attorney general of the state in which the business is located or incorporated. A trademark protects the company's name for twenty years and can be renewed for additional twenty-year periods.

Poor legal advice, no legal advice, or ignored legal advice can cause a business to fail and end up bankrupt. The Bankruptcy Act of 1978 contains eight odd-numbered chapters which explain debtor and creditor rights and responsibilities. If a bankrupt business cannot reorganize and become operational again, it is liquidated or sold to another buyer. We expect everyone who diligently reads this textbook to be successful and never to suffer the pain and embarrassment of bankruptcy.

Assembling the Pieces

Carol and Jacki knew they would need an attorney to assist them with some pre-startup activities. Like so many other startup entrepreneurs, they failed to conduct an objective search for the best attorney for their proposed business. Instead, they decided to use the services of a friend. Jacki and Carol first consulted their new attorney about the structure of the business. The owners thought that the corporate form was probably most appropriate because it would formalize their relationship, limit their liability, and make it easier for them to borrow money. The attorney suggested a C corporation, but their accountant, who had been recommended by the lawyer, suggested an S corporation. Jacki and Carol decided to accept the advice of their attorney and form a C corporation (only to regret it later).

Since the lawyer was Carol's friend, he said, "Let me do the incorporating as a friend" (a favor to Carol and Jacki). Neither owner could see how they had received any favors when the lawyer presented his bill. The next time Jacki and Carol called on their lawyer it was to help them negotiate a lease on the building they had selected. When the lawyer's negotiating efforts proved unsatisfactory, Carol's husband stepped in and completed the negotiations. (Carol and Jacki later changed lawyers.) Some of the pertinent lease provisions are presented in Figure 6.3.

Jacki and Carol planned a business that would have no proprietary products; therefore, they would not need to apply for any patents. Likewise, they had nothing that needed to be copyrighted. They did, however, have something that needed trademark protection—the name they had chosen for their shop. Jacki and Carol spent many hours trying to select a name for their business that would let customers know what merchandise the shop sold. They also wanted a name that would be easy to remember and would help create an "up-scale" image. They finally decided to name their business In Good Taste, a name they considered to be unique as well as descrip-

(continued on page 172)

FIGURE 6.3
Shopping Center Lease for Orange Grove Plaza

THIS SHOPPING CENTER LEASE, made and entered into as of the ______ day of ______________ 198_, by and between ORANGE GROVE ASSOCIATIONS, A SOUTH CAROLINA PARTNERSHIP (hereinafter sometimes referred to as "Landlord"), and Tenant as hereinafter defined.

WITNESSETH:

In consideration of the rent to be paid, the mutual covenants and agreements herein contained, and of other good and valuable considerations, the receipt and legal sufficiency of all of which are hereby acknowledged by both parties hereto, Landlord hereby demises and rents unto Tenant, and Tenant hereby leases from Landlord, certain premises in Landlord's shopping center known as Orange Grove Plaza, upon the terms, covenants and condition hereinafter contained.

ARTICLE 1

Fundamental Lease Provisions and Exhibits

Section 1.1 *Fundamental Lease Provisions.*

A. LANDLORD (including mailing address):
Orange Grove Associates
c/o Bailey & Associates
114 Doughty Street
Charleston, SC 29401

B. TENANT (including mailing address):
In Good Taste

C. LEASED PREMISES: A portion of the Orange Grove Plaza shopping center premises identified and/or outlined in red on Exhibit "B", having dimensions of approximately
______ feet × ______ feet, and containing approximately ______ square feet, known as space number ______.

D. PERMITTED USES:

E. LEASE DURATION: ______years (original term).

F. FIXED RENT: $______ per year in equal monthly installments of $______ .

G. (i) PERCENTAGE RENT RATE: ______(%) percent.
(ii) BASE GROSS SALES AMOUNT: ______.

H. COMMON AREA MAINTENANCE CONTRIBUTION: $______ per year, adjusted annually.

I. RENTAL COMMENCEMENT DATE: March ___, 198___ .
In the event the leased premises have not been constructed or completed, the Rental Commencement Date shall be determined pursuant to ARTICLE XIV.

J. RENTAL PAYMENT PLACE:
Bailey & Associates
114 Doughty Street
Charleston, SC 29401

K. PRO RATA SHARE: ______ percent, representing the percentage of the total rentable space in the shopping center represented by the number of rentable square feet in the Leased Premises as of the date of this lease.

L. SECURITY DEPOSIT: $______ .

M. RENEWAL OPTIONS:

N. BASE YEAR: 1988___ .

Note: The entire lease is twenty-one pages long.

tive of their business. It was not totally unique, as it turned out, for another company in California had already registered a similar name with the U.S. Commissioner of Patents. However, Jacki and Carol were able to register the name they had selected with the attorney general of South Carolina, which gave them the legal right to use the name In Good Taste in their trade area. ■

---

entrepreneur's checklist

PREINCORPORATION CHECKLIST

1. Who serves as the incorporators? Where do they live?
2. In what state will the business be incorporated?
3. Will the corporation's existence be perpetual or limited in duration?
4. What name will the corporation have? Has it been reserved?
5. Where will the principal place of business be? Will it be owned or leased? Who owns it or has the lease now? Will it be transferred to the corporation? In exchange for what?
6. Where else will the corporation operate? Will it own property or have operations in other states? When?
7. What is the nature of the business to be conducted? Is that likely to change?
8. Will the new corporation receive any patents or copyrights? From whom and for what?
9. Will the corporation need any state or local licenses? Are any licenses to be transferred to it? By whom? How long will this take? Can the corporation hold such a license or permit?
10. What will be the initial investment in the corporation? Will it be in cash or in some other form?
11. How many shares will be authorized by the corporation? How many will be issued? To whom? For what consideration?
12. Will there be more than one class of stock? For each class of stock, will there be preemptive rights? Restrictions on transfer? Cumulative voting?
13. Who will subscribe to the initial issue of stock? How many shares will they get? What will they pay in terms of cash or property?
14. When will the corporation begin business?
15. Who will execute the articles of incorporation and file them?
16. Will the articles of incorporation provide for indemnification of officers and directors? For the removal of directors by shareholders at any time, with or without cause?
17. How many directors will there be?
18. Who will serve on the first board of directors?
19. When will the directors hold their first meeting?
20. What will be the agenda of the organizational meetings of the incorporators and the directors?
21. Who will be the initial officers?
22. When will the annual meeting of the shareholders be held? Where? On what notice?
23. How will special meetings of the shareholders be called?

24. What kind of quorum will be needed for a meeting of shareholders?
25. How many days notice will be needed to call a meeting of the directors? What will be the quorum for a meeting of the directors?
26. What is the fiscal year of the corporation going to be?
27. How will the bylaws be amended: by the directors or the shareholders?
28. Where will the corporation open its bank account?
29. Who will keep possession of the minutes and records of the board and shareholders and prepare needed materials?
30. Who will keep the books and accounts of the business and be responsible for all tax filings?

Source: Reprinted by permission of the publisher from Carolyn Vella and John McGonagle, Jr., *Incorporating: A Guide for Small Business Owners* (New York: AMACOM, a division of the American Management Association, 1984), pp. 66–67. © 1984 The Helicon Group, Ltd. All rights reserved.

OWNERSHIP CHECKLIST

Instructions:

Step 1. Circle the P's and enlarge the x's in each column for those questions relevant to your business. (See code below.)
Step 2. Review results of Step 1 to determine if there is one form of doing business that is clearly the best. If yes, go to step 6. If no, go to Step 3.
Step 3. Determine if some enlarged X's are irrelevant to your plans. If so, cross them out and go back to Step 2.
Step 4. If Step 3 does not clearly indicate a choice, underline the A's in each column.
Step 5. Determine if the combination of P's and A's more clearly indicates a choice (i.e., fewer X's in a column with more P's and A's). If yes, go to Step 6. If no, go to Step 6.
Step 6. Regardless of whether or not you believe the choice is clear, contact your tax and legal advisor.

Code:

P Preferred form of doing business.
A Acceptable, but not preferred, form of doing business.
N Not the most desirable, but objective can be achieved by adopting this form of doing business.
x This form of doing business will not work.
NA/NM Not applicable or irrelevant

	Proprietorship	*Partnership*	*S*	*C*
1. Will there be only one, noncorporate owner:				
With product or service liability a significant risk?	N	N	P	P
With product or service liability not a significant risk?	P	N	A	A

	Proprietorship	*Partnership*	*S*	*C*
2. Will there be more than one, but fewer than thirty-five noncorporate owners?	x	A	P	A
3. If debt will be significant:				
Will the owners need to guarantee it?	N	A	A	A
Can it be nonrecourse, collateralized by specific related property?	N	P	A	A
4. Will there be nonbank debt or equity from sources outside of the original owners/investors?				
Debt	N	A	A	A
Equity	x	A	A	P
5. Is it anticipated that the company will go public (widely held)?	x	A	x	P
6. Will there be losses in early years to shelter owner's other income?	A	A	A	x
7. Will cash be retained in the business even when income is earned?	N	N	N	P
8. Will income/loss be divided in a ratio different from that of capital ownership?	x	P	N	N
9. Is more than one class of ownership being considered?	x	N	N	P
10. Is motivating employees a consideration?	N	N	A	P
11. Will management be nonowners?	x	A	N	P
12. Is the ultimate goal to sell the business or merge with another?	N	N	N	P
13. Is a fiscal year-end different from that of the owners desirable?	x	N	N	P
14. Will portions of ownership change frequently?	x	N	A	P
15. Will income be primarily passive?	A	A	A	N
16. Will tax-exempt income be significant?	P	P	A	N
17. Will dividend income subject to the 85 percent exclusion be significant?	N	x	x	P
18. Are capital gains or losses expected?	A	A	A	N
19. Will management be centralized?				
Yes	A	N	P	P
No	x	P	N	N
Summarize in each column, the number of				
P's	_____	_____	_____	_____
x's	_____	_____	_____	_____

	Proprietorship	*Partnership*	*S*	*C*
If Step 3 was completed, revise,				
x's	____	____	____	____
A's	____	____	____	____

Source: Robert Engle, "How to Choose the Right Form of Doing Business," *Management Accounting,* January 1985, pp. 46–47. Used with permission.

Questions for Review and Discussion

1. What are the advantages of using a large law firm?
2. How should startup entrepreneurs select a lawyer?
3. Do you think that punitive damages awarded to consumers are excessive? How would you limit the amount of money awarded to consumers?
4. How can owners of new companies judge the performance of their lawyers?
5. What are advantages and disadvantages of sole proprietorships?
6. What clauses should be included in a partnership agreement?
7. If you were starting a business, why might you choose an S corporation rather than a C corporation?
8. Explain the concepts of limited liability and double taxation.
9. What are the requirements of a valid contract?
10. How many different types of leases might a new business have?
11. If you were starting a business, would you register your company's name? With whom?

Notes

1. Mark Rollinson, "Small Company, Big Law Firm," *Harvard Business Review,* November–December 1985, pp. 6–14.
2. William Hancock, *The Small Business Legal Advisor* (New York: McGraw-Hill Book Co., 1982), p. 188.
3. Patricia Amend, Joshua Hyatt, Bruce Posner, and Steven Solomon, "Avoiding Punitive Damages," *Inc.,* May 1987, p. 139.
4. Mark Rollinson, "Small Company, Big Law Firm," pp. 6–14.
5. Patricia Bellew Gray, "More Lawyers Reluctantly Adopt Strange New Practice—Marketing," *The Wall Street Journal,* 30 January 1987, p. 25.
6. Marisa Manley, "How to Control Legal Costs," *Inc.,* April 1987, pp. 115–116.
7. Marc Lane, *Legal Handbook for Small Business* (New York: AMACOM, 1977), pp. 102–103.
8. Howard Stern, *Running Your Own Business* (New York: Crown Publishers, Inc., 1986), pp. 164–165.
9. William Hancock, *The Small Business Legal Advisor,* p. 8–10.
10. Ronald Alsop, "Firms Create Unique Names, But Are They Pronounceable?" *The Wall Street Journal,* 2 April 1987, p. 31.
11. Carolyn Vella and John McGonagle, Jr., *Incorporating: A Guide for Small-Business Owners* (New York: AMACOM, 1984), p. 49.

12. Marisa Manley, "Let's Shake on That," *Inc.,* June 1986, pp. 131–132.
13. Ibid.
14. Arnold Goldstein, *The Small Business Legal Problem Solver* (Boston: *Inc.*/CBI Publications, 1983), p. 131.
15. ———, "Allowing the Start-up to Fight Back," *Inc.,* December 1986, p. 14.
16. Mark Ivey, "Dear Hallmark: See You In Court. Best Wishes, a Competitor," *Business Week,* 8 December 1986, p. 42.

CHAPTER 7

Choosing the Location

Learning Objectives

After you have read this chapter, you will be able to do the following:

- Understand how selecting the wrong site can doom a business.
- Determine how startup entrepreneurs select regions, states, and cities in which to locate.
- Evaluate sites.

Nothing dooms a startup to failure quicker than selecting the wrong location. Entrepreneurs may have a unique product or service, adequate capital, reliable suppliers, motivated employees, but the wrong location. Chances are excellent that the entrepreneur will start the venture only to learn too late that the business should have been on the other side of the road, in an industrial park, in an incubator, in another part of town, or in another city. Entrepreneurs who realize after it opens that their business is in the wrong location find it very difficult to correct their mistake. Adequate planning and site evaluation will enable entrepreneurs to avoid making such location mistakes.

Some entrepreneurs trust consultants, real estate brokers, or others to find the ideal site for their new venture. While it is acceptable to use outside sources, all entrepreneurs should themselves be involved in the site selection process. In the end, it is the startup entrepreneur who must live with the location decision, and it provides little comfort to be able to say that "someone else chose this unsuitable site for me because I was too busy attending to other matters." Startup entrepreneurs can obtain site selection assistance and advice (see Chapter 4) from city hall, the chamber of commerce, and other helpful groups and individuals, but only the entrepreneur can make the final decision.

This chapter will provide startup entrepreneurs with the information and tools necessary to make successful site selections. We will discuss the selection of regions, states, and cities in which to locate, and we will examine the process of selecting the specific site for the business.

SELECTING THE REGION

We are assuming that most startup entrepreneurs are not likely to create new ventures in other countries, with the exceptions of Canada and Mexico. Although entrepreneurs can earn substantial profits overseas, it is easier to start and establish a business in the United States than it is abroad. Therefore, the first choice startup entrepreneurs must make is the region of the country in which they want to locate.

Many startup entrepreneurs do not have to decide which region would be best for their business because they are already committed to their hometowns; however, others may have no personal or family commitment to any particular area of the country. Outplaced managers, retired military personnel, recent college graduates, and others may decide to locate their new business in what they consider to be the best region, regardless of where they currently reside. For example, when Gian Carlo Menotti decided to bring his Spoleto festival to the United States, he felt free to choose any city in the country to be its host. He wanted a city that had the right "feel"—one that strongly resembled Spoleto, Italy. After many cities had been considered, the field was narrowed to New Orleans and Charleston, South Carolina. Menotti finally decided that Charleston would be the best place for his festival.

For many entrepreneurs, the initial selection of region is often based on one of two major criteria—proximity to raw materials or to customers. Businesses such as steel companies, which are heavy users of bulky raw materials, are likely to be located near the primary source of their most important raw material. Other businesses, such as beer companies, locate their breweries near their customers. By selecting sites near raw materials or customers, companies minimize their transportation costs and provide better service to their customers. As in many other cases, the more general decisions are often the easiest to make. It is the narrowing down of suitable particular locations that becomes difficult. Selecting states, cities, and, finally, the specific site is usually more difficult than identifying the appropriate region of the country.

SELECTING THE STATE

Once entrepreneurs have decided which region of the country is best for their startup business, they need to determine which state in that region offers the most benefits. Nearly every state has an office or a government official who is responsible for attracting new business to that state. Some states aggressively court all businesses, whereas others may be more selective. For example, every state tries to attract "clean" businesses that do not threaten the environment, such as computer or other high-tech companies, but many states actively discourage "dirty" manufacuring companies. Regardless of which companies they are trying to attract, states spend large amounts of money on advertising or propaganda explaining why they offer better locations than other states.

Importance of Selecting the Right State

Not all states are equally suitable for different types of business; therefore, it is important for startup entrepreneurs to select the best state for their particular company. A firm which scanned a number of sites in a dozen states found the following differences:

1. Between two of the locations there was a difference of 4.5 years in median school years completed among the general population.
2. There was a 700 percent spread in the number of scientists and engineers per 1,000 population.
3. There was a difference of 77 cents per hour in manufacturing wage rates.
4. The urban crime rate at one location was forty times that of another.
5. Per capita debt was $350 in one location and less than $1 in another.
6. Unionization of workers was six times greater in one location than in another.
7. Work stoppages were twelve times as great at one site as at another.
8. The accidental death rate was four times greater at one location than at another.[1]

In order to avoid costly locational mistakes, startup entrepreneurs must be willing to spend the time and money required to thoroughly evaluate prospective states.

Facts About the States

Startup entrepreneurs need information from the states about the location factors they consider important. However, the information provided by the states is often biased because each state tends to emphasize its strengths while minimizing its weaknesses. Entrepreneurs should consider the information provided by each state's development office, but they should rely more heavily on that provided by disinterested sources.

One disinterested source which provides information on the ability of states to stimulate entrepreneurial activity is *Inc.* magazine. Every year, *Inc.* rates all fifty states on the basis of their attractiveness to new businesses. Using the basic measures of new jobs, new companies, and the climate for business growth, *Inc.* places Arizona at the top of its list and Wyoming at the bottom. The following are the fifteen top-ranked states:

Arizona	Massachusetts
New Hampshire	Nevada
Maryland	Tennessee
Georgia	Texas
Virginia	North Carolina
Florida	South Carolina
Delaware	Utah
California	

In addition to ranking the states, the author of the *Inc.* study also explains what makes the top-ranked states appealing. For instance, Massachusetts (#9) has more than sixty-five institutions of higher learning; New Hampshire (#2) attracts people who want low-to-no taxes; Maryland (#3) and Virginia (#5) benefit from the service and technology growth around the nation's capital; California (#8) continues to profit from the engineering prowess of its universities and the spin-off activities among its technology companies; and Georgia (#4), with its impressive universities, Atlanta's expanded airport, and extensive interstate highways, has positioned itself as a regional hub for the entire fast-growing Southeast.[2]

The selection process would be so easy if startup entrepreneurs could decide which state was most appropriate for their new business simply by consulting the *Inc.* ranking. Unfortunately, it is not that simple. As informative as the *Inc.* ranking is, it is limited by the criteria it uses to rank states. Therefore, entrepreneurs also need to consider rankings done by other organizations using different criteria. For example, using the equality of men and women as a measure, sociologists derived the following ranking of the best and worst states:[3]

Top 10 States		*Bottom 10 States*	
Oregon	59.9*	North Dakota	34.1
Michigan	56.1	Wyoming	33.5
Alaska	55.5	Oklahoma	32.7
Maine	54.7	Louisiana	31.2
Maryland	53.9	Texas	30.5
Minnesota	52.5	Vermont	29.7
California	51.8	Arkansas	27.6
Connecticut	51.6	South Carolina	24.0
Hawaii	51.3	Alabama	20.1
Massachusetts	50.6	Mississippi	19.2

*100 = full equality

Some states, such as Arizona (#1) and New Hampshire (#2), ranked high on the *Inc.* list do not even appear on the sociologists' list; however, others, such as Wyoming (#50), North Dakota (#49), and Oklahoma (#47), which are low on the *Inc.* list, are also low on the sociologists' list. This list comparison illustrates the importance of using as many rankings as possible.

Factors to Evaluate

After considering information provided by states and distinterested sources, startup entrepreneurs need to make their own evaluation based on the factors, qualities, and characteristics that are important to them. It is difficult to determine which of these will be important to individual entrepreneurs; however, the following are among those factors that should be considered by all entrepreneurs:

- Availability and price of land
- State taxes
- Quantity and quality of labor
- Transportation systems
- State laws and regulations
- Environmental-control regulations
- Ability of government officials
- Prevailing economic conditions
- Quality of educational institutions

- Financial incentives offered, such as state loans, state grants, industrial development bonds, enterprise zones, etc.
- Quality of life

SELECTING CITIES

Within each state there are many cities that might be suitable locations for a new business. Startup entrepreneurs need to determine which city will be the best. Larger cities, like most states, have employees who are paid to attract new business to the city. Cities with relatively large development budgets are able to spend a substantial amount advertising their benefits and advantages (see Figure 7.1). Smaller cities, with less money, rely on personal contacts and less-expensive advertising. Regardless of size, some cities go to extraordinary lengths to acquire new businesses (see The Inside View 7-1). As with the states, location information on cities comes from biased and unbiased sources. Understandably, cities will present themselves in the best possible light, whereas disinterested sources will provide more balanced, less biased information.

Facts About Cities

Startup entrepreneurs will find that they need as much or more location information about cities than that for states. The collection of this information should begin with

7-1 *The Inside View*

CITIES BUY AND MOVE FIRMS

For Duluth, Minnesota, nothing was working. The timber and mining industries were in critical condition, and unemployment was as high as 50 percent in some areas. Efforts to recruit companies to Duluth by offering tax concessions and other aid were unsuccessful. "We had to admit that we were not exactly in the mainstream of commerce," says Jerry Udesen, a local executive. Udesen and other businesspeople did something unusual—they purchased companies and brought them to Duluth. Now other cities—Grand Junction, Colorado, and Great Falls, Montana—have adopted the same strategy.

Udesen's group, Duluth Growth Co. (DGC), sold $2.7 million worth of stock, mostly to local investors. DGC searched for companies that could capitalize on the Great Lakes fishing industry. It bought the assets of The Erwin Weller Co., a Sioux City, Iowa, maker of fishing tackle, and those of BC Electronics, a Seattle producer of electronic monitoring devices used by fishermen, and moved both to Duluth, creating fifty-one jobs.[4]

FIGURE 7.1

Meet Jennifer.
Dedicated. Involved. One of the reasons the state of the arts in the State of St. Louis is alive and well. Alive in our world class symphony. The Muny Opera, Missouri Concert Ballet, Casa, the Opera Theatre, Repertory Theatre, The Fox, The Art Museum.
Talented hands.
Lots of them. In the arts. In our booming high tech industries. With 60,000 skilled scientists, engineers and technicians utilizing the $1 billion we've invested in research and development. After all, not everybody can dance.
Jackhammer.
Sculpting the new face of St. Louis with four new luxury hotels, a convention center, the new Union Station development and the St. Louis Centre—a shopping complex to stretch three city blocks.
Legwarmers.
You'll need them sometimes. But we have a better weather index than Chicago, New York, Baltimore, Atlanta, Raleigh, Jacksonville and Seattle. When it's good, it's great. When it's bad, we kick a little.
Headband.
Because you'll work up a sweat at over 50 health clubs and 70 golf courses. That's just the warm-up. Try fishing, swimming, boating, floating, camping, ballooning, waterskiing.
Leotard.
Light and flexible. One of those times when less is more. Like St. Louis corporate tax rates. Up to 80% lower than other major metro areas. With opportunity for investment tax credits. Less taxes. More profit. That's the bottom line.
THE STATE OF
St. Louis
It's not what you'd expect.
Take a look at St. Louis. You'll like what you see. A Missouri/Illinois bi-state area. Home for over 2.4 million people. A central location, contemporary lifestyle, growing economy, stable work force. And a great place to raise a family.
That's the State of St. Louis.
If your business is interested in getting the big picture about St. Louis, write or call:
St. Louis Regional Commerce and Growth Assn., Ten Broadway, St. Louis, MO 63102, 314-231-5555.

city agencies and offices. As discussed in Chapter 4, city hall can provide a wealth of information about the city. Another good source of information is the chamber of commerce, which often employs location and development specialists.

For unbiased information, entrepreneurs can turn to the same sources they consulted for location information on states. For example, there is an *Inc.* listing of the top cities in the country. Using growth in jobs, business startups, and percent of fast-growing companies, *Inc.* identifies the following cities as the most conducive to new ventures:[5]

Austin, TX	Nashville, TN
Manchester-Nashua, NH	Tucson, AZ
Orlando, FL	Portsmouth-Dover, NH
Phoenix, AZ	Albuquerque, NM
Atlanta, GA	Tampa-St. Petersburg, FL
Raleigh-Durham, NC	Pensacola, FL
Huntsville, AL	Fort Myers, FL
Washington, DC	South Bend, IN
Dallas-Fort Worth, TX	Charleston, SC
San Diego, CA	Norfolk-Portsmouth, VA

We have listed the top 20 cities on the *Inc.* list, which includes a total of 156. The following are the last 20 cities on the list (numbers 137 to 156):

New Orleans, LA	Charleston, WV
Erie, PA	Huntington, WV
Shreveport, LA	Reading, PA
Columbus, GA	Davenport, IA
Johnson City, TN	Oklahoma City, OK
Beaumont, TX	Canton, OH
Amarillo, TX	Peoria, IL
Lubbock, TX	Duluth, MN
Utica-Rome, NY	Lafayette, LA
Springfield, IL	Odessa-Midland, TX

As the list illustrates, cities dependent on the oil and mining industries have experienced severe unemployment, which has dampened entrepreneurial activity.

City officials who are dissatisfied with their ranking on or omission from a particular list can always look for another list. The following list of "boomtowns" identifies five cities not included in the *Inc.* list:

- Rochester, Minnesota: Medical technology will help make it the Midwest's hottest city.
- Reno, Nevada: Industry is attracted by its low cost and strategic location.
- Santa Rosa-Petaluma, California: Exiles from San Francisco are fueling diverse economic growth.

- Gainesville, Florida: The University of Florida is a powerful high-tech magnet.
- Spring Hill, Tennessee: GM's new plant may be the beginning of auto-magic growth.[6]

The other cities ranked in this list are also on the *Inc.* top-twenty list of cities. Before selecting from any list of favorable cities, entrepreneurs should know what criteria were used to evaluate them. It is also important to make sure that the list is current because cities that were good locations for new ventures in the past may not be as hospitable now (see The Inside View 7-2).

Entrepreneurial Cities

Older, established cities like Detroit and New York are suitable for large, well-established companies. For new ventures, however, they may not be the ideal place. On the other hand, vibrant growth cities, such as Austin, Texas, seem to attract more than their share of startups. The following test can help those interested in starting a business measure a city's entrepreneurial climate:

1. When the mayor and business leaders meet, are there equal numbers of chief executive officers from mid-size growth firms and major corporations?
2. Are entrepreneurs invited to join the best social, athletic, and country clubs?
3. Does the local paper devote as much coverage to the fortunes of startups and mid-size companies as it does to major corporations?

7-2 *The Inside View*

NEW YORK: STILL THE GATEWAY TO THE "AMERICAN DREAM"?

For years, New York has attracted wave after wave of immigrants, each seeking the American dream in one of the nation's greatest cities. Many have realized their dreams by means of their own ability and enterprise. But today's immigrants are now finding a city no longer congenial to the entrepreneur. Typical of the hard-working immigrants are the Koreans, who own approximately 6 percent of the city's small businesses. These businesspeople have seen the rent for a typical 750-square-foot store grow from $1,500 to $3,500 in just a few years. Sung Soo Kim, president of the Korean American Small Business Service Center of New York, Inc., complains: "My business does only $300,000, and the landlord wants to take $90,000 off the top. This is becoming a city only for the rich." All small-business owners in New York face soaring rents and deteriorating services.[7]

4. Can innovative companies recruit most of their professional work force locally?
5. Is there a sizable, visible venture-capital community?
6. Does the local university encourage its faculty and students to participate in entrepreneurial spin-offs?
7. Do growth-company CEOs and venture capitalists hold even a quarter of the seats on the boards of the three largest banks?
8. Does the municipal economic development department spend as much time helping local companies grow as it does recruiting new companies or subsidiaries of major corporations?
9. Is there decent, affordable office and factory space available for new firms in the central business district?
10. Can you quickly think of ten recent spin-offs—growth companies started by entrepreneurs who have left large companies?[8]

Assign ten points to each "yes" answer, and consider sixty a passing score. Cities that score above sixty are more entrepreneurial than those with scores below.

Factors to Evaluate

When choosing a city in which to locate a new business, entrepreneurs have as much or more informaton to evaluate as they did when selecting the state. It is not possible to identify all of the factors that startup entrepreneurs need to evaluate; however, the following list provides an idea of the information needed to select the best city:

- Ability of local elected officials
- Competence of city managers and employees
- Availability and price of land
- Local taxes
- Availability of trained workers
- Transportation systems
- Quality of service from financial institutions
- Crime
- Quality of police and fire services
- Number and strength of competing businesses
- Public transportation
- Quality of school system
- Attitude of residents to business
- Financial incentives offered, such as direct or city guaranteed loans
- Sporting and cultural events
- Quality (see The Inside View 7-3)

SELECTING THE SITE

Choosing the site for a new venture is the last, and probably the most crucial, location decision which startup entrepreneurs need to make. Nearly everyone has heard of the successful businessman who named LOCATION, LOCATION, and LOCATION as the three principal reasons for his success. That response may seem trivial, but it

7-3 *The Inside View*

THE Q FACTOR

The key factor in choosing a city in which to start a business is quality, not cost. New businesses and established companies are choosing areas offering the qualitative advantages that permit an increasingly service-oriented, brain-dominated collection of companies to attract needed workers. A city no longer needs a natural harbor, a surplus of labor, and abundant sunshine in order to prosper, but quality universities, quality workers, quality airports and telephone systems, and quality government. For example, Dallas has built itself into a cultural and transportation center; Louisville has upgraded its substandard school system by gradually putting a computer in every classroom; Charleston, South Carolina, has revitalized an old southern port; and Orlando has built a thriving high-technology industry on the base of its Disney boom.[9]

is indicative of how important location is to most businesses. For some businesses, such as wholesalers, appliance-repair services, and exterminators, location might not be crucial; however, for any business that directly serves customers in its facility, choosing the right site is imperative.

In choosing the best region, state, and city in which to locate a new venture, relatively few entrepreneurs willingly consider relocating. A study conducted by Srully Blotnick, the author of *The Corporate Steeplechase*, indicated that 94 percent of the people questioned planned to start a new business where they were currently living.[10] In the past, according to Blotnick, it was common for no more than 70 percent of entrepreneurs who thought of entering a comparable variety of fields to stay at home. All startup entrepreneurs must consider every important factor in selecting the best site for their new venture.

Importance of Selecting the Right Site

There are numerous stories of people who have selected and purchased sites for their businesses only to discover that the area was subject to frequent flooding, the previous owner did not have clear title to the land, the neighborhood was deteriorating, road traffic patterns were being changed, a competitor was planning to locate next door, the site had been polluted (see The Inside View 7-4), etc. In order to avoid these mistakes, startup entrepreneurs should thoroughly investigate the sites under consideration. The investigator can use an elaborate evaluation checklist or one as simple

7-4

The Inside View

POLLUTED SITES

It was the ultimate nightmare for any company buying a piece of land. A lubricating-oil company bought property for $48,000 and finalized plans to build a warehouse. But its bulldozers soon uncovered an awful surprise: The prior owner, a solvent-recycling company had polluted the soil with toxins. The estimated cost to eliminate the pollutants was $2 million. According to the federal law that established Superfund, liability for hazardous-waste cleanup follows land ownership, or, in other words, the owner of the land, not the polluter, is responsible for cleanup. Therefore, pollution experts are urging companies to do their homework before buying land. Before signing any papers, many companies are testing soil for evidence of toxic waste, and some are requiring an indemnification clause protecting buyers from liability if toxic waste is discovered on the property later.[11]

and functional as the one illustrated in Figure 7.2. The startup entrepreneur should not rush the selection process and should use all the tools at his or her disposal, including the services of a location specialist.

If entrepreneurs choose to hire a location consultant, they should select a consultant who is a Certified Industrial Developer (CID). CIDs must have eight years of experience in development and must pass the Certification Board's testing procedures to receive the CID designation. There are approximately three hundred and fifty Certified Industrial Developers in the United States. Members of the Society of Industrial Realtors are also able to assist with site selection. Like CIDs, members of this association have passed a rather rigorous examination and need several years of experience before they can be certified. Management consultant Otto P. Geier suggests the following reasons for using outside consultants:[12]

1. Consultants will maintain the confidentiality needed to keep competitors or real estate firms from knowing which sites are under consideration.
2. Consultants are likely to be less biased than startup entrepreneurs.
3. Consultants are likely to make important business issues other than real estate considerations a part of their recommendations.
4. Consultants have access to local professionals and experts who can provide relevant information.
5. Consultants who have had years of site-selection experience can do the job in less time than inexperienced startup entrepreneurs can.

FIGURE 7.2 Rating Sheet on Sites

Grade each factor: 1 (lowest) to 10 (highest).
Weigh each factor: 1 (least important) to 5 (most important).

Factors	*Grade*	*Weight*
1. Centrally located to reach my market.	____	____
2. Raw materials readily available.	____	____
3. Quantity of available labor.	____	____
4. Transportation availability and rates.	____	____
5. Labor rates of pay/estimated productivity.	____	____
6. Adequacy of utilities (sewer, water, power, gas).	____	____
7. Local business climate.	____	____
8. Provision for future expansion.	____	____
9. Tax burden.	____	____
10. Topography of the site (slope and foundation).	____	____
11. Quality of police and fire protection.	____	____
12. Housing availability for workers and managers.	____	____
13. Environmental factors (schools, cultural, community atmosphere).	____	____
14. Estimate of quality of this site in years.	____	____
15. Estimate of this site in relation to my major competitor.	____	____

Source: Fred Weber, Jr., *Locating or Relocating Your Business* (Washington, DC: U.S. Small Business Administration, 1986) Management Aids, Number 2.002.

Facility Review

Startup entrepreneurs or their consultants should perform a facility review of every site under consideraton. The primary concern of this review is the environmental condition of the site, and since it is the owner of the site, not the polluter, who is liable for cleanup, its conclusions are critical. They will determine if a site merits further consideration. The following are some of the components of a facility review:

1. ***An operational history.*** This historical review will reveal if any toxic material has been processed, stored, or disposed of on the site. It will also describe the condition of any buildings on the site.

2. ***Environmental procedures and guidelines.*** All relevant health, safety, and security policies should be scrutinized. It is important to identify the weakest link in that chain.

3. ***Regulatory history and status.*** Entrepreneurs should determine whether the previous owner of a site has had any problems with regulatory authorities. It is also important to try to determine if any pending regulations such as zoning, environmental, etc., might have an impact on a site.

4. ***Titles, licenses, and permits.*** Anyone planning to purchase a site should determine the existence of permits, licenses, or titles that will convey with the property. Entrepreneurs must be absolutely certain that the seller has legal title to the land and that the purpose for which it is being purchased does not violate any existing regulations.

5. ***Local citizens' groups.*** Entrepreneurs should find out if local groups have complained about pollution problems associated with the site.

6. ***Neighbors.*** It is possible that the site under consideration is environmentally sound but that neighbors have polluted water that runs on or under the site. If this should be the case, the entrepreneur purchasing the site could be required to clean up the water.[13]

Factors to Evaluate

There are hundreds of factors that should be evaluated when selecting a site; however, the discussion in this section will be limited to the most important. (Consult the Entrepreneur's Checklist at the end of the chapter for other important criteria.) The following are the three major categories of site-selection criteria: (1) *critical:* factors such as ample electricity and water—prerequisites for site selection; (2) *objective:* factors such as cost of land and traffic count, which can be quantified; and (3) *subjective:* factors such as leisure activities and quality of schools, which are difficult to quantify.

Critical Factors. It is easy to evaluate sites based on the factors that are critical to site selection. For example, if a company is a heavy user of water and electricity, then only those sites that have ample supplies of power and water can be considered. If a business relies heavily on rail transportation, any site not served by a major railroad cannot be considered. Once the sites lacking the critical factors have been eliminated, the task of evaluating objective criteria begins.

Objective Factors. It is relatively easy to obtain objective data from the chamber of commerce, city hall, local realtors, etc., for sites under consideration. Some of the more important objective factors that startup entrepreneurs should consider include the following:

Cost of the site
Site preparation and development costs
Cost of transportation to the site
Cost of transportation from the site
Zoning ordinances
Traffic count
Physical characteristics, such as flooding
Crime rate
Proximity of competition
Property taxes
Potential for future expansion
Environmental quality
Proximity to customers and suppliers
Proximity of police and fire stations
Access

These and other factors can be evaluated for each site and fairly accurate numbers derived. If these numbers could be used to make the final site-selection decision, the process would be simpler and more straightforward. However, the process is complicated by the need to evaluate the subjective factors.

Subjective Factors. Evaluating subjective factors is difficult because personal opinions and feelings are involved. The following are some of the subjective factors that startup entrepreneurs should evaluate:

Desirability of neighborhood
Attitude of government officials
Quality of schools
Leisure and recreational activities
Community attitude toward business
Quality of potential employees
Reputation of surrounding businesses

Once entrepreneurs have considered all of the critical, objective, and subjective factors for each site, they should be able to determine where to locate their new business. Astute entrepreneurs will obtain advice from as many sources as possible before making the final selection because an incorrect decision can be disastrous.

Retail-Business Locations

In the preceding sections we have presented a generic site-selection process that can be used for any type of business. In this section, we will discuss the importance of site selection to entrepreneurs who are planning to start a retail business. We have chosen to focus on retail establishments because the selection of the best site is absolutely critical to the success of any business selling to the public.

Most entrepreneurs planning to start a retail business are usually not interested in buying raw land, developing it, and then constructing their own building. Instead, they look for a site with an existing building that suits their needs or that can be modified. To make the selection process as reliable as possible, startup entrepreneurs should answer the following questions:

- How much retail, office, storage, and workroom space is needed?
- Is there adequate parking space available?
- Does the site have high visibility?
- Is there good accessibility for shipping and receiving?
- Is the location served by public transportation?
- Is the site easily accessible?
- Will zoning restrict growth?
- Is there adequate fire and police protection?
- Will sanitation or utility supply be a problem?
- Will the landlord assist with improvements?
- Is exterior lighting adequate?
- Is the lease or sale price realistic and affordable?
- Does the area have growth potential?
- Are there customer restrooms?
- Will crime insurance be too expensive?
- Is the population density sufficient?

- Is there sufficient traffic flow?
- Where are competitors located?
- Are complementary businesses located nearby?
- Does the location have future resale potential?
- Can space be sublet?
- What interior structural alterations are allowed?
- What exterior alterations are permitted?
- Are there specific hours during which business can be conducted?

Once these and other location questions have been answered, entrepreneurs can decide which available location is the best for their retail business. We have stressed the need to select a site that is attractive and accessible because failure to do so can quickly end a business. The following example will make this point more meaningful:

> Jerry "discovered" a new recipe for biscuits and decided to open a restaurant that specialized in sausage biscuits for breakfast. Jerry acquired a building that had housed a chain restaurant that failed. He modified it and opened for business. The primary-target customers were the thousands of employees who worked at a nearby government facility. Breakfast business did not materialize, and Jerry realized that he had selected the wrong location. The people driving to work in the morning were on the side of the street opposite the restaurant, and there was a concrete median dividing the road. Everything Jerry did to improve business was fruitless, and his restaurant failed within the year.

Multiply Jerry's case thousands of times, and it becomes evident why the right location is so important to customer-dependent businesses.

SPECIAL LOCATIONS

Entrepreneurs planning to start a new business have a seemingly limitless number of locations to evaluate. Many sites can be eliminated early in the selection process because of deficiencies in terms of critical factors previously discussed. Others can be eliminated only after exhaustive analysis. The selection process can be expensive and time consuming; however, there are some sites, tailor-made for startups, which can save entrepreneurs time and money. These sites may also increase the survival odds for new businesses.

Incubators

Incubators have been in existence for about twenty years; however, about 90 percent of the 200 operating incubators are less than seven years old. Incubators are large buildings, generally owned by large corporations, such as Control Data Corporation or local governments, that offer space to new businesses usually at below-market rents (see The Inside View 7-5). In addition to space, incubators offer small businesses services such as secretarial, copying, and consulting at reasonable rates. Startup entrepreneurs can minimize their overhead by paying only for the services they use rather than for a secretary or copying machine that is not fully utilized.

Incubators, more formally known as technology centers or enterprise villages, are credited with the success of many small businesses that might have failed if their

7-5 **The Inside View**

INCUBATORS

Gilda Brouthers, a commercial and industrial real estate agent, decided to change careers. The sixty-one-year-old Brouthers turned her hobby—making hand-dipped chocolates—into a business. She formed Charleston Confection Company and located it in an incubator. The new business occupies space in a Control Data Corporation Business and Technology Center that is actually a renovated cigar factory in a revitalized area of Charleston, South Carolina. Brouthers pays about $5 per square foot for her space, including utilities and other services, and says the going market rate for such space is about $15 per square foot. Gilda Brouthers credits her early success to the services and support provided by the incubator.[14]

owners had chosen other locations. There are some estimates that approximately 70 percent of the businesses located in incubators are successful. Incubators themselves are so successful that there is now an association, the National Business Incubation Association (NBIA), that represents many established and starting incubators. The executive director of the NBIA, Carlos Morales, predicts that there will be more than a thousand incubators by 1990.[15]

Initially, incubators rented space to any new business that met certain requirements. However, several incubators are now specializing and renting space only to certain types of new ventures. For example, the Spokane Business Incubation Center in Washington has established the Kitchin Center, which is a state-approved facility for small food-processing companies. Similarly, the Massachusetts Innovation Center in Worcester will focus on biotechnology firms; San Diego is planning one incubator with an aerospace orientation and another for auto-repair ventures; and Florida International University and the city of Miami have established the Biomedical Research and Innovation Center in downtown Miami.[16]

In areas with more than one incubator, startup entrepreneurs need to choose the one most appropriate for their new business, and in some instances, they may find that incubators are not suitable for their new business. Before choosing to locate in an incubator, entrepreneurs should answer the following questions:

1. Is the location suitable? A blighted area suits some tenants but not others. Is a central location necessary? Is it important to have immediate access to major highways?
2. What services are provided? What management assistance is available? Is group

health insurance offered? Will the business need typing, data and word processing, a receptionist, a conference room, or a copier?

3. Will the space accommodate growth? If the business needs twice as much space three months from now, will it be available? Is storage adequate?
4. What is the track record of the incubator's manager? Will he or she keep the facility running smoothly?
5. Is the physical plant adequate? Is there a loading dock? Is there enough parking? Can interior modifications be made? Is security sufficient?
6. What types of tenants are in the incubator? Are there opportunities to learn from one another? Are there potential customers and suppliers in the incubator?
7. What is the incubator's graduation policy? Will the business have to relocate after a certain period of time? Will the rent increase to market level once the business is profitable?[17]

Enterprise Zones

Enterprise zones are disadvantaged neighborhoods, usually in inner cities, where most business and property taxes have been waived by government to induce businesses to locate there. Startup entrepreneurs need to weigh the risks and inadequacies of these locations against the benefit of negligible business and property taxes. In these zones, crime rates and unemployment often are high, and there is a shortage of skilled labor. For most entrepreneurs, the risks will outweigh the benefits. Even many major corporations have not been successful in their attempts to establish plants in enterprise zones (see The Inside View 7-6). If established companies have difficulty operating in enterprise zones, what chance would a startup business have?

7-6 *The Inside View*

ENTERPRISE ZONES

The Boston-based conglomerate EG&G Inc. opened a metal fabrication plant in the predominantly black area of Roxbury. EG&G wasn't prepared to take on what one company official calls a "totally unskilled labor force." After two years of uneven production rates, quality-control problems, and several million dollars in losses, EG&G closed the plant. An Aerojet General tent-making plant in Los Angeles ran into similar problems. Many new employees had never had a job before and had to be coaxed into just getting to work on time. After four years of operations, Aerojet decided to sell the plant.[18]

Free-Trade Zones

Any entrepreneur planning a business that uses raw materials or parts imported from other countries should consider locating in a free-trade zone (FTZ). A free-trade zone (also referred to as foreign-trade zones) is a so-designated area in which importers can defer payment of customs duty until they have completed assembly or production of goods. To be effective, FTZs must be located either at or near an international port, on major shipping routes, or within easy traveling distance to a major airport. The major benefits of locating in a free-trade zone include the following: (1) companies pay the customs duty (tariff) only when their products are ready to market; (2) manufacturing costs are lower because no taxes (corporate or income) are levied; and (3) while still in the zone, the manufacturer has the opportunity to repackage the goods, grade them, and check for spoilage, thus reducing waste.

Industrial Parks

Industrial parks are large areas, usually on the outskirts of a city, which have been developed to provide companies with space. These parks usually have paved roads, utilities, adequate lighting, access to road and rail transportation, prepared sites, and sometimes even security in the form of fences and guards. A site in an industrial park might be an ideal location for a new manufacturing business or a company that sells products or services to manufacturing firms. For example, a young entrepreneur who wanted to open a printing business chose a location in an industrial park because he had targeted manufacturing companies as his major customers. His decision must have been correct because his business has expanded and is very profitable.

Piggyback Arrangements

Some entrepreneurs, especially those with a novel product or service and little startup capital, are locating within other businesses. For example, Larry Margolis offers car phones from locations inside automobile dealerships and at car washes. Marie Mahan is selling cookies in Arby's restaurants, hotel lobbies, and a hospital. And Robert Johnson ships packages nationwide out of retail stores owned by others. Overhead is reduced and the store-within-a-store usually pays a percentage of revenues to its host in exchange for taking up what is most often less than one hundred square feet of space.[19]

Shopping Centers and Malls

Many new businesses will be successful if their owners choose to locate in shopping centers or malls. Shopping centers and malls offer new businesses the following advantages:

- Heavy traffic
- Ample parking
- Other complementary businesses
- Security

- Professional management
- Attractive surroundings
- Shared advertising support
- Space modifications to meet tenant's needs
- High visibility
- Prestige location

While the advantages of shopping-center locations are numerous, there are some disadvantages which must be considered. For example, rents are usually higher than in comparable non-shopping-center sites; leases may be longer; required opening hours may be excessive; required advertising may be costly; and competitors are often able to locate in the same center.

Startup entrepreneurs should evaluate several different kinds of shopping centers. There are large regional centers which attract customers from several counties. There are also smaller shopping centers, such as community shopping centers, mini-malls, small regional malls, and strip shopping centers. The target market of the new business will determine the type of shopping center.

Summary

Selecting the wrong site can be disastrous. We cannot emphasize too strongly that site selection is one of the most critical decisions startup entrepreneurs have to make. Some entrepreneurs, with no locational preference, will choose to locate their new business on the best site, regardless of where it is; others will prefer to remain in their home state and city. For those willing to relocate, it is necessary first to determine which state or states offer the most assistance to new ventures. Information about states can be acquired from the states themselves and from disinterested sources such as *Inc.* and other magazines.

In evaluating the desirability of various states, entrepreneurs should consider the following factors: the availability and price of land; taxes; availability of labor; transportation; laws and regulations; economic conditions; educational institutions; financial incentives; and the quality of life. It is also advisable to evaluate the general political climate in target states.

Once a state has been selected, entrepreneurs need to decide which cities and which sites in those cities should be considered. Demographic data are available from the chamber of commerce, city hall, real estate agencies, etc., all of which can help entrepreneurs choose the most appropriate city and site. It is necessary to evaluate each target city and site in terms of the following factors: cost of land, local taxes, crime rate, location of competitors, quality of fire and police protection, leisure and sporting facilities, and the quality of life.

Some entrepreneurs may find it advantageous to locate their new ventures in one of several "special" locations. Those locations most suitable for a new business include the following: incubators, enterprise zones, free-trade zones, industrial parks, and shopping centers and malls.

Assembling the Pieces

Because of family ties and job obligations, Carol and Jacki had to locate their new business within a relatively limited area. They decided to locate somewhere in Charleston County because that is where most of their target customers lived or worked. Carol and Jacki first considered sites in downtown Charleston, but eliminated them because they lacked parking and they had competing shops. Once they eliminated downtown, Carol and Jacki used census data, information from realtors and the chamber of commerce, and information gained through personal observation to determine that the best location was most likely to be in the western part of the city.

The major road in the western suburbs, Highway 7, connects the interstate and Highway 17, a major north–south throughway. The first site Carol and Jacki considered was a regional mall at the intersection of highways 7 and 17. They chose not to locate in this mall for the following reasons: space was too expensive; the mall was not generating enough traffic; the mall operators imposed too many restrictions on tenants; the people who frequented the mall were not likely to be customers of In Good Taste; and the mall just did not have the right "feel."

Having decided against a mall site, Carol and Jacki decided to consider free-standing buildings. A thorough search of the area failed to turn up a suitable building, and Carol and Jacki were not interested in constructing their own facility. They also concluded that their business should be located in a shopping center in order to benefit from traffic generated by other stores.

Carol and Jacki evaluated five relatively small shopping centers before finally selecting the best site. They eliminated four of the shopping centers because there was insufficient traffic, poor visibility, poor management, and competitive shops, or because the sites were almost inaccessible or too expensive. The shopping center finally selected by Carol and Jacki is a relatively small center located near a major intersection about a mile from the interstate. They selected this site for the following reasons: it was highly visible; it had good management; the space available was fairly priced; the landlord was willing to modify the building; there was a restaurant adjacent to the facility (patrons would be likely to shop at In Good Taste); it was located on the "going-home-from-work" side of the street; and the facility had the right "feel." ■

entrepreneur's checklist

SITE-SELECTION CHECKLIST

1. Does the labor force have deep community roots? _____
2. Is the labor force mainly permanent? _____
3. Has labor history been satisfactory? _____
4. Is the area union oriented? _____
5. Has a labor-availability survey been conducted? _____
   Typical factors:
   - **a.** Population at last census
   - **b.** Population density per square mile
   - **c.** Percentage employed in agriculture

   - **d.** Total employed in manufacturing
   - **e.** Total employed in nonmanufacturing
   - **f.** Countywide potential employment
   - **g.** Unemployed available workers
   - **h.** Willingness of workers to work different shifts
   - **i.** Distribution of available labor among skilled, semi-skilled, and unskilled groups

6. Is the community subject to seasonal labor variations? _____

7. Does an adequate labor pool exist within reasonable distance? _____

8. Do young people leave the area to find jobs? _____

9. Would better job opportunities keep them at home? _____

10. Has there been an evaluation of the factors that affect wages and working conditions:

   - **a.** Wage rates, by skills
   - **b.** Working hours
   - **c.** Shift patterns
   - **d.** Hourly or piece rates
   - **e.** Benefits
   - **f.** Degree of competition for skills
   - **g.** Pattern of year-end bonuses
   - **h.** Degree of unionization
   - **i.** Quality of union leadership
   - **j.** Degree of union loyalty
   - **k.** Pattern of productivity
   - **l.** Seniority provisions
   - **m.** Layoff provisions
   - **n.** Grievance patterns

11. Do state corporate taxes compare favorably with those of other states? _____

12. Does the state have a personal income tax system? _____

13. Are there state property taxes? _____

14. Is there a state sales tax? _____

15. Does the state permit the deduction of federal income tax? _____

16. Is the community tax burden shared equally by residential, industrial, and commercial sectors? _____

17. Are community taxes reasonable and fair? _____

18. Do unrealistically low taxes imply inferior schools, streets, or services? _____

19. Is there too much tax-free property? _____

20. Are community tax inducements offered to prospective businesses? _____

21. If so, is there evidence that high taxes later will wipe out initial tax advantage? _____

22. Is the site at or near a "trucking gateway" to reduce in-transit times? _____

23. Are state laws governing truck size and weight reasonable? _____

24. Are there good access roads, bridges, and culverts for trucks? _____

25. Is the pattern of recent increases in truck freight rates reasonable? _____

26. Does the state government function as well as those of other states? _____

27. Are state salaries high enough to attract and retain good employees? ____
28. Is the workmen's compensation picture satisfactory? ____
29. Are there any "hidden" restrictive laws? ____
30. Is there adequate electricity, natural gas, fuel oil, and coal? ____
31. Are power rates satisfactory? ____
32. Are off-peak rates available? ____
33. Is natural gas a competitive fuel in the area? ____
34. Is gas available on a steady basis? ____
35. Is coal a competitive fuel in the area? ____
36. Any delivery problems? ____
37. Are water requirements compatible with water resources? ____
38. Is there an adequate public water supply? ____
39. If water treatment is needed, are costs in line with those of other site locations? ____
40. If streams are the logical source, will the flow be adequate during dry months? ____
41. Will good business practice plus local or state ordinances call for waste treatment? ____
42. Are necessary raw materials close enough? ____
43. Are raw material sources reliable? ____
44. Are raw material prices satisfactory? ____
45. Is the cost of transport to the site reasonable? ____
46. Is the attitude of local officials toward existing and new industry sympathetic? ____
47. Does the record of local government reflect a high degree of honesty, efficiency, and ethical behavior? ____
48. Is the community industrially diversified? ____
49. Are the community's industries growing? ____
50. Does the community have an active city planning commission? ____
51. Can protection against undesirable neighbors be expected? ____
52. Do building inspectors have a reputation for honesty and integrity? ____
53. Can managers be recruited locally? ____
54. Are specialized skills available? ____
55. Have local people responded well to in-plant training? ____
56. Are there sufficient schools and personnel? ____
57. Are there opportunities for vocational, trade, and apprentice training? ____
58. Are colleges near enough to offer special courses to key personnel? ____
59. Are there adult education programs? ____
60. Do police department and fire departments have high standards of personnel, equipment, training, etc.? ____
61. Are private security services or uniformed detective agencies available? ____
62. Is the incidence of crime as low as or lower than that in surrounding areas? ____
63. Is the overall impression of residential areas an attractive one? ____
64. Are there satisfactory health and medical services? ____
65. Is there a variety of local outdoor attractions? ____

66. Are there family recreational areas, parks, and playgrounds? _____
67. Is the community near popular resort areas? _____
68. Is there much media activity, including dailies, weeklies, radio, and TV?[20] _____

Questions for Review and Discussion

1. What kinds of entrepreneurs do you think would be most likely to relocate to any site in the United States?
2. What factors would you consider when selecting a state in which to locate?
3. How would you acquire information about states in which you were considering locating?
4. What incentives do you think a state should offer to new companies to get them to locate in that state?
5. What makes cities attractive to new ventures?
6. How important do you think colleges and public school systems are to entrepreneurs looking for the best site?
7. How can consultants help entrepreneurs select a site?
8. Do you think it is fair to make the purchaser of a site clean up hazardous material left there by previous owners?
9. What kinds of businesses do you think should locate in special places such as incubators and industrial parks?

Notes

1. McKinley Conway, "To Compete Globally, Business Must Choose Optimum Sites," (*Site Selection Handbook* 1987), p. 4.
2. Joshua Hyatt, "Coast to Coast," *Inc.,* October 1987, pp. 76–86.
3. ———— "Equality: Rating the States," *Newsweek,* 6 October 1986, p. 4.
4. Greg Critser, "Cities Try New Plan: Buy and Move Firms," *Inc.,* April 1986, p. 19.
5. ———— "Hotspots: *Inc.*'s Annual Ranking of America's Cities," *Inc.,* March 1988, pp. 74–76.
6. Walter Updegrave, "Ten Boomtowns You Can Bet On," *Money,* November 1985, pp. 74–80.
7. Joel Kotkin, "Now That They Have Fixed Miss Liberty, Who Will Fix New York?" *Inc.,* July 1986, pp. 81–86.
8. David Birch, "Thriving on Adversity," *Inc.,* March 1988, pp. 80–81.
9. David Birch, "The Q factor," *Inc.,* April 1987, pp. 53–54.
10. Srully Blotnick, "There's no Place like Home," *Forbes,* 5 November 1984, pp. 294–295.
11. Lisa Sheeran, "Hidden Poisons," *Inc.,* February 1986, p. 97.
12. Otto Geier, Jr., "Site Selection and the Outsider," *American Industrial Properties Report,* December 1978, pp. 22–23.
13. Darryl Miller, "The Components of a Facility Review," *Industrial Development,* March/April 1986, p. 4.

14. Sharon Nelton, "Incubators for Baby Businesses," *Nation's Business,* November 1984, pp. 40–44.

15. Sallie Hofmeister, "The Clubs," *Venture,* September 1985, p. 22.

16. Steven Galante, "Business Incubators Adopting Niche Strategies to Stand Out," *The Wall Street Journal,* 13 April 1987, p. 27.

17. Ibid.

18. Alex Beam, "Why Few Ghetto Factories Are Making It," *Business Week,* 16 February 1987, pp. 86–89.

19. Paul Brown, "Piggyback," *Inc.,* August 1988, pp. 92–93.

20. Jon Browning, *How to Select a Business Site* (New York: McGraw-Hill, 1980), pp. 23–30 and 163–165.

CHAPTER 8

Designing Facilities

Learning Objectives

After you have read this chapter, you will be able to do the following:

- Determine whether it is more advantageous to lease or buy a building.
- Evaluate basic building considerations, such as space requirements, noise control, lighting, etc.
- Determine the best layouts for factories, stores, and offices.
- Set up offices in homes.

It is important for startup entrepreneurs to locate the best site because it can mean the difference between success and failure. However, once the site has been selected, entrepreneurs must make sure that their factory, store, office, etc., is laid out efficiently. Inefficient layouts can cause bottlenecks, poor traffic patterns for customers or employees, or extra product handling. Correct facility layout ensures operating efficiency, which makes companies more profitable and successful. While entrepreneurs will surely want to be involved in the design of their facilities, it is advisable to hire professionals to supervise all phases of design and construction. Architects, interior designers, lighting specialists, and landscape architects should be used to lay out a company's space.

In this chapter, we will illustrate the positive and negative effects of different types of designs on the efficiency of factories, stores, and offices. A poorly designed building will decrease business efficiency and, in turn, will decrease profits. We will also discuss the pros and cons of building versus modifying a facility and buying versus leasing. We will examine some basic environmental considerations and determine the best way to design buildings for different types of businesses.

TO BUILD OR NOT TO BUILD

Ideally, startup entrepreneurs will locate the most desirable site, make the necessary site preparations, and then construct a new facility to meet their exact specifications. In reality, most entrepreneurs select sites with existing buildings that can be modified to meet their requirements.

Building a New Structure

Entrepreneurs who are fortunate enough to locate an empty site on which to construct their own building will benefit from the following advantages:

- The building can be designed specifically to meet the company's needs.
- All new technologies can be incorporated in the structure.
- The structure will meet all local building codes.
- There will be no "hidden" flaws.
- Everything will be new.
- The building can be designed to allow for future expansion.
- The design of the building can create a company image.
- The interior can be designed for maximum efficiency.

Modifying Existing Structures

In most cases, startup entrepreneurs will select a site that already contains a building for their new venture; however, even existing structures usually need to be remodeled to suit the needs of new tenants. Remodeling limits the design possibilities for existing buildings, but, with imagination and expert assistance, most buildings can be laid out to meet the needs of a new business. The following are some of the advantages of remodeling an existing structure:

- Remodeling is usually less expensive than building a new facility.
- It takes less time to remodel than to build.
- Remodeling usually does not require the assistance of as many outside experts as building a new structure does.
- Much remodeling can be done by the entrepreneurs themselves (referred to as "sweat equity").
- Serviceable equipment and fixtures can be recycled.

PURCHASING OR LEASING FACILITIES

Once the decision to build or renovate has been made, startup entrepreneurs need to determine whether they should purchase or lease their facility. Entrepreneurs who have chosen a vacant site on which to construct their building can choose to own or lease the facility. For example, it is quite common for grocery chains to design stores that are built and owned by other companies or individuals who lease the building to the grocery chain. For those entrepreneurs who have selected a site with an existing facility, the buy or lease option may be made by the building owner.

Purchasing a Facility

Entrepreneurs who can afford to buy a facility should first evaluate the advantages and disadvantages of doing so. The following are some of the advantages of buying a building:

- Owners can make whatever modifications they wish without consulting landlords.
- Unlike lease payments, mortgage costs remain relatively stable.
- Depreciation, interest payments, and property taxes are treated as business expenses for tax purposes.
- Business owners cannot be evicted by a landlord who needs the building for other tenants.
- The property usually appreciates in value.

The advantages of owning a building should be weighed against the following disadvantages:

- The initial capital outlay required to buy a building is usually considerably greater than that required to lease.
- Owning a building can limit an entrepreneur's mobility.
- The owner of a building must pay for all maintenance and remodeling costs.
- If a neighborhood begins to deteriorate, the value of a building will decline.

Leasing a Facility

Entrepreneurs should consider the advantages and disadvantages of leasing their facility before taking the plunge. The following are some of the advantages of leasing a building:

- There is usually no large initial capital outlay.
- Landlords are often responsible for maintenance and repairs.
- It is easier for business owners to relocate if they do not have to sell their building first.
- Most lease expenses are tax deductible.
- The building owner usually pays the insurance premiums for the facility.
- If the value of the building declines, it does not directly affect the lessor.

The following are some of the disadvantages associated with leasing premises:

- The rent paid to landlords is usually increased on a regular basis.
- Tenants can be evicted if the landlord wants the building for other purposes.
- Some landlords allow their buildings to deteriorate.
- Landlords may restrict tenant activities.

BASIC DESIGN CONSIDERATIONS

In this section, we will consider some of the more basic design elements as well as some that are specific only to certain types of businesses. People starting any new business need to consider factors such as space requirements, noise control, lighting, etc., which are important to both remodelers and builders.

Space Requirements

Determining how much space is required for a new business is relatively easy, but forecasting future space requirements is considerably more difficult. All entrepreneurs who are sufficiently optimistic believe that their company will grow and prosper; therefore, they must base their space requirements on this expectation. Whether building or remodeling, it is advisable to have more space than that initially required because the business will most likely expand to occupy the space. Excess space can be leased temporarily to other tenants with the understanding that their lease will be terminated when the owners need the space for expansion.

In addition to determining how much space a business will need, owners should also consider personal space requirements. Most employees want to exercise some control over their "personal space." It may not be possible to provide all employees with complete privacy; however, good planning can ensure some privacy for most. Entrepreneurs who want to provide as many of their employees as possible with privacy should take the following measures:

- Identify each employee's work space. Nameplates, movable partitions, and the like, can delineate a person's territory.
- Provide lockable storage space.
- Avoid traffic bottlenecks or congestion.
- Give employees some control over light, temperature, etc.
- Provide window views for as many employees as possible.
- Allow employees to personalize their work space.
- Provide for ease of cleaning.[1]

Noise control

To promote efficiency in the workplace, it is important to control noise. Environmental Protection Agency (EPA) regulations set noise limits for different workplaces. The unit of measurement for sound levels is the decibel, or dB, which is based on the logarithmic comparison of a measured value to a reference value. (Table 8.1 lists noise measurements taken in different settings.) When considering the use of materials such as carpets and curtains, it is important to know their noise reduction coefficient (NRC), a number between zero and one which represents the amount of energy absorbed by the material. The higher the number, the more energy absorbed. Therefore, by using the right materials when building or remodeling, it is possible to reduce noise to acceptable levels.

Lighting

Adequate lighting, like acceptable noise levels, makes workplaces more comfortable and employees more efficient. Light is measured in footcandles, and different areas require different amounts of light. For example, areas where work is done will require

Table 8.1 Decibel Levels of Commonplace Sounds and Activities

Apparent Loudness	*Examples*	*dBA*
Deafening	Jet aircraft	140
	Threshold of feeling	130
Very loud	Thunder	120
	Noisy industrial plant	100
	Loud street noise	90
Loud	Average street noise	70
	Average office/department store	60
Moderate	Moderate restaurant clatter	50
	School classroom/private office	40
Faint	Bedroom	30
	Rustling leaves	20
Very faint	Normal breathing	10
	Threshold of audibility	0

more light than other areas. (See Table 8.2 for lighting requirements of different areas.) Proper lighting is essential for all businesses, but it is particularly important to businesses that sell consumer goods. It is very difficult, for example, to determine the color of clothes in poorly lighted stores.

An effective lighting plan will accomplish the following:

1. Motivate customers to purchase. (A successful lighting plan will heighten the sense of excitement and discovery.)
2. Expose "hidden" merchandise. (Items that cannot be seen cannot be sold.)
3. Organize the merchandise area.
4. Help direct shoppers to the merchandise.
5. Minimize structural deficiencies.
6. Accurately render the color of merchandise and flatter customers.
7. Make shoppers and employees feel comfortable.
8. Eliminate boredom.[2]

HVAC

Heating, ventilating, and air conditioning (HVAC) systems are important for the comfort and safety of employees. Interior climate control is necessary not only for the comfort of employees but also for the protection of sensitive equipment and fixtures.

Table 8.2 Lighting Level Requirements

Task Lighting		*Footcandles*
Reading:	Simple (high-contrast) copy	50
	Difficult (low-contrast) copy	70
Writing:	Short periods of time	50
	Long periods of time	70
Typing:	From good-quality originals	50
	From poor-quality originals	70
	Accounting areas	100
	Drafting boards	100
	CRT screens (display terminals)	50
General (Ambient) Lighting		*Footcandles*
	Workstation, nontask areas	25 to 30
	Circulation (corridor) areas	10 to 20
	Conference rooms, nontask areas	25 to 30
	Lounge and waiting areas	25 to 30
	Filing areas	30 to 40

Adequate HVAC systems are particularly necessary in many modern buildings, which have windows that cannot be opened. It is also mandatory to have ventilating systems that can eliminate noxious fumes and unpleasant odors from factories, stores, and offices.

Color

Color schemes selected for buildings play an important part in the comfort and well-being of employees and customers. As with lighting, color schemes are particularly important in retail establishments. The following characteristics are associated with different color groups:

1. ***Timeless color palettes.*** Neutrals—beige, cream, off-white, gray, and tan—do not compete with merchandise and are always in good taste.

2. ***Accent and jewel colors.*** Ruby, burgundy, emerald, navy, and turquoise should be used sparingly because customers may tire quickly of very bright or dark colors used over large surfaces.

3. ***Cool color schemes.*** Gray, blue, blue-green, gray-green, and blue-violet are conservative, soothing, and relaxing.

4. ***Warm color schemes.*** Red, orange, and yellow are friendly and cheerful, and add excitement to an area.

5. ***Pastels.*** Peach, mauve, and lavender are flattering to complexions and are good for areas where lingerie and jewelry are sold.[3]

FACTORY LAYOUT

Startup entrepreneurs planning a new manufacturing venture will have to choose from the following types of basic factory layout: product, process, and fixed.

Product Layout

A business engaged in the mass production of single or limited numbers of products would use a *product layout*. In this layout, all the equipment involved in producing an item is arranged sequentially, as in an assembly line (see Figure 8.1). Products are moved, usually by a conveyor system, to each machine until the manufacturing process has been completed. While this layout is not always practical for new ventures, it does offer the following advantages: affords more efficient use of floor space, reduces manufacturing costs, minimizes product handling time and costs, reduces production

FIGURE 8.1
Product Layout

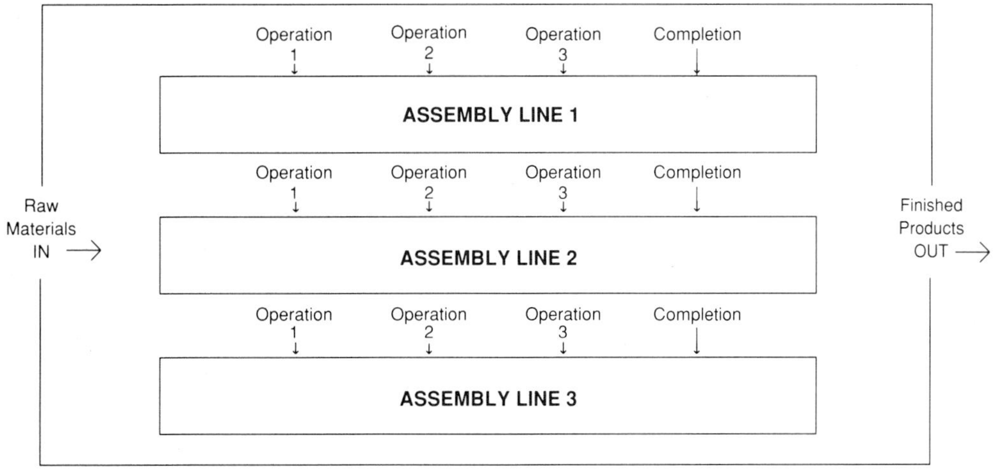

time, reduces employee-training time, provides smoother flow of materials, and reduces waste.

The major disadvantage of this layout is that machines are dependent on each other. If one machine becomes inoperable, the assembly line comes to a halt. The machines are also expensive and often are idle. Assembly line jobs are among the most tiring and boring in many industries.

Process Layout

Small plants that produce several different items generally use a *process* or *"job shop" layout*. This layout requires that all similar machines and equipment be located in the same area (see Figure 8.2). For example, products that need to be sanded and painted are taken first to an area where all sanding machines are located and then moved to another area where they are then painted. Process layouts offer the following benefits: greater utilization of machinery, ability to shift work when a machine is not functioning, better control of intricate processes, less initial capital investment, lower production costs for small numbers of items, and easier maintenance.

FIGURE 8.2
Process Layout for Window Manufacturer

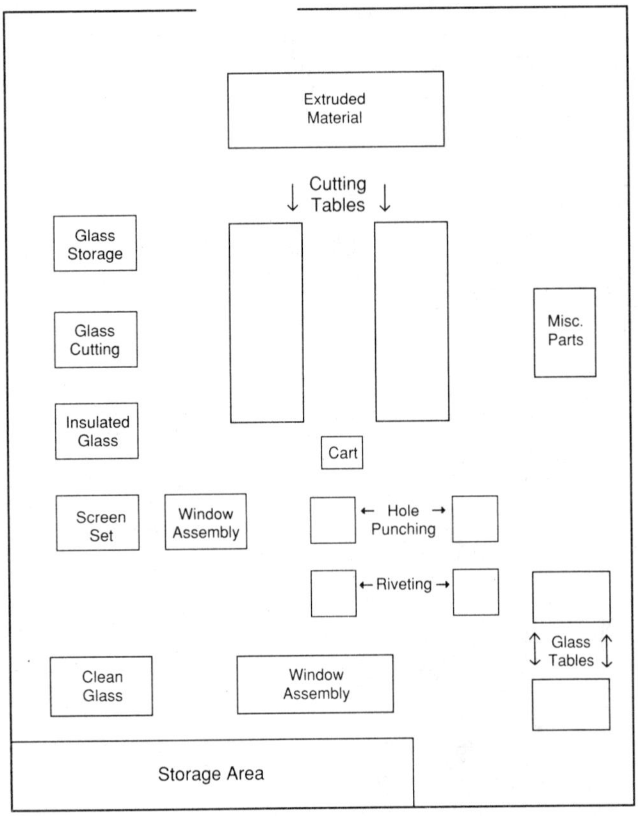

Fixed Layout

In a manufacturing plant with a *fixed layout*, the product remains in one place, and the workers and machinery move to perform their part of the manufacturing process. This layout, which is not common to startups, is used for large products, such as airplanes and locomotives, which cannot be moved easily.

STORE LAYOUT

Many retail businesses with quality merchandise and helpful employees have failed because their layouts were not "customer friendly." Proper store layout attracts customers, directs their movement through the store, and makes them want to spend time in the store. A number of items must be considered and questions answered before the best layout can be determined.

Questions and Considerations

Following is a list of some important considerations and questions:[4]

A. General considerations
  1. Exterior environment
    a. What is the nature of the surrounding neighborhood? Define the adjacent commercial area: shopping center or block, strip or free-standing stores?
    b. How will existing colors, textures, architectural styles, and graphics affect your store's design? Is traffic mainly vehicular or pedestrian?
  2. Characteristics of the merchandise
    a. What will be sold in the store?
      (1) Clothing: men's, women's, children's
      (2) Accessories: belts, scarves, hats, etc.
      (3) Shoes
      (4) Home furnishings: furniture, carpeting, lamps and lighting, wall decor
    b. What will be the range of styles?
      (1) Basic, classic
      (2) Trendy, promotional
      (3) Seasonal
      (4) Impulse or big ticket
      (5) Full markup or discount
    c. Financial breakdowns
      (1) Percentage of total sales represented by each category
      (2) Sales per square foot for each category
      (3) Stock turns per year
  3. Who are the store's customers?
    a. Age
    b. Geographical distribution
    c. Income level
    d. Size range

- **B.** Characteristics of the store
  1. Type of service
     - a. Full-service
     - b. Self-service
     - c. Combination
  2. Floor plan
     - a. Linear
     - b. Open
     - c. Enclosed
     - d. Random
     - e. U-shape
  3. Siting considerations
     - a. Proximity of merchandise to front, perimeter, or rear of store
     - b. Location of cashier in relation to merchandise
     - c. Customer's view of merchandise
- **C.** Merchandising
  1. Quantity
     - a. Number of different styles and colors
     - b. Number of items
  2. Seasonal
     - a. Weather
     - b. Holidays
     - c. Calendar considerations (back-to-school, cruisewear, etc.)
  3. Item pricing
     - a. Hang tags
     - b. Stickers
  4. Signs
     - a. Position (floor and counter)
     - b. Use of name brands
- **D.** Merchandising: Define how much flexibility is needed to display and stock the merchandise
  1. Wall displays, accessible by sales personnel
  2. Wall displays, above eighty inches
  3. Island displays
  4. Secure displays, under glass
  5. Manufacturer's displays
- **E.** Stock
  1. Concealed in floor displays
  2. Stored in drawers or behind doors
  3. Stockroom and backup areas
  4. Remote storage

Layout Types

Since there is considerable variation in the size and shape of stores, it is difficult to prescribe one or two distinct layouts which will satisfy all requirements. However, the following are some suggestions for designing an optimal layout:

- Display cases and other fixtures should not create a cluttered look.
- Furniture and fixtures should be low enough so that employees can see customers at all times.
- Similar kinds of merchandise should be displayed in the same area.
- Aisles should be wide enough to accommodate customers.
- Cash registers should be located near the exit.
- Impulse items should be displayed near the cash register.
- Customers should walk past "nice-to-have" items to reach necessities.
- Nonselling space should be kept to a minimum.

Once owners and their consultants know what is to be sold, who will be buying, etc., they can choose a layout that best suits the store's needs. The following are some of the more common store layouts (see Figure 8.3):

Straight Plan. This layout utilizes walls and projections to create smaller spaces. This plan lends itself well to pulling customers to the back of the store.

Pathway Plan. This plan is most appropriate for stores with more than 5,000 square feet of space all on one floor. An effective architectural organizer, this plan gets shoppers smoothly from the front to the rear of the store. This is an ideal layout for apparel stores because it minimizes the cluttered feeling that tends to discourage shoppers.

Diagonal Plan. This plan is ideal for self-service stores because it places cashiers in a central location from which they can see all areas of the store. This plan has a dynamic quality. Since it is not based on a straight line, it encourages movement and circulation.

Curved Plan. For salons, boutiques, or high-quality stores, the curved plan creates a special customer environment. This plan costs more than comparable angular or square store layouts.

Varied Plan. A variation of the straight plan, it provides enough space for box or carton storage off the main sales floor. This plan is most appropriate for retail businesses that require backup merchandise (shoes, men's shirts, etc.) stored near the sales area.

Geometric Plan. Designers position showcases, racks, or gondolas in a geometric plan so that space for fitting rooms is created without wasting square footage, making it ideal for clothing stores.[5]

The Checklist for Interior Arrangement and Display (at the end of the chapter) will help entrepreneurs determine which layout is most appropriate for a specific type of store and how merchandise should be displayed.

Arrangement of Merchandise

Once the basic store layout has been designed, entrepreneurs need to decide how to arrange their merchandise. Because customers generally enter a store, proceed to their right, and circulate in a counterclockwise direction, the front of the store is usually

FIGURE 8.3
Alternate Store Layouts

a.

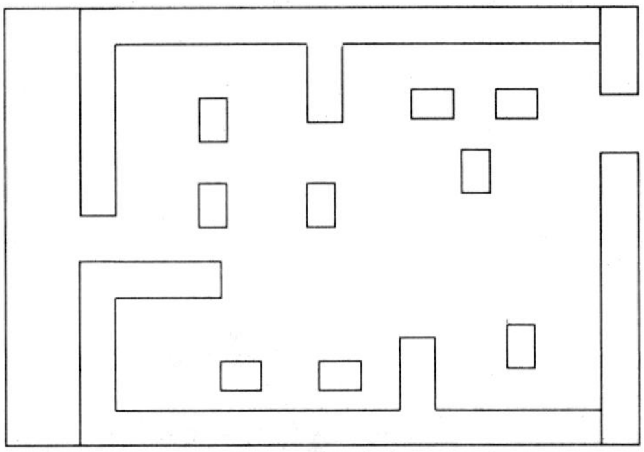

This straight plan uses walls and projections to create smaller spaces and is economical.

b.

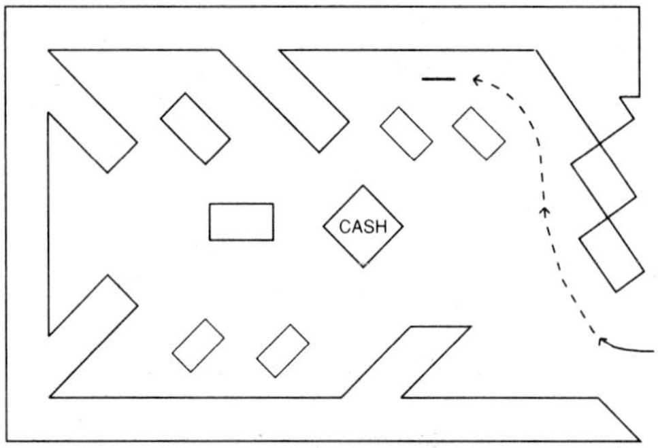

This diagonal pattern permits angular traffic flow and creates perimeter design interest and excitement in movement. The central placement of the cash-wrap permits security and vision.

c.

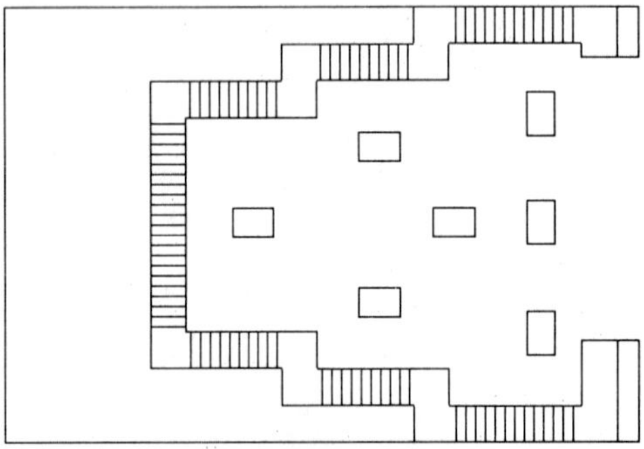

This varied plan illustrates added variety of forms which can work to a designer's advantage.

d.

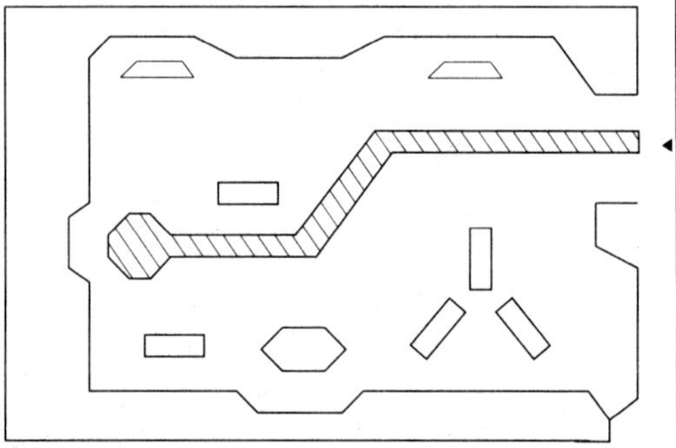

This pathway plan pulls patrons through the store to the rear without interruption by floor fixtures. The merits of such a layout are that the path can take any shape and that it creates a design pattern.

e.

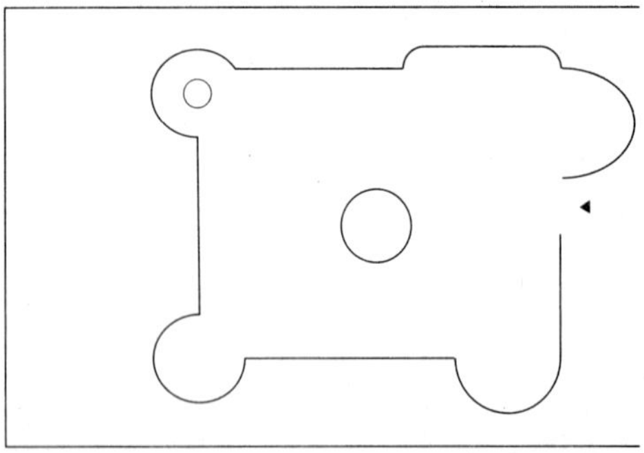

People respond to circular and curved shapes such as those shown here, which soften the angular and square plan.

f.

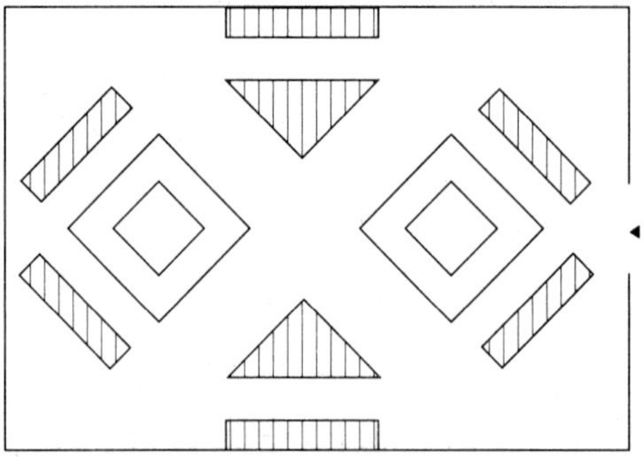

A geometric plan can establish interest without excessive cost, if the store's product can accept it. Ceiling and floors can be lowered or raised to create zones and departments.

more productive than the rear. Therefore, merchandise should be arranged in a manner that will take advantage of traffic patterns (see Table 8.3). Impulse goods and convenience items should be placed near the cash register at the front of the store. Staples should be placed at the rear of the store, and prime selling space should be allocated to the most expensive and hard-to-sell merchanidse.

OFFICE LAYOUT

Many startup entrepreneurs create new ventures that provide businesses and individuals with services. These new companies do not need retail or manufacturing space; rather they need attractive, efficient office space. The layout of offices is just as critical as that of factories and stores because an effective layout increases productivity. There are two basic layout plans—*closed* and *open*—which can be used effectively in different circumstances. Regardless of which plan entrepreneurs favor, they should be aware of the following findings of the Buffalo Organization for Social and Technological Innovation (BOSTI):

- In general, workers in enclosed spaces (even if the enclosure is only a movable panel) perform better than workers in bull pen environments.
- Clerical workers who are constantly supervised are no more productive than workers who are not.
- Most employees prefer to work near a window; however, the presence or absence of a window has little effect on job performance.

Table 8.3 Arrangement of Merchandise in Retail Stores

Kind of Merchandise	*How or Why Bought*	*Placement in Store*
Impulse goods	Because of attractive visual displays	Small store—near entrance Large store—on main aisle
Convenience goods	With frequency in small quantities	Easily accessible locations along main aisle
Necessities or staple goods	Because of need	Rear of single-level stores, upper floor(s) of multilevel stores (not a hard-and-fast rule)
Utility goods	For home use—brooms, dustpans, etc.	As impulse items, up front or along main aisle
Luxury and major expense items	After planning and much "shopping around"	Some distance from entrance

SOURCE: *Small Business Location and Layout* (Washington, DC: Small Business Administration, 1980), p. 6.

- About one-third of U.S. workers complain that the temperature in their offices fluctuates too frequently.
- If office space is reduced by more than 25 percent, job satisfaction drops considerably.[6]

Closed Offices

Traditionally office layouts called for a design that segregated management and staff in small, enclosed offices (see Figure 8.4). Each employee worked in an office separated from others by fixed walls. The size of the office often signified a person's rank or importance in the company. This layout afforded privacy, but it also allowed employees to waste time unobserved by management. The traditional office has now been replaced to a large extent by open offices.

Open Offices

Originally open offices reflected a basic bull pen design, with the majority of workers occupying one large room that was bordered by smaller private offices for the man-

FIGURE 8.4
Closed Offices

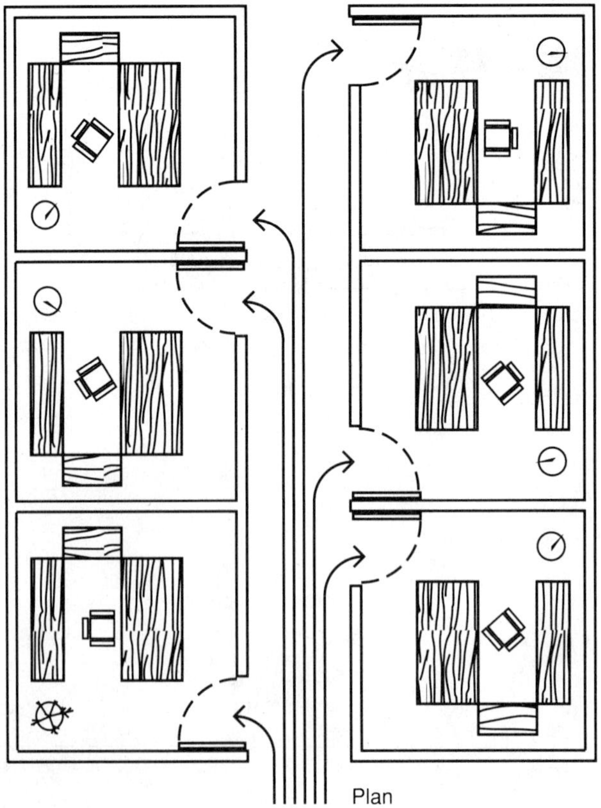

agers along the building's perimeter. Modern open offices now afford workers a slightly greater degree of privacy. These days the chief distinction between closed and open offices is a simple one: partitioning. In closed offices, partitions are usually interior walls that extend from floor to ceiling. In the open office (see Figure 8.5), partitions do not extend to the ceiling, are usually portable, and may or may not be flush with the floor. There is evidence that the desire for privacy in open offices is raising the level of partition heights now used in the interior construction of offices. The trend is toward 65-inch-tall partitions, which afford visual privacy, whether a worker is standing or sitting.[7]

Entrepreneurs considering open-office layouts should be aware of the following environmental requirements:

- The design of the workplace should be flexible enough to accommodate the formation of new work groups.
- All work groups must be identifiable as groups.
- Acoustical systems must be able to accommodate user rearrangement.
- Workers should be able to communicate confidentially.

FIGURE 8.5
Open Offices

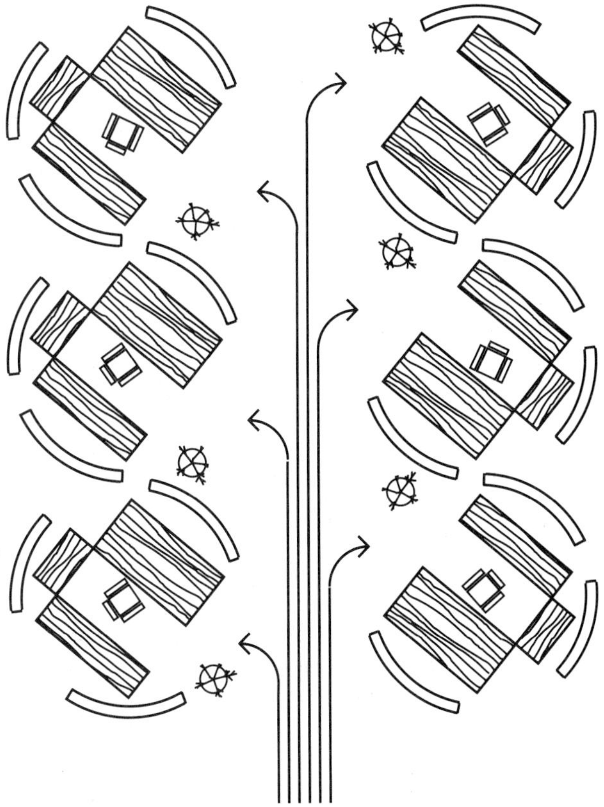

- There should be adequate lighting for areas in which conventional tasks are performed.
- Storage areas in each workplace should be within a worker's reach when he or she is seated at the desk.
- Work surfaces should be nonreflective.[8]

8-1 *The Inside View*

CIRCULAR WORKSTATIONS

Crimson Travel Service in Cambridge, Massachusetts, was rapidly running out of space. To solve the dilemma, president and owner David Paresky turned to the circular workstation, a configuration gaining popularity with small, overhead-conscious enterprises. In the typical open office, clustering workers creates space for 25 to 40 percent more people. In addition, the wraparound design of the desks creates 50 percent more work surface for each person. For example, five people who sit in a cluster occupy about the same space as four who sit in a rectilinear pattern.[9]

In laying out open offices, some designers have even substituted circular workstations for the traditional square ones (see The Inside View 8-1). Interior designers and architects are doing whatever is necessary to lay out offices that are functional, efficient, and attractive.

Linda Keir, President of Environmental Space Planning, Inc., in New York, advises entrepreneurs to answer the following questions before selecting an open office layout:

Do you plan to add people, or expand or contract departments often?
Is part of your operation noisy or air-polluting?
Do any employees use equipment that causes unusual vibrations?
Do you want to encourage interaction among personnel?
Does management want to see and be seen?
Are there particular groups of people who often work overtime?[10]

Home Offices

Many startup entrepreneurs will not need formal office space. For them, an office in their home will suffice (see The Inside View 8-2) and in some cases, might even be more efficient. With the price of copiers and fax machines approaching $500, entrepreneurs will not have unusually high setup costs if they choose to equip a home office. The ready availability of personal computers and modems enables people to work

8-2 *The Inside View*

HOME OFFICES

When Jim Hughes and his two partners started a software company in Cambridge, Massachusetts, two years ago, he was living more than an hour's commute away in Windham, New Hampshire. Knowing what long hours entrepreneurs devoted to their work, Hughes realized that he had two options—move to the Boston area or work at home. "I never seriously considered moving," he recalls. "I couldn't face the Boston-area housing costs, the traffic, and the parking problems." For the first year, home offices enabled the three partners to maintain the company's lean budget while they developed their primary products. They avoided renting office space and hiring support staff until money came in from their first sale.[11]

anywhere in the country and still maintain contact with company headquarters. Entrepreneurs who choose to work at home must designate specific facilities for their office and should have regular work hours. In this way, family and friends will not interrupt or lay claim to the entrepreneur's time simply because he or she is at home.

To create office space that is totally separate from living space—a requirement for income tax purposes—entrepreneurs need to do the following:

- Find some way to close off the office if it is not in a separate room.
- Buy a computer, preferably one with a hard disk, as well as a good printer—laser or other letter-quality type.
- Add a modem to transfer data over telephone lines.
- Subscribe to a public electronic-mail network, like MCI Mail or CompuServe, to minimize telephone costs.
- Buy a good answering machine.
- Buy a fax machine and an inexpensive copier—budget permitting.
- Install one or two separate phone lines.
- Install call waiting or a second phone with a hold button.
- Obtain an automatic call-forwarding system if absences are prolonged.[12]

Summary

Some entrepreneurs might select a vacant site on which to construct a building to suit their needs; however, most will select sites with existing buildings. Either way, entrepreneurs need to decide whether they should buy or lease their facility. The major benefit of buying is that entrepreneurs can control their own facility without having to consult with landlords; however, disadvantages include the following: initial capital outlay, limited mobility, and possible decline in building value. Some of these disadvantages can be avoided by leasing; however, leasing is not without its own disadvantages. For example, rents usually escalate, tenants can be evicted, some landlords neglect their buildings, and landlords can restrict a tenant's activities.

Whether entrepreneurs choose to build or remodel, they should anticipate the basic needs of their facility. Entrepreneurs should estimate how much space they will need for the next five years, plan on making the work space comfortable by eliminating unnecessary noise, and maximize the productivity of employees by providing enough light and appropriate color schemes. All of these elements plus the basic facility layout should contribute not only to employee productivity but also to employee job satisfaction.

For manufacturing facilities, a product (assembly-line) layout or a process (job-shop) layout are most common and most efficient. In cases of products that are difficult to move, a fixed layout might be necessary. Retail-store layouts should be designed to facilitate customer traffic and provide pleasant surroundings for employees. Well-planned stores encourage customers to browse, allow employees to see customers at all times, display merchandise to its best effect, and maximize selling and storage space. Offices should also be designed to maximize employee productivity. The basic configuration for most offices is either an open or closed plan; however, variations, such as circular workstations, are possible.

Assembling the Pieces

When Carol and Jacki leased space for In Good Taste, they had 1,100 square feet in which to accommodate an office, a lavatory, a cooking-demonstration area, and their merchandise. Jacki's husband, who is an architect, was able to provide a layout (see Figure 8.6) that maximized the available space, and he and Carol's husband built all the necessary shelving and display cases. This assistance allowed Carol and Jacki to lay out and equip their shop at a cost of approximately $1,200.

Carol and Jacki knew that customers usually enter a shop and move to their right; however, in their shop, the front door almost touches the right wall. To overcome this problem, Carol and Jacki decided to line the right wall with various wines so that customers could walk down that aisle looking at wine while venturing further into the store. In an effort to peak customer interest, Carol and Jacki placed their spices and coffee near the front of the shop, where anyone entering would be able to smell them.

Other important layout considerations included the following: The cash register was centrally located to provide employees with a view of the entire shop; work spaces were designed to serve several purposes—space used for the demonstration of cooking techniques also served as an area in which to wrap merchandise; office and storage space was kept to a minimum; and shelves and display cases were built low enough so that they did not obstruct the floor view of employees. ■

FIGURE 8.6
Store Layout of In Good Taste

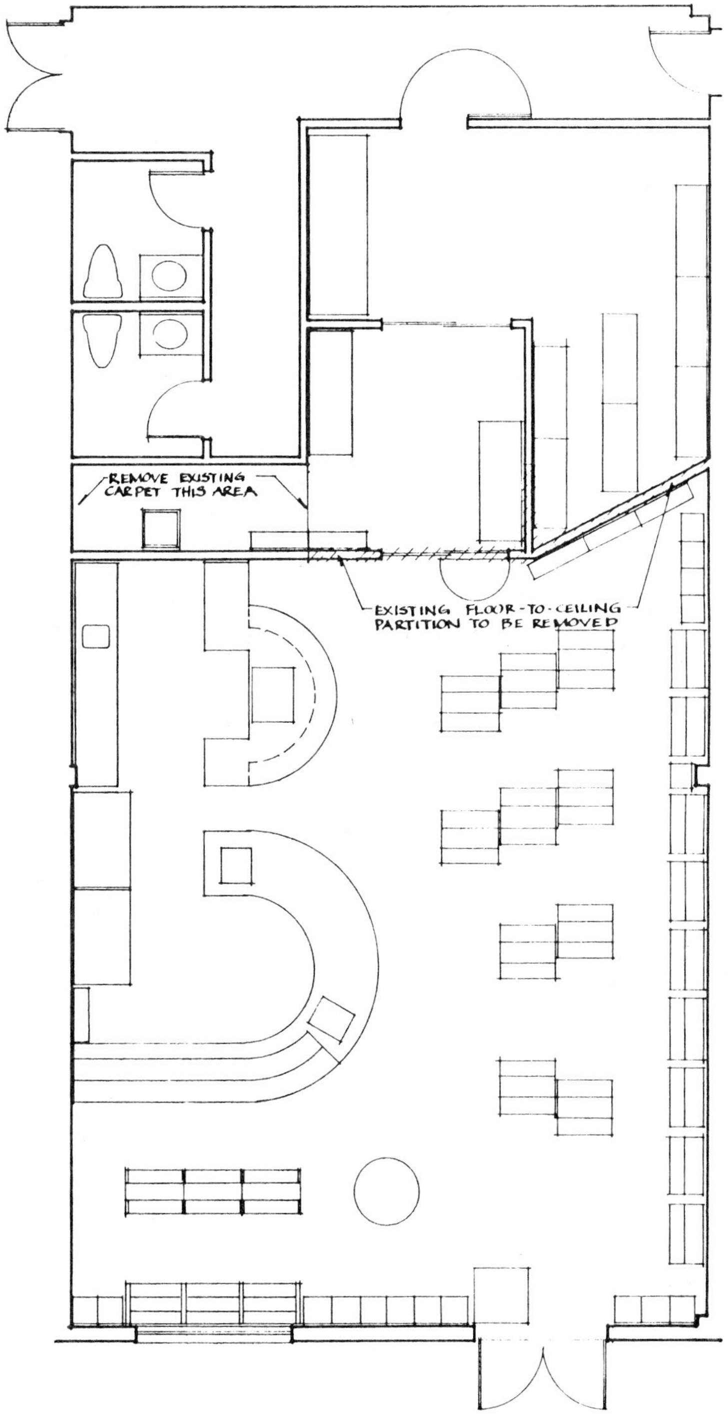

REMOVE EXISTING CARPET THIS AREA
EXISTING FLOOR-TO-CEILING PARTITION TO BE REMOVED

entrepreneur's checklist

CHECKLIST FOR INTERIOR ARRANGEMENT AND DISPLAY

Layout	Yes	No
1. Are fixtures low enough and signs so placed so that customers have a bird's-eye view of the store and can see where to go for desired goods?	____	____
2. Do aisle and counter arrangements tend to stimulate a circular traffic flow through the store?	____	____
3. Do fixtures, signs, lettering, and colors all create a coordinated and unified effect?	____	____
4. Is the use of hanging signs limited to special sale events?	____	____
5. Are counters and aisle tables overcrowded with merchandise?	____	____
6. Are ledges and cashier–wrapping stations kept free of boxes, unneeded wrapping materials, personal effects, and odds and end?	____	____
7. Are trash bins kept out of sight?	____	____

Merchandise Emphasis	Yes	No
1. Do signs referring to specific items contain important information rather than general facts such as the names and prices of the products?	____	____
2. Are advertised and nonadvertised specials prominently displayed at the ends of counters as well as at the point of sale?	____	____
3. Are national and private brands highlighted in arrangements and window displays?	____	____
4. Wherever feasible, is the more colorful merchandise given preference in display?	____	____
5. In the case of apparel and home furnishings, do the items that reflect the store's fashion sense or fashion leadership get special display attention at all times?	____	____
6. In positioning merchandise in the store, is the productivity of space (vertical as well as horizontal) considered?	____	____
7. Is self-service merchandise arranged to attract customers and assist them in their selection by the following means:		
a. Is each category grouped under a separate sign?	____	____
b. Is the merchandise in each category arranged according to its most significant characteristic—color, style, size, etc.?	____	____
c. In apparel categories, is the merchandise arranged by price lines or zones to assist customers in making a selection quickly?	____	____
d. Is horizontal space usually devoted to different items and styles within a category (with vertical space used for different sizes—smallest at the top, largest at the bottom)?	____	____

Source: J. Wingate and S. Helfant, *Small Store Planning for Growth* (Washington, DC: Small Business Administration, 1977), pp. 100–101.

Questions for Review and Discussion

1. What are the advantages of selecting a vacant site? A site with an existing building?
2. What are the advantages and disadvantages of leasing facilities?
3. If you were starting a business, under what conditions would you choose to buy a building?
4. Why should entrepreneurs be concerned about lighting, noise control, heating systems, color, and other physical features, when designing their facilities?
5. Explain the benefits of the different factory layouts.
6. What are the benefits of selecting the most appropriate store layout.
7. Question several people who work in offices to determine whether open or closed layouts are more desirable.

Notes

1. C. M. Deasy and Thomas Lasswell, *Designing Places for People* (New York: Billboard Publications, Inc., 1985), p. 33.
2. Vilma Barr and Charles Broudy, *Designing to Sell* (New York: McGraw-Hill, 1986), pp. 81–82.
3. Ibid.
4. Vilma Barr and Charles Broudy, *Designing to Sell* (New York: McGraw-Hill, 1986), pp. 29–31. Used by permission.
5. Vilma Barr and Charles Broudy, *Designing to Sell,* p. 43.
6. Barry Tarshis, "State of the Office," *Inc. Office Guide,* July 1988, p. 6.
7. Stevens Anderson, "Open Office Systems Gain Flexibility," *Architecture,* June 1988, pp. 119–122.
8. David Harris, Alvin Palmer, M. Susan Lewis, David Munson, Gershon Meckler, and Ralph Gerdes, *Planning and Designing the Office Environment* (New York: Van Nostrand Reinhold, 1981), p. 27.
9. Robert Mamis, "Office: Business in the Round," *Inc.,* February 1987, p. 11.
10. Linda Keir, "Choosing the Best Open Space Plan," *Management Review,* July 1985, pp. 44–46.
11. Sarah Glazer, "Setting Up an Office at Home," *Inc. Office Guide,* July 1988, pp. 28–32.
12. Ibid.

CHAPTER 9

Determining Financial Needs

Learning Objectives

After reading this chapter, you will be able to do the following:

- Use the business plan to help determine financial needs.
- Calculate expenses by budgeting.
- Interpret forecasts to help in predicting asset requirements.
- Analyze break-even points.

Before making the final decision to start a new business, entrepreneurs need to determine the amount of capital required to launch and sustain their business during its first three to six months. Producing a great product or service, being in the right location, and having a great marketing plan are all plusses, but without sufficient capital, even the best plans will fail. In this chapter, the process of determining the financial needs of the startup firm will be examined, and in the following chapter, the problem of securing the needed capital will be addressed.

Determining the financial needs of the startup enterprise is a difficult task, primarily because doing anything the first time with no prior experience or model is difficult. The financial needs of a new restaurant are very different from those of a new retail store, and even more complicated is the calculation of the startup funds for a company involved in the manufacture of a new high-technology product. By starting a business similar to an existing business, such as a restaurant or a retail store, the entrepreneur can use historical data to help determine the capital needed, but a new technology, like biotechnology, has no historical record for comparison.

This chapter will concentrate on methods that will help the startup entrepreneur determine the initial capital outlay needed to start and operate a firm for three to six months. To accomplish this goal, the chapter is divided into [a brief introduction and] four major sections as follows:

1. Using the business plan
2. Budgeting
3. Forecasting asset requirements
4. Break-even analysis

INTRODUCTION

Why plan? Planning is hard work and takes valuable time from the tasks that entrepreneurs consider to be the "real" work of starting a new enterprise: ordering equipment and materials, interviewing, hiring employees, training new personnel, and planning an advertisement campaign. The so-called real work, however, will be for naught if the funds to purchase equipment and pay new employees are unavailable.

Many entrepreneurs are so sure that their enterprise will be successful that they simply cannot believe that obtaining capital will be a problem. They believe that once lenders and venture capitalists hear about their new product or service, the necessary capital will be readily advanced. Unfortunately, many startup entrepreneurs are naive in this belief—a condition caused in part by the media, which tend to cover only success stories (and the spectacular failures) and to ignore the great number of failures. Typical of popular press coverage are the articles on startup companies in *Venture*, *Inc.*, *Money*, or *Forbes*, which stress success and present those who succeed as smart, resourceful entrepreneurs with the superb management ability to overcome their startup problems. If a problem with startup capital did exist, the usual culprit was a local banker who would not advance the necessary capital. However, in most stories, there is another, more understanding banker who, unlike his less creative fellow, saves the day.

Certainly, startup entrepreneurs must be optimistic about their chances of success, and, just as certainly, should believe in the profitability of their product or service, but planning for the capital needed to get the business off the ground is even more important. The key to the successful startup is simple: Offer a good product or service, let consumers know about it, and have the capital necessary to keep the doors open long enough to establish a reputation that brings in more and more customers. To be the most effective, all the methods presented in this chapter require the use of common sense. For example, a budget should include funds for such things as stock, equipment, raw materials, the people who must be paid, and the salary upon which the owner will live. It should also be checked thoroughly for omissions.

USING THE BUSINESS PLAN

The Chapter 5 discussion of business-plan development emphasized the importance of the planning that potential entrepreneurs do in the process of writing their business plans. The business plan should include both the pro forma income statement and pro forma balance sheet, from which startup entrepreneurs can project what their total assets will be at the end of the first reporting period.

From the information presented in Chapter 5, what were the estimated financial needs of In Good Taste for the first six months? Given the fact that this firm was building a new clientele, its owners needed to be cautious in estimating how much business they would do during the first six months. This firm, like most other new firms, should not have expected to be profitable during its first month, or even its first year, in business. The goal of a new venture should be to build a profitable business and to have the funds needed to stay in operation until the firm becomes profitable.

In Good Taste

The owners of In Good Taste had prior experience in the same line of business as that in which they wanted to start their venture. Using their previous experience with Charleston Spice Rack, they were able to estimate their startup costs fairly accurately. Their figures were based on an estimate of the cost of the initial inventory, the cost of leasehold improvements to the store they would rent, and the cost of operations. (See Table 9.1 for the cost of the initial inventory.)

In Table 9.2, the startup cost estimate for In Good Taste is presented. Note that the figures are based on a combination of known and estimated costs. The known costs include rent, insurance, fixtures and equipment, utility deposits, and the cost of licenses and permits. All other costs were estimated, although most estimates were based on quotes the owners had been given by contractors. Other estimates, such as the "opening promotion," were based on the known cost of local advertising and on projections of how long and to what extent the campaign would be continued.

Table 9.1 Initial Inventory

Coffees and coffee flavorings	$ 350
Cheeses	1,000
Wine	1,000
Silver Palate condiments	2,000
Gadgets and related items:	3,000
Coffeepots, grinders, pepper mills, mortar & pestles, cheese knives, hand tools, books	
Spices/Herbs	700
Oils	200
Potpourri	135
Teas	1,000
Ethnic or specialty items:	2,000
Maple syrup, extracts, Chinese, Italian, Greek, Jewish	
Reserve for new items	2,000
Total Startup Inventory	$13,385

Table 9.2 Startup Cost Estimate*

	Monthly	*Reserve*
Salaries of owner–managers	$1,700	$ 3,400
All other salary & wages	700	2,100
Rent	850	2,550
Advertising	500	1,500
Delivery expenses (restaurants)	40	120
Supplies		
General	200	600
Direct Charge	400	1,200
Telephone	60	120
Utilities	120	360
Insurance		
Life on partners	40	200
Business	100	600
Loan repayment	1,000	3,000
Maintenance	200	600
Accountant		150
Miscellaneous	1,000	1,000
Subtotal	6,910	17,500
Startup Costs Paid Only Once		
Fixtures and equipment		6,315
Decorating and remodeling		10,000
Installation of fixtures and equipment		2,400
Starting inventory		13,385
Deposits for public utilities		525
Legal & professional fees		650
Licenses and permits		480
Opening promotion		1,000
Cash		10,000
Subtotal		44,755
Estimated Cash Needed for Startup		$62,255

*Based on sales of $155,000/year.

Included in the estimated startup costs is an operational reserve for almost three months. A reserve of this length of time allows the company enough working capital to continue operating for an extended period while it builds a profitable business. Too many startup firms overlook the need for sufficient working capital to keep the firm operational over the critical first few months. As a result, they experience a severe cash flow problem before they have a chance to establish the viability of their business.

Developing Pro Forma Financial Statements

The business plan may be used to determine the financial needs of a startup enterprise, but many entrepreneurs do not have enough experience in the particular sphere of business they are entering to make accurate estimates. For these entrepreneurs, a pro forma estimate of income statements and pro forma balance sheets can be an excellent method of determining startup costs. The most common **method of developing** pro forma, financial-statement information can be found in public information sources such as those published by Robert Morris Associates (primarily *RMA Annual Statement Studies*), Dun & Bradstreet (several different publications), and Prentice-Hall (Troy's *Almanac of Business and Industrial Ratios*). These three companies collect financial data from thousands of firms in dozens of different industries—from advertising displays to water, sewer, and pipeline construction. From this information, averages are obtained for each SIC (Standard Industrial Classification—a term frequently used to define specific industries) category.

Pro Forma Income Statement

An example of the information available to entrepreneurs who are preparing pro forma income statements is shown in Table 9.3, which contains income and ratio data from Troy's *Almanac* for eating and drinking establishments. Broad size classifications, ranging from firms with zero assets to those with over $250 million, are included. From this information, a pro forma income statement may be derived.

For example, assume that an entrepreneur is planning to start a restaurant that will serve lunch and dinner six days a week and will have seating capacity for 45 people. Also assume that from information developed from the marketing plan, the owner can expect to average sixty customers for lunch, with the average meal costing $7.20, and fifty for dinner, with the average meal costing $11.50. From these estimates, monthly sales revenue should be $26,180, or $314,160 per year.

Potential Problems with Pro Forma Income Statements

Using the averages given in Table 9.3, the pro forma income statement shown in Table 9.4 was developed. In the course of preparing their own statements, entrepreneurs need to be aware of the potential problems. First, the estimate of sales revenue is critical to this entire process. Too many startup entrepreneurs overestimate their sales revenue, particularly during their first six months to one year of operations. They see other similar businesses that have been in business for several years and assume they can start out at or near their level of sales. Normally sales will be lower than that expected for the first three to six months. To see what effect lower sales revenue would have on the firm, startup entrepreneurs should prepare an estimated pro forma income statement as prescribed and then prepare another statement based on sales revenue of only 50 percent of that expected to see what impact lower sales revenues will have on the profitability of the firm. Entrepreneurs will then be able to determine if they can stay in business should sales be lower than expected.

Table 9.3 5800 Retail Trade: Eating and Drinking Places

Item Description for Accounting Period 7/83 Through 6/84	Size of Assets in Thousands of Dollars (000 Omitted)												
	A	B	C	D	E	F	G	H	I	J	K	L	M
	Total	Zero Assets	*Under 100*	*100 to 250*	*250 to 500*	*500 to 1,000*	*1,000 to 5,000*	*5,000 to 10,000*	*10,000 to 25,000*	*25,000 to 50,000*	*50,000 to 100,000*	*100,000 to 250,000*	*250,000 and over*
1. Number of Enterprises	53,434	1,435	26,437	13,830	6,750	3,197	1,506	143	69	30	22	9	7
2. Total receipts (in millions of dollars)	54,284.5	524.0	6,084.4	8,389.6	7,284.6	6,226.8	6,785.2	2,346.8	1,935.9	1,883.6	2,576.8	2,763.2	7,483.5
Selected Operating Factors in Percent of Net Sales													
3. Cost of operations	44.4	45.2	42.2	45.7	43.3	43.0	48.4	42.9	50.0	44.3	45.7	50.4	19.6
4. Compensation of officers	3.1	2.7	4.9	4.1	4.4	4.2	3.2	1.7	1.9	1.2	1.2	0.5	0.5
5. Repairs	1.5	2.3	1.4	1.4	1.4	1.4	1.4	1.6	1.3	1.4	1.5	1.4	1.8
6. Bad debts	0.1	0.1	0.3	0.1	0.2	—	0.1	0.1	0.2	0.2	0.2	0.1	—
7. Rent on business property	5.6	5.6	6.6	5.3	5.6	5.4	4.6	7.2	4.9	4.9	5.7	3.0	7.2
8. Taxes (excl. federal tax)	3.8	3.2	4.3	4.0	4.1	4.0	3.3	3.5	3.4	4.1	3.7	2.5	4.2
9. Interest	1.7	1.3	0.8	1.0	1.3	1.7	1.3	1.5	1.7	1.8	1.7	1.5	4.0
10. Deprec./Deplet./Amortiz.*	3.8	2.4	2.5	2.8	3.2	3.5	3.2	3.7	3.9	4.8	4.4	4.8	7.3
11. Advertising	2.6	2.7	1.8	2.0	2.2	2.4	2.7	2.8	2.4	2.2	2.8	2.3	4.6
12. Pensions & other benefit plans	0.8	0.5	0.2	0.4	0.8	0.8	1.2	1.1	0.8	1.6	1.2	0.9	1.1
13. Other expenses	31.9	30.9	32.1	30.3	31.4	31.9	29.0	34.6	30.7	34.1	33.4	32.1	35.2
14. Net profit before tax	0.7	3.1	2.9	2.9	2.1	1.7	1.6	#	#	#	#	0.5	#

Table 9.3 5800 Retail Trade: Eating and Drinking Places (*Continued*)

Item Description for Accounting Period 7/83 Through 6/84	*Size of Assets in Thousands of Dollars (000 Omitted)*												
	A *Total*	B Zero Assets	C *Under 100*	D *100 to 250*	E *250 to 500*	F *500 to 1,000*	G *1,000 to 5,000*	H *5,000 to 10,000*	I *10,000 to 25,000*	J *25,000 to 50,000*	K *50,000 to 100,000*	L *100,000 to 250,000*	M *250,000 and over*
Selected Financial Ratios (Number of Times Ratio Is to One)													
15. Current ratio	1.0	—	1.2	1.2	1.1	1.0	1.2	0.9	1.1	1.1	1.2	1.2	0.6
16. Quick ratio	0.6	—	0.8	0.9	0.8	0.7	0.8	0.5	0.8	0.6	0.6	0.8	0.2
17. Net sales to net wkg capital	—	—	78.9	57.1	116.5	—	59.7	—	56.6	145.5	46.0	46.2	—
18. Coverage ratio	4.1	—	7.0	5.1	3.8	3.2	4.2	4.0	3.9	3.5	5.1	4.8	3.6
19. Asset turnover	2.0	—	—	—	—	—	2.4	2.2	1.8	1.7	1.5	1.9	0.7
20. Total liability to net worth	1.5	—	2.4	2.1	1.8	2.0	1.5	2.1	1.5	1.8	1.2	1.2	1.1
Selected Financial Factors in Percentages													
21. Debt ratio	59.2	—	70.5	67.7	63.7	66.5	59.3	67.6	59.5	64.2	53.5	54.5	53.4
22. Return on assets	10.1	—	22.9	15.6	10.9	10.1	10.4	10.0	8.9	7.7	10.3	10.4	6.8
23. Return on equity	17.7	—	—	43.5	25.5	25.4	18.5	19.7	14.2	12.1	12.1	12.5	8.0
24. Retained earnings to net income	84.0	—	98.0	88.0	91.7	91.8	97.4	97.0	90.9	90.3	77.1	65.2	54.9

*Depreciation largest factor.
SOURCE: From Leo Troy, *Almanac of Business and Industrial Ratios*, 1987 edition, Prentice-Hall, 1987, p 261. Used by permission. Prentice-Hall, Inc., Englewood Cliffs, NJ.

Table 9.4 Pro Forma Income Statement—Restaurant

	Percentage of Sales	*Dollar Estimate (per month)*	
Sales*	100%		$26,180
Cost of operations	44.4	$11,624	
Compensation	3.1	812	
Repairs	1.5	393	
Bad debts	0.1	26	
Rent	5.6	1,446	
Taxes	3.8	995	
Interest	1.7	445	
Depreciation	3.8	995	
Advertising	2.6	680	
Benefits	0.8	209	
Other expenses	31.9	8,351	
Total	99.3		$25,996
Net profit	0.7		$ 184

*Sales estimate is based on a restaurant that will be open six days per week from 11 AM to 11 PM. Owner expects to serve meals for lunch at an average price of $7.20 per meal, and fifty meals for dinner at an average price of $11.50 per meal.

The extent to which all other planning depends on the accuracy of the sales revenue estimate is so great that it is not a number ever to be guessed at. To illustrate its importance, consider the case of an entrepreneur who opened a sailboating sales, repair, and supply company based on excellent estimates of the potential business in the Charleston, South Carolina, area. For the first three months of operation, the estimated figures proved to be accurate. Then the recession of the early 1980s hit, and one day sales plummeted to a new low of $1.50—the price of a single fishing lure. The firm managed to stay in business by drastically cutting expenses during the recession and later went on to become very successful, but this episode shows that sales estimates can be very inaccurate, and that owners must have a contingency plan if sales do not grow as quickly as expected.

Second, entrepreneurs will not find the averages presented here very encouraging. Is this business as profitable as that envisioned? Certainly the figures shown in Table 9.4 do not indicate that the average restaurant is very profitable. In fact, the averages shown in Table 9.3 are from those businesses that showed a net profit, but according to statistics which included all eating and drinking establishments, both profitable and unprofitable, the average firm lost about three cents for every dollar in sales.

With these statistics firmly in mind, startup entrepreneurs must clearly determine why their business will be different from the average. According to Table 9.3, the "other" expenses category is the second largest expense item. This would indicate that most restaurants have many small expenses that add up to a major expenditure, thereby reducing the profitability of the business.

How is the necessary amount of startup capital determined from the information contained in the pro forma income statement? Based on the figures presented in Table 9.4, the business should be able to cover its operating expenditures from sales revenues. This may not be true for all new businesses because expenses may be greater than revenues during the first few months. In such cases, the operating losses must be covered by additional funds. The biotechnology industry is an extreme example of large cash outflows in the early phase of the business startup. In their early years, almost all of the companies, from well-known Genentech to lesser-known Calgene, suffered huge losses that were funded largely through the sale of stock to a public that believed in their future profitability.

Pro Forma Balance Sheets

In addition to the pro forma income statement, the pro forma balance sheet is equally vital in determining the amount of startup capital needed. One method of obtaining an estimate of the various asset and liability accounts is to use averages derived from a number of similar businesses, such as those given in *RMA Annual Statement Studies* (see Table 9.5). Notice that in the fifth column of this table, labeled "All," assets and liabilities are given as a percentage of total assets.

For example, to develop the amount of total assets needed for a business, use the Sales/Total Assets ratio. From the information given, sales were estimated to be about \$314,000. If the Sales/Total Assets ratio is 2.9, total assets would be about \$110,000 (total assets = sales/2.9 = \$314,000/2.9). (The 2.9 Sales/Total Asset ratio represents the average for all restaurants surveyed. The 4.6 figure represents the average for the top 25 percent of the restaurants surveyed, and the 1.8 figure, the average for the lower 25 percent.)

Assuming that total assets are \$110,000, a pro forma balance sheet (such as that shown in Table 9.6 can be developed. This pro forma balance sheet provides startup entrepreneurs with an excellent starting point from which to develop a pro forma balance sheet for their own business plans. It is important to remember that it is only a starting point, since Table 9.6 represents an average and does not reflect the specific situations faced by individual entrepreneurs. However, using this pro forma as a guide, startup entrepreneurs can modify their statements to account for those items that are peculiar to their own situations. For example, if the restaurant will be in a building owned by the entrepreneur, the figure for net fixed assets will be much higher than the \$62,700 shown in Table 9.6, and if the building is secured by a mortgage, then the long-term debt figure would be much greater than \$35,310.

The figures for categories such as "other current assets" and "other current liabilities" cover those unknown and, therefore, usually overlooked items that can surprise startup entrepreneurs. These as well as all other assets and liabilities for which no known figures are available should be included in the estimate.

According to Table 9.6, it takes \$110,000 to start the average restaurant. The entrepreneur, however, does not have to supply the entire amount. For example, assume that the notes payable (\$14,300) represent a bank loan on some of the equip-

Table 9.5 Retailers—Restaurants

RETAILERS - RESTAURANTS SIC# 5812 — 273

Current Data					Type of Statement	Comparative Historical Data				
31	51	22	13	117	Unqualified				148	117
2	5	6	1	14	Qualified				15	14
85	50	2		137	Reviewed	DATA NOT AVAILABLE			162	137
263	67	4		334	Compiled				288	334
100	45	7	1	153	Other				185	153
327(6/30-9/30/85)		428(10/1/85-3/31/86)				6/30/81-3/31/82	6/30/82-3/31/83	6/30/83-3/31/84	6/30/84-3/31/85	6/30/85-3/31/86
0-1MM	1-10MM	10-50MM	50-100MM	ALL	ASSET SIZE	ALL	ALL	ALL	ALL	ALL
481	218	41	15	755	NUMBER OF STATEMENTS	745	805	653	798	755
%	%	%	%	%	**ASSETS**	%	%	%	%	%
12.1	10.4	5.8	6.4	11.2	Cash & Equivalents	10.7	10.9	10.2	10.4	11.2
4.3	4.9	5.3	2.4	4.5	Trade Receivables - (net)	5.1	5.0	4.9	4.6	4.5
7.6	6.5	6.0	3.4	7.1	Inventory	7.6	6.8	6.5	6.9	7.1
2.5	2.0	5.1	1.8	2.5	All Other Current	2.1	2.0	2.4	2.5	2.5
26.6	23.7	22.2	14.0	25.3	Total Current	25.6	24.6	24.0	24.4	25.3
56.3	57.9	56.6	66.7	57.0	Fixed Assets (net)	57.7	58.7	59.9	59.0	57.0
4.5	3.6	6.5	3.0	4.3	Intangibles (net)	3.8	3.9	4.1	4.0	4.3
12.6	14.9	14.7	16.3	13.4	All Other Non-Current	12.9	12.8	12.0	12.5	13.4
100.0	100.0	100.0	100.0	100.0	Total	100.0	100.0	100.0	100.0	100.0
					LIABILITIES					
7.7	5.4	4.4	1.8	6.7	Notes Payable-Short Term	5.0	5.8	5.8	6.7	6.7
6.8	5.7	5.3	2.2	6.3	Cur. Mat.-L/T/D	6.3	6.1	5.8	5.8	6.3
12.1	11.6	8.5	7.1	11.6	Trade Payables	11.4	11.5	11.3	11.2	11.6
1.4	.9	.8	.3	1.2	Income Taxes Payable	–	–	–	1.3	1.2
11.9	9.0	7.2	5.8	10.7	All Other Current	12.6	13.4	13.4	11.7	10.7
40.0	32.5	26.2	17.2	36.6	Total Current	35.3	36.7	36.2	36.7	36.6
32.8	30.8	32.3	31.7	32.1	Long Term Debt	31.9	30.2	31.6	32.5	32.1
.2	.7	2.2	2.7	.5	Deferred Taxes	–	–	–	.6	.5
2.8	2.7	2.6	11.1	2.9	All Other Non-Current	3.0	3.8	3.7	2.5	2.9
24.3	33.3	36.6	37.2	27.8	Net Worth	29.8	29.3	28.5	27.6	27.8
100.0	100.0	100.0	100.0	100.0	Total Liabilities & Net Worth	100.0	100.0	100.0	100.0	100.0
					INCOME DATA					
100.0	100.0	100.0	100.0	100.0	Net Sales	100.0	100.0	100.0	100.0	100.0
56.2	53.8	46.5	53.0	54.9	Gross Profit	54.2	54.8	53.8	54.1	54.9
52.6	49.6	38.9	47.6	50.9	Operating Expenses	49.2	49.5	49.2	49.4	50.9
3.7	4.2	7.5	5.4	4.1	Operating Profit	5.0	5.2	4.6	4.7	4.1
1.6	2.2	2.8	4.1	1.9	All Other Expenses (net)	1.9	2.1	1.6	2.1	1.9
2.1	2.0	4.7	1.3	2.2	Profit Before Taxes	3.1	3.1	3.0	2.7	2.2
					RATIOS					
1.3	1.2	1.3	1.1	1.3		1.2	1.2	1.2	1.2	1.3
.7	.8	.7	.9	.7	Current	.7	.7	.7	.6	.7
.3	.4	.4	.6	.4		.3	.3	.3	.3	.4
.8	.9	.7	.7	.8		.8	.9	.8	.8	.8
(475) .4	(217) .4	.3	.6	(748) .4	Quick	(740) .4	(796) .4	(646) .4	(787) .4	(748) .4
.2	.2	.2	.2	.2		.1	.1	.2	.2	.2
0 INF	0 904.8	2 212.0	2 230.2	0 INF		0 INF	0 INF	0 INF	0 INF	0 INF
1 451.0	3 143.1	5 79.0	4 90.1	2 215.0	Sales/Receivables	2 162.1	2 172.6	2 188.3	2 237.7	2 215.0
5 74.9	9 40.8	17 21.5	10 35.8	6 59.3		8 46.4	7 51.7	7 51.7	7 51.0	6 59.3
8 46.1	8 45.2	7 53.6	11 33.4	8 45.5		9 38.6	9 42.8	9 42.2	9 42.2	8 45.5
13 27.4	13 29.1	12 29.6	20 18.3	13 27.6	Cost of Sales/Inventory	15 24.0	14 26.5	13 27.5	14 26.1	13 27.6
23 16.1	23 16.1	33 11.1	26 14.0	23 15.7		25 14.7	23 16.2	23 16.1	22 16.5	23 15.7
8 45.2	19 19.4	19 19.6	17 21.6	12 30.9		14 26.7	14 25.4	15 23.6	13 27.8	12 30.9
22 16.5	32 11.4	34 10.6	52 7.0	25 14.5	Cost of Sales/Payables	28 13.1	27 13.5	29 12.7	26 13.8	25 14.5
38 9.5	54 6.7	56 6.5	66 5.5	47 7.8		46 7.9	45 8.2	46 8.0	45 8.1	47 7.8
51.0	46.3	22.6	90.5	47.8		48.7	59.3	51.2	66.1	47.8
−38.5	−41.9	−26.0	−93.3	−38.5	Sales/Working Capital	−35.9	−32.6	−29.4	−29.8	−38.5
−12.1	−11.6	−11.9	−16.5	−11.9		−11.9	−10.9	−11.3	−10.8	−11.9
4.9	4.4	5.0	4.3	4.8		5.1	5.0	5.1	5.2	4.8
(416) 2.0	(194) 2.3	(37) 2.2	(14) 1.5	(661) 2.0	EBIT/Interest	(646) 2.3	(686) 2.2	(580) 2.4	(689) 2.2	(661) 2.0
.4	.9	1.4	.2	.6		1.2	1.0	1.0	.9	.6
4.5	5.0	6.1	10.0	4.6		4.4	5.5	4.7	5.1	4.6
(203) 1.6	(136) 2.7	(32) 2.6	(12) 3.8	(383) 2.2	Net Profit + Depr., Dep., Amort./Cur. Mat. L/T/D	(389) 2.1	(375) 2.3	(352) 2.1	(400) 2.4	(383) 2.2
.7	1.4	1.3	1.7	1.0		1.1	1.2	1.1	1.1	1.0
1.0	1.1	1.1	1.1	1.1		1.1	1.1	1.2	1.2	1.1
2.7	2.2	2.1	2.0	2.4	Fixed/Worth	2.3	2.1	2.4	2.4	2.4
−18.3	5.3	4.3	4.4	27.1		7.2	10.5	9.1	15.3	27.1
1.0	1.0	1.1	1.2	1.1		1.1	1.0	1.2	1.2	1.1
3.2	2.5	2.3	2.7	2.8	Debt/Worth	2.6	2.5	2.6	2.9	2.8
−26.2	7.0	6.9	4.5	31.0		9.6	13.1	12.5	19.2	31.0
62.1	44.9	43.8	20.8	52.1		57.1	54.9	60.3	54.3	52.1
(347) 23.1	(191) 19.1	(36) 19.4	10.4	(589) 20.2	% Profit Before Taxes/Tangible Net Worth	(619) 25.5	(657) 27.4	(529) 25.7	(635) 24.6	(589) 20.2
4.6	4.3	9.3	−14.6	4.9		8.0	6.8	6.9	4.6	4.9
17.1	12.7	14.7	7.6	14.9		17.3	16.6	16.0	15.6	14.9
5.3	5.6	6.1	3.7	5.4	% Profit Before Taxes/Total Assets	6.9	7.3	8.0	6.9	5.4
−3.1	−.1	2.0	−3.8	−1.5		1.0	.0	.3	−.2	−1.5
14.1	7.0	4.6	2.7	10.4		9.4	9.4	8.3	9.7	10.4
6.8	4.5	3.0	1.8	5.3	Sales/Net Fixed Assets	4.9	5.2	4.8	4.9	5.3
3.2	2.5	2.4	1.4	2.7		2.9	2.7	2.6	2.6	2.7
5.2	3.4	2.2	1.5	4.6		4.1	4.1	4.0	4.4	4.6
3.5	2.5	1.7	1.3	2.9	Sales/Total Assets	2.8	2.8	2.7	2.8	2.9
2.2	1.7	1.3	.9	1.8		1.9	1.8	1.8	1.8	1.8
2.2	2.9	3.1	4.0	2.5		2.1	2.2	2.3	2.3	2.5
(440) 3.4	(204) 3.9	(39) 4.4	(14) 4.6	(697) 3.7	% Depr., Dep., Amort./Sales	(703) 3.1	(751) 3.3	(610) 3.5	(753) 3.5	(697) 3.7
5.1	5.2	5.2	5.8	5.2		4.3	4.7	4.8	4.7	5.2
3.4	1.9			2.9		3.4	3.1	2.9	2.7	2.9
(229) 5.4	(60) 3.5			(292) 5.0	% Officers' Comp/Sales	(323) 5.3	(339) 5.0	(245) 5.0	(306) 4.9	(292) 5.0
8.8	6.1			8.1		7.8	7.5	7.3	7.3	8.1
585887M	1600378M	1610696M	1455067M	5252028M	Net Sales ($)	6328514M	7072588M	6610038M	7170353M	5252028M
167181M	668837M	964334M	1084219M	2884571M	Total Assets ($)	3036465M	3595183M	3701365M	3329698M	2884571M

M = $thousand MM = $million

See Pages 1 through 13 for Explanation of Ratios and Data

SOURCE: *RMA Annual Statement Studies*, Robert Morris Associates, 1986, p. 273. Reprinted with permission.

Table 9.5 Retailers—Restaurants (*Continued*)

RETAILERS - RESTAURANTS - FAST FOODS SIC# 5812

Current Data					Type of Statement	Comparative Historical Data				
57	33	16	9	115	Unqualified				125	115
3	3	2		8	Qualified				8	8
52	35	1		88	Reviewed	DATA NOT AVAILABLE			78	88
131	27	4		162	Compiled				147	162
58	22	5	4	89	Other				101	89
181(6/30-9/30/85)		281(10/1/85-3/31/86)				6/30/81-3/31/82	6/30/82-3/31/83	6/30/83-3/31/84	6/30/84-3/31/85	6/30/85-3/31/86
0-1MM	1-10MM	10-50MM	50-100MM	ALL	ASSET SIZE	ALL	ALL	ALL	ALL	ALL
301	**120**	**28**	**13**	**462**	**NUMBER OF STATEMENTS**	**183**	**340**	**412**	**459**	**462**
%	%	%	%	%	**ASSETS**	%	%	%	%	%
14.9	12.8	8.0	6.3	13.7	Cash & Equivalents	9.8	11.4	11.9	12.8	13.7
1.9	1.2	3.7	3.0	1.9	Trade Receivables - (net)	2.3	2.6	2.9	2.0	1.9
4.8	3.7	3.5	3.6	4.4	Inventory	4.2	4.7	4.5	4.2	4.4
2.6	2.7	1.5	2.6	2.6	All Other Current	1.4	2.3	2.6	2.7	2.6
24.2	20.3	16.7	15.5	22.5	Total Current	17.6	21.0	22.0	21.7	22.5
53.0	58.1	69.1	63.7	55.6	Fixed Assets (net)	60.5	58.9	56.7	56.5	55.6
6.2	6.5	2.2	5.2	6.0	Intangibles (net)	5.1	7.3	6.6	7.4	6.0
16.5	15.1	12.0	15.6	15.9	All Other Non-Current	16.8	12.7	14.7	14.4	15.9
100.0	100.0	100.0	100.0	100.0	Total	100.0	100.0	100.0	100.0	100.0
					LIABILITIES					
6.2	4.2	1.5	2.3	5.3	Notes Payable-Short Term	4.2	3.3	5.1	4.8	5.3
6.9	7.3	5.7	2.8	6.8	Cur. Mat.-L/T/D	5.8	6.4	6.9	7.3	6.8
10.1	11.6	8.2	7.7	10.3	Trade Payables	9.7	9.9	10.8	10.9	10.3
1.8	.8	.5	.3	1.4	Income Taxes Payable	–	–	–	1.0	1.4
13.7	8.9	8.0	6.2	11.9	All Other Current	12.6	11.0	12.6	11.9	11.9
38.6	32.7	23.8	19.3	35.6	Total Current	32.3	30.6	35.3	35.9	35.6
35.6	33.3	44.4	32.9	35.4	Long Term Debt	36.1	37.3	34.7	33.9	35.4
.6	.6	1.0	3.0	.7	Deferred Taxes	–	–	–	.7	.7
1.5	2.8	1.6	5.5	2.0	All Other Non-Current	3.8	4.0	3.5	2.7	2.0
23.7	30.7	29.1	39.4	26.3	Net Worth	27.8	28.1	26.5	26.8	26.3
100.0	100.0	100.0	100.0	100.0	Total Liabilities & Net Worth	100.0	100.0	100.0	100.0	100.0
					INCOME DATA					
100.0	100.0	100.0	100.0	100.0	Net Sales	100.0	100.0	100.0	100.0	100.0
60.7	57.3	52.0	40.3	58.7	Gross Profit	56.4	57.0	57.8	58.0	58.7
55.0	52.3	46.9	37.4	53.3	Operating Expenses	50.9	51.3	52.7	52.1	53.3
5.7	5.0	5.1	2.9	5.4	Operating Profit	5.5	5.7	5.2	6.0	5.4
2.7	1.2	2.4	1.2	2.3	All Other Expenses (net)	2.4	2.2	2.0	2.1	2.3
3.0	3.8	2.7	1.8	3.1	Profit Before Taxes	3.2	3.4	3.1	3.9	3.1
					RATIOS					
1.2	1.1	.9	1.0	1.1		1.0	1.2	1.1	1.1	1.1
.6	.6	.7	.8	.6	Current	.5	.6	.6	.6	.6
.3	.3	.5	.4	.3		.2	.3	.3	.3	.3
.9	.8	.7	.7	.8		.7	.8	.8	.8	.8
(299) .4	.4	.5	.4	(460) .4	Quick	.3	(335) .4	(409) .4	(454) .4	(460) .4
.1	.2	.3	.2	.1		.1	.2	.1	.1	.1
0 INF	**0** INF	**1** 529.5	**2** 191.6	**0** INF		**0** INF	**0** INF	**0** INF	**0** INF	**0** INF
0 INF	**0** 999.8	**5** 72.9	**4** 90.1	**0** INF	Sales/Receivables	**0** INF	**0** 999.8	**0** 999.8	**0** 999.8	**0** INF
1 507.1	**2** 169.9	**9** 39.7	**9** 41.7	**1** 253.8		**2** 169.0	**2** 167.3	**2** 160.7	**2** 196.1	**1** 253.8
6 59.6	**6** 61.6	**8** 47.2	**7** 55.5	**6** 59.8		**7** 53.1	**7** 49.0	**8** 48.2	**6** 57.4	**6** 59.8
9 42.7	**8** 43.8	**11** 33.6	**8** 43.7	**9** 42.5	Cost of Sales/Inventory	**10** 36.4	**11** 34.5	**11** 34.0	**9** 39.4	**9** 42.5
13 28.2	**13** 27.7	**20** 18.3	**37** 9.9	**13** 27.6		**18** 20.8	**19** 19.3	**15** 23.8	**13** 27.3	**13** 27.6
9 38.7	**21** 17.3	**19** 18.8	**19** 19.4	**14** 25.2		**18** 19.9	**15** 24.4	**16** 23.2	**14** 25.7	**14** 25.2
21 17.6	**34** 10.8	**33** 11.2	**35** 10.3	**25** 14.7	Cost of Sales/Payables	**27** 13.3	**27** 13.3	**27** 13.5	**25** 14.5	**25** 14.7
36 10.2	**52** 7.0	**54** 6.7	**58** 6.3	**41** 9.0		**41** 8.9	**42** 8.6	**43** 8.4	**43** 8.4	**41** 9.0
56.2	256.0	−128.9	221.6	140.0		999.8	71.9	94.4	194.5	140.0
−31.4	−22.4	−35.2	−42.0	−28.6	Sales/Working Capital	−19.7	−29.6	−24.8	−28.4	−28.6
−11.8	−10.4	−16.4	−12.4	−11.7		−10.0	−12.8	−11.5	−11.0	−11.7
5.9	7.0	3.5	2.8	5.9		4.5	4.7	4.8	5.8	5.9
(265) 2.5	(112) 2.8	(25) 1.6	(12) 1.4	(414) 2.5	EBIT/Interest	(169) 2.4	(293) 2.4	(374) 2.5	(408) 2.7	(414) 2.5
1.0	1.3	1.1	.3	1.1		1.4	1.4	1.4	1.5	1.1
5.4	6.1	3.2		5.3		4.5	4.6	4.7	5.4	5.3
(152) 2.4	(84) 2.4	(22) 2.4		(267) 2.4	Net Profit + Depr., Dep., Amort./Cur. Mat. L/T/D	(114) 2.6	(195) 2.3	(236) 2.3	(260) 2.6	(267) 2.4
1.2	1.2	1.2		1.2		1.3	1.4	1.3	1.5	1.2
1.1	1.3	1.6	1.3	1.2		1.2	1.5	1.3	1.3	1.2
3.0	2.4	2.4	1.9	2.6	Fixed/Worth	3.0	2.8	3.1	2.8	2.6
−10.6	8.9	4.5	3.1	±INF		18.9	10.6	46.1	−42.3	±INF
1.2	1.3	1.5	1.0	1.3		1.2	1.4	1.4	1.3	1.3
3.8	2.9	2.3	2.4	3.3	Debt/Worth	2.9	3.2	3.9	3.6	3.3
−14.5	12.7	6.0	4.3	±INF		41.8	16.4	INF	−86.5	±INF
81.6	62.6	43.2	29.2	70.6		48.5	62.5	68.1	80.0	70.6
(215) 36.7	(95) 32.7	(24) 18.8	10.4	(347) 32.7	% Profit Before Taxes/Tangible Net Worth	(141) 29.2	(269) 33.9	(310) 35.2	(336) 38.5	(347) 32.7
15.9	11.1	3.1	−7.2	10.6		11.8	12.3	11.5	19.9	10.6
20.0	19.6	9.1	8.5	19.0		14.8	15.9	16.1	19.8	19.0
9.6	8.7	3.9	3.7	8.7	% Profit Before Taxes/Total Assets	8.3	8.2	8.4	9.9	8.7
1.0	1.2	.6	−2.1	.7		2.9	2.0	2.4	3.4	.7
12.0	6.5	3.9	3.1	9.8		7.9	8.1	9.3	9.5	9.8
6.9	4.4	2.8	1.8	5.7	Sales/Net Fixed Assets	4.8	4.8	5.3	5.6	5.7
4.1	2.9	1.9	1.4	3.2		2.4	2.6	2.8	3.4	3.2
5.1	3.5	2.4	1.6	4.5		3.6	3.8	4.1	4.4	4.5
3.3	2.5	1.8	1.3	3.0	Sales/Total Assets	2.6	2.6	2.8	3.0	3.0
2.4	1.8	1.5	1.2	2.0		1.8	1.8	1.8	2.0	2.0
2.2	2.8	3.4		2.5		2.4	2.5	2.5	2.5	2.5
(285) 3.3	(117) 3.6	(26) 4.2		(437) 3.5	% Depr., Dep., Amort./Sales	(178) 3.2	(323) 3.5	(393) 3.7	(441) 3.6	(437) 3.5
4.6	4.8	5.2		4.8		4.4	4.6	4.7	4.7	4.8
3.2	2.6			2.8		2.2	2.4	2.5	1.9	2.8
(131) 5.0	(35) 3.5			(171) 4.4	% Officers' Comp/Sales	(58) 4.5	(114) 4.1	(136) 4.2	(172) 3.8	(171) 4.4
7.5	4.9			7.1		8.0	6.8	8.0	6.7	7.1
416307M	**1090303M**	**1366815M**	**1401458M**	**4274883M**	Net Sales ($)	**2033802M**	**4544753M**	**4305321M**	**4215769M**	**4274883M**
126237M	**421437M**	**568642M**	**1010881M**	**2127197M**	Total Assets ($)	**1087833M**	**2212919M**	**2322025M**	**2168081M**	**2127197M**

M = $thousand MM = $million

See Pages 1 through 13 for Explanation of Ratios and Data

Table 9.6 Pro Forma Balance Sheet—Restaurant

Cash	$ 12,320	Notes payable	$ 14,300
Trade receivables	4,950	Trade payables	12,760
Inventory	7,810	Taxes payable	1,320
Other current assets	2,750	Other current liabilities	11,770
Total current assets	$ 27,830	Total current liabilities	$ 40,150
Net fixed assets	$ 62,700	Long-term debt	$ 35,310
Other noncurrent assets	19,470	Deferred taxes	550
		Other noncurrent	3,190
		Net worth	30,800
Total assets	$110,000	**Total liabilities net worth**	$110,000
Financial Needs		*Sources*	
Total assets	$110,000	Bank loan on equipment	$ 14,300
Total sources	64,240	Mortgage debt	35,310
Total needed	$ 45,760	Trade & other payables	14,630
		Total sources	$ 64,240

ment of the firm, that the long-term debt ($35,310) is debt secured by some mortgaged property, and that trade and other payables ($14,630) represent supplier credit. Under these circumstances, the startup firm will need to raise a total of $64,240 through debt, and the entrepreneur will have to raise $45,760 ($110,000 − $64,240) from his or her own resources. (The next chapter will cover funding sources.)

Although these calculations sound simple, it is important to remember that they are based on estimates that represent averages only and that the figures for each individual firm will vary, sometimes drastically, from the averages. Prebusiness courses and all the relevant literature emphasize the fact that despite careful calculations of startup costs, most entrepreneurs obtain figures that are too low. For example, the estimate of the cost per square foot of building shop space was too low, the air conditioning system was $10,000 more than originally estimated, or the inventory ordered just did not fill up the store and more stock had to be ordered. The best advice is to estimate startup costs as accurately as possible and then to add 20 percent to the total.

Pro forma financial statements are excellent tools for estimating the amount of capital needed to start and run a firm for the first three to six months. From the income statement entrepreneurs will know whether or not operating funds will be required to keep the firm in business until it is profitable and the cash flow from operations becomes positive. From the balance sheet, they will know what the total assets of the firm are, how much they can expect to raise from debt (both current and long-term), and how much (the balance) they need to raise on their own. The more homework entrepreneurs do at this point, the better are their chances of having sufficient capital for a successful startup.

BUDGETING

Budgeting has two primary purposes in determining the financial needs of the startup firm. The first purpose is to help startup entrepreneurs project when the firm can expect to be profitable. A *profit plan* is the budgeting device designed for this purpose. If the firm expects to be unprofitable during the startup period, then additional funds will be needed to finance the operations of the firm until it becomes profitable. If the firm is expected to be profitable from the beginning, then the need for startup funds will be reduced.

The second purpose of budgeting is to help startup entrepreneurs determine the cash flow expected from the operations of the firm. The budgeting device used for this purpose, the *cash budget,* is designed to forecast the short-term cash flow of the firm and to indicate if additional funding is needed.

Profit Plan

In its simplest form, a profit plan is a detailed list of expected sales revenue and expected expenses over the planning period. The planning period for a startup firm should be at least one year and can be as long as three to five years. The shorter planning period is appropriate for those firms that will generate immediate cash flow from sales, such as most retail or personal-service businesses. A longer planning period is needed for manufacturing firms, particularly those that will have a long cash-conversion cycle. The *cash-conversion cycle* is the time between when the firm has to pay for the materials it has purchased and when the firm receives cash for the goods sold. (The cash-conversion cycle is discussed in detail in Chapter 14.)

The profit plan is not designed to be a restraint on spending, as too many entrepreneurs believe, but a plan that will enable entrepreneurs to set profit goals and to determine the steps necessary to reach those goals. The first step is to list all production expenses and then determine which expenses are necessary to generate the desired level of sales or which are inadequate.

The determination of the number of salespeople to employ is one important part of the profit plan. How many salespeople are needed to produce the sales expected and to give customers the quality of service that will build repeat business? Sometimes the answer to this question is simple. For example, in some businesses, such as restaurants, the determination of the number of waiters or waitresses needed to adequately serve the type of customers expected is straightforward. For the manufacturing firm that produces new, high-technology equipment having no existing market, the answer is not so obvious. In this case, the sales force must make many calls that are both educational and sales oriented, making an accurate forecast of the sales generated per person very difficult.

Estimate of Sales Revenue

Entrepreneurs can begin their profit plan with an estimate of the sales revenue expected and work down to the profit estimate, or they can start with the profit estimate and work up to see what level of sales is required to produce the anticipated profits. Some prefer the former method, because it is usually more accurate than the latter, but studies have shown that most startup service businesses use the latter method. Why is the former method more accurate? Basically, entrepreneurs are less likely to seriously overestimate potential sales and less likely to underestimate expenses in their first draft of a profit plan.

The first draft of the profit plan is something like the first calculation of our income taxes: After we see what the tax payment will be, we tend to review Form 1040, checking each and every line, and then we reread the tax instructions for possible clues to reducing our taxes. Similarly, entrepreneurs will draft their first profit plan, and then when the indicated profit is not as great as that anticipated, they review the plan, checking the accuracy of the figures and calling additional suppliers to renegotiate better prices or estimates. The beauty of this process, in both cases, is that business owners, like taxpayers, are much more serious the second time through and will check expert sources to obtain better and more accurate information.

The profit plan is designed to provide entrepreneurs with a method of quantifying their plan of operation. It is a detailed plan of future receipts and expenditures, and as such, requires that planners determine the *actual* amount of each expenditure. For example, the estimate given for a restaurant in Table 9.4 was derived from a prediction of revenues for the first three months that was based on the expected number of meals and the average price per meal to be served during that same period of operations. The estimate of expenditures was based on national averages of all restaurants. This is a good starting point, but surely the resulting profit estimate is too small to tempt an entrepreneur into starting this business. Thus, a closer look at the pro forma income statement is indicated.

Original Estimated Budget

The original budget for the restaurant is presented in Table 9.7. The objective of the entrepreneur is to increase the net income figure by examining each of the expenditures listed. The first item is the cost of operations, which includes the cost of the food, all kitchen and dining room supplies, utilities, and laundry. For example, of these items, the entrepreneur knows from experience that food costs are very close to 26 percent of sales. Utilities have been estimated by the local utility company, or by the engineering firm that designed the building, to average $3,200 per month. Supplies and laundry have been estimated at $540 and $330 per month, respectively. The entrepreneur's estimate of the cost of operations (shown below) is less than the average given in the preliminary estimate shown in Table 9.7.

Estimate of the Cost of Operations

Food costs @ 0.26	=	$ 6,807
Utilities	=	3,200
Supplies	=	540
Laundry	=	330
		$10,877

The estimate of salaries and wages is based on the planned hiring of four waiters/waitresses who will work seven hours each at $4 per hour, two cashiers/receptionists

Table 9.7 Budget Estimate Based on Averages

	Budget (per month)
Sales	$26,180
Cost of operations	11,624
Gross margin	$14,556
Expenses	
Salaries and wages	$ 9,163
Rent	1,466
Depreciation	995
Advertising	680
Interest	445
Repairs	393
Benefits	209
Bad debts	26
	$13,377
Net income before taxes	1,179
Taxes	401
Net income	$ 778

who will each work seven-hour shifts at $5 per hour, and two dishwashers who will each work seven hours per day at $4 per hour. There will be two chefs who will each work seven hours per day at $10 per hour and two assistant chefs at $6 per hour. The total estimated monthly expenditure for salaries and wages is as follows:

Waiters/waitresses	4 @ $4/hr. (168 hrs.)	=	$ 2,688
Cashiers/receptionsts	2 @ $5/hr. (168 hrs.)	=	1,680
Dishwashers	2 @ $4/hr. (168 hrs.)	=	1,344
Chefs	2 @ $10/hr. (168 hrs.)	=	3,360
Assistant chefs	2 @ $6/hr. (168 hrs.)	=	2,016
			$ 11,088

Obviously this estimate is almost $2,000 greater than the average given in Table 9.7. What can the startup entrepreneur do to reduce these expenditures? First, the sales revenues are those typical of a startup business and thus are based not on the capacity of the restaurant but on the expected number of patrons and the average price per meal during the first three months. After the first three months, sales are expected to grow to the capacity of the restaurant without increasing the need for additional employees. To save money during the first three months of operation, the entrepreneur plans to work one shift as a chef and spend his or her remaining time in a management capacity, thereby reducing wages and salaries to $9,408 during the initial three-month startup period.

Budget Revisions

The startup entrepreneur will then revise the budget to reflect the specific circumstances of the enterprise by replacing where possible the original estimates based on national averages with more exact figures based on his or her knowledge and local conditions. The result (see Table 9.8) is a budget that includes all known costs plus estimates from national averages for those expenses not known with certainty.

The changes from Table 9.7 reflected in Table 9.8 include rent of $1,100 per month, a figure that came from a three-year contract signed by the owners of the building. This figure also covers all property taxes and insurance, including $1 million liability insurance coverage. Depreciation, which was estimated at $810, based on the depreciation schedule of the equipment purchased, and advertising (newspaper and radio spots planned for the first three-month period), which was $560, were also changed.

The change in interest expense was an exact figure from the loan agreement. No

Table 9.8 Budget Revision Based on Known Expenses

	Original Budget	*Revised Budget*
Sales	$26,180	$26,180
Cost of operations	11,624	10,877
Gross margin	$14,556	$15,303
Expenses		
Salaries and wages	$ 9,163	$ 9,408
Rent	1,466	1,100
Depreciation	995	810
Advertising	680	560
Interest	445	451
Repairs	393	393
Benefits	209	209
Bad debts	26	26
	$13,377	$12,957
Before-tax income	1,179	2,346
Taxes	402	798
Net income	$ 778	$ 1,548

other expense figures were known with certainty, so the original estimates were retained in the budget revision. The result of these changes was an income before taxes that was almost double that of the original estimate. Assuming a tax rate of 34 percent, the net income came to $1,548, a much more encouraging number than the original estimate of $184.

In summary, the purpose of the budget process is to develop a profit plan that reflects actual expenses as accurately as possible. In addition, entrepreneurs must carefully analyze whether or not the planned enterprise has a high enough probability of success, and whether or not it will yield reasonable profits in terms of the time and capital invested.

Cash Budget

For most startup entrepreneurs, a profitable business is a successful business. Unfortunately, many a profitable firm has gone bankrupt because it did not have the cash to fulfill its obligations. Thus, profitability is not enough, and, for the startup firm, cash flow is more important than profitability.

Cash is critical to the startup firm. Ultimately, almost every transaction involves a receipt or a payment of cash. Before the first sale is made, cash is needed to pay the rent, utilities, and insurance. Employees must be hired, trained, and paid. After the firm opens, there will be ongoing expenses that require cash, from payments for advertising to sales and income taxes. The objective of cash budgeting is to plan for the cash needs of the firm. When, and for what, will cash be needed? With a cash budget, entrepreneurs plan (budget) their cash expenditures for a three- to six-month period.

Budgeting Process

The budgeting process is designed to make entrepreneurs think about all the expenses their firm will incur in the first few months of operation. The task of constructing the budget forces entrepreneurs to think about the expenses of the firm and thereby facilitates planning for its future cash needs. Table 9.9 is a typical cash budget for the first three months of operation (the startup quarter) of a new restaurant. Note that the cash budget is divided into two sections. The first section is for net cash receipts. In this case, net cash receipts are total sales minus expected bad checks. The second section is for cash payments and includes all known cash expenses. Noncash items, such as depreciation, are not included in the cash budget.

The difference between cash receipts and cash payments is the firm's *net cash flow* (or *net cash outflow*) for the period under consideration. In this example, the firm expects a positive cash inflow for each month. Thus, no additional operating funds will be needed. If the net cash flow had been negative, then additional funds would be necessary to keep the firm operating.

Example of Cash Budget

To illustrate negative cash flows and to demonstrate the second primary purpose of the cash budget, the actual cash flows from the first month are presented in Table 9.10. The actual cash receipts for the first month of operation were not as great as

Table 9.9 Cash Budget

	August	*September*	*October*
Cash Receipts	$26,154	$27,200	$28,300
Cash Payments			
Food	$ 6,807	$ 7,072	$ 7,358
Utilities	3,200	3,300	3,400
Supplies	540	550	570
Laundry	330	345	360
Salary & wages	9,408	9,408	9,408
Rent	1,100	1,100	1,100
Advertising	560	560	560
Interest	451	451	451
Repairs	393	393	393
Benefits	209	209	209
Total payments	$22,998	$23,388	$23,809
Net cash flow	3,156	3,812	4,491
Beginning cash	5,000	8,156	11,968
Ending cash	8,156	11,968	16,459
Minimum cash desired	5,000	5,000	5,000
Surplus (deficit) cash	$ 3,156	$ 6,968	$11,459

anticipated even though the number of meals served was higher than the budgeted figure. An analysis of the receipts indicated that although most other payments were very close to the budgeted figures, the introductory two-for-the-price-of-one meals offered to first-time customers increased food expenditures well beyond the budgeted amount. Instead of the expected positive cash flow of $3,156, the result was a net cash outflow of $2,856.

Although the negative net cash outflow was a rude surprise, the fact that the advertised opening specials attracted more customers than anticipated was interpreted as a very strong sign of interest on the part of diners who could become regular customers in the future. On the negative side, the outflow meant that the firm would need a cash infusion to maintain a minimum cash balance of $5,000, required by the bank to compensate for a loan. The owners, therefore, had to either borrow more money from the bank or put up additional cash.

Cash budgets are designed to help entrepreneurs plan for the cash needs of their firms. From the cash budget, entrepreneurs should be able to determine if the firm will need additional cash in the near future. The cash budget also indicates when

Table 9.10 Actual Cash Flows—August

	Budget	*Actual*
Cash receipts	$26,154	$22,104
Cash payments		
Food	$ 6,807	$ 8,240
Utilities	3,200	3,108
Supplies	540	618
Laundry	330	280
Salary & wages	9,408	9,640
Rent	1,100	1,100
Advertising	560	580
Interest	451	470
Repairs	393	684
Benefits	209	240
Total payments	$22,998	$24,960
Net cash flow	3,156	(2,856)
Beginning cash	5,000	5,000
Ending cash	8,156	2,144
Min. cash desired	5,000	5,000
Surplus (deficit) cash	$ 3,156	($ 2,856)

positive cash flows will be large enough to start the repayment of loans. In either case, the cash budget will provide entrepreneurs with a very important planning tool that can help them make changes as actual results differ from budget predictions.

FORECASTING ASSET REQUIREMENTS

Assets are needed to produce sales, and in most cases the higher the expected sales, the greater the required assets. This section presents a method of forecasting asset requirements.

For most businesses, the size of the firm during the startup period is limited by the size of the existing physical plant. A restaurant, for example, will accommodate only a fixed number of people, regardless of how many may wish to dine there. However, this does not mean that the financial needs of the firm do not continue to grow as the business moves from startup to capacity. To see why this is true, we will reexamine the pro forma balance sheet presented earlier in this chapter in Table 9.6.

This pro forma balance sheet was developed to help the entrepreneur determine the financial resources needed for the startup of a new business. By forecasting, the balance sheet is extended beyond the startup to cover the period in which the firm grows to its physical capacity. In this case, assume that the entrepreneur wished to know what his or her additional financial needs would be as the firm grew from the startup phase to 80 percent capacity during the second three months of business. A common method of determining the need for additional funds during this period is the percentage-of-sales method. This method assumes that asset requirements grow in proportion to the growth in sales.

Percentage-of-Sales Method

To illustrate how the percentage-of-sales method is employed, the information in Table 9.6 has been repeated in the first column of Table 9.11. In the second column, all assets that will increase as sales increase are given as a percentage of sales. For the startup firm, sales were estimated at $26,180 per month, or $314,160 annually. As sales

Table 9.11 Percentage-of-Sales Method of Forecasting

	Balance Sheet with Present Sales	*As Percentage of Annual Sales*	*Balance Sheet with 20% Sales Increase*
Cash	$ 12,320	3.9	$ 14,703
Receivables	4,950	1.6	6,032
Inventory	7,810	2.5	9,425
Other C.A.	2,750	0.9	3,393
Total C.A.	$ 27,830	8.9	$ 33,553
Net fixed assets	$ 62,700	N.A.	62,700
Other noncurrent assets	19,470	6.2	23,374
Total assets	$110,000	15.1	$191,627
Notes payable	$ 14,300	N.A.	$ 14,300
Trade payables	12,760	4.1	15,457
Taxes payable	1,320	0.4	1,508
Other C.L.	11,770	3.8	14,326
Total C.L.	$ 40,150	8.3	$ 45,591
Long-term debt	35,310	N.A.	35,310
Deferred taxes	550	0.2	754
Other noncurrent	3,190	N.A.	3,190
Net worth	30,800	N.A.	36,362
Total Liability & Net Worth	$110,000	8.5	$121,207
		Additional Funds Needed	$ 70,420

increase, so will the need for cash, trade receivables, inventory, and other current assets, but the need for fixed assets will not change. If sales were expected to increase 20 percent, then all the current assets would also increase by 20 percent. (The assumption is that the firm is making efficient use of its assets and that as sales increase, there must be a corresponding increase in all the current assets.) This increase is shown in column three.

What happens to the liability side of the balance sheet when assets increase? Obviously, as the assets increase, so will the liabilities, since a balance sheet must balance. But which liabilities? Just as the current assets were expected to increase along with sales, so were some of the current liabilities. Notes payable will not increase along with sales unless the entrepreneur requests additional funds from a lender, but a proportional increase in all other current liabilities can be assumed. None of the long-term liabilities will increase with sales, but net worth will increase with sales if the firm is profitable and if the profits are retained by the firm and not paid out as dividends.

In the second column, those liabilities that were expected to increase with sales are given as a percentage of sales, the same as in the case of current assets. Those liabilities that did not increase along with sales are so indicated by an "N.A." (not applicable). The figures from the pro forma balance sheet are in the third column. Note that the liabilities that did not increase concomitantly were recorded at their original figures.

The pro forma is now complete except for the change in net worth. Based on the information given earlier in Table 9.8, profits during the second quarter would be $5,562. If none of these profits is paid out as dividends, then the net worth of the firm would increase by $5,562. The forecasted total liabilities and net worth are shown to be $121,207—$70,420 less than total assets. The difference is the amount of additional funds that were raised to finance the increase in sales that was expected in the second quarter.

The percentage-of-sales method is an excellent tool for helping the entrepreneur determine the financial needs of the firm beyond the startup phase. Unfortunately, many entrepreneurs do not plan beyond the startup phase, and as the business starts to grow, they are forced to scramble for additional funds. Planning for financial needs through at least the first six months is an absolute must to avoid the potential cash squeeze that may occur just as the business is starting to grow and be successful.

Problems with the Percentage-of-Sales Method. The major problem with the percentage-of-sales method is the fact that in reality all assets do *not* increase proportionately with sales. For example, a restaurant may be able to obtain a 50-percent increase in sales while experiencing only a 10-percent increase in accounts receivable and a 20-percent increase in inventory. On the other hand, a retail store may find that both accounts receivable and inventory will increase proportionately with sales.

In addition, the increase in fixed assets tends to have a step-function relationship with sales, particularly in businesses with production operations. As the full capacity of existing equipment is reached, incremental increases cannot be made to accommodate the increases in sales because capacity can be increased only through a major addition to plant and equipment. Such an addition will be all that is required until full capacity is again reached.

These problems indicate that each entrepreneur must analyze the relationship between assets and sales for his or her particular industry. The percentage-of-sales method, however, is an excellent method for the initial estimation of asset requirements.

BREAK-EVEN ANALYSIS

Break-even analysis is the last technique presented in this chapter to help the entrepreneur determine the financial needs of his or her startup firm. Break-even analysis in its simplest form is the determination of the number of units sold, or the dollar volume of sales, that must be generated before the firm covers all its operating costs or, in other words, before it breaks even. Break-even, however, can be much more than just a simple tool for the discovery of break-even points; it may also be a technique for projecting future results, a screening device, and an approach to dealing with uncertainty. Before delving into its various applications, however, a basic understanding of break-even is required.

Break-Even Equation

A typical problem faced by the startup firm is the determination of the number of units, or the dollar volume of sales, that is required for the firm to break even. Obviously the firm wishes to do more than break even, but the determination of the break-even point is an indication of the minimum sales needed to cover the cost of production. For example, if a firm produces a single product, how many units must be sold to cover the operating costs? In making these calculations, management must understand the relationship between contribution margin, fixed costs, and variable costs.

Contribution margin is the difference between revenue and variable cost. In equation form, contribution margin may be expressed as follows:

Contribution margin = Revenue − Variable costs

Therefore, this equation indicates that the contribution margin is the contribution of each unit sold to cover either the fixed costs of the firm or to produce profits. Before explaining this important concept further, entrepreneurs must understand *fixed* and *variable costs.*

Fixed Costs. The income statement breaks down the expenses of operating a business into the following four categories:

1. Direct materials and supplies—those that go directly into the service or product produced by the firm.
2. Direct labor—the cost of labor that is employed directly in the production of the final product.
3. Overhead cost—the allocation for depreciation, insurance, and other expenses that are charged to production.
4. Indirect costs—those not directly related to the production of goods or services.

This categorization of expenses helps management understand that some expenses are allocated directly to the production of goods or services and, therefore, vary with the number or amount of goods or services produced. Other expenses are not directly related to the production of goods or services and so do not vary with production. These latter expenses are fixed costs and include such liabilities as rent, insurance, depreciation, property taxes, advertising, and salaries of most management, staff, and sales personnel. These are costs that must be paid regardless of the volume of sales.

Fixed costs are those costs that result from long-term management decisions. The decision to hire an accountant is a management decision, and the salary of the accountant is a fixed expense that will not vary with changes in sales levels. The decision to borrow long-term funds creates an interest expense that, regardless of sales, is fixed. Similarly, the decision to rent office space, advertise, purchase insurance, and so forth, are all costs that will not vary with sales. The total amount of fixed costs, therefore, is controlled by management, which can choose to have relatively high or relatively low fixed costs. Whatever management decides, fixed costs will have a major impact on the firm's operating leverage (presented in the next section) and ultimately on the firm's profit potential.

Variable Costs. Some expenses vary directly with changes in sales levels. The cost of materials used in the manufacture of goods is an obvious example of a variable cost. As more goods are produced, the cost of materials used will increase as will the cost of the labor required to produce these goods. If funds are borrowed to purchase inventory or to support accounts receivable, then the interest on these funds is a variable cost. Variable costs are, therefore, all of those expenses that vary directly with sales. Variable expenses are sales driven and, therefore, do not depend upon past management decisions.

Semivariable Costs. Certainly some expenses cannot be identified as either fixed or variable. Utility expenses are an example. The cost of telephones, water, electricity, and gas will increase with sales, but even if sales drop to zero, these expenses will remain. Individuals who have gone on vacation are well aware of the fact that the telephone bill must be paid although no calls were made, but the cost of long-distance calls will increase when the individual returns. The same is true for the electric and water bills.

In allocating expenses for the purposes of break-even analysis, management will need to decide arbitrarily how much of these semivariable expenses to allocate to fixed costs and how much to allocate to variable expenses. Obviously such allocation is not going to yield an exact breakdown between fixed and variable expenses, but the error should be so negligible in comparison to the amount of known fixed and variable expenses that the analysis will not be seriously affected.

Break-Even Point

The break-even point is the point at which the sales revenue equals both the fixed costs and the variable costs of generating a given volume of revenue. The break-even point, therefore, is that point at which the firm does not earn any profit nor suffer any loss. The actual break-even equation is derived from the following profit equation:

$$\textbf{Profit} = \textbf{Revenues} - \textbf{Total costs}$$

in which total costs comprise fixed costs and variable costs. Thus, profits are zero at the break-even point, which is calculated as follows:

$$\textbf{Profits} = 0 = \textbf{Revenues} - \textbf{Fixed costs} - \textbf{Variable costs}$$

Revenues are unit sales times the selling price per unit, and variable costs are the variable costs per unit times the number of units produced. Therefore, the per unit contribution margin (CM) equals the sales price per unit minus variable costs per unit. The break-even point in units may be calculated as follows:

$$0 = \textbf{Revenues} - \textbf{Fixed costs} - \textbf{Variable costs}$$
$$0 = \textbf{Price} \times \textbf{Units sold} - \textbf{Fixed costs} - \textbf{Variable costs per unit} \times \textbf{Units sold}$$

If P = price per unit sold
and

$$Q = \text{units sold}$$

and

$$V = \text{variable costs per unit}$$

the break-even in units may be expressed as follows:

$$0 = P \times Q - \text{Fixed costs} - V \times Q$$

and

$$\text{Fixed costs} = Q(P - V)$$

and the break-even in units is

$$Q = \text{Fixed costs}/(P - V)$$

A simple example may help explain the concept. Assume that a firm is thinking about manufacturing an intruder alarm. The alarm will be produced in a rented plant with total fixed costs estimated at \$1.4 million and variable costs at \$25 per unit. If the selling price is budgeted at \$95, the break-even point may be calculated as follows:

$$\begin{aligned}\textbf{Break-even point} &= \text{Fixed costs}/(\text{Price} - \text{Variable costs})\\ &= \$1{,}400{,}000/(\$95 - \$25)\\ &= 20{,}000 \text{ units}\end{aligned}$$

From a managerial viewpoint, the firm should proceed with its plans to manufacture the alarm if its marketing research projects sales of at least 20,000 or more units over the budgeted period.

What will the expected profits be if the firm actually sells 25,000 units? Using the profit equation shown on page 245, the expected profits can be calculated as follows:

$$\begin{aligned} \textbf{Profits} &= \textbf{Total sales} - \textbf{Fixed costs} - \textbf{Variable costs} \\ &= \$95 \times 25{,}000 - \$1{,}400{,}000 - \$25 \times 25{,}000 \\ &= \$2{,}375{,}000 - \$1{,}400{,}000 - \$625{,}000 \\ &= \$350{,}000 \end{aligned}$$

Break-even analysis, therefore, is the determination of the cost–volume–profit relationship, which is expressed graphically in Figure 9.1. As a general rule, the higher the fixed costs, the higher the break-even point and the greater the profit per unit sold above the break-even point. In comparing companies within the same industry, those with higher fixed costs usually have lower variable costs per unit, since the higher fixed costs are usually due to more automated equipment. The higher-fixed-cost company, therefore, is said to have higher *operating leverage.*

High operating leverage has both positive and negative impact on a company. As long as it is operating above the break-even point, high leverage means that the company will reap large operating profits per unit, but if it falls below the break-even point, then the operating losses will be greater than those incurred if the company had lower operating leverage. To better understand operating leverage, see Figure 9.2. Note that the top graph represents a high-fixed-cost company and that the difference between sales and total costs is much greater than that in the lower graph. In

FIGURE 9.1
Break-even Graph

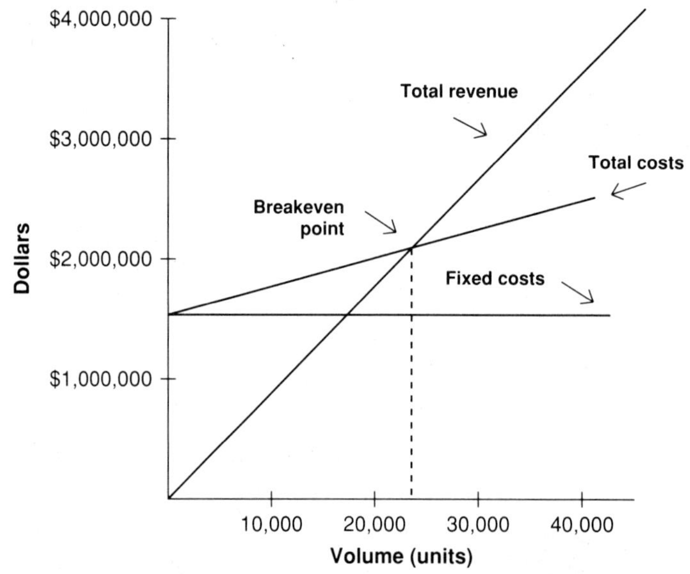

FIGURE 9.2
Operating Leverage

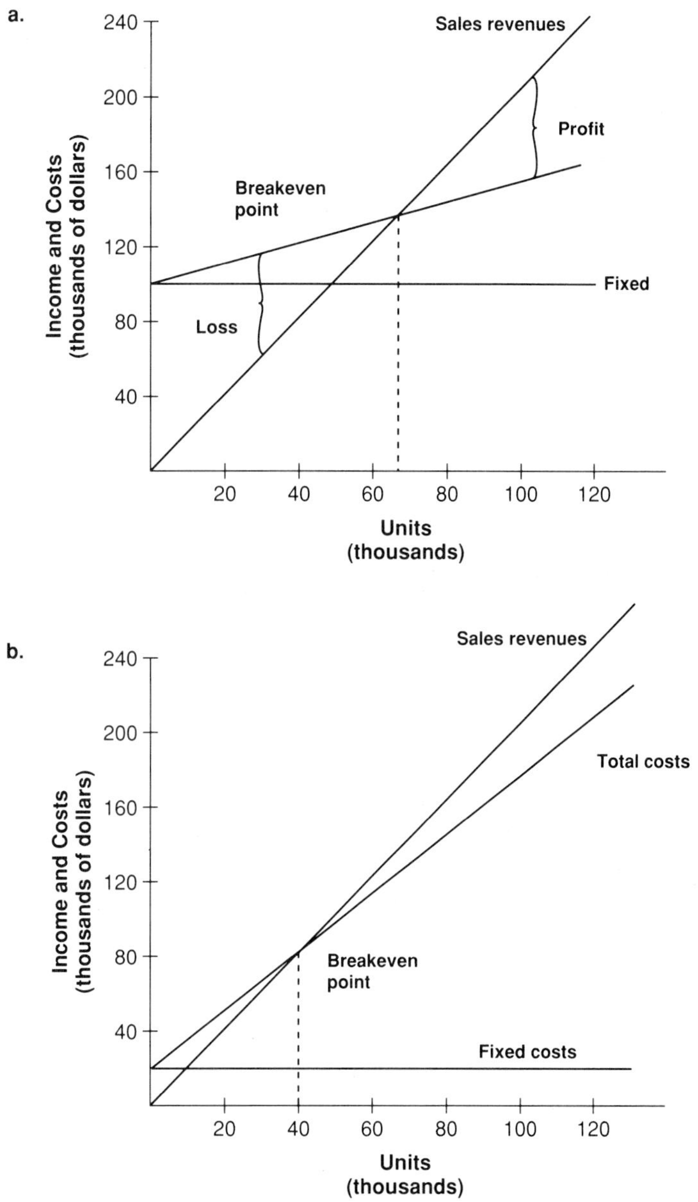

the low-fixed-cost firm, the break-even point is much lower, as will be the potential profits should the firm operate above break-even. However, should sales fall below the break-even point, the potential operating losses will be much less than those of the higher-leveraged firm.

Break-Even Example

A break-even point for the restaurant in our examples can be derived from the information already developed in this chapter. Using the budget information on the restaurant given in Table 9.9 and the depreciation expense from Table 9.7, the fixed costs and variable costs may be allocated as follows:

Fixed Costs		*Variable Costs*	
Salary & wages	$1,600	Food	$6,807
Rent	1,100	Utilities	1,600
Utilities*	1,600	Supplies	540
Advertising	560	Laundry	330
Benefits	209	Repairs	393
Depreciation	995		$9,670
	$14,323		

Although this breakdown of expenses is subjective, entrepreneurs will still have a better idea of which startup costs are fixed and which are variable. The point is to allocate all expenses, as accurately as possible, to either fixed or variable expenses.

Before the break-even point can be calculated for the restaurant, the average price per meal and the variable cost per meal must be determined. Using the estimates from Table 9.4, the average number of meals sold per day was 110, and the average price per meal was $9.15. The average price was derived from weighting the estimated number of meals sold as follows:

60 lunches × $7.20 = $ 432
50 dinners × $11.50 = $ 575
$1,007

Average price per meal = $1,007/110 = $9.15

In a similar manner, the average variable price per meal can be calculated by dividing the total variable cost ($9,670) by the 2,860 meals (from 110 meals per day times the estimated 26 operating days per month) expected to be served during the month.

Average variable costs = $9,670/2,860 = $3.38

The break-even point can be calculated as follows:

Break-even point = Fixed costs/(Sales price − Variable costs)
Break-even point = $14,323/($9.15 − 3.38) = 2,482 meals

This figure is below the expected 2,860 meals; therefore, the firm should operate above the break-even point.

It is important to note that if the number of meals served is only 400 less than that estimated, the firm will be below the break-even point. Four hundred meals sounds like a big drop but, in fact, represents only a 14-percent drop in the estimated number of meals served. However, for every meal (customer) served over the break-even point, the firm will make $5.77. Therefore, if the firm serves 400 more customers than estimated, its profits will increase by $2,308.

---

*Half of the cost of utilities was estimated as a fixed cost and half as a variable cost.

Problems with Break-Even Analysis

There are several problems with break-even analysis to address. First, break-even analysis assumes a linear (straight-line) relationship between volume and sales. This assumption is incorrect in most business situations in which additions to sales are the result of a reduction in the selling price. Firms cannot expect to continue increasing sales at a set price. Break-even analysis, however, is a short-term technique, and price over the short term can be expected to remain stable.

A second problem associated with break-even analysis is the failure of entrepreneurs to properly evaluate expected cash flow—a problem stemming from their use of break-even analysis as a capital budgeting technique. Since break-even analysis indicates at what volume of sales a business will be profitable, some managers rely on this technique to determine the acceptance or rejection of a new project. This use of break-even is inappropriate because capital decisions should be based on projections of cash flow over the entire life of a project. Again, break-even analysis is intended for short-term analysis only and should not be used for any long-term planning.

A third problem is that break-even analysis represents a short-term static relationship between costs and sales volume. Any variation in the conditions that affect costs will immediately affect the relationship. In other words, the break-even graph represents a relationship at a specific point in time, so a change in conditions can change that relationship.

Uses of Break-Even Analysis

The foregoing example has demonstrated the importance of break-even analysis and the *contribution margin.* The break-even point indicates the volume of sales the firm needs to cover its fixed costs, which, in turn, indicates how risky the startup phase will be for the firm. If the break-even point is close to the best sales projections for the firm, then the risks are high that the firm will not be able to cover its fixed costs and will be unprofitable. The contribution margin, therefore, is the contribution of each sale to cover fixed costs *below* the break-even point and is the contribution to profits *above* the break-even point.

Contribution margin may also be used to price one-time large orders. Assume that the owner of the intruder alarm system mentioned earlier in the chapter was invited to submit a bid to a government contractor for the one-time sale of 5,000 alarms. What price should the entrepreneur bid? To determine the correct price, he or she must answer the following questions. First, given existing plant capacity, can the order be filled without curtailing normal production? Second, can the order be filled without overtime? If the answer to both of these questions is yes, then the bid price should be $25 per unit plus whatever profit the entrepreneur wishes to make on each unit sold.

A bid price that just covers the variable cost production often causes concern among business owners. The oft-heard complaint is that the units being sold should be priced to cover some of the firm's fixed costs. What is overlooked is the fact that the one-time bid is an addition to the normal operations of the firm for which fixed costs are already covered. The units for which the bid has been made are *incremental sales*, so their sale price needs to cover only their *incremental costs*. Incremental costs are those incurred by producing just the next unit (increment). The fixed costs do not increase because of the extra units being produced for the bid; that is why they are called fixed. The entrepreneur should not plan to cover any fixed costs through one-time sales.

Summary

In this chapter entrepreneurs learn how to determine the amount of capital they need to start and operate a business for the first three to six months. After entrepreneurs decide what type of business they want to have and make all the necessary plans for starting that business, they need to determine how much capital is required to launch it.

To determine their financial needs, startup entrepreneurs should consult their business plan. A most important tool, the business plan will usually contain a pro forma balance sheet, from which entrepreneurs can calculate the total assets needed. From this figure, the assets that are already in hand are subtracted to find the amount of funds that still need to be obtained for the startup.

If a business plan is not available, startup entrepreneurs can develop a pro forma balance sheet and income statement from data that are available in most public libraries. These financial statements will represent averages that can be adjusted as more accurate information becomes available.

Budgeting is used to develop a *profit plan* and a *cash budget*. The profit plan is a detailed list of expected sales revenue and expected expenses for the planning period. The profit plan indicates how profitable a firm is likely to be. In the event that profits are not as high as expected, it also provides a written guideline that can be used to analyze problems and to evaluate proposed solutions.

The objective of the cash budget is to plan ahead for the cash needs of the firm. The budgeting process is designed to help startup entrepreneurs plan for all the expenses the firm will incur during the startup period. If the difference between cash inflow and net cash outflow is negative, sales must be increased and/or expenses must be reduced to avoid having to raise additional funds to keep the firm operating.

Forecasting is a technique used to determine the need for funds beyond the initial startup period. As sales increase, additional assets will be needed to support the growth. The percentage-of-sales forecasting method assumes that all current assets and some of the current liabilities will increase proportionately in relation to the increase in sales. Since current assets are usually greater than current liabilities, additional funds will be needed to support the increase in current assets. These funds may come from the profits of the firm.

Break-even analysis is the last method described in the chapter to help entrepreneurs determine their needs for funds. *Break-even analysis* is the determination of the cost–volume–profit relationship. The main purpose of break-even analysis is to indicate the number of units that must be sold by a firm to just cover its operating expenses. If the break-even point is higher than the level of expected sales during the startup period, the firm will need to obtain additional funds to cover its operating losses.

As a general rule, the higher the fixed costs, the higher the break-even point and the greater the profits per unit. Lower fixed costs yield lower profits per unit but run less risk of operating at a loss. One of the problems with break-even analysis is the determination of which costs are fixed and which are variable, particularly when some of the costs are semivariable.

Break-even analysis may also be used to predict profit or loss from the addition of a new product or service as well as to determine the price of a one-time contract for a single large order.

Assembling the Pieces

The determination of the financial needs (see Tables 9.1 and 9.2) for the startup of In Good Taste came from the business plan developed by Jacki and Carol. Their plan reflected initial startup costs and the expected negative cash flow of the first three to six months of operation. Interestingly, they based their estimate of financial needs on a best-, average-, and worst-case sales scenario. In the best case (sales of $200,000), estimated cash needs were $50,000; in the average case of $150,000, they would be $55,000; and in the worst case (sales of only $100,000), they would need $60,000.

Break-even sales were estimated at $66,600 per year, or $5,550 per month. Jacki and Carol even determined daily break-even sales of $222. ■

Questions for Review and Discussion

1. What are some of the problems of using averages, like those found in *RMA Annual Statement Studies,* to develop pro forma financial statements?
2. What is a profit plan?
3. Why is cash flow more important than profitability for startup firms?
4. What are the two primary purposes of the cash budget?
5. What is the purpose of forecasting?
6. The percentage-of-sales method assumes that all current assets will change proportionately in relation to sales. Why is this a valid assumption?
7. What are some of the uses of break-even analysis?
8. Name some fixed costs for the operation of a day-care center.
9. A firm that manufactures a single product (fried pies) has fixed costs of $240,000. If the selling price per pie is $.25 and the variable cost is $.08, what is the break-even point? What is the profit (loss) if sales are 1,800,000? 1,200,000?
10. If a proposed automated production facility for the firm in Problem 9 will raise the fixed cost to $520,000 and lower the variable costs to $.05, should the firm purchase the facility?
11. Develop a pro forma income statement and balance sheet using information from Robert Morris Associates, Dun & Bradstreet, or Troy's for a business you would like to start.
12. How would you prove that the break-even point found in Problem 9 was correct?

CHAPTER 10

Sources of Financing

Learning Objectives

After reading this chapter, you will be able to do the following:

- Identify the major sources of startup financing.
- Locate sources of funding.
- Describe the characteristics of each funding source.

Where can entrepreneurs obtain the capital necessary to start up their own business? This is the question every entrepreneur must answer before startup. This chapter will identify the various funding sources that are available to the startup entrepreneur, describe the characteristics of each, and help the entrepreneur determine which sources are most appropriate for different startup situations.

The sources of startup capital presented in this chapter include the following:

The entrepreneur's personal assets
Bootstrapping
Friends and relatives
Partners
Commercial banks
Small Business Administration
Small Business Investment Companies
Trade financing
Leasing
Venture capital
Franchisors
Miscellaneous sources

INTRODUCTION

Before launching a new business, the entrepreneur should estimate as realistically as possible the amount of capital needed to start the business and keep it operating for at least three or, preferably, six months—a process discussed at length in the preceding chapter. With this information, the entrepreneur is ready to locate sources of financing for his or her startup.

Two types of capital are generally needed to start a business: *permanent* and *working* capital. Because they do not always come from the same sources, it is important to understand the difference between these two types of capital before attempting to obtain financing. *Permanent,* or *long-term, capital* includes funds for land, buildings, equipment, furniture, and fixtures. Financing for these items should come from long-term sources, such as mortgage or term loans; from equity, in the form of the owner's capital or the sale of stock; from equity and/or long-term loans from partners or venture capitalists; or from long-term leasing arrangements.

Working capital, or *short-term funds,* include capital for cash, inventory, and accounts receivable. Financing for these items will come from commercial banks and other financial institutions in the form of notes payable, accounts receivable financing, inventory financing, lines of credit, and personal loans; from trade credit in the form of accounts payable; and from credit unions and life-insurance companies in the form of intermediate loans.

Another way of differentiating sources of financing is by how they are raised—either by debt or by equity. Funds raised through debt must eventually be paid off, usually on a schedule stipulated in a contract. Individuals and financial institutions lending funds to a firm expect to be reimbursed in the form of principal and interest payments over the period the loan is outstanding. Short-term debt is repaid from the liquidation of current assets, and long-term debt is repaid from the earnings of the firm. Understanding the difference in how debt will be repaid is of paramount importance to entrepreneurs, since most lending institutions will judge all loan requests on that basis.

Equity funds come from individuals and institutions who invest money without expecting a specific rate of return on that money or a specific date by which the money will be returned. Sources of equity financing expect to be rewarded from the earnings of the firm in the form of dividends and/or the increase in the value of the firm and its stock. Individuals and institutions who purchase equity are more interested in the long-term profitability of the firm than in the shorter-term cash flow, unlike the short-term debt holders, who are very interested in the cash flow.

Before examining the various sources of funding, the entrepreneur should be aware of what these sources want to know about his or her firm before they will commit their funds. Basically they want answers to the following questions:

1. ***How much capital is needed?*** The information in the previous chapter will help the entrepreneur specify how much capital is needed for setup costs and how much is needed for monthly operating costs to keep the firm in business until it is profitable.

2. ***How will the funds be spent?*** Before requesting funds, the entrepreneur must be able to specify the purposes for which the funds are intended. To say simply that funds are needed for the operation of the firm is the same as admitting that the firm is not in control of its spending. The entrepreneur must submit a detailed list of expenses that will include items such as supplies to build up inventory for the Christmas season, specific equipment needed for startup, the training of service personnel, and the like.

3. ***How long will the money be needed.*** Will the funds be needed for one month or ten years? Lenders of capital are very interested in how long their funds will be tied up in a particular business venture.

4. ***How will the money be repaid?*** When will money be collected from the sale of goods and services? The cash-flow statements and the profit plans developed in the previous chapter will help provide the answer to this question.

With ready answers to these questions, the entrepreneur can confidently approach various funding sources with a much greater probability of success.

THE ENTREPRENEUR'S PERSONAL ASSETS

Most business startups begin with the owners using personal funds to pay for the preliminary investigative steps, which include attending seminars, taking courses, visiting similar businesses, taking individuals out to lunch, travel, and, sometimes, consulting fees. The closer the entrepreneur is to startup, the more funds he or she needs. Recent data from the Census Bureau indicate that 40 percent of business owners used their own cash or other assets to provide startup capital for their firms. A survey by *Venture* magazine, which verified the Census Bureau data, showed that **45 percent** of business owners used their own funds to start their own companies.[1]

Sources

Where does an individual find the necessary funds? Most individuals have more assets than they realize. To be considered for a loan or a loan guarantee, the entrepreneur must fill out a personal financial data sheet (see the section on the Small Business Administration presented later in this chapter). From this sheet, several possible sources of funds are evident.

Cash. The individual entrepreneur should have some cash available in his or her checking and/or savings account. This is the most obvious source of funds. In addition, the entrepreneur may be able to borrow money by using a savings account as collateral or simply to obtain a personal loan from the bank with which he or she is presently doing business. If the entrepreneur belongs to a credit union, he or she may be able to borrow money from them to obtain startup capital (see Figure 10.1).

Stocks. Additional sources include the sale of stocks or bonds that the entrepreneur owns. The entrepreneur originally purchased the stocks and bonds as investments and now is merely cashing in one investment for another, hopefully more personally gratifying, investment—his or her own business. The entrepreneur can sell any real-estate holdings to raise cash for the startup, or if a homeowner, he or she can take out an equity loan to obtain needed capital.

Life-Insurance Policies. Another source of capital is that of borrowing on the cash value of a life-insurance policy. This may be an excellent source of funds for two major reasons: First, the interest charged on the loan is usually very low—in the range of 5 to 8 percent. Second, the loan can be considered to be the owner's personal funds and as such, does not require repayment. If the money is not repaid, then the value is subtracted from the face value of the life-insurance policy in the event of the owner's death.

FIGURE 10.1
Sources of Financing to Start or Purchase a Business

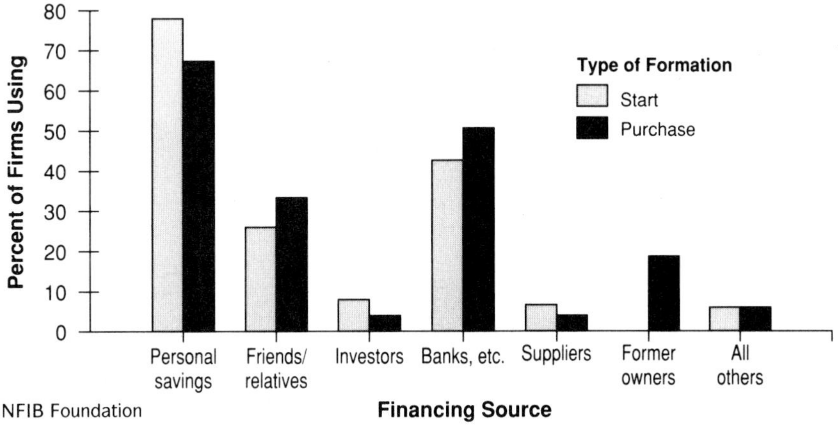

Data Source: The NFIB Foundation

It is clear from the foregoing discussion that most individuals have access to more potential sources of startup capital than they realize, but they need to be willing to tap these sources. If they are not willing to risk their own savings and investments to raise startup capital, then they cannot expect others to be willing to invest in their venture. Simply expressed, if entrepreneurs are not willing to risk their own money in the startup, then they should not be surprised when others refuse to risk theirs.

BOOTSTRAPPING

Bootstrapping is the practice of using funds from the entrepreneur and the firm to finance the firm's own startup and operation. Some of the sources of bootstrap financing include trade credit, customers, real estate, and equipment. Consider the individual who needed $25,000 to start a service firm but had only $7,000 in his own checking and savings accounts. This person applied for and was granted four different VISA and MasterCard accounts, which he then used to obtain cash advances. With the cash advances, the entrepreneur started a very successful firm and used the cash flow generated from the business to pay off the credit-card loans.

Trade Credit

Trade credit is a typical source of bootstrap financing. Many suppliers are willing to extend credit to a new business through the use of normal trade credit or through extended terms. To obtain trade credit from major suppliers, entrepreneurs should meet with suppliers, give them a copy of the business plan, show the suppliers how much of their product will be needed now and in the future, and then ask for credit.

The odds are high that the suppliers will either grant the firm trade credit or give it extended terms during the startup period in order to secure the firm's goodwill in the future. Startup entrepreneurs, like individuals, remember best those who helped them when they really needed help and tend to be very loyal to them.

Customers

Customers may also be an excellent source of bootstrap financing. One entrepreneur used this type of financing when he was installing a distribution system for his first customer. The entrepreneur did the design and installed the system, but the customer purchased all the materials, thereby eliminating the entrepreneur's need for and expense of obtaining credit to purchase them. Another way to obtain bootstrap financing is to have customers pay partial or progress payments on jobs that extend over a long period of time—an arrangement that should be included in the contract before it is signed. This method is typical of new firms, particularly those starting in the contracting or construction business.

Real Estate

Real estate may be prohibitively expensive for the startup firm. Many entrepreneurs want to own the land and the buildings in which their businesses are housed, but purchasing real estate should not be the primary consideration of the startup entrepreneur. The primary consideration is the long-term success of the business, and leasing or renting may require less capital than purchasing, thereby saving needed startup capital.

The use of already owned real estate, however, should not be overlooked as a source of bootstrap financing. Loans on commercial or industrial property can be written for up to 75 percent of the appraised value and may be amortized over a 10- to 25-year period. If the entrepreneur does not own commercial property, he or she may own residential property that has appreciated in value.

For example, assume that a house was purchased for $75,000 five years ago and that the owner still owes $60,000 on the mortgage. Today the house may be appraised at $125,000, and the owner may obtain a second mortgage on part of the increase in equity value of the home. Interest on the first mortgage will remain at the original rate, but the second mortgage would be at the current rate. The owner could also *refinance* the home, which would mean, in effect, paying off the first mortgage, getting the difference between the old and the new mortgage loan in cash for the business, and obtaining a new mortgage based on the current value of the home.

Furniture and Fixtures

If equipment, furniture, or fixtures are needed for the startup firm, several bootstrapping methods should be considered. First, new equipment is not a requirement for a startup firm. Used equipment may do the job just as well and will certainly cost less. Second, rather than paying for equipment with personal funds, the owner should consider obtaining an equipment loan. These loans have the advantage of allowing the entrepreneur to obtain needed equipment while retaining needed working capital. Depending on the expected life of the equipment, these loans may be paid off over a

2- to 7-year period. Finally, equipment leasing should be considered. Leasing reduces the need for startup capital and spreads the payments out over a number of years as an equipment loan does. Leasing normally is more expensive than financing through an equipment loan, but if the equipment loan is not available, then leasing is an alternative.

Many startup entrepreneurs do not watch their costs as closely as they should, and too much precious capital is lost to poor management. In a television interview, Steven Jobs, co-founder of Apple Computer, lamented this very fact when describing the startup of NEXT, the firm he founded after leaving Apple. In explaining how much money was spent during the startup period he said, "We aren't acting like a startup firm. We act like we have plenty of money . . . not asking for discounts on computers, not carefully managing our personnel costs, not scrounging for equipment. We are signaling deep pockets."

Bootstrap financing may be as unorthodox as borrowing from a credit card or as common as seeking trade credit, but if the entrepreneur really wants to finance the startup of his or her own firm, there is a way. Bootstrap financing requires that the entrepreneur take risks and control startup costs. Too many successful businesses have been started with little or no capital for anyone to ever use insufficient capital as an excuse for not starting his or her own business.

FRIENDS AND RELATIVES

The National Federation of Independent Businesses found that 27 percent of new businesses were at least partially financed by friends and relatives of startup entrepreneurs. Friends and relatives are an excellent source of startup capital for several reasons: First, they have access to many of the same sources of capital that the entrepreneur does; therefore, the amount of capital that can be raised increases with the number of individuals who are contributing to the business. Second, friends and relatives are usually more willing to risk capital in a firm where they know the owner and his or her abilities and aspirations than in businesses where they do not know the principals involved. Finally, friends and relatives derive a certain sense of satisfaction from helping someone they know start a business as well as a feeling of involvement that they do not get from putting money into the bank or into stocks and bonds of large corporations.

Obtaining capital from friends and relatives involves a type of risk that is not inherent in other sources of capital, and that is the risk of losing friends and angering relatives if the enterprise is unsuccessful. All those who invest money in a new business think they understand the risk involved, but too often they tend to blame failures on the individual to whom they entrusted their money. The entrepreneur can take steps to avoid this problem. The entrepreneur should explain to all investors the potential risks involved and should point out the fact that there is a chance that the firm may not be a success. This is a very difficult task for startup entrepreneurs who are necessarily optimistic about their chances for success, or they would not go into business in the first place.

The parties should have a written agreement stating the schedule of repayments and the interest to be paid if the funds are in the form of a loan. If it is an equity investment, the agreement should state how many shares are involved, when and how the shares may be redeemed, and what the possibilities are for dividends. These steps may not eliminate all points of disagreement, but they will reduce them.

Finally, the entrepreneur should not overlook other potential sources of startup capital from professionals who already know something about the firm. Several excellent sources include lawyers, accountants, consultants, and financial planners with whom the entrepreneur has worked during the planning stages of the enterprise. If they are not interested or do not have available funds, they may be willing to recommend the business to other professionals they know.

PARTNERS

Taking on a partner or partners in a startup firm has the advantage of increasing access to funds needed for startup but also has the disadvantage of involving additional people in making decisions about how the firm should be run. Partners are basically of two types, those who wish to actively participate in the firm's operation and those who merely take an equity position. From the standpoint of financing sources, partners increase potential sources of funding. In addition, they have friends and relatives who are also potential sources of financing for the startup firm.

COMMERCIAL BANKS

Commercial banks are generally much maligned by startup entrepreneurs, who see banks as having capital available but as unwilling to extend any of it to their startup firms. This reputation is not without a measure of truth, but in reality, both entrepreneurs and banks alike simply do not take the time to understand each other's needs. The fact is that most banks do not put up venture capital for startup firms, but they do lend funds based on assets. The main objective of this section will be to explain this distinction and clear up the general misconception about how banks operate.

This misconception about banks was vividly illustrated in one prebusiness seminar where, during a discussion of potential sources of funding, a budding entrepreneur stated that banks would not lend her any money for the startup of a service firm. Questioned further, she explained that she expected the bank to put up the entire $25,000 she needed for the startup and did not intend to put up any money herself. She was not willing to take money out of her savings account, sell any of her stocks, or use her home as collateral. From her viewpoint, the bank should be willing to take the risk, but she should have no obligation to risk any of her assets—"That's what banks are for."

Purpose of Commercial Banks

If banks will not take risks, what are banks for? Banks are in the business of making money, and so they are very concerned with how they will be paid back. Individuals who have entrusted banks with their money, expecting both a return of their capital as well as a return on their capital, are also interested in the bank's lending procedures. Banks, therefore, are obligated by their customers (savers) to be prudent in their lending habits (see The Inside View 10-1). This does not mean that banks won't lend money to any startup firms but that banks will lend money only to *qualified* firms. The question is what does "qualified" mean?

If an entrepreneur goes to a commercial bank with his or her business plan in hand and asks for a loan, what are the chances that a loan will be granted? To qualify for a loan, bankers will look over the business plan for the current and/or fixed assets of the business. Bankers will lend money that is secured by some type of marketable collateral. If the firm does not have any marketable collateral, then the bank will ask the entrepreneur for personal assets to use as collateral. If the entrepreneur does not have any assets either, then the chances of obtaining a loan are indeed slim. Thus for the startup firm to obtain a loan, either the firm's or the entrepreneur's assets will be needed for collateral. Therefore, to secure a loan, the entrepreneur should plan to submit both a personal financial statement and at least the pro forma balance sheet of the startup firm, if not the entire business plan.

The Attitude of Commercial Banks Toward Small Businesses

Different banks have very different attitudes toward small-business loans. Some banks, usually large ones, simply do not wish to spend the time necessary to review loan applications from small startup firms (see The Inside View 10-2). Other banks may have special small-business loan departments that cater to, and attempt to attract, small and startup firms. Their attitude is based on the concept of service to the community and on the fact that small firms can be a source of business for the bank for many years. The entrepreneur should check to see which banks in the community have a record of supporting small businesses.

10-1 *The Inside View*

WHAT BANKERS EXPECT

At a venture-capital conference, a group of entrepreneurs challenged Roger Smith, President of Silicon Valley Bank, to explain why bankers were so averse to risk, while venture capitalists seem to accept risk as a fact of life. Mr. Smith replied, "We're like Hertz Rent-A-Car. When they rent you a car, they charge you for usage, and they expect to get the car back. When we give you a loan, we charge interest, and we expect to get our money back."[2]

10-2 *The Inside View*

SOME BANKS SERVE SMALLER FIRMS

Banks are learning that small businesses can be as profitable as big businesses, and they are making special efforts to serve them. For example, Shawmut Corporation Bank has opened thirty-seven Business Banking Centers, which cater to small and mid-sized firms. Among the services offered is an easy-access, revolving line of credit that is renewed annually. Florida National has also developed a revolving line of credit based on any equity the entrepreneur has in real estate or in his or her firm. Citytrust Bank has a Center for Business Planning to help entrepreneurs develop business plans, and they also provide other financial services geared to the smaller business. What these and many other banks are realizing is that small companies are not only profitable but also may be very important to their future.[3]

Banks can offer the startup entrepreneur a number of valuable services, including the following:

1. Bankers know a lot about the business community in the bank's area. This knowledge can be an invaluable source of information and contacts for the startup firm. Bankers know who is in what business, how they are doing, and what their needs are. They also know which businesses are growing and which are declining.
2. Bankers may also be an excellent source of business advice. They have seen many businesses come and go, and they know what mistakes have caused their demise. Therefore, they can help the startup firm avoid some common mistakes. They have an interest in keeping the startup firm in business, for only an operating firm can be a source of income to the bank.
3. A bank can offer needed services to the startup firm. For example, the bank can suggest setting up a separate (from the entrepreneur's) checking account for the firm or explain the requirements for and the actual extention of a line of credit. Banks also can explain how personal loans are structured and what kinds of collateral are acceptable for short-term loans.

Banks as a Source of Information

Even if a bank turns down the startup entrepreneur's loan request, valuable information can be gained. The entrepreneur should always ask why the loan was rejected before going to the next bank with the same request. Some bankers are willing to explain, for example, that the cash-flow projections do not indicate adequate coverage for the requested working capital loan but that if the request had been structured as an equipment loan, the chances of acceptance would have been much better. In addition, these bankers, who see hundreds of loan requests, may spot a flaw in the request that the entrepreneur needs to correct before going on to the next financing source.

What type of loans do banks grant? There are four basic types of bank loans: (1) short-term commercial loans, (2) long-term loans, (3) current-asset finance loans, and (4) specialized loans. It is important for the entrepreneur to be aware of the criteria for each type of loan.

Short-Term Commercial Loans

The short-term commercial loan is the primary source of funds for day-to-day operating expenses. Short-term loans are used to take advantage of supplier discounts, to purchase inventory, or to cover seasonal cash-flow shortages. These loans are normally unsecured (granted without any specific collateral) and are based primarily on the firm's financial statements. If the financial statements indicate that the firm is somewhat weak, then some type of security may be required. Banks will accept stocks, bonds, certificates of deposit, and sometimes just the personal guarantee of the entrepreneur.

Short-term loans are usually repaid within 30 to 180 days, and repayment is normally in a lump sum that includes the principal plus interest. If the loan exceeds a specified amount, generally between $50,000 and $100,000, the bank may require that the borrower maintain a *compensating balance* in the firm's checking account. A compensating balance is a minimum or average amount that must be maintained in the firm's checking account. The effect of a compensating balance is to raise the actual (as opposed to the stated) interest rate, since a portion of the loan is not available to the firm.

Line of Credit. A line of credit is also a type of short-term loan. A *line of credit* is usually an agreement between the firm and the bank indicating the maximum amount of credit the bank is willing to extend to the firm. (Individuals have a line of credit if they have a bank charge card, such as VISA or MasterCard, that extends credit up to a specific limit such as $5,000.) The beauty of a line of credit is that the entrepreneur does not have to negotiate with the bank each time a loan is needed but simply borrows from the account until the agreed-upon limit is reached. For example, if a firm has a line of credit for $75,000 and needs $25,000 to purchase supplies, the entrepreneur would merely sign a promissory note for the $25,000, which is called *taking down* $25,000 of the total line of credit. With a line of credit, the amount taken down does not have to be repaid before additional funds can be borrowed.

Receivable Financing. Accounts receivable is another type of short-term loan granted by commercial banks. Some portion of the sales of most firms is credit rather than cash transactions and, for this reason, is called *accounts receivable*. In a typical accounts receivable loan, the bank will advance the firm 65 to 80 percent of the approved receivables, with repayment made as the accounts are collected. Thus if a firm had $20,000 in accounts receivable, it would be able to borrow $16,000 from the bank. Note that banks will not grant loans based on the total amount of the accounts receivable but only on *approved* receivables. Banks normally do not approve loans based on receivables that are over 90 days old, nor do they grant loans on receivables they consider to be poor risks.

One type of accounts-receivable financing that is used by some firms is factoring. *Factoring* is not an actual loan but the sale of the accounts receivables to a factor—a financial institution that purchases accounts receivables. Factoring is appropriate for a firm that has very few but relatively large customers. Some commercial banks have factoring departments that will approve the buyer's credit before credit is granted. After the sale, the seller will be paid, and the buyer will be notified that payments are to be made to the factor, not to the seller. This procedure is similar to that of accepting major bank credit cards rather than cash as payment for goods or services. With credit cards, the seller receives payment from the bank, and the buyer pays the bank. In both cases the seller receives a discounted payment, with the difference between the discount and the invoice representing the factor's, or the bank's, commission.

Inventory Financing. The remaining short-term loan extended by commercial banks is an inventory loan. An *inventory loan* is secured by a firm's inventory and is generally about 50 percent of the value of the inventory. The inventory loan may be secured with a *blanket lien*, which gives the bank a lien against all the borrower's inventories. *Trust receipts* are another form of security for inventory loans. Trust receipts are generally offered as security for the purchase of easily identifiable and expensive items, like automobiles. In effect, a trust receipt is an instrument stating that the goods are held in trust for the lender and that the proceeds of the sale of the goods must be remitted to the lender.

Long-Term Loans

Long-term loans are loans that are extended for more than one year and that are normally used for the purchase of real-estate and other fixed assets. Loans of this type include equipment loans, equipment leasing, and real-estate loans. Long-term loans are usually repaid in monthly or quarterly installments that include principal and interest, and funds for repayment are derived from the profits of the firm as opposed to short-term loans, which are repaid from cash flow. This point is important. Lenders will scrutinize the pro forma income statement before deciding whether or not to grant a long-term loan, but it is the cash-flow statement they will examine in the case of a short-term loan.

Equipment Loans. *Equipment loans* are long-term loans secured by the equipment being purchased. Typically, the bank will lend 60 to 80 percent of the cost of the equipment, with payments scheduled over the expected usable life of the equipment. Equipment leasing is the fastest-growing financing source. With a lease, the business has the use of the equipment, but the lender maintains title to the equipment. At the end of the lease period, the lessee (the firm leasing the equipment) usually has the right to purchase the equipment.

There are two major types of equipment leases: operating leases and financial leases. In the case of an *operating*, or *service*, *lease*, the lessor provides both the financing and the maintenance. This type of lease is common in computer, office equipment, automobile, or truck leasing. It is important to note that the typical operating lease does not amortize the cost of the equipment. Thus, the operating lease is very much like a short-term rental. In contrast, the *financial,* or *capital, lease,* does not provide for maintenance and is fully amortized. (*Fully amortized* means that the lease payments cover both the cost of the equipment and the interest charges.)

Real-Estate Loan. The final type of long-term loan presented in this section is the real-estate loan. Real-estate loans are written for longer periods of time than the normal equipment loan and may be for as long as twenty-five years. The typical loan is for 75 percent of the market value of the property. The benefit of real estate, and other long-term loans, is that the entrepreneur obtains the use of property and equipment for a relatively small monthly payment. Thus, scarce capital is not tied up. The important point to remember is that the entrepreneur does not need to own the property and equipment but merely have use of it.

Specialized Loans

The final category of commercial bank loans is the specialized loan. A well-known specialized loan is *flooring* or *floor-planning.* Flooring is typically used by retailers of so-called big-ticket items such as large appliances (refrigerators, washers, dryers, and televisions), boats, mobile homes, and automobiles. In flooring, the bank finances the firm's purchase of the expensive goods but maintains a security interest until the merchandise is sold and the loan paid off.

A similar type of specialized financing is *indirect collection,* which is also used for big-ticket items. Indirect-collection is a type of accounts-receivable financing, whereby the bank advances 70 to 80 percent of the value of each item when it is sold. The retailer repays the advance plus interest as the purchaser pays each installment.

Bank-Loan Criteria

What do bankers look for before they grant a loan to the startup entrepreneur? Bankers look at four primary items before deciding to extend credit to a customer.

1. ***Good character.*** Does the borrower have a good credit history? Individuals with a past history of paying off loans on time have a much better chance of obtaining loans than do individuals with poor credit histories. An individual's credit record includes a history of payments of credit cards, personal loans, revolving credit with retail stores, utility bills, and, if the individual has been in business before, repayments of business debts.
2. ***Capacity to repay.*** Good character is necessary, but the individual also must have the capacity to pay off the loan. The cash-flow budget may be an excellent indicator of capacity.
3. ***Collateral.*** Collateral is often a prime factor in the determination of whether a loan will be granted or not. If there is sufficient marketable collateral, the chances of securing a loan are greatly increased.
4. ***Appropriate purpose.*** Bankers like to know that the funds are earmarked for a particular purpose, like financing a seasonal inventory buildup or purchasing specific

raw materials or equipment, and not "to pay bills." Before asking for a loan, the entrepreneur should specify exactly how the money is going to be used.

There are three important facts entrepreneurs need to know when considering commercial banks as a source of financing. First, banks are the most frequent source of temporary funds for the small business; therefore, entrepreneurs need to know what a bank looks for in a loan application and then attempt to provide that information. Second, startup entrepreneurs may have better luck with a small bank than a large bank. The small startup operation means very little to a large bank, but many local small banks give preference to local small businesses in their immediate area. Finally, there are some banks that will not lend money for startups (see The Inside View 10-3). Startup entrepreneurs must recognize this and look for banks that have shown an interest in startups.

SMALL BUSINESS ADMINISTRATION

The Small Business Administration (SBA) is a federal agency created in 1953 to provide small businesses with both advice and financial aid. The SBA provides advice through numerous workshops, publications, and personal counseling (for more about advice, see Chapter 4) and financial aid through either direct or indirect loans. A *direct loan* is one made by the SBA; however, very few are actually granted. *Indirect loans* are those actually granted by another financial institution, normally a bank, and guaranteed by the SBA.

10-3 *The Inside View*

NO STARTUP ENTERPRISES ACCEPTED HERE

Many banks will not lend money for startups in some industries like restaurants. Kevin Hay and two friends launched a new restaurant in Ann Arbor, Michigan, with $28,000 from their own savings after being turned down by virtually every bank in Ann Arbor. The Southside Grille quickly became one of the most popular restaurants in town with revenues of $450,000. Did this success change the attitude of the local bankers?

Kevin Hay went back to the banks with plans to open a second restaurant. He proposed putting up $100,000 and borrowing $100,000, but again he was turned down. Undaunted, he raised capital from friends and relatives, got a low-interest loan from a community organization, and now has a second successful restaurant.[4]

Before seeking financial assistance from the SBA, the entrepreneur should recognize what the SBA is attempting to accomplish. First, the SBA's goal is to help small businesses by providing management assistance and aid at little or no cost to the business. Second, the SBA wants to help as many businesses as possible, and this means that the quantity and quality of help extended to any single business is somewhat limited. Finally, the SBA, through its social mandate, makes a special effort to provide help in economically depressed areas, in cleaning up the environment, and in aiding businesses owned by minorities and females.

About 90 percent of the SBA's loan activity involves indirect loans through bank participation, or guaranteed loans. Since the SBA is not in competition with local lending institutions, it will not consider bank participation until the entrepreneur has been turned down by at least two banks. Thus, to be considered by the SBA, the small business must be unable to obtain local financing. This fact should give the startup entrepreneur reason to stop and reflect on the wisdom of starting a new business. In effect, he or she cannot obtain a loan because the entrepreneur is viewed as too risky by individuals and institutions in the business of judging risk. It is true that banks and bankers have been wrong in the past, but the entrepreneur should at least consider the reasons for rejection.

Even if the entrepreneur has been turned down by the banks, the SBA will not automatically consider a loan guarantee. Before participating in a bank loan, the SBA expects startup entrepreneurs to contribute 50 percent of the startup capital from their own funds, although there are exceptions to this rule. In addition, the SBA will want collateral, and this may mean the entrepreneur's own assets, such as his or her home or other real and personal property. The SBA also expects the loan applicant to have a good credit rating and the capability to succeed.

Forms Required by SBA

If the entrepreneur wishes to apply to the SBA for a loan or loan guarantee, he or she must remember that the SBA is a large bureaucratic organization requiring a lot of paperwork and, as such, moves slowly. The extensive paperwork required by the SBA includes the following:

Loan application—SBA form (see Appendix B)
Personal history of principals—SBA form (see Figure 10.2)
Personal financial statement—SBA form
Current balance sheet
Pro forma income statement for one year
Business plan
Business lease and terms (if applicable)
Federal tax returns (previous two years)
Profit and loss statements of business to be purchased (if applicable)
Proposed bill of sale and schedule of inventory, equipment, furniture, and fixtures to be purchased with the loan

Two things should be evident from the foregoing: First, the entrepreneur must really want to go into business to be willing to fill out all the necessary forms. Second,

FIGURE 10.2
Personal Financial Statement

OMB Approval No. 3245–0188
Exp. Date: 10–31–87

PERSONAL FINANCIAL STATEMENT

As of ____________________ 19 _____

Complete this form if 1) a sole proprietorship by the proprietor; 2) a partnership by each partner; 3) a corporation by each officer and each stockholder with 20% or more ownership; 4) any other person or entity providing a guaranty on the loan.

Name ____________________ Residence Phone ____________________

Residence Address ____________________

City, State, & Zip ____________________

Business Name of Applicant/Borrower ____________________

ASSETS	(Omit Cents)	LIABILITIES	(Omit Cents)
Cash on hand & in Banks	$	Accounts Payable	$
Savings Accounts		Notes Payable (to Bk & Others (Describe in Section 2)	
IRA		Installment Account (Auto) Mo. Payments $	
Accounts & Notes Receivable (Describe in Section 6)		Installment Account (Other) Mo. Payments $	
Life Insurance—Cash Surrender Value Only		Loans on Life Insurance	
Stocks and Bonds (Describe in Section 3)		Mortgages on Real Estate (Describe in Section 4)	
Real Estate (Describe in Section 4)		Unpaid Taxes (Describe in Section 7)	
Automobile—Present Value		Other Liabilities (Describe in Section 8)	
Other Personal Property (Describe in Section 5)		Total Liabilities	
Other Assets (Describe in Section 6)		Net Worth	
Total	$	Total	$

Section 1. Source of Income		Contingent Liabilities	
Salary	$	As Endorser or Co-Maker	$
Net Investment Income		Legal Claims & Judgments	
Real Estate Income		Provision for Fed Income Tax	
Other Income (Describe)*		Other Special Debt	

Description of Items Listed in Section I ____________________

*(Alimony or child support payments need not be disclosed in "Other Income" unless it is desired to have such payments counted toward total income.)

Section 2. Notes Payable to Banks and Others

Name & Address of Noteholder	Original Balance	Current Balance	Payment Amount	Terms (Monthly-etc.)	How Secured or Endorsed—Type of Collateral

SBA Form 413 (10-86) Use 11-84 edition until exhausted Refer to SOP 50 10

(Response is required to obtain a benefit)

Section 3. Stocks and Bonds: (*Use separate sheet if necessary*)

No. of Shares	Names of Securities	Cost	Market Value Quotation/Exchange	Date Amount

Section 4. Real Estate Owned. (*List each parcel separately. Use supplemental sheets if necessary. Each sheet must be identified as a supplement to this statement and signed*).

Address—Type of property	Title is in name of	Date Purchased	Original Cost	Present Value	Mortgage Balance	Amount of Payment	Status of Mortgage

Section 5. Other Personal Property. (*Describe, and if any is mortgaged, state name and address of mortgage holder and amount of mortgage, terms of payment, and if delinquent, describe delinquency.*

Section 6. Other Assets, Notes & Accounts Receivable (Describe)

Section 7. Unpaid Taxes. (*Describe in detail, as to type, to whom payable, when due, amount, and what, if any, property the tax lien attaches*)

Section 8. Other Liabilities. (*Describe in detail*)

Section 9. Life Insurance Held (*Give face amount of policies—name of company and beneficiaries*)

SBA/Lender is authorized to make all inquiries deemed necessary to verify the accuracy of the statements made herein and to determine my/our creditworthiness.

(I) or (We) certify the above and the statements contained in the schedules herein are a true and accurate statement of (my) or (our) financial condition as of the date stated herein. This statement is given for the purpose of: (*Check one of the following*)

- ☐ Inducing S.B.A. to grant a loan as requested in the application, to the individual or firm whose name appears herein.
- ☐ Furnishing a statement of (my) or (our) financial condition, pursuant to the terms of the guaranty executed by (me) or (us) at the same time S.B.A. granted a loan to the individual or firm, whose name appears herein.

Signature | Signature | Date

SOCIAL SECURITY NO. | SOCIAL SECURITY NO.

SBA Form 413 (10-86)

*U. S. GOVERNMENT PRINTING OFFICE:1986- 716-533

the importance of planning through the use of past and pro forma financial statements cannot be overemphasized.

If the entrepreneur qualifies and wishes to pursue a loan or loan guarantee from the SBA, the good news is that the interest rates are set by Congress, and they are usually lower than bank rates. The entrepreneur can increase his or her chances of obtaining favorable results from the SBA by remembering three points:

1. The loan request should be for a relatively small amount.
2. Fill out all forms carefully, completely, and correctly.
3. Emphasize political considerations: Are there female or minority founders? Is the proposed business located in an economically depressed area? Is the business engaged in cleaning up the environment?

In spite of the paperwork, the SBA has been the favorite source of startup capital for many enterprises who may not otherwise have been able to obtain capital. SBA offices are located in almost every major city in the United States, and their locations can be found in the telephone directory under Federal Government. In addition, a list of the state headquarters is given in an appendix at the end of Chapter 4.

SMALL BUSINESS INVESTMENT COMPANIES

Small Business Investment Companies (SBIC) and Minority Enterprise Small Business Investment Companies (MESBIC) were set up by the federal government with the objective of increasing the number of private companies willing to invest in small businesses. Both SBICs and MESBICs operate along the lines of venture-capital firms, and the resources of the firms are augmented by federal loan programs. Both are licensed and regulated by the Small Business Administration. SBICs authorized by an act of Congress in 1958, must invest only in small businesses, making either an equity investment or a long-term (five years or more) loan. However, the investment in a single firm is limited to 20 percent of the SBIC's combined capital.

In 1969, the SBA, in cooperation with the U.S. Department of Commerce, created Minority Enterprise Small Business Investment Companies, or 301(d), licensees. MESBICs must make all their investments to minority entrepreneurs, including blacks, Hispanics, Indians, and Eskimos. More than 50 percent of the business must be owned by a minority or a socially and economically disadvantaged American. By law, a MESBIC may not invest more than 30 percent of its capital in a single firm.

SBIC and MESBIC Investors

SBICs and MESBICs are formed by relatively wealthy individuals, corporations, or financial institutions, although a few are publicly owned. They must be privately capitalized with at least $500,000, but once capitalized, they are eligible for three to four dollars in SBA funding for every dollar of private capital. Obviously the leverage potential is what makes them attractive to investors and a fine source of startup capital (see The Inside View 10-4).

Like venture-capital groups, individual SBICs and MESBICs tend to concentrate their investments in a relatively small geographic or industrial area. Some specialize

10-4 **The Inside View**

THE SBIC 100

Like their better-known counterparts, the Fortune 500, even SBICs have their own rankings. The top 100 SBICs and MESBICs invested a total of $558.2 million last year in 2,894 different ventures for an average investment of $192,875. Fifty-five percent of the total invested was in the form of debt, while 45 percent was in equity.

Bank-affiliated SBICs led by Citicorp Capital Ltd., invested $262.6 million in 603 ventures, or almost 47 percent of the total invested. There were 17 MESBICs among the top 100, an increase of 2 from the previous year.[5]

in the entertainment industry, others in aerospace, and others in health-related fields. Most prefer to invest in expanding businesses rather than in startups, but some prefer the startup enterprise. Generally, SBICs and MESBICs expect better than a 15 percent compounded annual rate of return.

A directory of the over three hundred SBICs and MESBICs is available from local SBA offices, or interested individuals can write to the following organization:

National Association of Small Business Investment Co.
1156 Fifteenth Street, N.W.
Washington, DC 20005

The 28-page directory *(The Directory of Operating Small Business Investment Companies)* costs $1.00 and provides the location, investment policies, industry perference, and financing limits of each investment company.

TRADE FINANCING

Trade financing, like debt financing, is essentially the buying of materials, merchandise, or equipment on credit. Typically, most entrepreneurs think of trade credit simply as requesting suppliers to extend terms and do not consider trade credit as a source of funds. Although not a direct source of funds, trade credit does alleviate the need to find additional funds and, as such, should be part of a firm's total funding plans. For example, the owner of a startup mail-order business asked her major supplier, a printing firm, to waive its normal cash-on-delivery policy and wait 90 days for payment. She was then able to use her limited cash to pay for the postage and mailing of the catalogs, and to pay the printer from sales. Without the printer's trade credit, the business may not have gotten off the ground.

When asking for unusual terms from a major supplier, entrepreneurs should show the supplier the business plan, explain the business to the supplier, and solicit his or her help in the startup. In many cases, suppliers remember the problems they had with obtaining startup financing. Depending on the entrepreneur's credit rating, some suppliers may be persuaded to extend credit on items such as inventory, furniture, fixtures, and equipment. For example, purchasing equipment through trade credit usually requires a down payment of 20 to 30 percent, with the remainder paid in monthly installments over a one- to two-year period.

LEASING

Leasing is the fastest-growing source of financing in the United States and is a long-term agreement to rent equipment, land, buildings, or any other asset. With leasing, the user (lessee) makes periodic payments to the owner (lessor) of the asset. The lessee has almost all of the benefits of ownership without the higher outlay of funds normally required in purchasing the asset.

Advantages of Leasing

Leasing affords the startup firm several advantages. First, leasing does not require a down payment, whereas securing a loan to make purchases often requires a 20- to 25-percent down payment. Some leasing companies do require an advance payment or a security deposit, but others offer 100 percent financing if the lessee's credit is good. Another advantage is that the total cost of leasing may be lower than the purchase price because the leasing company can borrow at a lower rate than the startup firm and may pass these savings on to the lessee.

Since many leasing companies are affiliated with large major banks, manufacturers, or insurance companies, they have better access to financial markets than smaller firms, and as a result they can borrow at much lower rates. In addition, these firms can buy equipment at lower prices because not only do they have greater buying power, they also purchase in greater quantities. The larger leasing firms can also take advantage of depreciation deductions that would not be available to a startup firm.

Startup firms also benefit from a lower periodic payment when they lease, since payments may be spread over a longer period than a loan would permit. The leasing firm probably has more knowledge of the equipment and its maintenance. With this knowledge, the lessor can provide excellent technical advice on which equipment is best suited to the startup firm's operations and can help in setting up maintenance schedules.

The remaining advantage of leasing is that leasing reduces the risk of obsolescence. For example, if a startup firm purchased a computer that was made obsolete through rapid growth of the firm or through technical improvements, the firm simply allows the lease to expire and leases a computer that is better suited to its needs. The same applies to a construction firm that needs heavy equipment for a construction project but does not wish to be saddled with the payments, or the equipment, after the project is completed. The short-term lease alleviates this problem.

Disadvantages of Leasing

Certainly leasing is not always advantageous to the lessee. One of the disadvantages is that the lessee loses certain tax advantages that go with ownership. However, if the lessee cannot take advantage of the available tax advantages because the startup firm does not have sufficient tax liabilities, then this disadvantage is negated.

A second disadvantage is that the lessee loses the economic benefit of the asset at the end of the lease. With many leases, the lessor retains ownership of the asset at the end of the lease period. Since lease payments are calculated to provide payment for the equipment minus any salvage value at the end of the lease period, the residual reverts to the lessor if the market value is higher than the estimated salvage value.

The remaining disadvantage is that a lease is a legal obligation that cannot be cancelled just because a project is completed earlier than expected or because the need for equipment never materialized. The legal obligation means that payments must be made on the lease for the entire lease period and that failure to continue payments can force a firm into bankruptcy.

Startup entrepreneurs should carefully consider all the advantages and disadvantages before deciding whether or not a lease is the best means of financing. If it is likely that the asset will be used for its entire life, leasing will probably not be the best choice. Obviously, if it is not likely that the asset will be used over its entire life, then leasing makes sense.

VENTURE CAPITAL

There is a mystique surrounding venture capital that all entrepreneurs must do is send their business plan to a venture capitalist and the startup money they need will arrive in the return mail. In fact, most venture-capital firms do not provide funds for startups, and few will provide funds based primarily on a business plan. Despite the common belief that venture capitalists are able to spot profitable deals, some have overlooked several lucrative opportunities (see The Inside View 10-5).

The venture-capital industry consists of firms that manage risk capital for other investors, including individuals and corporations. Venture-capital firms are willing to invest in companies that have more risk than that most individuals are willing to take, but individuals are willing to spread their risk in a group of firms. Managers of venture-capital firms are individuals who are able to evaluate risky propositions. In return for evaluating and taking risk, venture capitalists are looking for very high returns. Usually the objective of a venture-capital firm is to help a company grow very rapidly and then sell out. This usually means that a firm accepting venture-capital funds must be willing to go public or be acquired by a bigger firm.

Venture-capital firms usually specialize in particular industries. Some invest in startup firms, and others only invest after startup, when prospects for high growth are present. Before investing funds in a firm, venture capitalists look for experienced management, preferably in a high-technology industry, a growth industry, or an essential-services industry. Investments in retail operations, however, are practically zero. Venture capitalists can provide guidance in marketing and product development as well

10-5 The Inside View

VENTURE CAPITALISTS DO MAKE MISTAKES

Venture capitalists realize that they do not always see tomorrow's best bet when they read the business plans of some startup entrepreneurs. For example, venture capitalist Jacqueline Morby was just not impressed by an IBM clone and turned down an opportunity to invest in Osborne: "I could have made 100 times my money," she recalled with chagrin. In the case of another high-tech startup, Steven Merril—along with eighty other venture capitalists—passed up Printronix, Inc. and lost an opportunity for the 20 to 1 return that was realized by those few intrepid venture capitalists who did take the risk.

Bank of America's venture group turned down Tandem Computer: "They just didn't understand what a fail-safe computer that doesn't lose information would mean for transaction-oriented use." For that lack of understanding, Bank of America and other venture capitalists lost the chance to own stock worth $32 per share that they could have purchased for only six cents.

The list goes on and on, including such well-known firms as Federal Express, Seagate Technology, and Daisy Systems, where the returns to the astute venture capitalist have been as much as 100 to 1. On why some great ideas are overlooked one venture capitalist said, "I've hit more than my share, and I've blown more than my share."[6]

as additional financing and management consultation to help the firm during its high-growth period. The startup entrepreneur must realize that there is a potential conflict with the venture capitalist: Typically venture capitalists are more interested in the short-term growth of the firm, because they want to cash in their investment in four to seven years. On the other hand, the entrepreneur may wish to build a business that will produce substantial income for a long time.

Approaching Venture-Capital Firms

Should the startup entrepreneur approach a venture-capital firm for funds? The answer is an unqualified yes if:

1. The entrepreneur is willing to offer an equity investment.
2. The prospects are excellent for extremely rapid growth.
3. The startup is of the correct size (neither too large nor too small).

4. The venture-capital firm specializes in the area the entrepreneur is planning to enter.
5. The entrepreneur plans to make the firm's stock liquid within five to ten years.

If the entrepreneur can answer yes to these five questions, then how does he or she find the venture-capital firm likely to be interested in his or her firm? Among the best sources of help in locating a venture capitalist are the entrepreneur's accountant or lawyer or other entrepreneurs who are already in the same or similar business. These individuals can introduce the entrepreneur to the venture capitalist, who will expect to receive a copy of a business plan.

Lacking a personal introduction, the entrepreneur can always send his or her business plan directly to the venture capitalist. This method does not have a high probability of success; however, it is better than doing nothing and missing the chance to obtain the capital needed to start a firm.

Venture List

Each year *Venture* publishes a list of the top 100 venture-capital firms. The list, accompanied by articles on entrepreneur–venture-capitalist relationship, shows the name and location of the venture-capital firm, the size in total investments and number of deals, and whether or not the firm invests in startup, later-stage, or follow-on investments. In 1986, for example, the leading startup investment-capital firm was Edwards Capital Company of New York. Edwards, which invested in 457 startups, was far ahead of the second-place firm, Transportation Capital Corporation, which negotiated 102 deals.[7] In addition, *Venture* also publishes *The Venture Capital Directory* biannually. Some of the firms that invest in startups are listed in Appendix A at the end of this chapter.

FRANCHISORS

In 1987, a record number of franchised establishments (352,495) opened their doors. Franchisors are learning to fuel this growth by helping entrepreneurs locate financing for what, in some cases, are very costly startups; with those in the fast-food and hotel chains among the most expensive. The lowest cost of opening a Hampton Inn, for example, was about $2.3 million, and the lowest cost of opening a popular McDonald's, about $340,500. Other franchises are in the same range, with an Econo Lodge requiring $1.8 million and a Jack-in-the-Box restaurant costing $306,300 to start. Fortunately, other franchises are very inexpensive to start, with Packy the Shipper and Stork News requiring no startup capital at all. Nevertheless, the cost of starting most popular franchises is in the $50,000 to $400,000 range.[8]

Given such high startup costs, many would-be franchisees have a difficult time finding necessary capital. Franchisors are realizing that they can help promote the growth of their chains by helping potential franchisees locate the capital, and many lending institutions are realizing that franchises are potentially profitable lending opportunities. The needs of these three groups are being met more often now as lenders work with franchisors. For example, Citizens and Southern National Bank has a separate bank division for franchised businesses. Credit and leasing companies, such as Great Western, Westinghouse Credit, and General Electric Credit, are also providing capital and leasing arrangements especially for franchise chains.[9]

Many franchisors will finance 60 to 70 percent of the total startup costs. Franchisors also provide help by guaranteeing bank loans that the franchisee may have been unable to obtain without the financial strength of the franchisor.

As the foregoing examples indicate, locating startup capital to open a franchise business may now be much easier, given the common needs of the franchisors, franchisees, and lending institutions. In their desire to expand their franchise, many franchisors have developed the capital backing that helps potential franchisees acquire necessary startup capital.

MISCELLANEOUS SOURCES

There are several other financing sources available to the startup entrepreneur, including consumer finance companies, life-insurance companies, state and local governments, individual venture capitalists (sometimes known as "angels"), and credit cards. In this section the role of each of these sources in providing startup capital will be described.

Consumer Finance Companies

Consumer finance companies are known for their activities in granting consumer loans at rates higher than those of commercial banks, but they also will lend funds based on personal property, accounts receivable, and inventory, and some finance companies specialize in factoring. Sometimes the rates are lower than commercial bank rates. For example, when Pacific Envelope Company wanted to purchase some used production equipment for $400,000, the firm's bank would finance only 80 percent of the purchase price at a floating rate of $1\frac{1}{2}$ points over the prime rate, the rate banks charge their "best" customers. After shopping around, Bob Cashman, the firm's president, was able to borrow the full $400,000 with a fixed rate of 11 percent from C.I.T. Corporation, a consumer finance company.[10] This example indicates that entrepreneurs should shop around for their capital because unusual sources may have some excellent deals for them.

Life-Insurance Companies

Life-insurance companies are not major sources of capital for startup firms, but they have purchased small, privately placed bond and convertible bond issues. Insurance companies have huge amounts of cash to invest, and they look for excellent returns on their investments. Although they tend to be very-low-profile investors, insurance companies do purchase privately placed bonds and convertible bonds. Normally, they will purchase only through an investment banker and rarely have any direct contact with the entrepreneur until the complete financing package is ready to be closed. An added advantage for those lucky enough to obtain one of these loans is that the interest rates are usually lower than those of bank loans.[11]

State and Local Governments

State and local governments have also entered the financing act by providing capital for homegrown companies. State and local governments understand two important facts about helping small startup firms: First, small firms provide the majority of new jobs in their area, and, second, small homegrown firms tend to stay put. Thus, new firms provide jobs that tend to stay within the local community. In recognition of these facts, over half the states have formed business and industrial development corporations, sometimes called *bidcos*, whose objective is to help finance firms that have promise but are too risky for banks and do not have enough growth potential to attract venture capitalists.

Some states, like Maryland, concentrate on helping minority, women, and handicapped entrepreneurs set up franchised businesses. Others, like Pennsylvania, Ohio, and Massachusetts, concentrate on funding technology firms.[12] For example, Pennsylvania set up the Ben Franklin Partnership, which provided almost $80 million to state-based technology projects. Still other states, like Michigan and California, attempt to spur growth by providing seed financing. Although seed financing does not have a precise definition, these states are providing the initial backing for product innovators at their earliest stages.

As more and more states form bidcos, entrepreneurs have another source of financing for their startup firms. To find out whether or not their state or local government has a bidco, interested entrepreneurs can look under the name of their local or state government in their local directory.

Angels

For many startup entrepreneurs, informal investors, also known as *angels*, represent the best source of capital. Angels create an informal venture-capital market that ". . . is composed of a diverse and diffuse population of individuals of means, many of whom have created their own successful ventures."[13] These individuals tend to be self-made entrepreneurs who wish to put capital back into the system that helped them. The typical angel has substantial business and financial experience and a net worth of about $1 million. There are about 250,000 angels in the United States, and they have invested about $50 billion in startup and small-growth firms.

How do investors find firms in which to invest without being subjected to requests from hundreds of entrepreneurs? In some areas, venture-capital networks (VCN) have been formed to provide a central point of communication between the two groups. Probably the best known VCN is in Durham, New Hampshire. This VCN is directed by Professor William Wetzel, Jr., of the University of New Hampshire, through whose efforts additional VCNs have been formed (see The Inside View 10-6).

In the typical VCN, investors are sent profiles of firms that match the size and industry category in which they have expressed an interest. The investors can then directly contact those that look promising. The typical investment is about $250,000 from three or more private investors. For more information on VCNs, entrepreneurs should write VCN, P.O. Box 882, Durham, NH 03824.

10-6 The Inside View

PIEDMONT ENTREPRENEURS NETWORK

Piedmont Entrepreneurs Network (PEN) is a typical support group formed by entrepreneurs. The purpose of PEN is to encourage and assist entrepreneurial development throughout the Central Piedmont area of North Carolina—an area including the cities of High Point, Greensboro, and Winston–Salem.

To accomplish its purpose, PEN offers programs and services including the following:

1. Monthly meetings that include a presentation by successful entrepreneurs or experts in areas that would be helpful to business owners
2. Newsletters that focus on local entrepreneurial activities and development, and on sources and availability of private, state, and federal funding
3. Membership directories
4. An entrepreneurs' roundtable, consisting of individuals willing to serve as advisors and mentors to startup and/or established businesses
5. An investment contact network

Credit Cards

The use of credit cards was briefly mentioned earlier in the chapter. Although expensive, many entrepreneurs use credit cards as a source of cash when other sources have been reluctant to advance them credit. Entrepreneurs find that obtaining several credit cards is relatively easy and that each card typically allows them to obtain cash advances of $3,000 to $5,000. This ready source of cash has been a major source of capital for many startup firms. In fact, the director of a small-business incubator in Chicago estimates that 50 percent of her 83 tenants use credit cards to finance their companies.[14]

The use of credit cards has two major disadvantages. First, the rate of interest charged on cash advances is relatively high, usually ranging between 18 and 22 percent. Second, there is a high degree of risk involved because the entrepreneur is personally liable for the debt. In spite of these risks, credit cards may be the only available source of cash, and struggling entrepreneurs are willing to accept these risks as the price of launching their dream.

Sale of Stock

The sale of stock, a seemingly obvious source of capital to be included in a chapter on financing sources, is very seldom used to provide startup capital for small firms. Although there have been a few spectacular exceptions, like Genentech, the majority of firms are not able to sell stock until they have some operating history. For this reason, the sale of stock is not presented as a source of financing for the startup firm.

Summary

Locating the capital necessary to start a business can be a demanding and frustrating task. This chapter identifies the basic sources of financing for the startup business. In seeking funds, the entrepreneur must know the difference between permanent and working capital because they do not always come from the same source. Sources of funds may also be classified as either debt or equity.

The entrepreneur's personal funds are a major source of startup capital. The entrepreneur has his or her own savings and other assets, such as stocks, bonds, and real estate, which can be either sold or used as collateral for loans. The entrepreneur may also borrow from his or her bank, credit union, or life-insurance policy. In addition, the entrepreneur can use bootstrap financing as a method of financing a startup.

Friends, relatives, and partners are excellent sources of funds because they increase the assets and funding available to the individual entrepreneur. Commercial banks are a major source of working capital and tend to be willing lenders of funds that are secured by marketable collateral. There are four basic types of bank loans: (1) short-term commercial, (2) long-term, (3) current asset, and (4) specialized.

The Small Business Administration (SBA) is a federal agency created to provide small businesses with both advice and financial aid. Financial aid is provided by means of direct and bank-participation loans. The SBA also licenses and regulates Small Business Investment Companies and Minority Enterprise Small Business Investment Companies—two groups formed to provide capital for startup and small businesses.

The use of trade credit is a source of funds because the extension of credit by a supplier reduces the need for additional funds from another source. Similarly, leasing is a source of funding because, unlike buying, leasing reduces the entrepreneur's need for capital.

The venture-capital industry consists of firms that manage risk capital for other investors. Venture-capital firms generally take an equity interest in ventures that have high risk and the potential for high returns. In addition to providing capital, venture capitalists can provide guidance in marketing and product development as well as management consultation.

Many franchisors are helping to provide startup entrepreneurs with capital through arrangements with major lending institutions. In addition, some franchisors will finance up to 70 percent of the startup costs, and others will provide help by guaranteeing bank loans. There are also several miscellaneous sources of startup capital, including consumer finance companies, life-insurance companies, state and local governments, and angels.

Assembling the Pieces

Like most startup entrepreneurs, Carol and Jacki went to their local banks expecting to obtain their startup capital. Despite the fact that they had five years of business experience in a similar business, their original request for $60,000 (see Chapter 9 for a description of how they arrived at that figure) was rejected by five local banks. One bank finally agreed to loan them $40,000, based on a second mortgage on all of their real property.

After securing initial startup funds, Carol and Jacki needed to resort to short-term borrowing only on two occasions: once for pre-Christmas sales and once for a cash-flow crisis. Despite their initial rejection by the banks, after establishing their business, they never had any additional loan request rejected.

Their financial sources, therefore, came from a $40,000 loan that was based on their real property and their own personal savings. ■

Questions for Review and Discussion

1. What is the difference between permanent and working capital?
2. What are the primary sources of equity funds? How do these sources expect to be rewarded for supplying equity funds?
3. What four basic questions must the entrepreneur answer before starting to seek funds?
4. What is bootstrapping? What is a major problem with bootstrapping?
5. Why should a customer be willing to help finance a startup operation?
6. What is a major risk in obtaining funds from friends and relatives?
7. What are some of the typical short-term loans that are offered by commercial banks?
8. What are the primary differences between operating and financial leases?
9. What are the four primary items bankers look at before extending credit to a customer?
10. What is the SBA attempting to accomplish with its mandate from Congress?
11. Why is leasing more advantageous than buying?
12. Why are venture capitalists willing to accept high risk on startup firms?

Notes

1. Marilyn Pollock, "Financing Your Business," *Venture,* October 1986, p. 24.
2. "Quote of the Month," *Inc.,* September 1986, p. 99.
3. Mary-Margaret Wantuck, "Banks Rush to Serve Smaller Firms," *The Nation's Business,* October 1985, p. 16.
4. Sarah Bartlett, "It Will Get a Bit Easier to Find Startup Cash," *Business Week,* 3 November 1986, pp. 100–104.
5. Michele Fleischer, "More Deals for the Bucks," *Venture,* October 1985, pp. 50–54.
6. Margaret Mahar, "Who's Sorry Now?" *Venture,* August 1986, pp. 30–36.
7. Frances Marshman, "More Capital, Less Risk," *Venture,* August 1987, pp. 36–40.
8. David Roth, "The Secret? Easy Does It," *Venture,* November 1987, pp. 36–47.

9. Ken Condon, ''Financing a Franchise,'' *Inc.*, April 1987, pp. 89–95.
10. ''The Commercial Finance Alternative,'' *Inc.*, August 1986, p. 84.
11. Rachel Meltzer, ''The Private Deals Nobody Talks About,'' *Venture*, September 1986, pp. 100–101.
12. Udayan Gupta, ''States Play Expanding Role in Funding Technology Firms,'' *The Wall Street Journal*, 9 November 1987, p. 29.
13. ''Starting Up Without Borrowing,'' *In Business*, December 1987, p. 48.
14. Buck Brown, ''Companies Stay Afloat By Using Credit Cards,'' *The Wall Street Journal*, 20 May 1988, p. 29.

Appendix A

STARTUP VENTURE-CAPITAL DIRECTORY

The following list of venture-capital firms includes those appearing in the December 1987 issue of *Venture*. *Venture* publishes a biannual venture-capital directory that ". . . is designed to put qualified entrepreneurs who need venture financing in touch with venture capitalists." The firms listed all have a preference for startup ventures.

Firm	Geographic Preference	Industry Preference
AVI Management Inc. 3000 Sand Hill Road Bldg. 3, Suite 280 Menlo Park, CA 94025	Far West	Technology, industrial and professional electronics
Advanced Tech. Ventures 10 Post Office Square Suite 970 Boston, MA 02109	None	High technology
Bancboston Ventures 100 Federal Street Boston, MA 02110	U.S.A.	High technology, health care, and consumer products
Crosspoint Venture 1951 Landings Drive Mountain View, CA 94043	Southwest & Far West	Medical, telecommunications, software, & semiconductor devices
Edison Venture Fund 90 Nassau Street Princeton, NJ 08542	Northeast & Mid-Atlantic	No preference
IEG Venture Management 401 North Michigan Ave. Suite 2020 Chicago, IL 60611	Midwest	Technology-based companies
Merrill Lynch Venture 717 Fifth Avenue New York, NY 10022	No preference	No preference

Firm	Geographic Preference	Industry Preference
Corning Venture 125 Pearl Street Boston, MA 02110	No preference	Technology, medical
New Enterprise Assoc. 1119 St. Paul Street Baltimore, MD 21202	No preference	Technology, medical & specialty retailing
Orien Ventures, Inc. 36 Grove Street New Canaan, CT 06840	No preference	Biotechnology, advanced materials, & communications
Senmed Venture Group 100 Techne Center Drive Milford, OH 45150	No preference	Medical technology
S/L Health Care Ventures 1250 Broadway New York, NY 10001	No preference	Health care
Venture Founders Corp. One Cranberry Hill Lexington, MA 02173	Northeast, Southeast, Europe	Biotechnology, information systems, industrial products
TA Associates 45 Milk Street Boston, MA 02109	No preference	Electronics, software, & process control
Warburg, Pincus Ventures 466 Lexington Avenue New York, NY 10017	No preference	No preference
U.S. Venture Partners 2180 Sand Hill Road Menlo Park, CA 94025	Northeast & Far West	High technology, specialty retailing, consumer products
Wood River Capital 645 Madison Avenue New York, NY 10022	No preference	No preference

Appendix B

U.S. Small Business Administration:

APPLICATION FOR BUSINESS LOAN
(*See pages 281–283*)

OMB Approval No. 3245-0016
Expiration Date: 10-31-87

U.S. Small Business Administration

Application for Business Loan

Applicant	Full Address			
Name of Business				Tax I.D. No.
Full Street Address				Tel. No. (Inc. A/C)
City	County	State	Zip	Number of Employees (Including subsidiaries and affiliates)
Type of Business			Date Business Established	At Time of Application ________
Bank of Business Account and Address				If Loan is Approved ________ Subsidiaries or Affiliates ________ (Separate from above)

Use of Proceeds: (Enter Gross Dollar Amounts Rounded to Nearest Hundreds)	Loan Requested	SBA USE ONLY
Land Acquisition		
New Construction/ Expansion/Repair		
Acquisition and/or Repair of Machinery and Equipment		
Inventory Purchase		
Working Capital (Including Accounts Payable)		
Acquisition of Existing Business		
Payoff SBA Loan		
Payoff Bank Loan (Non SBA Associated)		
Other Debt Payment (Non SBA Associated)		
All Other		
Total Loan Requested		
Term of Loan		

Collateral

If your collateral consists of (A) Land and Building, (D) Accounts Receivable and/or (E) Inventory, fill in the appropriate blanks. If you are pledging (B) Machinery and Equipment, (C) Furniture and Fixtures, and/or (F) Other, please provide an itemized list (labeled Exhibit A) that contains serial and identification numbers for all articles that had an original value greater than $500. Include a legal description of Real Estate offered as collateral.

	Present Market Value	Present Loan Balance	SBA Use Only Collateral Valuation
A. Land and Building	$	$	$
B. Machinery & Equipment			
C. Furniture & Fixtures			
D. Accounts Receivable			
E. Inventory			
F. Other			
Totals	$	$	$

PREVIOUS SBA OR OTHER GOVERNMENT FINANCING: If you or any principals or affiliates have ever requested Government Financing, complete the following:

Name of Agency	Original Amount of Loan	Date of Request	Approved or Declined	Balance	Current or Past Due
	$			$	
	$			$	

SBA Form 4 (2-85) Previous Editions Obsolete

INDEBTEDNESS: Furnish the following information on all installment debts, contracts, notes, and mortgages payable. Indicate by an asterisk (*) items to be paid by loan proceeds and reason for paying same (present balance should agree with latest balance sheet submitted).

To Whom Payable	Original Amount	Original Date	Present Balance	Rate of Interest	Maturity Date	Monthly Payment	Security	Current or Past Due
	$		$			$		
	$		$			$		
	$		$			$		
	$		$			$		

MANAGEMENT (Proprietor, partners, officers, directors and all holders of outstanding stock — 100% of ownership must be shown). Use separate sheet if necessary.

Name and Social Security Number	Complete Address	% Owned	*Military Service		*Race	*Sex
			From	To		

* This data is collected for statistical purposes only. It has no bearing on the credit decision to approve or decline this application.

ASSISTANCE List the name(s) and occupation(s) of any who assisted in preparation of this form, other than applicant.

Name and Occupation	Address	Total Fees Paid	Fees Due
Name and Occupation	Address	Total Fees Paid	Fees Due

Signature of Preparers if Other Than Applicant

THE FOLLOWING EXHIBITS MUST BE COMPLETED WHERE APPLICABLE. ALL QUESTIONS ANSWERED ARE MADE A PART OF THE APPLICATION.

For Guaranty Loans please provide an original and one copy (Photocopy is Acceptable) of the Application Form, and all Exhibits to the participating lender. For Direct Loans submit one original copy of application and Exhibits to SBA.

Submit SBA Form 1261 (Statements Required by Laws and Executive Orders). This form must be signed and dated by each Proprietor, Partner, Principal or Guarantor.

1. Submit SBA Form 912 (Personal History Statement) for each person e.g. owners, partners, officers, directors, major stockholders, etc.; the instructions are on SBA Form 912.

2. Furnish a signed current personal balance sheet (SBA Form 413 may be used for this purpose) for each stockholder (with 20% or greater ownership), partner, officer, and owner. Social Security number should be included on personal financial statement. Label this Exhibit B.

3. Include the statements listed below: 1, 2, 3 for the last three years; also 1, 2, 3, 4 dated within 90 days of filing the application; and statement 5, if applicable. This is Exhibit C (SBA has Management Aids that help in the preparation of financial statements.) All information must be signed and dated.

1. Balance Sheet
2. Profit and Loss Statement
3. Reconciliation of Net Worth
4. Aging of Accounts Receivable and Payable
5. Earnings projections for at least one year where financial statements for the last three years are unavailable or where requested by District Office.
   (If Profit and Loss Statement is not available, explain why and substitute Federal Income Tax Forms.)

4. Provide a brief history of your company and a paragraph describing the expected benefits it will receive from the loan. Label it Exhibit D.

ALL EXHIBITS MUST BE SIGNED AND DATED BY PERSON SIGNING THIS FORM.

SBA Form 4 (2-85) Previous Editions Obsolete

5. Provide a brief description of the educational, technical and business background for all the people listed under Management. Please mark it Exhibit E.

6. Do you have any co-signers and/or guarantors for this loan? If so, please submit their names, addresses and personal balance sheet(s) as Exhibit F.

7. Are you buying machinery or equipment with your loan money? If so, you must include a list of the equipment and cost as quoted by the seller and his name and address. This is Exhibit G.

8. Have you or any officers of your company ever been involved in bankruptcy or insolvency proceedings? If so, please provide the details as Exhibit H. If none, check here: ☐ Yes ☐ No

9. Are you or your business involved in any pending lawsuits? If yes, provide the details as Exhibit I. If none, check here: ☐ Yes ☐ No

10. Do you or your spouse or any member of your household, or anyone who owns, manages, or directs your business or their spouses or members of their households work for the Small Business Administration, Small Business Advisory Council, SCORE or ACE, any Federal Agency, or the participating lender? If so, please provide the name and address of the person and the office where employed. label this Exhibit J. If none, check here: ☐ Yes ☐ No

11. Does your business, its owners or majority stockholders own or have a controlling interest in other businesses? If yes, please provide their names and the relationship with your company along with a current balance sheet and operating statement for each. This should be Exhibit K.

12. Do you buy from, sell to, or use the services of any concern in which someone in your company has a significant financial interest? If yes, provide details on a separate sheet of paper labeled Exhibit L.

13. If your business is a franchise, include a copy of the franchise agreement and a copy of the FTC disclosure statement supplied to you by the Franchisor. Please include it as Exhibit M.

CONSTRUCTION LOANS ONLY

14. Include a separate exhibit (Exhibit N) the estimated cost of the project and a statement of the source of any additional funds.

15. File the necessary compliance document (SBA Form 601).

16. Provide copies of preliminary construction plans and specifications. Include them as Exhibit O. Final plans will be required prior to disbursement.

DIRECT LOANS ONLY

17. Include two bank declination letters with your application. These letters should include the name and telephone number of the persons contacted at the banks, the amount and terms of the loan, the reason for decline and whether or not the bank will participate with SBA. In cities with 200,000 people or less, one letter will be sufficient.

EXPORT LOANS

18. Does your business presently engage in Export Trade?
Check here ☐ Yes ☐ No

19. Do you plan to begin exporting as a result of this loan?
Check here ☐ Yes ☐ No

20. Would you like information on Exporting?
Check here ☐ Yes ☐ No

AGREEMENTS AND CERTIFICATIONS

Agreements of Nonemployment of SBA Personnel: I/We agree that if SBA approves this loan application I/We will not, for at least two years, hire as an employee or consultant anyone that was employed by the SBA during the one year period prior to the disbursement of the loan.

Certification: I/We certify: (a) I/We have not paid anyone connected with the Federal Government for help in getting this loan. I/We also agree to report to the SBA office of the Inspector General, 1441 L Street N.W., Washington, D.C. 20416 any Federal Government employee who offers, in return for any type of compensation, to help get this loan approved.

(b) All information in this application and the Exhibits are true and complete to the best of my/our knowledge and are submitted to SBA so SBA can decide whether to grant a loan or participate with a lending institution in a loan to me/us. I/We agree to pay for or reimburse SBA for the cost of any surveys, title or mortgage examinations, appraisals etc., performed by non-SBA personnel provided I/We have given my/our consent.

I/We understand that I/We need not pay anybody to deal with SBA. I/We have read and understand Form 394 which explains SBA policy on representatives and their fees.

If you make a statement that you know to be false or if you over value a security in order to help obtain a loan under the provisions of the Small Business Act, you can be fined up to $5,000 or be put in jail for up to two years, or both.

If Applicant is a proprietor or general partner, sign below:

By: ______________________________ Date

If Applicant is a Corporation, sign below:

____
Corporate Name and Seal Date

____

By: ______________________________
Signature of President

Attested by: ______________________________
Signature of Corporate Secretary

ALL EXHIBITS MUST BE SIGNED AND DATED BY PERSON SIGNING THIS FORM.

THE CASE OF THE CONFUSED INVESTOR

"All right, now tell me how this idea for a new restaurant came about." Jim Wells sat back in his chair and drew deeply on his pipe. This investment proposal was intriguing. He had received the written proposal a week ago and had analyzed it carefully. It sounded like something new in the restaurant business, and he had thought that there could be nothing new under the sun in that industry. Something about the plan bothered him, but he had been unable to identify a problem or inconsistency. (See Exhibit 1.) That was one of the reasons he had asked to meet with the principals. He had wanted to hear them present the plan, discuss it with them, and learn something about them. It was a shame that only one of the four had shown up. (See Exhibit 2.) He wondered about that. There was another thing that he wondered about: For youngsters putting a project together, they sure had a lot of money up front. He didn't like that.

Jim Wells hadn't become wealthy by putting money into deals that gave returns only to other people. In his sixty-odd years he had retired twice, the last time for good, and for the last ten years had driven his accumulated capital even higher by a series of shrewd investments. One thing he had learned was how to get people to talk. They would give away all kinds of secrets and uncover all kinds of loopholes in their plans if you just let them talk. If a proposal wasn't well planned, that too would come out. Besides, he wanted to know how their minds worked. If they were going to be running a business that he financed, he would need to know how they thought. Still, with all his experience, there was something about this plan that did not seem to fit.

Ron Glass sat forward in his chair and took a moment to collect his thoughts. He was on firm ground now, he knew. The logic behind this business plan was impeccable. He and his three partners had painstakingly developed every aspect. The concept was destined to make money—big money. All they had to do was persuade a few well-heeled investors to put their money in it. The principals knew that Wells could easily take the entire investment if he wanted. Glass had prepared for this. He could deliver a twenty-minute speech off the cuff. That's why his three partners had sent him to this meeting alone. They didn't come across as smoothly as he did, and they knew it. Glass was the salesman in the group. He took one more breath and launched into his presentation.

"In the last five years, nostalgia has taken over the country. Clothing styles, haircuts, convertible cars, you name it, and people are demanding the good things of yesteryear. A very few people have recognized that this can be good for the restaurant business. We can't return to the days of the 5-cent hamburger, but we can give VALUE for money. Fast food was born in the '50s, but it's been inflationed to death in the '80s. Look at a typical hamburger: It starts out with a raw weight of ¼ pound, but it's nowhere near that when it's cooked, despite the fact that it costs two bucks or so. And talk about cooking, they say you can have it your way, but that turns out to be like Henry Ford. He would give you a Model T in any color you wanted as long as it was black. These folks will give you a hamburger any way you like it as long as it's cooked when they want to cook it. That can be anywhere from ten minutes ago to two hours. I'm convinced that some of them even keep cooked burgers overnight. At least they taste like it! What do you think people would say if you gave them a burger that was ¼ pound after it was cooked and was cooked to order when they ordered it, and was reasonably priced to boot? They would jump on it, that's what! Add to that the fast-food approach so that they don't have to waste time, and they'll come in droves.

"For icing on the cake, we'll let them have a cold beer or a glass of wine, or whatever they want to drink. If they want Cokes, then we'll give them Cokes, not those fountain

---

This case was prepared by James Carland, JoAnn Carland, and Raymond Crepeau, Western Carolina Univerity. Used by permission.

EXHIBIT 1

Investment Proposal for Ritchie's restaurant

This proposal is offered as a limited partnership between the Developers (General Partners) and up to six qualified limited partners. The Limited Partners will invest up to $300,000, and the General Partners will furnish 100% of the operational needs and expertise to develop the project.

This limited partnership is being offered on a first-come, first-served basis. Approved investors will be required to deposit their contribution simultaneously with the execution of the subscription agreement. The proposal is understood to be for a single restaurant location and not the actual restaurant concept.

The development strategy is based on the remodeling of an existing facility. Allowing for competitive bidding on modifications and improvements, site development should begin 30 to 60 days following execution of the subscription agreement. Total time from agreement to opening date is expected to be 5 to 7 months.

The Developers believe that there is potential to achieve an 18% return on investment for the Limited Partners in addition to a positive cash flow, appreciation in equity, and tax benefits. Net cash flows will be distributed on a 75%/25% basis, with the Limited Partners receiving 75% until such time as their investment is returned. Thereafter, the participation ratio will be 50%/50%.

Source and Use of Development Funds	
Source of Funds	
Limited partners	$300,000
Use of Funds	
Equipment and renovation	$225,000
Utility deposits, licenses, and fees	10,000
Initial salaries	15,000
Initial inventory	10,000
Preopening startup costs	20,000
Opening promotion	10,000
Beginning cash	10,000
Total Uses	$300,000

These results are subject to achieving the projections contained in the five-year forecasts of earnings. Investors should understand the risks associated with this or with any similar investment.

EXHIBIT 2

Resumés for the General Partners

Morris J. Stern

Mr. Stern is the Operations Director for O'Malley's Restaurants. He is the cofounder and developer of O'Malley's. A native of St. Louis, Mr. Stern attended Dade County Junior College. His love of and dedication to the food-service industry dates back over thirteen years, when he began washing dishes and doing some occasional cooking in a small California restaurant. He eventually worked his way up to a cooking position with the Victoria Station chain and from there into upper management. He spent the last six years prior to opening O'Malley's in various management positions with Victoria Station.

Davison M. Johnson

Mr. Johnson is the Food and Beverage Director for O'Malley's Restaurants. He is the cofounder and developer of O'Malley's. Mr. Johnson received a B.A. degree in economics from Emory University and has over ten years of experience in the food-service industry. He spent the eight years prior to opening O'Malley's working his way up the corporate ladder with several national restaurant chains, such as TGI Friday, Bennigan's, Steak and Ale, etc.

Anthony D. McDonald

Mr. McDonald is the Director of Personnel and Human Resources for O'Malley's Restaurants. He graduated from California State University with degrees in hotel and restaurant management and other related management studies. He has received various honors and awards for scholastic achievement. Starting as a part-time cook, he has worked his way up the corporate ladder. Prior to joining O'Malley's, Mr. McDonald spent five years in restaurant management with Victoria Station.

Ronald L. Glass

Mr. Glass is Comptroller for O'Malley's Restaurants. He graduated from Clemson University with a degree in accounting. He has held various management positions with restaurants and other firms and has over ten years of business experience.

drinks made with syrup. We'll give them a real Coke in a glass bottle, the way they used to come. We'll have whatever kind of soda pop they want.

"We're going to throw in an atmosphere. Not that stainless steel and plastic stuff, but a casual, comfortable place with wooden tables and chairs and real upholstered booths. We'll have green plants and wood paneling with lots of brick and soft, natural colors. We'll have young people waiting tables so there's no line to stand in to get your food, and we'll still get them in and out if they're in a hurry. If they want to linger and gab with their friends, we'll have a bar where they can do that, too.

"We'll put some pizzazz in the menu, too! We'll have your hamburger, any way you want it, including mushrooms and pizza burgers if you want, and believe me it will be a VALUE PLUS burger! But we'll have steaks and seafood, too. We'll do this with a daily special so we don't have to stock a lot of food to cover a broad menu. We'll choose something each day based on what looks good at the market, and we'll buy enough for one day at a time. That will be the special of the day. It may be salmon, or rib eyes, or king crab, but it'll be fresh, and it'll be good, and a good buy, too." Ron was hitting his stride now. This was going better than he had expected.

"Slow down a minute!" Wells was beginning to like this young fellow. He was certainly enthusiastic. "Who is it that you're shooting for? Certainly not me, doesn't sound like my kind of place at all." Wells smiled and puffed on his pipe.

"Oh, we're shooting for the baby boomers. Guys who were in high school in the '50s and '60s. They're the largest market these days, and they're the ones who are changing the restaurant business. People have been coming up with all kinds of things to try to make them happy. You know, fries with the skins on, salads with pasta, light foods, sprouts, and all that. We'll give them exactly what they want. We'll have photos on the wall from high school proms and football games—stuff from the '50s. We'll have their kind of music playing and all kinds of memorabilia. We'll get all the pictures and things from the people in the local area, and we'll rotate the stuff. Everyone will want to have a chance to give us something to display."

"Just like the soda fountains, huh? 'Cept with booze and steaks to take the place of malteds and cheeseburgers." Wells chuckled. When he had read the proposal, he had thought there might be a market for this but it would have to be well managed. Those baby-boomer folks might like to talk about their high school days, but their tastes had changed whether they admitted it or not.

"Yeah, but we'll have cheeseburgers and malteds, too, if they want them."

"OK, tell me something about the prices." Wells was beginning to be more intrigued, but he knew that something like this could easily bomb and prices were one place where that could happen.

"Everything will be value plus. Burgers will start at $1.95, and that's for a gourmet burger. We'll go up to $6.95 for the most expensive thing on the menu, except for the daily special. That'll depend on costs for the item that day in the market. We think that may hit $10 or $12 on occasion. But the basic menu, which will have burgers, salads, soups, several different kinds of sandwiches, desserts, and appetizers, will top out at $6.95. The soup will be homemade, a different kind each day, and we'll have a dessert special every day as well. We figure the average ticket will be five bucks at lunch and $7.50 for dinner. A lot of this stuff is in the written proposal, Mr. Wells." (See Exhibit 3.)

"Yeah, well, I'll look that over, but for now I want you to tell me about it." Wells was convinced that such a discussion would point up how well the principals knew their own proposal. "How about the people in this thing? Tell me about them." He drew deeply on the pipe.

"Well, the proposal has a brief resumé on each of us. But, I'll be running the shop while Dave will handle the buying. You know we already have an established restaurant, a traditional one, which we'll keep running. Morris and Tony will be the senior officers, they're the ones that started the first restaurant, and they'll do the planning for us and provide advice and assistance. What do you want to know about us?" This was one area in which Glass was shaky. He really wasn't terribly happy that his partners would be equal owners with himself

EXHIBIT 3

Description of the Operation

Ritchie's has been specifically designed and created to target the 21- to 49-year-old market, which controls two-thirds of disposable income. Demographics indicate that the median age of the population is 30.6 years. This is the generation that was raised on fast food—the "me" generation that wants things their way. Current restaurant themes have left a large gap between fast food and casual adult dining establishments. This gap will be filled by restaurants positioned to appeal to both singles and families alike with high-quality food and drink, served quickly in comfortable surroundings.

Experts say that if the burger market is now $20 billion, gourmet burgers could easily reach 15% of that amount, or $3 billion, allowing for at least 2,500 units at $1 million or more each. At present, this market is highly fragmented, with no major standout. What makes a gourmet burger? Experts say it is the size, quality, and freshness of the meat and cooking to order that makes a burger worthy of the title "gourmet."

Ritchie's will penetrate this market as "the place to go" for good fast food. Emphasis will be placed on unique foods and quick, attentive service. Ritchie's will be that much-needed halfway point between fast food and full-menu theme restaurants, with a strong family appeal as well as the business lunch.

The menu will feature the gourmet burger as well as other proven winners. In addition, so-called trend items will be introduced as the market dictates, i.e., light foods, fajitas, tacos, baked potatoes, etc. The menu will reflect Ritchie's general theme and concept. It will feature old-fashioned quality, with emphasis on "homemade from scratch." It will be billed as "light, continental" and will range in price from $1.95 to $6.95. All entrées will be served with homemade potato chips and a garnish of fresh fruit. Most of the menu will be permanent, with daily or weekly special selections of soups, hamburgers, and sandwiches. The specials will be presented on a large, centrally located chalkboard. These specials create perceived variety by regular customers without necessitating a large permanent menu and corresponding kitchen staff. Beer, wine, and liquor service are important aspects of the concept, but they will not dominate the restaurant. Ritchie's will offer a large selection of imported and domestic beers, house wines, and expertly served mixed drinks.

The critical difference between Ritchie's and its competition will be not only what is served but how it is prepared, cooked, and presented. The limited menu will allow the kitchen staff to concentrate preparation time on fewer items and therefore make all salad dressings from scratch, spend the three hours daily to hand-bread fried cheese, trim and grind fresh hamburger meat, etc. All meats and fresh fish will be broiled over mesquite or similar open flame, reflecting today's healthier trend in cooking. Even potato chips will be sliced from fresh Idaho potatoes and fried on the premises. This menu will be exclusively a "basket or bowl" menu. There will be no plates or dishwashers. There will be only one style dinner bowl, plus forks and spoons, and one style of glass mug, which will require washing.

Surveys show that the largest complaint restaurant customers have is indifferent service. Knowing how important the quality of service is, Ritchie's will place heavy emphasis on employee training. All servers and bartenders must undergo intensive training prior to going on the floor as well as attend periodic classes and training meetings. Service will be attentive, friendly, and quick. Ritchie's will not just preach these philosophies but will live them on a day-to-day basis.

The decor will consist of wood paneling and furniture, and soft, natural colors. Pictures from school proms, pep rallies, homecomings, graduations, and other school and local sports events will be featured. In addition, authentic pictures and replicas from the '50s and '60s will be used. All memorabilia will be taken from the local market area. The entire package will serve to give the customer that friendly, local, "good-old-days" feeling, while placing special emphasis on basic goodness, old-fashioned values, homemade quality, neighborly service, and the gourmet burger.

The Developers believe that the restaurant business is one of long-term success or failure and that word-of-mouth reputation is the only truly successful marketing strategy. Taking care of the customer will not only bring them back but will bring them back with their friends. Ritchie's success will be the result of executing the basics of good food, service, and atmosphere better than the competition. Priority in maintaining customer satisfaction will insure Ritchie's success.

Richie's will allocate 2% of sales to a time-proven in-house promotion plan. The plan will include: complimentary desserts, appetizers, and other food promos given out at server's discretion; participation in community-service activities and fundraising drives; advertising specialties such as matches, bumper stickers, balloons, and T-shirts.

The key to market penetration will be the opening four-day, dry run period. During this time, over 1,000 prominent people from all of the local surrounding businesses and residential communities will be invited for a complimentary meal. This will insure immediate market awareness of Ritchie's as the new place in town.

since he was going to be doing all the work.

"You plan to coordinate buying with the existing restaurant, is that right? But the two will be separate companies, and you just want me to buy into the new one?"

"Yessir, we'll get better prices on everything that way. But the new company won't be just one restaurant. (See Exhibit 4.) As soon as we get the first one down and running good, we'll start another one. You'll be in on the ground floor. We want six of these things inside five years." Glass and his partners were convinced that their expected rate of growth would perk up any investor.

"Yeah. What's 'running good'? When will you be able to say that the first one has proven itself?" Wells was accustomed to this kind of thing: Everybody always wanting to talk about growth, wanting to run before they walked. He discovered that his pipe had gone out.

"Well, we think we can reach break-even within six months. We plan to give it a full year, though, before we start the second one." (See Exhibits 5 and 6.)

"Yeah. You going to have any duties with the existing restaurant?" Wells tamped out the dottle from his pipe and proceeded to reload it.

"Well, yeah, some. I'm comptroller now, and there's not that much to it, so I'll keep on doing that while I run the new shop. I'll be hiring a whole new staff, and I intend to get first-class people. My wife will be working in the new shop with me, and she'll cover things when I have to go downtown. I don't think I'll need more than a couple of hours a day in the old shop, and I'll do that in the mornings while the new shop is being cleaned up for opening." It was clear in the proposal that none of the other partners were slated to do double duty, except for the buyer, who would simply be buying slightly larger quantities.

"Uh-huh." Wells proceeded to light his pipe. It took two matches and he had to tamp the tobacco in between. "And it's your partners' expertise that entitles them to $50,000 up front and a 10-percent management fee as well as a cut of the profits." The pipe was burning well now. Wells tamped it again. (See Exhibit 7.)

"Yeah. Well, the 50K is for the development costs of the project to date, like the proposal says. The management fee is really quite reasonable since all of the management and planning will be handled by the partners. We're going to take a reduced cut of the profits until the investors recoup their investment, and thereafter we'll be equal partners." Glass had not been in favor of that up-front take because he knew it would be hard to sell. This was when Morris should be here, to see what problems it created.

"Of course, your salary as manager will come out of the restaurant. Right?" Wells was almost completely obscured in smoke.

"Yeah. Of course, I'll draw a reduced salary from the existing restaurant to cover the comptroller duties. But my primary salary will be from the new shop. If we didn't have me, we would have to hire a manager, so there's really not any difference, costwise."

"Uh-huh. How much of those salaries on the proposal are for you?" Wells really didn't see anything wrong with this salary business. It was quite normal. Of course, you had to be careful that one of your partners didn't take his cut that way instead of as part of the profits. But he knew the question was expected in these situations.

"Well, that's not firmed up yet." Glass was thinking about taking up pipe smoking. It sure seemed a good cover for getting your thoughts together, or for shaking the concentration of people you were interviewing. "It'll be about what you'd have to pay to get a good, experienced manager. Probably be in the mid-thirties."

"Yeah. How much say-so do you intend to give the investors?" Wells' pipe required more tamping.

"Well, we'll be the managing partners—that's what you're paying us for—but we'll have regular meetings of the limited partners, and we'll be sure that they're all happy with what we're doing." The principals really did not want a great deal of managerial involvement from the investors. They felt that their own expertise was adequate.

"Uh-huh. Well, it's getting late. I'll take a careful look at the proposal and maybe call you next week. I appreciate your taking the time to come

(*continued on page 294*)

EXHIBIT 4

Site Analysis

The Developers believe that the success of Ritchie's will be determined by its reputation for excellent and unique food preparation and its in-house marketing strategy. Several factors have been pinpointed in determining the targeted market and proper location for Ritchie's. They are:

Density The selected site should be in an area with a high mixed density of business/office and residential populations.

Restaurant Row Studies have shown that locating a restaurant within proximity of several others immediately increases customer awareness of the new restaurant. This awareness generates higher sales for the good restaurants, while the poorer ones get the overflow.

Market-Area Growth All Ritchie's units should be located in areas of either high growth potential or a stable established population. Great care will be taken to avoid "changing" neighborhoods.

High Visibility Since Ritchie's will rely heavily on word-of-mouth advertising, as well as location, the site selected should have maximum visibility by local traffic, preferably one on a major thoroughfare.

Ease of Access This factor is very important because the entire concept is based on good food—fast. Very careful planning will be given to traffic patterns, entry, and exit at all units.

Adequate Parking This factor is a prerequisite of any site considered for a Ritchie's unit. If necessary, shared parking will be secured to meet the needs of a particular unit.

A location in Southern Tifton, Georgia, has been selected. At this time, a tentative commitment has been made with the landlord. This site meets all the requirements listed above. Current traffic counts directly in front of the site, according to the Department of Transportation's latest findings, are 17,000 cars northbound and 18,000 cars southbound per 24-hour period. Assuming 50% of this to be commuter traffic, approximately 80% of this commuter traffic travels between the hours of 8:00 AM and 8:00 PM. This location will have a peak exposure of 14,000 cars or 21,000 people (1.5 per car) per 24-hour period, or 98,000 per week.

EXHIBIT 5

Sales Forecast

Projected sales are $20,000 per week or $1 million for the year:

Lunch: 60%	=	$12,000	Average ticket of $5.00
Dinner: 40%	=	8,000	Average ticket of $7.50

Covers per meal:	Lunch	2,400
	Dinner	1,067
Total covers:		3,467, or 3.5% of weekly traffic

Seating capacity is 130. Assuming table turns of 35 minutes for lunch and 60 minutes for dinner, maximum volume would be:

Lunch: 8.5 covers × $5.00 × 130 seats × 7 days =	$38,675
Dinner: 7.0 covers × $7.50 × 130 seats × 7 days =	$47,775
Total maximum weekly capacity	$86,450

Operating at only 25% of the maximum weekly capacity would result in a gross volume of $21,612. This figure is above the minimum projection of $20,000.

Sales are projected to increase by 15% per year for each of the next four years.

Expense Forecast

All variable expenses are based on relationships to sales experienced at O'Malley's restaurant.
Cost of goods sold is based on a 35% food cost and 26% liquor cost, with a sales mix of 70% food, 30% liquor.
Depreciation is based on ACRS for $225,000 of depreciable assets.
Salaries, including managers' incentive bonuses, are 30% of sales.
Payroll taxes are 15% of salaries.
Rent is based on landlord quotations and is $25,000 per year plus an overage of 5% of sales in excess of $500,000.
Repairs and maintenance are 0.5% of sales.
Advertising is 2% of sales.
Supplies are 1% of sales.
Credit-card commissions are 0.85% of sales.
Uniforms and laundry expenses are based on 0.5% of sales.
All fixed expenses are based on present experience with O'Malley's restaurant and are forecast to grow at 5% per year.
Miscellaneous expense is set aside to cover unexpected expenses.

EXHIBIT 6

Pro Forma Income Statements

	Year 1	Year 2	Year 3	Year 4	Year 5
Net sales	$1,000,000	$1,150,000	$1,322,500	$1,520,875	$1,749,006
Cost of sales	323,000	371,450	427,168	491,243	564,929
Gross profit	677,000	778,550	895,333	1,029,632	1,184,077
Gen. & admin. exp.	517,500	587,375	667,191	758,754	863,692
Cash flow	159,500	191,175	228,141	270,879	346,620
Mgt. fee (10%)	15,950	19,118	22,814	27,088	34,662
Net cash flow	143,550	172,327	205,327	243,791	311,958
Depreciation	29,850	41,050	38,800	38,150	38,150
Taxable inc.	113,700	131,008	166,527	205,641	273,808
Ltd. partners	88,912	110,495	152,960	121,895	155,979
Gen. partners	54,638	61,832	52,367	121,896	155,979

Cumulative Cash Flows

Ltd. partners	88,912	199,407	352,367	474,262	630,241
Gen. partners	54,638	116,470	168,837	290,733	44,6712

General and Administrative Expenses

Salaries	300,000	345,000	396,750	456,263	524,702
Payroll Taxes	45,000	51,750	59,513	68,439	78,705
Rent	50,000	57,500	66,125	76,044	87,450
Repairs & main.	5,000	5,750	6,613	7,604	8,745
Advertising	20,000	23,000	26,450	30,418	34,980
Supplies	10,000	11,500	13,225	15,209	17,490
Credit card exp.	8,500	9,775	11,241	12,927	14,867
Uniforms & laundry	5,000	5,750	6,613	7,604	8,745
Utilities	25,000	26,250	27,563	28,941	30,388
Insurance	11,000	11,550	12,128	12,734	13,371
Telephone	2,000	2,100	2,205	2,315	2,431
Dues & subscrip.	2,000	2,100	2,000	2,000	2,000
Professional fees	2,500	2,625	2,756	2,894	3,039
Contract services	5,000	5,250	5,513	5,788	6,078
Printing	5,000	5,250	5,513	5,788	6,078
Service charges	4,000	4,200	4,410	4,631	4,862
Auto expense	5,000	5,250	5,513	5,788	6,078
Alarm/fire	2,000	2,100	2,205	2,315	2,431
Freight/postage	1,000	1,050	1,103	1,158	1,213
Entertainment	2,500	2,625	2,752	2,894	3,039
Miscellaneous	7,000	7,000	7,000	7,000	7,000
Total	517,500	587,375	667,191	758,754	863,692

EXHIBIT 7

Concept Development Cost

The Concept Development Cost is a one-time cost not considered as part of the original investment. This amount is $50,000 and represents out-of-pocket expenses incurred in the research and development of the Ritchie's concept and compensation of the Developers for the following intangible assets they bring to the partnership:

Over 40 years collectively in the food service business
Operational experience in all facets of the constantly changing restaurant industry
Numerous contacts and favorable purchasing advantages
A reputation in the local market area for the highest degree of quality in food and customer service
Use of "proven winners" from O'Malley's menu, access to their recipe files, and written restaurant manuals

The Concept Development Cost will be returned at the rate of 50% per year as a "first out" of cash flow and has been reflected in the General Partners' share of net cash flows on the projected income statement.

The Developers will receive a 10% management fee based on unit profitability. No royalties on sales will be required. Therefore, the payment of this fee will depend solely on management's ability to operate profitably.

and see me like this. Tell your partners I said that. 'Course, I'll want to meet with them at some point if we decide to go further with this." Wells thought that it really did sound like a good idea, but he wondered about the ongoing management. This young fellow seemed to be capable.

"Oh, I was happy to do it. We appreciate your interest and your taking the time to talk to us." Glass was suddenly relieved. Maybe it hadn't gone so badly after all. "My partners will be glad to meet with you anytime. Tonight was a bad night at the restaurant, and they couldn't get away. Most of the plans were mine anyway, and they thought I could answer most of your questions. Is there anything in the prospectus you have a question about?" Glass knew that proposal backwards and forwards. After all, he had developed every piece of information and had written every word.

"I'll give you a call if anything comes up. Thanks again."

After Glass had left, Wells leaned back in his chair and continued to puff on his pipe never realizing that it had gone out again. He pondered the presentation that he had just witnessed and the question of whether or not he wanted to make this investment of $300,000 dollars under these conditions. The only thing he was sure of at this point was that he was either going to be the sole investor or not at all. This would require some serious concentration.

The concept and proposal were well prepared. Wells had

known that from the start, but that strange something about the plan bothered him, and he still couldn't put his finger on it. He was half convinced that the project could be successful given good management. He was confused about whether there was a problem in that area, and he was still concerned about that up-front fee to the partners. It would take some more thought, before putting $300,000 in this venture. He wondered whether there could be any dealing on that number and on the fees. He was certain that he would have to have veto power over salaries to partners before he would invest. It was an interesting plan though. He could afford the risk, but he was proud of his record. He had never invested in a business that failed, and he didn't intend to start now. He hadn't gotten to a 50-percent income tax bracket by being foolish.

REFERENCES

"The Gourmet Hamburger," *Restaurants & Institutions*, 7 November 1984, pp. 103–128.

"Behind the Gourmet Hamburger Boom," *Restaurant Business*, 1 November 1984, pp. 121–137.

QUESTIONS

1. What do you feel from the interview?
2. Is any pertinent information missing from the resumés of top management?
3. Do you sense an undercurrent that could foretell future problems with the management team? If so, what is it?
4. If you were Mr. Wells, what would be your major concern about this prospectus?
5. Would you make the investment at this point following the interview?
6. If you were one of the Developers, what would be your major concern about this prospectus?

CHAPTER 11

Staffing

Learning Objectives

After reading this chapter, you will be able to do the following:

- Understand the major laws protecting the rights of employees.
- Recruit suitable workers for a startup business.
- Determine how entrepreneurs can select the best employees.
- Train new employees to succeed.
- Create effective compensation plans.

Most businesspeople concede that employees are their most valuable asset. Untrained, unmotivated employees can cause a business to fail just as surely as strong competitors or economic downturns. It is imperative, therefore, that startup entrepreneurs carefully plan the staffing of their business. If the right people are recruited, selected, and trained, the new business will very likely be successful.

In this chapter, we will discuss the proper way to acquire employees. We will begin with an examination of the laws affecting the personnel function and continue with the steps in the employment process, which normally include the following: recruiting, interviewing, testing, and training. Since money is important to most employees, we will discuss how startup entrepreneurs can establish a fair compensation system in their new business.

LABOR LAWS

In order to do business legally, startup entrepreneurs need to be aware of the rights and protection employees now enjoy because of federal and state legislation. Employers can no longer discriminate against employees, terminate employees without due cause, or sexually harass employees. The laws that protect employees generally apply to businesses employing fifteen or more people; however, startup entrepreneurs need to be familiar with these laws because their businesses could start with fifteen or more people and exceed that size within a few months. As in all other situations, ignorance of the law is not an acceptable excuse for illegal behavior.

The Civil Rights Act of 1964

Title VII of the Civil Rights Act may be one of the most important and comprehensive laws protecting employee rights. The provisions of this law pertain to businesses with more than fifteen employees. This is the law that makes discrimination in any form illegal. Employers cannot refuse a person employment, promotion, pay increases, training, or other employment-related activities because of race, color, religion, sex, or national origin.

The only way employers can legally discriminate against people is to show that their requirements are Bona Fide Occupational Qualifications (BFOQs). For example, if height, weight, and physical ability are used as selection criteria, employers must prove that those qualifications are BFOQs and not simply discriminatory requirements. The following are some additional examples of how the Civil Rights Act has been interpreted:

1. ***Ability Tests.*** Any abilities required for employment must have a relationship to successful job performance. Typing ability is a BFOQ for a secretary, but being over six feet tall is not necessarily a BFOQ for a police officer.
2. ***Education.*** Employers must show that a degree or program of study is required for success in a job before it can be required of all applicants.
3. ***Wages.*** Equal work requires equal pay, regardless of an individual's race, color, religion, sex, or national origin.

Employers cannot publish employment advertisements that indicate a preference for or discrimination against anyone based on their race, color, religion, sex, or national origin, unless such is a BFOQ.

We have only briefly covered the rather comprehensive provisions of the Civil Rights Act. Any entrepreneur planning a new business would be well advised to read the entire law because it is possible to discriminate unintentionally. The Equal Employment Opportunity Commission Discrimination Quiz at the end of the chapter demonstrates how employers can unknowingly discriminate.

The Equal Pay Act of 1963

The purpose of this law is: ". . . to prohibit discrimination on account of sex in the payment of wages by employers engaged in commerce or in the production of goods for commerce." Congress enacted this law because it found that wage differentials based on sex do the following:

1. depress wages and living standards necessary for the health and efficiency of employees
2. prevent the maximum utilization of the available labor resources
3. tend to cause labor disputes, thereby burdening, affecting, and obstructing commerce
4. burden commerce and the free flow of goods in commerce
5. constitute an unfair method of competition

Some employers changed job titles and job descriptions in order to continue paying men more than women. In order to rectify this condition, legislation was introduced (yet to be passed by Congress) to pay men and women the same for similar types of jobs. This concept, known as *comparable worth*, has been accepted by some state governments. Jobs with similar skill, education, ability, and experience requirements pay the same for men and women. For example, if it is determined that a female secretary's job is comparable to a male shipping clerk's job, both should receive the same wages. Wage differentials based on seniority, education, and so forth, are still acceptable and legal.

The Fair Labor Standards Act of 1938

This act requires the following:

1. ***Payment of minimum wage:*** Employers (with some exceptions) must pay their employees the minimum wage established by Congress.

2. ***Maximum forty-hour workweek:*** Employees receive additional compensation (at least one-and-one-half times regular wages) for any work performed beyond forty hours per week.

The provisions of the Fair Labor Standards Act do not apply to the following:

1. Any employee employed in a bona fide executive, administrative, or professional capacity, or in the capacity of outside salesperson
2. Employees of some retail or service establishments
3. Employees of amusement or recreational establishments, organized camps, or religious or nonprofit educational conference centers that operate less than seven months in any calendar year
4. Fishing-industry employees
5. Agricultural employees are exempt if the employer did not use more than five hundred man days of agricultural labor in any calendar quarter of the preceding year
6. Anyone employed in connection with the publication of any weekly, semiweekly, or daily newspaper with a circulation of less than four thousand most of which is within the county where published or counties contiguous thereto
7. Switchboard operators employed by an independently owned public telephone company that has less than 750 stations
8. Anyone employed as a seaman on a vessel other than an American vessel
9. Casual domestic babysitters or companions for those who cannot care for themselves

The Age Discrimination in Employment Act of 1967

This act (as amended) states:

> It is therefore the purpose of this act to promote employment of older persons based on their ability rather than age; to prohibit arbitrary age discrimination in employment; to help employers and workers find ways of meeting problems arising from the impact of age on employment.

This law does not protect all employees from job discrimination because of age. Only those employees between the ages of forty and seventy are protected by the Age Discrimination in Employment Act.

The Vocational Rehabilitation Act of 1973

Section 503 of this act requires employers who have federal government contracts of $50,000 or more and fifty or more employees, to actively seek, through affirmative action programs, to hire handicapped individuals. Employers cannot discriminate against mentally or physically handicapped persons for jobs they are qualified to do. Handicapped individuals must meet reasonable standards for employment that are job-related and consistent with job necessity and safe performance of duties. Companies must make efforts to accommodate physical and mental limitations of applicants and employees, unless they can show that such accommodation would constitute an "unusual hardship."

Vietnam Era Veterans Readjustment Act of 1974

Section 402 of this act requires contractors who have federal contracts in excess of $10,000 to take affirmative action to employ and advance in employment qualified disabled veterans and veterans of the Vietnam era.

Miscellaneous Laws

There are numerous other laws, such as Workers' Compensation laws, the Environmental Protection Act, and the Occupational Health and Safety Act, that protect employees once they have been hired. Startup entrepreneurs should familiarize themselves with the provisions of these laws so that they operate their businesses legally.

Immigration Laws

The new immigration law signed by former President Reagan in 1986 demonstrates how complex a seemingly simple regulation can be—and how costly it can be if startup entrepreneurs are unaware of its provisions and penalties.

Provisions. In an effort to keep illegal aliens **from finding work** in the United States, the new law requires most employers to check the documents of all new hires (documents need not be checked for people hired before November 1986). For the first time, it is actually against the law to hire illegal aliens. This seems like a relatively simple law, but it has far-reaching consequences for startup entrepreneurs. For example, employers cannot hire illegal aliens, yet it is very difficult in some states to determine a person's national origin. If employers refuse to hire all "foreign-looking" people, they will violate the Civil Rights Act. Employers will not be considered guiltless if they hire illegal aliens who presented forged documents, nor will they be allowed to claim innocence because they hired an illegal alien who was referred by an agency that certified the individual as legal.

Coverage. All employers must check the documentation of all employees hired after November 1986. Companies in the following industries employ the most illegal immigrants.

Apparel and textiles	12.25 percent
Agriculture	8.20
Restaurants	7.39

Construction	6.46
Food processing	4.02
Metals industry	3.92
Electrical machinery	3.06
Transportation equipment	2.40
Education	2.26
Retailing	2.20[1]

Employers in these industries must be especially vigilant against hiring illegal aliens, and employers in states with large illegal-alien populations will also have to be especially diligent in verifying documents. The following states have the most illegal immigrants:

California	49.8 percent of illegal aliens
New York	11.4
Texas	9.1
Illinois	6.6
Florida	3.9[2]

What Employers Must Do. Employers must check documents for all new hires and complete Form I-9 (see Figure 11.1), which must be available for inspection by Immigration and Naturalization Service (INS) personnel. The form certifies that the employer has seen proof that the employee is legally eligible to work in the United States. The company does not have to keep copies of the proof, but INS inspectors can demand to see the company's I-9 forms without a search warrant or subpoena.

The most reliable proof of legal resident status for employers is a U.S. passport, INS-issued certificate of U.S. citizenship or naturalization, or resident alien cards with photographs. Driver's licenses, birth certificates, and Social Security cards can also be used as proof of legal resident status.

Penalties. The new law levies a number of sanctions against employers who hire illegal immigrants. The first time an employer is caught hiring an illegal alien, he or she can be fined up to $2,000 per worker. A second violation means fines up to $5,000 for each illegal immigrant, and for additional violations, up to $10,000 per worker. The provisions and penalties of the new immigration law have already affected hiring practices (see The Inside View 11-1).

Startup entrepreneurs need to familiarize themselves with this and all other laws pertaining to employee rights. It would be wise for entrepreneurs to consult with their attorneys before initiating hiring, training, or promoting policies.

THE HIRING PROCESS

Once startup entrepreneurs become familiar with employment laws, they can begin the process of hiring the people they will need to operate their new business. Since employees do have considerable protection under the law, it is very difficult and expensive to terminate unsuitable workers. Therefore, entrepreneurs should devote ample time and effort to the hiring process to ensure that they select the very best

FIGURE 11.1
Employment Eligibility Verification (Form I-9)

EMPLOYMENT ELIGIBILITY VERIFICATION (Form I-9)

1 EMPLOYEE INFORMATION AND VERIFICATION: (To be completed and signed by employee.)

Name: (Print or Type) Last	First	Middle	Birth Name
Address: Street Name and Number	City	State	ZIP Code
Date of Birth (Month/Day/Year)		Social Security Number	

I attest, under penalty of perjury, that I am (check a box):

- ☐ 1. A citizen or national of the United States.
- ☐ 2. An alien lawfully admitted for permanent residence (Alien Number A ____________).
- ☐ 3. An alien authorized by the Immigration and Naturalization Service to work in the United States (Alien Number A ____________ or Admission Number ____________, expiration of employment authorization, if any ____________)

I attest, under penalty of perjury, the documents that I have presented as evidence of identity and employment eligibility are genuine and relate to me. I am aware that federal law provides for imprisonment and/or fine for any false statements or use of false documents in connection with this certificate.

Signature	Date (Month/Day/Year)

PREPARER/TRANSLATOR CERTIFICATION (To be completed if prepared by person other than the employee). I attest, under penalty of perjury, that the above was prepared by me at the request of the named individual and is based on all information of which I have any knowledge.

Signature	Name (Print or Type)		
Address (Street Name and Number)	City	State	Zip Code

2 EMPLOYER REVIEW AND VERIFICATION: (To be completed and signed by employer.)

Instructions:
Examine one document from List A and check the appropriate box, ***OR*** examine one document from List B ***and*** one from List C and check the appropriate boxes. Provide the ***Document Identification Number*** and ***Expiration Date*** for the document checked.

List A Documents that Establish Identity and Employment Eligibility	List B Documents that Establish Identity	**and**	List C Documents that Establish Employment Eligibility
☐ 1. United States Passport ☐ 2. Certificate of United States Citizenship ☐ 3. Certificate of Naturalization ☐ 4. Unexpired foreign passport with attached Employment Authorization ☐ 5. Alien Registration Card with photograph	☐ 1. A State-issued driver's license or a State-issued I.D. card with a photograph, or information, including name, sex, date of birth, height, weight, and color of eyes. (Specify State) ____________) ☐ 2. U.S. Military Card ☐ 3. Other (Specify document and issuing authority) ____________		☐ 1. Original Social Security Number Card (other than a card stating it is not valid for employment) ☐ 2. A birth certificate issued by State, county, or municipal authority bearing a seal or other certification ☐ 3. Unexpired INS Employment Authorization Specify form # ____________
Document Identification # ____________	***Document Identification*** # ____________		***Document Identification*** # ____________
Expiration Date (if any) ____________	***Expiration Date (if any)*** ____________		***Expiration Date (if any)*** ____________

CERTIFICATION: **I attest, under penalty of perjury, that I have examined the documents presented by the above individual, that they appear to be genuine and to relate to the individual named, and that the individual, to the best of my knowledge, is eligible to work in the United States.**

Signature	Name (Print or Type)	Title
Employer Name	Address	Date

Form I-9 (05/07/87)
OMB No. 1115-0136

U.S. Department of Justice
Immigration and Naturalization Service

FIGURE 11.1 *(Continued)*

Employment Eligibility Verification

NOTICE: Authority for collecting the information on this form is in Title 8, United States Code, Section 1324A, which requires employers to verify employment eligibility of individuals on a form approved by the Attorney General. This form will be used to verify the individual's eligibility for employment in the United States. Failure to present this form for inspection to officers of the Immigration and Naturalization Service or Department of Labor within the time period specified by regulation, or improper completion or retention of this form, may be a violation of the above law and may result in a civil money penalty.

Section 1. Instructions to Employee/Preparer for completing this form

Instructions for the employee.

All employees, upon being hired, must complete Section 1 of this form. Any person hired after November 6, 1986 must complete this form. (For the purpose of completion of this form the term "hired" applies to those employed, recruited or referred for a fee.)

All employees must print or type their complete name, address, date of birth, and Social Security Number. The block which correctly indicates the employee's immigration status must be checked. If the second block is checked, the employee's Alien Registration Number must be provided. If the third block is checked, the employee's Alien Registration Number ***or*** Admission Number must be provided, as well as the date of expiration of that status, if it expires.

All employees whose present names differ from birth names, because of marriage or other reasons, must print or type their birth names in the appropriate space of Section 1. Also, employees whose names change after employment verification should report these changes to their employer.

All employees must sign and date the form.

Instructions for the preparer of the form, if not the employee.

If a person assists the employee with completing this form, the preparer must certify the form by signing it and printing or typing his or her complete name and address.

Section 2. Instructions to Employer for completing this form

(For the purpose of completion of this form, the term "employer" applies to employers and those who recruit or refer for a fee.)

Employers must complete this section by examining evidence of identity and employment eligibility, and:

- checking the appropriate box in List A ***or*** boxes in both Lists B and C;
- recording the document identification number and expiration date (if any);
- recording the type of form if not specifically identified in the list;
- signing the certification section.

NOTE: Employers are responsible for reverifying employment eligibility of employees whose employment eligibility documents carry an expiration date.

Copies of documentation presented by an individual for the purpose of establishing identity and employment eligibility may be copied and retained for the purpose of complying with the requirements of this form and no other purpose. Any copies of documentation made for this purpose should be maintained with this form.

Name changes of employees which occur after preparation of this form should be recorded on the form by lining through the old name, printing the new name and the reason (such as marriage), and dating and initialing the changes. Employers should not attempt to delete or erase the old name in any fashion.

RETENTION OF RECORDS.

The completed form must be retained by the employer for:

- three years after the date of hiring; or
- one year after the date the employment is terminated, whichever is later.

Employers may photocopy or reprint this form as necessary.

U.S. Department of Justice
Immigration and Naturalization Service

OMB #1115-0136
Form I-9 (05/07/87)
☆ U.S.G.P.O. 1987- 183-918/69085

For sale by the Superintendent of Documents, U.S. Government Printing Office
Washington, D.C. 20402

11-1 *The Inside View*

THE EFFECT OF THE NEW IMMIGRATION LAW

The new law is already affecting the hiring patterns of some industries, particularly those that have historically hired illegal aliens, such as restaurants. In Houston, Antonietta Hernández, coordinator of the AFL-CIO's Texas Union Immigrant Project, says wages for restaurant workers seem to be rising. Similarly, Leo Matteucci, co-owner of Armando's in Chicago, says fewer people want dishwashing jobs, forcing him to raise wages to $4 an hour from $3.35. Chris Carson, co-owner of another Chicago restaurant, says he has refused to hire fifty applicants for summer jobs because they did not have the necessary documents. They were, he says, "mostly Mexican kids."[3]

employees available. Staffing new ventures is particularly difficult because people should be employed not only for their current skills and ability but also for their potential to grow with the company and accept more responsible positions.

The hiring process will be most efficient if startup entrepreneurs follow basic guidelines and proceed in an orderly and timely manner. In this chapter, we will discuss the steps in the hiring process, which include:

- Needs assessment
- Recruitment
- Job application
- Interviews
- Test administration
- Reference checks
- Physical exams
- Job offer

This may seem like an awful lot of work just to hire a few people for a new business, but following these steps may keep entrepreneurs from hiring the wrong person.

NEEDS ASSESSMENT

Determining how many people are required to initially staff a new business is not particularly difficult. Every entrepreneur should be able to describe the jobs that need to be filled in the new firm and the skills that successful applicants should possess. Entrepreneurs who developed a complete business plan should already know what jobs their company will need filled. What is then necessary is the completion of descriptions of each job and its specifications.

Job Descriptions

Job descriptions are basic listings of the duties performed by people in their respective positions. These descriptions should be simple and as brief as possible. It is not possible to cover all of the functions of each job; however, those duties that are a routine part of the job should be described. The following is an example of a job description for a secretary/receptionist:

Title: Secretary/Receptionist
Duties: Greets and assists customers; answers telephone when necessary; takes dictation, types letters and other documents, and files important items; arranges managers' meetings, appointments, etc.; and performs other assorted duties as needed
Reports to: Owner

A job description for a salesperson could include the following information:

Title: Salesperson
Duties: Greets and assists customers; explains merchandise; records sales; writes up charge slips; packages merchandise; stocks shelves; follows store opening and closing procedures; and performs other duties as necessary.
Reports to: Store manager

Most good job descriptions contain a clause stating that employees will perform unspecified duties when instructed to do so. This statement is particularly necessary when firms grow and employees are not sure of their responsibilities or claim that they are not responsible for duties not specified in their job description.

The job descriptions presented here are very simple and basic. It should be noted that as jobs become more complex, so too their descriptions. Job descriptions for technical employees could be several pages long.

Job Specifications

Once the duties of a job have been described, it is possible to determine the skills a person should possess to perform competently that job. As with job descriptions, it is possible to compile either simple or elaborate job specifications. The following job specifications are for the secretary/receptionist position previously described:

Title: Secretary/Receptionist
Requirements: Applicants should have at least a high school diploma and be able to type seventy words per minute with two or fewer mistakes. They should be able to learn how to use standard office machines. Applicants should have a pleasant personality and be able to work closely with others. They should have initiative and be able to assume more responsibility as the firm grows.

Similarly, the job specifications for the salesperson could include the following:

Title: Salesperson
Requirements: Applicants must be good at arithmetic and be bondable. They should be personable and have a genuine interest in helping customers. Applicants should be

able to stand up for several hours and be available to work nights and on weekends. It would be helpful if applicants had previous sales experience.

The job descriptions and specifications presented are very simple, but much more detailed descriptions and specifications can be established for jobs and applicants. It is possible, for example, to write specifications that only one person, known to the employer, can satisfy. This allows an employer to hire a friend or family member without having discrimination charges filed by other applicants. The following are some additional areas for which job specifications can be established:

Intelligence	Emotional stability
Analytic ability	Assertiveness
Creativity	Enthusiasm
Intellectual flexibility	Leadership ability
Communication skills	Motivation level
Education	Health
Experience	Ambition
Resourcefulness	Honesty
Perseverance	Interpersonal skills
Performance	Interests

Entrepreneurs planning to develop lengthy job specifications should remember that skills or attitudes required of successful job applicants need to be Bona Fide Occupational Qualifications. It would also be necessary to use valid instruments to measure characteristics such as creativity, resourcefulness, perseverance, or other specified traits.

Determining Personnel Needs

Once job descriptions and specifications have been written, it should be possible to determine how many employees will be needed to open and operate a new business. One pitfall entrepreneurs should avoid is the urge to hire enough full-time employees to staff the business for peak production or selling times. New firms will be more efficient if their owners hire a core of qualified full-time employees and supplement their staff with part-time employees during peak operating periods. Some new business owners should even consider using part-time people to fill key positions until the company can justify a full-time person (see The Inside View 11-2).

RECRUITMENT

Having determined how many employees the new business needs, entrepreneurs must decide next which sources of employees will be the most fruitful. Several sources, some more efficient and less expensive than others, can provide startup companies with employees. Entrepreneurs should evaluate each source and decide which one or ones will best suit their needs. It is generally not a good practice to become dependent on only one source of workers because good employees available through other sources will be overlooked.

11-2 The Inside View

PART-TIME OFFICERS

In May, Brad Howe walked into five companies on five successive days and said, "I'm your new chief financial officer." Brad Howe is not excessively mobile; he just happens to have a thriving business as part-time CFO for six small companies. A growing number of small-business owners are turning to part-time officers to complete their management teams. Unlike regular consultants who work on a specific project, part-timers manage the daily operations of the companies that hire them. Many part-timers specialize in startups. For example, part-timer Patricia Mapps gets referrals from venture capitalists and often works for high-technology startups run by scientists who have little experience starting and managing a business. A part-time arrangement is a very logical approach that can expand from a few hours a week to a full-time position.[4]

Advertisements

Many new ventures can be staffed by advertising for employees in the local newspaper. If only a few workers with relatively common skills are needed, an appealing ad placed in the local paper should attract more than enough qualified applicants. The ad should probably be in the Sunday paper to be seen by the greatest number of readers, and it should describe the job, the company, and the incumbent's growth potential. In some cases, it might also be necessary to state the salary range and describe the benefits package.

If the positions to be filled require people with specialized skills, it might be necessary to advertise in regional or national newspapers such as the *Atlanta Journal*, the *Los Angeles Times*, or the *Wall Street Journal*. If the new venture needs professionals such as engineers or scientists, advertisements placed in professional journals are likely to be quite productive. Ads should be well written, descriptive, and appropriately placed. Finally, the advertisements must be absolutely accurate, or employees can sue the business for false advertising.

Networks

Entrepreneurs who choose not to make their staffing needs public can find employees through their own informal networks. Friends and family members can recommend suitable employees who may be reluctant to respond to newspaper advertisements. Entrepreneurs can also make their staffing needs known to social acquaintances, members of their fraternal organizations, members of their church, and so forth. The advantage of these informal sources is that entrepreneurs can evaluate a potential employee without making formal contact with the individual. Unqualified people would not even know they had been considered for the job, and the entrepreneur would not have to tell candidates why they were not hired.

Private Employment Agencies

Private agencies maintain rosters of job applicants who can be referred to startup entrepreneurs. These agencies can prescreen potential employees by referring only those candidates who meet the employer's specific criteria. Like the employer, employment agencies are also subject to the provisions of the Civil Rights Act and can be prosecuted if they are party to discriminatory practices. The excuse that they were sending only those applicants with employer's requisite qualifications does not protect employment agencies from prosecution under Title VII of the Civil Rights Act. If the employer hires an individual referred by an employment agency, either the employer or the person hired pays the agency a fee of between 5 and 15 percent of the person's yearly salary.

Public Employment Agencies

State employment offices, in conjunction with the U.S. Employment Service, maintain lists of people actively seeking jobs. The primary difference between private and public agencies is that the latter do not charge employers or job applicants a fee for their services. In some cases, companies will not hire any workers who have not been referred by the local public employment agency.

Schools

Colleges, universities, vocational schools, and high schools are excellent sources of qualified employees. These institutions usually have placement counselors who can refer suitable students to prospective employers. Entrepreneurs can take advantage of the intern or work-study programs available at many schools to employ students on a temporary basis. If student-employees prove to be capable, the employer can then make the short-term arrangement permanent.

Temporary Agencies

As we mentioned earlier, startup entrepreneurs may not know precisely how many full-time employees they will need to open and operate their businesses. Temporary agencies can provide startup firms with trained employees for a few days, weeks, or months. Once the new company's work force has stabilized, temporary employees can be dismissed or offered full-time employment. Most agencies attempt to make it difficult for their part-time employees to accept a permanent position with another employer; however, it is not impossible to hire away a qualified person.

THE JOB APPLICATION

If the recruiting process is successful, entrepreneurs will have more applicants than positions to fill. Then the process of elimination begins, at the end of which all positions should be filled with the best qualified applicants. The selection process should be closely monitored so that no applicant is refused a job on discriminatory grounds.

By following federal and state hiring guidelines, from the completion of the job application form to the selection of the best candidate, entrepreneurs can avoid discrimination charges. (Later in this chapter, we will discuss the construction of an acceptable application form that provides as much information as possible without violating an applicant's rights.) Questions that cannot be included in an application form also cannot be asked in an interview; however, most of the disallowed questions can be asked after a person is hired.

Potentially Discriminatory Information

Current antidiscrimination laws now make it illegal to ask many questions which traditionally had appeared on application forms in the past; however, if those questions pertain to Bona Fide Occupational Qualifications, they still can be included in the application form. Information pertaining to the following characteristics should generally be eliminated from application forms:

Race
Sex
Age
Marital Status
Names and number of dependents
Names and addresses of any relatives
Job title and occupation of spouse
Height
Weight
Religion
National origin

In certain cases, it is acceptable to ask questions relating to some of those characteristics. For example, applicants can be asked where they live, if they are fluent in any foreign languages, if they have relatives already employed by the company, and if they are in the United States on a visa that would not permit them to work in this country.

Constructing a Legal Application Form

With so many questions now considered discriminatory, many startup entrepreneurs believe that there isn't anything they can include in their application form. True, many items of "interest" have been eliminated; however, it is still possible to collect some important information about a person from the application form. The application form included here (see Figure 11.2) is an example of a legal two-page document that provides employers with necessary information about applicants. The question pertaining to age—"are you under 18?"—is not discriminatory since people under eighteen are excluded from some occupations, and special work rules apply to younger people. Similarly, the new immigration laws require employers to have proof of a person's legal resident status.

INTERVIEWS

As application forms have lost some of their value because of the limited information they can provide, interviews have become more important. During an interview one can visually determine an applicant's race, sex, approximate age, height, weight, etc., without violating any federal or state laws. Interviews also provide an opportunity to probe an applicant's background, character, capabilities, and intentions. Personal

FIGURE 11.2
Application for Employment

Application for Employment

Please Complete in Your Own Handwriting.
Employment is subject to a satisfactory check of references.

Position applied for ______________________ Date __________

Referred by ______________________

PERSONAL

Name ______________________ Soc. Sec. No. __________
LAST FIRST MIDDLE

Address ______________________ Telephone __________
STREET AND NUMBER CITY ZONE STATE

Citizen of United States ☐ Yes ☐ No Are you under 18 ☐ Yes ☐ No

Do you have any health problem that might interfere with your ability to perform the job for which you have applied? ☐ Yes ☐ No

Have you ever been convicted of a crime? ☐ Yes ☐ No If yes, describe

Have you any relatives or friends in our employ? ☐ Yes ☐ No If yes, please name

Person to be contacted in case of emergency

______________________ NAME ______________________ RELATIONSHIP

______________________ ADDRESS ______________________ TELEPHONE

EDUCATION List schools in order attended
Include any special training such as business or evening school

NAME AND ADDRESS OF SCHOOL	COURSE TAKEN OR MAJOR SUBJECT	CERTIFICATE OR DEGREE RECEIVED	AVERAGE GRADE

ARE YOU ATTENDING SCHOOL NOW? ☐ Yes ☐ No IF YES, GIVE NAME OF INSTITUTION, COURSE AND HOURS OF STUDY.

DESCRIBE BRIEFLY WHAT YOU CONSIDER TO BE YOUR MAIN QUALIFICATIONS FOR BEING SUCCESSFUL IN THE JOB FOR WHICH YOU HAVE APPLIED.

DESCRIBE BRIEFLY ANY ADDITIONAL SKILLS, KNOWLEDGE, AND EXPERIENCE YOU HAVE WHICH YOU BELIEVE MAY BE OF VALUE FOR A CAREER AT THIS FIRM. (INCLUDE OFFICE MACHINES YOU CAN OPERATE, TYPING, STENOGRAPHY, ETC.)

FIGURE 11.2 *(Continued)*

EMPLOYMENT HISTORY

List former employers in reverse order, beginning with the last.
Include information on any armed forces service and any periods of unemployment.

DATES FROM (MO. YEAR)	DATES TO (MO. YEAR)	NAME AND ADDRESS OF EMPLOYER	TYPE OF BUSINESS	NAME OF SUPERVISOR	JOB TITLE OR RANK AND KIND OF WORK YOU DO	WEEKLY SALARY STARTING	WEEKLY SALARY LEAVING	SPECIFIC REASON FOR LEAVING
		NAME ADDRESS						
		NAME ADDRESS						
		NAME ADDRESS						
		NAME ADDRESS						
		NAME ADDRESS						
		NAME ADDRESS						

If your application is considered favorably, what salary would you expect?__________ per__________. On what date would you be available for work?__________

Signature ____________________

interviews have become one of the key steps in the selection process; however, entrepreneurs should not devote too much time to applicant interviews. If interviews are properly planned, structured, and executed, entrepreneurs can solicit as much information as they need in a relatively short period of time.

Preparing for Interviews

Well-planned interviews will minimize the amount of time entrepreneurs need to spend with prospective employees. Adequate planning and preparation also ensure that laws will not be violated and that the maximum amount of information will be acquired. The following are some time-saving steps that startup entrepreneurs should take before interviewing applicants.

Know the Job. It may seem unnecessary to suggest that interviewers thoroughly familiarize themselves with the job description and specifications before an interview; however, some interviewers fail to hire the candidates of their choice because they were unable to provide any specifics about the available jobs. In an interview, information flows both ways. Employers want to know about applicants, and applicants want to know about the company they might work for and the specific job for which they have applied.

Determine What Information Is Important. Interviewers should know what information is important and how to acquire it. While small talk is necessary to put the interviewee at ease, it is not the primary purpose of the interview. Entrepreneurs should know what information they need and how to interpret that information.

Select the Location. The proper physical setting for an interview is quite important. The location should be quiet, comfortable, and free of distractions. A room with no traffic and no telephones would be the ideal location for a serious, private interview.

Decide How Long Interviews Should Last. Interviews for most positions last between thirty and sixty minutes. Interviews that last too long waste valuable time and usually provide little useful additional information. In some cases, interviews of key employees will last more than an hour, but even these interviews should not drag on and become exercises in the collection of trivia.

Structuring Interviews

Interviews can be structured or unstructured; that is, the same questions can be asked of all applicants, or each applicant can be asked different questions. In most cases it is preferable to have one set of questions prepared for all applicants. With all applicants providing the same information, they can be evaluated more systematically. Questions asked of candidates will vary for different jobs; however, there are some fairly standard questions good interviewers ask. The following are some typical interview questions:

- Can you describe a typical day in your current job?
- What has been your most significant contribution to your current job?
- What do you think it takes for a person to be successful in the job for which you are applying?

- What do you consider to be your major strength?
- What do you consider to be your major weakness?
- Why are you leaving your current position?
- How far do you think you can advance in the next five years?
- How much do you expect to be earning in the next two years?
- What were your favorite subjects in school (college)?
- What portion of your education was paid for by you?
- What are your favorite leisure activities?

Conducting Interviews

Successful interviews require preparation and structure, but conducting the interview intelligently and efficiently is perhaps the most important aspect of the interviewing process. Entrepreneurs who use the following guidelines will perform more efficiently and conduct more productive interviews:

Establish Rapport. Job applicants who are tense and nervous are not likely to make a good impression or provide necessary information. The interview should begin with small talk. Discuss topics of mutual interest such as sports or hobbies. Once the interviewee relaxes, the meaningful questions can be asked.

Let the Interviewee Talk. As we mentioned earlier, the interview is a two-way process of providing information; however, the interviewee should be given the opportunity to do most of the talking. It is important for the interviewer to provide information about the company and the job, but it is more important for the interviewee to provide information about himself or herself.

Ask Insightful Questions. The interviewer should ask the questions prepared before the interview of all candidates. He or she should not ask questions that were selected but do not appear to be appropriate and should avoid questions that can be answered with a yes or a no or a brief statement. The more useful questions are those that give interviewees ample opportunity to respond in depth.

Listen Actively. Too often, interviewers fail to take the time to listen effectively to the information provided by an interviewee. Interviewers might be thinking about follow-up questions or contemplating a previous answer, and they do not really hear what the applicant is saying. Entrepreneurs who do not listen effectively should spend more time developing their ability to really hear what people are saying to them.

Active listening enables interviewers to determine if questions have embarrassed or offended candidates and to sense when candidates are not being completely truthful. The following is a list of behaviors indicating that applicants may not be at ease or that their answers may not be completely accurate or truthful:

Blushing
Responses that are too long and involved
Sudden loss of what had been good eye contact

Noticeable change in pace (speeding up or slowing down)
Suddenly higher or lower voice
Inappropriate use of humor
Voice suddenly becoming louder or softer
Sudden twitching, stammering, frowning, or drumming of fingers
Inconsistency between what is said and nonverbal behavior
Sudden loss of rapport
Grabbing suddenly for something to drink
Perspiring for no apparent reason
Unusually long pauses[5]

Take Notes. Some managers believe that taking notes during an interview is distracting and contributes to ineffective listening. Not taking notes, however, usually means that the interviewer may forget important information, especially if several interviews take place the same day. Notes should be brief and should include only the most important facts. Tape-recording the interview might be preferable to taking notes, but the presence of a tape recorder often inhibits the free flow of information.

Terminate and Summarize the Interview. Good interviewers know instinctively when to end an interview. Once all the important questions have been answered, the interview should not be prolonged unnecessarily by small talk. Immediately after each interview, the interviewer should write a summary of the session, including general observations on the candidate's demeanor, ability to answer questions, apparent honesty, and suitability for the job. Such summaries help to refresh the entrepreneur's memory when he or she finally has to decide who should be offered the job.

Notify All Applicants. After all interviews are completed, the successful candidates are offered the position or asked to come in for tests, physical exams, etc.; however, unsuccessful applicants are often ignored. It is disconcerting to be interviewed for a job and then never hear from the interviewer. The "don't call us, we will call you" attitude should be avoided by all startup entrepreneurs. Common courtesy dictates that *everyone* be informed of the outcome of his or her interview.

Interviewer Errors

Once the interview is completed, interviewers should evaluate their own performance to make sure that the interview was as effective as possible. Interviews are usually effective if the interviewer has not committed any of the following errors:

Misunderstand the real nature of the job
Overlook important specifications
Fail to ask important questions about work habits and management style
Ask misleading questions
Forget responses to important questions
Forget just when the interviewee was nervous, awkward, and uncomfortable
Form biases/prejudices/stereotypes[6]

TEST ADMINISTRATION

Testing has traditionally been one of the pillars of the selection process; however, recent laws and court cases have questioned the value of some tests. For example, in the landmark case of *Griggs* vs. *Duke Power Company*, the court ruled that selection tests and other promotion criteria that are not job-related are unacceptable. The major complaint about tests is that they are not valid or reliable. To be valid, tests must actually measure qualities and characteristics needed for a job. Tests should be validated by the company using them, not by the company producing the tests, and they should be revalidated at regular intervals, such as semiannually or annually.

While companies tended to use tests less frequently in the 1960s and 1970s because of validity problems, they seem to be using tests more often now that determining validity is becoming a more rigorous process. A recent survey of 390 companies conducted by the American Society for Personnel Administration (ASPA) found that companies are using or planning to use selection tests more frequently than in the past. Approximately 24 percent of the companies reported that they are testing more now than a year ago; 39 percent are testing more now than five years ago; and 44 percent are planning to increase the amount of testing that they currently do.

Administering Tests

How a test is administered can be as important as which test is used. Startup entrepreneurs who do not feel that they know enough about administering tests can leave the job to professionals. For example, psychologists or trained personnel consultants can administer the tests for a startup company, or the company can rely on assessment centers. Normally used to assist companies in their selection of key executives, these centers administer and evaluate the results of a battery of tests and report their findings to the company. Regardless of who does the testing, it is necessary to implement some basic safeguards against discrimination.

First, startup companies should use standardized, validated tests. Most startup entrepreneurs will not have the knowledge and experience to create their own tests; therefore, relying on tests used by other companies is advisable. Second, everyone except those who seem marginal should be tested; selective testing can lead to lawsuits claiming discrimination. Third, tests should be administered in an appropriate place. As with interviews, tests should be administered in a quiet, isolated, comfortable room. Finally, test scores should not be used as the only basis for selecting employees. Tests are only a part of the selection process, and they should not have inordinate weight in determining who is hired.

Types of Tests

Selecting the tests to use is as important as administering them correctly. In fact, companies are more likely to be sued for selecting inappropriate tests than for administering them incorrectly. The following are some of the more common types of tests used by employers:

Personality Tests. Tests such as the Minnesota Multiphasic Personality Inventory (MMPI) provide information about an individual's personality. This test claims to "scale" a person in areas such as paranoia, hysteria, schizophrenia, depression, and mania. Personality tests give some indication of how well a person will relate to other employees in a new business.

Aptitude Tests. These tests, taken by most people in high school or college, indicate what occupations are most appropriate for each person. The results of these tests are often questioned because many people have excelled in occupations for which the test indicated they had no aptitude.

Skills Tests. Skills tests are probably the least challenged of all selection tests. These tests measure a person's ability to perform certain tasks. For example, people applying for secretarial positions should expect to be asked to take a typing test, and they may be asked to demonstrate that they can operate common office machines.

Intelligence Tests. Basic intelligence tests are not commonly used by employers because few people have found a strong correlation between intelligence and job performance. If it could be demonstrated that only people with IQs in excess of 110 can perform a certain job competently, intelligence tests would be acceptable. However, until such correlation can be established, entrepreneurs should not rely on IQ tests.

Honesty Tests. These tests are important because all employers want to hire honest employees and because they are so controversial. There are basically two types of honesty tests—polygraph tests and pencil-and-paper tests. The former are probably the most controversial. Since polygraph tests have been called invasive and unreliable, they have been banned or restricted in twenty-two states. These tests have the added disadvantage of being relatively expensive—they cost anywhere from $40 to $100 and require a trained operator to administer them. In addition to administration costs, companies face huge court-ordered settlements if incorrect results cause an employee to lose his or her job (see The Inside View 11-3). To counter the criticisms of polygraph tests, companies that produce selection tests have developed pencil-and-paper tests that purportedly measure honesty.

Several companies have developed fairly simple tests that reportedly can spot dishonest people. There are approximately twenty such tests, the most frequently used of which are: the Reid Report by Reid Industrial Psychologists, Chicago, IL; The Stanton Survey by the Stanton Corp., Charlotte, NC; the Personnel Selection Inventory (PSI) from London House, Inc., Park Ridge, IL; and the Trustworthiness Attitude Survey by Personnel Security Corp., Oak Brook, IL. These tests, which cost about $10, are simple to administer and take little time to complete. The following are sample questions from the Stanton test:

- Did you ever lie to a teacher or a policeman?
- When you are wrong, do you usually admit it?
- Is it very important for you to be trusted?
- Do you think you are sometimes too honest?
- Do you agree with this: Once a thief, always a thief?

While the producers of these tests claim that they do identify dishonest people, other disinterested people are not completely convinced. Paul Sackett, a psychologist

11-3 *The Inside View*

LIE DETECTORS

After working ten years for Papa Gino's of America, John J. O'Brien was an area supervisor in charge of twenty-eight restaurants and about five hundred employees. He refused to promote a company director's son and was charged, several weeks later, with drug use. The company gave O'Brien two choices: take a polygraph test or be fired. He took the test and was fired because Papa Gino's said the results proved that he lied. O'Brien sued the company and won. He was awarded $595,000, a settlement that was later upheld by a federal appeals court. Now a renovator of houses in New Hampshire, O'Brien feels the false charge of drug abuse will always be with him: "People in the company avoided me like the plague when they spread that around, and I think I'll always carry the stigma."[7]

at the University of Illinois at Chicago, examined nineteen different tests and found the accompanying validity data wanting. He cautions that such tests are an exercise in "playing the odds" and do not necessarily reveal something absolute about a person. If entrepreneurs choose to use these tests, Sackett suggests the following guidelines:

1. Don't overrely on them. Use other screening devices in conjunction with these tests.
2. Use test results as an additional piece of information, not as a way to make or break someone's career.
3. Periodically retest employees at all levels. People change.
4. Use tests at the end of the preemployment screening process, once the number of candidates has been reduced to the few best choices.[8]

Graphology. The study of a person's handwriting is also a form of testing. Used more often in Europe than in the United States, graphology is a kind of testing that describes an individual's personality. Approximately four to five thousand U.S. companies have used handwriting analysis as a part of their selection process.

REFERENCE CHECKS

Most application forms ask job candidates to list several references who can provide occupational and personal information about them. There are two types of references—personal references and past employers or professional references. Few employers give much credence to personal references because they know that most applicants would not list anyone who would give them an unfavorable recommendation. Preachers, teachers, and friends are not a likely source of objective information upon which employers can base their selection decisions.

Previous employers and professional references are a more objective source of information about an applicant's potential than are personal references. Before a potential employer can contact a previous employer, applicants must give their permission in writing. Once contact is made, inquirers can expect to receive very little information about the applicant. Fear of discrimination suits has caused many employers to provide information only about the length of time an applicant was employed. It is very difficult to convince a previous employer to discuss an applicant's job performance, salary, or reasons for the termination of employment.

Because of the sensitive nature of employee information, many employers no longer write to previous employers for such information. People are aware that written records can be easily used as evidence in any litigation; therefore, they may be more willing to provide information in person or over the telephone. Even if the telephone is used, entrepreneurs should not expect to receive much useful information. Telephone reference requests should be structured (see Figure 11.3) in order to conserve time and record important information.

FIGURE 11.3
Telephone Reference

Candidate ____________ Position ____________

Previous employer ____________

Spoke to ____________

1. Dates of employment: From ____________ To ____________
2. Job title ____________ Duties ____________

____

3. Job attendance: Good ________ Average ________ Poor ________
4. Job performance: Good ________ Average ________ Poor ________
5. Worked without close supervision: Yes ________ No ________
6. Number of promotions ________ Number of pay raises ________
7. Beginning salary ____________ Ending salary ____________
8. Reason for leaving ____________
9. Would you rehire? Yes ________ (if not, why not?) ____________

____

Date ____________

PHYSICAL EXAMS

Physicals should be one of the last tests administered to prospective applicants. They are expensive, and the results should be used only to determine if a person is physically capable of performing the job for which he or she has applied. Entrepreneurs who use physical exams to determine what jobs an applicant can perform are not likely to have discrimination lawsuits filed against them.

THE JOB OFFER

Once the selection process has been completed, interviewers should make a formal job offer to successful applicants and should also formally notify unsuccessful applicants that they were not selected. The employer can notify successful candidates of their selection by telephone; however, he or she should also mail a formal job offer to them. The offer can be structured to suit the employer, but it should contain at least the following information:

Short congratulatory message from the business owner
Title of the job
Where the applicant will be working and the name of his or her immediate supervisor
Hourly wages or annual salary
Brief description of the company benefits program
Normal working hours
Date by which a reply is expected

The interviewer should have conveyed most of this information to applicants during the interview, so a response should not require lengthy deliberation.

HIRING PITFALLS

We have devoted a lot of attention to the various steps in the hiring process because selecting the right employees is so important to the startup firm. It is very expensive to hire the wrong person, and is becoming increasingly difficult to terminate unsuitable employees. So it is appropriate to conclude this section with a list of hiring pitfalls suggested by Lester Tobias, President of Psychological Services International:[9]

- Hiring expediently under the pressure of time—the "buy now, pay later" approach
- Hiring on the basis of product knowledge instead of ability
- Deciding to hire the "best of the batch" out of desperation
- Using the "don't some of us have to be Indians and not chiefs?" rationale to justify lower standards
- Hiring a well-known company's castoffs
- Assuming that a track record is a guarantee of future performance
- Explaining away inconsistencies in someone's record or presentation
- Hiring with the hope that someone will change
- Hiring for a specific position only and ignoring promotability

- Ignoring personal feelings and hiring someone only on the objective facts
- Relying only on first impressions
- Hiring an underachiever on the assumption that the entrepreneur's energy and success will be contagious

TRAINING

Even startup entrepreneurs with an uncanny ability to select the best employees hire people who need to be trained. All new employees, regardless of their individual skills and abilities, will need to be trained in company operating procedures in order to become part of the team. The American Society for Training and Development (ASTD) estimates that businesses spend approximately $31 billion to train and educate their employees. Most of that money is spent to make employees more productive and more committed to their jobs and companies. The first part of the training program for which entrepreneurs should prepare is the orientation of new employees.

Orientation

Almost everyone hired to staff a new venture will be somewhat confused and uncomfortable at first; therefore, it is the entrepreneur's responsibility to familiarize all new employees with their surroundings as well as with their jobs. Many studies have shown that employees who receive no formal orientation take longer to adjust to their new company and job than do those who have been through an orientation. Orientations, which should be conducted by startup entrepreneurs, give new employees an opportunity to learn about company policies and philosophy.

It is difficult to specify exactly what information should be provided to new employees during an orientation; however, the following are some general topics which should be included: normal working hours, holidays, compensation policies, absences from work, grievance procedures, performance evaluations, line of authority, work rules, and other company procedures. In addition, employees should be introduced to each other and their supervisors, and they should be given a tour of the facilities. Some employers try to complete the entire orientation in a few hours or one morning; however, employees absorb and retain more information if the orientation is spread out over a few days.

Basic Training

After the orientation, most employees will need additional training to familiarize them with company procedures and their specific jobs. Once the company is fully operational, employees will need additional refresher training and specialized training to equip them for more responsible jobs.

Training methods. For most new companies, on-the-job training (OJT) is probably the most effective and least expensive training method, for it enables entrepreneurs or their assistants to train new employees to perform their jobs the "right" way without acquiring any undesirable work habits. If several new employees are to be trained to perform similar jobs, they can be trained in a classroom setting rather than on the job.

Trainers. In most cases, someone within the new firm will be responsible for training; however, if such is not the case, or if specialized training is needed, the entrepreneur can hire outside trainers. A training consultant can provide specific training programs, or employees can enroll in local vocational schools or colleges in order to receive the necessary training.

COMPENSATION

Deciding how much employees should be paid, including both cash and benefits, is difficult for any employer, but it is especially so for entrepreneurs who are just starting a business. Startup entrepreneurs do not want to offer salaries significantly above what other employers pay, nor do they want to offer salaries too low to attract capable employees. Determining the appropriate salary for each position in a new firm seems to require the wisdom of Solomon; however, lesser men and women can usually establish equitable pay rates if they consider basic job-related factors. Before deciding how much to pay employees, entrepreneurs should determine which compensation method to use.

Compensation Methods

Entrepreneurs can choose to pay employees either for the number of hours they work or for the amount of product they produce. Most companies pay their employees for the amount of time they work because it is the easier of the two methods. Employees keep track of the number of hours they work, and they are paid accordingly at the end of the pay period. Employers who want to eliminate clock-watching can pay all their employees on a salary basis that guarantees them a stipulated sum of money each year. Payment for time worked essentially eliminates or minimizes discrimination, but it may not motivate employees to work to their maximum potential.

To encourage employees to maximize their output, employers can pay them on an incentive, or pay-for-output, basis. There are several different incentive plans all based on the assumption that it is possible and useful to tie pay directly to performance. One of the earliest incentive plans used, the piecework system, bases an employee's wages on the number of items or pieces he or she has produced. For many retail employees, commissions paid for merchandise sold is a form of the piecework system. Entrepreneurs who want their employees to be committed to the company may use profit-sharing and stock-ownership plans. Such deferred-compensation programs are less expensive for startups than paying high salaries, and they encourage employees to stay and grow with the company. It is considerably easier to create incentive systems for salaried workers than for hourly wage earners; however, one small company has developed such a system for its hourly workers (see The Inside View 11-4).

Factors Affecting Wages

Startup entrepreneurs may not be able to decide how much each job in their new company is worth, but some factors can serve as guidelines for establishing wages.

11-4

The Inside View

CREATING INCENTIVES FOR HOURLY WORKERS

Parsons Pine Products Inc., a small firm in Ashland, Oregon, developed a four-point plan for "positive reinforcement" of hourly workers. The plan includes:

- *Safety pay.* Each employee who works for one month without a lost-time accident receives a bonus equal to four hours' pay.
- *Retro pay.* The workers share any money the company receives when its workers' compensation premiums go down because of a reduced accident rate.
- *Well pay.* Employees have no sick days. Instead, they receive monthly "well pay," equal to eight hours' pay, provided they have been neither absent nor tardy.
- *Profit pay.* Earnings above 4 percent after taxes are distributed to employees whose share is determined by multiplying their wages times a job rating that is based on attendance, productivity, and leadership.

Since the plan was introduced, the accident rate, which was 86 percent above the state average, dropped to 32 percent below that average; turnover is minimal; tardiness is rare; and absenteeism has dropped to almost zero.[10]

The following factors affect wages:

Supply and Demand. If the demand for various types of workers is greater than the supply, wages will be higher than they should be and vice versa.

Area Pay Practices. In most communities there is a "going rate" for jobs established by local custom. Employers try to pay their workers wages that are in line with those earned by workers doing comparable jobs in other companies.

Type of Work Performed. Skilled jobs demand higher pay rates than unskilled jobs, but other adjustments are made to compensate for dangerous work, jobs performed in undesirable work environments, and jobs nobody wants to do.

Legislation. We have already discussed the Equal Pay Act and the Fair Labor Standards Act, both of which affect compensation. There are two other laws that are important to startup entrepreneurs, especially those who plan to do business with the federal government. The first, the Davis-Bacon Act, stipulates that companies doing construction work for the federal government in excess of $2,000 pay wages comparable to those prevailing in the area as determined by the Department of Labor. The second, the Walsh-Healy Act, requires employers with federal contracts in excess of $10,000 to pay wages comparable to those prevailing in the area as determined by the Department of Labor.

Benefits

Money represents only a portion of an employee's total compensation. The compensation package also includes the benefits (noncash items) provided by the company. In the past, the term fringe was used with *benefits* because they were often an insignificant part of the compensation package; however, now the U.S. Chamber of Commerce calculates that benefits cost 39.3 percent of payroll. They are no longer fringes. We cannot identify all benefits offered by different companies, but the following list contains some of the major benefits that startup entrepreneurs should consider:

Group insurance (life, health, etc.)
Paid holidays
Paid vacations
Jury duty pay
Paid sick leave
Pension plan
Profit-sharing plan
Sponsored recreational programs
Workers' compensation
Unemployment insurance
Tuition reimbursement

Employers can choose which benefits their employees receive; however, it might be more appropriate to allow employees to select their own benefits. Flexible benefit programs, known as "cafeteria" plans, allow each employee to "spend" a stipulated amount of money to "buy" the benefits most important to her or him. For example, a female employee may have health and life insurance through her husband's plan, so profit sharing or tuition reimbursement may be more important to her. Each employee puts together a benefit plan that suits his or her own personal needs.

Regardless of how benefit plans are developed, entrepreneurs should make certain that employees know the value of their plan in real dollars. Unfortunately, too many employees believe that their benefits are not worth much because nobody has told them the cost of all the benefits. Beginning with the orientation and continuing at regular periods thereafter, employers should tell their employees what their benefits cost the company (see The Inside View 11-5).

Performance Appraisals

Most employees begin working at similar jobs earning the same salary; however, as the new firm grows, some employees earn more than others. Deciding how to allocate raises is not always easy, but startup entrepreneurs will be ahead of the game if they establish fair, objective performance-appraisal systems before their company starts operations. During orientation, employers should tell their employees what is expected of them and how their performance will be evaluated. Evaluation systems should be consistent and objective, but they need not be overly complicated (see Figure 11-4).

Finally, employers should use evaluations. People who perform better than their peers should advance faster and be paid more than less capable employees. Employees should be evaluated more than once a year, and the results of the evaluation should

11-5 *The Inside View*

COMMUNICATING BENEFITS

Companies should begin explaining what they provide in the way of benefits as well as how much they pay for them. Most companies do an atrocious job on both counts, with the result that most employees are unaware of what they are receiving or what their benefits are worth. There is a fairly simple solution to the problem: Give each employee a customized booklet that spells it all out in plain English. One company, BenePlus Inc. will produce such booklets for as little as $14.50 each, depending on the number of employees involved. Each booklet includes the employee's salary; the overall value of the benefits, both in dollars and as a percentage of salary; and a breakdown of those benefits, with clear explanations and figures showing how much each one is worth.[11]

be communicated to them. Companies that let their employees know how they are doing should have no trouble retaining the good employees they worked so hard to recruit, hire, and train.

Summary

One of the most critical tasks facing startup entrepreneurs is the selection of capable employees. One reason it is so important to hire the right people is that the government has made it very difficult to terminate employees. Federal legislation such as the Civil Rights Act of 1964, the Equal Pay Act, the Fair Labor Standards Act, the Age Discrimination in Employment Act, the Vietnam Era Veterans Readjustment Act, and the new immigration laws protect employees' rights and allow employers to terminate workers only for just cause. That being the case, employers should devote enough time to the selection process to ensure that they select the best people to work for their startup companies.

Once entrepreneurs have determined how many employees they need, they should develop recruiting programs that will attract qualified job candidates. Interviews, tests, and reference checks should identify those candidates who are best suited to the available jobs. Entrepreneurs should understand that they are hiring people for current jobs who can also grow with the business. Even qualified employees will need training; therefore, entrepreneurs should install effective training programs. Trained and competent employees expect to be equitably compensated for their contribution to the new firm.

FIGURE 11.4
Performance Review: Non-Exempt Salaried Personnel

PERFORMANCE REVIEW
NON-EXEMPT SALARIED PERSONNEL

NAME ______________________ JOB TITLE ______________________

DIVISION ______________ DEPARTMENT ________ LOCATION ______________

TIME IN CURRENT JOB ______________________________

RATING SCALE:

1. SUPERIOR 2. VERY GOOD 3. SATISFACTORY 4. FAIR 5. UNSATISFACTORY

PERFORMANCE FACTORS – Circle the appropriate rating.

QUALITY OF WORK:	Consider accuracy, thoroughness, and general acceptability.	1	2	3	4	5
QUANTITY OF WORK:	Consider the volume of work produced within reasonable time limits.	1	2	3	4	5
JOB KNOWLEDGE:	Consider mastery of skills and duties required for the job.	1	2	3	4	5
INITIATIVE:	Consider how often he seeks additional responsibility.	1	2	3	4	5
COMMUNICATIONS:	Consider skills exhibited in expressing himself and in listening effectively.	1	2	3	4	5
DEPENDABILITY:	Consider consistency of meeting work schedules and deadlines.	1	2	3	4	5

REMARKS AND SUMMARY EVALUATIONS:

____

____

____

____

REVIEW DISCUSSION Held on: ______________________

Summarize his reactions to the review. Did he concur with your conclusions? Did he offer ideas for improving his performance?

____

____

____

____

______________________ ______________________

REVIEWER'S SIGNATURE/DATE SIGNATURE OF REVIEWER'S SUPERVISOR/DATE

Startup entrepreneurs need to determine the best method of compensating their employees, the rate of compensation, and the benefits they should offer. Employees can be paid for the time they work or for the amount of goods they produce. The salary or wage an employee receives is determined by such factors as supply of available workers, area pay practices, type of work performed, and federal legislation. To complete a compensation package, entrepreneurs can offer benefits such as group insurance, paid holidays and vacations, paid sick leave, profit-sharing, workers' compensation, and tuition reimbursement.

Assembling the Pieces

When Jacki and Carol were planning In Good Taste, they intended to have no full-time employees. They thought that they would be able to manage the business and deal with customers. Since the business would be somewhat seasonal, Jacki and Carol planned to hire part-time employees to assist them during Christmas and other busy seasons. The part-time workers to be employed were friends of Jacki and Carol; therefore, no recruiting, testing, etc., would be necessary. Soon after startup, Carol and Jacki realized that they would have to rethink their original decision.

Within a few months after startup, it became apparent that if Jacki and Carol were the only full-time employees of In Good Taste, the business would always be just another "mom-and-pop" company. The owners were so busy with day-to-day activities that they had no time to plan, make contacts, participate in professional organizations, maintain adequate records, go on buying trips, or expand the business. The company would grow only if Carol and Jacki were able to spend time planning, buying, and so forth; therefore, they decided to hire one full-time employee and at least two part-time employees who could be used as needed.

The full-time employee was hired at a starting wage of $3.50 per hour and was given incremental raises. The new employee received her training on the job and attended special courses at local colleges and the technical school. There are no benefits, other than merchandise discounts, for part-time or full-time employees, nor are there any other incentives or bonuses. As the company grows, Jacki and Carol know that they will have to make some adjustments to their personnel policies (see Chapter 20). ■

entrepreneur's checklist

THE EQUAL EMPLOYMENT OPPORTUNITY COMMISSION DISCRIMINATION QUIZ

An employer

	True	False
1. can refuse to hire women who have small children at home.	____	____
2. can generally obtain and use an applicant's arrest record as a basis for non-employment.	____	____

	True	False
3. can prohibit employees from conversing in their native language on the job.	____	____
4. whose employees are mostly white or male, can rely solely upon word of mouth to recruit new employees.	____	____
5. can refuse to hire women to work at night because he or she wishes to protect them.	____	____
6. may require all pregnant employees to take a leave of absence at a specified time before delivery date.	____	____
7. may establish benefits—pension, retirement, insurance, and health plans—for male employees that are different than those for female employees.	____	____
8. may hire only males for a job if state law forbids employment of women in that capacity.	____	____
9. need not attempt to adjust work schedules to permit an employee time off for a religious observance.	____	____
10. only disobeys the Equal Employment Opportunity laws when he or she is acting intentionally or with ill motive.	____	____

ANSWERS TO EEO QUIZ: All answers are false.

Questions for Review and Discussion

1. What protection do people receive from the Civil Rights Act of 1964?
2. The Equal Pay Act requires employers to pay women the same wage they pay men for the same job. Why do women continue to earn less than men for the same work?
3. Which sources of employees do you think entrepreneurs should use to acquire workers for their new companies?
4. Ask any company you are familiar with for one of its application forms. What questions, if any, do you think are illegal or potentially discriminatory?
5. What should entrepreneurs do to conduct successful interviews?
6. Which of the different types of tests do you feel are least likely to be discriminatory?
7. Can you make a case for using polygraph tests to select employees?
8. Of what value are company orientations?
9. Should entrepreneurs plan to pay their employees for the time they work or for their output?
10. Do you think that employees are really aware of the value of the benefits their employers provide?
11. What factors affect employee wages?

Notes

1. Dianna Solis, John Emshwiller, and Alfredo Corchado, "New Immigration Law Brings Much Anxiety," *The Wall Street Journal,* 5 June, 1987, p. 1.
2. Ibid., p. 18.

3. Thomas Ricks, Pauline Yoshihashi, and Robert Johnson, "Even Though They Hate the Paperwork, Most Firms Obey New Immigration Law," *The Wall Street Journal,* 28 April, 1987, p. 21.

4. Virginia Inman, "Small Companies Hire Part-time Officers," *Inc.,* September 1985, p. 11.

5. Bradford Smart, *Selection Interviewing* (New York: John Wiley & Sons, 1983), p. 125.

6. Ibid., pp. 188–189.

7. John Hoerr, Katherine Hafner, Gail DeGeorge, Anne Field, and Laura Zinn, "Privacy," *Business Week,* 28 March, 1988, pp. 61–68.

8. Ron Zemke, "Employee Theft: How to Cut Your Losses," *Training,* May 1986, pp. 74–78.

9. Lester Tobias, "Hiring for Excellence," *Industry Week,* 20 April, 1987, p. 71.

10. Bruce Posner, "Creating Incentives for Hourly Workers," *Inc.,* July 1986, pp. 89–90.

11. Patricia Amend, Donna Fenn, Joshua Hyatt, and Bruce Posner, "Communicating Benefits," *Inc.,* December 1986, p. 120.

CHAPTER 12

Marketing

Learning Objectives

After reading this chapter you will be able to do the following:

- Understand the importance of marketing research.
- Recognize the value of effective packaging.
- Calculate the right price for products and services.
- Develop promotional and sales campaigns.
- Understand the value of advertising.

To be successful, startups need effective marketing programs. Startup entrepreneurs can develop unique products, devise a more efficient way of providing a service, or assemble a winning management team, but they will not see their firms succeed unless they can convince consumers to buy their product or service. *Marketing* is the art and science businesses use to convince consumers to patronize them. For startups, effective marketing is critical because they are unknown and must create or capture market share. Therefore, it is absolutely necessary for startup entrepreneurs to develop a successful marketing program before they open their new business.

Most successful marketing programs incorporate the four P's: product, price, place, and promotion. *Product* is the term used for the activities involved in creating, developing, producing, and packaging goods and services. *Price* is the amount of money customers are willing to pay for products or services. *Place* is the method of distributing the product or service to customers. *Promotion* includes all information and advertising activities used to convince customers to buy a firm's product or service.

The four P's of marketing will serve as the primary focus of this chapter. There will also be a discussion of marketing research, packaging, pricing, advertising, and other miscellaneous marketing activities as well as an explanation of why these functions can make or break a new venture. While we stress the importance of an effective marketing program, we are not suggesting that every startup entrepreneur must create an original or unique marketing program. In fact, there is nothing wrong with

12-1 *The Inside View*

COPYCAT MARKETING

There is basically nothing new about marketing. All the important techniques were invented long ago. So how does an entrepreneur determine what type of marketing to use? Management consultant Jack Falvey's answer to that question is: Be a copycat marketer. "Find out what works for other companies, particularly the leaders in your field, and do the same." Falvey points out that real marketing, the kind that successful small companies do, is not a glamorous activity: "It's done one-on-one with key customers at sporting events, in restaurants, and around hospitality suites. It's hard work, requiring long hours and careful follow-up, and it won't get you into the next business best-seller. But it might get you three new accounts and pay for a part of a new building."[1]

using the successful programs of other companies if they are appropriate and adaptable to a new venture (see The Inside View 12-1).

Using marketing programs developed by other companies is an acceptable business practice, but there are some other practices to be avoided. For example, the following are some of the most common unethical activities businesspeople would like to eliminate: (1) gifts, gratuities, bribes, and companions who provide sexual favors; (2) price discrimination and unfair pricing; (3) dishonest advertising; (4) miscellaneous unfair competitive practices; (5) cheating customers, unfair credit practices, and overselling; (6) price collusion by competitors; (7) dishonesty in making or keeping a contract; and (8) unfairness to employees and prejudice in hiring.[2] It is important to note that five of the eight most important ethical problems relate to marketing activities.

MARKETING RESEARCH

In Chapter 2, we discussed how startup entrepreneurs can use marketing research to determine whether or not a need for their products or services exists. In this chapter, we will consider how marketing research can determine who the customers are and what it will take to convince them to patronize a new firm. Now startup entrepreneurs need to answer the following questions: Who are our customers and where are they located? How great is the demand for our products or services? How should we package the product? What channels of distribution should we use? How much should our products or services cost? How can we give value to our customers? How should we advertise and promote our products?

Learning as much as possible about customers is one of the primary reasons for undertaking marketing research. Customers are real people who patronize those businesses that treat them courteously and offer quality products or services at fair prices. Before trying to identify and categorize customers, startup entrepreneurs should consider what James Cash Penney said about customers in 1913:

- The customer is the most important person in any business.
- The customer is not dependent on the business—the business is dependent on the customer.
- The customer is not an interruption of work—he or she is the purpose of it.
- The customer is doing the business a favor by calling—the business is not doing a favor by serving him or her.
- The customer is part of the business—not an outsider.
- The customer is not a cold statistic—he or she is a flesh-and-blood human being with feelings and emotions.
- The customer is always right.
- The customer is a person with wants—it is the job of the business to satisfy them.
- The customer deserves the most courteous and attentive treatment the business can supply.
- The customer is the lifeblood of this, and every other business.

Conducting Marketing Research

To answer the foregoing questions, startup entrepreneurs need to collect as much pertinent information as possible. They do not need to spend numerous hours collecting data, nor do they need to spend huge sums of money for the information they need. It is possible to use the results of other research and to get free information from several sources (see The Inside View 12-2). Suppliers, brokerage houses, and trade associations are all ideal sources of free information.

When free sources cannot provide all the needed information, entrepreneurs will have to pay for additional data; however, purchased data need not be unduly expensive. The following techniques will keep the price of information down:

Do some of the work yourself: You can do the counting yourself and have the researcher tell you what your findings mean. Doing the grunt work yourself will lower the bill.

*Do not hold the researcher to a useless **standard of care:*** You can hire a researcher who will give you a "best guess," based on less-than-total data.

Buy pieces of a study: Pay only for those parts of bigger studies that apply to your own product and market.

Offer the researcher equity: If your business looks like it will be successful, researchers may be willing to trade you extremely reduced fees for a small part of the action.[3]

Market Segmentation

No business can manufacture or sell a product that appeals to everyone; therefore, startup entrepreneurs have to identify their target market. *Segmentation* is the process used to determine just who will be the new firm's customers. Markets can be segmented by using geographic variables, such as urban, suburban, rural, etc.; demo-

12-2 *The Inside View*

INEXPENSIVE MARKETING RESEARCH

When Phil Kelly left Marshall Field & Company to start his own shop, he needed marketing research but could not afford to pay very much for his information. Kelly began his information hunt by reviewing all the research he had absorbed over his nearly thirty years in retailing, including "the decline of discounting, the growth of specialty stores, and the steady drop in department-store market share." Next, Kelly approached clothing manufacturers for information about the size of his target market. The free data they showed Kelly revealed that 21 percent of clothes buyers prefer suits costing $200 to $299. Kelly decided that these men would be his customers. The decision to target that market—arrived at with the help of someone else's research—dictated a large part of Kelly's merchandising strategy.[4]

graphic variables, such as age, sex, education, income, etc.; or psychographic variables, such as life-style and personality. Startup entrepreneurs should also decide what type of consumer is most likely to patronize the new business. The basic consumer types and their percentage of total buyers are: innovators (2 to 3 percent), early adopters (12 to 15 percent), early majority (33 percent), late majority (34 percent), and laggards (12 to 15 percent).

Innovators. Innovators are willing, and have the income, to buy new products. These consumers are usually upper-class, well-traveled, and self-confident. They do not need peer approval for the products or services they purchase.

Early Adopters. Usually well-educated and upper-middle-class, early adopters are those consumers who have earned their own wealth and are willing to spend it for quality products. These consumers are not confident enough to purchase new products until they see someone else buy them. However, once they see innovators using new products, they quickly follow suit.

Early Majority. These consumers are less-well-educated and not as wealthy as innovators or early adopters. They may be small-business owners or nonmanagement, white-collar workers who identify strongly with their own kind. This group, influenced by the early adopters, will only purchase new products after they have seen other people using them for some time after introduction.

Late Majority. This group is composed of skilled workers who are basically upper lower-class. They lack the confidence to purchase new products, so they wait until the product has been purchased by a considerable number of people (the early majority) before they make their decision.

Laggards. Laggards are people with unskilled or menial jobs who tend to live only for the present. They purchase mainly necessities.

Having identified the target market (see the Entrepreneur's Checklist on customer analysis), startup entrepreneurs can then proceed to determine how to attract those consumers to their new business. It is important to understand that advertising and promotion will have to be specifically tailored to the target market. Advertising that appeals to early adopters will probably have little effect on laggards.

PACKAGING

Many startup entrepreneurs will need to decide how to package their product or service to make it appealing to consumers. Package design, once a relatively minor consideration, has become a major element of marketing strategy. Many consumers base their purchasing decision on the package that contains the product they want. For example, the Point-of-Purchase Advertising Institute (POPAI) reports that 80 percent of supermarket purchases now result from in-store decisions, up from 65 percent just ten years ago. This has led companies to spend nearly $5 billion annually to upgrade package designs. Much of that money is spent by small firms for whom the market shelf has become the great leveler in their competition with industry giants.

Purposes of Packaging

Packaging serves purposes other than the basically utilitarian function of containment. For example, effective packaging serves to identify the product (the Coca-Cola bottle) and to provide consumers with necessary information. Packaging can also satisfy the aesthetic and status needs of customers. Finally, by using different size packages, sellers can offer goods in the quantity desired.

While the size and shape of packages help meet the functional requirements of sellers, color also enhances the effectiveness of packages. Different colors convey different messages to consumers. For example, green is symbolic of safety and youth; red denotes danger, warmth, and power; and white symbolizes cleanliness and purity. Entrepreneurs who choose the wrong color for their packages will confuse consumers and will probably not enjoy the sales levels they would have had the color chosen reinforced the written or spoken message.

Graphic Design

Size, shape, and color are important packaging considerations; however, the package is not complete until it has been labeled. Graphic designers have primary responsibility for creating appealing and functional labels. Some specific modern packaging and graphic-design trends include the following:

- The accurate, photographic representation of the product on the package when possible—to communicate honestly.

entrepreneur's checklist

CUSTOMER ANALYSIS

	Yes	No
Who are your target customers and what are they seeking?		
Have you profiled your customers by age, income, education, occupation, etc.?	____	____
Should you try to appeal to the entire market rather than a segment?	____	____
Are you familiar with your customers' life-styles?	____	____
Are there new customer segments or special markets that deserve attention?	____	____
Have you considered that among your target customers changes may take place that could significantly affect your business?	____	____
Do you know where your customers live?	____	____
Do you use census data from your city or state (e.g., neighborhood tracts, income, population)?	____	____
Are you aware of the reasons why customers shop at your store? (convenience, price, quality products, etc.)?	____	____
Do you stress a special area of appeal, such as lower prices, better quality, wider selection, convenient location, or convenient hours?	____	____
Do you ask customers for suggestions on ways to improve your operation?	____	____
Do you know which products or services your customers prefer?	____	____
Do you belong to a trade association or local chamber of commerce?	____	____
Do you subscribe to important trade publications?	____	____
Do you know what seasons and holidays most influence the buying behavior of your customers?	____	____
Have you considered using a consumer questionnaire to aid you in determining customer needs?	____	____
Do you know at what other types of stores your customers shop?	____	____
Do you visit trade shows and conventions to help anticipate customer wants?	____	____

Source: Michael Little, *Marketing Checklist for Small Retailers* (Washington, DC: U.S. Small Business Administration, 1985), Management Aids, Number 4.012, p. 2.

- The "natural look" or concern for naturalness in a product, suggested by natural props used in conjunction with the **product**—to communicate the product's natural qualities.
- The simplification of all graphic material on the package—to communicate quickly.
- The selection of high-contrast color combinations—to communicate legibly.
- The promise of the product, such as warranties or guarantees, displayed on the package.[5]

Packaging Creativity

Mundane, utilitarian products that have no inherent customer appeal should be attractively packaged to generate interest. It is not always possible to create exciting packages; however, those entrepreneurs who succeed in designing unusual packages can beat their competition. An example of very unusual and genuinely creative packaging is seen in The Inside View 12-3.

PRICING

For many startup entrepreneurs, determining the right price to charge for their products or services is not easy. The bankruptcy of Contextural Design Inc. serves as an example of what happens to startups that do not charge the right price. Contextural Design was founded in 1977 to manufacture furniture. The owners set up a production line that took rough lumber and sawed, clamped, glued, tenoned, planed, routed, mortised, and sanded it into unfinished components that were shipped to about 800 furniture components outlets.

Given such an involved production process and the machines and space it required, how were prices calculated? The partners decided that 50 percent gross "felt like it would work," not only taking care of overhead but returning a comfortable net profit as well. So they simply added direct labor and raw materials, and multiplied by two. Sales increased, but the company had difficulty earning a profit. Over the years, Contextural Design was not able to find the right price for its products. By 1984, the

12-3 *The Inside View*

CREATIVE PACKAGING

Remember when condoms were hidden behind drugstore counters and inside teenagers' wallets? Now some people are displaying them openly—on their ears. A firm in Austin, Texas, has introduced a line of earrings made of packaged condoms mounted on cardboard squares. In three months the company, called Wear and Share, has sold more than 1,200 pairs for $4.50 each through hair salons, clothing stores, and novelty shops from Washington, D.C., to San Francisco. Austinites Marsha Malgesini, a gynecological nurse, and business partner Patricia Jackson started the venture out of their homes in hopes of easing inhibitions in the age of AIDS. The original run of earrings was red, yellow, blue, and green. Since then, they have added a $10 designer line decorated with beads and glitter.[6]

company showed payables at $454,322 versus receivables of $189,025 and a 4 percent pretax loss—$95,431 on sales of $2,393,090. The company struggled on for a few more months, but on June 19, 1985, the company filed for bankruptcy.[7]

Pricing Objectives

Like the owners of Contextural Design Inc., many startup entrepreneurs do not establish realistic pricing objectives. They want to make money but are unaware of other pricing objectives. The following are some other legitimate pricing objectives:

- Cover all costs.
- Ensure profitability.
- Make the product or service competitive.
- Discourage other firms from entering the market.
- Impart a quality image.
- Gain market share.
- Assure longevity.

Once startup entrepreneurs understand the importance of establishing the correct price, they can select the appropriate strategy for its determination.

Pricing Strategies

In certain instances, startup entrepreneurs will find that they have no choice of the price they charge for their goods; however, if the product should be unique or new, there will be considerable pricing latitude. Following are some basic pricing strategies:

Cost-Plus Pricing. One of the most common pricing strategies is to simply add a set percentage to the cost of a product in order to earn the company an acceptable profit. The difference between the cost of the merchandise and the retail price is called the *markup* (sometimes also referred to as *mark-on*). Markup can be calculated as follows:

$$\text{Dollar markup} = \text{Retail price} - \text{Cost of merchandise}$$

$$\text{Percentage markup} = \frac{\text{Dollar markup}}{\text{Retail price}}$$

For example, if an item costs $6.50 to produce and an entrepreneur believes that customers will buy it for $10.00, the dollar markup is $3.50, which is $10.00 − $6.50. The percentage markup is 35 percent, which is $3.50 divided by $10.00. While this procedure is relatively simple, it has the following drawbacks:

- It is often difficult to determine such costs as construction expenses and material price changes before they are incurred.
- It is difficult to allocate joint costs to individual products.
- It ignores elasticity of demand.
- It generally ignores competition.
- It does not differentiate between out-of-pocket and "sunk" costs.
- It is not always easy to determine "fair" return.
- It ignores capital requirements and return on investment.[8]

Competitive Pricing. If goods or services are essentially undifferentiated, new business owners will probably be forced to charge about the same price as their competitors.

Status Pricing. When customers are unable to evaluate product quality, they often equate quality with price. The equation of quality with price occurs when these three conditions exist: (1) consumers must be able to acquire information about price more easily than information about quality; (2) their desire for high quality must be strong enough to make them risk buying the high-priced product with no assurance of correspondingly high quality; (3) there must be a sufficiently large number of informed consumers who appreciate quality and will pay a high price only for the high-quality product.[9]

Penetration Pricing. When a firm is trying to establish its products in a new market, it might choose to use lower-than-normal prices to attract customers.

Opportunistic Pricing. Some companies might choose to charge artificially high prices during periods of severe product shortage. This strategy may be profitable in the short run; however, when the shortage is over, customers will probably choose to buy from competitors because they feel "ripped off" by the opportunistic pricer.

Skimming. If a company is the only maker or seller of a product, it can afford to charge a high price for that product. However, once other makers or sellers enter the market, a competitive pricing strategy will usually be necessary.

Loss-Leader Pricing. Some companies cut the price of selected products in order to attract customers who might also buy other products. Leader pricing is an accepted business practice, but startup entrepreneurs should avoid the closely related "bait-and-switch" strategy. Firms cannot advertise low prices for their products with the intent of forcing customers to "trade up" to higher-priced products.

Introductory Pricing. Startup companies trying to establish their products might offer "special introductory" prices that are lower than the regular price will be once the company and its products have been accepted by consumers.

Oddball Pricing. Many companies have found that for special sales or promotions, oddball prices are effective: offering three items for $1 may sell many more products than pricing each item at $0.33.

Odd-number Pricing. Many products are priced at odd numbers such as $19.99 or $99.99 because customers perceive these prices as being less than $20 and $100, thereby reducing their resistance to purchasing items with odd-number prices.

Discounting. Startup entrepreneurs often decide to charge less for the same product available at competing companies in order to gain market share. The plan is relatively simple: Customers will patronize the new business because it has prices lower than those of competitors, and they will remain with the new business even though it eventually raises its prices to match the competition. For the uninitiated, this simple formula of selling more for less can be a fatal trap (see The Inside View 12-4).

12-4

The Inside View

DISCOUNT PRICING

When Thomas McKiernan started Printing Images Corp., he fell headfirst into the trap of viewing sales growth as a measure of success. Besides, he believed that cutting prices was the only way for his startup company to distinguish itself from others in the printing business. Discounting his services brought in considerable business. Printing Images went from zero to $725,000 in annual sales in four years, but the company was losing more and more money each year. Here is an example of what was wrong: The selling price of a particular product was $100. The variable costs, including production and labor, were 53 percent of the selling price, or $53. Fixed costs were $40, which left a $7 profit on each unit sold. If that unit were to be discounted to $80, with the variable costs remaining at $53 and the fixed costs at $40, the business would be $13 in the hole for each unit sold. McKiernan changed his pricing strategy to ensure his company's profitability.[10]

Determining the Right Price

We have described several alternative pricing strategies; however, we have not indicated how startup entrepreneurs can determine the right price for their products or services. The appropriate price can only be determined after entrepreneurs have answered questions specific to their product, customers, and competition. Some pertinent questions (see the Entrepreneur's Checklist on pricing for a more complete list of questions) include the following:

- Is the product unique?
- Can other entrepreneurs easily copy the product?
- Is the product protected (patent, trademark, etc.)?
- Is the product a "fad" item?
- How much are customers willing to pay?
- What is the demand for the product?
- What are the customers' buying habits and motives?
- Do customers shop around for this type of product?
- What is the degree of price awareness?
- How will competitors react to this price?
- What is the availability of competing and substitute items?

entrepreneur's checklist

PRICING

	Yes	No
Have you established a set of pricing policies and goals?	____	____
Have you determined whether to price below, at, or above the market?	____	____
Do you set specific markups for each product?	____	____
Do you set markups for product categories?	____	____
Do you use a one-price policy rather than bargain with customers?	____	____
Do you offer discounts for quantity purchases or to special groups?	____	____
Do you set prices to cover full costs for every sale?	____	____
Do the prices you have established earn the gross margin you planned?	____	____
Do you clearly understand the market forces affecting your pricing methods?	____	____
Do you know which products are slow movers and which are fast movers?	____	____
Do you take this into consideration when pricing?	____	____
Do you experiment with odd or even prices to increase your sales?	____	____
Do you know which products are price sensitive, that is, when a slight increase in price will lead to a big dropoff in demand?	____	____
Do you know which of your products draw people when put on sale?	____	____
Do you know the maximum price customers will pay for specific products?	____	____
If the prices on some products are dropped too low, do buyers hesitate?	____	____
Is there a specific time of year when your competitors have sales?	____	____
Do your customers expect sales at certain times?	____	____
Have you determined whether or not a series of sales is better than one annual clearance sale?	____	____
Have you developed a markdown policy?	____	____
Do you take markdowns on a regular basis, or as needed?	____	____
Do you know what role you want price to play in your overall retailing strategy?	____	____
Are you influenced by the price changes of competitors?	____	____
Do any of your suppliers set a minimum price below which you cannot go?	____	____
Does your state have fair trade practice laws that require you to mark up your merchandise by a minimum percentage?	____	____
Are you sure you know all the regulations affecting your business, such as two-for-one sales and the like?	____	____
When sale items are sold out, do you issue "rain checks" to customers so they can purchase them later at sale price?	____	____

Source: Michael Little, *Marketing Checklist for Small Retailers* (Washington, DC: U.S. Small Business Administration, 1985), Management Aids, Number 4.012, pp. 3–4.

After answering these questions, startup entrepreneurs should be able to determine the right price for their products. It is important to remember that once established, prices are not permanently fixed, because as the startup firm gains market share, it may want to raise its prices to reflect increased costs, decreased competition, and other variables.

Increasing Prices

Higher prices should increase net profit; however, entrepreneurs should not raise prices indiscriminately. To make price increases effective and palatable, entrepreneurs should take the following steps: (1) raise prices when everyone else does; (2) do not raise prices too much at any one time, and do not raise them too often; (3) try to reduce some prices when increasing others; and (4) let customers know why prices have been increased. For entrepreneurs reluctant to increase prices, here are ten ways to increase prices without actually increasing prices:[11]

1. Revise the discount structure.
2. Change the minimum-order size.
3. Charge for delivery and special services.
4. Invoice for repairs on purchased equipment.
5. Charge for engineering, installation, and supervision.
6. Make customers pay for overtime required to get out rush orders.
7. Collect interest on overdue accounts.
8. Produce less of the lower-margin models in the product line.
9. Write escalator clauses into contracts.
10. Change the physical characteristics of the product.

PROMOTION AND SELLING

New businesses will not succeed if they are unable to attract and retain customers. Startup entrepreneurs should plan their promotional programs before they actually open their doors. Special promotions differ from advertising in that they are usually one-time special events while advertising is a continuous campaign. Special promotions are used to introduce a new company or product or to inform consumers of some special event, such as a sale or relocation.

Developing Promotional Programs

Since startup entrepreneurs will rely heavily on promotional programs to announce the opening of their new business, they should allocate enough time and effort to the development of a program to ensure its success. Effective promotional programs can be created (see the Entrepreneur's Checklist on promotion) by taking the following developmental steps:

- Analyze the firm's marketing objectives.
- Isolate the role of promotion.
- Develop promotional objectives.
- Define the target audience.

entrepreneur's checklist

PROMOTION

	Yes	No
Are you familiar with the strengths and weaknesses of various promotional methods?	____	____
Are the unique appeals of your business reflected in the store image (e.g., low prices, quality product, special services, and the like)?	____	____
Have you considered how various media and promotional methods might be used by your firm?	____	____
Do you know which of your items can be successfully advertised?	____	____
Do you record sales of advertised merchandise?	____	____
Do you check store traffic?	____	____
Do you know which of the media (radio, TV, magazines, newspapers, yellow pages, billboards) can most effectively reach your target market?	____	____
Do you know what can and cannot be said in your ads (truth-in-advertising requirements)?	____	____
Can you make use of direct mail?	____	____
Do you have a mailing list? If so, has it been updated recently?	____	____
Is a customer list available through customer checks or credit cards?	____	____
Do you use coupons in your print ads?	____	____
Are your promotional efforts fairly regular?	____	____
Do you concentrate your efforts on certain seasons?	____	____
Are certain days of the week better than others?	____	____
Do you use trade journals and out-of-town newspapers for promotional ideas?	____	____
Have you considered specialty advertising?	____	____
Do you participate in the activities of your chamber of commerce, merchants' association, better business bureau, or other civic organizations?	____	____
Have you considered customer seminars and classes?	____	____
Are cooperative-advertising funds available from vendors/suppliers?	____	____
Do you join with other merchants in area-wide promotional programs?	____	____
Do you ask customers to recommend your business to their friends and relatives?	____	____
Have you looked for ratios to estimate what similar firms are spending on promotion?	____	____
Do you make use of community projects or publicity?	____	____
Would a newsletter be effective in contacting customers or in reminding them of your business?	____	____
Do you study the advertising of other successful firms as well as that of your competitors?	____	____

	Yes	No
Do you know which of your items have unusual eye appeal and can be effective in displays?	____	____
Have you determined the best locations for displays?	____	____
Have you a schedule for changing various displays?	____	____
Do you display attention-getting items where they will call attention to other products?	____	____
Do signs in your business provide useful price and product information?	____	____
Do you know which items are bought on impulse and therefore should be placed in high-traffic areas?	____	____

Source: Michael Little, "Marketing Checklist for Small Retailers," (Washington, DC: U.S. Small Business Administration, 1985), Management Aids, Number 4.012, pp. 4–5.

- Analyze alternative approaches.
- Select optimum use of elements of promotion.
- Determine general message content and desired image.
- Select appropriate media.
- Implement the plan.
- Measure results and provide feedback.[12]

It is important to remember that the purpose of promotional programs is to make products appealing to consumers. This can be accomplished by using the following types of appeal: status, humor, statistics (studies, surveys, etc.), sex, economics, natural ingredients, youth, and health. It is possible to develop a promotional program that uses more than one type of appeal, and it is possible to develop a program that uses a type of appeal unsuccessfully. For example, a company may develop a program with a humorous appeal only to discover that its campaign is not funny.

Promotion Techniques

New businesses can promote themselves and their goods or services by offering customers samples, product demonstrations, coupons, premiums (gifts customers receive with their purchase), rebates, extended warranties or guarantees, and free service contracts. However, some of these giveaways may not have the desired effect and can even reduce the company's sales. For example, the owner of a dress shop provided reduced-price coupons to a firm that did bulk mailing to households in the shop's market area. Very few coupons were redeemed because recipients discarded their "junk" mail without even opening the envelope. The owner later learned that many people are suspicious of the quality of merchandise sold by stores that offer discount coupons.

Selling

Every business is involved in selling something. Some sell manufactured products; some sell handcrafted goods; some sell buildings and land; and some sell services.

Some businesses sell to other businesses; some sell to wholesalers; some sell to customers who come to their stores; some sell to customers in their homes (direct selling); some sell by telephone; and some sell by mail. Regardless of the product or service being sold or the method of selling, new ventures will not be successful if their owners and their staff are unable to sell. Therefore, it is important that new business owners recruit individuals who can be trained to become successful salespeople.

It is difficult to spot individuals who can sell successfully; however, there are some recognizable traits that are common to effective salespeople. First, they have a thorough knowledge of their customers, markets, and competition. Second, they always want to learn more selling skills and techniques. Third, they handle customer objections well because they are aware of the value of personal service. Fourth, they understand company policy. Last, they have positive attitudes.

Selling is likely to become more challenging in the future. In their study of eighty companies, the Yankee Group, a consulting firm, identified the following as the sales challenges of the 1990s:

Distinguishing between similar products and services. Lack of distinction among products is causing buyer confusion; therefore, companies need salespeople who can explain to customers how their products or services differ from those of their competitors.

Offering groups of products to gain greater consumer appeal. Selling product "packages" or "bundles" to satisfy buyer needs is a challenge for the marketing and sales forces of the future.

Handling a better educated buying population. Customers will work harder to purchase products that maximize value; therefore, salespeople will have to work harder to make a sale.

Mastering the art of consultative selling. Salespeople will have to convince customers that the service or product offered is exactly what they need.

Managing a team-selling approach. More sales will be made by teams of people who will draw upon the knowledge of technical staff, support personnel, marketing staff, and other experts.

Knowing the customer's business. In the future making sales will require better knowledge of the customer's business operations.

Adding value through service. Companies can differentiate their products and add value by offering services such as business consulting and ongoing support for their products.[13]

ADVERTISING

Effective advertising is crucial to the survival of new ventures. Startup entrepreneurs need advertising first to inform their target customers that their business will soon be operational and then to persuade customers to buy their products or services and to patronize the business. Finally, advertising should constantly remind customers that the company is in business to serve them and that it appreciates their patronage. If advertising campaigns created for new ventures fail to inform, persuade, and remind, the new company will have difficulty surviving.

Purchasing Motives

People need to be persuaded to purchase most products and services. We all instinctively purchase the goods that we absolutely need such as food, clothing, shelter, and the like, but it is other nonessential goods, such as TVs, stereo equipment, and luxury automobiles, that we need to be persuaded to purchase. What motivates people to buy items they do not really need? The following emotions prompt people to buy products and services:

Pride. An appreciation of personal worth or a statement of personal style.
Vanity. An enhancement of self- or public image.
Status. A sense of accomplishment or social recognition.
Cupidity. The joy of possession, for show or for security.
Love and libido. The belief that a given product will bring or earn love, or lead to libidinal gratification.
Fear. The fear of losing friends, security, station, respect, life, and so forth.
Pleasure. The absence of pain. The desire to be entertained, amused, soothed, and thrilled.
Envy. The need to keep up with or to surpass the Joneses.
Power. The need to influence the lives of others.
Sense of mission or conscience. The expression of patriotic, religious, or charitable feelings.[14]

Regardless of what motivates people to buy, entrepreneurs must trigger something in customers to convince them to purchase goods or services. For most consumers, buying is not always a simple procedure (see Figure 12.1); they need to have a latent desire to purchase products; they search for and evaluate suitable products; they make their purchase; and finally they evaluate the whole process. The result of that evaluation determines whether or not they will continue to patronize a business or switch to competitors.

The Usefulness of Advertising

Advertising will not solve all the problems encountered by new ventures. Therefore, startup entrepreneurs should be aware of what advertising can and cannot do. For example, advertising *can* do the following:

Introduce a new company
Introduce a new product
Improve an image
Suggest new uses for products
Tell customers about product availability
Create product awareness
Increase consumption of a product
Increase frequency of purchase or use
Provide warranty and guarantee information
Tell customers about a special sales promotion

FIGURE 12.1
A Simplified Model of Consumer Purchasing

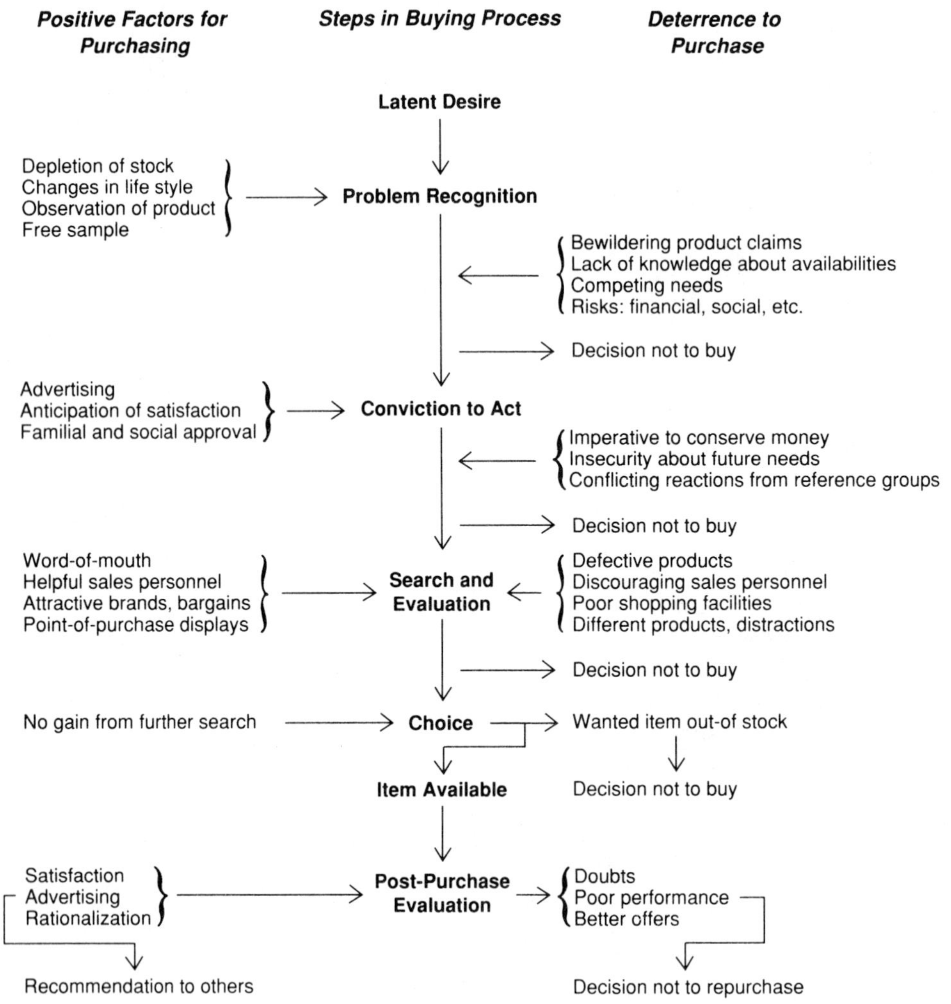
Positive Factors for Purchasing
Steps in Buying Process
Deterrence to Purchase
Latent Desire
Depletion of stock
Changes in life style
Observation of product
Free sample
Problem Recognition
Bewildering product claims
Lack of knowledge about availabilities
Competing needs
Risks: financial, social, etc.
Decision not to buy
Advertising
Anticipation of satisfaction
Familial and social approval
Conviction to Act
Imperative to conserve money
Insecurity about future needs
Conflicting reactions from reference groups
Decision not to buy
Word-of-mouth
Helpful sales personnel
Attractive brands, bargains
Point-of-purchase displays
Search and Evaluation
Defective products
Discouraging sales personnel
Poor shopping facilities
Different products, distractions
Decision not to buy
No gain from further search
Choice
Wanted item out-of stock
Item Available
Decision not to buy
Satisfaction
Advertising
Rationalization
Post-Purchase Evaluation
Doubts
Poor performance
Better offers
Recommendation to others
Decision not to repurchase

Source: Harold Fox, *Understanding Your Customers* (Washington, DC: U.S. Small Business Administration, 1985), Management Aids Number 4.001, p. 5.

However, advertising *cannot* perform miracles such as:

Sell an inherently bad product, service, or business
Bolster a basically inadequate marketing program
Sell a product for which no want or need exists
Sell a product for which need cannot be created[15]

12-5 *The Inside View*

ADVERTISING ASSISTANCE

For two years Gary Copp did all his company's advertising himself. Today his oil-change and tune-up outlets are number 1 in Louisiana. However, Copp now admits that he could have used some help: "At first I wrote all my own advertising—including a few direct-mail pieces that lost money," he says, acknowledging that some of his creative work was not effective. Copp did not want to hire an advertising agency because ". . . the trouble with ad agencies is that they don't know anything about your business. You have to train them and work with them closely." Nevertheless, Gary Copp eventually gave in and hired an outside agency.[16]

In-house Advertising

Entrepreneurs who need to be in control of all aspects of their business also choose to control the firm's advertising campaign. A study conducted by *Venture* revealed that 95 percent of the responding entrepreneurs took active roles in their companies' advertising, from writing their own copy to organizing publicity events. Some entrepreneurs are successful advertisers, and some are not. Even successful advertisers sometimes admit that they could have benefitted from using professional advertising services (see The Inside View 12-5).

Being familiar with the business, knowing the merchandise, and saving money are some of the benefits of in-house advertising. However, lack of expertise and time are reasons entrepreneurs should consider using outside agencies to handle their advertising. Another reason to use a professional ad agency is that few entrepreneurs and laypeople are creative enough to develop effective advertisements. The following are qualities characteristic of creative people:

- Gives up immediate gain to achieve long-range goals.
- Channels tremendous amount of energy into productive effort.
- Perseveres despite obstacles and opposition.
- Exercises great initiative.
- Pursues many hobbies, skills, and interests.
- Welcomes new experiences.
- Criticizes himself or herself more than others do.
- Is not afraid to ask questions that show ignorance.
- Competes with self rather than others.
- Wants to integrate utility with the aesthetic.
- Moves toward solutions using intuition.[17]

Entrepreneurs who do not possess these traits should hire professionals to handle their advertising.

Advertising Agencies

Ad agencies provide all the services new ventures need. They write copy, prepare layouts and artwork, select appropriate media, and evaluate the effectiveness of the advertisement. Entrepreneurs who do not need all of these services can hire more specialized agencies. Media agencies, for example, only help companies determine the most effective media for their advertising program, and other agencies only prepare artwork or write copy. Finally, radio and TV stations, magazines, and newspapers will provide their clients with advertising assistance.

Advertising Budgets

No matter who does it, startup entrepreneurs themselves or their agencies, advertising is not inexpensive. The problem most entrepreneurs face is determining how much to budget for their advertising programs. There are several relatively simple ways of determining how much money to spend on advertising. First, a certain percentage of sales can be allocated to advertising. Second, entrepreneurs can choose to match their competition and spend as much on advertising as they do. Third, entrepreneurs can decide to spend "whatever it takes." Or, they can allocate any money that is left after paying other expenses to advertising. Following is a list of different businesses showing the typical size of their advertising budgets (as a percentage of sales) and the media they use most frequently.

Type of Business	Average Budget (%)	Favorite Media
Bicycle shops	1.5 to 2.0	Newspapers
Bookstores	1.5 to 1.6	Newspapers, yellow pages
Drugstores (independent)	1.0 to 3.0	Local newspapers
Gift stores	2.2 →	Weekly newspapers
Home-furnishings stores	1.9 to 3.2	Newspapers
Liquor stores	0.5 to 0.6	Point-of-purchase displays
Mail-order firms	15.0 to 25.0	Newspapers & magazines
Pet shops	2.0 to 5.0	Yellow pages
Restaurants	0 to 3.2	Newspapers, radio, transit, yellow pages
Shoe stores	0.5 to 0.8	Newspapers, direct mail, radio[18]

Advertising Media

To have an effective advertising program, startup entrepreneurs need to select the right media or combination of media for their advertising. To announce the creation of new firms entrepreneurs use printed media (direct mail, leaflets, newspapers, etc.); broadcast media (television and radio); position media (billboards and transportation advertising); point-of-purchase displays; and word of mouth. Properly used, all of these media can be effective; however, we will discuss the advantages and disadvantages only of the media most commonly used by new businesses.

Yellow Pages. Most startup entrepreneurs will buy advertising space in the yellow pages of their telephone directory. The following dos and don'ts should help entrepreneurs maximize their yellow-page advertising:

- Do list as many important facts about your business as feasible.
- Do make your ad look and "feel" sophisticated.
- Do treat the ad like a personal communication, not a cold listing.
- Do let folks know if you accept credit cards or offer other methods of finance.
- Do gain the reader's attention with a strong headline.
- Do let people know all the reasons they should buy from you.
- Don't let the staff of the yellow pages write your ad.
- Don't run small ads if your competitors run big ads.
- Don't make your ad look or sound boring.
- Don't forget to use graphics to communicate handsomely.
- Don't list your business in too many directories or categories.
- Don't treat your ad less seriously than a full-page magazine ad.[19]

Direct Mail. Entrepreneurs can mail announcements of the impending opening of their business to potential customers living or working in the new firm's market. Relatively inexpensive, direct mail is sent only to targeted customers and is not intrusive. The major disadvantage is that many recipients might consider the mailer to be junk mail and will not read the message.

Leaflets. Like direct mail, leaflets can be distributed to those people most likely to patronize a new business. They are inexpensive to produce and distribute, and they can include cents-off coupons or other devices to induce people to patronize a new business. Unfortunately, leaflets share the same disadvantage as direct mail: People often discard them without reading them.

Newspapers. Startup entrepreneurs use this advertising medium more often than others because it is timely, provides good market coverage, and is relatively inexpensive. In addition, coupons and inserts can be included in newspapers. The disadvantages of newspaper advertising relate to *segmentation* and *clutter*. It is not possible to use newspapers to reach only a select group of potential customers, and a new firm's advertisement might not be read because it is clustered with so many others. Consumers often read newspaper ads for price-comparison shopping; therefore, quality-oriented products should be advertised in other media (see The Inside View 12-6).

Radio. Radio advertising is usually more expensive than printed advertising, but it does have some advantages startup entrepreneurs should consider. First, ads can be targeted to a specific audience. Second, selecting appropriate time slots exposes the same audience to the same ads several times. Third, good copy can hold a listener's attention, and announcers can add personality to an advertisement. Finally, listeners cannot "skip over" or ignore radio ads as easily as they can printed advertisements. However, there are negatives: Ads usually cannot exceed sixty seconds; there is com-

12-6 *The Inside View*

AVOIDING THE NEWSPAPER TRAP

Barry Knowles, owner of a ValCom Computer Center in Harrisonburg, Virginia, spent a year and several thousand dollars advertising in local newspapers before he realized that he was using the wrong medium: "We were positioning ourselves as a high-performance business center," he says, which did not leave room to compete on price. Knowles built a new advertising strategy on the product-information seminars that he conducted in local hotels. He advertised the seminars in local newspapers, but there was no mention of price in the ads and no hard sell at the seminars. This strategy proved to be much more successful than newspaper advertising.[20]

petition for the best time slots; and listeners who are working or driving do not pay careful attention to radio advertising.

Miscellaneous. The following are less frequently used advertising media that might help new businesses get started:

- Billboards and signs on buses or subways.
- Ads displayed in sports arenas.
- Ads in programs for cultural events.
- Free speeches or seminars.
- Complimentary T-shirts.
- Giveaway calendars, pens, matches, etc.

Writing Advertisements

Regardless of the media selected, to be effective, advertisements must be well written. Startup entrepreneurs can write their own copy, or they can hire professionals. The following tips should help entrepreneurs write advertisements that sell their products or services:

Make it easy on the reader. Write short sentences and use familiar words.
Don't waste words. Do not be verbose or try to wax eloquent.
Stick to the present tense, active voice. It is crisper.
Don't hesitate to use personal pronouns. Remember, you are trying to talk to just one person, so talk as you would to a friend.
Clichés are crutches. Learn to get along without them.
Don't overpunctuate. It kills copy flow. Excessive commas are the chief culprits.
Use contractions whenever possible. They are fast, personal, and natural.

Don't brag or boast. Translate those product features you are so proud of into consumer benefits that appeal to customers.
Be single-minded. Don't try to accomplish too much with one advertisement.
Write with flair. Make sure the enthusiasm you feel comes through in your copy.[21]

Advertising Mistakes and Misconceptions

Not all advertising is effective. Sometimes the copy is not good; sometimes the wrong medium is selected; and sometimes the firm's advertising philosophy is inappropriate. The following are some advertising mistakes and misconceptions:

- Advertising can sell anything, anywhere, anytime.
- The customer needs and wants our product.
- Clever copy is thoroughly read.
- "Big" equals "better" in advertising.
- Anything our competitor does, we should do bigger.
- Advertising agencies are too expensive.
- Humor can sell anything.
- Sex can sell anything.
- Less expensive media will save us money.
- Sales are down, so cut the advertising budget.
- Sales are up, so cut the advertising budget.
- The customer knows us by now.
- Our target market includes everybody.
- Our customers are educated; they will understand.
- Our customers are dumb; talk down to them.
- Nobody reads long copy.
- We paid for thirty seconds; speak faster.
- Research is expensive; we know the ads are working.[22]

Effective advertising can be achieved by using the *AIDA* formula. *A* stands for attention: An ad must capture the attention of the target market. *I* stands for interest: Once customers have begun to read, look at, or listen to an ad, they must be kept interested in order to "get the message." *D* is for desire: Good advertising makes people want the advertised product or service. Finally, *A* stands for action: If an ad does not motivate a person to buy the product or service, it has failed.

Truthful Advertising

Entrepreneurs may periodically pay for advertising that does not achieve the desired end; however, they should not engage in untruthful or misleading advertisements. By following these guidelines, entrepreneurs will stay on the right side of the law:

1. Don't make specific representations or statements unless they can be verified by scientific tests or other reliable means.
2. Don't advertise a product as "new" unless it is less than six months old.
3. Don't imply that a product had a country of origin unless it was actually produced in that country.

4. Don't suggest that a product is endorsed by any person or group unless that endorsement is in writing.
5. Don't advertise a "limited" supply unless the supply is actually short. The FTC (Federal Trade Commission) takes the position that this places undue pressure on the consumer.
6. Don't compare products with those of a competitor unless you give a full and fair comparison of all relevant points.
7. Check every word in the advertisement for truthfulness and accuracy.[23]

Regulatory Agencies

Because entrepreneurs have a tendency to exaggerate the benefits or qualities of their products, there are several government agencies that regulate advertising. No single agency is responsible for guaranteeing truth in advertising; however, several agencies have as one of their functions the protection of consumers from false or deceptive advertising. A few of the agencies that monitor advertising are the Federal Trade Commission (FTC), the Food and Drug Administration (FDA), the Consumer Products Safety Commission (CPSC), the Federal Communications Commission (FCC), and the Office of Consumer Affairs (OCA).

Summary

Startup entrepreneurs who fail to appreciate the value of marketing are not likely to enjoy successful business careers. It is a fact that most businesses are market driven; that is, without demand for products or services, businesses will fail. Before starting a new venture, entrepreneurs should do some basic research in order to understand who their customers are, where they live, why they buy, how often they buy, and other important characteristics. Sound marketing research is one of the underpinnings of most successful businesses.

To get the attention of consumers, products and services must be attractively packaged. Packaging can identify the product, protect the product, satisfy status needs, and provide consumers with convenience and protection. The use of color and professional graphic design enhances a package's attractiveness to consumers. Once entrepreneurs know what they are selling, they need to determine how much to charge for their goods and services. Some pricing strategies to consider include cost-plus pricing, competitive pricing, status pricing, skimming, penetration and introduction pricing, and discounting.

After products have been packaged and priced, entrepreneurs need to decide how they are going to attract their patrons. Various promotion techniques can help generate consumer interest in new businesses. New business owners can give customers samples, cents-off coupons, product demonstrations, extended service contracts, or rebates to promote patronage of their companies. Special promotions, which are usually one-time affairs, can initially attract customers to a new business, but sustained advertising is usually required to keep customers coming back on a regular basis.

Advertising can introduce a new company or product, improve a firm's image, create product awareness, and increase consumption of a product. However, advertising cannot sell an inherently bad product, a product for which no want or need exists, or a product for which need cannot be created. Startup entrepreneurs can choose to do their own advertising, or they can hire advertising agencies. Entrepreneurs or their agents need to decide which advertising media are likely to be most successful. They can advertise in print, broadcast, or position media, or they can rely on point-of-purchase displays or word of mouth.

Assembling the Pieces

Jacki and Carol selected the name *In Good Taste* for their new business because it enhanced the image of quality they were trying to project. They wanted everything about their business—products, layout, packaging, advertising, and service—to be of the highest quality. Their promotion and advertising programs also were designed to strengthen their quality image. First, Jacki and Carol designed their logo—a cluster of grapes—to indicate that fine wine was one of their primary products. Second, they decided that the name of the business, the title of the newsletter, and other text would be printed in script rather than block letters. Third, they decided on a color scheme—burgundy and silver—that would be used for their ribbons, wine bags, and other items. Fourth, Carol and Jacki decided that their packages (spices, cheese trays, gift baskets, etc.) should be distinct enough that recipients would recognize their origin. Carol and Jacki also wanted to create an advertising program that would be in keeping with their image.

Pricing the products sold at In Good Taste was not difficult. Prices for major items such as wine, cheese, and coffee were usually "manufacturer's suggested retail price" or those suggested by wholesalers. Other items were marked up an average of approximately 50 percent. Finally, some unique items, such as the specialty herbs and spices, were priced at "what the market would bear." Jacki and Carol were always careful to keep their prices in line with those of their competitors. They hoped to "outsell" the competition by providing better service and by developing an effective advertising campaign.

Jacki and Carol decided that the best advertising for their business would be word of mouth, so they made sure that all their friends, acquaintances, and professional associates were fully informed about In Good Taste. Since word of mouth is not always reliable, Jacki and Carol decided also to advertise in the local newspaper and to prepare brochures for distribution in their target market. Jacki and Carol wrote most of the advertising copy themselves; however, they did rely on professionals for some special advertisements.

In addition to word-of-mouth and newspaper advertising, Jacki and Carol decided to use a special promotion for the opening of the business. Coupons entitling customers to price discounts were included in a mass mailing of other coupons and discount offers, but the response was so negligible that the promotion was not repeated. Special promotions after startup were limited to reduced prices on particular product lines, such as wine, cheese, coffee, and the like.

Since direct mail seemed to be the most effective advertising for In Good Taste, Jacki and Carol bought a mailing list compiled by the chamber of commerce. They also used the mailing lists of professional and social organizations to which they belonged. One of their first projects after startup was to compile a mailing list consisting of all the people who entered their shop whether their purpose was to buy or just to browse. Each month or so, Carol and Jacki send everyone on the mailing list a copy of the newsletter they publish, which contains recipes, other items of interest, and news of upcoming events such as special sales, group tours, or cooking classes. ■

Questions for Review and Discussion

1. Explain why effective marketing programs are so important to startup entrepreneurs.
2. What questions is marketing research supposed to answer?
3. What are the characteristics of different types of consumers?
4. What functions does packaging perform?
5. Can you name packages, like Coca-Cola bottles, that identify products?
6. Explain the different pricing strategies.
7. Do you think skimming and opportunistic pricing are unethical?
8. What promotion techniques can startup entrepreneurs use?
9. Explain what advertising can and cannot do.
10. If you were starting a business, how would you choose the appropriate media for your advertising?

Notes

1. Jack Falvey, "Follow the Leader," *Inc.*, July 1986, pp. 93–95.
2. R. C. Baumhart, "How Ethical Are Businessmen?" *Harvard Business Review*, 39:6–9, 156–157.
3. Paul Brown, "On the Cheap," *Inc.*, February 1988, pp. 108–110.
4. Ibid., pp. 108–110.
5. Bruce Bradway, Mary Frenzel, and Robert Pritchard, *Strategic Marketing: A Handbook for Entrepreneurs and Managers* (Reading, MA: Addison-Wesley, 1982), pp. 121–122.
6. Annetta Miller and Carolyn Friday, "Condom Earrings: Kitsch with a Message," *Newsweek*, 28 March 1988, p. 50.
7. Robert Mamis, "The Price Is Wrong," *Inc.*, May 1986, pp. 159–164.
8. John Winkler, *Pricing for Results* (New York: Facts on File, 1984), p. 44.
9. Gerard Tellis, "Beyond the Many Faces of Price: An Integration of Pricing Strategies," *Journal of Marketing*, October 1986, pp. 146–160.
10. Mary Rowland, "Avoiding the Discount Trap," *Venture*, November 1985, pp. 33–34.
11. John Winkler, *Pricing for Results*, p. 46.
12. William Cohen and Marshall Reddick, *Successful Marketing for Small Business* (New York: AMACOM, 1981), p. 62.
13. ————, "Selling Today," *Training and Development Journal*, March 1988, pp. 38–41.
14. Ken Delmar, *Winning Moves* (New York: Warner Books, 1984), pp. 166–167.
15. Bruce Bradway, Mary Frenzel, and Robert Pritchard, *Strategic Marketing: A Handbook for Entrepreneurs and Managers*, pp. 63–64.
16. Nancy Madlin, "Creating an Image," *Venture*, March 1986, p. 24.
17. Eugene Raudsepp, "Are You a Creative Executive?" *Management Review*, February 1978, pp. 10–15.
18. Mike Cantor, *Open and Operate Your Own Small Store* (Englewood Cliffs, NJ: Prentice-Hall, Inc., 1982), pp. 80–81.
19. Jay Levinson, *Guerrilla Marketing* (Boston: Houghton Mifflin Company, 1984), pp. 110–111.

20. Donna Fenn, Teri Lammers, and Bruce Posner, "Avoiding the Newspaper Trap," *Inc.*, January 1988, p. 85.

21. David Malickson and John Nason, *Advertising: How to Write the Kind That Works* (New York: Charles Scribner's Sons, 1982), p. 81.

22. Bruce Bradway, Mary Frenzel, and Robert Pritchard, *Strategic Marketing: A Handbook for Entrepreneurs and Managers,* p. 92.

23. Arnold Goldstein, *The Small Business Legal Problem Solver* (New York: *Inc.*/CBI Publications, 1983), pp. 130–131.

CHAPTER 13

Purchasing and Inventory Control

Learning Objectives

After reading this chapter, you will be able to do the following:

- Describe the purchasing function.
- Locate and select suppliers.
- Explain how to maintain good supplier relations.
- Measure supplier performance.
- Describe how to control purchasing.
- Apply inventory-control techniques and systems.

Goods and materials are the major expenditure of most startup businesses. For example, almost 60 percent of the total cost of manufactured goods in the United States is the cost of materials, and the cost of wholesale goods represents almost 55 percent of the average retailer's total costs. Obviously, any reduction in either of these costs will have a significant impact on profitability. For this reason, the focus of this chapter is on obtaining, and having on hand, the correct quantity and quality of goods and/or materials needed for the efficient operation of the firm.

There are two major sections in this chapter. The first section contains a discussion of the purchasing system and its relationship to the overall profitability of the firm. Other topics presented in this section include the following: how to locate and select suppliers, how to develop and maintain good supplier relationships, how to measure supplier performance, and how to control the purchasing system. The second section focuses on the inventory system, including the management and control of inventory, and a presentation of different inventory systems. Also included is a list of inventory danger signals.

THE PURCHASING FUNCTION

Nearly all small businesses need to purchase goods and services. Retail and wholesale firms, which make up almost 37 percent of all small businesses, obviously must purchase the goods that they sell to their customers. The price and quality of these goods will be a major factor in the long-run success and profitability of these firms. Likewise, manufacturing and construction firms, which make up almost 22 percent of all small businesses, must purchase the materials they use in the manufacturing and construction process.

The cost and quality of these materials will affect not only the profitability but also the quality of the goods produced. In fact, the results of a survey of 81 small businesses in Pennsylvania indicated the importance of purchasing activities to the performance of those firms. On the survey it was noted that the job of purchasing was usually performed by the entrepreneur and that this activity consumed an average of five-and-one-half hours per week. This was not wasted time, however, as the survey findings showed that these entrepreneurs saw a strong positive correlation between the number of hours spent in purchasing activities and profitability.[1]

Purchasing is not, however, just the simple buying of goods and materials based only on cost and quality. Purchasing also includes obtaining goods, materials, and services in the right quantity at the right time. Buying four times the amount of a product needed just because the price is right is not a practice that will lead to the long-term viability of the startup enterprise. Purchasing is, therefore, obtaining goods and services at the right price, in the right quantity, of the right quality, at the right time.

The Right Price

The right price means that the cost of the goods or services is competitive but not necessarily the lowest available. Price should not be the only criterion in the purchasing decision, for both quality and quantity should be considered.

The Right Quantity

The right quantity means that the seller has the capability to deliver the specified quantity of the goods or materials sold. In the hope of obtaining an order and worrying later about meeting an agreed upon schedule, many suppliers promise more than they can deliver (see The Inside View 13-1).

The Right Quality

The right quality means that the product or service is suitable for its intended use. Notice that the term "right quality" was used and not "best quality." For most applications, the best quality is neither needed nor desired. For example, a firm that produces printed "tourist" T-shirts does not necessarily need the best quality cotton T-shirts.

The Right Time

Finally, the right time means that the product or material purchased will arrive when requested by the purchaser. Products arriving ahead of schedule tend to take up valu-

13-1

The Inside View

SALES VERSUS PRODUCTION

Salespeople have been known to promise more than production can deliver. Consider the case of a mill that produced animal feed and operated 24 hours a day for about 362 days each year. All machines were scheduled to operate 100 percent of the time, except for scheduled maintenance, which consisted of about 2 hours per day.

The sales force, which was based in another city, signed contracts to deliver feed to a new group of customers who required about 20 percent of the total production capacity of the mill. They then proudly presented their accomplishment to the mill's management. When the sales manager was informed that the plant simply did not have the capacity to produce any any more feed, he was totally amazed. The sales force had not thought of that problem before signing the contracts.

The problem was solved by producing a concentrate at the mill and by building a satellite mill to produce the finished product near some of the major buyers. In this case, the buyer was unaware of the potential problem, and the terms of the contract were satisfied. Unfortunately, many firms promise more than they can deliver in their efforts to increase sales. After obtaining the sales, they then attempt to balance production against sales by shipping partial orders and/or shipping late.

able warehouse or storage space, and products arriving late may be too late to have any value. We know of one new business that ordered $10,000 worth of posters to sell during a special two-week cultural event. The posters arrived two days after the event was over and were virtually worthless.

Suppliers as Sources of Information

Certainly securing goods and services at the right price, in the right quantity, of the right quality, and at the right time is important to startup entrepreneurs. However, few startup entrepreneurs have the time to research purchases, seek alternative sources, and/or negotiate lower prices. For these reasons, they are dependent on their suppliers to provide a high degree of service, product knowledge, technical support, and, sometimes, even financial support. Obviously this dependency can also be a trap for entrepreneurs since they may depend so much on their current suppliers that they do not become aware of better-quality products, lower prices, better service, or newer technological innovations. Because of this potential problem, startup entrepreneurs must guard against the habit of buying from the same suppliers without exploring alternative sources.

Startup entrepreneurs should also be aware that professional salespeople are trained to convince the potential buyer of the superior quality of their products. The buyer, therefore, must learn enough about the product being purchased to determine its true quality. One way to make this determination is to check the quality of other products by taking the time to listen to the presentations of different suppliers. Some startup entrepreneurs accomplish this by obtaining information from competitive suppliers by telephone. (Other methods for the location and selection of suppliers will be presented in a later section of this chapter.)

The Importance of Purchasing

How important is the function of purchasing to the startup enterprise? Without careful consideration of the quality, price, and timing of purchases, the future of the firm will not be bright. However, excellent purchasing techniques alone do not insure the success of a new business. This difference may best be illustrated by the tale of two restaurants.

Two family-style steak restaurants opened at about the same time and within two blocks of each other in Charleston, South Carolina. The two restaurants were almost identical in all respects: Both were franchises of nationally known chains; the prices in both were equal; and the service and decor were almost the same. However, one restaurant had waiting lines by the end of the first month, and the other seldom had more than a half dozen customers. The former is still in business many years later, and the other went bankrupt within a year.

What was the difference between the two restaurants? The owner of the successful restaurant purchased steaks of better quality (fresh rather than frozen) than those of the owner of the other, and customers could discern this difference in quality. Interestingly, the owner of the failing restaurant never understood the problem. He tried to increase his declining customer base with a variety of promotional and advertising campaigns that brought customers to the restaurant for their first visit but then failed to capture very much repeat business. Unfortunately, the owner of the failed restaurant never considered the quality problem because all his steaks were shipped (frozen) from a central warehouse, and he assumed they were okay—a practice that was true in other cities where the competition did the same.

Impact on Profits

In addition to the impact on the viability of the firm, purchasing can have a direct impact on the profitability of the firm. If the cost of materials accounts for about fifty cents of each sales dollar and profit is about five cents, a 1-percent reduction in the purchasing cost of materials could result in a 10-percent increase in profits. For example, consider the income statement of a firm with sales as follows:

	Original COGS	*COGS Reduced 1%*
Sales	$600,000	$600,000
Cost of goods sold (COGS)	300,000	297,000
Gross profit	300,000	303,000
General & admin.	170,000	170,000
Selling	100,000	100,000
Profit before taxes	30,000	33,000
Income tax (34%)	10,200	11,220
Net profit	$19,800	$21,780

The 1-percent decrease in the cost of goods, to $297,000, resulted in a 10-percent increase in profit before taxes, to $33,000. A 5-percent decrease in the cost of goods sold would have resulted in a 50-percent increase in profits. This example dramatizes the impact of purchasing on profits and indicates why entrepreneurs must spend time on the location and selection of their suppliers.

LOCATION AND SELECTION OF SUPPLIERS

Understanding the relationship of purchasing to the profitability of the startup firm is important, but the startup entrepreneur must know where to locate suppliers. Some entrepreneurs start their businesses already knowing the local suppliers, so their search process is as short as the time it takes to telephone these suppliers. However, most entrepreneurs must locate and select all, or at least some, of their suppliers and must develop a working relationship with them. Following is a list of sources of suppliers.

Sources of New Suppliers

1. ***Previous experience.*** Many entrepreneurs have previous work experience in the industry in which they start a business. From this experience, they have met and are familiar with many of the suppliers of the goods and services needed by their firms. This knowledge, however, can be a trap, in that the entrepreneur may rely on suppliers with whom he or she is comfortable and not seek out alternative, possibly superior, sources.

2. ***Experience of other members within the firm.*** In addition to the owner, other members of the startup firm may have had previous work experience that has brought them into contact with suppliers of goods and services needed by the startup firm.

3. ***Yellow pages.*** Many startup entrepreneurs completely overlook this handy and easy-to-use source of suppliers of many of the goods and services needed by their startup firms. The yellow pages are an excellent place to find local contractors, wholesalers, equipment-repair specialists, and suppliers of specialized equipment for many industries.

4. ***Sales representatives.*** Sales representatives (reps) are individuals who represent the products of one or more firms. Although they generally sell noncompeting products, sales reps tend to have a broad general knowledge of competing products. As a group, sales reps can be valuable sources of information on the strengths and weaknesses of various products. From the standpoint of the sales rep, if he or she can help a customer locate a needed product, even a competing product, then that grateful customer will be more receptive to the products offered by that sales rep.

5. ***Local chamber of commerce.*** Few organizations know the products and services offered in the community better than the local chamber of commerce. Typically, the chamber of commerce will furnish startup entrepreneurs with a directory of all local businesses that are members of the chamber. Entrepreneurs can obtain more specific information from the individual within the chamber of commerce designated to help new businesses.

6. ***Trade journals.*** Almost every industry has its own trade journal. These journals are full of advertisements and articles on new products, equipment, and services that are of interest to the industry. Trade journals, thus, serve both as a source of information on competing products and as a means of locating suppliers of those products.

7. ***Trade shows.*** Several industries hold semiannual or annual trade shows which offer entrepreneurs an outstanding opportunity to see and compare different types of products and services. The entrepreneur may place orders directly with the exhibitors or may just establish contact for possible future business connections. Some of the best known trade shows are North Carolina's Furniture Mart and Comdex, the semiannual computer show in Atlanta.

8. ***Merchandise markets.*** Merchandise markets are permanent markets that display merchandise throughout the year. Three of the best known are the Merchandise Mart in Chicago, Atlanta's Merchandise Mart, and the Trade Mart in Dallas.

9. ***Industry directories.*** Industry directories or catalogs of the products and services available in almost every major industry are other excellent sources of suppliers. Similarly, manufacturers' directories list the major manufacturers in the various industries. A list of these directories can be found in the *Thomas Register* or *U.S. Industrial Directory*. The *Thomas Register*, for example, is published annually in 21 volumes. Volumes 1–12 contain an alphabetical list of available products and services.

10. ***Cooperative buying.*** Some wholesalers, retailers, and end users have formed cooperative buying groups to reduce costs. The cooperative is owned by the businesses that form the group and is operated exclusively for the benefit of the members who may join by paying dues to the organization. A buying group is similar to a cooperative, but it is not owned by the members. A buying group is an organization of businesses that combine for the purpose of buying in large quantities in order to obtain reduced prices. For some of the pros and cons of a buying group, see The Inside View 13-2.

13-2 *The Inside View*

BUYING GROUPS

Small businesses are forming buying groups to gain the purchasing clout necessary to compete with the prices offered by larger corporations.[2] These buying groups include wholesalers, retailers, and end-users. For example, in 1986 the Independent Drug Wholesalers Group of Chicago purchased more than $2.2 billion in merchandise for its fifty-five members. Among hospitals, schools, and nursing homes, end-user buying groups are experiencing a tremendous growth in membership.

Buying groups are most prevalent in those businesses in which customers (buyers) can get the same quality from many sources and, therefore, buy on the basis of price. As small wholesalers and retailers are forced into competition with national chains in a price-sensitive market, a buying group can mean survival. In addition to providing buying clout, buying groups can provide logistical services and promotional materials like ad mats, catalogs, and fliers.

Buying groups also have some disadvantages. Firms who join buying groups can lose the close relationships they have enjoyed with their suppliers. In addition, members of a buying group may have to pay for some of the group's services that they do not need. Members may also find that they need long purchasing lead times or that the group may have restrictive covenants penalizing members who buy elsewhere. Finally, the initial fee for joining a buying group may be high, with typical costs ranging from $10,000 to $50,000.

Multiple Supply Sources

After locating the initial suppliers necessary to start the new enterprise, entrepreneurs should continue to develop multiple supply sources. There are three excellent reasons for developing multiple supply sources:

1. Competition leads to lower prices and/or better service. With only one supplier, entrepreneurs are accepting the price and services offered by that supplier, but if there is more than one supplier, entrepreneurs have a basis for comparing both the prices and the services available.

2. Dealing with multiple suppliers reduces the risk of missed shipments. With only one supplier of an important material or product, the new business could be in serious financial trouble if the supplier were to suffer a strike, a fire, or a truck wreck. Although these events are rare, they can also be devastating to new businesses that do not have alternative sources.

3. One business "fact of life" is that there are business cycles. There are times when cash and credit are tight, and suppliers may be forced to limit the credit available to customers. Often during these tight credit times, the purchasers who have their credit limited are the newer and smaller ones.

Single Sourcing

In some cases, entrepreneurs should consider single sourcing rather than purchasing from multiple sources. *Single sourcing* means that the buying firm chooses to purchase all of the material required for a particular item from a single firm. One of the major benefits of single sourcing is the potential for improved communication between the buyer and the supplier. When buyers are depending upon a single source, they tend to provide the supplier with much more accurate purchase-requirement data. The supplier, in turn, tends to provide much more helpful feedback about production capabilities, available alternatives, possible design modifications, and other details.

The disadvantages of single sourcing include the potential loss of bargaining power. Certainly single sourcing has both positive and negative aspects, and experts are divided on whether entrepreneurs should ever adopt this practice. However, where a truly cooperative relationship can be formed between buyers and suppliers, single sourcing does have the potential to be beneficial to both parties.[3]

SUPPLIER RELATIONS

There is more to the supplier–purchaser relationship than that of simply transacting business. The axiom that a "small business is only as strong as its suppliers" indicates that the relationship may even impact on the success of the new firm. What, then, should entrepreneurs do to develop strong supplier relationships? The key to strong supplier relationships is the golden rule: Treat others as you would have them treat you. Entrepreneurs should be strong in requiring that the terms of a contract be met; by the same token, they should be fair by not making unreasonable demands on the supplier and by paying on time.

Startup entrepreneurs must realize that suppliers are in the business of selling goods and/or services just like they are. The only difference is that the supplier is selling to other businesses whereas entrepreneurs are usually selling to a larger number of individual customers. They are, however, dependent on one another. Buyers/entrepreneurs depend on suppliers for the on-time delivery of the correct quantity and quality. Sellers/suppliers depend on buyers for on-time payment for those products and timely notification of any changes in expected delivery schedules.

The Buyer's Viewpoint

What are buyers looking for from sellers/suppliers? Buyers could evaluate what they expect from suppliers based on the following criteria:

1. ***Quality.*** Do suppliers deliver the quality promised in accordance with the terms of the contract, or is the number of rejections too high? Buyers have a right to expect consistent quality.

2. *Quantity.* Are suppliers able to deliver the quantity promised, or is the number of partial shipments too high? A percentage of the order shipped in the initial delivery is one method of evaluating a supplier's performance.

3. *On-time delivery.* Do suppliers ship on time, or do they have the reputation for shipping late?

4. *Technical support.* Do suppliers provide technical support? Technical support is necessary for some products, and buyers should expect enough support to enable them to effectively market that product.

5. *Expediting.* Expediting is requesting that an order, or part of an order, be shipped early. Are suppliers willing to expedite orders, or are suppliers unwilling to change their production and/or shipping schedules?

6. *Financial stability.* Are suppliers financially strong? It is just as important for buyers to check on the financial standing of their suppliers as it is for them to check on the financial standing of their own credit customers. A bankrupt supplier can leave the buyer in a very precarious position.

Some firms set up formal performance reviews of their suppliers and rank them by using various criteria (see The Inside View 13-3). What buyers expect from suppliers, then, is that suppliers meet the terms of a contract and provide technical and financial support when needed.

The Supplier's Viewpoint

Suppliers want customers who are able to plan orders far enough in advance of the expected shipping date to enable the suppliers to meet those dates without unnecessary production or scheduling changes. In addition, suppliers expect the buyers to pay on time for the goods or services received and not to make unreasonable demands on the supplier.

What is most evident from both the buyer's and the supplier's viewpoint is that each needs the other in order to be successful, and they can, therefore, create symbiotic relationships that are mutually beneficial. Each needs to understand and respect the situation of the other and to work toward their mutual goals.

Negotiation

Most small-business owners do not think they have the buying power or the necessary skills to negotiate with their suppliers. If owners do negotiate, they do so on price only. However, negotiation may also include terms, discounts, advertising support, freight costs, delivery schedules, warranty provisions, and return provisions. Each of these items can improve the long-run success of the firm.

Negotiation is a technique that all entrepreneurs must develop, and it starts simply with asking questions. For suppliers, sample questions might be: "Do you offer advertising support?" "What are your return provisions?" From questions as simple as these, buyers and sellers can negotiate the specifics of a contract. Negotiation is nothing more than a mutual agreement that ensures a better understanding between buyers and sellers. Without negotiation, both parties are left assuming that the other understands what is expected.

13-3

The Inside View

SUPPLIER PERFORMANCE

Small businesses that rely on a large number of suppliers for the products they resell, need to attract and retain high-caliber suppliers. To accomplish this, firms must have a way to accurately evaluate the performance of their suppliers. Miller Business Systems (MBS), a regional distributor of office products and furniture, initiated a rigorous supplier rating program that used the following criteria to rate supplier performance:

Accounting: Credit policies and billing accuracy.

Administration: Product-line acceptability, product quality, and responsiveness.

Advertising: Promotion flexibility and advertising allowance.

Purchasing: Fill percentage, lead time, representatives' performance, pricing, and minimum order.

Receiving: Packing list accuracy and quality of shipments.

For each performance criterion, suppliers are rated on a scale of 1 to 5, with 5 being the highest rating. Ratings for each supplier are calculated, and suppliers are compared by product category. The top suppliers are notified and thanked for their excellent service; lower-ranked suppliers are also notified and given an opportunity to improve. Interestingly, suppliers' response to the program has been positive, as it gives them some insight into what kind of performance MBS expects.[4]

Discounts. Discounts should be part of the negotiation process. There are four different types of discounts suppliers can offer. First, *trade discounts* are reductions from the list price that are available to various classes of buyers. A second type of discount is the *quantity discount*, where additional quantities may be purchased at a lower per unit cost. A third type of discount is the *seasonal discount*, which is the purchase of goods now but being billed later (in season), and the last type is the *cash discount* for payment by a certain date.

Ethics

This section could have been called *purchasing policy*, but "ethics" is an even more appropriate heading because all contact with a supplier should be ethical and professional. However, individuals often have different ideas about what is ethical, so entrepreneurs must have standard procedures to avoid misunderstandings and potential legal problems.

The policies regarding ethical standards for those involved in purchasing should include statements on the following:

1. Within each firm, it should be clear who has the authority to purchase material and services. This person (or persons) should also have the authority to select suppliers and sign supplier contracts.
2. Reciprocal buying should be avoided.
3. Other purchases by employees of the firm should be discouraged. Similarly, personal purchases in behalf of employees should be avoided.
4. Purchases from any firm in which an employee has an interest can cause a conflict of interest which is not beneficial to the buyer.
5. No employee should accept gifts, gratuities, or loans from any present or potential suppliers. Obviously the acceptance of lunch or dinner may be acceptable, but there should be written rules regarding what is considered excessive.
6. Employees should not discuss competitors' quotes, terms of a purchase agreement, or any other confidential information with outside suppliers.

The foregoing is only a partial list of items concerning purchasing and the relationship of a firm's employees and suppliers. Even a startup business needs a written set of procedures concerning the conduct of purchasing unless only the owner controls all purchasing.

CONTROL OF PURCHASING

Since the objective of purchasing is to obtain goods and services at the right price, in the right quantity, of the right quality, and at the right time, a method of controlling and coordinating these efforts is necessary. The basic document used to control purchasing is the purchase order form. The purchase order (P.O.) should be used by all businesses, no matter how small. The P.O. form provides a written record of all goods and material ordered and specifies prices and delivery expectations. In addition, the P.O. form functions as an internal control document, reducing or eliminating unauthorized purchases and serving as an aid in verifying that the proper material is received.

Purchase Order Form

A typical purchase order form is shown in Figure 13.1. Although some businesses may wish to design their own P.O. form, perfectly adequate P.O. forms can be purchased from the local business supply store or from a standard-form firm. The typical form contains three, four, or five parts (copies). For most startup businesses, the three-part form is adequate. The original should go to the vendor, the second copy used for control purposes, and the third copy used as an accounting copy to match with the supplier's invoice.

All P.O.'s should be consecutively prenumbered, and suppliers should be requested to use the appropriate P.O. number on all shipments, packing lists, invoices, and correspondence. Many potential problems can be eliminated by following this simple procedure. For example, a call to a supplier to request the addition of 100 one-

FIGURE 13.1
Purchase Order

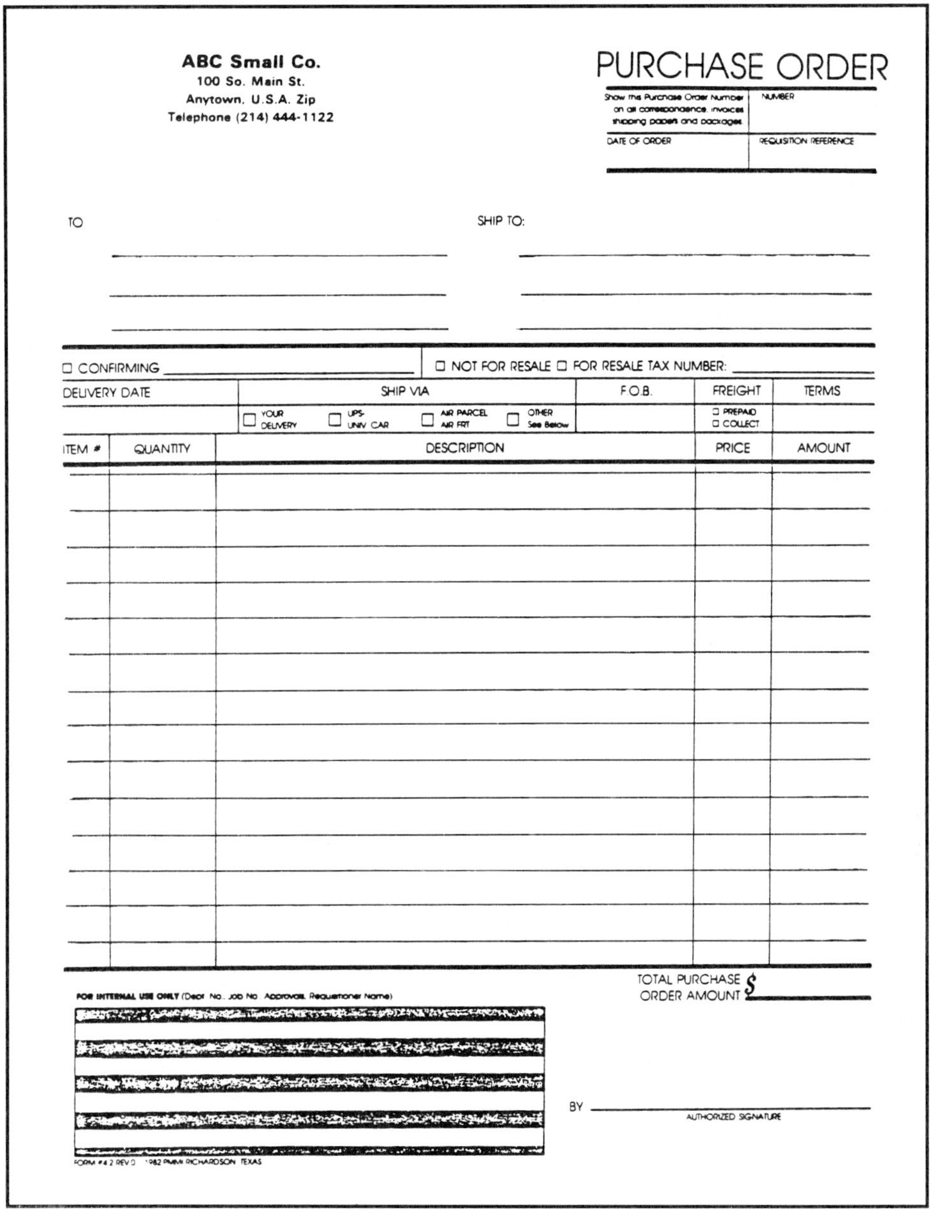
ABC Small Co.
100 So. Main St.
Anytown, U.S.A. Zip
Telephone (214) 444-1122

PURCHASE ORDER

Show this Purchase Order Number on all correspondence, invoices, shipping papers and packages.

NUMBER

DATE OF ORDER

REQUISITION REFERENCE

TO

SHIP TO:

☐ CONFIRMING

☐ NOT FOR RESALE ☐ FOR RESALE TAX NUMBER:

DELIVERY DATE	SHIP VIA	F.O.B.	FREIGHT	TERMS
	☐ YOUR DELIVERY ☐ UPS-UNIV CAR ☐ AIR PARCEL AIR FRT ☐ OTHER See Below		☐ PREPAID ☐ COLLECT	

ITEM #	QUANTITY	DESCRIPTION	PRICE	AMOUNT

FOR INTERNAL USE ONLY (Dept. No., Job No., Approvals, Requisitioner Name)

TOTAL PURCHASE ORDER AMOUNT $

BY

AUTHORIZED SIGNATURE

Source: William E. Dollar, *Effective Purchasing and Inventory Control for Small Business* (Van Nostrand Reinhold Co., 1983). Reprinted by permission.

horsepower motors to the next shipment has a much greater chance of success if the buyer refers to a specific P.O. number. A call about "my order" may result in another confirmation of Murphy's Law.

Other Purchase-Order Requirements

Following is a list of items that should be included on all purchase orders:

1. ***Date of order.*** The date that the P.O. was written and sent to the supplier is critical. If the order was telephoned in, then that date should be used and not the date that the order was actually written.

2. ***Requisition reference.*** The name of the individual who requested the purchase should be indicated on the P.O. This reference can reduce the time required to locate to whom, or where, the shipment should be sent once it arrives.

3. ***Supplier.*** The name and address of the supplier should be included on each purchase order.

4. ***Items.*** Each item should be numbered for reference purposes.

5. ***Quantity.*** The writer should be specific. A term such as "box" may mean a box of 5000 staples to one person, or a box of twelve boxes to another.

6. ***Description.*** An excellent method of eliminating possible errors is to use the noun first and then adjectives (e.g., Stapler, Bates 550).

7. ***Price.*** This is either the price from a current catalog or the agreed upon price. This helps eliminate problems with a quantity order if the price is shown as a unit price and then the total amount of the order is indicated.

8. ***Total amount.*** The total price of each item ordered should be shown as well as the total number of all items ordered.

9. ***Authorized signature.*** The person who authorized the order should sign the P.O. This signature can help eliminate unauthorized purchases.

10. ***Terms.*** The terms of the purchase should be specified and agreed upon with the seller in advance of submitting the P.O.

11. ***Shipping address.*** The address of where the purchase is to be shipped should be included on all P.O.'s. Normally the address would be that of the firm's only place of business, but the shipping address could be to a branch office or to a construction site.

12. ***Delivery date.*** A specific date should be given. Terms such as "As Soon as Possible" (ASAP) have little meaning.

13. ***Ship via.*** The preferred method of shipment should be indicated. On some P.O.'s, the party responsible for shipping costs is also indicated here. *F.O.B.* (free on board) *shipping point* means that the buyer owns the goods in transit, pays the freight charges, and files claims (if any) with the carrier. *F.O.B. destination, freight prepaid,* means that the seller owns the goods in transit, pays the freight charges, and files claims (if any) against the carrier.

14. ***Tax ID number.*** The buyer's tax ID number should be used on orders that are exempt from local or state sales taxes. If a business purchases goods for resale, no sales taxes need be paid, for only the end-user pays the sales taxes. To avoid double taxation, the purchaser for the new firm should obtain a state tax ID number.

The Contract

The purchase order is a legal contract with the seller. The purchaser, therefore, is an agent authorized to make valid contracts of purchase for the company. Since purchase orders are contracts and are legally binding, it should be clear who has the authority to sign them. For example, typical company policy specifies the maximum dollar amount for which various individuals are authorized to sign. In some startup firms, any purchase order over $1,000 must be signed by the owner, but any order for an amount under $1,000 may be signed by other employees.

To be enforceable, a contract must meet several requirements. First, both the offer and the acceptance must be in identical terms. Second, the contract must impose an obligation on both parties. This typically means that the seller is obligated to sell specified merchandise, and the buyer agrees to pay for said merchandise. Third, the contract may not be in conflict with existing federal, state, or local laws. Last, the contract is invalid if fraud was perpetrated by either the buyer or the seller in arriving at the agreement. Fraud is defined as any act, deed, or statement made by either party before the purchase contract is signed or completed (that is likely to deceive the other party).

Buying, therefore, is more complicated than determining what products and services a firm needs and purchasing them in the correct quantity and quality. Buying also includes an awareness of the legal and financial implications of purchasing agreements that may cause the firm financial embarrassment.

INVENTORY MANAGEMENT AND CONTROL

After locating and selecting suppliers and determining what to purchase, the next decision is when and how much to purchase. Inventory management and control focuses on this decision. Inventory control is the necessary informal or formal record-keeping system that insures that an adequate quantity of material and/or merchandise is available for the profitable operation of the firm. Inventory management is the buying of goods and/or services of appropriate quality in the correct quantity at the right time and the evaluation of the supplier's performance.

Most of the material and supply requirements of manufacturing operations have a repetitive pattern that can be forecast well in advance by using bills of material for the end product, sales projections, and past experiences. Purchases for many retail-sales firms, however, are made on a seasonal basis, so there are some special difficulties in the forecasting of sales by style or size. Similarly, in the case of custom, special, and single-order supplies or requirements, the decision of when and how much to purchase is determined on a case-by-case basis. In all cases, however, the goal is to have the correct quantity on hand when needed without having too much inventory.

Inventory as an Investment

Inventory represents a major capital investment in either material or merchandise. In fact, many entrepreneurs look at their inventory and think of it as stacks of money. The objective should be to earn a fair return on this investment. Inventory has a carrying cost that includes such items as interest on the inventory investment, handling and warehousing costs, depreciation, obsolescence, taxes, and insurance. Having too much inventory means that the carrying cost is higher than is necessary, which results in lower profits to the firm. One method of determining if inventory is too high is to calculate the inventory turnover ratio.

The inventory turnover ratio is calculated by dividing total annual sales by the actual inventory valuation as follows:

$$\text{Inventory turnover} = \frac{\text{Total annual sales}}{\text{Actual inventory evaluation}}$$

The resulting ratio should be compared to other firms of comparable size in the same industry by consulting Troy's *Almanac of Business and Industrial Ratios* or *RMA Annual Statement Studies*.

The following example illustrates how a low inventory turnover increases the expenses of a firm. Assume that a firm has annual sales of $300,000 and an annual inventory carrying cost of 25 percent of the inventory:

Inventory Turnover	Investment	Carrying Cost
1	$300,000	$75,000
2	150,000	37,500
3	100,000	25,000
4	75,000	18,750
5	60,000	15,000
6	50,000	12,500

The savings in carrying cost translate into increased profit for the firm, because the reduction in expenses increases profits before taxes by an equal amount. In this example, increasing the inventory turnover from one to three turns per year results in a $50,000 decrease in carrying costs. One obvious method of increasing turnover is to reduce the amount of inventory; however, the cost of having insufficient inventory is not as easy to calculate because it is in the form of intangibles such as lost sales, costly production downtime, and rush orders.

Inventory control, therefore, presents entrepreneurs with the difficult task of keeping inventory levels low, but not too low, and not so high that unnecessary inventory costs are incurred. Determining when inventory levels are too low is easy. The levels are too low if the firm runs out of an item that is needed either for the production process or for a customer request. But when is the inventory level too high?

Inventory Danger Signals

There are several danger signals that indicate the inventory of some items is too high. These danger signals include the following:

1. Inventories are climbing faster than sales.
2. There is a noticeable shifting in inventory mix.
3. Back orders and lead times are increasing significantly.
4. Write-offs for obsolete materials are increasing in proportion to inventory investments.

5. Customers complain frequently about back orders and missed deliveries.
6. Machine setup costs are increasing at a significant rate.

Usually there will be more than one danger signal indicating that inventory problems exist, but danger signals are meaningless unless entrepreneurs are aware of them. This is why proper inventory management and control systems are so important. In other words, a system is worthless unless it is used for its intended purpose.

When inventory problems exist, keeping the inventory in stock is a profit drain on the firm. The problem inventory wastes money because: (1) it ties up company funds in an unproductive asset; (2) it requires additional record keeping; (3) it takes up space that could be used for productive assets; and (4) it has a high risk of obsolescence. For these reasons, a reduction in problem inventory can have a major positive impact on a firm's profitability.[5]

What can entrepreneurs do when inventories build up? Certainly for most retailers the most common solution is to have a sale. For the sale to be effective, the prices of the overstocked items must be reduced sufficiently to attract customers. Clothing stores have semiannual sales to clear seasonal clothes in order to reduce the excess inventory on last season's clothes and to make room for the new season's clothes. Like clothing stores, many other retail stores and even manufacturing firms can and should have sales to reduce excess inventory.

A second method of reducing inventory is to return excess stock to the original supplier. This is not possible in many cases, but in others it is not only possible but much better than having customers expect periodic price reductions. The right to return excess inventory is something buyers should attempt to obtain during the negotiating phase of purchasing. A return policy is common in some industries, such as the retail book/magazine business.

A third method of reducing inventory is to trade inventory with another firm or to convert the inventory into items that are more in demand. An alternative to trading is to sell the excess inventory to wholesalers or firms that specialize in overstocked or out-of-date inventory.

Inventory Control—Simple Systems

For most startup firms, a simple inventory-control system is all that is required for the efficient operation of the firm. Four very simple systems are: visual control, the two-bin reorder point, ABC management, and blanket orders.

Visual Control. For entrepreneurs who work with the firm's inventory each day or for those who can quickly check all the inventory, the visual-control method is very effective. *Visual control* is the simple visual check of all inventory and the notation of which items need to be ordered. This system works best in those small (one-to-five-person) firms for which the entrepreneur is both the main salesperson and the buyer. In these cases, entrepreneurs are aware of what is selling, what the customers are looking for, where these items may be purchased, and the lead time required between ordering and delivery.

The Two-bin System. The *two-bin system* is an inventory-control system that works best for small items that are sold in large quantities. Hardware items such as nails, screws, or bolts of different sizes would be a typical example. Two bins of each item are maintained, usually one on top of the other. When one bin is sold out, store personnel open the second bin and, at the same time, place an order for the quantity sold. This system works very well for small items with low unit costs. A variation of this system is the placement of a reorder card in the inventory at the point where additional merchandise should be ordered. Many bookstores, for example, utilize this variation by placing a reorder card in a stack of books. When the book, which is near the end of the stack, is sold, the card is removed and an order is placed for additional books.

ABC Management. The first step in ABC management is to determine what items need to be closely watched and what items require minimal attention. Usually a small percentage of the total number of items in the firm's inventory accounts for the majority of inventory costs, while a greater percentage of items accounts for a minority of costs. In recognition of this, the ABC method for inventory control classifies inventory items according to their relative impact on cost as follows:

Group A consists of items that make up 70 percent of the total dollar value of items in inventory.
Group B consists of items that make up the next 20 percent of inventory dollar value.
Group C items are the remaining inventory items.

Typically these items are inexpensive and require minimal handling.

After groups have been established, time and resources can be allocated to each group. For example, Group A items require frequent inventory checks, whereas Group B items require less frequent inventory checks. The method used for ordering also should be different for each group. Group A items should be ordered by the most cost-effective method available, while Group B items can be ordered in quantity and Group C items ordered only as needed. Storage of the three items should also be different. Group A items should be stored in the most accessible areas, Group B in less accessible areas, and Group C can be stored in relatively inaccessible areas.[6]

Blanket Orders. A *blanket purchase order* is a general agreement between the buyer and the supplier listing a description of the items covered, the price, and the period of time over which the agreement extends. A blanket order is used for items frequently reordered, such as film, shampoo, razor blades, pastries, and the like. The advantages of blanket orders are: (1) they fix a price for a specified period of time; (2) they act as an inflation hedge; and (3) they reduce the buyer's paperwork for repetitive items. In many firms these items are ordered through a company catalog.

A similar technique is *stockless purchasing*. With stockless purchasing, the supplier agrees to maintain the inventory of specified items on the buyer's premises. The inventory belongs to the supplier and is charged to the customer only as it is used. Stockless purchasing is typical of many grocery store items such as bread, milk, magazines, and soft drinks.

Inventory Control—Formal Systems

For startup firms in sales or manufacturing for which certain items are either relatively expensive or vital to the operation of the firm, a more formal inventory system is needed. A formal system is one that keeps an up-to-date record of each item being inventoried. Thus, entrepreneurs need only look at the inventory record to determine the number of units on hand and the time to order additional units.

The *formal inventory record,* sometimes called a *perpetual inventory record,* also indicates when additional units have been ordered, when they were received, and when they were used. A typical inventory record card is shown in Table 13.1. Although inventory record cards, or inventory systems, are available in most office supply stores, entrepreneurs can develop a simple system to provide just the amount of information their firm needs. In addition, there are some excellent specialized computer inventory systems (see The Inside View 13-4). For example, there are programs for video rental stores, point-of-purchase systems for retail stores, and others. These will be discussed in greater detail in Chapter 16.

Inventory Record Card. The inventory record card in Table 13.1 has several features that should be part of any perpetual inventory-record system. First, the inventory item should have a clear and unambiguous description. Adding a catalog number, even if there is only one supplier, also helps eliminate the possibility of ordering the wrong item.

Second, a notation of the minimum-order quantity, the reorder point, and the expedite point, can be helpful to the person who does the ordering. In the example in Table 13.1, the order quantity is based on the economic-order quantity. (*Economic-order quantity* will be explained in the next section of this chapter.) The *reorder point* is the inventory level at which an order should be placed for an additional 300 units. In Table 13.1, when inventory reaches 100 units, an order should be placed for an additional 300 units. The reorder point is based on the estimated amount of usage and the normal shipping time between the placing of an order and actual receipt of the

Table 13.1 Inventory Record Card*

Item: Motor, $\frac{1}{2}$ hp, 240 volt AC, explosion proof

Order Quantity 300
Reorder point 150
Expedite point 50

Date	*Rec'd.*	*Sold/Used*	*Balance*	*Note*
5/23		20	130	
5/25		50	80	Ordered 300 P.O. # 1021
5/27		20	60	
6/1		30	30	
6/1			27	Physical inventory
6/3	300		327	

*Additional information such as the name, address, and telephone number of the supplier, and expected lead time can be easily added to the inventory record card.

13-4 The Inside View

COMPUTERIZED INVENTORY BOOSTS PROFITS

To increase profits in an increasingly competitive environment, many firms have found that an automated inventory system is one area in which they can obtain impressive results. For example, Dominion Automotive Industries increased margins by more than 10 percent after installing an automated inventory- and production-control system. On-hand inventory was reduced by 54 percent, and the firm discovered that production runs could be reduced through better inventory control. With the reduction in production runs, the firm was able to reduce labor costs by 28 percent.

The increase in the firm's profits was even more impressive, considering that sales during the period were down 6 percent. According to Dan Huskey, the production- and inventory-control manager, "The computer eliminates part shortages that used to shut down production lines every day." The system helps Dominion Automotive reduce the number of hours required to produce each finished product by 40 percent over a two-year period. As a result, the firm is much more efficient than it was before the installation of the automated inventory-control system.[7]

ordered items. The *expedite point* is the point at which extra effort must be made to have the order, or at least part of the order, delivered as quickly as possible. In the example, the expedite point occurs when the inventory has been reduced to 25 units.

Transactions are recorded on the third part of the inventory record card. This section is a history of the usage of the item and a running balance. In addition to the date, there should be columns to show receipt of the item, the amount used or sold, the balance, and comments or notations. Table 13.1 indicates that a physical inventory was conducted on June 1.

A physical inventory is necessary because people use the wrong item, do not record usage, discover damaged items (which are either discarded or returned), or find that items have been stolen. The physical inventory reveals discrepancies between reported inventory and actual inventory. If the difference between the recorded inventory and the actual inventory is large, entrepreneurs must investigate to determine the cause.

Economic-Order Quantity

The inventory systems presented help answer the question of when to order, but there still remains the related question of how much to order. The economic-order quantity is a simple technique that has proven to be relatively accurate, cost effective, and easy to use. The economic-order quantity helps solve the problem of the trade-off between the ordering cost and the carrying cost.

The ordering cost—the cost of actually placing the order—includes the managerial and clerical time required to process an order, the cost of communicating with the supplier, the cost of receiving, and the accounting cost of recording and paying for the shipment. The cost of placing a single order is about the same whether 20 or 200 units are ordered; therefore, fewer and larger orders result in smaller total ordering costs and lower cost per unit. For example, if the ordering cost for a particular item was $40, then the cost per unit ordered if 50 units are ordered is 80¢ per unit, but only 20¢ per unit if 200 units are ordered.

The carrying cost, on the other hand, represents the cost of carrying the inventory. Carrying costs include the cost of financing the inventory, the warehousing or storage cost, shrinkage (losses due to damage, production deterioration, pilferage, etc.), taxes, and insurance. Inventory carrying cost is usually calculated as a percentage of the cost of the inventory. For example, the inventory carrying cost for electric monitors may be 15 percent (on an annual basis) of the cost of the motors. Obviously the carrying cost will be lower, the smaller the size of the inventory.

These two costs are graphically represented in Figure 13.2. The ordering cost is inversely related to the size of each order, while carrying costs are directly related to the size of each order. The total cost (order cost plus carrying cost) is an additive function of these two costs. The economic-order quantity model determines the minimum total cost point, which is the lowest point on the total cost curve.

Economic-Order Quantity Model. The economic-order quantity helps solve this trade-off between ordering cost and carrying cost. The economic-order quantity (EOQ) is calculated by using a formula that may be stated as follows:

$$EOQ = \sqrt{\frac{2NS}{PI}}$$

where:

EOQ = economic-order quantity in units
N = number of units needed each year
S = ordering cost per order
P = price per unit
I = annual inventory carrying cost, in percent

For example, assume that an entrepreneur has determined that he will need 4,500 $\frac{1}{2}$-horsepower motors for production for the next year. Also assume that the average cost to process an order is $40 and the price of each motor is projected to be $25. If the firm's carrying cost of its inventory is 15 percent, what is the economic-order quantity?

$$EOQ = \sqrt{\frac{2 \times 4{,}500 \times 40}{25 \times .15}} = 309.84, \text{ or } 310 \text{ units}$$

FIGURE 13.2
Graphic Representation of *EOQ* Model

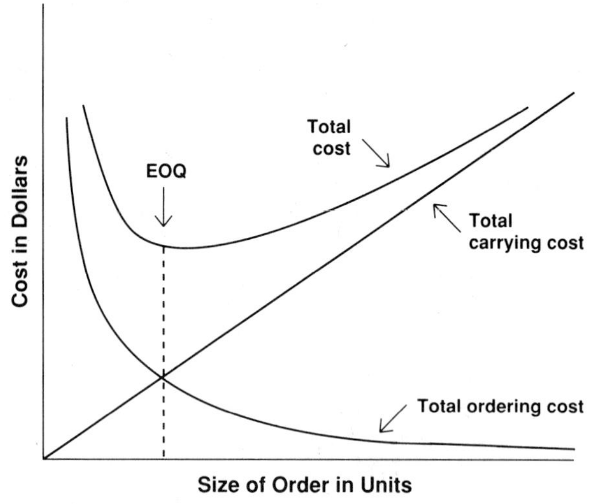

There are two points to remember when considering the EOQ model. First, ordering too little usually costs much more than ordering too much because of lost production time or lost sales. Second, a change in the carrying cost has a big effect on the EOQ. If interest rates increase dramatically, as they did in the late 1970s and early 1980s, the carrying cost will also increase, causing a significant drop in the EOQ. In addition, purchasers must remember that the EOQ is not a number that should be blindly obeyed. For example, the item to be ordered may be shipped only in lots of 50 or 100, or there may be significant cost savings from quantity discounts (see the section on quantity discounts presented later in this chapter).

The EOQ model should not be used to calculate every item in inventory; rather it should be employed for only those items that have a high cost or are especially critical to the operation of the firm. One of the simple systems mentioned previously, such as visual control, two-bin system, or blanket order, should be used for low-cost and noncritical items.

Potential Problems with the EOQ Model. There are several potential problems with using the EOQ model. First, the results of the model should be interpreted logically. For example, actual warehouse space may be inadequate, shipping time could reduce the need for large orders, or the shelf life of the product may require small orders. These and other facts should be taken into consideration in determining the actual order quantity.

A second potential problem concerns the calculation of the order cost. Very few companies have accurate order-cost information for each type of product ordered and, therefore, obtain the average order cost by dividing their total annual ordering cost by the number of orders written. A calculation of this type does not reflect the additional cost that may be attributed to certain types of orders.

A third potential problem involves the standard shipping unit. A standard shipping unit may consist of units, a truckload, or the number of units, rolls, cartons, or barrels. Thus, although the EOQ may call for 350 units, a standard shipping unit may be 250 units, and the shipping cost for a broken unit may be more than the cost of shipping a standard unit.

A fourth potential problem with the EOQ model concerns changes in unit price. The EOQ model assumes that the cost per unit does not change, regardless of the number of units ordered. For those products that do have quantity discounts, the EOQ model is not appropriate, but the lowest-cost order quantity could be determined by calculating the total cost for each price break.

For example, assume that the price per unit decreases as shown in column 1 of Table 13.2. In addition, assume that 4,500 units will be ordered next year, that the average cost to process an order is $40, and that the firm's carrying cost is 15 percent of the total inventory value. As can be seen in Table 13.2, the lowest total cost is to order 400 units. Although this order size is very close to the same cost as the EOQ of 300 units calculated in the previous section, this example is only intended to show how to determine order quantity when a firm is offered quantity discounts.

Reorder Point

While the EOQ is the determination of how much to order, the reorder point indicates when to place the order. The reorder point (RP) may be expressed mathematically as follows:

$$RP = (\textbf{Lead time} \times \textbf{Daily usage}) + \textbf{Safety stock}$$

Lead time is the average number of days between the placing and receiving of an order. Lead time includes the order processing time of both the buyer and the seller, the time to produce the product, and the time required for shipping.

Table 13.2 Order Quantity with Volume Price Discounts*

(1) Order Size	(2) Cost per Unit	(3) Number of Orders	(4) Average Inventory (1) /2 × (2)	(5) Carrying Cost (4) × .15	(6) Ordering Cost (3) × $40	(7) Total Cost (5) + (6)
50	29	90	$ 725	$109	$3,600	$3,709
100	27	45	1,350	203	1,800	2,003
150	26	30	1,950	293	1,200	1,493
200	25	23	2,500	375	920	1,295
300	24	15	3,600	540	600	1,140
400	23	11	4,600	690	440	1,130

*Assume 4,500 units/yr.

Safety stock is the amount of stock carried to absorb random fluctuations in purchasing, production, or sales. The amount of safety stock depends on two major factors. First is the risk (probability) of being out of stock. For example, if there is a high probability of having several large orders processed at the same time, the firm will require a safety stock larger than that required if there is a low probability of processing several large orders at the same time.

The second factor concerns cost. What is the cost of being out of stock? If the cost is low, then the safety stock may be low, but if the cost is high, then a higher safety stock is required. Cost, in this case, includes the cost of lost sales, the cost of changing production schedules, and the cost of lost time.

A graphical representation of the inventory usage and reorder point is shown in Figure 13.3. The graph assumes that inventory usage is the same each day and that the lead time is known. In this example, the usage is assumed to be 100 units per five-day week and the lead time is five days. If the EOQ is 300 units, an order is placed every fifteen working days when the inventory reaches 150 units.

Summary

Purchasing is the buying of goods and materials needed by the firm for its efficient operation. Selection is based primarily on price, quality, quantity, and service. Service includes on-time delivery as well as technical, financial, and marketing support.

Entrepreneurs may locate their suppliers by using several sources, including the following: (1) their own previous experience, (2) the previous experience of their employees, (3) the yellow pages, (4) sales representatives, (5) the chamber of commerce, (6) trade journals, (7) trade shows, (8) merchandise markets, (9) industry direc-

FIGURE 13.3
Graphic Representation of Inventory Behavior

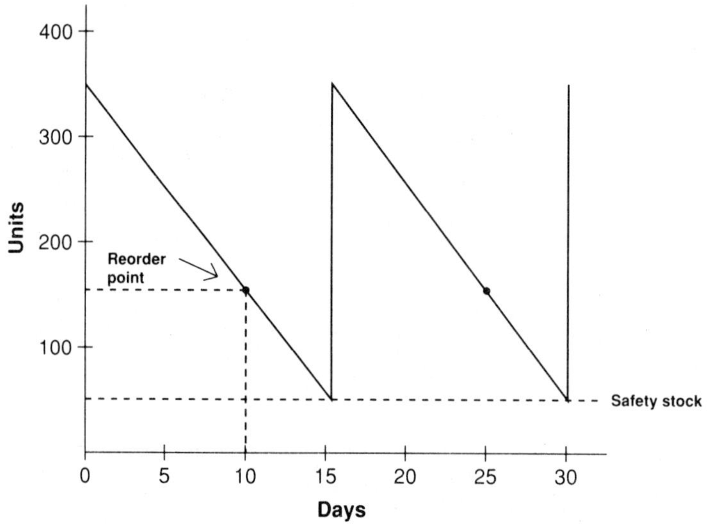

tories, and (10) cooperative buying. Although the selection of suppliers is time-consuming, entrepreneurs should develop multiple supply sources in order to obtain competitive prices and services, to reduce the dependence of the firm on a single source, and to increase the sources of available credit.

The buyer–seller relationship should be mutually beneficial, in that both parties expect that each will fulfill the terms of the contract. Developing a strong relationship with a supplier does not preclude negotiating for better prices, quality, or service, but it does include developing a standard procedure that describes the policies concerning the ethical standards expected for those involved in purchasing.

The purchase order form is an excellent method of controlling purchases since it provides a written record of all goods and materials ordered and specifies prices and delivery expectations.

Inventory control is the necessary record-keeping system that insures that an adequate quantity of material and/or merchandise is available for the successful operation of the firm. Inventory management is the buying of goods and/or services of appropriate quality in the correct quantity at the right time and the evaluation of the supplier's performance. In maintaining control, the owner must determine the best inventory level for the firm.

Once the inventory level is determined, the owner can control the quantity of many items through a simple control system, such as the visual control system or the two-bin system. Inventory that is vital to the operation of the firm or that has a high unit cost should be controlled through a more formal system, such as the perpetual inventory system.

The economic-order quantity is a model designed to determine how much to order. The model balances the trade-off between the order cost and the carrying cost. There are, however, several potential problems with the EOQ model.

Assembling the Pieces

The owners of In Good Taste determine how much to purchase based upon a cash budget and the time of the year. Purchases are increased for the Christmas season and decreased for the summer months. The determination of what to buy is more subjective. The owners keep records of what customers request, and they purchase goods from what they see at trade shows and in trade publications. In their purchasing decision, Carol and Jacki look primarily for quality, reliability, and then cost.

Inventory is controlled by keeping perpetual inventory records. In the future, they hope to purchase a point-of-sale inventory system, but at this time the cost of the system is prohibitive. In the meantime, they are comfortable with their present system since they are the primary salespeople, and they know what is selling and what their customers are requesting.

In Good Taste has six suppliers for the four major products it carries. Wine is purchased locally through three distributors: Associated Wine Distributors; Palmetto Wines; and Ben Arnold, Fine Wines. Food products are purchased through A and A Richter in New York; cheese is secured from Long Island Cheese Company; and coffee is supplied by Seven Hills Company of Cincinnati, Ohio. ■

Questions for Review and Discussion

1. If the cost of materials accounts for 60¢ out of each sales dollar and profits are about 5¢, what is the impact on profits of a 5-percent reduction in the purchasing cost of materials?
2. What are the four primary variables upon which purchasing selections should be based?
3. Using your local yellow pages, locate several different potential suppliers for the restaurant business.
4. Why should a firm develop multiple supply sources?
5. Develop a system that would be useful in evaluating a supplier.
6. Why are standard procedures needed in order to develop an ethical purchasing policy?
7. What are the requirements of an enforceable contract?
8. Why is a shift in inventory mix a signal that some inventories may be too high?
9. How can management help reduce inventory levels?
10. If a supply firm expects to sell 3,400 pumps a year, what is the EOQ for the pump? Assume that the cost of processing an order is $40 and the carrying cost is 20 percent.
11. What are the potential problems with the EOQ model?
12. Go to the library and find the *Thomas Register.* Locate the suppliers for abacuses and/or actuators: photoelectric.

Notes

1. Marc Dollinger and Michael Kolchin, "Purchasing and the Small Firm," *American Journal of Small Business,* Winter 1986, pp. 33–43.
2. Kenneth Hardy and Allan Magrath, "Buying Groups: Clout For Small Business," *Harvard Business Review,* September–October 1987, pp. 16–24.
3. Mark Treleven, "Single Sourcing: A Management Tool for the Quality Supplier," *Journal of Purchasing and Materials Management,* Spring 1987, pp. 19–24.
4. "Rating Vendor Performance," *Small Business Report,* April 1988, pp. 48–49.
5. Glenda Paquin, "Dealing with Problem Inventory," *P&IM Review,* May 1988, pp. 40–41.
6. "Inventory Management," *Small Business Report,* August 1987, pp. 50–53.
7. "Plant Boosts Profits 10 Percent with Computerized Inventory, Production Control," *P&IM Review,* April 1988, pp. 40–41.

CHAPTER 14

Managing Cash Flow

Learning Objectives

After reading this chapter, you will be able to do the following:

- Set up and utilize a cash budget.
- Understand the value of working-capital management.
- Show how to use credit lines.
- Describe sources of working capital.

For the startup business, the management of cash flow is more important than profitability: If the firm does not have the cash to cover its liabilities, it will not be able to remain in operation long enough to become profitable. A startup firm that grows slowly and gradually becomes profitable will usually not have a cash-flow problem; however, a startup firm that is immediately successful and grows rapidly, as most entrepreneurs hope their businesses will, is likely to have a cash-flow problem. The objective of this chapter is to present methods for preventing cash-flow problems.

CASH BUDGET

Almost every business will have to borrow money at some time during its startup phase. Lenders, usually from the local bank, willingly lend money if they believe there is a high probability the money will be repaid on time. A cash budget is the prime financial statement indicating when funds flow into and out of a firm and, therefore, when funds are expected to be available to pay off loans. (Profit and loss statements do not show when funds will be available.)

The main purpose of a cash budget, therefore, is to help the entrepreneur plan the best use of the firm's cash. The second purpose of a cash budget is to facilitate the firm's ability to borrow capital. Cash is an asset, but, unlike inventory, accounts receivable, and plant and equipment, it is a relatively sterile asset on which no return is earned. A cash budget can help reduce the cash balance to an absolute minimum in order that funds may be better utilized to earn a profit.

Cash Flow Versus Profit

The difference between cash flow and profit is a concept that many businesspeople do not understand. Even for businesses that operate on a cash-only basis, a substantial difference between cash flow and profits may exist. Basically, depreciation is an expense included on the profit and loss statement, but since depreciation does not require the payment of cash, it does not show up on the cash-flow statement. A very simple example is shown in Table 14.1.

It should be noted that in the example the difference between cash flow and profits for the period was $9,000—the amount of the depreciation expense; the firm's obligations are paid with cash, not profits. It is true that cash flows are profits plus depreciation expenses, but even profits do not fully indicate how much cash a firm has on hand. If we assume, for example, that a startup firm has sales of $4,000 the first month

Table 14.1 Cash Flow Versus Profit

Profit and Loss Statement		
Net Sales		$120,000
Cost of goods sold		72,000
Gross profit		$48,000
Operating expenses:		
General and administrative expenses	$15,000	
Depreciation	9,000	24,000
Operating profit		$24,000
Interest		750
Profit before taxes		$23,250
Taxes (34%)		7,905
Net profit		$15,345
Cash Flow		
Cash inflows		$120,000
Cash outflows:		
Cost of goods sold	$72,000	
General and administrative expenses	15,000	
Interest	750	
Taxes	7,905	$95,655
Net cash flow		$24,345

it is in business and that those sales double each month for the first four months, the company has a perfect situation. If we also assume that the firm's cash sales are 15 percent of net sales, all other customers buy on credit, 45 percent of the customers pay in thirty days, 25 percent pay in sixty days, 12 percent pay ninety days, and 3 percent never pay, what is the firm's cash-flow situation? The profit-and-loss statement and the cash-flow statement for the first four months are shown in Table 14.2.

The information presented in Table 14.2 is typical of the situation in which many firms find themselves when they start a successful business. The firm is profitable and looks like a going concern on paper. Management has done an excellent job of holding

Table 14.2 Problems with Growth

Profit and Loss Statement

	April	*May*	*June*	*July*
Net sales	$4,000	$8,000	$16,000	$32,000
Cost of sales (60%)	2,400	4,800	9,600	$19,200
Gross profit	$1,600	$3,200	$ 6,400	$12,800
G & A expense	500	750	1,000	1,250
Depreciation	500	500	500	500
Interest	100	120	140	160
Taxable profit	$ 500	$1,830	$ 4,760	$10,890
Taxes	170	622	1,618	3,703
Net profit	$ 330	$1,208	$ 3,142	$ 7,187

Cash Flow

Cash inflows:				
Cash sales (15%)	$ 600	$1,200	$ 2,400	$ 4,800
Paid in 30 days (45%)		1,800	3,600	7,200
Paid in 60 days (25%)			1,000	2,000
Paid in 90 days (12%)				480
Total inflows	$ 600	$3,000	$ 7,000	$14,480
Cash outflows:				
Cost of sales	$2,400	$4,800	$ 9,600	$19,200
General and administrative expenses	500	750	1,000	1,250
Interest	100	120	140	160
Taxes	170	622	1,618	3,703
Net cash flow	($2,570)	($3,292)	($ 5,358)	($ 9,833)

down costs as sales have risen. For example, general and administrative expenses have risen only $250 per month while sales have skyrocketed. Over the four-month period, the firm has made a net profit of $11,867. Cash flow, however, indicates a serious problem.

As sales have taken off, so has the firm's need for more cash. Each month the net cash outflow has increased, until after four months, it totals $21,053. As long as sales continue to increase, so will the firm's need for cash. What the entrepreneur sees is a firm that is going places; therefore borrowing cash to help finance the growth should be easy. What a commercial banker sees, however, is a firm that is out of control and headed for potential disaster. The solution is simple, but difficult for most entrepreneurs to implement. The firm must reduce the rate of growth of sales to a more manageable level. This is the key to cash budgeting and understanding the difference between profitability and cash flow. The Inside View 14-1 illustrates this situation.

Cash Cycle

In order to discuss cash budgeting as a method of managing growth, it is necessary to understand the cash cycle. The *cash cycle* may be defined as the length of time between the payment for the purchase of materials (raw materials or finished goods) and the receipt of cash for the sale of those same materials. For the service firm, the cash cycle would be the length of time between the payment for expenses incurred in rendering a service (office, administrative, labor expenses, etc.) and the receipt of cash for those services. Obviously the longer the cash cycle, the greater the need for cash.

The length of the cash cycle is determined by three variables. First is the *inventory-conversion period*, which may be defined as the average length of time between the receipt of raw materials or finished goods and the sale of those materials. The inventory-conversion period may be calculated by dividing 360 days by the inventory turnover ratio (which is sales divided by the average inventory). Thus, for a firm with annual sales of $240,000 and an average inventory (beginning inventory plus ending inventory divided by 2) of $40,000, the inventory-conversion period would be 60 days (360/6).

The second variable is the receivables-conversion period. The *receivables-conversion period* is the average length of time between the sale of goods and materials and the receipt of cash for those goods. For the firm with only cash sales, the receivables-conversion period is zero. For those firms that sell on credit, the conversion period is the length of the average collection period. The average collection period may be calculated by dividing receivables by average daily sales (sales divided by 360). For a firm with annual sales of $240,000 and receivables of $36,000, the average collection period is 54 days.

The remaining variable is the accounts-payable period. The *accounts-payable period* is the length of time between the purchase of materials and labor and the payment for them. No simple formula exists for this calculation, but most managers know approximately how long they take to pay for their purchases.

14-1 The Inside View

RUNNING INTO BANKRUPTCY[1]

Too often, startup firms grow faster than the amount of cash available to support their fast start. The startup entrepreneur must control the growth rate of the new enterprise so that the firm does not become financially overextended. Many entrepreneurs do not heed this advice. Bill Rodgers & Co. (BRC) was one of them.

Bill Rodgers, four-time winner of the Boston Marathon, is one of the best-known distance runners in the United States. He started a retail clothing and shoe store in Boston in 1977 that was a modest commercial success, grossing about $1 million in annual sales. His next venture was the design, production, and sales of running apparel. In 1981, BRC had $3 million in sales and was growing fast. Revenues were $6.5 million in 1983 and $8.4 million in 1984. Although BRC was profitable, its growth was not generating enough cash to keep up with production demands.

The Bank of Boston granted BRC a term loan of $350,000 to finance office improvements and new equipment, and a $200,000 line of credit to cover seasonal production requirements. These loans were secured by a lien on inventory. Even with these loans, BRC, through a combination of bad luck and bad management, slipped into deeper financial trouble.

BRC attempted to establish an operation in Great Britain that ended up as a $400,000 loss. Competition from large shoe manufacturers—Nike, Adidas, New Balance—started squeezing profit margins. Credit-control policies were poor, and BRC kept shipping to delinquent accounts. By the end of 1985, BRC owed the Bank of Boston $2.5 million, in addition to the growing trade debt.

Demands by the bank for immediate payment left BRC in a desperate position. If cash received from sales went to the bank, none would be left for working capital, and the firm would be out of business. BRC explored many alternatives, but the bank forced the issue by demanding full payment on a $1.3 million loan. When BRC could not meet this demand, bank officers and security guards arrived early one morning and padlocked BRC's office and warehouse. The inventory valued at cost for $660,000 was sold by the bank with unreasonable haste for $125,000 net. Interestingly, BRC had an outside offer on the inventory for $475,000, which the bank ignored. To settle the remaining debt, Bill Rodgers lost his house, which had been used to secure a loan, and agreed to represent the bank at a number of public functions.

The length of the cash cycle is the net of these three variables. In equation form, the cash cycle could be expressed as follows:

Cash cycle = Inventory conversion period + Receivables period − Accounts payable period.

To illustrate how the equation works, suppose that a firm takes an average of forty days to sell its inventory, has an average receivables period of forty-five days, and takes about twenty-five days to pay for materials and labor received. The cash cycle for this firm would be sixty days.

The purpose of this exercise is twofold. First, the cash cycle indicates the length of time for which a firm must be able to finance the purchase of materials and labor and the extension of credit to customers. If the cash cycle is extended for any reason, such as the lengthening of the average inventory life or the lengthening of the credit period, for example, additional financing will be required. The second purpose of the cash cycle is to indicate the length of the individual periods so that the entrepreneur (analyst) can choose the most effective measures to reduce the cash cycle.

Why are either of these purposes important? A firm whose purchasing averages $2,000 worth of materials and labor each day to produce the goods it sells and whose cash cycle is sixty days is responsible for financing $120,000 worth of materials and labor. If the cost of capital is 12 percent, the annual cost to the firm is $14,000. If the cash-conversion cycle can be reduced by ten days, the savings to the firm is $2,400 (10 × $2,000 × 0.12). Conversely, if the cash cycle increases by ten days, the additional cost to the firm is $2,400.

Preparation of a Cash Budget

A cash budget can help alleviate cash-flow problems and facilitate borrowing to cover temporary cash-flow shortages, the use of a cash budget is nothing more than a projection of cash inflows and cash payments expected over the next planning period. This planning period could be for one month, three months, or even a semiannual or annual period. The objective is to forecast both the sales and the expenditures over that planning period as accurately as possible, thereby enabling the manager to plan when he or she will need to make short-term loans and when those loans can be repaid.

The cash budget is made up of three sections. The first section contains a forecast of sales over the budgeted period, with an estimate of when cash from these sales will be received. The second section is an estimate of all cash expenditures. One of the positive aspects of developing the cash budget is that entrepreneurs are forced to contemplate what they expect their firm to spend over the budgeted period. The final section is the calculation of cash flows, showing the expected cash surplus generated or the amount of borrowing that is expected.

To illustrate a cash budget, assume that a startup firm, SRA Inc., had sales of $24,000 in April, $28,000 in May, and $32,000 in June. The owner estimates that sales will continue to grow at a rate of $4,000 per month through September, at which time growth will slow to $2,000 per month until December, when sales are estimated to total $56,000. In setting up the cash budget, the estimate of sales over the budgeting period is extremely important if the budget is to be of any value in the planning process. In this example, the estimates are based on the rate of growth during the first three months of operation, with an expected reduction in growth during the early fall and then a big increase during the Christmas sales period.

Sales Forecast. Estimates of forecasted sales for the startup firm should come from the business plan and reflect the entrepreneur's reasonable expectations of the potential for the product or services offered by the firms. Estimates, however, are just estimates and are not intended to be precise; however, they are meant to provide a reasonable guideline for planning and decision making.

After forecasting sales, the entrepreneur needs to estimate how quickly the sales will be converted into cash. An estimate could come from the experiences of similar firms located in the same general area. For our example, SRA Inc. expects 20 percent of its sales will be for cash, 50 percent of its customers will pay in thirty days, 20 percent will pay in sixty days, 8 percent will pay in ninety days, and 2 percent of all sales will be written off as bad debts. The total cash inflows for the next six months, given these assumptions, are shown in Table 14.3.

Payments. To complete the cash budget, entrepreneurs must also estimate their payments (cash outflows) over the same budgeted period. Again, the estimates should come primarily from business plans, but if business plans are not available, then the entrepreneur should estimate cash expenditures over the planning period as accurately as possible. The estimates for SRA Inc. are shown in Table 14.3. Note that only cash payments are included; therefore, the cash budget is not a profit and loss statement for two major reasons. First, the cash budget shows only cash receipts and expenditures, unlike most profit and loss statements, which are based on accrual accounting. With accrual accounting, sales are shown as revenues on the date of the sale, and expenses are shown as expenses as of the date of the liability. Second, the profit and loss statement shows noncash expenses, such as depreciation, as an expense. The cash budget would not show depreciation as an expense since there is no cash expenditure.

Net Flows. The remaining section of the cash budget is the calculation section. The first calculation is the determination of the net cash flow. The *net cash flow* is the difference between the cash inflows and the total payments for the period. For the month of July, the expected net cash flow is $2,300, but in August, the net flow is a negative cash flow of $600.

The firm began operating in July with $3,000 in cash, so this amount is added to the $2,300 positive cash flow to show an ending cash balance of $5,300. SRA Inc. has determined that it must maintain a minimum cash balance of $3,000 in order to have the liquidity suggested by its commercial banker. With the $3,000 minimum, SRA Inc. has a cash surplus of $2,300.

During August, SRA has a negative net cash flow but is able to show a cash surplus of $1,700 because of the surplus remaining from July. The large negative cash flow in September and October, when SRA Inc. is stocking up for the fall and Christmas seasons, results in the firm having to borrow $200 in September and $5,600 in October for a total of $5,800 in loans. By November, SRA Inc. is again forecasting a

Table 14.3 SRA Inc.: Cash Budget (thousands of dollars)

	July	Aug.	Sep.	Oct.	Nov.	Dec.
Forecasted sales	$ 36	40	44	46	48	56
Cash inflows:						
Cash sales (20%)	7.2	8.0	8.8	9.2	9.6	11.2
Paid in 30 days (50%)	16.0	18.0	20.0	22.0	23.0	24.0
Paid in 60 days (20%)	5.6	6.4	7.2	8.0	8.8	9.2
Paid in 90 days (8%)	1.9	2.2	2.6	2.9	3.2	3.5
Total cash inflows	$30.7	34.6	38.6	42.1	44.6	47.9
Payments:						
Purchases	$19.2	21.6	28.0	30.4	27.6	28.8
Wages	5.4	5.8	6.2	6.2	6.4	7.0
Rent	0.8	0.8	1.0	1.0	1.0	1.0
Utilities	0.4	0.6	0.4	0.4	0.5	0.6
Selling exp.	1.3	1.3	1.3	1.3	1.3	1.3
Admin. exp.	0.2	0.2	0.2	0.2	0.2	0.2
Interest	0.5	1.5	1.0	1.5	0.5	1.0
Taxes	0.4	3.2	0.2	4.5	1.2	0.2
Misc.	0.2	0.2	2.2	2.2	0.5	0.5
Total payments	$28.4	35.2	40.5	47.7	39.2	40.6
Net cash flow	2.3	(0.6)	(1.9)	(5.6)	5.4	7.3
Beginning cash	3.0	5.3	4.7	2.8	(2.8)	2.6
Ending cash	5.3	4.7	2.8	(2.8)	2.6	9.9
Min. cash desired	3.0	3.0	3.0	3.0	3.0	3.0
Cumulative borrowings			.2	5.8	.4	
Surplus cash	$ 2.3	1.7				6.9

positive cash flow and can start paying off the short-term loans. By the end of November, SRA Inc. expects to be able to repay all but $400 of the $5,800 loan.

Thus, one of the advantages of the cash budget is that it allows management to forecast when funds will be needed and when those loans can be paid off. With this information, managers can set up a line of credit before the need arises. Bankers are much more willing to lend short-term funds to a firm that can show, in advance, when it expects to need funds and when it expects to be able to repay those loans. Bankers are reluctant to lend funds to firms that wait until they need the money before requesting a loan. In the first case, they assume the owner is in control of his or her firm, but in the second case, they are not certain that the manager is on top of the financial situation. To conclude the illustration, SRA Inc. expects to have a cash surplus of $6,900 by the end of December. This cash is available to pay off long-term loans, pay bonuses, or invest in additional assets.

Monthly Expense Report

In conjunction with the cash budget, a monthly expense report should be maintained. The cash budget is designed as a planning standard on which management can base borrowing and repayment plans. Since the budget is a plan, and since actual results may vary from the plan, management may have to adjust the firm's expenditures. If, for example, sales are below budget, purchases need to be reduced and other expenses adjusted to fit the reality of actual sales. A firm that expects to sell $1 million worth of goods a month but finds that actual sales are only $600,000 would be well advised to adjust its expenses down to the lower figure.

An example of an expense report is presented in Table 14.4. In this example, which was calculated at the end of October, the budgeted and actual receipts and expenses are shown along with their corresponding year-to-date figures. The value of a monthly expense report is twofold. First, the expense report provides a format the owner can and should use to control the firm's level of expenses in order to maintain them in the proper proportion to actual sales. Thus, if sales exceed the budget, then expenditures, such as purchases, supplies, and wages (commissions), will be over budget also. However, if sales do not meet expectations, then management can look at the expense report and determine which expenses should be reduced. Actually the reduction in sales may be due to lack of proper advertising, and, if such be the case, advertising expenses may need to be increased.

Table 14.4 SRA Inc.: Monthly Expense Report

	October			Year to Date		
	Budgeted	*Actual*	*Difference*	*Budgeted*	*Actual*	*Difference*
Receipts	$42,100	$38,660	($3,440)	$242,000	$236,110	($5,890)
Expenses:						
Purchases	$30,400	$32,300	($1,900)	$152,000	$157,300	($5,300)
Wages	6,200	6,350	(150)	31,000	34,200	(3,200)
Rent	1,000	1,000	0	6,000	6,000	0
Utilities	440	390	50	3,080	2,840	240
Advertising	200	240	(40)	1,600	1,900	(300)
Supplies	900	620	280	4,500	3,400	1,100
Travel	200	310	(110)	850	620	230
Interest	1,500	1,440	60	9,000	10,450	(1,450)
Insurance	200	200	0	1,000	1,000	0
Taxes	4,500	4,310	190	14,500	12,790	1,710
Maintenance	500	240	260	2,000	1,810	190
Office exp.	1,200	1,430	(230)	3,600	4,020	(420)
Misc.	460	510	(50)	1,500	880	620
Total	$47,700	$49,340	($1,640)	$230,630	$237,210	($6,580)

Monthly expense reports also provide entrepreneurs with regular, up-to-date reports on all expenditures for the firm. Analyzing these reports and comparing the results to expected figures provide managers with an opportunity to look at each category of expenditures to determine if firms are utilizing their assets efficiently. For example, are purchases as projected, or could entrepreneurs find the same quality at lower prices from another dealer? Is the maintenance figure too high and climbing each month? Does a piece of equipment need replacing rather than constant repair? Questions similar to these can help entrepreneurs spot costly expenditures early enough to take corrective action in order to maintain efficiency.

WORKING-CAPITAL MANAGEMENT

Good working-capital management is vital to the success of the startup firm, yet many entrepreneurs do not understand the full range of possible working-capital policies available to them. Following is a discussion of working-capital management and an explanation of the differences between aggressive and conservative working-capital policies.

Working capital is a firm's investment in current assets—cash, marketable securities, inventories, and accounts receivable. *Net working capital* may be defined as the difference between current assets and current liabilities. *Working-capital policy* is management policy (philosophy) regarding the level of current assets. Thus, working-capital management involves the maintenance of the level of current assets in relation to current liabilities within the policy guidelines of the firm. Working-capital management, therefore, is basically the determination of the level of current assets the firm desires to maintain.

Working-capital management is particularly important to the startup firm, which must obtain both current and fixed assets through a combination of current and long-term debt and owners' equity. The problem faced by most startup firms is limited access to long-term capital. To solve this problem, many entrepreneurs reduce their need for long-term capital by renting or leasing the plant and equipment, but they cannot reduce their short-term capital needs for current assets in a similar manner. Their need for short-term capital makes them rely heavily on trade credit and short-term bank loans, both of which affect working capital. Finally, there is a direct relationship between sales growth and current assets. Therefore, growth in sales must be financed with increases in trade credit and short-term bank loans. For these reasons it is important for startup entrepreneurs to understand working-capital management and the various alternative working-capital policies.

Alternative Working-Capital Policies

The working-capital policy of a firm may be conservative or aggressive. The firm that adopts a conservative policy will maintain a high degree of liquidity, meaning that current assets will be relatively high. Those who adopt a more aggressive policy are attempting to keep current assets at a relatively low level. Since operating with a low level of current assets is risky, the adoption of this approach would indicate that management is willing and able to operate more efficiently than firms that adopt the conservative approach.

An illustration of the differences in working-capital policies is presented in Table 14.5. Basically the goal of the conservative approach is to maintain a high degree of liquidity. For example, a firm with a conservative working-capital policy will have more cash and inventory available than the firm with a more aggressive policy. In this case, "conservative" means that management chooses to have enough cash available for almost any contingency and enough inventory available so that stock-outs are a rare event. In addition, those customers whose accounts are past due are not aggressively reminded of the past due date; therefore, accounts receivable are relatively high.

Cash. Firms with a more aggressive working-capital management approach reduce cash to a minimum. This approach requires the use of daily (for large firms), weekly, or monthly (for most small startup firms) cash budgets that enable management to know when cash is expected and when liabilities are due. The aggressive manager

Table 14.5 Alternative Working-Capital Policies

	Conservative	*Middle*	*Aggressive*
Cash	$ 100	$ 75	$ 50
Accounts receivable	300	225	150
Inventories	350	280	175
Total current assets	$ 750	$ 580	$ 375
Fixed Assets	600	600	600
Total assets	$1,350	$1,180	$ 975
Accounts payable	$ 200	$ 200	$ 200
Accruals	50	50	50
Total current liabilities	$ 250	$ 250	$ 250
Long-term debt, 12%	425	340	237.5
Common stock	425	340	237.5
Retained earnings	250	250	250
Total liabilities & equity	$1,350	$1,180	$ 975
Net sales	$1,500	$1,500	$1,500
Less variable costs	600	600	600
Less fixed costs	670	670	670
Operating earnings	$ 230	$ 230	$ 230
Interest expense	51	40.8	28.5
Earnings before taxes	$ 179	$ 189.2	$ 201.5
Taxes @ 40%	71.6	75.7	80.6
Net income	$ 107.4	$ 113.5	$ 120.9
Current ratio	3	2.3	1.5
Return on investment	15.9	19.2	24.8
Debt to total assets	50%	50%	50%

tries to have the arrival and the disbursement of cash coincide so that the need for short-term loans is reduced to a minimum. Firms with a more conservative policy try to keep enough cash on hand so that cash budgets are either not required or are used only for long-term planning and management-control purposes, not for tracking the date of arrival and the date of disbursement of cash flows. Conservatives also have more cash available for emergencies than those who favor a more aggressive approach.

Inventories. The goal of a more aggressive approach is to reduce inventories to a minimum through an inventory-management system that indicates which items are selling and which are moving more slowly. Although inventory-control systems were discussed in greater detail in the previous chapter, it must be emphasized that the aggressive approach is a management philosophy that implies that inventories can be maintained in sufficient quantity so that stock-outs will occur, but they will be of short duration. In such cases, inventory turnover rates are high. For a production operation, for example, aggressive inventory management is the use of "just-in-time" inventory management. Thus, inventories arrive when they are needed and are not stockpiled in the storeroom for long periods of time.

The goal of a more conservative management approach is to have relatively high inventory levels and low turnover rates. Those who espouse this philosophy are afraid of stock-outs and believe that if customers do not find what they want in the store, they will go to a competitor's store, never to return. The result is a high level of inventories and the accompanying high cost of financing them.

Accounts Receivable. Like cash and inventory, the aggressive approach to accounts receivable is to maintain a low level of accounts receivable. To obtain a low level of accounts receivable, management must be willing to set up and maintain accurate, up-to-date records on all credit customers. These records should indicate all customers who are past due and their current balance. Management must be willing to follow up on these overdue accounts quickly, without letting time pass before requesting payment. (For more on credit policies, see Chapter 15.) This aggressive approach to collections will cause the firm to lose a few customers, but in most cases they will be less profitable customers.

Accounts receivable must be financed by the seller. Allowing accounts receivable to build up means that the firm is incurring additional financing costs and, in addition, must absorb the expense of the cost of following up on the slow-paying customers. These costs include the salary of the individual(s) working in credit and collections, the additional office expenses, and, in some cases, the legal expenses of collecting past due accounts.

The more conservative approach is to be less exacting in accepting credit customers and to be more patient with slow-paying customers. With this approach, accounts receivable will be higher than with the more aggressive approach, but sales will also be somewhat higher. The cost of extending credit and collecting past due accounts will also be higher.

Summary. The difference between the aggressive and the conservative approaches to working-capital management is that with the former, management is willing to work hard to maintain control of, and reduce to a minimum, all current assets. With the conservative approach, however, management does not maintain control over current assets and believes that its time is better spent on other aspects of the business.

HOW TO USE CREDIT

The days of operating a legal business on a cash only basis are over for all but the smallest operations. Cash business has too many problems, including the inability to properly document income and expenditures for the IRS. For individuals and businesses there is the expectation that credit will be offered. In fact, there is a direct relationship between the amount a customer spends and the credit offered. The smaller the sale, the more likely the sale will be in cash; the larger the sale, the more likely it will involve credit. Since almost all businesses are both providers and users of credit, the key is to learn how to use credit.

Individual Credit

One way to understand how businesses use credit is to understand the way individuals use credit. Many items can be purchased for cash or for credit. If there is no difference in the price, the buyer should always use credit instead of cash for all those purchases he or she would have made regardless of the method of payment. Why? The use of credit normally allows the purchaser to pay at a later date, and the time value of money enables the purchaser to earn interest on the funds until payment is required. For the user of the typical bank credit card, a period of about thirty to forty-five days will elapse between the time of purchase and the time of payment. Over the period of a year, the interest earned on this delay in payment can be substantial.

The problem with credit is that many individuals tend to purchase items that they would not have purchased if cash had been required at the time of purchase. Credit allows them to obtain the use of some goods or services now and put off the pain of paying until later. For these individuals, credit works to their disadvantage in two ways. First, they tend to purchase more goods and services than they would have had credit not been available. Second, the cost of these additional purchases tends to be greater than the individual's ability to pay for them, so many remit partial payments and incur high interest charges on the unpaid balance until they complete payment.

Individuals can use credit wisely for personal benefit, or they can misuse it by making unnecessary purchases and incurring unneeded interest charges. Similarly, the startup business can use credit both for the benefit or the detriment of the business.

Trade Credit

The terms of most sales include trade credit. In most industries, trade credit is taken for granted, for very few suppliers ask for cash on delivery (COD) unless the firm has a very poor credit history. A typical trade-credit term with a cash discount is "2/10, net 30." This terms means that a 2-percent cash discount may be taken if the invoice is paid within ten days of the billing date, or the net amount of the invoice is due within thirty days of the billing date.

When trade credit is offered with a cash discount, it has two parts: a free credit period and a costly credit period. The free credit period in the foregoing example is the first ten days during which no cost is incurred by the buyer. The costly period is the last twenty days, when there is a cost to the buyer.

Cost of Trade Credit. An example may help explain the cost. Assume that a firm's purchasing averages \$500,000 worth of goods and services each year. If the terms for these purchases are 2/10, net 30, the net purchases are \$490,000 for the year, or \$1,361 per day. If the firm takes the discount and pays by the tenth day, payables will average (10 × \$1,361) \$13,610. If the firm does not take the discount, payables will average (30 × \$1,361) \$40,830. The cost to the firm for not taking the discount is (0.02 × \$500,000) \$10,000, the amount of additional cash the firm must pay its suppliers. The increase in payables for extending the payment period from day ten to day thirty, a period of twenty days, is (\$40,830 − \$13,610) \$27,220. The cost for this credit extension of twenty days is calculated as follows:

$$\text{Credit cost} = \$10{,}000/\$27{,}220 = 36.7\%$$

This is a very expensive way to obtain a twenty-day credit extension. (There is also the question of whether accounts payable should reflect gross purchases or purchases net of discount. Generally Accepted Accounting Principles (GAAP) permits either treatment. We choose to show purchases as net of discount under the assumption that most well-managed firms would always take this course.)

A quick method of calculating the cost of not taking a cash discount that is offered is as follows:

$$\text{Approx. cost} = \frac{\text{Discount percentage}}{100 - \text{Discount percentage}} \times \frac{360}{\text{Costly credit period}}$$

Using the example with terms of 2/10, net 30:

$$\text{Approx. cost} = \frac{2}{100 - 2} \times \frac{360}{30 - 10} = 36.7\%$$

What does this cost of 36.7% mean? It means that if firms can borrow funds that cost less than 36.7 percent from any source, they should do so and use them to pay within the discount period—on the tenth day. The borrowed funds should be repaid at the end of the credit period (thirty days in the above example) when the full invoice would have been paid anyway.

Line of Credit

Although trade credit is the major source of short-term funds for the startup business, a line of credit from a bank is a close second. Most individuals have a personal line of credit if they have a bank credit card. Bank credit cards have some charge limit which is, in effect, a line of credit. If the limit is \$2,000, then the bank has granted the holder a \$2,000 line of credit. Thus, the holder can charge up to \$2,000, but credit will not be granted for purchases over that amount. (Actually banks allow credit card holders to charge between 10 and 20 percent over the stated limit, but this fact is not advertised.)

If an individual has purchased $500 on the bank card, then the individual has $1,500 remaining on his or her personal line of credit. For the startup business that has been granted a line of credit by a bank, the financial arrangement is much the same. A line of credit is an agreement between the bank and the borrower on the amount of credit that will be extended to the borrower during a specified period. Credit lines can be informal or formal lines of credit.

Informal Line of Credit. The informal line of credit is the typical type of credit extended by local banks to small businesses. For example, if a bank has granted a startup firm a $50,000 line of credit, then the firm may borrow up to $50,000 during the period of the agreement. The agreement will specify the interest rate to be charged on borrowed funds and the repayment schedule. If the firm needs $30,000 in order to take a cash discount on material purchased, then the firm asks the bank to transfer that amount to its checking account. The firm is said to have "taken down" $30,000 of the total line of credit. (Some banks will require that a promissory note be signed at the time the funds are transferred, but other banks will have obtained a written agreement before the first funds are transferred.)

Interest charges start accumulating on the date that the funds are transferred, and the firm can write checks on the borrowed funds. The firm can still borrow up to an additional $20,000 at some future date, even if none of the $30,000 loan has been repaid. If $5,000 of the $30,000 loan has been repaid, then the firm will have a borrowing limit of $25,000 remaining.

The actual mechanics of the transfer of funds will vary from bank to bank, with the most informal being a type of instant loan whereby the bank transfers funds to cover checks written by the firm if the funds are not available in the firm's checking account. Typically, the bank loans funds in multiple amounts of $100. Thus, if a check for $450 arrives for presentation and the firm has only $405 in its checking account, then the bank will advance the firm $100 and clear the check. A more formal loan would require the firm to sign a promissory note for the amount borrowed before the funds were transferred to the firm's account.

Formal line of credit. Large businesses may obtain a formal line of credit. With the formal line of credit, the bank makes a formal commitment to lend the firm up to the amount specified in the loan agreement, and for this commitment, the firm pays a commitment fee. An example will help explain this type of loan agreement. If a startup firm has a formal line of credit from a bank to borrow up to $1 million over a two-year period, then the firm may borrow any amount up to $1 million any time over the two-year period. For this privilege, the startup firm will pay a commitment fee of about 0.25 percent on any unborrowed funds and a stated rate, usually in terms of the prime rate plus 1 to 3 percent, on the borrowed funds.

For example, if the agreement called for an interest rate of prime plus 2 percent, then if the firm borrowed $400,000, the firm would pay a commitment fee of 0.25 percent on the $600,000 remaining line of credit plus the prime rate at the time of the loan plus 2 percent on the $400,000 borrowed.

Note that the difference between the formal and informal types of commitment by the bank is that in the case of the formal line of credit, the bank has a legal obligation to honor the loan agreement and charges for a fee for this commitment. This legal obligation does not exist with the more informal line of credit, and the bank can terminate the line of credit before the end of the agreement period.

Promissory Note

Rather than obtain a line of credit, many firms will borrow a specified amount of money to be used for startup expenses such as purchasing materials. In such cases, when banks loan funds to a startup firm, they usually will have the firms sign a promissory note. A *promissory note* is a signed agreement between the bank (the lender) and the startup firm (the borrower) specifying the amount of the loan, the interest rate, the repayment schedule, the collateral required, the amount the note is discounted (if any), and the amount of a compensating balance, if any is required.

If, for example, a beginning firm borrows $300,000 for startup expenses, the bank may charge a 10-percent interest discounted rate, with a single payment of the principal due in twelve months and collateral consisting of the personal assets of the borrower as well as a compensating balance of 20 percent.

Discounting. If a note is discounted, the interest is subtracted from the principal, and what the borrower receives is the discounted balance. Thus, in the foregoing example, the interest of $30,000 is subtracted from the principal of $300,000, and the borrower actually receives only $270,000; however, the entire $300,000 is due at the end of the twelve-month term of the agreement. This increases the actual rate of interest since the borrower is paying $30,000 in interest expenses but only borrowing $270,000. The actual effective rate of interest is calculated as follows:

$$\text{Effective rate} = \frac{\text{Interest paid}}{\text{Amount received}} = \frac{\$30{,}000}{\$270{,}000} = 11.1\%$$

Thus, the effective rate of 11.1 percent is quite a bit more than the stated, or nominal rate, of 10 percent.

Collateral. *Collateral* is the pledging of an asset or assets of the firm to secure a loan. In pledging assets, the borrower is giving the lender a claim on those assets in the event the firm defaulted on the loan. For the startup firm, the assets may be the real estate or the plant and equipment that the firm owns, or they may be the personal assets of the owner. Typically, owners may have to pledge personal securities or the homes in which they live. Since startup firms seldom have accounts receivable, these cannot be used as collateral. Firms that have been in business long enough to have sizable accounts receivable often use them as collateral for short-term loans.

Compensating Balance. As a condition for obtaining a loan, banks will sometimes require that borrowers maintain compensating balances. If the compensating balance in the example is 20 percent, then the borrower must maintain a checking account balance of at least $60,000 ($300,000 × 0.20) with the lender. The compensating balance has two purposes. First, the bank maintains control over a portion of the loan (the compensating balance that is in the checking account), thereby reducing some of the risk. Second, the compensating balance increases the effective rate being charged and, thus, increases the bank's profits.

To illustrate how the effective rate of a loan is increased assume that \$300,000 is borrowed at 10 percent interest and that a 20-percent compensating balance must be maintained. The effective rate of interest is calculated as follows:

$$\text{Effective rate} = \frac{\$30{,}000}{\$300{,}000 - \$60{,}000} = 12.5\%$$

Of course, if the firm already maintains a checking account balance of \$60,000 or more, then the compensating requirement would not have the effect of increasing the stated rate of interest. Few startup firms, however, have the luxury of maintaining large checking account balances.

Discounting and Compensating Balances. Some lending institutions will require compensating balances and discount the loan, increasing the effective cost of the loan. If the startup firm in the example borrows \$300,000 at 10 percent and if the loan is discounted and the bank requires a 20-percent compensating balance, then the effective rate of interest of the loan would be calculated as follows:

$$\text{Effective rate} = \frac{\$30{,}000}{\$300{,}000 - 30{,}000 - 60{,}000} = 14.29\%$$

The examples presented in this section show that the effective rate of a loan can be much higher than the stated rate of interest. For this reason, the entrepreneur should compare rates offered by different lending institutions.

SOURCES OF WORKING CAPITAL

In addition to the sources of working capital already discussed in this chapter, there are others. Although commercial banks are the prime lending source for businesses, they are not always willing to grant loans to startup businesses. Commercial finance companies and personal finance companies are other possible sources of working capital for the startup firm.

Commercial Finance Companies

Commercial finance companies are more willing to take risks than most commercial banks and, therefore, may be willing to lend funds to a startup firm that was refused credit by a commercial bank. As should be expected, commercial finance companies normally charge a higher rate of interest than commercial banks. Interestingly, with the increasing deregulation of the nation's banks, commercial finance companies have become much more rate competitive and are competing aggressively in many areas of the working-capital loan business. Entrepreneurs should be aware, however, that commercial finance companies are not subject to the same rules and regulations that apply to commercial banks. Most commercial finance companies base their lending limits on the value of the borrowers' assets in what is known as *asset lending* (see The Inside View 14-2).

Commercial finance companies are corporations that are in the business of raising funds through the sale of commercial paper or attracting funds from pension plans,

14-2 The Inside View

ASSET-BASED LENDING

Many startup businesses find that bankers want to see profit and loss statements, balance sheets, and net worth statements before they will extend a loan. Since few startup businesses have healthy financial statements, obtaining a commercial bank loan is almost impossible. Asset-based lenders, like commercial finance companies, will grant working-capital loans backed by inventories or receivables, assets which the lender can seize immediately if the borrowers fall behind on their payment plans.

Asset-based lending has increased rapidly in the past few years, growing from $30 billion in 1982 to $68 billion in 1986. Because of the higher risks involved, asset-based lenders normally charge higher interest rates than commercial banks and tend to keep a tighter grip on their loans. They are also quick to claim their collateral. However, for some companies like Otis Spunkmeyer, Inc., a firm that could not obtain any other type of loan, asset-based lenders may be the only available source of working capital.[2]

insurance companies, and other financial institutions and loaning these funds (at a profit) to businesses. While this may sound exactly like what a commercial bank does, and from a lending standpoint it is, commercial banks primarily use their customers' deposits as their lending base. For this reason they are subject to federal banking regulations and commercial finance companies are not. Unfortunately a few finance companies have taken advantage of the naiveté of their customers by charging very high rates of interest and requiring extraordinary collateral security. For these reasons, therefore, the entrepreneur should be sure to select a well-established commercial finance company with a good reputation.

Accounts Receivable Financing

Commercial finance companies lend funds for working capital primarily through accounts receivable financing, factoring, and inventory financing. *Accounts receivable financing* is the lending of funds based on the accounts receivable assets of the borrowing firm. For example, if the startup firm had $100,000 in accounts receivable, the commercial finance company may take all of those receivables as collateral but only lend funds on 75 percent of the total value, or $75,000 in this example. The amount of the loan will typically vary from 60 to 85 percent of the receivables, depending upon their quality. The borrower pays off the loan as the receivables are collected. If the receivables are not collected, however, the borrower still has the obligation to pay off the loan.

Factoring

Factoring is the actual sale of a firm's accounts receivable. When factoring is used as a source of working-capital funds, the seller of the goods sells the receivables to the factor, who purchases the receivables at a discount. The factor normally notifies the buyer that payments for the goods are to be sent to the factor and not to the seller. Before purchasing the receivables, the factor will usually check the credit standing of the buyer. Those buyers who do not measure up to the factors' standards will not be accepted. In cases where the seller sells all of his or her receivables to a factor, the seller will not make a sale until the factor has checked the credit history of the buyer and has agreed to factor the account.

The factor, therefore, can save the seller the cost of maintaining a credit department or, at least, reduce the cost of the credit department. For the startup enterprise, a factor can provide a source of working capital with the immediate cash proceeds from a sale and a reduction in costs from the reduced need for a credit and collection department. As mentioned previously, if sellers are accepting payment by bank credit cards, the bank issuing the credit card is, in effect, acting as a factor. The bank checked the credit history of the card holder before issuing the card, and the bank will purchase, at a discount, the credit purchases of the card holder.

Inventory Financing

Inventory financing is the use of inventories as security to obtain working-capital loans. Inventories, for many firms, are the largest single current asset and, as such, may be used to secure additional capital. Both commercial banks and commercial finance companies will advance loans based on the value of a firm's inventories. Blanket liens, trust receipts, and warehouse-receipt financing are the three major types of inventory financing.

Blanket Liens. With a blanket lien, the borrower pledges all of his or her inventories as security for a short-term loan. The lender will grant a loan based on the cost or the market value of the inventory. Typically, the lender will grant a loan for between 60 and 80 percent of the value of the inventory. The borrower is free to sell the inventory and is expected to pay off the loan from the proceeds of the sales.

Trust Receipts. In the case of the blanket lien, it is possible for the lender to find that after some inventory has been sold, the value of the remaining inventory is less than the level that existed when the loan was granted. An inventory loan that gives the lender better control of the inventory being pledged as security is the *trust receipt*. With a trust receipt, the borrower acknowledges that the inventory is being held in trust for the lender and that the lender must be paid as soon as the seller is paid by the buyer. The trust receipt is typically used for expensive items that can be individually identified, such as automobiles, trucks, large appliances, and farm equipment.

One of the disadvantages of the trust receipt is that a representative of the lender must visit the premises of the borrower and personally identify the items held in trust, usually by serial or registration numbers. This process is time consuming and explains why trust receipts are not used for small, inexpensive inventory items.

Warehouse-Receipt Financing. Warehouse-receipt financing is another method of reducing the capital needed for the startup business. The use of warehouse-receipt financing involves three parties: a lender, a borrower, and a warehousing company. In transactions that involve warehouse-receipt financing, the lender employs a third party to take control of the borrower's inventory and to act as an agent of the lender. Typically the inventory may be held in a public warehouse or on the seller's premises in what is known as a *field warehouse.*

In a field warehouse arrangement, the warehousing company sets up a warehouse on the company's premises. The supplier ships merchandise that is marked for the warehousing company to the customer. In addition, the invoice and bill of lading is sent to the warehouse representative, who secures the merchandise in an enclosed area on the customer's property. Only the agent (sometimes a bonded employee) is allowed to remove the merchandise from the enclosed area.

For example, a startup firm that builds fourteen- to twenty-two-foot fiberglass inboard/outboard boats may not have the capital to purchase the motors that are an integral part of the finished product. The boat builder could enter into an arrangement with a motor manufacturer, whereby boat motors would be shipped to and kept on the builder's premises within an enclosed area. The motors would remain the property of the manufacturer until they were removed from the enclosed area and placed in the boats. The manufacturer's agent, or a bonded employee, would be the only person allowed access to the warehouse area. The boat motors would be considered "sold" as they were removed from the warehouse area.

This type of arrangement benefits both the boat builder and the motor manufacturer. The builder does not have to pay for the inventory of boat motors until the motors are actually needed, thus reducing the amount of capital needed for the manufacturing process. The builder also has quick access to a wide range of sizes and types of motors. The motor manufacturer obtains a steady customer and an inexpensive warehouse, saving regional warehousing costs and the cost of having to ship the motors twice: once to the regional warehouse and once to the boat builder. Since the title does not pass to the buyer until the motors are removed from the warehouse, the motors legally belong to the manufacturer and are not subject to court action in the event of bankruptcy.

There are two basic methods of making payments for materials removed from a field warehouse. With the first method, the buyer would pay for the materials as they are removed. With the second, for example, the manufacturer may ship the boat builder $50,000 worth of motors and, after $25,000 worth of motors have been removed, may require the builder to pay for those motors before removing any additional motors.

Public Warehouse. A *public warehouse* is an operation independent of the buyer and seller engaged in storing goods. The public warehouse may be used in one of two ways by a startup firm to reduce short-term capital needs. First, a startup firm may store finished products in a public warehouse and use the warehouse receipt as collateral to obtain additional loans. For example, a frozen orange juice operation has to cope with a very short operating season, and very high outlay of capital to pay for the raw material (oranges). The cannery may store frozen orange juice in a public warehouse and obtain additional operating capital by using the warehouse receipts as collateral.

The second method involves the purchase of raw materials. With this method, the manufacturer would purchase raw materials and have them stored in a public warehouse. The manufacturer could then use the warehouse receipts to obtain additional capital to purchase additional raw materials.

Personal Finance Companies

The last source of short-term capital for the startup entrepreneur to be discussed is the personal finance company. Personal finance companies are in the business of loaning money to individuals of higher risk than those who deal with commercial banks and, as expected, also charge a higher rate of interest on their loans. Most of their loans are granted on a secured basis, which normally means that the borrower will have the loan secured by a lien on his or her personal property. (Personal finance companies should be considered as a possible source of funds only after all the other aforementioned sources have been explored.)

Summary

For startup businesses, cash flow is more important than profitability. Cash is needed to purchase inventories, pay employees, and purchase all the supplies needed to start up a business. The profit and loss statement indicates the profitability of firms, but accounting profits may not give a true picture of the firm's cash flow. The cash cycle for a firm is the length of time between the payment for the purchase of materials and labor and the receipt of cash for the sale of goods and services. The longer the cash cycle, the more critical cash-flow management becomes.

To alleviate potential cash-flow problems, cash budgets showing expected cash inflows and outflows over a three-to-twelve-month period are suggested. Cash budgets promote managerial planning for the borrowing and repayment of working-capital funds. In addition to cash budgets, monthly expense reports should be maintained. Whereas cash budgets show expected cash flows, the expense reports provide a format that can be used to control expenses and maintain their proper relationship to sales.

Working-capital management is the management of the level of a firm's current assets and current liabilities. Management may adopt a working-capital policy that varies from conservative to aggressive. With a conservative policy, firms maintain a higher level of liquidity than those with a more aggressive approach. Therefore, firms adopting the more aggressive approach must maintain close control of cash, inventories, and accounts receivable.

The efficient management of credit is vital to startup firms. Trade credit is extended to firms by suppliers, whereas accounts receivable represent credit that firms have extended to their customers. Both have costs to the firm that entrepreneurs should analyze in order to determine their effective cost. Banks may extend short-term credit to the startup firm in the form of loans and/or line of credit. The effective cost of a bank loan may be increased if the loan is discounted or if a compensating balance is required.

Additional sources of working capital may be obtained from commercial finance companies and personal finance companies. Both commercial banks and commercial finance companies extend credit based on a firm's accounts receivable and/or inventory, and both will factor a firm's accounts receivable. The need for capital may also be reduced through the use of a field warehouse. An alternative source of capital for working-capital funds is personal finance companies.

Assembling the Pieces

Carol and Jacki developed a cash-flow budget based on estimated sales of three different levels. The budget included an initial three- to six-month period of operating below break-even while sales were being promoted through a well-designed advertising campaign. During this period, they planned to develop a reliable customer base.

Expenditures during the startup phase included the normal expenditures for rent, utilities, inventory, loan repayment, advertising, and insurance of $6,910 per month. In addition, a one-time startup cost for fixtures and equipment, decorating, starting inventory, deposits, legal and professional fees, and the opening promotional was projected to be $44,755. The objective of the cash budget was to help plan the firm's cash expenditures from the loan commitment in late July to the opening of business in mid-October through the first three to six months of business. Interestingly, the actual expenditures were almost exactly the same as the budgeted figures as a result of Carol and Jacki's efforts to keep spending in line with the funds available. Happily, sales were much better than expected, and they stopped using the cash budget. Unfortunately, the result was a less efficient use of their time and money. Recognizing these ill effects, they went back to using the cash budget and now make the information it contains a large part of their weekly meetings. ■

Questions for Review and Discussion

1. Why are there major differences between a firm's reported profits and its cash flow?
2. What are the three variables that determine the cash cycle?
3. Why should a firm have both a cash budget and an expense report?
4. Of what value to management is the monthly expense report?
5. What is the cost of not taking the discount in the case of each of the following terms? Assume that the payment will be made on the due date.
   (a) 3/10, net 90
   (b) 2/15, net 60
   (c) 1/10, net 30
   (d) 2/10, net 40

6. SRA Inc. is considering borrowing $100,000 for one year to finance a permanent increase in working capital. First National Bank is offering to extend a discounted loan at an 11-percent rate of interest. First State Bank's rate is 10 percent, but First State requires a 20-percent compensating balance. Which bank has the lower effective rate?
7. What factor could make the First State Bank's offer more attractive?
8. Extend the example given in Table 14.2 for three additional months. Prepare a profit and loss statement and a cash-flow statement. Assume sales grow only $8,000 per month, G&A expenses grow by $250 per month, and interest expenses increase only $20 per month.
9. What did you learn from the exercise in problem 8?
10. SPR Inc. had sales of $420,000, an average inventory of $50,000, accounts receivable of $44,000, and forty days to pay its accounts payable. What is the length of SPR's cash cycle?

Notes

1. Joseph Kahn, "Heartbreak Hill," *Inc.,* April 1988, pp. 68–78.
2. Edmund Andrews, "The Cookie Dough Also Rises," *Venture,* December 1987, pp. 94–95.

CHAPTER 15

Accounting and Control Systems

Learning Objectives

After reading this chapter, you will be able to do the following:

- Understand the rationale and need for control systems.
- Determine which records are the most useful for the new business and know how to maintain them.
- Control expenses.
- Establish credit policies.

Imagine going to a basketball game where the scoreboard did not work. The spectators would have to try to keep score in their heads or just keep track of who they think is scoring the most points. If the game were close, what should the team do as the game nears the end? Should the team slow the game down or try to score on three-point shots? Without knowledge of the actual score, both players and fans would be extremely frustrated. Starting up and running a new business without accurate and appropriate records is just about the same as not keeping score at a basketball game, and the entrepreneur will soon be just as frustrated as the basketball spectator.

This chapter is about record keeping: what records are needed, how they are maintained, and how they are used by the entrepreneur to help control what is happening. In addition, there is a section on the establishment of sound credit policies.

Mismanagement is the most oft cited reason for business failure. Many times mismanagement is the result of inaccurate or inadequate information. Entrepreneurs normally do not mismanage their companies on purpose, but they often make decisions based on incomplete information that causes the firm to misprice a product, bid too low on a project, or purchase unneeded equipment. With well-designed, well-kept records, management has a much better chance of making the correct decisions.

THE RATIONALE AND NEED FOR CONTROL SYSTEMS

Many times individuals starting a new business consider record keeping to be an unjustifiable waste of time because they think that they know all that is going on. They know what has been ordered and when it will arrive. They know who has been hired, when they will be paid, and how much they will be paid. They keep this information in their heads. Unfortunately, memories can fail, and the owner is not always at the business when an employee needs the answer to a particular question. Well-known entrepreneur Paul Hawken believes that records should be started when the business is started and that the records must be accurate and should be used. He argues, "The best time to start keeping a daily log is at the very beginning." Unfortunately most people do not. Instead, they delegate the task to experts and wind up hopelessly out of touch with what's happening in the business.[1]

Mr. Hawken's comments indicate two major points about record keeping. First, records should be kept from the very beginning, and, second, entrepreneurs must know what the records are and what they show. The records should not be designed by an accountant to make the accountant's job easier; the purpose of records is to help run firms. Accountants want the records set up so that the job of keeping the books is easier for them, but this is not the main purpose of the records. Certainly entrepreneurs should listen to qualified accountants concerning record keeping, but they must not delegate to the accountants the responsibility of deciding which records are needed and how they should be kept. Too often, when record keeping is designed by professional record keepers, entrepreneurs will not understand them and will not use them. Simply put, entrepreneurs will not be in charge of their own businesses.

Why Keep Records?

Determining which records the startup firm needs and maintaining them is a necessary part of operating a successful business. Records are also required by local, state, and federal regulations. The IRS, for example, simply will not accept an estimate of a firm's expenses, nor can sales tax be paid on an estimate of sales.

Why keep records? First, certain records are required by law. The IRS requires detailed records of revenues and expenses. Both federal and state regulations require the maintenance of personnel records, and local governments require sales tax records. Second, records help entrepreneurs keep their objectives in mind. Records tell what the score is. Whether the objective is sales per month or profit per quarter, records give an indication of when these objectives are reached. A third reason for keeping records is that they help managers spot trends by answering questions. Are sales increasing faster than anticipated, or are sales and administrative expenses growing faster than the rate of sales? Are unit costs increasing? The last reason for keeping records is tax planning. Recording depreciation expenses is but one example of records that are needed for tax planning. Other tax related reasons are explained in detail in Chapter 17.

The Qualities of Good Records

What are the qualities of good records? The qualities of good records include the following:

1. Good records are those an owner can understand, which means that good records must be kept simple. There is nothing to be gained by having a complex analysis of variance if the owner only understands and needs to know by how many dollars actual sales varied from budgeted sales.
2. Records must be kept so that periodic information is available. For one business, this may mean on a weekly, monthly, or quarterly basis, and for another, a cash record may be needed on a daily basis.
3. Records should be set up so that they are easily kept up to date. Some of the best records are those that are updated with each entry—like a checkbook.
4. Records must be accurate. Good records do not fool the person using them. A useful record is one that accurately describes what is recorded.

Having established the reasons for keeping records and having indicated some of the qualities of useful records, it is now time for entrepreneurs to determine what records their startup firms really need.

RECORDS FOR THE NEW BUSINESS

Determining what records are needed for the new business and how they should be set up will vary from firm to firm. For example, a firm that sells only for cash, such as a grocery store or a fast-food restaurant, does not need an accounts receivable record. Most of the records presented in this section, however, may be utilized by most firms. In addition, records will be divided into two groups. The first group presented in this section is called managerial records. The second group, presented in the following section, is accounting records.

Although all records could be classified as accounting records, managerial records are those used primarily by management to make managerial decisions, while accounting records are those used primarily to develop the firm's financial statements. Managerial records include the following: (1) sales records, (2) financial records, (3) inventory records, and (4) personnel records.

Sales Records

Sales records should be designed to show simply, at a glance, the sales for each department and the total sales for each day. An example of a daily sales record is shown in Figure 15.1. For the startup firm, this daily sales record should have certain specific characteristics. First, the sales record should be simple to maintain and simple to understand. Second, the record should be easily modified to suit any business. For example, if the business were a grocery store, the column headings could be changed to show sales by department: meat, produce, bakery, general grocery, and nongrocery. For a restaurant, the column headings may be bar, food, catering, and private groups.

Finally, the daily sales record should have a daily sales summary that allows man-

FIGURE 15.1
Daily Sales Records

DAILY SALES RECORDS

Firm ______________ Month ________ 19 ____

Day	Retail	Wholesale	Service	Contract	Total
1					
2					
3					
4					
5					
30					
31					

agement to see at a glance how each department is doing. There are additional refinements, such as a column for weather for a restaurant and, for one cafetaria, a column for each main dish and a column for the weather. In the last case, the manager found a high correlation between the sales of certain meats and the weather and based his menu on the day of the week (Friday was the biggest day) and the weather (the colder the weather, the higher the percentage of beef dishes).

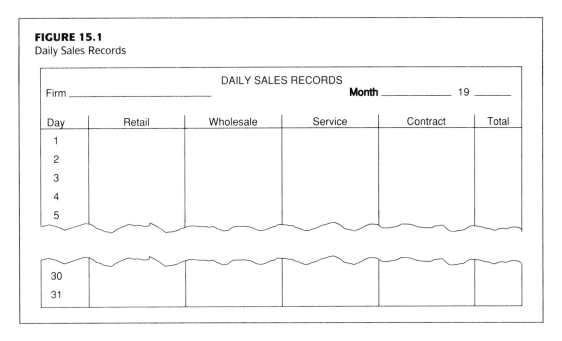

An important point to remember about sales records is that all receipts for each day should be deposited in a bank. The deposit should be the exact amount received. If cash is needed for the business, the cash should come from the petty-cash fund, and a check should be drawn periodically to replenish the petty-cash fund. Petty-cash funds should be used for payments of very small amounts, and all other payments should be paid by check.

Financial Records

The only financial record listed here as a managerial record is the checkbook. (All other financial records are classified as accounting records, and they will be presented in the next section of this chapter.) The checkbook is probably the first, and certainly one of the most important, financial records that startup businesses should have. A checking account should be opened in the name of the business before the first bill is paid. One of the most common errors entrepreneurs make when starting a business is to use their own personal checking account to pay the bills of the firm. This common practice causes the problem of comingled funds and makes reconciling the checkbook difficult.

Comingled Funds. The first problem concerns the determination of which checks were paid for business expenses and which were for personal expenses. At the time they write checks, entrepreneurs are certain which are personal and which are business; later, however, they cannot always remember. The comingling of funds can cause serious problems with the IRS even when the name and account number of the payee is written on the check. For example, was the check written for the telephone bill for company business or personal use? The second problem stems from the temptation to use funds from the business for personal use. With most startups, entrepreneurs use their own funds to pay the initial expenses of the business, and then, to balance the accounts, start paying personal expenses from the funds flowing into the business. This all too common practice is the reason the IRS becomes suspicious if personal and business funds are comingled.

A checking account should be opened before the first funds are spent for the new enterprise, and all subsequent expenses should be paid from this account. Entrepreneurs can, and usually will, deposit funds from their personal checking accounts in the checking account of the new firm to keep the two funds separate. This arrangement makes accounting for expenses easier and, not inconsequentially, makes the IRS happy. When writing each check, the purpose of the check should be entered in the checkbook with the name of the payee, the amount, the check number, and the date.

Reconciling the Checkbook. At the end of each statement period, usually each month, the bank balance should be reconciled, a task necessary for two important reasons. First, the bank considers the statement correct unless they are notified promptly, usually within thirty days, of any errors. Second, just going through the checks each month provides owners with a quick check of the firms' expenses. Owners, therefore, have an opportunity to ascertain that checks are being written only for business purposes and, it is hoped, to spend some time thinking about how funds are being allocated.

There is a simple method for reconciling the bank statement each period. The reconciliation is simply making sure that what the bank says the firm has in its checking account is the same amount as the firm thinks it has in its checking account. The method for accomplishing the reconciliation can be shown as follows:

Bank balance	\$
Add deposits not recorded by the bank	\$
Subtract all outstanding checks	\$
Subtract any bank charges	\$
Balance	\$

The final balance should be the same as the checkbook balance.

The main problem with reconciling bank statements is the float. The *float* is the time between the date a check is written and the date the check is presented to the firms' banks for payment. This time can vary from one day to more than two weeks. A second problem is that the bank's statement date is on, say, the twentieth of the month, but the firm does not receive the statement until the thirtieth. Given these these two problems, the balances to be reconciled can be far apart. However, the foregoing method merely collects all the checks written by the firm, but not presented to the bank, as a single total, greatly reducing the problem of reconciliation. (A bank-reconciliation problem is included at the end of the chapter.)

Petty-Cash Fund. A petty-cash fund should be set up and used to make payments for expenses that are both small in dollar amount and for which there is no invoice. A typical example would be money needed to pay for a few stamps or for making a few copies of a document. The entrepreneur should start the petty-cash fund by drawing a check for the amount he or she thinks is sufficient to cover such small cash disbursements, usually about $50, and placing this money in a separate drawer, box, or envelope. When money is withdrawn from the petty-cash fund, a record of the expenditure should be maintained in a petty-cash fund record book. This book can be a simple spiral notebook. When the fund becomes low, a check should be drawn for the amount of the petty-cash expenditures to date, and a new page in the petty-cash record should be started. In this manner, the amount in the petty-cash fund plus the listed expenditures should always equal the amount of the fund. In this example, that amount should always be $50.

Inventory Records

Entrepreneurs should keep records on both major equipment and materials purchased. An equipment inventory record should be maintained on all major-equipment purchases. Major-equipment purchases include all the equipment that has a life of more than one year and will be depreciated for tax purposes. The record should have a description of the equipment, the date purchased, the name of the supplier from whom it was purchased, and the cost (including shipping and installation). It should also indicate how it was paid for (record check numbers) and show individual payments if it was purchased on an installment plan. A simple but excellent system is to keep a card for each item of equipment and have a maintenance record on the back of the card. These records provide a basis for calculating depreciation in addition to providing supporting data for fixed-asset accounts.

In addition to major-equipment records, the firm should maintain records on all raw materials purchased for use in manufacturing. These records should show the date and quantity ordered, date and quantity received, and the date and quantity used. Material received should be checked against purchase orders. (This topic was covered in much greater detail in Chapter 13.)

Personnel Records

There must be a file for each employee. The file should include a record of the employee's initial interview and the terms of his or her employment. In addition, an interview record should be maintained for each person interviewed for employment by the startup firm. These interview records are of vital importance should a person who was not hired or who was hired but not promoted as quickly as someone else claim discrimination.

In addition to the interview records, owners of firms must see that accurate records are kept on the hours each employee works. This record could be a simple time card or similar record of both the regular and overtime hours the employee has worked. Employees should be paid by check, and a record of each check should be part of their record. (The maintenance of a payroll record for each employee is required by both the federal and state regulations.)

If the firm has personnel policies, a copy of these policies should be given to each employee, and these policies should be explained to the employee before he or she is hired. A signed statement that the employee has read these policies and understands them can be invaluable when problems arise over firings, promotions, and even retirement.

A copy of local, state, and federal laws should be included as part of the firm's personnel records. To learn what these laws are, entrepreneurs can call the nearest office of the U.S. Department of Labor, which will provide firms with a copy of the necessary requirements. In addition, in most areas, the Internal Revenue Service regularly offers courses on the records necessary to satisfy the federal requirements.

ACCOUNTING RECORDS

Accounting is the scorekeeping for the business enterprise. Just as spectators cannot tell the score at a basketball game without a scoreboard, neither can entrepreneurs tell where their businesses are without accounting records. Other individuals besides the entrepreneur want to know what the business score is. These people include all the suppliers of capital to the firm. Although accounting is an activity that most entrepreneurs want someone else to do, some knowledge of accounting and accounting records is required if a business is to be successful. Several surveys have shown that most of the small businesses that fail have very poor operating records. Many small firms that fail operate without any records, with single-entry accounting records, or with only a checkbook as a record system.

An adequate financial record keeping system is a means of collecting, summarizing, analyzing, and reporting financial information on the firm. The basic accounting records include the cash receipts journal, cash disbursements journal, general journal, and the general ledger. Before presenting a discussion of these records, however, entrepreneurs need to understand a few accounting principles.

An account represents a single category of business transactions, such as employees' wages, cash, interest expenses, or sales expenses. All business transactions are, therefore, recorded in some account. For example, when an employee is paid, the amount is recorded in the employee-wage account. The simplest form of account is called a T account, with cash flowing into the account shown on the left (debit) side of the T and cash flowing out of the account shown on the right (credit) side (see Figure 15.2). The account balance is derived by totaling both sides and subtracting the right-side total from the left-side total.

Double-Entry Accounting. Double-entry accounting means that for every transaction, two entries are recorded. For example, when an employee is paid, the employee-wage account is increased and the cash account is decreased. In the case of a retail store, when an item is sold for cash, the cash account increases and the inventory

FIGURE 15.2
T Account

Cash		*Month*	*January*
	Increases		*Decreases*
Beginning balance	$7,432		$240
	389		662
	1,210		3,180
	147		
	$9,178		$4,082
New balance	$5,096		

account decreases. With double-entry accounting for each transaction, the total increases must equal the total decreases—the debits must equal the credits. Thus, for each recorded transaction there must be at least one debit entry and one credit entry.

Debits and Credits. *Debits* are entries on the left side of an account, and *credits* are entries on the right side of an account. A common misconception is that debit means to subtract and credit means to add. This is not always true, as shown in the following chart.

Debit and Credit Entries

Type Account	*Increases Are Entered As*	*Decreases Are Entered As*
Asset	Debit	Credit
Liability	Credit	Debit
Capital	Credit	Debit
Revenue	Credit	Debit
Expense	Debit	Credit

Journals

Entries from the different records are entered into journals, often called the books of original entry. The original entry is the entry of the transaction into the accounting system. Journals are simply a chronological record of financial transactions; when they occurred and the amount.

Cash Receipts Journal. All transactions involving the receipt of cash are entered in the cash receipts journal. The number and headings of the various columns are tailored to meet the needs of the individual business. An example of a page from a cash receipts journal is shown in Figure 15.3.

At the close of each day's business, a summary of all cash deposits, sales, and

FIGURE 15.3
Medical Eye Lasers, Inc: Cash Receipts Journal

Date	Account Title	Cash Deposited (debit)	Sales (credit)	Sales Tax (credit)	Accounts Receivable (credit)
March 1	Daily cash report	880	420	36.00	424.00
1	Jim Jones	180			180.00
1	Sam Head	290			290.00
2	Daily cash report	681	330	16.50	334.50
Monthly Totals		121,740	82,620	4,131	34,989.00

individual accounts should be entered in the cash receipts journal. For those firms that have cash sales, such as retail stores and some service businesses, the daily cash report is the total of all the sales from the different cash registers. It is important for each cash register to be reconciled each day or at the end of the operator's shift on each register. In addition to the daily cash report, sales to major accounts should also be recorded in the cash receipts journal each day. For different firms, the cash receipts journal may have a column for sales tax, a miscellaneous column for minor sources of income, a column for service revenues, or a column for any other major source of income.

At the end of the month, each column in the journal is totaled. The total in the "cash deposited" column should equal the sum of all the remaining columns; thus, the total of the debt column should equal the total of the credit columns. These totals are then posted to their respective accounts in the general ledger (explained later in this chapter).

Cash Disbursements Journal. The cash disbursements journal is designed to provide an accounting of all payments made by the firm. If all invoices and bills are paid by check, then the journal summarizes all checking-account activity on a single page. This format provides entrepreneurs with a concise picture of the firm's expenses and in this way may be helpful in management analysis. Figure 15.4 is an example of a cash disbursements journal for Medical Eye Lasers, Inc.

The cash disbursements journal illustrated has a minimum number of columns, but like the cash receipts journal, the column headings can be changed to suit the type firm for which journal is being set up. For example, headings could include columns

FIGURE 15.4
Medical Eye Lasers, Inc.: Cash Disbursements Journal

Date	Account Title	Cash (credit)	Purch. Dis. Taken. (credit)	Acc'ts. Pay. (debit)	Purchases (debit)	Misc. (debit)
March 1	Utilities expense	270				270
1	Cornea, Inc.	564	12	576		
2	Cash purchases	120			120	

for the different payroll deductions. At the end of the month, each column is totaled, and again, the total of the credit columns should equal the total of the debit columns. The totals are then posted to their respective accounts in the general ledger.

General Journal. Both the cash receipts journal and the cash disbursements journal are known as special journals. For larger firms, other special journals may be needed to better account for either the revenues or expenses in different categories. Examples of other special journals include the following: sales journals, sales returns and allowances journal, purchases journal, or a purchases returns and allowances journal. For most small startup firms, however, infrequent cash receipts and disbursement transactions are recorded in the general journal. The date of the transaction, the amounts to be debited and credited, the amounts of the debit and credit entries, and an explanation of each transaction are recorded in the general journal. The general journal for Medical Eye Lasers, Inc. is illustrated in Figures 15.5.

Credit sales and purchases represent the most common type of transaction recorded in this journal. Both are financial transactions that do not involve the immediate exchange of cash. Another example of a transaction not involving cash that is recorded in the general journal is the accounting for bad debts. Bad debts are written off in the general journal, and if payment for the debt is received later, the entry is reversed. Additional examples of financial transactions that are recorded in the general journal include the recording of equipment depreciation, correcting entries, and the adjusting and closing of entries (see Figure 15.5).

General Ledger. The purpose of the general ledger is to provide a central collection point for all the financial information contained in the various journals of the firm and to provide a method of collecting accounts before the firm's financial statements are prepared. General-ledger accounts are usually arranged in the sequence in which they will appear in the financial statements: assets first, followed by liabilities, stockholders'

FIGURE 15.5
Medical Eye Lasers, Inc.: General Journal

Date	Account Titles and Explanations	Acct. No.	Debit	Credit
Feb 1	Cash	300	20,000	
	I.C. Wu, Capital			20,000
	Owner invested cash into business			
1	Office supplies	104	400	
	Accounts payable			400
	Purchased office supplies on account from Caroline Office Supply Company.			
1	Accounts receivable	102	350	
	Office equipment			350
	Sold used printer to Jim Small, Inc. (Full amount due March 1.)			
28	Equipment rental revenues	401	2,300	
	Income summary			2,300
	To close the revenue account			
28	Office supplies expense	506	48	
	Office supplies			48
	To record office supplies used during Febuary			
28	Depreciation expense: building	509	120	
	Accumulated depreciation: building			120
	To record depreciation of office building			

equity, revenue, and finally expenses. Two pages from the general ledger of Medical Eye Lasers, Inc., are shown in Figure 15.6.

In Figure 15.6, the equipment-rental revenues page shows the date and amount of rental income received. In addition, at the end of the month, the account is closed, with the total amount of rental revenues ($2,300) shown as a closing entry in the general journal. (See Figure 15.5 for the closing entry.) The second account that is presented in Figure 15.6 is the office supplies expense. In the example, the charge to the account for office supplies for the month of February was $48. Again, the general-ledger account was closed at the end of the month and was posted in the general journal (Figure 15.5).

Before concluding this discussion of the general ledger, some additional com-

FIGURE 15.6
Medical Eye Lasers, Inc.: General Ledger

Equipment Rental Revenues, Account No. 401

Date	Explanation	Jr. Ref.	Debit	Credit	Credit Balance
Feb. 5		3		410	410
16		3		730	1,140
20		4		500	1,640
24		5		600	2,300
28		5	2,300		0

Office Supplies Expense, Account No. 506

Date	Explanation	Jr. Ref.	Debit	Credit	Debit Balance
Feb. 28		5	48		48
28		5		48	0

ments should be made without attempting to explain accounting procedures—a process best left to accounting textbooks. The general ledger consists of many pages similar to the two illustrated in Figure 15.6. In addition, the general ledger provides a running balance of the various accounts. It should be noted that each account has been given a number. These account numbers will vary from firm to firm, but the accompanying chart of accounts is typical.

Chart of Accounts

Assets	Liabilities
101 Cash	201 Accounts payable
102 Accounts receivable	202 Notes payable
103 Inventory	203 Sales taxes—payable
105 Materials and supplies	205 FICA taxes—payable
107 Prepaid expenses	208 Fed. withholding taxes
108 Buildings	210 State withholding tax
110 Land	212 Unemployment tax
120 Accumulated depreciation	220 Long-term debt
122 Equipment	
130 Furniture and fixtures	

Revenues	*Expenses*
400 Retail sales	500 Salaries and wages
401 Wholesale sales	501 Payroll taxes
402 Sales-service	502 Utilities
404 Miscellaneous income	503 Rent
	504 Interest
	505 Supplies
	508 Maintenance
	510 Depreciation
	520 Travel & entertainment
	530 Miscellaneous expenses

Financial Statements

The information obtained through each of the accounting journals is, in effect, a scoreboard for only a part of the total financial picture. The cash receipts journal, for example, indicates how the firm is doing in relationship to cash but does not indicate how sales or expenses are performing. In terms of the basketball scoreboard analogy, the cash receipts journal only indicates the number of goals made but does not tell anything about the number of goals attempted, a vital statistic if one of the objectives is to improve the performance of the team.

Since improving the performance of the startup company must be one of the goals of the entrepreneur, all of the accounting journals are combined into financial statements that can be used to indicate how well the firm is doing. The information is taken from the various accounting journals and summarized in financial statements. The two most important of these are the income statement and the balance sheet. The income statement is a summary of the firm's income and expenses during a specific period of time (month, quarter, year). The balance sheet is a summary of the firm's assets, liabilities, and equity at a specific point in time (end of the month, quarter, or year). Thus, the former is a record of what happened over a period of time, and the latter is a record of where the firm is at a specific point in time.

Income Statement. An *income statement* is a financial statement summarizing the revenues, expenses, and net income (or net loss) of a firm for its accounting period. This statement is alternatively referred to as a statement of income, statement of earnings, profit and loss statement, or statement of operations. Net income can be expressed in a simple equation as follows:

Net income = Revenues − Expenses

The major objective of the startup firm is to sell goods or services to customers at a price higher than the cost of producing those goods and services. The income statement indicates just how well the firm is meeting that objective.

An illustration of a typical income statement is shown in Figure 15.7. The income statement is for the first month of the firm's operation. Note that, unlike almost every

FIGURE 15.7
Medical Eye Lasers, Inc.: Income Statement for Month Ended February 28

			As a Percentage of Revenues
Revenues:			
Service revenue		$3,100	
Equipment rentals		2,300	
Total revenues		$5,400	
Expenses:			
Employees wages	$6,120		113.3
Utilities expense	384		7.1
Rent expense	750		13.9
Supplies	48		0.1
Depreciation expense	120		2.2
Insurance expense	115		2.1
Telephone expense	45		0.1
Van expense	345		6.4
Interest expense	270		5.0
Miscellaneous expense	210		3.9
Total expenses		$8,407	
Net Income (loss)		($3,007)	

textbook example, a net loss is shown. This was done to emphasize that the first few months of most startup firms are not profitable, but, it is hoped that the loss will decrease each month until the firm eventually does become profitable.

The figures in the income statement can be presented as a percentage of sales in order to analyze how the firm is doing in comparison to similar firms in the industry. By expressing the different items in percentage form, an analysis of how the firm is performing can be made by comparing results with similar firms. Industry data are presented as percentages in Robert Morris Associates' *RMA Annual Statement Studies*, or Troy's *Almanac of Business and Industrial Ratios*. The comparison may indicate where the new firm is spending too much money, or where it is not spending enough. In addition, entrepreneurs can compare each month's result with those of past months to determine whether the firm has made any progress toward profitability.

Balance Sheet. Whereas the income statement shows what happened in the firm over a period of time, the balance sheet indicates where the firm is at a particular time, usually the last day of the reporting period. The balance sheet shows the assets of the firm on one side (the left side) and the liabilities and stockholders' equity on the other side. Thus, the balance sheet shows the resources of the firm and how those resources were financed.

The assets are divided into two categories, current assets and fixed assets. The current assets—those assets that are held only temporarily by the firm—are listed in order of their liquidity, from cash (the most liquid current asset) to inventory (the least liquid of the current assets). Fixed assets include the tangible property of a long-term or permanent nature that is owned by the firm. Liabilities are the debts (obligations) of the firm, with current liabilities those debts that are due within one year and long-term liabilities those debts that mature in more than one year. Stockholders' equity, or net worth, is the excess of assets over liabilities. Basically, stockholders' equity is capital invested in the firm at startup by the owner(s) plus any additions from retained income or additional infusions of capital. Stockholders' equity can decrease if the firm suffers any losses. The balance sheet for Medical Eye Lasers, Inc. is shown in Figure 15.8.

CONTROLLING EXPENSES

The accounting and financial statements serve two major purposes. First, they are required by the IRS as well as by entrepreneurs who use them as an aid in securing capital. Second, they can be used as a means of determining the financial health of the

FIGURE 15.8
Medical Eye Lasers, Inc.: Balance Sheet, February 28

Assets		*Liabilities*	
Current Assets		Current Liabilities	
Cash	$5,548	Accounts payable	$1,245
Receivables	540	Salaries payable	810
Inventory	4,330	Notes payable	2,000
Prepaid items	190		
Total current assets	$10,608	**Total current liabilities**	$4,055
Plant & Equipment	$50,650	Long-term debt	
Less depreciation	210	Note payable (due 1/31/1994)	$10,000
Net plant & equipment	$50,440	Bond payable	30,000
		Total long-term debt	$40,000
		Total liabilities	$44,055
		Stockholder's Equity	
		I.C. Wu, Capital	$16,993
Total Assets	$61,048	**Total Liabilities and Stockholder's Equity**	$61,048

firm. It is this second purpose that is the topic of this section: the use of accounting and financial statements as an aid in controlling expenses.

Financial and accounting statements can be used as an aid in controlling expenses because they indicate, in dollar terms, how the firm is utilizing its resources. The income statement indicates, for example, how productive the firm has been in utilizing its assets to produce a profit. If entrepreneurs begin studying the statements each month from the startup month on, they will develop a habit that will prove invaluable to the success of the firm. By starting when the statements are fairly simple to read, and asking the preparer questions about the various accounts presented, entrepreneurs will learn that these statements are not only simple to understand but also can yield valuable information about the firm.

The use of the income statement as a control device was mentioned in the previous section. There, the various expenses in the income statement were listed as a percentage of sales. By comparing the firm's expenses against those of similar firms, entrepreneurs can obtain an idea about how their firms are doing. In addition to the sources mentioned earlier, comparisons with other retail firms may be found in *Expenses in Retail Business*, published by NCR Corporation, and in the *Barometer of Small Business*, published by the Accounting Corporation of America. Comparisons of the different expense items may indicate if the firm's costs are out of line and, therefore, should be reduced. A word of caution on making point for point comparisons: Expense items may not always be comparable. For example, one firm may include civic club membership and donations to local charities as part of advertising expenses while another firm does not. Although such discrepancies do exist, comparisons with other firms still provide entrepreneurs with the means to determine whether any expenses are out of line. Often overlooked is the fact that below-average expenses may indicate potential problems. For example, low advertising expenditures may be part of the reason for low sales.

Ratio Analysis

The use of financial statements is important in ratio analysis. Ratios that are calculated from the income statement and balance sheet enable entrepreneurs to compare their results with those of similar firms. Sources of comparative industry ratios that are readily available in most public libraries include the following:

Dun & Bradstreet Corporation's *Key Business Ratios*
Robert Morris Associates' *Annual Statement Studies*
Leo Troy's *Almanac of Business and Industrial Financial Ratios*
Trade publications

Ratios may be grouped into four major categories: (1) liquidity, (2) asset management, (3) debt management, and (4) profitability.

Liquidity. The two major liquidity ratios are the current ratio and the quick ratio. The current ratio is calculated by dividing current assets by current liabilities. Using the balance sheet information in Figure 15.8, the current ratio for Medical Eye Lasers is 2.6, and the industry average (from Troy's *Almanac*) is 0.9. (All ratios and industry averages are shown in Figure 15.9.)

Since Medical Eye Lasers has a higher current ratio than the industry average, does this mean that the firm is doing better than other firms in the industry? In this case, the answer is no. The higher ratio is primarily the result of the high initial cash position provided by the owner of the firm, but the high ratio does indicate that the firm does not have a liquidity problem. Similarly, the quick ratio (current assets minus inventory divided by current liabilities) is a stronger indication of a firm's liquidity. For Medical Eye Lasers, the quick ratio is 1.5, and the industry average is 0.6. This comparison would indicate that the firm does not have a liquidity problem.

Generally, when a firm is developing a liquidity problem, it begins paying its bills later and later, increasing the accounts and notes payable. Thus, current liabilities rise faster than current assets, and liquidity ratios begin to deteriorate. Liquidity ratios, therefore, act as an indicator of the financial health of a firm. If the ratios are dropping, then an owner must look further at the financial statements to determine the reason and then work to correct the problem.

Debt Management. A second indication of the financial health of a firm comes from debt-management ratios. Debt-management ratios indicate the amount of debt the firm is incurring in relationship to its other assets. Typical indicator ratios are total debt to (divided by) total assets, total debt to net worth, fixed assets to net worth, and total assets to net worth. For example, the debt-to-net-worth ratio is a comparison of the amount of funds that lenders have invested in the firm to the funds that the owners have invested. While the ratio can vary greatly from industry to industry, lenders are wary of investing in a firm whose owners are not able, or willing, to invest.

The debt-to-total-asset ratio for Medical Eye Lasers is 0.72, compared to the industry average of 0.68, and its debt to net worth is 3.6 compared to the industry average of 2.3. Both these comparisons indicate that this firm's ratios are very close to

Figure 15.9
Ratio Analysis

Liquidity	*Medical Eye*	*Industry*
Current ratio	$\frac{10,608}{4,055} = 2.6$	0.90
Quick ratio	$\frac{6,278}{4,055} = 1.5$	0.60
Debt Management		
Debt/Total Assets	$\frac{44,055}{61,048} = .72$	0.68
Debt/New Worth	$\frac{44,055}{16,993} = 2.6$	2.30

the industry average. In analyzing debt-management ratios, entrepreneurs are looking at two major factors. First, if the firm has ratios that are much lower than the industry averages, the firm may encounter difficulty in borrowing additional funds. Many lenders will not lend additional funds until the ratios are improved. Thus, entrepreneurs must remember to analyze these ratios and attempt to improve them before lenders start demanding that they do so.

Second, if the firm's ratios are higher than the industry average, it may not be utilizing financial leverage to its advantage. Financial leverage is an advantage to the firm when borrowed funds earn a higher rate of return than the cost of those funds. Financial leverage is a disadvantage when the cost of borrowed funds is higher than the return from the use of those funds. Financial leverage, therefore, can have both a positive and negative effect on the profitability of the firm. Entrepreneurs should strive to use financial leverage to improve the firm's profitability.

Asset-Management and Profitability Ratios. Asset management and profitability ratios for Medical Eye Laser are not included in Figure 15.9. For only one month of operation, these ratios would be meaningless for two reasons. First, industry ratios are based on the results of an entire year. Therefore, asset-management ratios (e.g., sales to inventory and sales to total assets) and profitability ratios (e.g., profit divided by sales or profit divided by assets) simply cannot be calculated. Then why are they even presented in this chapter? The objective in presenting ratio analysis for startup firms is to familiarize entrepreneurs with the various ratios and to demonstrate that these ratios can provide an early warning of potential problems. The liquidity and debt ratios should be analyzed from the startup month on, and the asset-management and profitability ratios must be utilized after the firm has been in operation for a longer period of time.

Budgeting

Budgeting helps firms control expenses and, in so doing, accomplishes two purposes. First, the process of deciding how much should be spent on each expense item forces entrepreneurs to examine how much money they are planning to spend. This examination helps owners to question the value of each expenditure on a regular basis.

The second purpose of budgeting for the startup firm is to provide a means of communicating to all employees what management expects. For example, an advertising expense budget of $3,600 for the month states in unambiguous terms what can be spent for advertising. Too often startup firms operate without clear financial guidelines—a situation that often results in the expenditure of too much money. The budget should state the dollar amount of sales revenues expected and what amount the firm expects to spend to generate those revenues. The difference between the two is the expected profit for the budgeting period. For the startup firm, monthly budgets are imperative, and they should be reviewed during the first week of each month.

Sales budgets for startup firms can be broken into weekly sales forecasts so that progress can be measured each week. A simple, but very effective, method is illustrated in Figure 15.10. Here, expected sales are plotted on a cumulative basis, and actual month-to-date sales are plotted each week. A chart of this type, which is easy

FIGURE 15.10
Cumulative Sales vs. Plan: March

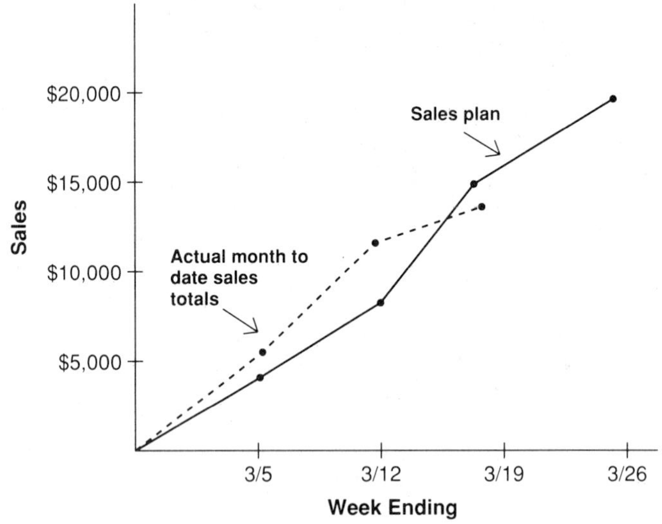

to construct, easy to keep current, and easy to use, is an indispensable management tool. If sales are lagging behind budget, the owner knows about it early in the month, when there is still time to take action, not at the end of the month, when it is too late. Effective managerial action could take the form of increased sales efforts, a reduction of expenditures, or a combination of the two.

Expenses cannot be broken down easily on a week-to-week basis because many expenses, such as rent and utilities payments, occur as a single payment during the month. Thus, it is necessary to maintain a monthly expense budget (see Figure 15.11). The monthly expense report is a useful tool for managerial control. By recording monthly expenses by line item, management can take corrective action before the year-to-date spending variance gets too far out of line.

Management Control

Management control is the process by which entrepreneurs insure that the resources of firms are properly utilized. For most firms, operating a profitable enterprise is their major objective, for without a profitable operation, few firms would last very long.

Since no manager can control everything, the goal is to decide what to control. When firms are very small, owners may think that they can control all operations, but, in reality, this is neither necessary nor good management. Since the entrepreneur's time is limited, only those aspects of the operation that have the greatest effect on the desired results of the firm really need to be controlled. For most firms, entrepreneurs should be in control of the product, people, and finances.

Product. The product or service offered by the startup firm is the one thing that makes it unique, and, as expected, successful entrepreneurs will maintain close control

FIGURE 15.11
Monthly Expense Report

SALES AND ADMINISTRATION EXPENSES — MONTH: JUNE

	Current Month			Year to Date		
	Actual Cost	Budgeted Cost	Spending Variance	Actual Cost	Budgeted Cost	Spending Variance
Salaries	$6,100	$6,100	$ 0	$32,500	$30,000	$(2,500)
Commision	1,120	1,400	280	6,250	6,000	(250)
Car allowance	305	300	(5)	1,810	1,600	(210)
Travel	429	400	(29)	2,140	2,400	260
Office rent	1,200	1,200	0	7,200	7,200	0
Utilities	484	450	(34)	2,840	2,700	(140)
Supplies	75	64	11	390	420	30
TOTAL COSTS	$18,600	$17,900	$(700)	$105,660	$102,000	$(3,660)

over their product or service. Most entrepreneurs who start a business want to provide a particular type of product or service that is either different from or better than those on the market. If this were not the goal of entrepreneurs, how would they be successful? This is true whether the product is a running shoe (Nike shoes were started in the home of one of the founders, using a waffle iron to make the distinctive "waffle" soles) or a service like the home delivery of rental videotapes. Entrepreneurs must always keep in mind what makes their company unique (why the firm was started in the first place) and make certain that all employees, and all contractors working for the firm, also do not lose sight of the primary goals of the company.

People. Entrepreneurs should devote most of their attention to the products produced by their firms; however, the major expense of most small firms is labor. The owner of a startup firm must control labor expenses from the beginning, or these expenses will grow out of control. Unfortunately, or maybe fortunately, owners of small firms have close contact with their employees and often think of them as individuals rather than as expenses. Startup entrepreneurs must treat their employees as individuals, but must also remember that unless the firm is profitable, none of these individuals will have a job.

To help properly manage labor expenses, entrepreneurs should periodically review the performance of each individual in the firm and assess his or her value to the profitable operation of the firm. One method of doing this is to imagine how well the business would operate without the services of that individual. Would he or she be replaced, could a part-time employee do the job, or is he or she so valuable that replacement would be very difficult? Asking these kinds of questions can help entrepreneurs manage their employees better. The next step, and a difficult one for most entrepreneurs, is to reduce unnecessary expenses, which often means terminating employees who are not performing up to the standards required by company policy.

In addition to assessing the value of the firm's employees, the manager can help improve the quality of output by rewarding quality work. Well-timed incentive rewards for outstanding work can do more to help all employees understand the owner's standards than all the memos, company newsletters, and bulletin board notices combined. Although the subject of staffing was discussed in Chapter 11 in much greater detail, entrepreneurs must realize that in order to control the business, they must properly manage their employees.

Financing. The last area over which entrepreneurs need to maintain control is that of finances. Although some entrepreneurs do not feel that they understand accounting statements and are embarrassed to ask their accountants "dumb" questions, the fact is that unless entrepreneurs maintain control of the financing, the firm is wide open to fraud and embezzlement.

A perfect example of what can occur if financing is not controlled is the case of Philip Crosby, founder of PCA, Inc. PCA is a quality-management consulting firm that prides itself on employing quality people and in being able to show client firms how to provide better-quality products, service, and people. In 1986, PCA hired John Nelson, who presented all the right credentials and was accepted as "the kind of honest individual we'd want to hire." Mr. Nelson was placed in charge of disbursements and within six months had embezzled $961,606 from PCA, Inc., almost bankrupting the firm. How was this possible? Basically, neither Philip Crosby nor any of the other top management people were really in control of financing, a fact Mr. Nelson soon learned and exploited. In addition, John Nelson was not even John Nelson; his real name was Robert Liszewski.[2]

The main reason, however, for maintaining control of a firm's financing, is to be able to manage the future of the firm. The second reason is to prevent fraud, which, of course, can also affect the future of the firm.

Control of the Future. The entrepreneur must learn to read and understand the numbers that indicate where the firm is heading. An article in *Inc.* (see The Inside View 15-1) explains how numbers can be used to gain control of the firm.

Without belaboring the point, entrepreneurs must learn to read the financial statements produced by the firm or by the firm's accountants and must ask questions about numbers they do not understand. According to an old Chinese saying, "'Tis better to ask a question and be thought of a fool for an hour, than remain silent and be a fool for a lifetime." Ask the accountant questions.

Control of Fraud. Just as there is no perfect system for preventing a car from being stolen, there also is no perfect system for protecting a business from fraud. However, several steps can be taken to reduce the possibility of fraud.[3]

1. Financial records should be complete.

15-1 ***The Inside View***

USE NUMBERS TO GAIN CONTROL

Success in business may depend on how well management can read its firm's financial numbers and how it reacts to them. The numbers come from the dozens of reports and statements produced by the business. Rather than get bogged down in analyzing everything, the manager may find a method called *exception reporting* to be more effective.

Basically, exception reporting is taking time to analyze only those items requiring immediate attention (the exceptions). For example, a manager does not need to know who is paying on time, only who is late. That is, where his or her time is best spent.

To have a control system that works, management needs to ask, "What do I really need to know about?" Successful managers should list the important parameters of the reports they receive, such as (1) receivables more than thirty days past due, (2) unusually high or low stock levels, or (3) products (or employees) having the greatest amount of quality rejects.

For example, Battery & Tire Warehouse began using exception reporting, and the president, Mr. Charles Bodenstab, could not be happier with the results. His accounts receivable printout listed 77 accounts (out of a total of 3,167) that needed attention. The report showed which customers were making their second and third appearances on the list, their record of payments, and their account balances. Armed with this information, Mr. Bodenstab now spends his time seeking answers from his credit manager and ". . . within forty-eight hours she's expected to have credible answers."

With exception reporting, management spends time where correction, follow-up, or some other action is needed. The result is an efficient and more profitable operation.[4]

2. Be sure the person responsible for the bookkeeping for an asset or event is not the same person who has physical custody of the asset or management of the event.
3. Before hiring, check the backgrounds of management and accounting employees thoroughly.
4. Require employees to take vacations.

Although there is no perfect system, these four rather simple steps can greatly reduce the possibilities of fraud and embezzlement. For the startup firm, they are very important, because they, least of all, need no additional problems.

CREDIT POLICIES

Even the owners of startup enterprises must consider whether or not to offer credit to their customers. Even for a so-called cash business such as a restaurant, owners must consider whether or not to accept major credit cards. In many businesses, such as manufacturing or wholesaling, acceptance of credit is a fact of life. The problem for startup firms is to determine whether or not to extend credit and, if extended, how to control accounts receivable.

Why sell on credit? First, selling on credit will normally increase sales. Second, if the industry or the local competition offers credit, then new firms must also offer credit in order to compete. Of course, startup firms may compete by selling below current market prices or by offering a superior product or service, but generally startup firms will have to offer credit if competitors do. Third, credit customers are more likely to become regular customers than are the cash customers. Cash customers tend to trade with the business that offers the lowest price, but credit customers tend to become regular customers who are more interested in quality and service than in price. Thus, extending credit enables firms to establish long-lasting bonds with credit customers that firms normally will not be able to establish with its cash customers.

Of course, selling on credit also has its disadvantages. The primary disadvantage is that extending credit costs money which startup firms may not have. When goods are sold on credit, it is as if the inventory never left the store. Firms are still financing the inventory just as if it were still on the shelf waiting to be sold. Thus, firms incur the cost of additional financing. There are other costs firms incur in extending credit, such as the cost of setting up a credit system and the cost of losses from bad debts. The owners of startup firms must weigh the advantages against the disadvantages of extending credit.

Extending Credit

The first question owners of startup firms must answer, then, is whether or not to extend credit. If they decide to extend credit, the second question is how to set up a reliable credit system.

To develop effective credit systems, the owners should do the following:

1. Establish a credit policy for the firm.
2. Prepare, or buy, a credit application form.
3. Investigate the applicant before extending credit.
4. Set a limit on the amount of credit to be extended to each customer.
5. Establish a system for monitoring credit customers.
6. Develop a standard collection policy for delinquent accounts.

Credit Policy. Credit policy is the determination of the credit terms, the length of the credit period, and the credit standards that are acceptable to the startup firm. Credit terms may be for a set number of days—typically thirty—and the discount, if any, that is being offered must be determined. In an attempt to reduce the average collection time, some firms offer discounts if the invoice is paid quickly. Terms of "2/10, net 30" mean that a 2-percent discount is received if the customer pays by the tenth day from the date of the invoice, and if the discount is not taken, then the entire amount is due in thirty days.

The term *credit standards* refers to the financial strength of customers required to qualify for credit. For example, customers must have a Dun & Bradstreet rating of B or better, no history of bad debts with the local credit bureau, or no current bad debts over thirty days past due. However, these standards should be flexible, for example, so that new customers can qualify for a smaller amount of credit until a credit history is developed.

Credit Application Form. Standard credit application forms can be purchased from an office supply store, but whatever their source, applications should include the following: (1) name, address, and telephone number; (2) information concerning present employment or business, including length of employment or age of business; (3) personal financial data, including salary (for individual accounts), business income, name of bank, and financial statement data, including a list of assets and liabilities; (4) details of credit history, including who they have (or had) credit with; and (5) a statement concerning any present unsatisfied claims against the applicants as well as a declaration concerning any past filing of bankruptcy.

Credit Investigation. A primary cause of bad debt loss is inadequate verification of the information requested in the credit application. Many firms go to the trouble of having customers fill out a credit application and then simply never check any of the data listed. Although credit investigations take time and cost money, not checking the information and accepting poor credit risks can cost a lot more time and money.

One of the earliest methods of verifying a customer's past credit history is to check with the local credit bureau, the customer's bank, other firms with which the customer does business, or simply to check that the business does indeed exist or that the telephone number is a working number.

Credit Limit. After individuals or firms have been investigated and have had their credit approved, a limit should be placed on each customer. The initial limit should be low and then increased as customers build a credit history with the startup firm. Under no circumstances should startup firms extend to a single individual or firm an amount of credit that they cannot afford to lose. In their desire to obtain business during the startup period, many entrepreneurs extend too much credit to a single firm, so that when the firm is slow in paying or does not pay at all, they may be faced with severe financial trouble.

Monitoring Credit Customers. Once credit is granted, firms need a system of monitoring credit customers. The first step in setting up a monitoring system is to mail the invoices to customers on time. This may be done once a month, the day the goods are shipped, or on some other regular schedule, but a timetable must be set and rigorously followed. The invoice must show the date of purchase; what was purchased; how much it cost; how much was paid, if anything; how much is owed; and when payment is due. A statement should also indicate any past-due balances and how long the balance has been outstanding. The first step, then, is simply prompt and accurate billing procedures.

The second step is the construction of a monitoring system that indicates which accounts are past due and what their outstanding balances are. A simple, but excellent, system is called the *aging of accounts receivable*. Typically, accounts are divided into those that are 0–30 days old, 31–60 days old, 61–90 days old, and over 90 days old. An accounts-receivable aging schedule is shown in Figure 15-12. Note that this breakdown shows the name of the account, the amount past due, and the number of days past due, all in a one-page format.

While the aging data shows individual accounts, the startup entrepreneur should also follow the aging trend for the whole company. One way to do this is to express the accounts receivable in terms of sales, known as *days sales outstanding* (DSO). DSO can be expressed mathematically as follows:

$$\text{DSO} = \frac{\text{Average A/R balance last 3 months}}{\text{Sales for last 3 months}}(90)$$

The combination of aging accounts receivable for individual accounts and DSO to show how the firm is doing overall enables entrepreneurs to monitor and control their credit accounts.

Collection Policy. The procedures the firm follows to collect past-due accounts constitute the firm's collection policy. A working policy might include the following:

1. Mailing a duplicate statement that is stamped "past due" to the customer when the account is ten days overdue.
2. Mailing a letter to the customer when the account is twenty days past due.
3. Calling the customer when the account is thirty days past due and inquiring into the circumstances concerning the lack of payment.

FIGURE 15.12
Accounts Receivable, March 31

Customer	*Total*	*0–30 Days*	*31–60 Days*	*61–90 Days*	*Over 90 Days*
A. Adass	$ 782.10	$ 511.50	$ 270.60		
D. Byerly	468.40	162.80	130.20	$ 175.40	
J. Denton	459.90				$459.90
M. Hanes	204.05	204.05			
C. Kearns	720.45			720.45	
D. Mooney	852.00	137.50	283.35	240.85	190.30
H. Prizer	139.10	139.10			
C. Sievers	97.40	97.40			
K. Weston	603.80		603.80		
Totals	$4,327.20	$1,252.35	$1,287.95	$1,136.70	$650.20

4. Mailing a more strongly worded letter when the account is forty-five days past due.
5. When the account is sixty days past due, mailing another letter requesting payment within ten days and stating that if payment is not received, the account will be turned over to an attorney or to a collection agency.
6. Turning the account over to an attorney or collection agency after it is seventy days past due.

This policy is not designed to work for all types of businesses but is presented merely to demonstrate the types of procedures that a collection policy should contain.

Summary

Startup entrepreneurs need accounting and control systems to help them keep up with how their firms are doing and to determine the most efficient use of the firm's resources. In addition, financial records are required by law. Good records should be: (1) easy to understand, (2) easy to keep up to date, (3) easy to produce on a regular basis, and (4) easy to keep accurate.

Owners of startup businesses should set up and maintain both managerial and accounting records. Managerial records include the following: (1) sales records, (2) financial records, (3) inventory records, and (4) personnel records. Sales records should show at a glance how the firm is doing from a sales standpoint, while checkbooks provide a quick view of the amount of cash available to operate the firm. The startup entrepreneur also needs to maintain inventory records on both equipment purchases and materials or goods purchased. There should also be a complete personnel file for each employee.

Accounting records are the way businesses keep score on how they are doing. The owners of startup enterprises should maintain the basic accounting records, including the cash receipts journal, the cash disbursements journal, the general journal, and the general ledger. Information from the accounting journals is combined in financial statements that indicate how well (financially) the firms are performing. The two most important of these financial statements are the income statement and the balance statement.

Budgeting is an excellent device for controlling expenses. Both sales and expense budgets are needed to properly control expenditures.

Management control is the process by which entrepreneurs ensure that the resources of the firm are properly utilized. Although entrepreneurs cannot control all of the firm's resources, they should always maintain control of the product, the people, and the finances of the firm. In addition, entrepreneurs can help control the future by understanding and analyzing the numbers contained in the firm's financial statements. Entrepreneurs must also take the steps necessary to protect the firm against the threat of fraud and embezzlement.

Most business owners must extend credit to attract additional sales. If credit is extended, then they must set up a sound credit system to accomplish the following: (1) establish a credit policy, (2) prepare a credit application, (3) provide for the investigation of credit applicants, (4) set credit limits, (5) provide an accurate monitoring system, and (6) establish a standard collection policy.

Assembling the Pieces

The accounting and control systems that Carol and Jacki set up and use include the general ledger, a sales record, a payroll record, and a cash-flow record. Jacki maintains these accounting records with the help of a local College of Charleston accounting student.

Carol and Jacki have not had positive experiences with accountants. This is typical for many small firms that find that their accountants do not give them first-class service but instead concentrate on their larger customers. The accountant for In Good Taste repeatedly failed to return original documents needed for the operation of the business and had unacceptable turn-around times on quarterly financial statements. The poor service prompted Carol and Jacki to keep their own records. The system they set up works much better for them than the original accountant's system, which was set up primarily to suit him. They do, however, have an accountant review their records.

All records are maintained on computer programs purchased by In Good Taste. Carol and Jacki started with a **VZ Calc** spreadsheet for sales records and then purchased the **Peachtree General Ledger Software** for their accounting records. The sales record spreadsheet has been modified over time. At first, Carol and Jacki wanted only a tally of weekly and monthly sales. Now they have sales divided into forty categories from the cash register. In addition, they maintain the sales and cost of goods sold in twelve broad categories. ■

Questions for Review and Discussion

1. Why should entrepreneurs keep records?
2. What are the qualities of good records?
3. What managerial records should a new business maintain?
4. What are the potential problems involved with the comingling of funds?
5. What is the difference between the checking account and the cash disbursements journal?
6. How can entrepreneurs use the income statement to analyze how their firm is doing?
7. If a firm has liquidity ratios that are below the industry average, does this indicate that the firm may have trouble paying its current liabilities? Explain your answer.
8. Are low debt ratios a positive sign for a firm? Explain.
9. What policy decisions can owners make to affect profitability ratios? Debt-management ratios?
10. What are the costs of extending credit?
11. A firm has a DSO that increases a few days each month. What does this mean?
12. You have just received your company's monthly bank statement. The bank balance, as of the twentieth of the month, is $5,482. You have outstanding a total of six checks that total $3,894 and a deposit of $6,400 that was made on the twenty-second. If there were no bank charges, what should your checkbook balance be?

Notes

1. Paul Hawken, "Mastering the Numbers," *Inc.*, October 1987, pp. 19–20.
2. Joshua Hyatt, "Easy Money," *Inc.*, February 1988, pp. 91–96.

3. Stephen Nelson, "To Catch a Thief," *Inc.,* January 1988, pp. 89–90.
4. Bruce Posner, "Hitting Your Numbers," *Inc.*, April 1987, pp. 106–108.

entrepreneur's checklist

SMALL-BUSINESS FINANCIAL STATUS: WHAT AN OWNER-MANAGER SHOULD KNOW

Daily

1. Cash is on hand.
2. Bank balance.
3. The daily summary of sales and cash receipts is complete.
4. All errors in recording collections on accounts are corrected.
5. A record of all monies paid out, by cash or check, is maintained.

Weekly

1. Accounts receivable (take action on slow payers).
2. Accounts payable (take advantage of discounts).
3. Payroll (Records should include name and address of employee, social security number, number of exemptions, date ending the pay period, hours worked, rate of pay, total wages, deductions, net pay, check number.)
4. Taxes and reports to state and federal government (sales, withholdings, social security, etc.).

Monthly

1. All journal entries have been classified according to like elements (generally accepted and standardized for both income and expense) and posted to general ledger.
2. A profit and loss statement for the month is available within a reasonable time, usually ten to fifteen days following the close of the month, and shows the expense incurred in obtaining the income and the profit or loss resulting. From this, take action to eliminate loss: Adjust markup? reduce overhead expense? pilferage? incorrect tax reporting? incorrect buying procedures? failure to take advantage of cash discounts?
3. A balance sheet accompanies the profit and loss statement.
4. The bank statement is reconciled.
5. The petty-cash account is in balance.
6. All federal tax deposits, withheld income and FICA taxes (Form 501), and state taxes have been paid.
7. Accounts receivable are aged, that is, 30, 60, 90 days past due. Work all bad and slow accounts.
8. Inventory control has been worked to remove dead stock and order new stock. (What moves slowly? Reduce. What moves fast? Increase.)

Source: From "Keeping Records in Small Business," Management Aides No. 1.017 (Washington, D.C.: Small Business Administration, 1974), pp. 5–6.

RUBBER DISPOSAL SYSTEMS, INC.

Rubber Disposal Systems, Inc. (RDS, Inc.) was incorporated February 16, 1984, in Steeleville, Illinois, with the following officers: James Sheible, President; Billy J. Clements, Vice President; Charles W. Watts, Secretary-Treasurer. The purpose of the business was to design and build equipment that could cut or shred discarded automobile and truck tires into smaller pieces so that they could be recycled and marketed to alternative markets, profitably. If feasible, the prototype shredding equipment could also be manufactured and marketed to landfills and tire disposers to facilitate environmentally approved disposal of discarded tires.

The idea for the business began in the spring of 1983 when Jim Sheible began talking to his friend, Charlie Watts, about ways discarded automobile and truck tires could be recycled. Jim had already gained some experience with the product. For several years, like other "jockies" in the region, he used his pickup truck to gather discarded tires from tire dealers and haul them to a recapper in Batesville, Mississippi. The fee the recapper paid him for each acceptable tire supplemented Jim's income from the local surface mine where he was employed as a coal miner. Because the tire dealers insisted that he take all the tires they had, and not just the ones acceptable for recapping, Jim ended up with a stockpile of tires. As his stockpile grew, he thought of the huge quantities of discarded tires that must be accumulating over the countryside and thought there had to be some way to profit from that situation.

Jim talked to a friend of his and fellow coal miner, Charlie Watts, about profiting from discarded tires. He knew that Charlie had been successful owning his own office machines maintenance business for 12 years in California. Charlie had sold out to return to Steeleville to be with a family member who had become ill, so Jim thought he might be interested in starting a business in southern Illinois. Discussions between Jim and Charlie continued informally for about a year before they decided to do some serious planning. Charlie's advice was to develop a plan beginning with identifying what this business could produce from discarded tires that would be of value to someone. He said they would also need a lawyer and an accountant, but not right away.

THE PRODUCT DECISION

Their first thought was of fuel. They knew rubber tires burned with a very hot flame and they thought some of the same customers who bought coal in large quantities might also be customers for tire-derived fuel (TDF). They heard of a generating plant near Sikeston, Missouri, that was doing just that, so they went there in the summer of 1983 to see for themselves. The Sikeston plant had a grate-fed furnace system that was capable of burning rubber as a fuel additive. They were receiving discarded rubber parts from the Gates Corporation, a nearby manufacturer of rubber hoses, belts, and similar items. The rejected hose and belt material was discarded in short sections that could be passed into the furnace along with coal in a ratio of about 10 percent rubber to 90 percent coal. Although only furnaces based on the chain grate-fed system could use rubber as a fuel additive, there were many other plants using that system in the region.

Everyone they talked to at the Sikeston plant was extremely pleased with the performance of the rubber product in the furnace. Not only did the rubber burn with a hotter flame than coal (approximately 14–15,000 BTU/lb. compared to 11–12,000 for coal), thus increasing the efficiency of the furnace, but the increased temperature also destroyed some of the undesirable pollutants associated with burning coal. Burning the rubber with coal in the prescribed concentration did not produce the odor commonly associated with burning rubber in the open, and the EPA (Environmental Protection Agency) had no objections to its use as an addition to coal. The plant superintendent told Jim and

Charlie the supply of rubber parts from the Gates Corporation was insufficient and he would be glad to take all the rubber products they could produce and suggested an initial order of 50 tons per week in order to evaluate the product. The results of this visit further solidified their resolve to proceed with plans for the emerging business.

With a product decided on for the business, it now became apparent that the problem was to develop a manufacturing system to produce the desired small rubber pieces from whole tires. Researching ways to manufacture the product became Charlie's responsibility. He investigated various government reports and business periodicals related to tire recycling and wrote to approximately 15 businesses already manufacturing shredding machines or parts. Charlie also investigated other uses for recycled tires.

He found that there are currently 1 to 2 billion scrap tires stockpiled nationally and each year over 200 million car tires and 40 million truck tires are discarded in the United States with the same geographical distribution as the population. Roughly 75% of scrap tires are landfilled while the remaining 25% are diverted to various resource recovery uses, including retreading, reclaiming, and recycling. Retreading takes 4% of the scrap tires. This amount is not expected to increase because retreads are considered inferior products by the consuming public. The percentage diverted to reclaim, which involves using recovered rubber to remanufacture rubber products, is not expected to increase because these products are also considered inferior. So, the recycling options left for consideration included asphalt-rubber, pyrolysis, landfill, and several other miscellaneous uses like landscaping cover, playground cover, and export.

POTENTIAL APPLICATIONS

In asphalt applications mesh-sized rubber crumb is mixed with asphalt to provide a more durable surface for concrete-based highways. Cryogenic production of the rubber mesh is needed to achieve the large volumes of metal free rubber. The cover is being used in Texas and Arizona, but wide-scale acceptance has not been achieved due to uncertainty about actual performance under varying conditions.

In pyrolysis, or destructive distillation, the rubber is heated under controlled conditions in order to recover chemicals present in the material such as carbon black, oil, gases, and scrap steel. Energy is given off as a by-product and can be utilized or sold. Several well-capitalized firms have developed technologically successful pyrolysis methods, but there are questions regarding the marketability of the recovered products because they are considered inferior to their originally manufactured counterparts. This process requires large volumes of mechanically produced rubber scrap.

Landfill operators should cut up or shred tires to dispose of them in an environmentally safe manner as recommended by the state and federal governments. Tires left whole and unburied provide ideal refuge for rats, mosquitoes, and other vermin. The air trapped in tires buried whole causes them to rise to the surface in a short time. Thus landfill operators should be the largest market for mechanical shredders or shredding services. But regulation of landfills has been left to local governments, and most do not require landfills to accept tires or dispose of them in an environmentally safe manner. Charlie discovered that the problem of tire disposal was of greater concern to tire dealers than it was to landfill operators. Locally, tire dealers are forced to cover the costs of transporting scrap to landfills that will accept them and then pay a disposal rate that exceeds the rate charged for other solid wastes. Several of the landfills in the more highly populated areas within a hundred mile radius of Steeleville have stopped accepting tires. Therefore tire dealers may be the better target for mechanical shredders or shredding services. Businesses offering shredding services using mobile shredding equipment have charged approximately $.25/tire or $25/ton.

DECIDING ON A PRODUCTION METHOD

From his survey of mechanical shredder manufacturers, he found that there are several types of mechanical shredders available that could be used to reduce tires. Some punched out chunks; others sliced, tore, or pulverized tires. Most used the hammermill principle to tear the tire into smaller pieces. Existing shredders are typically used to reduce a wide range of scrap items, including tires, for landfill disposal. Most shredder manufacturers recommended a two stage shredding process to produce chunks as small as the approximately 2 in. × 2 in. rubber chunks needed by the Sikeston plant. However, a two-step system would increase operating costs considerably, besides the fact that the shredding machines themselves were very expensive—starting at $250,000 and up. Charlie thought that they could come up with a design for a shredder that would achieve the needed size reduction and cost much less than shredders now on the market.

During the course of his research, Charlie discovered that removing the small steel cable in the bead ring in all tires would reduce wear and tear on the shredding equipment. However, there were very few debeading machines on the market. He did locate one business in Tennessee that debeaded tires by first splitting the tire longitudinally, punching out the bead ring, and selling the two debeaded sections. Despite his attempts he was unable to find out who their customers were or what use was being made of the product. Charlie was intrigued by this Tennessee business because they were the only processor using a machine to split the tire longitudinally and because their machine accomplished the splitting action in a single revolution. This was faster than Charlie had thought possible. Charlie thought there may be some opportunity to profit if they could design and build a debeader and a splitter (to be used in conjunction with the shredder) that would be superior to existing designs and much less expensive to build and maintain.

It was becoming increasingly apparent to them that they needed help from someone with mechanical engineering skill and experience. Since coal mining is a business using a lot of heavy equipment, several candidates who were experienced with the mechanical engineering of coal-mining equipment were considered, but the person they both thought would be the best for the job was Billy Clements. He agreed to go in with them.

THE PRODUCTION EQUIPMENT

The three of them began to work on the problem of shredder design. They decided on a two-stage process consisting of two sets of counter-rotating cylinders. The cylinders would meet in a tongue-in-groove fashion. Tire pieces would be caught in the counter rotation of the two cylinders and sheared into pieces as they were forced between the spaces of the tongue-in-groove pattern. Pieces from the first stage would be conveyed to a second stage of similar counter-rotating cylinders to be cut again into smaller pieces corresponding to the smaller spaces between the cylinders.

The primary stage on the shredder would consist of two counter-rotating cylinders—one with a 30-inch diameter and one with a diameter of 20 inches. The second stage would consist of two counter-rotating cylinders each with 10-inch diameters. The main consideration in arriving at the various diameters was to conserve the amount of steel needed to make the two stages of counter-rotating cylinders. The material used to make the cylinders consisted of a slab of steel eight by twenty feet and two inches thick costing $7,000. By using the different diameters, one could use almost the entire steel slab to make both stages and avoid the cost of purchasing an additional slab to build the second stage.

Plans for the four steel cylinders with the tongue-in-groove adaptation were taken to a machine shop in St. Louis. The shop owner agreed to build the cylinders as specified for $7,500 with delivery in six weeks. With this schedule in mind, plans were made to be in production and selling product in two months; however, some unforeseen problems arose. Instead of six weeks, the work required nine months and instead of $7,500 the cylinders cost $29,500. Since the order had been placed verbally, there was little to do but wait and pay. The result was a crunch on the finances of the business.

With the shredder parts almost ready to be assembled it was necessary to find a building to house the machinery and to start setting up the production process. The local bank was happy to rent them a roofed enclosure (with only two sides) for $500 a month. The fact that neither end of this building was enclosed, nor could it be enclosed easily because of the extra high ceiling required by the former occupant, made it impractical to carry on the assembly work of RDS, Inc., in this space during the winter. The former occupant was a failed business the bank had financed. It was obvious that a more suitable location would have to be found.

Charlie thought now was the time to hire the lawyer and accountant he had mentioned earlier. Their lawyer recommended investigating sources of federal, state, and local funding. In October 1983, Charlie contacted the state senator and congressman from his district. As a result, he met and talked to various governmental and public agencies including the Illinois Department of Commerce and Community Affairs (DCCA) where he learned of other possible sources of state funding. He submitted a request for $1,130,000 to DCCA that was based on cost and production projections prepared by the accountant. None of the agencies approached was able to provide funding immediately although all expressed an interest in the future possibilities of the firm.

Jim and Bill had been working on the construction of a debeader and splitter. They were able to build a splitter that splits car and truck tires in half, longitudinally, thus providing an edge that could be gripped more easily by the counter-rotating cylinders of the shredder's primary stage. It took 1 rpm per tire and was electric/hydraulic powered. They designed a debeader that could debead car and truck tires after they had been split. It was also electric/hydraulic powered and, unlike existing debeaders, allowed for easy changes in the blade size used in the cutting head to accommodate different size tires. It appeared that RDS, Inc. had indeed come up with original and superior designs for the splitter and debeader that may be patentable.

Once the splitter was completed, and just prior to the completion of the debeader, the tongue-in-groove shredder parts arrived form the machine shop. The shredder was quickly assembled. Everyone was anxious to test the performance, but before a trial run could be conducted it was necessary to split and debead the small stockpile of tires that had been collected. Instead of waiting to finish their own debeader, they decided to borrow one from a business in Texas, Tire Disposal, Inc., where Jim's brother, Ronnie, worked. TD, Inc. had recently completed a working model of a debeader and they were anxious to have it tested.

Using the borrowed debeader it was possible to debead and split enough tires to make a test run of approximately five tons through the shredder and still not lose any work time at the mine. The conclusion was that the primary stage worked fine, but the secondary stage was not performing as expected. Using one piece of sheet metal to construct the cylinders for the primary and secondary stages has resulted in a faulty design. In retrospect, trying to conserve on the amount of steel used was not such a good idea. Charlie estimated that correcting the problem with the second stage would now cost about $20,000. Their lawyer advised them that it was questionable whether their shredder could be patented even if the redesigned second stage was successful.

The existing shredding system was designed to work in the following way: A tire would be placed by hand on the splitter where foot-operated controls would rotate the tire tread against a cutting blade, which would split the tire in half; each half would be removed by hand and placed on the debeader, which would punch out the bead ring; the debeaded half tire would be placed by hand on a conveyor belt, which would convey the split tire to the primary stage about ten feet above the floor. The tire half would be dropped off the revolving conveyor belt into the primary stage of counter-rotating cylinders. After going through the primary stage, the 3 in. to 4 in. wide, shredded strips of tire would be conveyed down to the second stage to be sheared or sliced into pieces about two inches square. The pieces from the second stage would be conveyed to a portable bin where they would be washed and stored ready for sale. The problem that developed was that the pieces would not go through the second stage unless fed into it by hand. The pieces were supposed to go through this stage on their own; instead, the rubber chunks bounced along the top of the counter-rotating cylinders rather than being pulled by them through the tongue-in-groove openings. The 10-inch diameter of the cylinders was too small, resulting in a depression between the two counter-rotating cylinders too shallow to grip the rubber pieces and pull them through.

MARKET DYNAMICS

By hand feeding the tire pieces into the second stage, a sample of 2 in. to 3 in. chunks was obtained and was taken to the Sikeston plant in the summer of 1985. The product was well received by the plant supervisory personnel responsible for product purchase decisions. However, it was then that Charlie found out that the Gates Corporation did not charge the Sikeston plant for their rubber parts, because the Sikeston Plant was providing a cost-free method of disposal by hauling away Gates' rejected rubber parts. Therefore the management of the Sikeston plant was not willing to pay more than a nominal fee for RDS, Inc.'s rubber chunks. It became clear that Sikeston was not a potential customer.

Other generating plants with less favorable sources of rubber might be possible customers for RDS, Inc.'s product but the price of coal put a low ceiling on the price of TDF (tire-derived fuel). Current coal prices for utilities were approximately $30/ton including transportation for utilities and $40/ton for industrial users. The cost/ton of shredded tires was estimated to exceed these amounts. Also, utilities buy huge quantities of fuel and their purchasing methods are oriented to large volume producers. RDS, Inc.'s management concluded that it was questionable that any utility would be interested in the relatively untried rubber product from a small producer. Industrial users (factories, schools, prisons) may still be a possibility, but RDS, Inc.'s maximum tonnage could be used up by just a few users and the selling price would not cover the cost of shredding. For these reasons they decided that some other market had to be found to establish RDS, Inc.

When Ronnie heard that the Sikeston deal had fallen through, he suggested contacting Tire Disposal, Inc. about the possibility of selling debeaded tire sidewalls and tread sections to them. Charlie followed up the suggestion and was told by Tire Disposal, Inc. that they were selling this product to an exporter who in turn sold the product to a business in China. According to Tire Disposal, Inc. management, the exporter told them that the demand was limitless. The debeaded tire sidewall product did not require the use of the shredding machine; however, it did require the use of splitting and debeading equipment. The existing debeader, which Jim and Billy had now completed, was not equipped to separate the sidewall from the tread as required by the China customer, so they started to work on the required modifications, which they were able to accomplish quickly after work at the coal mine and using scrap pieces of metal.

The offer from TD, Inc. sounded pretty good to Charlie and the others, especially since the only equipment needed would be the splitter and debeader. Cash flow from this activity could help pay for the changes they now knew had to be made in the second stage of the shredder.

Charlie contacted TD, Inc. to finalize price and agree on quantities, schedules, delivery methods, and other contractual details. A tentative agreement was made in September 1985, and Charlie requested a routine letter of credit on the behalf of Tire Disposal, Inc. with a local bank to guarantee payment to Rubber Disposal Systems, Inc. for shipments. Tire Disposal, Inc. management agreed to have the letter sent within a week. After two weeks, the letter had not arrived. Upon inquiry, Charlie was told that Tire Disposal, Inc. had been sold to a Japanese firm and there was no longer any interest in pursuing the idea of purchasing rubber pieces for export to China. Following the disappointing news that the Sikeston plant would not buy the shredded product, except at scrap disposal prices, and the collapse of the proposed deal with Tire Disposal, Inc., it became necessary to think again about alternate uses of shredded tires.

There was one more promising alternative use for RDS, Inc.'s product. The principal of the local grade school was a friend of Charlie's and familiar with RDS, Inc.'s product. He suggested they sell it to his school as a playground cover. The principal knew of a similar playground cover made of rubber crumb from discarded tires that was marketed by a firm in Chicago. The principal was interested in putting a cover down under the playground equipment that would reduce injuries and permit all-weather playground use. But he thought the $2.13/sq. ft. (not including transportation and installation) price for the rubber crumb cover was prohibitive for his school. He thought Charlie's product might be a good substitute if the cost/ton were reasonable. So he suggested Charlie sell his rubber chunks to the local grade school. Charlie, Jim, and Billy thought $80/ton sounded like a good price. Because they had a pickup truck and some free time they agreed to include delivery and installation at no extra charge.

The five tons of rubber chunks that had been produced on the test run were sold to the local grade school in the fall of 1985. After about six months of use, the results were very good. The shredded 2 in. × 3 in. chunks provided a springy, cushioned ground cover that the children liked. The material stabilized quite well, which avoided the development of muddy spots during wet weather. The only problem was that the pieces were quite large and invited being thrown. It was concluded that smaller size rubber chunks would probably be more desirable in the playground cover market. Through word-of-mouth, several school administrators and day-care centers heard about and expressed an interest in RDS, Inc.'s playground cover. By mid-1986, approximately $8,000 in orders had accumulated.

Although smaller pieces could be produced by correcting the problem with the second stage of the shredder, the capital needed to complete this modification just was not available. A less costly alternative was considered. A commercial bark chipper was available and could be rented for $200 a month or purchased for $10,000. A test run on the 3 in. to 4 in. wide strips from the primary stage showed that the bark chipper could indeed produce smaller pieces (average ¾ in.) for the playground market, but the processing time was much slower than it would have been through the shredder if the second stage were operating properly.

PLAYGROUND MARKET

The playground market looked more and more like the market that would establish RDS, Inc.'s business. There had been a general heightened awareness of the need to provide "safe" playground environments. Several TV programs and periodicals had discussed the topic. This heightened awareness was largely due to the increasing number of lawsuits involving playground accidents. In most cases (approximately 60%) children were hurt when falling off playground equipment onto hard surfaces. Installing safer surfaces was expected to reduce the number of injuries, reduce playground operators' risk of being sued, and lead to lower insurance premiums for liability coverage. However the insurance industry was going through a transformation that made it increasingly difficult to get and maintain liability coverage. As a provider of the playground cover, RDS, Inc. would be exposing themselves to the same potential lawsuits faced by playground operators.

The primary target market for RDS, Inc.'s playground cover was thought to be grade schools and day-care centers; other potential targets included parks, campgrounds, and apartment complexes. The management of RDS, Inc. thought they could make use of the idle 5-ton dump truck one of them owned and include free delivery and installation in the price of their product. Because they were all from southern Illinois and knew the area and people, they felt that first targeting those portions of Illinois within a 100-mile radius of Steeleville would maximize initial sales. They estimated it would cost $1.00 per mile to deliver.

COMPETITIVE SITUATION

Competing products currently available included hard surfaces such as asphalt and concrete, and soft surfaces such as sand, pea gravel, wood chips, 1 in. rubber matting and cryogenically produced rubber crumb. Safety, all-weather conditioning, cleanliness, maintenance, life span, and cost per square foot of coverage are probably the most important product characteristics for the purchasers of soft playground surfaces. RDS, Inc. would have the first mechanically produced, rubber chunks sold to the playground market. For playground use only metal-free rubber can be used. Therefore, only the sidewalls of steel-belted tires can be used for rubber chunks.

The registered trademark for the crumb is "Cushion-turf" and it is sold exclusively by Reese Industries, Inc., a Chicago-based manufacturer's representative. They have done a good job penetrating the Chicago market, but have only one installation in downstate Illinois. "Cushion-turf" was manufactured by a cryogenic process whereby the tire is frozen into a brittle state and then crushed producing granulated rubber pieces about the size of pea gravel. All the metal in the tire is separated from the rubber automatically as a result of freezing and crushing. The cryogenic process has an important advantage over mechanical shredding operations, because debeading is unnecessary and the entire tire can be used whether steel belted or not. There are several commercial plants in the United States capable of producing rubber crumb by the cryogenic process, although only the one already mentioned sold rubber crumb to the playground market. The capital investment and operating costs for these plants far exceeded the costs for mechanical processing plants.

Sand was available in bulk from several southern Illinois sand and gravel companies. Woodchips could be bought in bulk or bags from many local landscaping nurseries. Pea gravel was available from rock quarries in St. Louis. They would deliver and install only in the St. Louis area. Illinois purchasers must arrange their own transportation and installation. Rubber matting could be purchased from several of the playground equipment manufacturers' representatives in St. Louis and Chicago, and shipped from the manufacturer.

The firms providing rubber matting and rubber crumb have developed marketing strategies consisting of brochures sent to potential customers and manufacturers representatives who call on prospective customers. Because the other playground covers have many uses besides playground cover, the firms selling these products had not actively promoted to the playground market.

A playground cover safety test was commissioned by the manufacturers and marketers of "Cushion-turf." They engaged a university lab to conduct a test using methods established by the National Bureau of Standards in compliance with the recommended testing procedures of the United States Consumer Product Safety Commission. The tests measured safety based on the amount of cratering effect created by falls from varying heights. Covers that minimized the amount of cratering decreased the chances of injury from falling off playground equipment. The marketers of "cushion-turf" recommended 4 in. depths for general play areas and 6 in. depths under playground equipment. Tests were conducted on 4 in. and 6 in. depths of sand, pea gravel, wood chips, 1⅛ in. rubber matting and rubber crumb. Results indicated the rubber crumb at 5 in. depth showed minimal cratering. It tended to restore its original contour due to stored elastic energy, even after multiple drops. The other covers fell within the safety range for concussion only on their first drop. These other covers do not have a tendency to restore their original contour and were unsafe after multiple drops. Therefore, rubber crumb was deemed safest for playground cover. Pea gravel, at a recommended 8 in. depth, had been found to be a safe playground cover in other independent tests.

The management of RDS, Inc. proposed that their product would be almost as safe as the rubber crumb, although they were not sure what should be the recommended depth. After approximately a year of use, the 3 in. depth selected for the Steeleville school performed very well. A 3 in. depth was used for their first installation because this was the size of the landscaping timbers used to outline the playground area. RDS, Inc.'s rubber chunks would have some advantages over rubber crumb. The chunks would not stick to clothing, it would be more stable than crumb and equal to crumb in low maintenance, all weather use, and long life. The chunks may be expensive when compared to other playground covers such as pea gravel, but the cost of rubber chunks would be much lower than rubber crumb.

Exhibit 1 presents the coverage cost of competing products based on a survey of firms selling these products. RDS, Inc.'s initial sales were quoted at $80/ton including delivery and installation. This price was set after considering the low price in the fuel market ($25/ton) and the very high price of rubber crumb ($320/ton), excluding delivery and installation. The coverage cost per ton of RDS, Inc.'s rubber chunk was estimated from the installation at the Steeleville grade school.

A few manufacturers' representatives of playground equipment were contacted in the St. Louis and Chicago areas. Conversations with these individuals indicated that some could be persuaded to carry the product and thought it would do well. Others had reservations about the safety of the product, particularly flammability and toxicity, and its ability to reduce injuries from falls. Some thought the $80/ton price might be too high.

PRODUCTION RATE AND EXPENSE PROJECTIONS

In the past, RDS, Inc. had to cover the cost of transportation to obtain tires. The 15,000 tires on hand were valued at $.14 each. A survey of local supply suggested that they could get a minimum of 10,000 tons per year of tires, delivered at no expense. However, management estimated the supply of tires would actually cost approximately $.07 each to obtain. For the first six months, the business would run 4 hours/day and 6 days/week, and on 8 hours/day and 5 days/week schedule after that. The owners of RDS, Inc. planned to donate their time to the business for the first six months. Mr. Watts planned to continue working on the business aspects and Mr. Sheible and Mr. Clements would devote themselves to getting the production process up and running. Initially the manufacturing process would require five general laborers. Arrangements have been made with two government job-training agencies to split the labor costs for the first year of operation. Labor costs were estimated to be $1.675/hour for the first six months, $2.25/hour for the second six months and minimum wage thereafter. One secretary would also be needed. Benefits to be paid by RDS, Inc. included: social security 7%; federal unemployment taxes 7.15%; and state unemployment taxes 7.15%. Workmen's compensation would cost $1,500 for the first six months and $3,000/year thereafter.

Maximum expected production capacity was uncertain because the production process had been operational on a testing basis. The management of RDS, Inc. had stated that average maximum output is in the range of 1 to 6 tons/hour, and 3 tons/hour was the most likely

Exhibit 1

Coverage Cost of Competing Playground Covers[1]

Cover	*Recommended Depth*[2]	*Price per Ton*	*Coverage per Ton*	*Coverage Cost Sq. Ft.*
¼ in. Pea Gravel	8 in.	$4-$5	20 Sq. Ft.	$.20–$.25
Course Sand	10 in.	$1–$3	25 Sq. Ft.	$.04–$.10
Wood Chips	12 in.	$100	150 Sq. Ft.	$.67
Rubber Mat	1⅛ in.	—	—	$.72
½ in. Rubber Crumb	5 in.[3]	$320	150 Sq. Ft.	$2.13
Rubber Chunks	3 in.	$80	200 Sq. Ft.	$.40

[1] FOB shipping point except for rubber chunks.
[2] Recommended depths suggested by independent testing or experience.
[3] An average based on the recommended 4 in. depth under general play areas and 6 in. under playground equipment.

rate. However, government research reports stated processing rates and equipment costs were not as important as other costs, like transportation and labor, to the bottom line. The mix of tires processed was estimated to be 70% truck (average weight 100 lbs. each) and 30% auto (average weight 20 lbs. each). Debeading was expected to create a yield loss for auto tires of 2.5 lbs. and 5 lbs. for truck tires. The average weight of tire input was estimated at 76 lbs. and average yield loss was estimated at 7% for non–steel-belted tires.

Production expenses were estimated based on the 3 tons/hour production rate. Power to run the debeading, shredding, and woodchipper-assumed use of 150 kw/hr. and $.08 per kw/hr., for a $12/hr. rate. Heat for the building was estimated to cost $100 per month for a woodburner using bead rings for fuel to be used only during the five coldest months of the year. Equipment maintenance costs were estimated to run 5% of equipment costs annually. Other miscellaneous production supplies were estimated at $1,000 annually. The depreciation schedule selected was a five-year double-declining balance method. Other expenses like office supplies, marketing, legal and accounting fees, insurance, telephone, taxes, and transportation expenses had to be estimated. RDS, Inc. expected to receive a $7,500 investment tax credit for their first operating year.

For playground use, it was essential that the resulting product be free of metal. RDS, Inc. would be restricted to shredding only the sidewalls of steel-belted tires when manufacturing the rubber pieces to be used as playground cover. The newly modified debeader could be used to remove the tire tread as well as the bead ring, thus separating the metal portions in most steel-belted tires before shredding. Sidewalls of most steel-belted tires could be used for producing playground chunks, but production rates would have to be revised. Separate production runs would have to be done for the tread and a market would have to be found for the chunks containing steel. The presence of steel did not impair the use of the chunks for fuel.

FINANCIAL SITUATION

Several assets were lent by the owners to RDS, Inc. to reduce operating expenses and capital investment costs. These assets on loan included a tractor with loader bucket, electric welder, gas welder, 5-ton truck, trailer, front-end loader, miscellaneous tools, chains, cables, and office equipment. Assets total $65,000 in equipment, including roughly $7,500 in the splitter, $10,500 in the debeader, $40,000 in the shredder, and $7,000 in conveyors. Assets also included $2,100 in tires. Liabilities included two notes with the local bank for $7,000 @ 10% and $45,000 @ 13.75%, which were due in January 1985. The three owners had invested $15,100 in the business and had exhausted their personal resources. Future funding from the bank and from state and federal agencies was dependent upon the provision of a comprehensive business plan that explained exactly how the business could justify a new loan of working capital to get the business started. A few private investors had expressed interest in the business but none had stepped forward.

The management of RDS, Inc. had come to the conclusion that their rubber chunk product could appeal to the playground market. They thought that entering the playground cover business was the best way to establish the business and support diversification into other lines of business, such as manufacturing shredding equipment and the sale of TDF fuel to specific users. It was becoming apparent that Charlie needed some help converting the business ideas into reality. He had devoted all of his spare time and money to the business over the last two and a half years, yet positive cash flows still seemed a distant prospect. It became necessary to move out of their rented enclosure to save cash and to store all of their equipment in Billie Clements' garage while they searched for capital to seed the business. Both the local bank and government lending agencies refused to lend any more money unless a convincing, formal business plan was prepared. The plan would have to explain in an objective manner exactly how the business could become established and become successful in the fu-

RUBBER DISPOSAL SYSTEMS, INC.
PROJECTED INCOME STATEMENT
3 TONS/HR. AND $80/TON

Income Statement	*1st 6 Mth*	*2nd 6 Mth*	*FY1 Totals*	*FY2*	*FY3*
OPERATING STATISTICS					
Tons Produced	1,800	3,000	4,800	6,000	6,000
Average Sales Price	$80	$80	$80	$80	$80
Average Sale in Tons	5	5	5	5	5
Tons of Input (93% yield)	1,935	3,226	5,161	6,452	6,452
Average Tire Weight (lbs)	76	76	76	76	76
Days Operated	150	125	275	250	250
Hours per Day	4	8		8	8
Number of Employees	6	6	6	6	6
Average Wage per Hour	$1.68	$2.25	$1.96	$3.35	$3.35
Value of Equipment	$65,000	$75,000	$75,000	$75,000	$75,000
INCOME STATEMENT					
Sales	$144,000	$144,000	$384,000	$480,000	$480,000
COST OF GOODS SOLD					
Raw Materials	$3,565	$5,942	$9,508	$11,885	$11,885
Labor—Direct	$6,030	$13,500	$19,530	$40,200	$40,200
Benefits—FICA and Unemployment	$1,744	$2,906	$4,650	$5,813	$5,813
Benefits—Workmens Comp Insurance	$1,500	$1,500	$3,000	$3,000	$3,000
Heat	$250	$250	$500	$500	$500
Rent for Building	$1,800	$1,800	$3,600	$3,600	$3,600
Rent for Equipment (Woodchip)	$1,200	$1,200	$2,400	$2,400	$2,400
Maintenance (5% of Equipment)	$1,625	$1,875	$3,500	$3,750	$3,750
Power (150kw Used @ $.08)	$7,200	$12,000	$19,200	$24,000	$24,000
Production Supplies	$500	$500	$1,000	$1,000	$1,000
Transportation (200mi rt)	$36,000	$60,000	$96,000	$120,000	$120,000
Depreciation	$6,500	$7,500	$14,000	$24,000	$18,000
Total Cost of Goods Sold	$67,914	$108,974	$176,888	$240,147	$234,147
Gross Margin	$76,086	$131,026	$207,112	$239,853	$245,853
SELLING AND ADMINISTRATIVE					
Officer Salaries and Benefits	$0	$17,123	$17,124	$34,245	$34,245
Office Supplies	$600	$600	$1,200	$1,200	$1,200
Marketing (10% of Sales)	$14,400	$24,000	$38,400	$48,000	$48,000
Legal and Accounting Fees	$500	$500	$1,000	$1,000	$1,000
Insurance	$500	$500	$1,000	$1,000	$1,000
Telephone Expenses	$1,200	$1,200	$2,400	$2,400	$2,400
Total Selling and Admin.	$17,200	$43,923	$61,123	$87,845	$87,845
Operating Income	$58,886	$87,104	$145,990	$152,008	$158,008

RUBBER DISPOSAL SYSTEMS, INC.
PROJECTED INCOME STATEMENT
3 TONS/HR. AND $80/TON *(Continued)*

Income Statement	*1st 6 Mth*	*2nd 6 Mth*	*FY1 Totals*	*FY2*	*FY3*
Interest Expense	$7,088	$7,088	$14,175	$14,175	$14,175
Income Before Taxes	$51,798	$80,016	$131,815	$137,833	$143,833
Taxes (Current and Deferred)	$23,827	$36,807	$60,635	$63,403	$66,163
Investment Tax Credit	$6,500	$1,000	$7,500	$0	$0
Net Taxes	$17,327	$35,807	$53,135	$63,403	$66,163
Net Income	$34,471	$44,209	$78,680	$74,430	$77,670

RUBBER DISPOSAL SYSTEMS, INC.
PROJECTED BALANCE SHEETS
FISCAL YEARS—0/1/2/3
3 TONS/HR. AND $80/TON

	FY0	*FY1*	*FY2*	*FY3*
CURRENT ASSETS				
Cash	$40,000	$77,529	$160,895	$256,565
Accounts Receivables	$0	$58,667	$73,333	$73,333
Inventory (Raw Materials)	$2,100	$1,584	$1,981	$1,981
Total Current Assets	$42,100	$137,780	$236,209	$331,879
PROPERTY AND EQUIPMENT				
Equipment	$65,000	$75,000	$75,000	$75,000
Less Accumulated Depreciation	$0	$14,000	$38,000	$56,000
Net Property and Equipment	$65,000	$61,000	$37,000	$19,000
TOTAL ASSETS	$107,100	$198,780	$273,209	$350,879
LIABILITIES AND PARTNERS' CAPITAL				
CURRENT LIABILITIES				
Notes Payable to Bank	$92,000	$105,000	$105,000	$105,000
Total Current Liabilities	$92,000	$105,000	$105,000	$105,000
PARTNERS' CAPITAL				
Paid-in Capital	$15,100	$15,100	$15,100	$15,100
Undistributed Cash Earnings	$0	$78,680	$153,109	$230,779
Total Partners' Capital	$15,100	$93,780	$168,209	$245,879
Total Liabilities and Partners' Capital	$107,100	$198,780	$273,209	$350,879

ture. He sought the help of a business consultant who prepared the following financial projections. The projections were based on the assumption that a new injection of $40,000 in seed capital, to get the business started again, could be obtained. Based on the financial projections, the $40,000 could be repaid in a timely manner. The consultant emphasized to Charlie that it was now up to him to decide what to do about the future of the business.

QUESTIONS

1. What market share would be required if RDS, Inc. were to meet its FY1 production goal by selling to the regional Illinois grade schools?
2. What market share would be required for RDS, Inc. to meet its future production goals by selling statewide to public elementary (grade) schools? How important would be the sales to day-care centers?
3. How important are interstate sales of the cubes to RDS, Inc.?
4. Can the concept of Marketing Management or Strategic Marketing be used to explain the situation in which RDS, Inc. presently finds itself?
5. Can the concept of Marketing Management or Strategic Marketing be used to recommend a future course of action for RDS, Inc.?

This case was prepared by Kendall A. Adams, Professor of Marketing, Southern Illinois University, and Patti McDonald, consultant. Copyrighted © 1988 by the authors. Used by permission.

CHAPTER 16

Determining Computer Needs

Learning Objectives

After reading this chapter, you will be able to do the following:

- Show how the computer can benefit a startup firm.
- Present some popular business software programs.
- Research the availability of basic computer hardware.
- Describe a software and hardware selection process.
- Discuss factors concerning the installation, maintenance, and security of the security system.

Computers of different sizes and costs have been successfully used in many small businesses. Takeme and Craft Works are two examples. Takeme is a gift store in San Francisco. After Takeme decided to computerize its operations, it experienced a reduction in inventory expense of almost 30 percent, while its business grew by 25 percent. The system Takeme installed cost almost $45,000, including the cost of new cash registers, computers, telephone system, and customized software.

Craft Works is a small manufacturer of store display fixtures and cabinets. For $1,500 Craft Works purchased a used computer that enabled it to computerize its business. The system Craft Works installed handles the firm's correspondence, contracts, financial reports, and mailing lists, and is used for spreadsheet and break-even analysis. Three years after Craft Works installed its computer system, income almost doubled.[1]

Both Takeme and Craft Works were successful in installing a computer system that was designed to help their particular business. Craft Works did not need an expensive system with unnecessary programs, and Takeme would have been in trouble with a less comprehensive system. This chapter is designed to help entrepreneurs determine if they should consider the installation of a computer system, and, if so, to supply some basic information on the major components of small-business systems.

COMPUTERS IN SMALL BUSINESSES

A recent survey of the members of the National Federation of Independent Business (NFIB) indicated that computer usage is very much a function of the size of the firm. Of the firms with 1 to 4 employees, only 26 percent had a computer, whereas 39 percent of the firms with 5 to 9 employees had at least one computer. Over 54 percent of the firms with 10 to 19 employees had a computer, and an impressive 95 percent of the firms with more than 100 employees had at least one computer. Firms in the manufacturing, wholesale trade, professional services, finance, insurance, and real-estate industries were the most likely to use computers, as over 55 percent of this group utilized at least one computer. In addition, the greater the sales growth rate, the greater the probability that the firm used a computer.[2]

Additional results of the survey indicated that the majority of those firms that had computers used IBM or IBM-compatible equipment. Although the average expenditure varied directly with the size of the firm, firms with fewer than 20 employees averaged spending less than $13,000 for computer hardware and less than $5,000 for computer software. The four most popular software applications were for accounting, word processing, spreadsheet analysis, and billing.

The primary reason for acquiring computers varied by industry. Firms in the finance, insurance, real estate, and professional services industries acquired computers primarily to increase productivity, whereas those in agriculture, construction, manufacturing, wholesale, and retail industries wanted computers to improve the quality of the information on their firms. Interestingly, no industry gave the reduction of cost as the primary reason for acquiring a computer by any industry. Of those that did acquire one or more computers, 81 percent perceived them as very useful, as opposed to only 1 percent that found them not useful.

Small-business owners relied on several different sources of information to learn about computers. Many sources were cited, but the two most popular sources of information were business associates (66 percent) and computer sales representatives (51 percent). Almost 47 percent used a business or computer magazine, and 39 percent took computer courses to increase their knowledge of computers. Other sources of information included trade shows, outside consultants, friends and relatives, and employees.

The Role of Computers in a Small Business

The results of the aforementioned survey indicate that small businesses purchased computers for several reasons. One-third of the businesses that acquired a computer did so primarily to help improve productivity. For example, word processing can double a typist's output, and a general ledger program can cut bookkeeping time in half. Firms that utilize mailing lists, can increase output ten to twenty times by using a data-base program coupled with word processing.

Another one-third of the small-business owners cited in the survey acquired computers primarily to obtain better information on their firms. Quicker and more accurate information flows facilitate better control of the business. In addition, higher sales and better profit margins result from improvements in information. Better information can also reduce delinquencies, pinpoint bad credit risks, and help speed up payments.

Among the roles the computer plays in the operation of a small business is that of time saver, enabling entrepreneurs to concentrate on the fundamentals of their business—selling, producing, providing services, etc. Entrepreneurs have more time because the computer can do many of the time-consuming tasks much faster than an individual can do them. Actually, there are very few jobs that a computer can do that an employee cannot, but the computer can do most of its jobs faster and more efficiently, with fewer errors than an individual employee can. Computers, therefore, bring speed and accuracy to many business tasks, freeing the entrepreneur for those jobs that the computer cannot do.

BUSINESS SOFTWARE

When businesspeople talk about what the computer is doing for their businesses, they really are referring to the results they are obtaining from a program (software) run on a computer. The computer, without software, is for all practical purposes worthless, since a computer needs instructions to tell it what to do. Business software programs provide these instructions. Because of the importance of the software program to the computer's capabilities, entrepreneurs should always select the software programs that their firms will find useful before selecting the computer (hardware). This point cannot be overemphasized: The software should be selected first; only then should the computer be chosen.

An analysis of the needs of the firm and asking questions will determine which software is most appropriate. For example, where are the bottlenecks, or potential bottlenecks, in the operation? What information is critical to the success of this firm? What information does the entrepreneur need that he or she is not receiving, or not receiving in time to be of any real benefit? Is too much time being spent on paperwork? Once the entrepreneur starts asking these types of questions, then the question of whether these needs can best be met through computer applications is easy to answer. The next task is to find a software program that will give entrepreneurs answers to their questions.

Very few small businesses have software programs written specifically for their firms; instead, they will purchase basic software programs that are applicable to most operations. The four most popular software programs are word processing, data-base management, spreadsheet analysis, and accounting.

Word Processing

A survey of entrepreneurs by *Venture* magazine showed that computers were most often used for word processing. Eighty-three percent of the respondents used the computer for word processing, making it easily the most popular of the programs purchased by entrepreneurial firms.[3] In addition, the NFIB survey indicated that word processing is the most popular software program for firms with one to four employees and is the easiest way to introduce a computer to the office. For the person who has never used a computer, word processing is an easy place to start by virtue of its similarity to typing.

A common rule of thumb is that if more than two hours per day are spent typing, then the firm should consider buying a word processor. As the name implies, word processing is the processing (i.e., inserting, deleting, and moving) of words. In addition, many word-processing programs check spelling and grammar or supply synonyms. Since mistakes are very easy to correct, the writer learns to be more creative about what is being written rather than to concentrate on writing without making mistakes. With word processing, sentences can be moved, paragraphs added or deleted, words underlined, and corrections made without having to retype the entire document.

Word processors may also be used to write "original" form letters. Word-processing software can be combined with a data-base program to send personalized letters to selected individuals. For example, the firm could send a letter to all customers who have not made a purchase within the last ninety days or to customers who are thirty days past due on their accounts. It could also send selected advertising to a group of customers known to be interested in a particular product. This use of word processing can make the firm more profitable since the advertising dollars are spent only on selected customers.

Accounting

Although word processing is the most popular software package among the smallest (one to four employees) firms, accounting software is the most popular among all small firms with fewer than one hundred employees, with more than 67 percent of these firms using some type of accounting software. A general rule of thumb is that an accounting software package should be considered when the following conditions exist:

1. There are over 50 accounts receivable invoices per month.
2. Over 125 checks are issued per month.
3. More than 35 employees are on the payroll.

In choosing an accounting software package for their firms, entrepreneurs should look for software that was developed for their particular industry (i.e., retail sales, wholesale, manufacturing, service, etc.) or for a standard accounting package. The standard accounting package should contain the general ledger, accounts payable, accounts receivable, and payroll reports. Many excellent accounting packages are available at most computer and computer-software stores. To select an accounting package that is just right for the firm, it is a good idea to have the individuals who are keeping the accounting records choose the program. They will know what they are doing now and what they should look for in an accounting program. Entrepreneurs should also obtain the assistance of the firm's accountant in the selection of the accounting package.

After an accounting program is purchased, the change from manual accounting to computerization of the accounting records should proceed slowly and with caution. The best method is to change one account at a time and maintain both the manual and the computer accounting until there are no discrepancies between the two systems. Accounts receivable is an excellent account with which to start the changeover.

Data-Base Management

While word processors allow the user to manipulate words, data-base programs allow the user to manipulate data. Data-base programs are designed to create file records initially and to add, delete, or modify file records later. Data-base management programs are capable of sorting records into a predetermined sequence according to one or more data fields in each record, or to use criteria specified by the user to find and display the contents of one or more records. In addition, the data-base management program is capable of preparing reports according to the user's specifications.

For example, suppose a list of all the firm's customers in Kansas City was needed for a special mailing. The data-base management program would search all the firm's records for customers in Kansas City and then print a list of these customers with their addresses. When combined with a word-processing program, an individual letter could be written to each customer.

Two words are the key to understanding data-base management programs: SEARCH and SORT. Data-base management enables the user to have the computer search through a large number of files, to find those files that meet a specified criterion, and then sort those files according to any of the given data fields, such as last name, amount of purchases, zip code, city, or state. The ability of the data-base management program to sort through a large list and find those customers or items that meet established criteria makes this software particularly valuable to many firms.

Spreadsheet Programs

Spreadsheet programs are useful to anyone who prepares numerical analyses involving a grid of numbers. For example, both budgeting and cash-flow planning require rows and columns (a grid) of numbers. The spreadsheet program is also useful to the business that does a great deal of estimating, such as financial forecasting or construction estimates. The value of the spreadsheet is its capability to calculate a "bottom line" for a set of calculations under different conditions, like the cost of a new warehouse, monthly cash flow, or even the amount of taxes due on April 15. For example, in calculating the cost of a new warehouse, the user can see what the cost would be if the price of bricks were to increase 10 percent, or if labor were to obtain a 15-percent increase in wages over the construction period. This kind of analysis is known as *sensitivity analysis*, or *"what if" analysis*.

Templates for spreadsheets are available for everything from income-tax forms to profit and loss statements. With templates, users simply add their own numbers to the format presented to see what results would be obtained. Different costs can then be changed to see what effect this would have on the results. Some of these formats have been developed specifically with the problems of startup or small businesses in mind (see The Inside View 16-1).

Integrated Software

In addition to the individual software packages for word processing, spreadsheets, and data-base management, there are some integrated programs that combine all three of these programs into one package. Some of these packages even include additional pro-

16-1 *The Inside View*

LOTUS COURTS SMALL BUSINESSES

Lotus Development Company realizes that financial planning can be more critical for small businesses than larger businesses because larger businesses can afford more mistakes than the small business. Lotus also knows that the most common cause of small-business failure is poor financial management. To help improve the financial management capabilities of small firms, Lotus markets the *1-2-3 Small Business Kit,* which contains the Lotus 1-2-3 spreadsheet and a selection of add-on applications that cover the basics of financial analysis and planning. Included in the price is six months of unlimited access to telephone support for this specific program.

The package includes templates that help answer such questions as, "When is my money going to run out?" and "What price must be charged for a product for it to break even?" or "What profits are expected if sales continue to grow 20 percent per year?" A manual that gives step-by-step instructions for analysis and planning is included. There are worksheets for cash flow, source and use of cash, basic financial ratios, and cost-profit-volume analysis. With these worksheets, entrepreneurs should have an accurate picture of the current financial health of their firms and be able to identify several areas in which their firms may need help.[4]

grams that combine graphics with the spreadsheet or data-base numbers. The main advantage of integrated software is that the user has to learn only one set of operating commands rather than the operating commands that are unique to each individual package. In addition, a single integrated package is much less expensive than several individual packages. However, the integrated systems are seldom as complete or as sophisticated as the individual programs, but for many startup businesses, the added features are not worth the additional costs.

Point-of-Purchase Software

Point-of-purchase software is available, inexpensive, and, in some cases, almost indispensable for **the startup firm.** Point-of-purchase software can give entrepreneurs an excellent idea of what is selling, what is not selling, and what is in stock. Part of the attraction of point-of-purchase software is the diversity of programs available for every type of business, from candy stores to video rental stores. These programs are advertised in the various trade journals and should be carefully considered. Some of the programs are almost worthless, and so the entrepreneur should not purchase a program without first learning more about its quality from others in the business or from reviews in the journals.

COMPUTER HARDWARE

After deciding what software the firm needs, entrepreneurs need to determine what hardware is required to run their software. Hardware is computer equipment such as the terminals, printers, disk drives, and modems. The hardware selection decision is complicated by several factors. First, most entrepreneurs do not know what their computer needs are. The first-time computer buyer is like many car buyers. Most car buyers are looking for a "nice" car, and they know about how much money they have to spend or are able to spend each month on payments. The purchase of a car should be based on such criteria as the amount of driving the owner will do, the type of road the car will be driven on, the average number of passengers, the size of the normal load carried or pulled, the maintenance record, and the resale value.

Second, most computer stores have sales personnel who know computers but who do not know much about what a business needs. Few computer salespeople know about payrolls, general ledgers, cash budgets, and the like, except what they can demonstrate on the particular software package they are selling.

Third, the gap between the first two factors is filled with terminology that neither the buyer nor the seller fully understands. The objective of this section is to help close that gap by providing entrepreneurs with a brief, but basic, description of microcomputer equipment.

Computer Terminals or Workstations

When most people think of computers, they really are referring to the computer terminal or work station. The computer terminal usually consists of the central processing unit (CPU), the keyboard, and the video screen or monitor. The system unit is a metal rectangular cabinet that contains the CPU, memory chips, plug-in boards, expansion slots, and sometimes disk drives. The heart of the microcomputer is the CPU, where information (data) is processed (sorted).

Microcomputers contain an 8-bit, 16-bit, or 32-bit CPU, which processes data in 8-bit, 16-bit, or 32-bit chunks, respectively. Computing power grows with the bit size. For example, the 16-bit computer can process data two to four times faster than the older 8-bit computers. The most popular systems for business uses contain a 16-bit CPU, although the growth of powerful 32-bit computers seems to indicate that they will be the most popular in the near future. A bit (for BInary digiT) is one yes or no character, and 8 bits equal a byte. It takes 8 bits to form a single character (a letter, number, or space).

Memory. *Computer memory* is a term used to describe the amount of data that can be stored within the computer. There are two types of memory, RAM and ROM. RAM, or random-access memory, is the temporary storage that can be accessed by the CPU. RAM is temporary because when the computer is turned off, the data in

RAM disappear. This memory is called "random" because the CPU can access any of the data stored there in any (random) order.

The size of the computer may be determined by its RAM memory. The minimum size a small business should consider is 256K (1,024 bytes is 1K, therefore 256K means that the memory can hold about 256,000 bytes of information). To put this number into perspective, a page of double-spaced, typewritten text contains about 2,000 (2K) characters (bytes).

ROM, read-only memory, is the other main type of memory in the microcomputer. ROM is permanently stored in the computer and is not lost when the computer is turned off. ROM, which cannot be changed by the user, contains portions of the disk operating system, which tells the computer how to operate.

Most computers have expansion slots, which allow the RAM to be increased by adding additional memory chips to a memory expansion board. Computers have a system board that contains a limited amount of RAM memory. For example, the IBM-PC computer has a system limit of 256 RAM. For most uses, this limit poses no problems, but some business programs may require more than 256 RAM. To alleviate this potential problem, the expansion board allows memory expansion, usually ranging from 64K to 512K.

Disk Drives

Any computer system that is being considered for business application should have either two disk drives, or a hard disk. For the small additional cost, the hard disk should be considered the standard for the business computer. A disk drive is required because the main memory (RAM) does not have the ability to permanently store information (data), and the data in RAM is lost when the computer is turned off. The disk drive provides permanent storage of data on computer disks.

The disk drive transfers data from a disk (sometimes called a floppy disk) to the computer's main memory and from the main memory to the disk. The storage medium is a plastic diskette on which magnetic impulses (those yes or no characters mentioned earlier) are stored. The disk drive is able to transfer data by "reading" information from the disk and sending this information to the computer or by "writing" information from the computer onto the disk. To accomplish this, the disk drive contains a read/write head located on a movable arm that "reads" or "writes" information on the disk, which is spinning under the head at about 300 rpm. (It works much like a record player, with the stylus "reading" from the spinning record.)

The two most popular disks are the 5¼-inch disk and the 3½-inch disk. The 5¼-inch disk is used most commonly with the IBM-PC, IBM-compatible computers, most of Radio Shack's Tandy computers, and the Apple II series of computers. The 3½-inch disk is more common with the Apple Macintosh series, IBM's PS/2 series of computers, the Commodore Amiga, and several laptop computers. The 3½-inch disks are rigid, not flexible like the 5¼-inch disks, and, therefore, are a safer storage medium. In addition, the 3½-inch disks hold more data.

Hard-Disk Drives. The hard-disk drive is an alternative to the two-disk drive system. The hard disk is a magnetically coated metal platter that operates like a floppy disk in that it spins under a read/write head—except about ten times faster. The hard disk, however, can store 30 to 120 times more data than the 5¼-inch disks, and the data retrival time is about ten times faster. Of course, hard-disk drives are more expensive than their floppy counterparts.

Because of the large memory storage required, a hard-disk drive is recommended for many popular accounting programs and for computer systems that connect more than one computer terminal. One of the best features of the hard-disk drive is that its storage capacity allows it to store most, if not all, of the firm's software programs, thereby eliminating the need to insert disks each time another program is run. The most common hard-disk size is the 10-megabytes (10 million bytes of data) drive, which will hold the equivalent of about thirty 5¼-inch disks.

If a hard disk is purchased, it should have the ability to recover from a power failure without losing all the data stored on the disk. In addition, if a hard disk is purchased, the buyer should also consider the purchase of a high-speed tape backup system. The tape backup copies the data stored on the hard disk onto a magnetic tape. The tape should be stored in a location different from that of the computer.

Keyboard

The typewriter keyboard is the most common device for sending data to the computer. (Other devices include the electronic mouse, light pen, joystick, and microphone.) Although there is no standard keyboard layout, there are substantial similarities between the keyboards of all computer manufacturers. Almost all keyboards are divided into three sections of keys as follows: (1) the alphabet (or typewriter) keys, (2) the numeric and cursor keys, and (3) the function keys. The layout of the alphabet keys should be in the standard "QWERTY" arrangement to allow easy transition from typewriter to computer keyboard.

The numeric section is usually located on the right-hand side of the keyboard and is similar in layout to a standard calculator. The cursor keys should be in a position that makes them easy to manipulate. (The cursor is the constantly blinking character on the computer screen that indicates where the operator's next character will be entered. The cursor keys are used to move the cursor up, down, left, or right on the monitor screen.) There are between ten and twenty function keys on the typical keyboard. The function keys send a set of instructions to the computer, such as print, underline, or move the cursor to a preset location. The function of these keys may vary from program to program, and in some cases, the function of the key may be programmed by the user. The function keys are usually located either on the left side or on top of the keyboard.

Video Screen Monitor

The video screen monitor is the last major hardware item required for a complete computer system. The video monitor is sometimes called the video display terminal, a CRT (for cathode ray tube), or simply the computer screen. Entrepreneurs should consider size, color, resolution, and ergonomics before purchasing a monitor.

Size. Most monitors used for business purposes are 12- to 14-inch (measured diagonally) screens. The screen should be able to display 80 characters (columns) and 24 or

25 (lines) rows. Larger monitors are useful for those applications that require more lines, such as a large spreadsheet. Some monitors will display 80 characters by 57 lines, which is almost the amount of information on an 8½-by-11 inch sheet of paper. This size is useful for word-processing applications. Even larger displays are available: one 17-inch screen will display 160 characters by 64 lines; however, special software is required to utilize this larger screen's display capabilities.

Color. One-color, or monochrome, screens typically come in white, green, or amber on black screens. Green is popular in the United States, while amber is popular in Europe. Monochrome screens are less expensive than color screens and display sharper letters and numbers. The monochrome screen is adequate for most graphs and charts.

Color monitors can greatly enhance the visual effect of business graphics, but there is usually a reduction in the legibility of textual information. There are two basic types of color monitors: RGB (for red-green-blue) and composite. The RGB color monitor is more expensive than the composite monitor and produces sharper color images. The composite monitor is more expensive than the monochrome monitors but less expensive than the RGB monitor. The color on the composite monitor is produced like the picture of a color television; the color, however, is not nearly as sharp. Some composite monitors provide audio output, which is useful if the system is to be used as a component part of a television system. For most business applications requiring a color monitor, the RGB monitor is the best choice.

Resolution. All images that are produced on the computer screen are made up of a number of small dots called pixels. A *pixel* is the amount of space assigned an individual dot. The more closely packed the dots, the sharper the image. Resolution may be measured in the number of pixels wide (horizontal) times the number of pixels high (vertical) on a computer screen. Thus, a resolution of 720 by 350 means that there are 720 dots in each row on the computer screen and 350 rows of dots, for a total of 252,000 pixels. The greater the number of pixels, the better the resolution and the less the eyestrain on the user.

Ergonomics. There has been growing concern regarding the environments in which individuals use computers. In particular, computer monitors have received adverse publicity because of their effect on the health and comfort of users. There are two guidelines concerning the use of monitors. First, the glare on a computer screen can cause eyestrain and severe discomfort. When purchasing a monitor, the buyer should look for one with an antiglare screen or one that can be fitted with an antiglare screen. Of course, the placement of the monitor within a room can also affect the amount of glare on the screen.

Second, studies have shown that a computer monitor should be at a level with or slightly below the user's line of sight. Since more than one person may be using a computer, monitors can be placed on stands that allow the monitor to be tilted up or down, or forward or backward, to suit each user. The tilting also allows the screen to be moved to reduce the glare and to accommodate people of different heights.

PERIPHERALS

In addition to the main computer components, entrepreneurs should consider at least two other hardware components for their computer system. The printer is almost a necessity for most businesses, and a communication device called a modem is required for communication with other computers and data bases.

Printers

Anyone who has ever used a typewriter will be impressed with the speed and accuracy of computer printers. In addition, the better-quality printers can produce copy that looks like it came from a print shop. Printers come in a bewildering number of speeds, quality, and price. There are, however, only four major types of printers that are used with microcomputers: (1) dot matrix, (2) letter quality, (3) laser, and (4) ink-jet printers.

Dot Matrix Printers. Dot-matrix printers are usually the least expensive printers available. They produce characters and pictures comprised of small dots in the same manner that numbers are formed on a scoreboard or that individual dots make up a photograph in a newspaper. The greater the number of dots in each character, the better the print quality. Dot-matrix printers are excellent for billing, invoicing, check printing, and graphics.

Dot-matrix printers are either unidirectional or bidirectional. The unidirectional printer prints from left to right and then returns to the left to print the next line, just like a typewriter. The bidirectional printer prints a line from left to right and then prints the next line from right to left, going back and forth over the page. In most cases, bidirectional printers are faster than unidirectional ones.

In addition to print quality, speed is the other primary consideration in the selection of a printer. Speed may be measured in characters per second (cps) or lines per minute. The cps of a printer is similar to the EPA gas mileage rating given to automobiles, in that the rating is a good comparison guideline but not necessarily what the individual user will obtain. Dot-matrix printer speeds vary from about 40 cps to more than 300 cps.

Letter-Quality Printers. Letter-quality printers print fully formed characters in the same manner as typewriters. The two major types of letter-quality printers are the daisy-wheel printer and the thimble-type printer. The daisy-wheel printers have a flat wheel with thin spokes that each contain a character extending from the center. In printing, the wheel spins the needed character beneath a tiny hammer that strikes the character against the ribbon, printing the character on the paper. The thimble printers work the same way as the daisy-wheel, except the characters are held on a thimblelike device. The printing speed of these two letter-quality printers is about twenty to eighty cps—slower than most dot-matrix printers. Letter-quality printers are needed if the primary use of the printer is for word processing.

Laser Printers. Laser printers are more expensive than either the dot-matrix or the letter-quality printers; however they produce both higher-quality print and higher speeds—between ten and fifty pages per minute. Laser printers work like a photocopy machine and can produce characters of typeset quality as well as excellent business graphics. Prices range from about $1,000 to over $100,000, suggesting that only those startup businesses that rely on the printed page as a major part of their business should consider this type of printer.

Ink-Jet Printers. Ink-jet printers are actually special dot-matrix printers that form characters by spraying dots on the paper with a high-precision ink jet. The quality of the print can range from the draft quality of the dot-matrix printer to almost typeset quality.

Other Types of Printers. In addition to the four major types of printers mentioned above, several special-purpose printers should be considered for their specific characteristics. The color printer is one type of special-purpose printer that may be useful for some startup businesses. Although color printing is still a developing technology, the current choice of color printers is limited to dot-matrix printers with a multicolored ribbon and a non-impact printer that uses thermal printing technology. Both printers are capable of producing a quality print of up to eight colors.

For firms that need to produce drawings or graphs, a plotter may be useful. A plotter is a special-purpose printer that "draws" with a mechanical arm with one or more pens attached. The pen(s) may be able to print in one or more colors. The quality of the drawing can vary greatly, but the best models can produce blueprint-quality graphics. For startup engineering firms that do drafting, the saving of time and the increase in quality can make the plotter a required piece of equipment.

Communications

The ability of computers to communicate with large external information data bases and with each other can be an important computer capability for the startup business. In fact, the intelligent use of the computer's communication ability can provide a firm with the competitive edge in today's fast changing global marketplace. The ability of computers to communicate requires a linking device, known as a modem, and software instructions. (The linking of several computers without the modem will be presented in the next section.)

The Modem. A modem is a device that enables the computer to be connected to telephone lines, and through telephone lines to other companies. The modem (from MOdulator/DEModulator) not only provides the physical link but also converts data from the binary output of the computer into the analog signals used by the telephone.

Communication software programs are needed to properly transmit and/or receive data from external sources. Communication between computers can be a problem because they may not all have the same protocols. The protocols that may be different include the transmission speed (measured in baud or bits per second), the parity (an error-checking procedure), the number of start and stop bits used to specify the beginning and the end of transmitted characters, and the transmission capability—either full- or half-duplex. Most modems are full duplex, which means that data can be sent as well as received at the same time, whereas half-duplex modems can either send or receive data at one time.

When purchasing a modem, the most important decision is that concerning the transmission speed. The most common transmission speeds are 300 and 1,200 bits per second (bps), with the 1,200 bps the most popular. Higher transmission speeds are available but are not commonly used by small businesses. The 1,200 bps modems cost more than the slower 300 bps modems, but if the modem is being used to access some of the large data-base systems, such as The Source, CompuServe, or Dow Jones News Retrieval, which charge by the time connected, then the faster transmission results in less connect time. Typically the cost for receiving data at 300 bps is one-half that of receiving at 1,200 bps, but the user is obtaining four times the amount of data at only twice the cost.

Entrepreneurs should consider other features before purchasing a modem, including the modem's ability to perform such tasks as dialing and/or answering the telephone, setting the transmission rate, and storing data in a buffer that enables the computer to read bigger blocks rather than just a character at a time. A modem may also be either an external or internal device, depending on whether it is connected outside the computer unit or placed inside the unit in one of the expansion slots.

The advantage of the internal modem is that space is saved in the computer work area. The advantage of the external modem is that it may be either acoustic or direct connect. The direct-connect type of modem connects directly to a telephone jack, whereas the acoustic modem requires an acoustic coupler in which the telephone handset is placed. Individuals who travel and/or use portable computers to connect them with other computers or data bases need the acoustic modem.

Multiuser Systems

A multiuser system consists of a central microcomputer with a hard-disk drive that is connected to one or more computer terminals. The central microcomputer has the firm's most commonly used programs on hard disk and has one or more peripherals attached. Multiuser systems enable the connected users to share these peripherals, such as printers or plotters, which results in an equipment savings. Another reason such systems are economical is that they require only one set of programs, which is stored on hard disk. The programs on hard disk are available to all connected users.

The multiuser system also results in an increase in efficiency because users can continually update the data on hard disk, which is instantly accessible to all. In the case of separate microcomputers, to enable others to use an updated file, the data had to be saved on a diskette, copied, and then physically handed to the next user. The only up-to-date copy would be the last one used, and other users may not be aware of it.

One of the main disadvantages of the multiuser system is that if the central computer goes down, then the entire system is down. With separate microcomputers, if one goes down, then only one workstation is affected. Thus, there is a trade-off between the equipment savings and potential downtime.

Local-Area Network. While the multiuser system links several terminals together through a central computer, a local-area network (LAN) is a communications system that enables computers and peripherals to share data and equipment with each other. A LAN, therefore, is a group of two or more computers that are physically connected.

With a LAN, hardware resources such as hard disks, printers, and modems may be shared among the microcomputers attached to the system. In addition, each computer in the network can also share data with all other computers in the network.

THE SELECTION DECISION

After entrepreneurs gain a basic understanding of computer software and hardware, the next step for them is to determine what components they need for their business. The three most common mistakes made in the selection process are:

1. Selecting the computer hardware first.
2. Not taking time to thoroughly analyze why the computer is being purchased.
3. Failing to do basic research on computers.

Entrepreneurs must determine their software needs prior to considering their hardware needs; the software will govern what hardware is required. The best way to start the process is to write a description of what the computer is expected to do. Is the computer expected to automate the accounting process, keep track of inventory, provide a list of past-due accounts, keep a mailing list up to date, or just handle word-processing chores? Simply writing a list of the functions the computer is expected to handle is an important first step.

The second step is to estimate the present and future size of each of the functions the computer is expected to perform. Size refers to the number of customer accounts and/or transactions, the number of items in inventory, the number of customers on a mailing list, or the number of accounts in the firm's chart of accounts.

Software Search

With the foregoing information, entrepreneurs can begin the search for the appropriate software. The first step in the search should start with the purchase of a few computer magazines that feature software articles and reviews of software. The articles will give readers a basic understanding of what the programs will do, and the reviews will point out what experts look for in a software program.

The second step should be to talk to business associates about their experiences with the software under consideration. Their experience in selecting software, especially if they are in the same industry, can provide valuable insight into features to look for and pitfalls to avoid. This step is even more important for entrepreneurs in specialized businesses. For example, there are software packages designed especially for gas stations, small construction firms, and retail operations. Some of this specialized software is excellent, and some is poor. A check on the results other businesses have had with a particular type of software can save entrepreneurs many hours of frustration and many dollars.

The third step is to visit computer stores. About 75 percent of all small-business owners buy their software from a computer retailer. For entrepreneurs the major advantage of purchasing from a local retail store is that they can provide a demonstration as well as answer questions concerning the software they sell. In addition, the local store can help with the installation and provide service support after the sale.

For their visit to the computer store, entrepreneurs should have prepared a list of questions concerning the needs of their firms. The objective is to buy a software system that matches their needs, not one that is merely close to them. Store personnel should understand that an entrepreneur's first trip to their store is an exploratory trip and that a demonstration of the software is appreciated. Store personnel should be prepared to demonstrate more than one program for each task the computer needs to perform and to explain the advantages and disadvantages of each.

The final step is to read the software literature and once again to read the computer magazine articles on the software under consideration. If some of the software packages are more well recommended than others (through reviews, business associates, or retail stores), then these are the programs that should receive more consideration. Entrepreneurs should remember, however, that the objective is to ascertain that the software under consideration is the best available software for the firm's needs. If more than one software package seems to meet all the firm's requirements, the program that has the greatest amount of excess capacity over the required amount is the one that should be purchased.

Hardware Search

The hardware search, like the software search, should begin with a description of the tasks the computer is supposed to perform. The basic requirements should include the following:

1. ***CPU/RAM memory.*** The absolute minimum should be 256K, but since the additional cost is so small, 512K is a better (safer) minimum.
2. ***Disk drives.*** There should be at least two disk drives, at least one of which should be a 10-megabyte hard-disk drive, if possible.
3. ***Keyboard.*** Be sure the keyboard has a standard typewriter layout, a numeric pad, and at least ten function keys.
4. ***Video monitor.*** The choice of color or monochrome should depend on the intended use, but the user should be able to view the screen comfortably for extended periods of time.
5. ***Printer.*** The choice between dot matrix and letter quality depends on the planned use of the printer. The buyer should see the print from the printer before purchasing it.
6. ***Modem.*** If a modem is required, a "smart" modem, one that checks protocols between senders and receivers, should be purchased.

With these basic criteria in mind, entrepreneurs should start shopping for their hardware in much the same manner as they did their software, by going through the same four basic steps. However, before making the final decision on hardware, entrepreneurs should consider four additional factors.

The first factor is the reliability of the equipment: Has the firm been in business long enough to have an established reputation for quality products? A startup business is not the place to try out a new product.

The second factor is the maintenance record for the equipment: Does the equipment have a reputation for maintenance-free operation? Articles in computer magazines, discussions with business associates, and the general reputation of the manufacturer will help determine the potential for a relatively maintenance-freelife.

A third factor to consider is the expandability of the computer: Does the computer have the ability to expand as the needs of the firm grow? The classic mistake is to purchase a computer that does not have room for expansion.

The last factor is that of compatibility. Is all the hardware under consideration compatible? Even more important, will the computer system run the software programs the firm has selected?

INSTALLATION, MAINTENANCE, AND SECURITY

After selecting and purchasing a computer system for their businesses, entrepreneurs should properly install the system, train employees in its efficient operation, see that the system is properly maintained, and ensure that the computer and the data produced on the computer are secure.

Installation

Installation of a computer can be as simple as taking the components out of a box and connecting them, or as complex as the building and wiring of separate rooms for the computer and related equipment. In either case, entrepreneurs should give some serious thought to where the computer system will be installed. Even with a single microcomputer, a few simple steps can help make the computer installation and initial operation go smoothly.

The first step is to select a location that is not subject to temperature extremes and that is relatively dust free. Heat, cold, and dust will cause problems, usually through lost data.

The second step is to determine whether the location will accommodate computer hardware. For example, will the keyboard be at a height that will enable users to efficiently operate them? Can the monitor be placed just below the eye level of the principal user?

The third step is the actual assembly of the computer and its components. If possible, have the seller assemble the computer system; if not, be sure to read the instructions before beginning the assembly process. The assembly process is slightly more complicated than installing a VCR, which means that a novice can do it.

The fourth step is to test the system by operating each device to ensure that it functions properly. One method that has proven to be an excellent test is to run a simple program, hopefully one that the tester has operated before.

Training

Just as a person would not drive a car for the first time without basic training and without operating it under the guidance of an experienced driver, so the first-time user of a computer system requires basic training and operating time under the guidance of a more experienced user. Many computer stores offer classes on the basic operation of the computer and on particular software they sell. These classes are relatively inexpensive, but their benefits, in the form of the increased efficiency of its users, far outweigh their cost. If classes are not available or not feasible, then the operator must take the time to read the manual, preferably before attempting to operate the computer or any software package. Time spent reading will save many hours of frustration.

Maintenance

The car analogy can be extended to include maintenance. No responsible owner would operate a car without occasional maintenance, and no computer should be operated without attending to a few maintenance details. Following is a brief summary of the maintenance required by each of the major components.

1. ***Computer unit.*** The CPU should be protected from temperature extremes and dust, because both can cause loss of data and unnecessary downtime.

2. ***Disk drive.*** Disk-drive heads should be cleaned on a regular basis, depending on the amount of usage. Cleaning kits are very inexpensive and can be purchased from any computer store. About once a year the disk heads should be checked for alignment and speed.

3. ***Hard disk.*** Hard disks are temperature sensitive; if they are moved from one temperature to another, the operators should wait at least twenty-four hours before attempting to operate the system. Temperature changes may cause temporary distortion of the disk, and premature operation could cause contact between the read/write head and the disk, resulting in lost data. Smoke also can harm a hard-disk drive; therefore, smoking should not be allowed in the vicinity of the hard-disk drive.

4. ***Video monitor.*** The monitor should be kept clean of dust and fingerprints.Cleaners are available from local computer stores.

5. ***Keyboard.*** The keyboard should be covered with a dust cover when not in use and cleaned periodically with a vacuum cleaner with a soft brush attachment.

6. ***Printer.*** The printer should also be covered when not in use. It should also be placed on a stable surface so that there is as little movement as possible during printing.

7. ***Diskettes.*** Data are magnetically saved on disks, and these magnetic "dots" can easily be lost if reasonable care of the disks is not taken. Care starts with keeping the disks in their paper envelopes when not in use. If the disk is to be carried around in a briefcase or carried just from one office to another, the disk should be placed in a rigid cardboard or plastic jacket to prevent its being bent or folded. The disk must be kept away from magnets and electromagetic devices, such as those in telephones and speakers, because magnetic devices will remove, or rearrange, the magnetically coded disks rendering them worthless. Disks must also be protected from dust, liquid, food, drink, and the like. More than one diskette has been ruined by an accidental coffee spill. The collection of disks should be kept in a nonmetallic file box. Finally, disks should be properly labeled with both a name and a date.

The objective of the maintenance of any system is to keep the system operating with as little downtime as possible. The aforementioned suggestions will help keep the startup firm's computer system up and running. The last maintenance chore—that of saving all work—is one that all users must turn into a habit. While entering data, the user should save the data to disk at least every fifteen minutes. If something happens and the system goes down, the most work that is lost is the last fifteen minutes. In addition, at the completion of a work session, a copy of the file should be saved and placed in a location different from that of the normal computer operations.

Security

The owners of most computers do not usually think about security, and in many cases, security procedures may not be needed. However, entrepreneurs should realize that valuable information is recorded on disks, and a single copy can contain a great deal of confidential information that they may not wish to lose or to have fall into the hands of competitors. Unfortunately, most entrepreneurs do not realize just how vulnerable their firms are to computer crime. According to Mr. Bequai, a lawyer specializing in industrial security, "Small companies . . . are concerned with growth and cash flow. They don't understand computer security and don't have money to implement it. They become prime targets (for computer crime).[5]

Computer security consists of controlling access to computer equipment as well as the computer's information. There are four items essential for controlling access to the computer area. These four items are: (1) sturdy door and locks, (2) fire alarm, (3) alarm, (3) burglar alarm, and (4) security training. Interestingly, a survey of small businesses found that 38 percent did not have even one of these items. In addition, 58 percent did not even back up their data daily—another method that can prevent the accidental loss of information. Even more interesting was the finding that over 25 percent of these businesses had suffered some type of computer-related loss.[6]

Summary

Computers are being employed with increasing confidence and positive results by the nation's small businesses. Owners of small firms purchase a computer primarily to improve productivity and to obtain better information on their firms. It is the software program that gives the computer its instructions, and entrepreneurs should always select the software program that meets their firm's specific needs before purchasing the computer hardware. The most popular software programs for small businesses are those for word processing, accounting, data-base management, and spreadsheet analysis. In addition, several integrated software programs combine two or more of these popular programs into a single package.

Computer hardware is the equipment required to operate the software programs. Computer hardware includes the system unit, keyboard, video monitor, printers, and modems. The system unit contains the central processing unit (CPU) and the main-memory storage. The size of a computer is determined by its main, or RAM, memory. Disk drives allow the permanent storage of data, since the computer's RAM memory is lost when the computer is turned off.

The keyboard is the most common device for sending data to the computer. Whereas the keyboard is an input device, the video monitor is an output device that displays data from the CPU. The features that entrepreneurs should look for in a monitor are size, color, resolution, and ergonomics. Printers display output from the

CPU in printed form. Printers vary greatly in the speed at which they operate and in the quality of the printing. The four most common types of printers used by small businesses are the dot-matrix, letter-quality, laser, and ink-jet printers.

Modems enable computers to communicate with each other and to access information from large data bases. Modems, however, are not needed for connecting computers in multiuser systems or local-area networks, because the computers in these systems are linked through cables and have the ability to share both data and equipment.

The entrepreneur should begin the software selection process by reading a few computer magazines to gain a basic understanding of what computer programs will do. The next step is to talk to business associates about their experiences with different software programs. The third step should be a visit to a computer store to see demonstrations of specific software. The final step is to read reviews of the specific software under consideration.

The selection of computer hardware should follow the same basic steps as that for software selection. Entrepreneurs should have basic hardware criteria in mind before starting to evaluate different systems. In addition, buyers should consider the reliability, maintenance record, and the expandability of the components under consideration.

After selecting and purchasing a computer system, entrepreneurs should plan for its installation and for basic training of those employees who will be operating the computer. Maintenance of the system and the security of both the equipment and the data generated should be given careful consideration.

Assembling the Pieces

From the beginning, sales records for In Good Taste were maintained on a spreadsheet program to obtain a weekly record of sales. For more specific information on sales, Jacki gradually modified the spreadsheet program to separate sales into forty categories. A computer was also used to maintain and process a mailing list of about 1,200 names, which enabled Carol and Jacki to optimize sales. For example, they found that 28 percent of their customers were ordering within seven to ten days after receiving their catalogs. They used Jacki's husband's Hewlett-Packard 86 computer (with 128K of memory) for their business. They admit it is not the best for the task, but the price was right.

In addition, shortly after startup they realized they needed up-to-date accounting information, so they purchased the Peachtree General Ledger Software program and computerized the manual system with the help of a local college accounting student. This system provided them with the timely information they needed to make financial decisions.

The computer system operates very slowly (because of limited memory), and the printer seems to take forever to print the results. In the future, the owners of In Good Taste plan to purchase a larger computer (an IBM or IBM-compatible) that will provide them with a better breakdown of sales by categories and given them room for expansion to other tasks. ■

Questions for Review and Discussion

1. Why should a startup firm consider the purchase of a computer?
2. Why do you think word processing is the most popular program among entrepreneurial firms?
3. What are some common uses of data-base programs?
4. Read and summarize a review article from a computer magazine on a software program that is of interest to you.
5. What RAM memory is required to run the program you read about in question #4?
6. Why would a hard-disk drive be required for a computer system?
7. When should the purchase of a high-resolution monitor be considered?
8. When should the purchase of a letter-quality printer be considered?
9. Determine the computer requirements for a startup firm in your area.
10. At which point in the selection search do you think most purchasers of computer software make mistakes?
11. What is meant by "the expandability" of the computer?
12. What is the most important part of a computer-maintenace program?

Notes

1. Daniel Goldsmith, "Automating Small Business," *Changing Times,* November 1986, vol. 40, no. 11, pp. 96–104.
2. Russell Rumberger and Henry Levin, *Computers in Small Business* (Washington, D.C.: Institute for Enterprise Advancement, 1986), pp.1–2.
3. Marilyn and John Pollock, "Are You Ready to Go On-Line?" *Venture,* September 1986, p. 16.
4. Peter Lewis, "Lotus Is Courting Small Business," *New York Times,* 8 May 1988, p. F11.
5. William Souder, "Computers Vulnerable in Small Companies," *Inc.,* October 1985, p. 22.
6. Norman Pendegraft, Linda Morris, and Kathryn Savage, "Small Business Computer Security," *Journal of Small Business Management,* October 1987, pp. 54–60.

CHAPTER 17

Paying Income Taxes

Learning Objectives

After reading this chapter, you will be able to do the following:

- Understand tax accounting for business.
- Explain basic tax accounting for sole proprietorships.
- Explain tax accounting for partnerships.
- Explain tax accounting for S corporations.
- Explain tax accounting for C corporations.

The purpose of this chapter is to help startup entrepreneurs understand some of the basic tax laws that will affect their businesses. Since the tax code covers some five thousand plus pages, there are a few items that will not be thoroughly covered in this chapter. In addition, the frequency of changes in the tax laws makes decision making even more difficult.

INTRODUCTION

Any introduction to taxes should begin with the statement that evasion of taxes is a crime for which the penalties are severe, but tax avoidance is legal. In keeping with this point of view, the tone for this chapter is best expressed by Judge Learned Hand's dictum: "There is nothing sinister in so arranging one's affairs to keep taxes as low as possible. Everybody does so, rich and poor; and all do right, for nobody owes any public duty to pay more than the law demands: Taxes are enforced exactions, not voluntary contributions."

What can startup entrepreneurs do to arrange the affairs of their businesses to keep taxes as low as possible? One of the obvious things is to pay taxes on their earnings only once, as some forms of businesses can do, rather than twice, as corporations must do. Another method is to shelter some of the income from taxes through employee benefit and retirement plans. Still another is to defer taxes through the use of accelerated depreciation. However, the very best method is to keep accurate records of all the firm's expenses so that all legitimate expenses may be claimed. Finally, entrepreneurs must recognize that paying taxes is part of doing business, just like selling and buying, and that knowledge of those tax laws that affect their businesses is just as important as keeping informed of the product or service in their industries. Once all expenses are paid, the remaining funds, called profits, go to two groups: the government, in the form of taxes, and to the owners. Thus, each dollar saved from taxes goes to the owner(s). What better incentive do entrepreneurs need in order to learn all they can about taxes?

The objective of this chapter on taxes is to provide a basic understanding of the tax laws affecting startup businesses and to help startup entrepreneurs understand what their accountants are telling them. With a basic understanding, entrepreneurs can better work with their firm's accountants to reduce taxes to a minimum. The major portion of the chapter deals with the taxes affecting sole proprietorships, partnerships, and S corporations, because these are the forms of business most startup firms assume.

One final warning before entering the heart of the chapter. Federal tax laws are very complex and subject to change by a Congress that seems to constantly make major changes in the tax laws. The information presented in this chapter is based on the Tax Reform Act of 1986 and, therefore, is applicable for tax returns for 1987 and later.

EMPLOYER IDENTIFICATION NUMBER

Before the actual startup date, entrepreneurs should obtain an employer identification number (EIN) from the IRS. This number is required for all businesses unless the owner is the only employee, and then the entrepreneur's social security number serves as the EIN. In most areas, the EIN may be obtained by a single telephone call to the nearest IRS regional office. Even if the EIN is obtained over the telephone, startup entrepreneurs must obtain and fill in Form SS-4, the formal application for the EIN. Finally, if a business changes from one type of organization to another, a new EIN must be obtained. Thus, if the entrepreneur changes from a sole proprietorship to a partnership or an S corporation, a new EIN is required.

TAX ACCOUNTING FOR BUSINESS

Tax accounting is the determination of when income and expenses are computed for tax purposes. This section contains a discussion of the cash versus the accrual method of accounting, long-term contract methods, installment sales, computation of the cost of goods sold, accounting for inventories, depreciation, and basic rules for business deductions.

The Cash Versus the Accrual Method of Accounting

Taxable income must be computed according to a taxpayer's normal accounting method, providing it clearly reflects income. The normal accounting method is not just cash or accrual but may be the percentage-of-completion method or the completed-contract method. For most businesses, the accrual method is required by the present tax code, although there are certain exceptions allowing the cash-basis method.

Cash-Basis Method. The cash-basis method of accounting is familiar to most taxpayers since that is the method used by most individuals in filing their personal income taxes. With the cash-basis method, individuals report only the actual cash (or its equivalent in services or property) received and claim deductions only for those items actually paid in the tax year. Thus, an individual who receives a check on January 3, that was mailed on December 31, does not claim the proceeds from that check as December income. However, the individual writing the check can claim the deduction as a December expense. In addition, any income constructively received by the taxpayer is considered taxable income. For example, interest income from a savings account is fully taxable to the depositor when credited to the account, although the taxpayer did not actually receive the cash.

Income may be in forms other than cash. If, for example, a tax accountant gave advice to an electrician in return for wiring a boat house, the value of the wiring job would be considered taxable income.

Who may use the cash method? The present tax law states that for most businesses, income shall *not* be computed under the cash-receipts-and-disbursements method of accounting. The exceptions to this rule are: (1) any farming business, (2) qualified personal service corporations, and (3) entities with average gross receipts of not more than $5 million. Thus, most startup businesses would qualify for use of the cash-basis method.

Accrual-Basis Method. Accrual-basis taxpayers report income when earned, even though not actually received, and deduct expenses when incurred, even if not actually paid. Thus, on the accrual basis, income is recognized when a service is rendered or a product is sold, even though the customer may not pay until a later date. An appliance repair firm, for example, will recognize the income from repairing a washing machine on the day the machine is repaired and returned to the owner, even though the customer may not pay for the repairs until the end of the following month. Similarly, expenses are recognized when incurred, although the bill may not be paid until the end of the next quarter.

Cash Versus Accrual. Which method is best for startup businesses—the cash or the accrual method? Generally, the best method is the one that the owner understands and that the IRS will allow. For most startup businesses, the cash method may be the best since it is the method that owners have used for their personal tax records for years. In addition, the cash method does allow the accumulation of substantial assets on which no income tax has been paid. For example, a service-oriented business may have $150,000 of accounts receivable on its books, which, according to the accrual method, would have to be recognized as income. According to the cash method, however, the income would not be recognized until received, allowing the deferment of taxes.

On the other hand, if the firm is using the accrual method for its financial-management accounting, then, for the sake of record keeping, the firm may wish to use the accrual method for tax purposes also. Basically, taxpayers may adopt either the cash or the accrual method for the first tax return of a new small business. Once that election has been made, the taxpayer may not change without obtaining the permission of the IRS. Startup entrepreneurs must realize that after the firm's earnings grow beyond $5 million, or if inventories are material in determining income, then the IRS will require the firm to adopt the accrual method.

Long-Term Contract Methods

The cash and accrual methods are satisfactory for most types of businesses, but what if the startup business is a building contracting firm: If a building is 60 percent completed at the end of the year, what does the contractor claim as income and expenses? Both the cash or accrual methods may impose serious practical problems. Costs are incurred as the work on the building progresses, but these costs really are just increases in work-in-process inventory. At the same time, the contractor may be billing, and being paid, as work on the building progresses. These billings, however, are not "sales" in the normal accounting sense of the word, since the costs incurred are not a specific determination of the amount of the billing.

The tax law provides two methods for determining income and expenses for long-term contracts. The first method is known as the percentage-of-completion method. With this approach, the percentage of the total contract completed is estimated. Revenue is calculated as a percentage of the contract price of the completed building. For example, if a building with a contract price of $200,000 is 60 percent completed at the end of the tax year, then the revenue would be $120,000. The costs are calculated from actual expenditures. Profit is the difference between the revenues and expenses.

The second method allows the contractor to wait until the project is finished. Profits (or losses) are the difference between the contract price and the expenses incurred. No interim profit and loss is estimated.

Installment Sales

There is another problem for the business that sells major appliances, furniture, automobiles or trucks, or other retailers who sell on the installment plan. When is the sale of a new car recorded if it is purchased in one year but paid for over a three-year period? Once again, the five thousand plus pages of the United States tax code come to the rescue. A business that normally sells merchandise on an installment basis is known as a dealer. Dealers may elect to recognize gross profit on a sale or as payments are received from the customer. For example, if the dealer normally operates with a gross profit margin of 40 percent, then 40 percent of all collections from the customer are recognized as gross income. Thus, the recognition of income is delayed until collected and not when sold. For those businesses that qualify, the installment method of reporting offers a legal way to defer taxes.

Computing the Cost of Goods Sold

The cost of goods sold (CGS) is an essential element in computing gross income for manufacturing and merchandising businesses, and all startup entrepreneurs should have a basic idea of how CGS is calculated. To illustrate the computation, assume that a retail firm has sales of $200,000. A shortened version of the income statement may be as follows:

Net sales	$200,000
Cost of goods sold	140,000
Gross profit	$60,000
Selling & admin. expenses	25,000
Profit before taxes	$35,000
Taxes @ 15 percent	5,250
Net profit	$29,750

In this abbreviated example, the cost of goods sold easily has a greater impact on profit than any other figure. But how is the CGS calculated? The CGS is computed by adding to the inventory at the beginning of the year the cost of merchandise and materials bought or produced during the year as well as all other costs related to obtaining and producing the merchandise. From this total, the inventory at the close of the taxable year is subtracted. The difference is the cost of goods sold. This relationship may be expressed as follows:

Beginning inventory + Purchases − Ending inventory = Cost of goods sold

For the sole proprietor, the computation is made in Part III of Schedule C (see Figure 17.1). Included in the cost of goods sold for a manufacturer are the costs of direct and indirect labor, materials, and supplies consumed. For both manufacturing and merchandising concerns, costs of goods sold include freight-in and a proportion of overhead expenses. Trade discounts should be subtracted from the purchase price of materials and supplies, but cash discounts may be shown either as a reduction of the purchase price or as other income. Most professional and service firms do not have to take inventories and, therefore, are not concerned about the cost of goods sold.

Accounting for Inventories

In computing the cost of goods sold, the ending inventory was subtracted from the beginning inventory, a simple enough computation. But where did the firm obtain the values used for the two inventory figures? Unfortunately, valuing inventories is not always so simple.

Inventories may be valued either by the first-in, first-out (FIFO) method or by the last-in, first-out (LIFO) method. (One colleague claims he uses the FISH—first-in, still-here method.) According to the FIFO method, the merchandise sold is assumed to be the oldest merchandise, whereas according to the LIFO method, the merchandise sold is assumed to be the newest merchandise. The difference between these two methods may not be trivial for tax purposes.

In times of rising costs, the use of LIFO will reduce the amount of taxes paid by

FIGURE 17.1
Schedule C

SCHEDULE C (Form 1040)
Department of the Treasury
Internal Revenue Service (0)

Profit or Loss From Business
(Sole Proprietorship)
Partnerships, Joint Ventures, Etc., Must File Form 1065.
▶ Attach to Form 1040, Form 1041, or Form 1041S. ▶ See Instructions for Schedule C (Form 1040).

OMB No. 1545-0074
1988
Attachment Sequence No. 09

Name of proprietor | Social security number (SSN)

A Principal business or profession, including product or service (see Instructions)
B Principal business code (from Part IV) ▶

C Business name and address ▶
D Employer ID number (Not SSN)

E Method(s) used to value closing inventory.
(1) ☐ Cost (2) ☐ Lower of cost or market (3) ☐ Other (attach explanation)

		Yes	No
F	Accounting method: (1) ☐ Cash (2) ☐ Accrual (3) ☐ Other (specify) ▶		
G	Was there any change in determining quantities, costs, or valuations between opening and closing inventory? (If "Yes," attach explanation.)		
H	Are you deducting expenses for business use of your home? (If "Yes," see Instructions for limitations.)		
I	Did you "materially participate" in the operation of this business during 1988? (If "No," see Instructions for limitations on losses.)		

J If this schedule includes a loss, credit, deduction, income, or other tax benefit relating to a tax shelter required to be registered, check here ▶ ☐
If you check this box, you MUST attach **Form 8271**

Part I Income

1a	Gross receipts or sales	1a	
b	Less: Returns and allowances	1b	
c	Subtract line 1b from line 1a. Enter the result here	1c	
2	Cost of goods sold and/or operations (from Part III, line 8)	2	
3	Subtract line 2 from line 1c and enter the **gross profit** here	3	
4	Other income (including windfall profit tax credit or refund received in 1988)	4	
5	Add lines 3 and 4. This is the **gross income** ▶	5	

Part II Deductions

6	Advertising	6		23	Repairs	23	
7	Bad debts from sales or services (see Instructions)	7		24	Supplies (not included in Part III)	24	
				25	Taxes	25	
8	Bank service charges	8		26	Travel, meals, and entertainment:		
9	Car and truck expenses	9		a	Travel	26a	
10	Commissions	10		b	Meals and entertainment		
11	Depletion	11		c	Enter 20% of line 26b subject to limitations (see Instructions)		
12	Depreciation and section 179 deduction from Form 4562 (not included in Part III)	12					
13	Dues and publications	13		d	Subtract line 26c from 26b	26d	
14	Employee benefit programs	14		27	Utilities and telephone	27	
15	Freight (not included in Part III)	15		28a	Wages		
16	Insurance	16		b	Jobs credit		
17	Interest:			c	Subtract line 28b from 28a	28c	
a	Mortgage (paid to banks, etc.)	17a		29	Other expenses (list type and amount):		
b	Other	17b					
18	Laundry and cleaning	18					
19	Legal and professional services	19					
20	Office expense	20					
21	Pension and profit-sharing plans	21					
22	Rent on business property	22				29	

30	Add amounts in columns for lines 6 through 29. These are the **total deductions** ▶	30	
31	**Net profit or (loss).** Subtract line 30 from line 5. If a profit, enter here and on Form 1040, line 12, and on Schedule SE, line 2. If a loss, you MUST go on to line 32. (Fiduciaries, see Instructions.)	31	

32 If you have a loss, you MUST check the box that describes your investment in this activity (see Instructions)
32a ☐ All investment is at risk.
32b ☐ Some investment is not at risk.

If you checked 32a, enter the loss on Form 1040, line 12, and Schedule SE, line 2. If you checked 32b, you MUST attach **Form 6198.**

For Paperwork Reduction Act Notice, see Form 1040 Instructions. **Schedule C (Form 1040) 1988**

FIGURE 17.1
(Continued)

Schedule C (Form 1040) 1988 Page **2**

Part III **Cost of Goods Sold and/or Operations (See Schedule C Instructions for Part III)**

1	Inventory at beginning of year. (If different from last year's closing inventory, attach explanation.)	1	
2	Purchases less cost of items withdrawn for personal use	2	
3	Cost of labor. (Do not include salary paid to yourself.)	3	
4	Materials and supplies	4	
5	Other costs	5	
6	Add lines 1 through 5	6	
7	Less: Inventory at end of year	7	
8	**Cost of goods sold and/or operations.** Subtract line 7 from line 6. Enter the result here and in Part I, line 2.	8	

Part IV **Codes for Principal Business or Professional Activity**

Locate the major business category that best describes your activity (for example, Retail Trade, Services, etc.). Within the major category, select the activity code that identifies (or most closely identifies) the business or profession that is the principal source of your sales or receipts. **Enter this 4-digit code on line B on page 1 of Schedule C.** (**Note:** *If your principal source of income is from farming activities, you should file* **Schedule F** *(Form 1040), Farm Income and Expenses.*)

Construction

Code

0018 Operative builders (building for own account)

General contractors

0034 Residential building
0059 Nonresidential building
0075 Highway and street construction
3889 Other heavy construction (pipe laying, bridge construction, etc.)

Building trade contractors, including repairs

0232 Plumbing, heating, air conditioning
0257 Painting and paper hanging
0273 Electrical work
0299 Masonry, dry wall, stone, tile
0414 Carpentering and flooring
0430 Roofing, siding, and sheet metal
0455 Concrete work
0471 Water well drilling
0885 Other building trade contractors (excavation, glazing, etc.)

Manufacturing, Including Printing and Publishing

0612 Bakeries selling at retail
0638 Other food products and beverages
0653 Textile mill products
0679 Apparel and other textile products
0695 Leather, footware, handbags, etc.
0810 Furniture and fixtures
0836 Lumber and other wood products
0851 Printing and publishing
0877 Paper and allied products
0893 Chemicals and allied products
1016 Rubber and plastics products
1032 Stone, clay, and glass products
1057 Primary metal industries
1073 Fabricated metal products
1099 Machinery and machine shops
1115 Electric and electronic equipment
1313 Transportation equipment
1339 Instruments and related products
1883 Other manufacturing industries

Mining and Mineral Extraction

1511 Metal mining
1537 Coal mining
1552 Oil and gas
1719 Quarrying and nonmetallic mining

Agricultural Services, Forestry, and Fishing

1917 Soil preparation services
1933 Crop services
1958 Veterinary services, including pets
1974 Livestock breeding
1990 Other animal services
2113 Farm labor and management services
2212 Horticulture and landscaping
2238 Forestry, except logging
0836 Logging
2279 Fishing, hunting, and trapping

Wholesale Trade—Selling Goods to Other Businesses, Government, or Institutions, Etc.

Durable goods, including machinery, equipment, wood, metals, etc.

2618 Selling for your own account

Code

2634 Agent or broker for other firms—more than 50% of gross sales on commission

Nondurable goods, including food, fiber, chemicals, etc.

2659 Selling for your own account
2675 Agent or broker for other firms—more than 50% of gross sales on commission

Retail Trade—Selling Goods to Individuals and Households

3012 Selling door-to-door, by telephone or party plan, or from mobile unit
3038 Catalog or mail order
3053 Vending machine selling

Selling From Store, Showroom, or Other Fixed Location

Food, beverages, and drugs

3079 Eating places (meals or snacks)
3095 Drinking places (alcoholic beverages)
3210 Grocery stores (general line)
0612 Bakeries selling at retail
3236 Other food stores (meat, produce, candy, etc.)
3251 Liquor stores
3277 Drug stores

Automotive and service stations

3319 New car dealers (franchised)
3335 Used car dealers
3517 Other automotive dealers (motorcycles, recreational vehicles, etc.)
3533 Tires, accessories, and parts
3558 Gasoline service stations

General merchandise, apparel, and furniture

3715 Variety stores
3731 Other general merchandise stores
3756 Shoe stores
3772 Men's and boys' clothing stores
3913 Women's ready-to-wear stores
3921 Women's accessory and specialty stores and furriers
3939 Family clothing stores
3954 Other apparel and accessory stores
3970 Furniture stores
3996 TV, audio, and electronics
3988 Computer and software stores
4119 Household appliance stores
4317 Other home furnishing stores (china, floor coverings, drapes, etc.)
4333 Music and record stores

Building, hardware, and garden supply

4416 Building materials dealers
4432 Paint, glass, and wallpaper stores
4457 Hardware stores
4473 Nurseries and garden supply stores

Other retail stores

4614 Used merchandise and antique stores (except used motor vehicle parts)
4630 Gift, novelty, and souvenir shops
4655 Florists
4671 Jewelry stores

Code

4697 Sporting goods and bicycle shops
4812 Boat dealers
4838 Hobby, toy, and game shops
4853 Camera and photo supply stores
4879 Optical goods stores
4895 Luggage and leather goods stores
5017 Book stores, excluding newsstands
5033 Stationery stores
5058 Fabric and needlework stores
5074 Mobile home dealers
5090 Fuel dealers (except gasoline)
5884 Other retail stores

Real Estate, Insurance, Finance, and Related Services

5512 Real estate agents and managers
5538 Operators and lessors of buildings (except developers)
5553 Operators and lessors of other real property (except developers)
5710 Subdividers and developers, except cemeteries
5736 Insurance agents and services
5751 Security and commodity brokers, dealers, and investment services
5777 Other real estate, insurance, and financial activities

Transportation, Communications, Public Utilities, and Related Services

6114 Taxicabs
6312 Bus and limousine transportation
6338 Trucking (except trash collection)
6510 Trash collection without own dump
6536 Public warehousing
6551 Water transportation
6619 Air transportation
6635 Travel agents and tour operators
6650 Other transportation and related services
6676 Communication services
6692 Utilities, including dumps, snowplowing, road cleaning, etc.

Services (Providing Personal, Professional, and Business Services)

Hotels and other lodging places

7096 Hotels, motels, and tourist homes
7211 Rooming and boarding houses
7237 Camps and camping parks

Laundry and cleaning services

7419 Coin-operated laundries and dry cleaning
7435 Other laundry, dry cleaning, and garment services
7450 Carpet and upholstery cleaning
7476 Janitorial and related services (building, house, and window cleaning)

Business and/or personal services

7617 Legal services (or lawyer)
7633 Income tax preparation
7658 Accounting and bookkeeping
7674 Engineering, surveying, and architectural

Code

7690 Management, consulting, and public relations
7716 Advertising, except direct mail
7732 Employment agencies and personnel supply
7757 Computer and data processing, including repair and leasing
7773 Equipment rental and leasing (except computer or automotive)
7914 Investigative and protective services
7880 Other business services

Personal services

8110 Beauty shops (or beautician)
8318 Barber shop (or barber)
8334 Photographic portrait studios
8516 Shoe repair and shine services
8532 Funeral services and crematories
8714 Child day care
8730 Teaching or tutoring
8755 Counseling (except health practitioners)
8771 Ministers and chaplains
6882 Other personal services

Automotive services

8813 Automotive rental or leasing, without driver
8839 Parking, except valet
8854 General automotive repairs
8870 Specialized automotive repairs (brake, body repairs, paint, etc.)
8896 Other automotive services (wash, towing, etc.)

Miscellaneous repair, except computers

9019 TV and audio equipment repair
9035 Other electrical equipment repair
9050 Reupholstery and furniture repair
2881 Other equipment repair

Medical and health services

9217 Offices and clinics of medical doctors (MDs)
9233 Offices and clinics of dentists
9258 Osteopathic physicians and surgeons
9274 Chiropractors
9290 Optometrists
9415 Registered and practical nurses
9431 Other licensed health practitioners
9456 Dental laboratories
9472 Nursing and personal care facilities
9886 Other health services

Amusement and recreational services

8557 Physical fitness facilities
9613 Videotape rental stores
9639 Motion picture theaters
9654 Other motion picture and TV film and tape activities
9670 Bowling alleys
9696 Professional sports and racing, including promoters and managers
9811 Theatrical performers, musicians, agents, producers, and related services
9837 Other amusement and recreational services

8888 Unable to classify

☆ U.S.G.P.O.: 1988- 205-113

increasing the value of the cost of goods sold. Similarly, in times of falling prices (e.g., when oil prices dropped drastically in the late 1970s), FIFO will reduce taxes by increasing the value of the cost of goods sold. Businesses cannot, however, switch back and forth between these two methods, depending on what is happening to prevailing prices.

To illustrate FIFO and LIFO inventories, consider the following example. Assume that a firm purchases emergency generators for resale. The firm begins the year with fifty generators that cost $500 each. During the year, the cost of copper wiring rises dramatically, and twenty generators purchased in April cost $550 each, twenty purchased in August cost $600 each, and twenty purchased in November cost $625 each, for total purchases of $35,500. If the firm sold sixty generators during the year for $48,000, what is the gross profit? The answer can vary dramatically, depending on the inventory method employed by the firm.

	FIFO		*LIFO*	
Sales		$48,000		$48,000
Less:				
Opening inventory	$25,000		$25,000	
Purchased	35,500		35,500	
	$60,500		$60,500	
Less:				
Closing inventory*	30,500		25,000	
Cost of goods sold		30,000		35,500
Gross Profit		$18,000		$12,500

*For FIFO, the closing inventory of fifty units is the value of the last fifty units purchased, and for LIFO, it is the value of the original fifty units.

The foregoing example clearly illustrates how the LIFO method will reduce the tax liability in a period of rising prices. But there are problems with using LIFO for valuing inventory. Note that profits are also reduced considerably. The reduction in reported profits can be a negative factor for those firms which pay managers a salary based on reported profits. In addition, if LIFO is used over a period of several years of rising costs, the book value of inventory will be a fraction of actual (present) value.

Before adopting the LIFO inventory method, firms must obtain approval from the IRS (using Form 970). Once adopted, the firm must continue using LIFO unless the IRS permits or requires a change. In addition, if LIFO is adopted for tax purposes, then LIFO must also be used for other financial reports issued by the firm.

Depreciation

New businesses are permitted to amortize the cost of startup over a sixty-month period, beginning with the month in which the business begins. Startup expenses include any amount paid or incurred in connection with investigating the creation or acquisition of an active business. Startup expenses also include the costs incurred prior to actual startup (e.g., hiring, training, labor, utilities, etc.).

Startup firms may own long-term assets, such as a building, machinery, or an automobile. How do the firms account for the cost and expense of these assets? The tax cost allows firms to charge a portion of the cost of long-term tangible property as an expense over a stated period of time, depending on its property class. The classes of property are three-, five-, seven-, ten-, fifteen-, and twenty-year property. In addition, most real property is classified as residential rental (depreciated over 27.5 years) or nonresidential real property (depreciated over 31.5 years).

Firms may, however, elect to use extended recovery periods that are specified by the tax code. For those electing the modified accelerated-cost-recovery system (MACRS), the tax code specifies the amount of the cost of the assets that may be charged to expenses each year. For example, the applicable percentage for a five-year class of property is 20 percent the first year, 32 percent the second year, 39 percent the third year, 12 percent the fourth and fifth years, and 5 percent the sixth year. Thus, if a piece of machinery cost $10,000 installed, the firm could charge $2,000 to depreciation expenses the first year, $3,200 the second year, $3,900 the third year, and so on.

Why should startup firms even be interested in MACRS? Remember, from Chapter 15, that cash flow is more important to the startup business than profits. By charging a higher amount for depreciation than the ordinary straight-line method, firms are claiming as expenses something for which no cash was needed. Thus, the firm's cash flow is increased by the amount of the depreciation, and MACRS yields more cash flow than the straight-line depreciation method—and cash is what most startup firms need.

Basic Rules for Business Deductions

There are specific provisions for business deductions in the tax code, which allows "as a deduction all the ordinary and necessary expenses paid or incurred during the taxable year in carrying on any trade or business." An ordinary expense is one that could be expected in other similar businesses. Expenses are "necessary" in the sense that the expense should contribute to the operation of the business or to the production of income. For the sole proprietorship, all business deductions are entered on Schedule C (Form 1040), Part II.

Some of the ordinary and necessary expenses that are allowed are listed on lines 6–30 of Schedule C. Most are self-explanatory, but a few require additional information. For example, car and truck expenses (line 9) can be the actual cost of operating a car or truck or a fixed cost per mile. The fixed rate is computed at 22.5¢ per mile for the first 15,000 miles and 11¢ per mile for each mile beyond 15,000 miles. The rate, however, is limited to 11¢ per mile if the vehicle has been fully depreciated. (A vehicle is considered to have a useful life of 60,000 miles.)

Employee benefit programs (line 14) include any contributions made by the business on behalf of employees to an employee benefit plan, such as life or health insurance. Payments to a pension or profit-sharing plan are not included here because those expenses are shown on line 21.

Freight (line 15) includes freight costs that are not included in computing the cost of goods sold. Insurance (line 16) includes the cost of premiums paid for fire, liability, crime, and other property insurance, but not that of insurance for the vehicles. (Insurance on the cars and trucks is covered under car and truck expenses mentioned earlier.)

Businesses cannot deduct the costs of "entertainment facilities." Thus, deductions for yachts, hunting clubs, fishing camps, swimming pools, and tennis courts are not allowed under the present tax code. Deductions for dues and fees to social, athletic, or sporting clubs or organizations are also not allowed. However, dues paid to civic and professional organizations are allowed as are dues paid to country clubs, if the facility is used primarily for business.

TAX ACCOUNTING FOR THE SOLE PROPRIETORSHIP

Most startup businesses are sole proprietorships: An individual who decides to go into business starts a business in which he or she is the sole owner. From a tax standpoint, all the profit from a sole proprietorship is taxable. Since profits are taxable, this section on sole proprietorships and the following sections on partnerships, S corporations, and corporations, examines only the tax aspect of the different forms of business. The interested reader may wish to refer to Chapter 6 for a full description and discussion of the different forms of businesses.

Although the individual owner assumes all tax liability for the sole proprietorship's profits, there is a big difference between the taxes paid by an individual and those paid by the sole owner of a business. Two of the differences are: (1) the sole proprietor has the ability to charge some expenses to the business that the individual taxpayer could not charge, and (2) the sole proprietor can put aside some of the profits in tax-deferred retirement plans. On the negative side, the sole proprietor also tends to have more problems with the IRS than the individual taxpayer.

Sole-proprietor taxpayers have a greater chance of being audited by the IRS because of the greater opportunity that the owner has either to reduce the amount of revenues that the business claims or to increase the expenses claimed. A few people go into business because they know there exists the opportunity to take cash from the business without claiming that cash as revenue. Some also claim expenses that never occurred, leaving the "cost" of the expenses as extra income for the owner. The IRS is aware of these and many other schemes and, therefore, tends to audit sole proprietors closely. Audits are costly and time consuming, and if the IRS finds any irregularities, large fines and/or imprisonment may result.

Rather than dwell on the negative aspects of potential problems with the IRS, we will consider the positive steps the sole proprietor should take. Problems with the IRS may be reduced to a minimum by taking the following steps: (1) always filing on time, (2) filing a complete, neat form, (3) complying with the tax code, and (4) hiring someone knowledgeable to compute the taxes. These steps are not a simple endorsement of honest behavior. They propose much more: Be honest, knowledgeable, accurate, and on time.

On the other hand, four practices that increase the probability of constant IRS attention are: (1) comingling personal and business funds, (2) having the firm pay personal bills, (3) using company assets for personal gain, and (4) failing to report outside income. All of these tend to make the IRS very suspicious. When the IRS becomes suspicious of the accuracy of a business's tax returns, it can make life most unpleasant for the owner. The bottom line is to simply follow the four steps in the previous paragraph.

The owner of a sole proprietorship should be familiar with three main federal income tax forms: (1) Form 1040-ES, (2) Schedule SE, and (3) Schedule C.

Form 1040-ES

Payment of an estimated tax with Form 1040-ES is required if the startup entrepreneur expects to owe (after subtracting withholding and credits) at least $500 in taxes for the current tax year. Form 1040-ES provides payment vouchers (see Appendix A) for the quarterly payments, which are due April 15, June 15, September 15, and January 15.

Schedule SE

The computation of social security self-employment tax is filed on Schedule SE. For social security coverage, self-employed entrepreneurs pay self-employment tax in place of the social security tax that is withheld from an employee's wages. Entrepreneurs are subject to self-employment tax if they have $400 or more of net earnings from self-employment income.

Schedule C

Sole proprietorships file Schedule C to report the profit (or loss) from their business or profession. This section will include an income statement for a retail firm operated as a sole proprietorship and then use the information to compute Schedule C. For example, the following is an income statement for Who's Limited, a small retail firm owned by William Who.

William Who
Who's Limited
Summary of Income and Expense
Year Ended December 31, 198X

Gross sales		$431,860
Less:		
Sales returns & allowances	$6,430	6,430
Net sales		$425,430
Cost of goods sold:		
Inventory, Jan. 1, 198X	$16,250	
Purchases	225,600	
Cost of goods available	241,850	
Inventory, Dec. 31, 198X	18,650	223,200
Gross margin		$202,230

Operating expenses:		
Sales salaries	$42,300	
Office salaries	14,500	
Advertising	6,450	
Rent	12,000	
Insurance	8,100	
Professional services	4,400	
Taxes	800	
Office expenses	3,300	
Utilities	7,200	
Interest	11,450	
Miscellaneous	2,500	$113,000
Net profit		$ 89,230

From the income statement, the business taxpayer can obtain most of the information that is needed to complete Schedule C. The income statement for Who's Limited was used to complete the version of Schedule C shown in Figure 17.2. In addition to the income statement, there are several other items that require explanation.

Inventory Valuation. On line E, the taxpayer is asked how the inventory of the firm is valued. Inventory may be valued either at cost or at the lower of cost or market value. The tax concept of market value is the current bid price prevailing at the date the inventory is taken. Some taxpayers are tempted to arbitrarily lower the value of their inventory. A quick glance at Part III of Schedule C shows why. If the ending inventory is reduced, the cost of goods sold is increased, lowering the gross income and, therefore, income taxes. For this reason, an important area of IRS audit interest is the inventory-valuation method.

Home Office. On line H, the taxpayer is asked about deducting expenses for a home office. Although almost all taxpayers do some work at home and although they may use a specific place at home they call an office, the IRS may not allow a deduction for home-office expenses. To qualify as a deduction, the home office must meet the following requirements:

1. Must be a specific part of the residence.
2. Must be used exclusively for business purposes.
3. Must be used on a regular basis.
4. Must be a principal place of business, or a place where the taxpayer meets with customers, clients, or patients.

A deduction for a home office may result in substantial tax savings, but the deduction will also result in an increase in the probability of an IRS audit. In the final analysis, the deduction for a home office is worth the tax savings and should be claimed by the taxpayer if the four requirements are clearly met.

FIGURE 17.2
Schedule C

SCHEDULE C (Form 1040) Department of the Treasury Internal Revenue Service (0)	**Profit or (Loss) From Business or Profession** (Sole Proprietorship) Partnerships, Joint Ventures, etc., Must File Form 1065. ▶ Attach to Form 1040, Form 1041, or Form 1041S. ▶ See Instructions for Schedule C (Form 1040).	OMB No. 1545-0074 **1987** Attachment Sequence No. 09

Name of proprietor: William C. Who	Social security number (SSN): 234 56 7890
A Principal business or profession, including product or service (see Instructions): Retail sales	B Principal business code (from Part IV) ▶ 3913
C Business name and address ▶ Who's Limited 100 Not Main St. Centerville, FL	D Employer ID number (Not SSN): 887766543

E Method(s) used to value closing inventory:
(1) ☒ Cost (2) ☐ Lower of cost or market (3) ☐ Other (attach explanation)

		Yes	No
F	Accounting method: (1) ☐ Cash (2) ☒ Accrual (3) ☐ Other (specify) ▶		
G	Was there any change in determining quantities, costs, or valuations between opening and closing inventory? (If "Yes," attach explanation.)		X
H	Are you deducting expenses for an office in your home?		X
I	Did you file **Form 941** for this business for any quarter in 1987?		X
J	Did you "materially participate" in the operation of this business during 1987? (If "No," see Instructions for limitations on losses.)	X	
K	Was this business in operation at the end of 1987?	X	
L	How many months was this business in operation during 1987? ▶	12	
M	If this schedule includes a loss, credit, deduction, income, or other tax benefit relating to a tax shelter required to be registered, check here ▶ ☐ If you check this box, you **MUST** attach **Form 8271**.		

Part I Income

1a	Gross receipts or sales	1a	431,860
b	Less: Returns and allowances	1b	6,430
c	Subtract line 1b from line 1a and enter the balance here	1c	425,430
2	Cost of goods sold and/or operations (from Part III, line 8)	2	223,200
3	Subtract line 2 from line 1c and enter the **gross profit** here	3	202,230
4	Other income (including windfall profit tax credit or refund received in 1987)	4	
5	Add lines 3 and 4. This is the **gross income** ▶	5	202,230

Part II Deductions

6	Advertising	6,450	23	Repairs	
7	Bad debts from sales or services (see Instructions.)		24	Supplies (not included in Part III)	
8	Bank service charges		25	Taxes	800
9	Car and truck expenses		26	Travel, meals, and entertainment:	
10	Commissions		a	Travel	
11	Depletion		b	Total meals and entertainment	
12	Depreciation and section 179 deduction from Form 4562 (not included in Part III)		c	Enter 20% of line 26b subject to limitations (see Instructions)	
13	Dues and publications		d	Subtract line 26c from 26b	
14	Employee benefit programs		27	Utilities and telephone	7,200
15	Freight (not included in Part III)		28a	Wages 56800	
16	Insurance	8,100	b	Jobs credit	
17	Interest:		c	Subtract line 28b from 28a	56,800
a	Mortgage (paid to financial institutions)		29	Other expenses (list type and amount):	
b	Other	11,450		Misc.	
18	Laundry and cleaning				
19	Legal and professional services	4,400			
20	Office expense	3,300			
21	Pension and profit-sharing plans				
22	Rent on business property	12,000			2,500

30	Add amounts in columns for lines 6 through 29. These are the **total deductions** ▶	30	113,000
31	**Net profit or (loss).** Subtract line 30 from line 5. If a profit, enter here and on Form 1040, line 13, and on Schedule SE, line 2 (or line 5 of Form 1041 or Form 1041S). If a loss, you **MUST** go on to line 32	31	
32	If you have a loss, you **MUST** answer this question: "Do you have amounts for which you are not at risk in this business?" (See Instructions.) ☐ Yes ☐ No If "Yes," you **MUST** attach **Form 6198**. If "No," enter the loss on Form 1040, line 13, and on Schedule SE, line 2 (or line 5 of Form 1041 or Form 1041S).		

For Paperwork Reduction Act Notice, see Form 1040 Instructions. **Schedule C (Form 1040) 1987**

FIGURE 17.2
(Continued)

Schedule C (Form 1040) 1987 Page **2**

Part III **Cost of Goods Sold and/or Operations (See Schedule C Instructions for Part III)**

1	Inventory at beginning of year (If different from last year's closing inventory, attach explanation.)	1	16,250
2	Purchases less cost of items withdrawn for personal use	2	225,600
3	Cost of labor. (Do not include salary paid to yourself.)	3	
4	Materials and supplies	4	
5	Other costs	5	
6	Add lines 1 through 5	6	241,850
7	Less: Inventory at end of year	7	18,650
8	**Cost of goods sold and/or operations.** Subtract line 7 from line 6. Enter here and in Part I, line 2	8	223,200

Part IV **Codes for Principal Business or Professional Activity**

Locate the major business category that best describes your activity (for example, Retail Trade, Services, etc.). Within the major category, select the activity code that identifies (or most closely identifies) the business or profession that is the principal source of your sales or receipts. **Enter this 4-digit code on line B on page 1 of Schedule C.** (**Note:** *If your principal source of income is from farming activities, you should file* ***Schedule F*** *(Form 1040), Farm Income and Expenses.)*

Construction

Code

0018 Operative builders (building for own account)

General contractors

0034 Residential building
0059 Nonresidential building
0075 Highway and street construction
3889 Other heavy construction (pipe laying, bridge construction, etc.)

Building trade contractors, including repairs

0232 Plumbing, heating, air conditioning
0257 Painting and paper hanging
0273 Electrical work
0299 Masonry, dry wall, stone, tile
0414 Carpentering and flooring
0430 Roofing, siding, and sheet metal
0455 Concrete work
0471 Water well drilling
0885 Other building trade contractors (excavation, glazing, etc.)

Manufacturing, Including Printing and Publishing

0612 Bakeries selling at retail
0638 Other food products and beverages
0653 Textile mill products
0679 Apparel and other textile products
0695 Leather, footware, handbags, etc.
0810 Furniture and fixtures
0836 Lumber and other wood products
0851 Printing and publishing
0877 Paper and allied products
0893 Chemicals and allied products
1016 Rubber and plastics products
1032 Stone, clay, and glass products
1057 Primary metal industries
1073 Fabricated metal products
1099 Machinery and machine shops
1115 Electric and electronic equipment
1313 Transportation equipment
1339 Instruments and related products
1883 Other manufacturing industries

Mining and Mineral Extraction

1511 Metal mining
1537 Coal mining
1552 Oil and gas
1719 Quarrying and nonmetallic mining

Agricultural Services, Forestry, and Fishing

1917 Soil preparation services
1933 Crop services
1958 Veterinary services, including pets
1974 Livestock breeding
1990 Other animal services
2113 Farm labor and management services
2212 Horticulture and landscaping
2238 Forestry, except logging
0836 Logging
2279 Fishing, hunting, and trapping

Wholesale Trade—Selling Goods to Other Businesses, Government, or Institutions, etc.

Durable goods, including machinery, equipment, wood, metals, etc.

2618 Selling for your own account
2634 Agent or broker for other firms—more than 50% of gross sales on commission

Nondurable goods, including food, fiber, chemicals, etc.

2659 Selling for your own account
2675 Agent or broker for other firms—more than 50% of gross sales on commission

Retail Trade—Selling Goods to Individuals and Households

3012 Selling door-to-door, by telephone or party plan, or from mobile unit
3038 Catalog or mail order
3053 Vending machine selling

Selling From Store, Showroom, or Other Fixed Location

Food, beverages, and drugs

3079 Eating places (meals or snacks)
3095 Drinking places (alcoholic beverages)
3210 Grocery stores (general line)
0612 Bakeries selling at retail
3236 Other food stores (meat, produce, candy, etc.)
3251 Liquor stores
3277 Drug stores

Automotive and service stations

3319 New car dealers (franchised)
3335 Used car dealers
3517 Other automotive dealers (motorcycles, recreational vehicles, etc.)
3533 Tires, accessories, and parts
3558 Gasoline service stations

General merchandise, apparel, and furniture

3715 Variety stores
3731 Other general merchandise stores
3756 Shoe stores
3772 Men's and boys' clothing stores
3913 Women's ready-to-wear stores
3921 Women's accessory and specialty stores and furriers
3939 Family clothing stores
3954 Other apparel and accessory stores
3970 Furniture stores
3996 TV, audio, and electronics
3988 Computer and software stores
4119 Household appliance stores
4317 Other home furnishing stores (china, floor coverings, drapes, etc.)
4333 Music and record stores

Building, hardware, and garden supply

4416 Building materials dealers
4432 Paint, glass, and wallpaper stores
4457 Hardware stores
4473 Nurseries and garden supply stores

Other retail stores

4614 Used merchandise and antique stores (except used motor vehicle parts)
4630 Gift, novelty, and souvenir shops
4655 Florists
4671 Jewelry stores
4697 Sporting goods and bicycle shops
4812 Boat dealers
4838 Hobby, toy, and game shops
4853 Camera and photo supply stores
4879 Optical goods stores
4895 Luggage and leather goods stores
5017 Book stores, excluding newsstands
5033 Stationery stores
5058 Fabric and needlework stores
5074 Mobile home dealers
5090 Fuel dealers (except gasoline)
5884 Other retail stores

Real Estate, Insurance, Finance, and Related Services

5512 Real estate agents and managers
5538 Operators and lessors of buildings (except developers)
5553 Operators and lessors of other real property (except developers)
5710 Subdividers and developers, except cemeteries
5736 Insurance agents and services
5751 Security and commodity brokers, dealers, and investment services
5777 Other real estate, insurance, and financial activities

Transportation, Communications, Public Utilities, and Related Services

6114 Taxicabs
6312 Bus and limousine transportation
6338 Trucking (except trash collection)
6510 Trash collection without own dump
6536 Public warehousing
6551 Water transportation
6619 Air transportation
6635 Travel agents and tour operators
6650 Other transportation and related services
6676 Communication services
6692 Utilities, including dumps, snowplowing, road cleaning, etc.

Services (Providing Personal, Professional, and Business Services)

Hotels and other lodging places

7096 Hotels, motels, and tourist homes
7211 Rooming and boarding houses
7237 Camps and camping parks

Laundry and cleaning services

7419 Coin-operated laundries and dry cleaning
7435 Other laundry, dry cleaning, and garment services
7450 Carpet and upholstery cleaning
7476 Janitorial and related services (building, house, and window cleaning)

Business and/or personal services

7617 Legal services (or lawyer)
7633 Income tax preparation
7658 Accounting and bookkeeping
7674 Engineering, surveying, and architectural
7690 Management, consulting, and public relations
7716 Advertising, except direct mail
7732 Employment agencies and personnel supply
7757 Computer and data processing, including repair and leasing
7773 Equipment rental and leasing (except computer or automotive)
7914 Investigative and protective services
7880 Other business services

Personal services

8110 Beauty shops (or beautician)
8318 Barber shop (or barber)
8334 Photographic portrait studios
8516 Shoe repair and shine services
8532 Funeral services and crematories
8714 Child day care
8730 Teaching or tutoring
8755 Counseling (except health practitioners)
8771 Ministers and chaplains
6882 Other personal services

Automotive services

8813 Automotive rental or leasing, without driver
8839 Parking, except valet
8854 General automotive repairs
8870 Specialized automotive repairs (brake, body repairs, paint, etc.)
8896 Other automotive services (wash, towing, etc.)

Miscellaneous repair, except computers

9019 TV and audio equipment repair
9035 Other electrical equipment repair
9050 Reupholstery and furniture repair
2881 Other equipment repair

Medical and health services

9217 Offices and clinics of medical doctors (MD's)
9233 Offices and clinics of dentists
9258 Osteopathic physicians and surgeons
9274 Chiropractors
9290 Optometrists
9415 Registered and practical nurses
9431 Other licensed health practitioners
9456 Dental laboratories
9472 Nursing and personal care facilities
9886 Other health services

Amusement and recreational services

8557 Physical fitness facilities
9613 Videotape rental stores
9639 Motion picture theaters
9654 Other motion picture and TV film and tape activities
9670 Bowling alleys
9696 Professional sports and racing, including promoters and managers
9811 Theatrical performers, musicians, agents, producers, and related services
9837 Other amusement and recreational services

8888 Unable to classify

☆ U.S.G.P.O. 1987 - 183-096

Bad Debts. Bad debts are a part of almost any business, except a cash-only business. If the business is using the accrual method of accounting, all sales are shown as gross receipts or sales. If the customer does not pay for the goods or services he or she has purchased, the business has incurred a bad debt. Bad debts are treated as a deduction from sales in one of two methods.

The first method is called the *direct write-off method.* According to the direct write-off method, the business waits until a specific customer fails to pay and then claims the outstanding amount as an expense. According to the second method, called the *reserve method,* the business estimates the amount of all credit sales that will be uncollectible. The estimate for the startup firm is based on the experience of similar firms in similar industries and should be adjusted as the firm gains experience with its own customers.

Employee Benefit Programs. Employee benefit programs afford both the employer and the employee tax advantages. Through employee benefit programs, the employer is providing a tax-deductible incentive to help retain the employee, and the employee is receiving a tax-free benefit. To be eligible for the tax deduction, the employee-benefit plans for group-term life insurance, accident, health benefit, and other fringe benefit plans must meet three strict nondiscrimination (discrimination regarding the treatment of more highly paid owner/managers versus that of other employees) rules. These requirements are as follows:

1. Nonhighly compensated employees must constitute at least 50 percent of the group of employees eligible to participate in the same plan with highly compensated employees or in a comparable plan. Alternatively, the percentage of highly compensated employees who are eligible to participate in the plan must not be greater than the percentage of nonhighly compensated employees who are eligible.

2. At least 90 percent of the employer's nonhighly compensated employees must be eligible for a benefit that is at least 50 percent as valuable as the benefit available to the highly compensated employees.

3. A plan may not contain any provision relating to eligibility to participate that by its terms, or otherwise, discriminates in favor of highly compensated employees.

These rules are rigorous and are intended to ensure the equitability of employee benefit plans. If a benefit discriminates in favor of highly compensated employees, then the allowable tax deductions of the benefit will be reduced.

Pension Plans. Most employers generally consider pension and profit-sharing plans as separate items; however, according to Schedule C, they constitute one deduction (on line 21). In this section, the two will be considered separately.

The tax laws do not require any employer to have any pension plan other than social security. If the employer does have a pension plan, the plan may be either "qualified" or "unqualified." The qualified pension plan affords the employer tax deductions, whereas the unqualified plan does not. To qualify, a plan must not discriminate in favor of employees who are officers, shareholders, or highly paid. In addition, at least 70 percent of the rank and file must be covered, and the plan must provide for accrued benefits to vest fully in five years or gradually over seven years.

There are three advantages to having a qualified plan. First, the employer's contributions to the plan may be deducted as an expense. Second, the earnings from the funds in the plan are not subject to current taxes. Third, employees do not have any recognized (taxable) income until distributions from the plan are made.

In addition, a plan may be either "contributory" or "noncontributory." In a contributory plan, both the employer and the employee put funds into the plan. Typically employees contribute 7 to 10 percent of their earnings to the plan, and this amount is matched by the employer. In a noncontributory plan, the employer is the sole contributor.

A Simplified Employee Pension (SEP) is similar to the more familiar Individual Retirement Account (IRA), except SEP permits higher annual contributions.The limit on SEP is $30,000 or 15 percent of the employee's compensation, or whichever is less. For a plan to qualify as a company SEP, at least 50 percent of the employees must elect coverage, and the employer cannot employ more than twenty-five employees at any time during the year.

Keogh, or H.R. 10, plans are for the self-employed individual. The maximum amount that an individual can contribute (to a Keogh plan) and deduct (from taxable income) is the lesser of $30,000 or 25 percent of earned income. (Note: The amount to be deducted for individual IRAs and Keogh contributions is on line 26 or 27 of Form 1040. Company contributions are listed on line 21 of Schedule C.)

In addition to the aforementioned pension plans, the tax law also permits some individuals to contribute to their own retirement account through an IRA. The contribution to an IRA account is limited to $2,000 per employee, or $2,250 for a spousal IRA. Employees are eligible for IRAs if neither they, nor their spouse, belong to a company-funded retirement plan and their adjusted gross income is less than $40,000. If the employee makes between $40,000 and $50,000, the deductible portion of the $2,000 annual contribution is reduced.

Profit-Sharing Plans. Employers can contribute to profit-sharing plans for the employees of the firm. One of the advantages of profit-sharing plans is that no set annual contributions are required and no set benefits are stipulated in the plan. The employer, however, cannot deduct more than 15 percent of the aggregate compensation of the employees covered under the plan. With a profit-sharing plan, the firm can make contributions when it earns a profit, and skip them when it does not. Interestingly, the firm is allowed to make contributions in years when there is no profit. Firms may, therefore, use profit-sharing plans as an incentive and contribute a percentage of their profits, or they may contribute to the plan regardless of whether the firm was profitable or not.

TAX ACCOUNTING FOR PARTNERSHIPS

A partnership is treated as a multiple proprietorship for tax purposes. The partnership does not pay taxes, but each partner pays taxes on his or her share of the partnership's net income, whether the income is distributed by the partnership or not. Although there are some limitations, each partner may also use his or her share of any partnership loss to reduce his or her own personal taxes. For tax purposes, the partnership, therefore, is merely a conduit that passes tax information to the individual partners. The partnership does file an income statement on Form 1065 (see Appendix A), but this form is used for reporting purposes only.

The partnership must use the same year end as the partner owning the majority interest of profits and capital in the partnership. The partnership, therefore, will use the same year end as the principal partner or, otherwise, a calendar year. If the partnership does not use a calendar year, partners must be able to show the IRS why they deviate from year-end accounting.

The partners' share of the income, or deductions, from a partnership are reported on Schedule K or K-1 (see Appendix A), which is filed with Form 1065. A simple example may help explain how partnership income is distributed. Assume, for example, that a four-person partnership has ordinary income of $120,000 for the year and $12,000 in capital gains. If the four partners have equal shares, then each partner will include $30,000 as his or her share of the ordinary income plus $3,000 of the capital gain. Thus, one partner may be able to use the capital gain to offset a capital loss and another partner may not.

Social-Security Tax

Since the income from a partnership flows directly to the partners, no "salaries" are paid to them. Does this mean that the partners are able to escape social-security taxes? If this were possible, the number of partnerships would increase dramatically. Partners report their share of partnership income on their individual income-tax returns and pay the social-security tax. The self-employment tax is computed on Schedule SE (Form 1040) and entered on line 51 of the individual's Form 1040. (For an example of Schedule SE, see Appendix A.)

Partnership Basis

Partnerships should not be formed without first obtaining legal advice. One of the main reasons for obtaining legal assistance is to establish the tax basis for the partnership. The *tax basis* is the tax equivalent of cost in calculating gain or loss on disposition. (Gain is the selling price less the tax basis of the property.) Tax basis is calculated by adding the original cost of the property to any additions or improvements (not including ordinary repair and maintenance) and subtracting any depreciation taken as a deduction.

To illustrate the computation of tax basis, consider the following example. Assume that four people, Axel, Billie, Charlie, and Dot, decide to form a partnership and start a new business making and selling fried pies. Axel contributes a building with a fair market value of $100,000, but the tax basis on the building is $50,000 to the partnership. Billie contributes $50,000 cash. Charlie contributes machinery with a fair market value of $35,000 but with a tax basis of $50,000. Dot has the knowledge and experience to run the operation, and her contribution will be the time she spends setting up the equipment and training the employees. Their respective basis for their new asset, an interest in the CABD partnership, is as follows:

Axel	$50,000
Billie	$50,000
Charlie	$50,000
Dot	No basis

As a general rule, no gain or loss can result from forming a partnership. The basis before the formation of the partnership becomes the basis to the partnership. Sweat equity (Dot's work) cannot be part of the basis. Therefore, in the above example, Axel cannot recognize a $50,000 gain, and Charlie does not recognize a $15,000 loss resulting from the transfer of their assets to the partnership. Likewise, the partnership will recognize no gain or loss. The partnership's basis in the three assets will be as follows:

Cash	$50,000
Building	$50,000
Machinery	$50,000

Obviously, this can create some inequities, and the tax law recognizes this fact by requiring the partnership to make adjustments between the partners so that they obtain equitable treatment. The law is fairly complex and beyond the scope of this chapter, but in this simple example, the deductions would be allocated in such a way that Axel would bear the tax brunt of the difference between the $100,000 fair market value of his building and the $50,000 tax basis. Axel would bear the brunt because the partnership loses the depreciation deduction of the fair market value.

After initial allocation of the partnership basis, the basis can change. The basis is increased by additional cash contributions, taxable income, and capital gains; by tax-exempt income; and by the partners' assumption of liabilities. Similarly, the basis may be decreased by distributions of cash or properties, operating losses, capital losses, the amount of nondeductible expenses, and by reductions in liabilities. The basis, therefore, is adjusted with changes in capital changes in the partnership. The basis is also used for calculating the gain or loss resulting from the sale of a partnership.

TAX ACCOUNTING FOR THE S CORPORATION

With both the sole proprietorship and with partnerships, the income earned by the business is taxed once—directly to the owner/partner. In C corporations (discussed later in this chapter), income earned by the business is taxed twice—once to the corporation and again when dividends are paid to the owners/shareholders. With S (or Subchapter S) corporations, the income earned by the business is taxed only once—directly to the owners/shareholder—and no income taxes are paid by the corporation. This elimination of double taxation combined with the flexibility of a partnership and the advantages, such as limited liability, of a corporation, makes the S corporation a form of business every startup firm should consider. The popularity of S corporations as a form of business for small firms is confirmed by the fact that there are 780,000 S corporations in the United States and 99.98 percent of them had assets of less than $10 million.[1]

The number of S corporations is expected to grow dramatically now that individual tax rates are lower than corporate tax rates. To see why, consider the following example. A small business is planning to pass through $10,000 in income to each owner/shareholder. At present, the individual tax rates are as follows:

For Married Couples Filing Joint Returns	
Taxable income up to $29,750	15%
Taxable income $29,751 to $71,900	28%
Taxable income $71,901 to $149,250	33%
Taxable income over $149,250	28%
For Corporations	
Taxable income up to $50,000	15%
Taxable income $50,001 to $75,000	25%
Taxable income $75,001 to $100,000	34%
Taxable income $100,001 to $335,000	39%
Taxable income over $335,000	34%

Assuming each owner/shareholder had other income and each dollar received would be taxed at the highest tax rate (28 percent), the S corporation owner would pay $2,800 in taxes. The C corporation owner would pay a total of $3,880 or 38.8 percent in taxes—15 percent at the corporate level and an effective personal rate of 23.8 percent (28 percent of the remaining $8,500) on the distributed earnings. The gap widens as the C corporation's tax rate increases from the 15 percent minimum rate to the maximum rate.

Disadvantages of S-Corporation Status

There are, of course, drawbacks to S-corporation status. S corporations are limited to thirty-five shareholders (all of whom must be U.S. residents); they cannot have corporate shareholders; and they cannot have incorporated subsidiaries. In addition, retirement and fringe benefits paid to shareholders are not deductible expenses. Finally, fourteen states and the District of Columbia do not recognize S corporations, and in those states, S corporations are required to pay state income taxes at corporate rates. Despite these drawbacks, many experts believe that owners of small businesses, and particularly those owners who expect their net income to exceed $75,000, should seriously consider forming or changing their form of business to an S corporation.[2]

Income Tax

An S corporation must divide its items of income, loss, expense, and credit into two categories: separately stated items, and nonseparately computed income or loss. *Nonseparately computed income* or *loss* consists of all gross income items of the S corporation minus all its deductible items, except the separately stated items. Separately stated items are those items whose separate treatment on the shareholder's income-tax return could affect the shareholder's tax liability. Separately stated items include the following: (1) capital gains and losses, (2) charitable contributions, (3) dividends, (4) tax-exempt interest, (5) recoveries of bad debts, (6) depletion on S-corporation oil and gas properties, (7) interest expense on investments, and (8) other similar items.

The income-tax return for an S corporation is filed on Form 1120S (see Appendix A). In addition, a Schedule K-1 is filed for each shareholder, just as required for partnerships. The separately stated items are allocated to the shareholders on a daily pro rata basis according to the number of shares of stock held by the shareholder on each day during the corporation's tax year. If, for example, there is no change in the relative interest in stock owned during the tax year, then shareholders are allocated their pro rata share of the separately stated items according to their ownership share of the corporation.

TAX ACCOUNTING FOR C CORPORATIONS

Almost 2.9 million corporations file income-tax returns each year, but only about 43,000 of these returns have a tax liability in excess of $100,000.[3] These statistics indicate that there are more than 2.8 million relatively small corporations and that the corporate form of business is very popular among small businesses. The reasons for the popularity and the advantages and disadvantages of the corporate form of business were given in Chapter 6. This section will present a discussion of the tax aspects of the corporation, beginning with its formation and ending with the income-tax return.

Forming the Corporation

As is true of partnerships, the transfer of property from individuals forming the corporation is tax free if the individuals acquiring the stock at the time the corporation is formed own at least 80 percent of the stock immediately after its transfer. The individuals may transfer cash or property as Axel, Billie, Charlie, and Dot did in the partnership example previously discussed. If the group forming the corporation should own less than 80 percent of the stock after the transfer of property, each person would recognize gain measured by the difference between the fair market value of the stock received and the adjusted basis of the property transferred. There is no recognition of recognition of losses. If cash is raised through the sale of stock, or securities, there is no income for tax purposes.

The individuals forming a C corporation may encounter some problems. The first is similar to that encountered by the CABD partnership, when Dot, a partner, was contributing no property other than her services to the partnership. In a corporation, if a person receives stock for services, management skills, contacts, or similar "nonproperty" considerations, those services do not qualify for tax-free treatment. Thus, if Dot performed services for stock in the new corporation, she would face a tax liability based on the market value of the stock received.

There may be another problem if the property that is transferred has a liability that is greater than the adjusted basis of the property. For example, assume that a building with a $100,000 adjusted basis but a $150,000 mortgage debt is transferred to the corporation. The transfer would not be tax free to the individual who transferred the building to the corporation. In this case, the individual must recognize a gain, although the gain would not be greater than $50,000.

Corporate Income Taxes

In all the forms of business presented so far, the income flows to the owners of the business, and the business does not pay income taxes. Corporations, however, do pay taxes on the income earned by the business. Basically, the corporation is a legal and taxpaying entity. In many ways the steps for computing the tax liability for a corporation are simpler than those for computing individual income taxes. Corporate tax liability is the gross income minus deductions.

Corporations file their income tax on Form 1120 (or short Form 1120-A, if eligible), whether or not they have any taxable income. Form 1120 (see Appendix A) is divided into three sections: (1) income, (2) deductions, and (3) tax payment. Total income is simply gross receipts minus the cost of goods sold, plus other income such as interest, rents, royalties, and any capital gains or losses. In the income section, line 8 (capital gain net income) needs further comment. After the net short-term and net long-term capital gain and loss are computed, the gains and losses are merged to produce a net capital gain or loss. A net capital gain is included in gross income. A net capital loss, however, is not deductible in the tax year but may be carried back three years and forward five years as a short-term capital loss to offset the capital gains in that period.

From total income, deductions are subtracted. Most of the deductions a corporation is allowed to take have been explained previously or are fairly straightforward business expenses. However, a few items warrant further comment. First, compensation of officers is entered on line 12. This information is transferred from Schedule E, which shows each officer's compensation. If the corporation's total receipts are less than $150,000, then Schedule E is not required. If salaries are considered unreasonable (to escape double taxation), then the IRS may treat the excess compensation as a taxable dividend.

Second, the rules have changed for the calculations of bad debts (line 15). According to the current tax laws, all corporations except financial institutions must use the specific charge-off method for computing the amount of bad debts. Contributions (line 19) is another area that warrants further comment. Contributions are limited to 10 percent of the firm's taxable income (computed without the contribution deduction, any net operating loss carryback, any capital loss carryback, or other special deductions).

Taxable income is calculated on line 30, and the actual tax computation is transferred from Schedule J (Form 1120). Full payment of income tax is due with the return. Although a request for extension of time for filing (Form 7004) will yield an extra six months to compute taxes, an estimated tax due must be filed with the request for extension. The penalties for late filing are high enough (up to 5 percent a month) that most business owners should give the task of preparing tax returns serious attention.

Since all income does not flow through to the owners of a corporation, the residual left after dividends are paid is called *retained earnings*. The quick student may think that leaving the retained earnings in the firm and not paying dividends is one way of escaping double taxation. This is correct except that a corporation is allowed to accumulate only $250,000 in retained earnings before the IRS questions why the firm is accumulating the earnings. If the firm is retaining the earnings for a reasonable business need, such as expected debt retirement or planned plant expansion, then the firm will be allowed to retain the earnings without additional taxes. However, if the firm cannot show an acceptable business reason for the accumulation of retained earnings, then the IRS will impose a penalty tax on the excess.

Alternative Minimum Tax

In the past, some corporations with relatively large financial-statement income have escaped paying income taxes through the use of various tax loopholes. The alternative minimum tax (AMT) is designed to ensure that all corporations with financial-statement income pay some income tax. The ATM is equal to regular taxable income plus tax preferences less certain deductions. The key here is tax preferences. Tax preferences include accelerated depreciation, capital gains, expensed intangible drilling costs, amortization of pollution-control facilities, and mining exploration and development costs. The resulting amount, called *alternative minimum taxable income,* is reduced by an exemption amount and then multiplied by the 28-percent rate. The amount of minimum tax owed is the amount by which the AMT exceeds the regular tax. If earnings are less than $100,000, AMT will have very little effect on taxes.

ADDITIONAL IRS FORMS

There are several additional forms that the startup entrepreneur is responsible for filing. Some of the most important are listed below with a brief description.

1. *Form 940.* Employer's annual federal unemployment (FUTA) tax return.
2. *Form 941.* Employer's quarterly federal tax return.
3. *Form W-2.* Employer must provide copies of the Wage and Tax Statement Form (W-2) to each employee from whom income tax was withheld.
4. *Form W-4.* Employer must have all employees complete a W-4 form, which is used to determine an employee's withholding allowance.

STATE AND LOCAL TAXES

Obviously state and local income taxes will vary from area to area and, therefore, cannot be covered in any textbook. The department of revenue of most state and local governments will provide the startup entrepreneur with the information he or she needs. Many will not only provide the necessary instructions and forms but also conduct short courses. The IRS also conducts short courses on the filing of federal income-tax forms in many areas. In both cases, good help may be as close as the phone. In fact, the IRS has a pamphlet titled "The Tax Guide for Small Business," which can be obtained by calling 1-800-424-FORM. The pamphlet and the telephone call are free, and the service is normally both pleasant and prompt.

Summary

Paying taxes is an unpleasant but necessary part of owning a business. The objective of this chapter was to give startup entrepreneurs some basic information on how taxes will affect their businesses. Armed with basic information, they should be able to make decisions that will reduce taxes.

Tax accounting is the determination of when income and expenses are taken. Most large businesses employ the accrual method of accounting. Most small startup enterprises, however, use the cash method of accounting. Percentage-of-completion and installment methods are two other methods of accounting that qualified firms are allowed to use.

There was a discussion of how several items from Schedule C are computed for a sole proprietorship. Gross profit is calculated by subtracting the cost of goods sold from net sales. Cost of goods sold is based mainly on the cost of the merchandise or materials sold. The inventory value of merchandise or materials can vary greatly, depending upon whether the business uses the first-in, first-out or the last-in, first-out method. Other expenses, such as depreciation, travel, employee benefit programs, and freight, were briefly examined.

Other items from Schedule C of which sole proprietors need to be aware, include the claiming of expenses for a home office and the methods of deducting bad debts. Employee benefit programs have tax advantages for both the employer and the employee, but to be eligible for the tax deduction, the benefit programs must meet strict nondiscrimination rules intended to ensure the equal treatment of highly and nonhighly compensated employees.

Tax laws do not require employers to have a pension plan, but if they have one, only "qualified" plans are tax deductible. To qualify, a plan must not discriminate in favor of employees who are officers, owners, or who are highly paid. Various types of pension plans are available, including the following: (1) individual retirement accounts, (2) simplified employee pension plans, and (3) Keogh plans.

Partnerships are treated as multiple proprietorships for tax purposes. Partnerships do not pay taxes, but partners pay taxes on their respective share of the net income. Partnerships, however, must file an income statement with the IRS. Partnerships also must calculate the tax basis for the partners—a complex calculation that usually must be made at least once a year.

S corporations offer the limited liability advantages of corporations and the complete flow-through of income to the owners. The division of income into separately stated items and nonseparately computed income or loss does, however, make the preparation of the tax return for an S corporation rather complex.

C corporations are legal entities that pay taxes. Income from the C corporation does not flow to the owners; instead, the corporation pays taxes and then may pay dividends to the owners, who are then subject to taxes on the dividend income received.

To reduce the difference between tax accounting and financial accounting, C corporations must compute the alternative minimum tax (AMT). The computed AMT is compared to the regular tax, and if the AMT is greater, then the difference is added to the regular tax.

Assembling the Pieces

Carol and Jacki first learned about taxes during the time they operated the Charleston Spice Rack—a shop open two days per week. Since they operated the Charleston Spice Rack as a partnership, they filed Form 1065 with their federal Form 1040. To file Form 1065, they followed the IRS instructions and did not need additional tax assistance.

After starting In Good Taste as an incorporated business, Carol and Jacki had less time to learn about new tax forms. They, like most business owners, knew they needed good tax advice so that all tax forms would be accurate, filed on time, and their tax liability reduced to a minimum. To solve their problem, they hired Thayer Boswell, a local CPA they both knew, to prepare their federal and state tax form and to assist them in setting up an accounting system.

Carol and Jacki maintain the records for In Good Taste and send the computerized results to Mr. Boswell every three months. He prepares their quarterly federal and state income-tax forms. Carol and Jacki prepare the state tax, unemployment, and social-security state forms. They also prepare and pay the local property-tax forms, and renew the various business and beer and wine licenses. ■

Questions for Review and Discussion

1. Which method of accounting is usually best for the startup firms, cash or accrual? Why?
2. If the cost of merchandise and materials is constantly increasing, which method of accounting for inventories will yield the lower tax payment?
3. Why is the use of MACRS of interest to the startup firm?
4. How is the sole proprietor able to reduce his or her taxes? Give some specific examples.
5. Inventory may be valued either at cost or at the lower of cost or market value. When could market value be lower than cost?
6. What are the advantages of employee benefit programs for the employer? For the employee?
7. What are the major differences between an IRA and a SEP?
8. In the CABD partnership example given in the chapter, Axel contributed a building with a fair market value of $100,000 but a tax basis of $50,000. How could the tax basis be less than the fair market value?
9. Since individual tax rates are lower than corporate tax rates, why are there not more S corporations in comparison to C corporations?
10. What is the rationale behind the alternative minimum tax?

Notes

1. Internal Revenue Service, *Statistics of Income Bulletin,* U.S. Department of Treasury Publ. 1135, vol. 5, no. 2, table 12 (Washington, DC: U.S. Government Printing Office, 1985), p. 93.

2. Stuart Weiss, "Small Companies," *Business Week,* 10 November 1986. p. 150.
3. Internal Revenue Service, *Statistics of Income Bulletin,* U.S. Department of Treasury Publ. 1136, vol. 4, no. 3, (Washington, DC: U.S. Government Printing Office, 1984–85), p. 31.

Appendix A

TAX FORMS

Form **1040-ES**
Department of the Treasury
Internal Revenue Service

1989
Payment-
Voucher

Return this voucher with check or money order payable to the Internal Revenue Service. Please write your social security number and "1989 Form 1040-ES" on your check or money order. Please do not send cash. Enclose, but do not staple or attach, your payment with this voucher.
File only if you are making a payment of estimated tax.

OMB No. 1545-0087
Expires 8-31-91

(Calendar year—Due Sept. 15, 1989)

1 Amount of payment
$ ----------------------
2 Fiscal year filers enter year ending

(month and year)

Please type or print

Your first name and initial	Your last name	Your social security number
(If joint payment, complete for spouse) Spouse's first name and initial	Spouse's last name if different from yours	If joint payment, spouse's social security number
Address (number and street)		
City, state, and ZIP code		

For Paperwork Reduction Act Notice, see instructions on page 1.

Form **1065**

Department of the Treasury
Internal Revenue Service

U.S. Partnership Return of Income

▶ **For Paperwork Reduction Act Notice, see Form 1065 Instructions.**

For calendar year 1987, or fiscal year beginning ________________, 1987, and ending ______________, 19___

OMB No. 1545-0099

1987

A Principal business activity	**Use IRS label. Other-wise, please print or type.**	Name	D Employer identification number
B Principal product or service		Number and street (or P.O. Box number if mail is not delivered to street address)	E Date business started
C Business code number		City or town, state, and ZIP code	F Enter total assets at end of tax year $

G Check accounting method: (1) ☐ Cash (2) ☐ Accrual (3) ☐ Other

H Check applicable boxes: (1) ☐ Final return (2) ☐ Change in address (3) ☐ Amended return

	Yes	No
I Number of partners in this partnership ▶ ____________		
J Is this partnership a limited partnership (see the Instructions)?		
K Is this partnership a partner in another partnership?		
L Are any partners in this partnership also partnerships?		
M Does the partnership meet **all** the requirements shown in the Instructions for **Question M**?		
N Was there a distribution of property or a transfer (for example, by sale or death) of a partnership interest during the tax year? If "Yes," see the Instructions concerning an election to adjust the basis of the partnership's assets under section 754		

	Yes	No
O At any time during the tax year, did the partnership have an interest in or a signature or other authority over a financial account in a foreign country (such as a bank account, securities account, or other financial account)? (See the Instructions for exceptions and filing requirements for Form TD F 90-22.1.) If "Yes," write the name of the foreign country. ▶ ______________		
P Was the partnership the grantor of, or transferor to, a foreign trust which existed during the current tax year, whether or not the partnership or any partner has any beneficial interest in it? If "Yes," you may have to file Forms 3520, 3520-A, or 926		
Q Was this partnership in operation at the end of 1987?		
R Number of months in 1987 that this partnership was in operation ▶ ________		

S Check this box if the partnership has filed or is required to file Form 8264, Application for Registration of a Tax Shelter ☐

T Check this box if this is a partnership subject to the consolidated partnership audit procedures of TEFRA. (See page 7 of the Instructions.) ☐

Caution: *Include* **only** *trade or business income and expenses on lines 1a–21 below. See the instructions for more information.*

Income	**1a**	Gross receipts or sales $ ____________ **1b** Minus returns and allowances $ __________ Balance ▶	1c	
	2	Cost of goods sold and/or operations (Schedule A, line 7)	2	
	3	Gross profit (subtract line 2 from line 1c)	3	
	4	Ordinary income (loss) from other partnerships and fiduciaries (attach schedule)	4	
	5	Net farm profit (loss) (attach Schedule F (Form 1040))	5	
	6	Net gain (loss) (Form 4797, line 18)	6	
	7	Other income (loss)	7	
	8	**TOTAL** income (loss) (combine lines 3 through 7)	8	
Deductions *(see instructions for limitations)*	**9a**	Salaries and wages (other than to partners) $ __________ **9b** Minus jobs credit $ __________ Balance ▶	9c	
	10	Guaranteed payments to partners	10	
	11	Rent	11	
	12	Deductible interest expense not claimed elsewhere on return (see Instructions)	12	
	13	Taxes	13	
	14	Bad debts	14	
	15	Repairs	15	
	16a	Depreciation from Form 4562 (attach Form 4562) $ ______________ **16b** Minus depreciation claimed on Schedule A and elsewhere on return $ ______________ Balance ▶	16c	
	17	Depletion (***Do not deduct oil and gas depletion.***)	17	
	18a	Retirement plans, etc.	18a	
	b	Employee benefit programs	18b	
	19	Other deductions (attach schedule)	19	
	20	**TOTAL** deductions (add amounts in column for lines 9c through 19)	20	
	21	Ordinary income (loss) from trade or business activity(ies) (subtract line 20 from line 8)	21	

Please Sign Here

Under penalties of perjury, I declare that I have examined this return, including accompanying schedules and statements, and to the best of my knowledge and belief, it is true, correct, and complete. Declaration of preparer (other than taxpayer) is based on all information of which preparer has any knowledge.

▶ ______________________ Signature of general partner ▶ __________ Date

Paid Preparer's Use Only

Preparer's signature ▶	Date	Check if self-employed ▶ ☐	Preparer's social security no.
Firm's name (or yours if self-employed) and address ▶		E.I. No. ▶	
		ZIP code ▶	

Form 1065 (1987) Page 2

Schedule A Cost of Goods Sold and/or Operations

1	Inventory at beginning of year	1	
2	Purchases minus cost of items withdrawn for personal use	2	
3	Cost of labor	3	
4a	Additional section 263A costs (see instructions)	4a	
b	Other costs (attach schedule)	4b	
5	Total (add lines 1 through 4b)	5	
6	Inventory at end of year	6	
7	Cost of goods sold (subtract line 6 from line 5). Enter here and on page 1, line 2	7	

8a Check all methods used for valuing closing inventory:

(i) ☐ Cost

(ii) ☐ Lower of cost or market as described in regulations section 1.471-4

(iii) ☐ Writedown of "subnormal" goods as described in regulations section 1.471-2(c)

(iv) ☐ Other (specify method used and attach explanation) ▶ ....

b Check if the LIFO inventory method was adopted this tax year for any goods (if checked, attach Form 970) ☐

c Do the rules of section 263A (with respect to property produced or acquired for resale) apply to the partnership? ☐ Yes ☐ No

d Was there any change (other than for section 263A purposes) in determining quantities, cost, or valuations between opening and closing inventory? If "Yes," attach explanation ☐ Yes ☐ No

Schedule H Income (Loss) From Rental Real Estate Activity(ies)

1 In the space provided below, show the kind and location of each rental property. Attach a schedule if more space is needed.

Property A ....

Property B ....

Property C

Rental Real Estate Income		Properties A	Properties B	Properties C	Totals (Add columns A, B, C, and amounts from any attached schedule)	
2 Gross Income	2				2	
Rental Real Estate Expenses						
3 Advertising	3					
4 Auto and travel	4					
5 Cleaning and maintenance	5					
6 Commissions	6					
7 Insurance	7					
8 Legal and other professional fees	8					
9 Interest expense	9					
10 Repairs	10					
11 Taxes	11					
12 Utilities	12					
13 Wages and salaries	13					
14 Depreciation from Form 4562	14					
15 Other (list)						
....						
....						
16 Total expenses. Add lines 3 through 15	16				16	
17 Net income (loss) from rental real estate activity(ies). Subtract line 16 from line 2. Enter total net income (loss) from all properties on Schedule K, line 2.	17				17	

Form 1065 (1987) Page 3

Schedule K **Partners' Shares of Income, Credits, Deductions, etc.**

	(a) Distributive share items		(b) Total amount
Income (Loss)	1 Ordinary income (loss) from trade or business activity(ies) (page 1, line 21)	1	
	2 Net income (loss) from rental real estate activity(ies) (Schedule H, line 17)	2	
	3a Gross income from other rental activity(ies) 3a $		
	b Minus expenses (attach schedule) 3b $		
	c Balance net income (loss) from other rental activity(ies) ▶	3c	
	4 Portfolio income (loss):		
	a Interest income	4a	
	b Dividend income	4b	
	c Royalty income	4c	
	d Net short-term capital gain (loss) (Schedule D, line 4)	4d	
	e Net long-term capital gain (loss) (Schedule D, line 9)	4e	
	f Other portfolio income (loss) (attach schedule)	4f	
	5 Guaranteed payments	5	
	6 Net gain (loss) under section 1231 (other than due to casualty or theft)	6	
	7 Other (attach schedule)	7	
Deductions	8 Charitable contributions (attach list)	8	
	9 Expense deduction for recovery property (section 179)	9	
	10 Deductions related to portfolio income (do not include investment interest expense)	10	
	11 Other (attach schedule)	11	
Credits	12a Credit for income tax withheld	12a	
	b Low-income housing credit (attach Form 8586)	12b	
	c Qualified rehabilitation expenditures related to rental real estate activity(ies) (attach schedule)	12c	
	d Credit(s) related to rental real estate activity(ies) other than 12b and 12c (attach schedule)	12d	
	e Credit(s) related to rental activity(ies) other than 12b, 12c, and 12d (attach schedule)	12e	
	13 Other (attach schedule)	13	
Self-Employment	14a Net earnings (loss) from self-employment	14a	
	b Gross farming or fishing income	14b	
	c Gross nonfarm income	14c	
Tax Preference Items	15a Accelerated depreciation of real property placed in service before 1/1/87	15a	
	b Accelerated depreciation of leased personal property placed in service before 1/1/87	15b	
	c Depreciation adjustment on property placed in service after 12/31/86	15c	
	d Depletion (other than oil and gas)	15d	
	e (1) Gross income from oil, gas, and geothermal properties	15e(1)	
	(2) Deductions allocable to oil, gas, and geothermal properties	15e(2)	
	f Other (attach schedule)	15f	
Investment Interest	16a Interest expense on investment debts	16a	
	b (1) Investment income included on lines 4a through 4f, Schedule K	16b(1)	
	(2) Investment expenses included on line 10, Schedule K	16b(2)	
Foreign Taxes	17a Type of income		
	b Foreign country or U.S. possession		
	c Total gross income from sources outside the U.S. (attach schedule)	17c	
	d Total applicable deductions and losses (attach schedule)	17d	
	e Total foreign taxes (check one): ▶ ☐ Paid ☐ Accrued	17e	
	f Reduction in taxes available for credit (attach schedule)	17f	
	g Other (attach schedule)	17g	
Other	18 Attach schedule for other items and amounts not reported above. See Instructions		

Form 1065 (1987) **Page 4**

Schedule L **Balance Sheets**

(See the instructions for Question M Before Completing Schedules L and M.)

Assets	Beginning of tax year (a)	(b)	End of tax year (c)	(d)
1 Cash				
2 Trade notes and accounts receivable				
a Minus allowance for bad debts				
3 Inventories				
4 Federal and state government obligations				
5 Other current assets (attach schedule)				
6 Mortgage and real estate loans				
7 Other investments (attach schedule)				
8 Buildings and other depreciable assets				
a Minus accumulated depreciation				
9 Depletable assets				
a Minus accumulated depletion				
10 Land (net of any amortization)				
11 Intangible assets (amortizable only)				
a Minus accumulated amortization				
12 Other assets (attach schedule)				
13 TOTAL assets				
Liabilities and Capital				
14 Accounts payable				
15 Mortgages, notes, bonds payable in less than 1 year				
16 Other current liabilities (attach schedule)				
17 All nonrecourse loans				
18 Mortgages, notes, bonds payable in 1 year or more				
19 Other liabilities (attach schedule)				
20 Partners' capital accounts				
21 TOTAL liabilities and capital				

Schedule M **Reconciliation of Partners' Capital Accounts**

(Show reconciliation of each partner's capital account on Schedule K-1 (Form 1065), Question I.)

(a) Capital account at beginning of year	(b) Capital contributed during year	(c) Income (loss) from lines 1, 2, 3c, and 4 of Sch. K	(d) Income not included in column (c), plus nontaxable income	(e) Losses not included in column (c), plus unallowable deductions	(f) Withdrawals and distributions	(g) Capital account at end of year

Designation of Tax Matters Partner

The following general partner is hereby designated as the tax matters partner (TMP) for the tax year for which this partnership return is filed:

Name of designated TMP ▶ Identifying number of TMP ▶

Address of designated TMP ▶

☆ U.S. Government Printing Office: 1987—183-166 23-0916750

SCHEDULE K-1 (Form 1065)
Department of the Treasury
Internal Revenue Service

Partner's Share of Income, Credits, Deductions, etc.

For calendar year 1988 or fiscal year
beginning , 1988, and ending , 19

OMB No. 1545-0099

1988

Partner's identifying number ▶ **Partnership's identifying number ▶**

Partner's name, address, and ZIP code

Partnership's name, address, and ZIP code

A Is this partner a general partner? ☐ Yes ☐ No

B Partner's share of liabilities:
Nonrecourse. $ ________
Other $ ________

C What type of entity is this partner? ▶ ________

D Is this partner a ☐ domestic or a ☐ foreign partner?

E Enter partner's percentage of:

	(i) Before decrease or termination	(ii) End of year
Profit sharing	%	%
Loss sharing	%	%
Ownership of capital	%	%

F IRS Center where partnership filed return ▶ ________

G Tax Shelter Registration Number ▶ ________

H(1) Did the partner's ownership interest in the partnership change after Oct. 22, 1986? ☐ Yes ☐ No
If yes, attach statement. (See Form 1065 Instructions.)

(2) Did the partnership start or acquire a new activity after Oct. 22, 1986? ☐ Yes ☐ No
If yes, attach statement. (See Form 1065 Instructions.)

I Check here if this partnership is a publicly traded partnership as defined in section 469(k)(2) ☐

J Check here if this is an amended Schedule K-1 ☐

K Reconciliation of partner's capital account:

(a) Capital account at beginning of year	(b) Capital contributed during year	(c) Income (loss) from lines 1, 2, 3, and 4 below	(d) Income not included in column (c), plus nontaxable income	(e) Losses not included in column (c), plus unallowable deductions	(f) Withdrawals and distributions	(g) Capital account at end of year

Reminder: If you received a 1987 Schedule K-1 that was for a short year and you chose to report the 1987 amounts over a 4-year period, be sure to include one-fourth of the short year amounts, in addition to the items reported on this Schedule K-1, on the appropriate lines of your 1988 Form 1040 and related schedules.

Caution: *Refer to attached Partner's Instructions for Schedule K-1 (Form 1065) before entering information from this schedule on your tax return.*

		(a) Distributive share item		(b) Amount	(c) 1040 filers enter the amount in column (b) on:
Income (Loss)	1	Ordinary income (loss) from trade or business activity(ies)	1		(See Partner's Instructions for Schedule K-1 (Form 1065))
	2	Net income or loss from rental real estate activity(ies)	2		
	3	Net income or loss from other rental activity(ies)	3		
	4	Portfolio income (loss):			
	a	Interest	4a		Sch. B, Part I, line 2
	b	Dividends	4b		Sch. B, Part II, line 4
	c	Royalties	4c		Sch. E, Part I, line 5
	d	Net short-term capital gain (loss)	4d		Sch. D, line 5, col. (f) or (g)
	e	Net long-term capital gain (loss)	4e		Sch. D, line 12, col. (f) or (g)
	f	Other portfolio income (loss) (attach schedule)	4f		(Enter on applicable lines of your return)
	5	Guaranteed payments	5		(See Partner's Instructions for Schedule K-1 (Form 1065))
	6	Net gain (loss) under section 1231 (other than due to casualty or theft)	6		
	7	Other (attach schedule)	7		(Enter on applicable lines of your return)
Deductions	8	Charitable contributions	8		Sch. A, line 14 or 15
	9	Expense deduction for recovery property (section 179) (attach schedule)	9		(See Partner's Instructions for Schedule K-1 (Form 1065))
	10	Deductions related to portfolio income	10		
	11	Other (attach schedule)	11		
Credits	12a	Credit for income tax withheld	12a		See Partner's Instructions for Schedule K-1 (Form 1065)
	b	Low-income housing credit: (1) Partnerships to which section 42(j)(5) applies	b(1)		Form 8586, line 5
		(2) Other	b(2)		
	c	Qualified rehabilitation expenditures related to rental real estate activity(ies) (attach schedule)	12c		(See Partner's Instructions for Schedule K-1 (Form 1065))
	d	Credit(s) related to rental real estate activity(ies) other than 12b and 12c (attach schedule)	12d		
	e	Credit(s) related to other rental activity(ies) (see instructions) (attach schedule)	12e		
	13	Other credits (attach schedule)	13		

For Paperwork Reduction Act Notice, see Form 1065 Instructions. **Schedule K-1 (Form 1065) 1988**

Schedule K-1 (Form 1065) (1988) Page **2**

		(a) Distributive share item		(b) Amount	(c) 1040 filers enter the amount in column (b) on:
Self-employment	14a	Net earnings (loss) from self-employment	14a		Sch. SE, Section A or B
	b	Gross farming or fishing income	14b		(See Partner's Instructions for Schedule K-1 (Form 1065))
	c	Gross nonfarm income	14c		
Tax Preference Items	15a	Accelerated depreciation of real property placed in service before 1/1/87	15a		Form 6251, line 5e
	b	Accelerated depreciation of leased personal property placed in service before 1/1/87	15b		Form 6251, line 5f
	c	Depreciation adjustment on property placed in service after 12/31/86	15c		Form 6251, line 4j
	d	Depletion (other than oil and gas)	15d		Form 6251, line 5c
	e	(1) Gross income from oil, gas, and geothermal properties	e(1)		See Form 6251 Instructions
		(2) Deductions allocable to oil, gas, and geothermal properties	e(2)		See Form 6251 Instructions
	f	Other (attach schedule)	15f		(See Partner's Instructions for Schedule K-1 (Form 1065))
Investment Interest	16a	Interest expense on investment debts	16a		Form 4952, line 1
	b	(1) Investment income included in Schedule K-1, lines 4a through 4f	b(1)		(See Partner's Instructions for Schedule K-1 (Form 1065))
		(2) Investment expenses included in Schedule K-1, line 10	b(2)		
Foreign Taxes	17a	Type of income ______			Form 1116, Check boxes
	b	Name of foreign country or U.S. possession ______			Form 1116, Part I
	c	Total gross income from sources outside the U.S. (attach schedule)	17c		Form 1116, Part I
	d	Total applicable deductions and losses (attach schedule)	17d		Form 1116, Part I
	e	Total foreign taxes (check one): ▶ ☐ Paid ☐ Accrued	17e		Form 1116, Part II
	f	Reduction in taxes available for credit (attach schedule)	17f		Form 1116, Part III
	g	Other (attach schedule)	17g		See Form 1116 Instructions
Other	18a	Total expenditures to which a section 59(e) election (relating to the optional 10-year writeoff of certain tax preference items) may apply (attach schedule)			(See Partner's Instructions for Schedule K-1 (Form 1065))
	b	Other items and amounts not reported on lines 1 through 17g, 19, and 20 that are required to be reported separately to you			
Recapture of Tax Credits	19a	Low-income housing credit: Partnerships to which section 42(j)(5) applies	19a		Form 8611
	b	Low-income housing credit: Other	19b		

20	Investment Tax Credit Property:	A	B	C	
a	Description of property (State whether recovery or nonrecovery property. If recovery property, state whether regular percentage method or section 48(q) election used.)				Form 4255, top
b	Date placed in service				Form 4255, line 2
c	Cost or other basis				Form 4255, line 3
d	Class of recovery property or original estimated useful life				Form 4255, line 4
e	Date item ceased to be investment credit property				Form 4255, line 8

Other Information Provided by Partnership:

★U S GPO 1988-0-205-180

SCHEDULE SE
(Form 1040)
Department of the Treasury
Internal Revenue Service (O)

Social Security Self-Employment Tax

▶ See Instructions for Schedule SE (Form 1040).
▶ Attach to Form 1040.

OMB No. 1545-0074
1988
Attachment Sequence No. **18**

Name of person with **self-employment** income (as shown on social security card)	Social security number of person with **self-employment** income ▶	

Who Must File Schedule SE

You must file Schedule SE if:

- Your net earnings from self-employment were $400 or more (or you had wages of $100 or more from an electing church or church organization); AND
- You did not have wages (subject to social security or railroad retirement tax) of $45,000 or more.

For more information about Schedule SE, see the Instructions.

Note: *Most taxpayers can now use the new short Schedule SE on this page. But, you may have to use the longer Schedule SE that is on the back.*

Who MUST Use the Long Schedule SE (Section B)

You must use Section B if ANY of the following applies:

- You choose the "optional method" to figure your self-employment tax. See Section B, Part II;
- You are a minister, member of a religious order, or Christian Science practitioner and received IRS approval (from **Form 4361**) not to be taxed on your earnings from these sources, but you owe self-employment tax on other earnings;
- You are an employee of a church or church organization that chose by law not to pay employer social security taxes;
- You have tip income that is subject to social security tax, but you did not report those tips to your employer; OR
- You are a government employee with wages subject ONLY to the 1.45% medicare part of the social security tax.

Section A—Short Schedule SE
(Read above to see if you must use the long Schedule SE on the back (Section B))

1	Net farm profit or (loss) from Schedule F (Form 1040), line 39, and farm partnerships, Schedule K-1 (Form 1065), line 14a	1		
2	Net profit or (loss) from Schedule C (Form 1040), line 31, and Schedule K-1 (Form 1065), line 14a (other than farming). See the Instructions for other income to report	2		
3	Add lines 1 and 2. Enter the total. If the total is less than $400, **do not** file this schedule	3		
4	The largest amount of combined wages and self-employment earnings subject to social security or railroad retirement tax (tier 1) for 1988 is	4	$45,000	00
5	Total social security wages and tips from Forms W-2 and railroad retirement compensation (tier 1)	5		
6	Subtract line 5 from line 4. Enter the result. (If the result is zero or less, **do not** file this schedule.)	6		
7	Enter the **smaller** of line 3 or line 6	7		
	If line 7 is $45,000, enter $5,859 on line 8. Otherwise, multiply line 7 by .1302 and enter the result on line 8		×.1302	
8	Self-employment tax. Enter this amount on Form 1040, line 48	8		

For Paperwork Reduction Act Notice, see Form 1040 Instructions.

Schedule SE (Form 1040) 1988 Attachment Sequence No. **18** Page **2**

Name of person with **self-employment** income (as shown on social security card)	Social security number of person with **self-employment** income ▶	

Section B—Long Schedule SE

(Before completing, see if you can use the short Schedule SE on the other side (Section A).)

A If your only self-employment income was from earnings as a minister, member of a religious order, or Christian Science practitioner, AND you filed **Form 4361,** then DO NOT file Schedule SE. Instead, write "Exempt-Form 4361" on Form 1040, line **48**. **However, if you** filed Form 4361, but have $400 or more of other earnings subject to self-employment tax, continue with Part I and check here. ▶ ☐

B If your only earnings subject to self-employment tax are wages from an electing church or church-controlled organization that is exempt from employer social security taxes and you are not a minister or a member of a religious order, skip lines 1–3b. Enter zero on line 3c and go on to line 5a.

Part I **Figure Social Security Self-Employment Tax**

1	Net farm profit or (loss) from Schedule F (Form 1040), line 39, and farm partnerships, Schedule K-1 (Form 1065), line 14a	1		
2	Net profit or (loss) from Schedule C (Form 1040), line 31, and Schedule K-1 (Form 1065), line 14a (other than farming). (See Instructions for other income to report.) Employees of an electing church or church-controlled organization **do not** enter your Form W-2 wages on line 2. See the Instructions	2		
3a	Enter the amount from line 1 (**or,** if you elected the farm optional method, Part II, line 10)	3a		
b	Enter the amount from line 2 (**or,** if you elected the nonfarm optional method, Part II, line 12)	3b		
c	Add lines 3a and 3b. Enter the total. If the total is less than $400, **do not** file this schedule. (**Exception:** *If you are an employee of an electing church or church-controlled organization and the total of lines 3a and 3b is less than $400, enter zero and complete the rest of this schedule.*)	3c		
4	The largest amount of combined wages and self-employment earnings subject to social security or railroad retirement tax (tier 1) for 1988 is	4	$45,000	00
5a	Total social security wages and tips from Forms W-2 and railroad retirement compensation (tier 1). **Note:** *Government employees whose wages are subject only to the 1.45% medicare tax and employees of certain church or church-controlled organizations should* **not** *include those wages on this line. See Instructions* — 5a			
b	Unreported tips subject to social security tax from Form 4137, line 9, or to railroad retirement tax (tier 1) — 5b			
c	Add lines 5a and 5b. Enter the total	5c		
6a	Subtract line 5c from line 4. Enter the result. (If the result is zero or less, enter zero.)	6a		
b	Enter your medicare qualified government wages if you are required to use the worksheet in the Instructions — 6b			
c	Enter your Form W-2 wages of $100 or more from an electing church or church-controlled organization — 6c			
d	Add lines 3c and 6c. Enter the total	6d		
7	Enter the **smaller** of line 6a or line 6d	7		
	If line 7 is $45,000, enter $5,859 on line 8. Otherwise, multiply line 7 by .1302 and enter the result on line 8		×.1302	
8	Self-employment tax. Enter this amount on Form 1040, line 48	8		

Part II **Optional Method To Figure Net Earnings** (See "Who Can File Schedule SE" in the Instructions.)

See Instructions for limitations. Generally, you may use this part **only** if:

A Your **gross** farm income[1] was not more than $2,400; **or**

B Your **gross** farm income[1] was more than $2,400 and your **net** farm profits[2] were **less** than $1,600; **or**

C Your **net** nonfarm profits[3] were less than $1,600 and also **less** than two-thirds (⅔) of your **gross** nonfarm income.[4]

Note: *If line 2 above is two-thirds (⅔) or more of your gross nonfarm income[4], or if line 2 is $1,600 or more, you may* **not** *use the optional method.*

[1]From Schedule F (Form 1040), line 12, and Schedule K-1 (Form 1065), line 14b.
[2]From Schedule F (Form 1040), line 39, and Schedule K-1 (Form 1065), line 14a.
[3]From Schedule C (Form 1040), line 31, and Schedule K-1 (Form 1065), line 14a.
[4]From Schedule C (Form 1040), line 5, and Schedule K-1 (Form 1065), line 14c.

9	Maximum income for optional methods	9	$1,600	00
10	**Farm Optional Method**—If you meet test A or B above, enter the **smaller** of: two-thirds (⅔) of gross farm income from Schedule F (Form 1040), line 12, and farm partnerships, Schedule K-1 (Form 1065), line 14b; **or** $1,600. Also enter this amount on line 3a above	10		
11	Subtract line 10 from line 9. Enter the result	11		
12	**Nonfarm Optional Method**—If you meet test C above, enter the **smallest** of: two-thirds (⅔) of gross nonfarm income from Schedule C (Form 1040), line 5, and Schedule K-1 (Form 1065), line 14c (other than farming); **or** $1,600; **or,** if you elected the farm optional method, the amount on line 11. Also enter this amount on line 3b above	12		

For Paperwork Reduction Act Notice, see Form 1040 Instructions. **Schedule SE (Form 1040) 1988**

☆U.S. Government Printing Office: 1988-205-135 23-0916750

Form **1120** — Department of the Treasury, Internal Revenue Service

U.S. Corporation Income Tax Return

For calendar year 1988 or tax year beginning ______________, 1988, ending ______________, 19____

▶ For Paperwork Reduction Act Notice, see page 1 of the instructions.

OMB No. 1545-0123

1988

Check if a—
A Consolidated return ☐
B Personal holding co. ☐
C Personal service corp. (as defined in Temp. Regs. sec. 1.441-4T—see instructions) ☐

Use IRS label. Otherwise, please print or type.

Name

Number and street (or P.O. box number if mail is not delivered to street address)

City or town, state, and ZIP code

D Employer identification number

E Date incorporated

F Total assets (See Specific Instructions.) Dollars | Cents
$

G Check applicable boxes: (1) ☐ Initial return (2) ☐ Final return (3) ☐ Change in address

Income

Line	Description	Box	Amount
1a	Gross receipts or sales ____ b Less returns and allowances ____ c Bal ▶	1c	
2	Cost of goods sold and/or operations (Schedule A)	2	
3	Gross profit (line 1c less line 2)	3	
4	Dividends (Schedule C, line 19)	4	
5	Interest	5	
6	Gross rents	6	
7	Gross royalties	7	
8	Capital gain net income (attach separate Schedule D)	8	
9	Net gain or (loss) from Form 4797, Part II, line 18 (attach Form 4797)	9	
10	Other income (see instructions—attach schedule)	10	
11	**Total** income—Add lines 3 through 10 and enter here ▶	11	

Deductions (See instructions for limitations on deductions.)

Line	Description	Box	Amount
12	Compensation of officers (Schedule E)	12	
13a	Salaries and wages ____ b Less jobs credit ____ c Balance ▶	13c	
14	Repairs	14	
15	Bad debts	15	
16	Rents	16	
17	Taxes	17	
18	Interest	18	
19	Contributions (**see instructions for 10% limitation**)	19	
20	Depreciation (attach Form 4562) — 20		
21	Less depreciation claimed in Schedule A and elsewhere on return — 21a	21b	
22	Depletion	22	
23	Advertising	23	
24	Pension, profit-sharing, etc., plans	24	
25	Employee benefit programs	25	
26	Other deductions (attach schedule)	26	
27	**Total** deductions—Add lines 12 through 26 and enter here ▶	27	
28	Taxable income before net operating loss deduction and special deductions (line 11 less line 27)	28	
29	**Less: a** Net operating loss deduction (see instructions) — 29a		
	b Special deductions (Schedule C, line 20) — 29b	29c	

Tax and Payments

Line	Description	Box	Amount
30	Taxable income (line 28 less line 29c)	30	
31	**Total tax** (Schedule J)	31	
32	**Payments: a** 1987 overpayment credited to 1988 — 32a		
b	1988 estimated tax payments — 32b		
c	Less 1988 refund applied for on Form 4466 — 32c ( ) d Bal ▶ 32d		
e	Tax deposited with Form 7004 — 32e		
f	Credit from regulated investment companies (attach Form 2439) — 32f		
g	Credit for Federal tax on fuels (attach Form 4136) — 32g	32h	
33	Enter any **penalty** for underpayment of estimated tax—check ▶ ☐ if Form 2220 is attached	33	
34	**Tax due**—If the total of lines 31 and 33 is larger than line 32h, enter amount owed	34	
35	**Overpayment**—If line 32h is larger than the total of lines 31 and 33, enter amount overpaid	35	
36	Enter amount of line 35 you want: **Credited to 1989 estimated tax ▶** ____ **Refunded ▶**	36	

Please Sign Here

Under penalties of perjury, I declare that I have examined this return, including accompanying schedules and statements, and to the best of my knowledge and belief, it is true, correct, and complete. Declaration of preparer (other than taxpayer) is based on all information of which preparer has any knowledge.

▶ Signature of officer — Date — ▶ Title

Paid Preparer's Use Only

Preparer's signature ▶ — Date — Check if self-employed ☐ — Preparer's social security number

Firm's name (or yours if self-employed) and address ▶ — E.I. No. ▶ — ZIP code ▶

Form 1120 (1988) Page 2

Schedule A **Cost of Goods Sold and/or Operations** (See instructions for line 2, page 1.)

1 Inventory at beginning of year	1	
2 Purchases	2	
3 Cost of labor	3	
4a Additional section 263A costs (see instructions—attach schedule)	4a	
b Other costs (attach schedule)	4b	
5 Total—Add lines 1 through 4b	5	
6 Inventory at end of year	6	
7 Cost of goods sold and/or operations—Line 5 less line 6. Enter here and on line 2, page 1	7	

8a Check all methods used for valuing closing inventory:
(i) ☐ Cost (ii) ☐ Lower of cost or market as described in Regulations section 1.471-4 (see instructions)
(iii) ☐ Writedown of "subnormal" goods as described in Regulations section 1.471-2(c) (see instructions)
(iv) ☐ Other (Specify method used and attach explanation.) ▶
b Check if the LIFO inventory method was adopted this tax year for any goods (if checked, attach Form 970) ☐
c If the LIFO inventory method was used for this tax year, enter percentage (or amounts) of closing inventory computed under LIFO | 8c |
d Do the rules of section 263A (with respect to property produced or acquired for resale) apply to the corporation? ☐ Yes ☐ No
e Was there any change in determining quantities, cost, or valuations between opening and closing inventory? If "Yes," attach explanation ☐ Yes ☐ No

Schedule C **Dividends and Special Deductions** (See Schedule C instructions.)

	(a) Dividends received	(b) %	(c) Special deductions: multiply (a) × (b)
1 Dividends from less-than-20%-owned domestic corporations that are subject to the 70% deduction (other than debt-financed stock)		70	
2 Dividends from 20%-or-more-owned domestic corporations that are subject to the 80% deduction (other than debt-financed stock)		80	
3 Dividends on debt-financed stock of domestic and foreign corporations (section 246A)		see instructions	
4 Dividends on certain preferred stock of less-than-20%-owned public utilities		41.176	
5 Dividends on certain preferred stock of 20%-or-more-owned public utilities		47.059	
6 Dividends from less-than-20%-owned foreign corporations and certain FSCs that are subject to the 70% deduction		70	
7 Dividends from 20%-or-more-owned foreign corporations and certain FSCs that are subject to the 80% deduction		80	
8 Dividends from wholly owned foreign subsidiaries subject to the 100% deduction (section 245(b))		100	
9 Total—Add lines 1 through 8. See instructions for limitation			
10 Dividends from domestic corporations received by a small business investment company operating under the Small Business Investment Act of 1958		100	
11 Dividends from certain FSCs that are subject to the 100% deduction (section 245(c)(1))		100	
12 Dividends from affiliated group members subject to the 100% deduction (section 243(a)(3))		100	
13 Other dividends from foreign corporations not included in lines 3, 6, 7, 8, and 11			
14 Income from controlled foreign corporations under subpart F (attach Forms 5471)			
15 Foreign dividend gross-up (section 78)			
16 IC-DISC and former DISC dividends not included in lines 1, 2, and/or 3 (section 246(d))			
17 Other dividends			
18 Deduction for dividends paid on certain preferred stock of public utilities (see instructions)			
19 Total dividends—Add lines 1 through 17. Enter here and on line 4, page 1. ▶			
20 Total deductions—Add lines 9, 10, 11, 12, and 18. Enter here and on line 29b, page 1 ▶			

Schedule E **Compensation of Officers** (See instructions for line 12, page 1.)
Complete Schedule E only if total receipts (line 1a, plus lines 4 through 10, of page 1, Form 1120) are $150,000 or more.

(a) Name of officer	(b) Social security number	(c) Percent of time devoted to business	Percent of corporation stock owned: (d) Common	(e) Preferred	(f) Amount of compensation
1		%	%	%	
		%	%	%	
		%	%	%	
		%	%	%	
		%	%	%	

2 Total compensation of officers	
3 Less: Compensation of officers claimed in Schedule A and elsewhere on return	( )
4 Compensation of officers deducted on line 12, page 1	

Form 1120 (1988) Page 3

Schedule J Tax Computation (See instructions.)

1 Check if you are a member of a controlled group (see sections 1561 and 1563) . . . . ▶ ☐			
2 If line 1 is checked:			
a Enter your share of the $50,000 and $25,000 taxable income bracket amounts (in that order): (i) $ (ii) $			
b Enter your share of the additional 5% tax (not to exceed $11,750) $			
3 Income tax (See instructions to figure the tax). Check this box if the corporation is a qualified personal service corporation (see instructions) ▶ ☐		3	
4a Foreign tax credit (attach Form 1118)	4a		
b Possessions tax credit (attach Form 5735)	4b		
c Orphan drug credit (attach Form 6765)	4c		
d Credit for fuel produced from a nonconventional source (see instructions)	4d		
e General business credit. Enter here and check which forms are attached: ☐ Form 3800 ☐ Form 3468 ☐ Form 5884 ☐ Form 6478 ☐ Form 6765 ☐ Form 8586	4e		
f Credit for prior year minimum tax (attach Form 8801)	4f		
5 Total—Add lines 4a through 4f		5	
6 Line 3 less line 5		6	
7 Personal holding company tax (attach Schedule PH (Form 1120))		7	
8 Recapture taxes. Check if from: ☐ Form 4255 ☐ Form 8611		8	
9a Alternative minimum tax (see instructions—attach Form 4626)		9a	
b Environmental tax (see instructions—attach Form 4626)		9b	
10 Total tax—Add lines 6 through 9b. Enter here and on line 31, page 1		10	

Additional Information (See instruction F.) — Yes | No

H Refer to the list in the instructions and state the principal:

(1) Business activity code no. ▶ ____________

(2) Business activity ▶ ____________

(3) Product or service ▶ ____________

I (1) Did the corporation at the end of the tax year own, directly or indirectly, 50% or more of the voting stock of a domestic corporation? (For rules of attribution, see section 267(c).) . .

If "Yes," attach a schedule showing: (a) name, address, and identifying number; (b) percentage owned; and (c) taxable income or (loss) before NOL and special deductions of such corporation for the tax year ending with or within your tax year.

(2) Did any individual, partnership, corporation, estate, or trust at the end of the tax year own, directly or indirectly, 50% or more of the corporation's voting stock? (For rules of attribution, see section 267(c).) If "Yes," complete (a) through (c) . . . .

(a) Attach a schedule showing name, address, and identifying number.

(b) Enter percentage owned ▶ ____________

(c) Was the owner of such voting stock a person other than a U.S. person? (See instructions.) **Note:** *If "Yes," the corporation may have to file Form 5472.* . . . . .

If "Yes," enter owner's country ▶ ____________

J Was the corporation a U.S. shareholder of any controlled foreign corporation? (See sections 951 and 957.) . . . . . .

If "Yes," attach Form 5471 for each such corporation.

Yes | No

K At any time during the tax year, did the corporation have an interest in or a signature or other authority over a financial account in a foreign country (such as a bank account, securities account, or other financial account)? . . . .

(See instruction F and filing requirements for form TD F 90-22.1.)

If "Yes," enter name of foreign country ▶ ____________

L Was the corporation the grantor of, or transferor to, a foreign trust which existed during the current tax year, whether or not the corporation has any beneficial interest in it? . . . . . .

If "Yes," the corporation may have to file Forms 3520, 3520-A, or 926.

M During this tax year, did the corporation pay dividends (other than stock dividends and distributions in exchange for stock) in excess of the corporation's current and accumulated earnings and profits? (See sections 301 and 316.) . . . . . .

If "Yes," file Form 5452. If this is a consolidated return, answer here for parent corporation and on **Form 851**, Affiliations Schedule, for each subsidiary.

N During this tax year did the corporation maintain any part of its accounting/tax records on a computerized system? . . . . .

O Check method of accounting:

(1) ☐ Cash

(2) ☐ Accrual

(3) ☐ Other (specify) ▶ ____________

P Check this box if the corporation issued publicly offered debt instruments with original issue discount . . . . . ☐

If so, the corporation may have to file Form 8281.

Q Enter the amount of tax-exempt interest received or accrued during the tax year ▶ ____________

R Enter the number of shareholders at the end of the tax year if there were 35 or fewer shareholders ▶

Form 1120 (1988) Page **4**

Schedule L Balance Sheets

Assets	Beginning of tax year (a)	(b)	End of tax year (c)	(d)
1 Cash				
2 Trade notes and accounts receivable				
a Less allowance for bad debts				
3 Inventories				
4 Federal and state government obligations				
5 Other current assets (attach schedule)				
6 Loans to stockholders				
7 Mortgage and real estate loans				
8 Other investments (attach schedule)				
9 Buildings and other depreciable assets				
a Less accumulated depreciation				
10 Depletable assets				
a Less accumulated depletion				
11 Land (net of any amortization)				
12 Intangible assets (amortizable only)				
a Less accumulated amortization				
13 Other assets (attach schedule)				
14 Total assets				
Liabilities and Stockholders' Equity				
15 Accounts payable				
16 Mortgages, notes, bonds payable in less than 1 year				
17 Other current liabilities (attach schedule)				
18 Loans from stockholders				
19 Mortgages, notes, bonds payable in 1 year or more				
20 Other liabilities (attach schedule)				
21 Capital stock: a Preferred stock				
b Common stock				
22 Paid-in or capital surplus				
23 Retained earnings—Appropriated (attach schedule)				
24 Retained earnings—Unappropriated				
25 Less cost of treasury stock		( )		( )
26 Total liabilities and stockholders' equity				

Schedule M-1 Reconciliation of Income per Books With Income per Return (You are not required to complete this schedule if the total assets on line 14, column (d), of Schedule L are less than $25,000.)

1 Net income per books		7 Income recorded on books this year not included in this return (itemize):	
2 Federal income tax		a Tax-exempt interest $	
3 Excess of capital losses over capital gains			
4 Income subject to tax not recorded on books this year (itemize):		8 Deductions in this tax return not charged against book income this year (itemize):	
5 Expenses recorded on books this year not deducted in this return (itemize):		a Depreciation $	
a Depreciation $		b Contributions carryover $	
b Contributions carryover $			
c Travel and entertainment $			
		9 Total of lines 7 and 8	
6 Total of lines 1 through 5		10 Income (line 28, page 1)—line 6 less line 9	

Schedule M-2 Analysis of Unappropriated Retained Earnings per Books (line 24, Schedule L) (You are not required to complete this schedule if the total assets on line 14, column (d), of Schedule L are less than $25,000.)

1 Balance at beginning of year		5 Distributions: a Cash	
2 Net income per books		b Stock	
3 Other increases (itemize):		c Property	
		6 Other decreases (itemize):	
		7 Total of lines 5 and 6	
4 Total of lines 1, 2, and 3		8 Balance at end of year (line 4 less line 7)	

CHAPTER 18

Evaluating Insurance Needs

Learning Objectives

After reading this chapter, you will be able to do the following:

- Introduce and define what insurance is.
- Supply alternatives to insurance.
- Describe the different types of insurance.
- Offer methods for determining insurance needs.
- Explain how to settle losses with insurance firms.
- Manage an efficient insurance program.

Determining the insurance needs of the startup firm is a matter of great importance to all entrepreneurs. Unfortunately, the insurance decision comes at a time when the startup is usually in a critical phase, so that entrepreneurs tend to devote insufficient time and thought to determining the insurance needs of their businesses. As a result, entrepreneurs often end up buying too much of one type of insurance and not enough of another, and remain unaware of the deficiency until they suffer a loss.

Businesses and business owners have always had to contend with risks, some inconsequential and some major. From the experiences of others, businesspeople realize that they, too, are subject to many of the same risks, such as fire, theft, and liability, and that they should secure protection from these risks. This desire for security is the basis of insurance. However, too many startup firms have insurance programs that resemble the insurance programs of some individuals. For example, consider a young executive who is in an airport and about to depart for a convention in another city. Realizing that she has no life insurance and that she has a teenage daughter just entering high school, she stops at the closest insurance counter and purchases $200,000 of life insurance.

This executive, like many business owners, has purchased insurance without determining how much she really needs and without thinking of the long term. She has also paid too much for the type of insurance she purchased. Rather than purchase insurance in a capricious fashion, she should determine the cost of supporting her daughter to age twenty-one, or through college, and should purchase enough life insurance to cover that need. This, in essence, is the basis of adequate insurance coverage: First determine the need in dollar terms, and then purchase insurance that will cover that need.

INSURANCE

The dictionary defines "insurance" as a contract binding a company to indemnify an insured party against a specified loss (or losses) in return for premiums paid. This definition implies that insurance is a legal contract between two parties, according to which one party (the insurance company) agrees to pay the insured a specified amount if a loss occurs from a specified cause. The insured agrees to pay the insurer a premium for this protection against the possible loss. As simple as this sounds, insurance is a complex subject and one that confuses many a startup entrepreneur. Because of the confusion, many owners purchase too much or too little insurance and leave gaps in their coverage that leave their firms vulnerable to loss and the possible imposition of a huge financial burden.

Risk

Risk is a concept that most individuals claim to understand but have difficulty explaining, although insurance is nothing more than risk management. The writer of an excellent article in *Science 85* illustrated this fact by asking practical questions such as: Which is riskier, flying on a commercial plane or driving a car? The answers revealed that most individuals perceive driving as less risky (because they are in control of the car) than flying when, in fact, their chances of being killed in an automobile are about ten times greater.[1] In another study, risk experts judged nuclear power to be safer than riding a bicycle, yet the general public perceived exactly the opposite. Planning for risks is called *risk management*. Risk management is the estimation of the probability and cost of potential losses, methods for meeting those risks, and their implementation. The major objective of risk management is to protect the entrepreneur and the firm against major losses.

The foregoing examples show that we as individuals do have trouble understanding risk. Yet risk is the very foundation of insurance. Risk may be defined as uncertainty. Risk is the uncertainty of a liability claim, loss from a fire, loss from a theft, or loss from an automobile or truck accident. If there is no uncertainty, there is no risk. Life insurance is a good example of uncertainty. Life insurance is purchased because of the uncertainty of when death will occur, not if it will, for that is certain. The executive purchasing life insurance in the airport is purchasing insurance against the uncertainty that death may occur during her trip and is betting, in fact, that death will not occur during that portion (95 percent) of her life when she is not going to a convention. Poor estimation of risks is how individuals make mistakes because, as we saw, we are ten times more likely to die driving a car (mile for mile) than flying, but we would not think of buying life insurance if we were driving to the same convention in our car.

The startup entrepreneur must learn to recognize risk and then learn to manage it. In fact, insurance is called risk management. Insurance is valuable because it reduces the loss from risk. This concept is important, since we cannot eliminate every risk. Purchasing insurance, therefore, allows the business enterprise to trade a large but uncertain loss for a small but certain loss, called a *premium*. For the cost of a small periodic premium, the owner of a business is insured against the uncertainty of incurring a large loss. This loss could be caused by the death of a key employee, a warehouse fire, a product-liability suit, or one of many other possible risks faced by the startup firm. In effect, the manager is trading uncertainty for a certainty, and this reduces risk.

Why is risk management important to the new business? A more illustrative question may be: What happens to the new business if a fire destroys the entire inventory and there is no fire insurance or the insurance that does exist covers only half the loss? A quick answer may be that the business could be wiped out, but this is not always the case. There are times when insurance does not pay and is not needed.

INSURANCE ALTERNATIVES

Before looking at the various types of insurance, an entrepreneur should realize that there are several alternatives to insurance, including the assumption of risk, the transference of risk, self-insurance, and loss prevention.

Assumption of Risk

One alternative to insurance is the assumption of risk, something individuals and businesses do every day because it is almost impossible to afford insurance against every conceivable loss. A firm should assume the risk of loss only when the potential loss is small, but it is extremely foolhardy for a firm to assume the risk of loss simply because the insurance premium is too high. Before assuming the risk, the entrepreneur should determine that the potential loss to the firm is not so severe that it could cripple the firm.

Transference of Risk

A second alternative is to transfer the risk to a third party. For example, never owning a building is avoidance of risk, but selling a building one owns and then leasing it is the transference of risk. A firm that leases a building is transferring risk by having the lessor maintain all the insurance on the building. Similarly, risk can be transferred by hiring temporary personnel from an employment agency rather than using one's own full-time employees for some jobs. Leasing automobiles and equipment under an agreement whereby the lessor maintains all the insurance is yet another example of risk transference.

Self-Insurance

Self-insurance is a third alternative to purchasing insurance. Self-insurance, however, is not non-insurance. A business with no insurance is assuming risk and doing nothing about it. In the case of self-insurance, a firm is setting aside funds, just as if it were paying an insurance premium, and using these funds to cover losses when they occur.

A typical example would be to have each outlet in a chain store firm contribute to a fund that would be used by headquarters to provide coverage in the case of a loss in one of the stores. Generally startup and small firms would not self-insure since they do not have several stores over which the risks could be spread, nor do they have the large amount of cash necessary to set aside to cover the potential loss.

Loss Prevention

The last alternative to insurance is loss prevention. Loss prevention includes programs that reduce the risk of loss. Programs to prevent fires (training programs, sprinkler systems, etc.) or the spread of fires (fire doors or fire barriers) and programs to protect against burglary (burglar alarms, video monitors, and dead bolt locks) are typical examples of preventing or reducing losses (see The Inside View 18-1). Loss prevention really is as simple as not cutting corners on construction, personnel training, and maintenance for the sake of saving a few dollars and taking the chance that nothing will happen. No parent would give the family car to their only son and tell him to go learn to drive without first giving him some instructions, yet some businesses do exactly that with their employees by putting them (without sufficient training) in situations that could have disastrous results for the firm.

THE INSURANCE INDUSTRY

Before describing the different types of insurance it is necessary to understand the nature of insurance, the insurance industry, and common insurance terms. Basically, insurance is a transfer device whereby risk is transferred from one individual or group

18-1 *The Inside View*

VIDEO CAMERAS INCREASE SALES

What happened to a well-known doughnut franchise is an interesting example of loss prevention. Several years ago, the management of Dunkin' Donuts decided to install video cameras in several of its stores that seemed to have a high risk of robbery. Their stated purpose was to prevent a robbery, since the cameras were in plain sight and any would-be robber would notice them and not risk being "caught" by the unblinking eye. The unexpected result was an almost 30-percent increase in sales. Management then decided to install the cameras in several additional stores. In this case, it seems like an ounce of prevention was worth a 30-percent increase in sales.

to another individual or group. For the farmer selling corn in the futures market, the risk of price fluctuations is transferred from the farmer to the buyer of the contract and, therefore, is insurance against adverse price changes. For the individual who belongs to a group health plan like Blue Cross/Blue Shield, the risk of incurring a major hospital bill is shared with other individuals who also subscribe to the plan. Each individual makes a relatively small contribution to the plan, providing a fund out of which those who incur large hospital or medical costs may be reimbursed.

From the insurance industry's standpoint, insurance is a contract in which the insurer agrees to reimburse the insured for any financial loss covered by that contract. The insurance firm is collecting premiums from a large group of insured individuals according to the probabilities of loss (known as underwriting), so that risk is distributed among a large group of individuals facing similar risks.

In providing insurance, the insurance firm enters into a legal contract (agreement) with its subscribers. To be valid, the contract must satisfy four conditions. First, the contract may not be in conflict with existing federal, state, or local laws. A policy to insure the delivery of illegal drugs from South America would not be considered a legal contract. Second, there must be a definite offer by one party and acceptance by the other. The offer from the insurance company is usually in terms of what it will pay for specified losses and what the premium will be for this insurance. Third, the contract must impose an obligation on both parties. For example, the insurance company agrees to pay for damages caused by a fire, if one occurs, and the insured agrees to pay a premium. Finally, the contract is invalid if fraud was perpetrated by either party in arriving at the agreement. A typical example is the gross misstatement of age or preexisting health problems on an insurance policy.

INSURANCE TERMS

Before delving into the different types of insurance, the entrepreneur must have a basic understanding of a few common insurance terms, for, without this understanding, purchasing the correct type and amount of insurance is difficult. With that in mind, this section will introduce the following concepts: insurable interest, indemnity, subrogation, representation, warranty, deductibles, coinsurance, and pro rata liability.

Insurable Interest

Under most insurance contracts, particularly property insurance, the insured must risk suffering a financial loss to be able to collect from an insurance policy. Thus, an individual cannot insure the building next door that is owned by another individual against a loss from a fire and collect if a fire does occur, because no financial loss was incurred by the insured. A general creditor, for example, has no property right to a living debtor's property and, therefore, no insurable interest. One does not have to own the property to have an insurable interest but simply must be able to show that one would suffer a financial loss if the property were damaged or destroyed. A repair shop may have another firm's equipment in for repair and have that equipment insured against loss from a fire. Certainly, in this case, ownership is not a requirement for a financial loss to occur.

Indemnity

According to the principle of indemnity, the insured can collect (be indemnified) only the cash value of the loss. In other words, the insured cannot profit from a loss. A fire-insurance policy for $100,000 on a building worth only $72,000 will pay only $72,000 in the event the building is destroyed by fire. This principle does not preclude the insurer from purchasing replacement-cost insurance, which allows the replacement of new materials for old materials that were destroyed or damaged. A property and liability insurance contract is generally a contract of indemnity while a life insurance policy is not.

Subrogation

According to the principle of subrogation, the insurer has the right to recover losses suffered by one of its insureds by collecting from the person or firm responsible for the loss. In the case of a loss from a fire that was caused by a negligent furnace repairman working for the oil company, the insurance company should first indemnify the insured for the loss but then has the right to collect (sue for) the amount of the loss from the oil company.

Representation

Representation is a statement (written or oral) in the insurance application process made by the individual seeking insurance. If, in the application, the individual gives false or misleading information that materially affects the risk factors involved, the insurance company may invalidate the contract. While the obvious example is falsifying information about the business, the omission of material information that affects the risks involved may also invalidate the insurance contract. For example, not mentioning that a store is located next to a fireworks factory is a misrepresentation that could invalidate a contract.

Warranty

A warranty is a statement by the insured that is incorporated into the written terms of the policy. If the insured breaches the warranty, the contract may be invalidated by the insurer even if the warranty concerns a fact that seems immaterial to the conditions of the contract. This is the major difference between a warranty and a representation, since the misrepresentation must be material before the breach of which would invalidate the contract. A typical warranty could include agreements on the maintenance of fire extinguishers and sprinkler systems or on having security personnel on the premises at all times.

Deductibles

Deductibles are the dollar amount or percentage of a loss that will not be paid by the insured. Automobile insurance is typical, in that most policies have a deductible amount of $50, $100, or $200. In case of an accident, the insurance company will cover the loss minus the deductible. Deductibles serve two purposes: They tend to reduce the amount of the premium by sharing any potential loss between the insurer and the insured and to eliminate small losses that are more likely to be the result of wear and tear than of perils that warrant insurance.

Co-Insurance

According to co-insurance, the insured has an obligation to share in the losses. Assume that a building is insured for $100,000 with an 80-percent co-insurance clause. If the building sustains a $20,000 loss in a fire and at the time of the fire the building was worth $150,000, how much will the insurance company pay? Without co-insurance, businesses tend to underinsure because, as in the aforementioned case, they assume that the insurance company will pay for the entire $20,000 minus any deductibles. In this case, however, with co-insurance the firm can recover only that proportion of the loss that the insurance taken ($100,000) bears to the insurance required ($120,000). The firm would receive 100/120 of the loss of $20,000 or about $16,667. If the firm had insured 80 percent of the building value as required ($120,000), all losses would have been paid by the insurance company minus any deductibles.

Pro Rata Liability

According to pro rata liability, the last insurance term, if the insured buys more than one policy and a loss occurs, then the various insurers pay only their pro rata share of the loss. For example, if a firm buys two $50,000 fire insurance policies on a building and sustains a loss of $20,000, each insurance company pays only half of the loss or $10,000. Thus, the pro rata liability principle reinforces the indemnity and subrogation principles.

THE MAIN TYPES OF INSURANCE COVERAGE

Although there are innumerable types of insurance, from fire to water damage, this section will cover some of the major types of insurance (to help entrepreneurs determine which type of insurance their startup businesses need. Fire, liability, automobile, workmen's compensation, crime insurance, and bonding are the major focus of this section.

Fire Insurance

Unlike most other forms of insurance, fire insurance is written by means of a standard policy prescribed by state laws that differ very little from state to state. The New York policy, with minor variations, is the standard policy used in most states. An advantage of a standard policy is that since all insurance companies use the same form of contract, it is easier for the insured to understand the meaning of the contract. Thus, discrepancies between different policies on the same risk are reduced, and agreement on loss settlements between the insured and insurer are easier than if standard policies were not used. Another advantage is that the number of lawsuits is greatly reduced.

Fire insurance policies insure "against all direct loss by fire, lightning, and by removal from premises endangered by the perils insured against in this policy except as herein provided." "Loss" means damage as well as destruction. "Direct loss" means that the property that is the subject of insurance must actually be damaged and excludes liability for such indirect losses as inability to operate, loss of sales, or loss of possible profits. (Coverage for these indirect losses is covered later in the chapter. See also the section on supplementary coverages.) To provide coverage against more than these three perils, the insured must add additional extensions to the basic policy. Other perils include hail, tornado, earthquake, windstorm, explosion, smoke damage, vandalism, water damage, freezing, motor vehicle damage, and falling objects.

Coverage may be suspended or canceled by either party. The policy may be suspended if the hazard to the business is increased by any means within the insured's control or knowledge or if the property is vacant for an extended period of time. For example, the coverage may be suspended if the insured starts a paint-mixing business on the second floor of a dry goods warehouse. The insurance company may cancel the policy for any reason by giving five days' notice, and the insured may cancel the policy at any time with no notice. In both cases, any advanced premium will be refunded on a pro rata basis, depending on the length of time to the expiration of the policy.

States regulate fire insurance rates through rating bureaus. These rating bureaus both inspect the properties before insurance is issued and develop a rate for each building. Fire insurance rate is the cost of $100 worth of insurance for one year. The premium is the rate multiplied by the number of hundred dollars of insurance face value. Almost all fire insurance rates can be divided into class rates and schedule rates.

Class Rates. With class rates, dwellings are classified according to the amount of insurance, construction (brick or frame) or state of occupancy, and the protection of the community (10 grades). The community class depends on the adequacy of water supply, fire departments, alarm systems, structural conditions, hazard ordinances, and the like. Communities are ranked in descending order from one to ten, with lower insurance rates going to those in the lower ranks.

Schedule Rates. Schedule rates are the results of surveys of the individual property. The survey includes an analysis of the building's construction, type of occupancy, exposure to risk, and protection from fire hazards. Results of this analysis are added to a basis rate, which is the rate for a standard building in the same city. These charges, or credits, are defined in a "schedule" and are the same for all properties subject to that particular schedule. Thus there may be schedules for hotels, lumberyards, grain elevators, and so forth, and the individual rate will depend on the schedule to which the building is subject.

Liability Insurance

Liability and liability lawsuits make the news almost every day. Like the weather, we all have opinions on liability lawsuits, and yet we always seem to disagree with the outcomes. Business owners must be aware of the threat of liability lawsuits and must try to protect themselves against that threat. A single lost case can close a small firm and has caused several very large corporations (e.g., A. H. Robbins with the Dalkon shield and Johns Mansville with asbestos) to declare bankruptcy. Part of the problem comes from our ignorance of the law, and part comes from the imponderables of the jury system. Examples are easy to find. In one case, a jury awarded over $1 million to a man who, in training for an athletic contest, strapped a refrigerator to his back and ran around a track. The strap broke and the refrigerator fell, injuring the athlete, who sued the manufacturer of the offending strap.[2] The cost of insuring against liability, for the strap maker and others, is high and getting higher. Almost nine cents of every dollar spent by purchasers for wooden ladders goes for the cost of liability insurance. Costs for liability insurance are added to everything consumers buy, from higher automobile prices to higher medical bills (see The Inside View 18-2).

What is liability? Liability involves the commission of a *tort,* which is a civil (as opposed to a criminal) injury. In a criminal injury, the injury is caused in violation of the law or with intent to harm. In a civil case, intent does not have to be proved, rather it is sufficient to find only that a product or service caused the injury. Liability is also the financial responsibility that one party has for another as a consequence of doing or failing to do something because of negligence or because of the terms of an existing contract agreement between two or more parties. In the second case, if one party signs a contract to purchase the services of another (for a movie or for accounting services), then that party has a liability to pay for those services whether they are used or not. Thus, after a contract is signed, one accounting firm cannot be replaced

18-2 *The Inside View*

WHAT PRICE INSURANCE?

The country is in the midst of a product liability-insurance crisis that is hitting startup firms and firms with new products very hard. In 1985, the average product-liability award was over $1.8 million. With these huge awards have come huge liability insurance premiums or, in many cases, an inability to obtain any liability insurance. Alcide Corp., a startup firm producing a disinfectant, has insurance premiums of $54,000 on sales of only $300,000. But they are luckier than CGS Aviation Inc., a manufacturer of ultralight aircraft, which had its insurance canceled. Even though the firm had a total of sixty firm orders, without insurance, banks would not lend it the funds for materials and expenses. Without operating funds, the firm is facing the prospect of having to go out of business.

Obtaining insurance, however, is something the startup firm must plan to do. Starting 120 days before the company needs coverage, the entrepreneur (and the insurance broker) should present information about the firm's products and/or services, including comments from independent testing agencies and any published research reports, to the insurer. Educating the insurance firm is the key, since many tend to refuse to insure or to quote very high rates to firms with new or different products. The entrepreneur must remember that insurance rates are based on past experience, so he or she must educate the insurance firm so that insurers can relate the product to something they know.[3]

by another that happens to offer a lower price. Negligence is a little more difficult to explain.

Negligence. Negligence legally obliges individuals and firms to exercise reasonable, or prudent, care, such that an innocent party is not personally injured nor property damaged. The problem with this straightforward definition is that there exists no widely accepted set of rules that define reasonable and prudent care. Since there is a legal duty to exercise reasonable care, an individual, or firm, can be negligent in several ways. First, is the failure to exercise care. Second, is the absence of an intent to cause injury. Third, is the injury of an innocent party a result of failure. Whatever the case, the injured party has the burden of proving that the defendant was negligent.

Liability insurance provides coverage against negligence suits and will pay for the loss from liability judgments, the expenses of investigating and defending lawsuits, and the cost of any court bonds or interest levied on judgments accrued during an appeal period. From the insured's standpoint, the fact that the insurance company handles the lawsuit from investigation to payment makes liability insurance worthwhile just for the handling of "nuisance" suits alone. Liability insurance does not cover the firm's obligations related to workmen's compensation laws (covered later in this chapter), damage to the property of others that is left in a firm's care, and liability resulting from war, nuclear energy, or blasting operations. The limitations of liability insurance are generally those set in the individual policy. A typical contract may state that the insurance firm will pay $150,000 per person injured, or a total of $500,000 in any one accident.

Types of Liability Insurance. The foregoing discussion of liability insurance is not intended to provide any more than background information on a very complex subject. A partial list of the many types of liability insurance available illustrates the complexity of the liability-insurance industry. These include the following: owners', landlords', and tenants' liability; manufacturers' and contractors' liability; products or completed-operations liability; contractual liability, catastrophe, or "umbrella" liability; water damage; sprinkler leakage; safe depository; libel; and several types of professional liability insurance for physicians, dentists, hospitals, accountants, and even lawyers.

Liability rates are based on the type of business seeking coverage and can vary dramatically from business to business and from firm to firm. Some firms even refuse to offer insurance to some types of businesses. More serious, however, is the fact that startup and young firms do not recognize the extent of their liability and do not have enough liability insurance. Too often they have a minimum amount of liability insurance when four times as much may cost only one-and-a-half times more. Yet one large judgment against such a firm could close it. The advice is simple: With the granting of huge awards in today's litigious society, the startup firm should not save money by purchasing too little liability coverage; one customer slipping on something dropped on the floor by another customer can financially cripple a firm. (Some firms are "solving" their liability-insurance problem by going bare. For example see The Inside View 18-3.)

18-3

The Inside View

GOING BARE

As more firms find their liability premiums increasing sharply, or eliminated altogether, they are looking for new ways of responding to the rising costs. A 1988 U.S. Chamber of Commerce survey found that 40 percent saw their insurance costs more than double and a quarter of those suffered increases of more than 500 percent. Nearly three companies in twenty could not get any liability coverage at all, and seven in twenty were considering "going bare" (without liability insurance).

One company that went bare was Sure-Grip International, an $80-million manufacturer of roller skates. After being told that the annual premiums for product liability insurance would jump 250 percent, Sure-Grip's president, Harry Ball, just decided to go without. In insurance terms, this meant going bare, and more and more firms are taking that route and assuming that risk. Mr. Ball recalls one product-liability case against his firm that he thinks is all too typical of why premiums have skyrocketed: "A woman was skating on our roller skates down a sidewalk . . . when she hit an upheaval and broke her ankle. She sued the city . . . the city, in turn, sued us. Part of the lawsuit was her contention that she had been caused sexual anguish. Our insurance company ended up having to pay her $45,000."[4]

Automobile Insurance

The risks involved in owning or operating an automobile, truck, or other moving vehicle are legal liability for bodily injuries or property damage and for damage to or loss of the insured's vehicle. The basic principles of liability insurance (see the previous section) apply to the liability that the startup business can incur in owning or using a vehicle. Whether employees of the firm are using company-owned, -rented, or -leased vehicles, or merely using the vehicles of their customers, the liability normally remains with the firm. To protect against liability losses and physical loss, most firms purchase a "comprehensive" insurance policy that insures against all types of physical loss except collision.

Collision is basically the damage to the insured's vehicle or to the vehicle operated by the insured that is caused by collision. Most collision policies are deductible collision, according to which a stated amount is deducted from each loss. Individuals and firms can realize significant savings on their premiums by determining the amount of the deduction that best meets their needs. For automobiles, the difference between a $50 deductible and a $300 deductible can be over $150 a year in premiums. Savings also can be realized for the vehicle worth less than $2,000. Is collision insurance for $400 needed if a vehicle seldom leaves the plant property? Is collision insurance needed even if the vehicle is out on the road?

Rates are set according to the territory in which the vehicle will be operating, the policy limits desired, miles driven per trip and per year, and the age and safety record of the driver and/or firm. Other rate factors include the size of the vehicle, the use of the vehicle, and the training given to the firm's drivers.

Workers' Compensation

Workers' compensation insurance is protection for employees in the event they are injured or disabled by a job-related accident. Workers' compensation is also liability insurance for the employer against lawsuits arising from employees' claims about working conditions that lead to disease, injury, or death. Although the law requires an employer to provide employees with a safe working environment, workers' compensation insurance was instituted because some industries are riskier than others. Universities hiring college professors are in a very low-risk industry, whereas coal mining firms are in a very high-risk industry. In compliance with state law, workers' compensation provides a specific payment for injuries rather than allow firms and their employees to dispute every injury case.

Workers' compensation does not cover all workers, however, because different state laws exempt some employers. In some states, employers hiring less than five people are not required to have workers' compensation, and in some states, covering employees is optional. Most states also exclude agricultural, domestic, and casual laborers from compensation laws. If employees are not covered, then they have the right of legal recourse through the courts.

Premiums for workers' compensation are based on the number of employees, the type of industry, and the safety record of the firm and the industry. Rates vary from 0.1 percent to over 20 percent of the payroll. The employer can, therefore, reduce his or her premium by reducing accidents. Accidents can be reduced by providing mechanical safeguards and protection where needed, educating employees about safe working practices, and convincing management that safety really does pay.

Crime Insurance

Most small-business owners are not familiar with crime insurance; they assume that loss from crime is part of doing business. All too prevalent is the belief that a major burglary could wipe out a business. Unfortunately there are no accurate facts on the losses businesses suffer each year because of criminal activity, but available figures do show that the dollar value of all losses may exceed the losses caused by fire.

Crime insurance offers protection against criminal acts committed by persons not connected with the business. The three major types of crime insurance are burglary, robbery, and theft. Burglary is the forcible entry into or exit from a business' premises for the purpose of stealing. Burglary insurance usually covers safes and inventoried merchandise. Robbery is the taking of property from a person by force or threat of force. Robbery insurance protects firms from a loss either on or off the firms' business premises and typically covers both physical losses and property damaged during the robbery. Theft (or larceny) is the taking of another person's property without his or her permission or with intent to defraud. Businesses like jewelry stores, whose inventory consists mainly of small items, should not be without crime insurance.

Several types of crime insurance are available, including the following very specific types: (1) burglary, (2) robbery, (3) mercantile theft, (4) safe burglary or payroll robbery, and (5) storekeeper's. There is also insurance for other types of crimes, including forgery and counterfeiting. Comprehensive policies covering losses from all types of crimes are available. Crime insurance premiums tend to be rather high, because businesses seeking this type of insurance are usually those in high-risk businesses.

Bonding

The two major types of bonds, fidelity and surety, both have distinctive purposes. Fidelity bonds protect a firm against losses from employee theft, whereas surety bonds guarantee that a firm will comply with the terms of a contract.

Fidelity Bonds. Each year firms lose more money to employee theft than to burglary, robbery, or larceny. Although embezzling causes huge losses each year, these losses do not show up in crime figures, because firms are reluctant to bring those responsible to trial for fear of bad publicity among customers or creditors. Fidelity bonds protect startup (and existing) firms from potentially crippling losses of employee theft (see The Inside View 18-4). Simply requiring that employees be bonded often discourages theft because the character investigation conducted by the bonding company may uncover information that helps the firm in its hiring and placement decisions.

Fidelity bonds are different from insurance contracts, in that the insurance contract involves two parties, whereas the fidelity bond is a contract among three parties. The fidelity-bond contract includes the bonding company (called the *surety*), the insured party (called the *obligee*), and the individual or entity assuming the obligation to the insured party (called the *principal*). With insurance, a covered loss of the insured party is paid by the insurance company. In bonding, if the event insured against should occur, the bonding company pays for the loss only if the principal fails to make good on a contractual agreement. The bond is thus a guarantee by the surety to the obligee that if the principal does not live up to his or her promise to the obligee, the surety will make good in his or her behalf. Most fidelity bonds cover the loss of property or money through "larceny, theft, embezzlement, forgery, misappropriation, wrongful abstraction, willful misapplication, or other fraudulent or dishonest act or acts."

There are three kinds of fidelity bonds: individual, schedule, and blanket. The specific person or persons who are named in the individual (or name) bond are bonded for a specified amount regardless of the position the individual holds within the firm or whether he or she moves from one position to another within the organization. A schedule (or position) bond lists all the names or positions to be covered and specifies the amount of coverage for each position, regardless of who occupies it.

18-4

The Inside View

EMPLOYEE CRIME

In a survey conducted by *Venture* magazine, 64 percent of the respondents reported that their companies had been the target of a crime. Unfortunately, employee theft is a significant part of the crime problem. According to the Council of Better Business Bureaus, nearly one-third of all business failures are caused by employee theft, making the startup company especially vulnerable.

Of the firms reporting crime problems, those with revenues under $2 million suffered an average loss of $87,213. For example, the office manager of a surveying equipment firm embezzled a total of $238,793 in her first year on the job. Interestingly, the owner of the firm had failed to check her references from a previous employer, who had accused her of embezzling. Tragic as this case is, it points out the need for preventive measures in reducing crime.

First, always investigate the background of job candidates for evidence of previous criminal activity. Second, keep tight controls on the accounting department. Third, have at least two people assume responsibility for issuing checks. Unfortunately, these three preventive measures are seldom taken until a problem has already occurred.[5]

The blanket bond covers all employees but does not identify them by name or position, thereby, in effect, providing group coverage. One advantage of the blanket bond is that coverage for losses is obtained without having to pinpoint which employee caused the loss. For example, losses from theft in a warehouse could be recovered without having to prove which person in the warehouse was guilty of the theft. Another advantage of the blanket bond is that new employees are automatically covered whether they are replacements or additional personnel.

Surety Bonds. Surety bonds guarantee that the named firm (the principal) will perform according to a plan or contract. Surety bonds are usually used in connection with construction contracts and help smaller firms compete against larger, better-financed firms. The insurance company (called a *surety*) guarantees that the principal (individual or firm) is honest and has the ability, and/or the financial strength, to perform according to the terms of a contract. Surety bonds are also used in connection with court actions and with those seeking permits or licenses. Court actions include fiduciary bonds; which name an individual who is appointed by the courts to carry out some task, and court bonds, which are filed by people engaged in litigation to obtain some restriction upon property or a release of some property from some restriction. Court bonds include garnishment, indemnity, and sequestration bonds.

SUPPLEMENTARY AND SPECIAL INSURANCE COVERAGE

In addition to the main types of insurance coverage, there are several types of supplementary and special-purpose programs that fit the specific needs of some companies.

Sprinkler-Leakage Insurance

Many buildings are equipped with automatic sprinkler systems to protect against the spread of fire. The pipes of these systems are usually located in the ceilings, with sprinkler heads located along the pipes at regular intervals. The valves of the sprinkler heads are heat sensitive and are set to open at a certain temperature. Unfortunately, these valves may open accidentally, they may open in response to non-fire-related high temperatures, thereby causing extensive property damage. Sprinkler-leakage insurance is designed to protect against the loss resulting from the accidental discharge of water from any part of the sprinkler system.

Water-Damage Insurance

Water-damage insurance is similar to sprinkler-leakage insurance but includes water damage from sources other than the sprinkler system. Hazards covered include damage from the air-conditioning system, the boiler and hot-water heating system, the plumbing system, or from the entrance of rain or snow through a broken window or roof. Water damage from rising waters, backed up drains, and floods are not included in this type of policy.

Glass Insurance

Glass insurance is one of the oldest and simplest of the casualty-insurance contracts, and its use has increased in recent years. Property covered by glass insurance includes plate-glass windows and doors, glass signs and lettering, glass countertops, and glass screens or panels. A comprehensive policy used by most firms excludes losses only from fire, war, and nuclear destruction.

Credit Insurance

With less than 5 percent of commercial transactions involving cash, the potential loss from extending credit is huge, particularly if a business has just a few large customers. Credit insurance is used to protect a wholesaler, jobber, or manufacturer against the failure of customers to meet their financial obligations. This type of insurance is not normally available to retailers or to those who lend money to commercial borrowers.

Rent Insurance

Rent insurance is designed to cover the loss of rent from property that is damaged by fire or some other peril. They are contracts of indemnity that do not allow the insured to recover more than the actual cash loss. Thus, expenses, like utilities, that do not occur because the renter is not occupying the rented space, are subtracted from the rent if the rent included utilities. The insured is also required to move with "due diligence and dispatch" in restoring the building to rentable condition.

Business-Interruption Insurance

Business-interruption insurance (similar to rent insurance) is designed to cover expenses due to the loss of the use of insured property while that property is being repaired because of damage from a fire or other insured peril. Typically business-interruption insurance covers the cost of continuing to pay some employees and scheduled expenses such as taxes, interest, insurance, advertising, and utilities. Firms can also obtain profits and commissions insurance to cover losses due to the loss of profits and/or commissions if goods are destroyed by fire or some other insured peril.

Transportation Insurance

Many firms transport a large portion of their products via truck, rail, airplane, or ship. Losses from spoilage caused by delays, theft, collision, fire, and other perils represent a substantial loss to the shipper; however, such losses can be covered with transportation insurance. A typical policy is the blanket motor-cargo policy, which includes insurance against losses due to all the perils previously mentioned as well as windstorm, flood, and explosion.

LIFE AND HEALTH INSURANCE

For the business startup, life and health insurance has three major purposes. First, life and health insurance provides needed protection for employees, the majority of whom have come to expect this benefit as part of their total compensation package. The firm that does not offer some form of employee life- and health-insurance package, will find high employee turnover. A second purpose of life and health insurance is to protect the firm from the death or disability of a key employee. The firm needs protection from the financial loss that can result from such a loss. The third reason is to aid in transferring ownership rights. Partnerships, sole proprietorships, and closely held corporations often need to purchase life insurance to ease the transfer of ownership or to keep control in the family when an owner dies. For these three purposes, there are several different kinds of life- and health-insurance plans available.

Group Insurance

From a total cost standpoint, group coverage is usually the best way to obtain life and health insurance. Group insurance can cover a large group like the employees of a single firm, or, for the very small firm, a group can be composed of other firms in the same type of business. For example, a two-person florist shop may be able to obtain group life and health insurance by joining an association of other florists in the same area. In this case, the group benefits would be available to all florists who belonged to the association. Group life and health insurance may be purchased from a single insurer or from two different insurers.

Group Life Insurance. Although employees tend to think of the total insurance package, life and health insurance are usually separate policies. Group life insurance is usually term insurance that covers employees during the term of the policy (which may be renewed periodically); however, at the end of the term (or employment), there is no further coverage and no accumulated cash benefit. These plans usually provide a stated amount of coverage that is normally related to the income of the employee. With most group life-insurance plans, the insurer requires that the insured group contain a minimum number but does not usually require medical examinations of the insured in such a group. In some plans (noncontributory), the employer pays all of the premium and all the employees are covered, whereas in other plans (contributory), the employees pay part of the premium and most of them must elect coverage. For the reduced term-insurance rates, the employer does much of the administrative work. That and the absence of a medical examination reduces the insurer's cost. Also the total selling expenses are less than those incurred in the case of an equivalent amount of individual insurance.

Life-insurance contracts contain none of the "indemnity" provisions characteristic of property- and liability-insurance contracts. Upon the death of the insured, life insurers pay a stated amount that may exceed the economic loss to the beneficiary.

Another way businesses use life insurance is to reward and retain valuable personnel. The split-dollar plan of life insurance is a good vehicle for this purpose both because the employer and employee pay a part of the premium for a whole life policy. The employer's share equals the annual increase in cash value, while the employee's share is the balance. Thus, each year the employee works, the cash value grows larger, and the employee pays less for his or her life insurance.

Businesses also use life insurance to maintain control of the firm. In a closed corporation, it is sometimes desirable to confine the control of the company to a limited group. To prevent the loss of control through the death of one of the major stockholders, each stockholder is insured, and the policies are given over to a trustee. The policies are accompanied by a trustee agreement to the effect that the proceeds are to be used to purchase the deceased's stockholdings and that the trustee is to divide them among the surviving stockholders.

Group Health Insurance. There are four major types of group health-insurance plans: (1) medical-expense insurance, (2) major medical insurance, (3) disability-income insurance, and (4) dental insurance. Medical-expense insurance is designed to protect the insured from financial loss due to medical costs. Some policies, like Blue Cross/Blue Shield, pay benefits directly to the provider of the medical service, whereas others, like most insurance companies, pay benefits directly to the insured.

Major-medical insurance plans are designed to provide protection from the cost of catastrophic illnesses. These plans provide medical-care coverage after the basic medical-expense insurance benefits have been exhausted. With major medical insurance, there is usually a substantial deductible amount for each claim but a high face amount of insurance. In addition, there may be a participation provision. For example, an employee who has had a heart attack is facing a $22,000 total medical-care bill. With a $500 deductible, an 80-percent participation provision, and a face amount of $50,000, the insured would owe only $4,800 plus the $500 deductible.

$22,000	Medical expense
−500	Deductible
$21,500	
17,200	Insurance coverage (21,500 × .80)
4,800	Amount owed by insured

Disability due to illness or accident may be the greatest threat to the financial security of employees; not only are they unable to earn an income, but they also may experience very large medical expenses at the same time. Disability-income insurance is designed to replace income that cannot be earned when employees are physically unable to work because of a long-term illness or disabling accident. Benefits are typically stated as a dollar amount per week for a stated number of weeks or as a certain percentage of the employee's annual salary. With most plans, there is a waiting period of from two to four weeks before the benefits begin. Health-insurance contracts that provide a specific periodic income to a disabled person are not contracts of indemnity, but they may contain provisions preventing duplicate recoveries from other insurance.

SETTLEMENT OF LOSSES

Very few businesspeople buy insurance hoping to collect the benefits; however, businesspeople do hope to be compensated for financial losses when they occur. In the event of a loss, the insurance contract states that "... the insured shall give immediate notice to this company of any loss" and, in the case of physical loss or damage, the insured shall "... protect the property from further damage...." These two statements are very important because the failure to comply with them can invalidate the insurance contract or result in a reduction of benefits. In addition, in the case of a fire loss, the insured must " ... furnish a complete inventory of the destroyed, damaged, and undamaged property, showing in detail quantities, costs, actual cash value, and amount of loss claimed." With a life-insurance policy, the proof of loss requires a death certificate or other documented evidence that the insured is deceased. With health insurance, proof of loss usually consists of doctors', hospital, or other medical bills.

What all of the foregoing indicates is that to collect, the insured must have good records to prove that a loss occurred. If a fire were to occur at an individual's apartment, home, or place of business right now, how would he or she prove what was lost? The sad fact is that most individuals could not remember everything in the building, let alone prove a loss. This fact points to the need, once again, for a complete set of accounting records. Adequate records should include original costs and purchase dates, costs and dates of improvements or additions, and up-to-date appraisals of the property. Up-to-date appraisals also help a manager determine how much insurance is needed, thus protecting against underinsuring. In addition, photographs, taken from several angles of each room or videotapes can provide evidence of ownership.

Although most claims for losses are handled quickly and to the satisfaction of the insured, most insurance contracts call for specific arbitration procedures if the insured and the insurer fail to agree on the amount to be paid for a loss. If agreement is not reached in this phase, then the insured may resort to a lawsuit.

In most cases, local insurance agents are authorized to settle small claims. Larger claims are usually handled by insurance adjusters whose job it is to evaluate the extent of the loss and to arrive at a settlement that will fairly compensate the insured in accordance with the terms of the policy. With most insurance policies, the insurer has three ways to settle a claim. The first is to make a cash payment. In accepting the cash payment, the insured normally forgoes the right to seek additional compensation. The second method is to repair the property or, third, to replace the property with other goods of equal quality, both at the insurer's expense.

MANAGING THE INSURANCE PROGRAM

From the many types of insurance coverages discussed in this chapter, it should be evident that with all the perils that exist (including many more not covered), most business owners will have a very difficult time determining the exact amount of insurance their businesses need. What, then, should be done? Basically, they should determine how the loss or damage of each of their resources would affect their ability to maintain control of their businesses and learn to manage risk. Risk management, in the broadest sense, is the determination of which risks the firm should insure against and for how much. Most risks, such as fire, death of a key person, a liability judgment, or theft are obvious, but others, such as the dishonesty of employees, are not as obvious. The problem is that no firm can insure against all eventualities, but most can do a better job than most firms are now doing.

Purchasing Insurance

There are two kinds of insurance agents: fire and casualty, and life and health. The fire-and-casualty agent can recommend what the firm needs. However, the manager must make the agent explain what he or she sees as the firm's needs and why. The agent should explain the firm's needs for liability coverage, workmen's compensation, bonds, and umbrella policies. The startup entrepreneur often overlooks this request for two simple reasons. First, startup owners are often so busy that they think they do not have time to be concerned about insurance—often a fatal mistake. Second, they assume that the insurance agent will design a policy that will be just right for their firm. Rather than ask questions about something they do not know, they delegate the future of their firm to an outsider who does not know the firm and its problems as well as they do. The bottom line is simple. Startup owners are paying very good money for insurance, so they should make the agent take the time to explain what they need and why. They should not be afraid to ask questions. In fact, this chapter was written to provide the startup owner with enough information so that he or she could ask relevant questions.

The life-and-health insurance agent can help design the firm's employee benefit package, provide key-person protection, assist with the personal insurance affairs of the entrepreneur, plan for the estate, and protect heirs. Again the agent must be asked to explain the details, and the entrepreneur must ask questions (see The Inside View 18-5).

In summary, the startup entrepreneur needs insurance but does not need to pay the insurance agent's mortgage. The following is a simple four-step plan: (1) Decide what risks the firm is exposed to. (2) Cover the largest loss exposures first and smaller ones as the budget permits. (3) Make proper use of deductibles. (4) Review insurance needs periodically. As a final note, a good insurance agent should visit the insured firm periodically in order to keep abreast of any changes in risk exposures.

18-5 *The Inside View*

INSURANCE FOR THE STARTUP FIRM

Obtaining insurance coverage for a startup firm is much more difficult today than it was a few years ago. The difficulty comes from much higher costs for most types of insurance and a dizzying array of coverage choices. According to Dennis Pillsbury, there are several steps the owner can take to obtain the correct amount and type of insurance needed for his or her firm.

1. Look at the commercial multiple-peril policies that are offered by many insurance companies. These policies provide most of the property and liability insurance needed by a small business in one package at a price that is substantially less than the sum of the premiums for the separate coverages.

2. Select your insurance agent carefully and consider using an independent agent who can offer a variety of insurance packages.

3. When buying liability insurance, utilize a sizable deduction to save on the premiums while sheltering the firm from a major liability loss.

4. Placing a real interest on safety and loss prevention can substantially reduce workers' compensation costs.

5. Several insurance firms market a small-business health package for organizations with one to ninety-nine employees. These packages offer substantial savings over individual coverage.[6]

Summary

Starting any new business entails a lot of risk. Some risks can be reduced through a good risk management (insurance) program. The objective of risk management is simple: Determine what risks the firm faces and reduce the chance of loss through insurance and loss-reduction techniques. There are several alternatives to purchasing insurance, including the assumption of risk, the transference of risk, self-insurance, and loss prevention.

Insurance is a contract according to which the insurer agrees to make good any financial loss covered by the contract that the insured may suffer. The insured agrees to pay a premium for the insurance and to try to prevent losses from occurring. The main types of insurance coverage that most startup firms should consider include fire, liability, automobile, workers' compensation, and crime insurance. In addition, some firms should consider having some employees bonded. There are also several types of special insurance coverage that fit specific situations.

Finally, the startup entrepreneur must consider life and health insurance. The three major purposes of life and health insurance are (1) to protect employees, (2) to protect the firm from the death or disability of a key employee, and (3) to aid in transferring ownership rights. Life and health insurance are normally purchased as group insurance to reduce the cost.

In the event of a loss, the insured must immediately notify the insurer and attempt to prevent any additional losses. Most insurance claims are paid quickly and to the satisfaction of the insured, but the insurance contract usually specifies the steps that must be taken should there be a disagreement between the insured and the insurer. Good insurance programs are developed when the entrepreneur takes the time to determine what risks the firm faces and then makes sure that the most important of these risks are covered.

Assembling the Pieces

As Jacki and Carol moved from their part-time operation (Charleston Spice Rack) to a full-time business (In Good Taste), they realized that they needed a good insurance (risk management) program. The potential risks they faced were the loss of one of the principal officers, property damage (from fire, theft, wind, water, etc.), and liability protection for both the business and the employees.

To protect themselves from these potential risks, they talked to two independent insurance agents and chose two insurance packages. The first provided \$100,000 term life insurance on each of the four officers of the corporation. This insurance was to help protect the firm from the financial loss that could result from the death of a key officer. The second package was a commercial multiple-peril policy that provided both property and liability insurance. Since they leased their store, the property insurance was based on the value of the inventory and the value of leasehold improvements—a total of \$100,000. Liability insurance provided a total of \$500,000 insurance, with a \$10,000 deduction clause. ■

Questions for Review and Discussion

1. What are four alternatives to insurance? Give an example of each.
2. An insurance contract is not valid unless four conditions are met. What are these four conditions?
3. What is the difference between risk avoidance and risk transfer? Provide an example.
4. Under what condition might a business decide to assume a risk?
5. Define "representation." Give an example of misrepresentation.
6. What is the difference between a warranty and a representation?
7. Assume a store is insured for $150,000 with an 80-percent co-insurance clause. If the building sustains a $90,000 loss in a fire, and, at the time of the fire, the building was worth $250,000, how much will the insurance company pay on the loss?
8. Fire insurance rates can be divided into class rates and schedule rates. Describe these two rates.
9. Use a recent local or national liability court case involving negligence to explain the grounds on which the plaintiff's attorney claims the defendant was negligent.
10. How is workers' compensation insurance different from liability insurance?
11. What are the three major types of crime insurance? Define each one.
12. Describe a local firm that would need to have its employees bonded. Which type of bond would it need? Why?
13. What are the three major purposes of life and health insurance?
14. How does a split-dollar plan of life insurance help a firm retain key employees?
15. What are the three ways an insurer settles claims?
16. As a class or student project, determine the potential risks faced by a nearby startup firm.

Notes

1. William Allman, "Staying Alive in the 20th Century," *Science 85,* October 1985, pp. 31–41.
2. Stephen Solomon, "Writing Policy," *Inc.,* February 1986, p. 17.
3. Jim Jubak, "Your Premium or Your Company," *Venture,* February 1986, pp. 40–44.
4. John Persinos, "Going Bare," *Inc.,* October 1985, pp. 72–85.
5. Nancy Madlin, "Crime and Your Business," *Venture,* February 1986, p. 26.
6. Dennis Pillsbury, "Insurance Alternatives for Growing Corporations," *Inc.,* June 1986, pp. 89–102.

Appendix A

INSURANCE CHECKLIST FOR SMALL BUSINESS

The following insurance checklist for small business was developed by Mark Greene, Professor of Insurance at the University of Georgia. This checklist enables entrepreneurs to discover areas in which their insurance program can be improved, costs can be saved, and the effectiveness of their insurance can be increased. It will also serve as a reminder of points to discuss with their insurance agent, broker, or other insurance counselor.

THE CHECKLIST

The points covered in the checklist are grouped under three general classes of insurance: (1) coverages that are essential for most businesses, (2) coverages that are desirable for many firms but not absolutely necessary, and (3) coverages for employee benefits. For each of the statements, put a check in the first answer column if you understand the statement and how it affects your insurance program. Otherwise, check the second column. Then study your policies with these points in mind and discuss any questions you still have with your agent.

Essential Coverages

Four kinds of insurance are essential: *fire insurance, liability insurance, automobile insurance,* and *workers' compensation insurance.* In some areas and in some kinds of businesses, crime insurance, which is discussed under "Desirable Coverages," is also essential.

Are you certain that all the following points have been given full consideration in your insurance program?

Fire Insurance

	No action needed	Look into this
1. You can add other perils—such as windstorm, hail, smoke, explosion, vandalism, and malicious mischief—to your basic fire insurance at a relatively small additional cost.	___	___
2. If you need comprehensive coverage, your best buy may be one of the all-risk contracts that offer the broadest available protection for the money.	___	___
3. The insurance company may indemnify you—that is, compensate you for your losses—in any one of several ways: (1) It may pay actual cash value of the property at the time of loss. (2) It may repair or replace the property with material of like kind and quality. (3) It may take *all* the property at the agreed or appraised value and reimburse you for your loss.	___	___
4. You can insure property you don't own. You must have an insurable interest—a financial interest—in the property *when a loss occurs* but not necessarily at the time the insurance contract is made. For instance, a repair shop or drycleaning plant may carry insurance on customers' property in the shop, or you may hold a mortgage on a building and insure the building although you don't own it.	___	___
5. When you sell property, you cannot assign the insurance policy along with the property unless you have permission from the insurance company.	___	___

6. Even if you have several policies on your property, you can still collect only the amount of your actual cash loss. All the insurers share the payment proportionately. Suppose, for example, that you are carrying two policies—one for \$20,000 and one for \$30,000—on a \$40,000 building, and fire causes damage to the building amounting to \$12,000. The \$20,000 policy will pay \$4,800; that is,

$$\frac{20{,}000}{50{,}000}, \text{ or } \frac{2}{5} \text{ of } \$12{,}000$$

No action needed | Look into this

The $30,000 policy will pay $7,200;

$$\text{that is, } \frac{30{,}000}{50{,}000}, \text{ or } \frac{3}{5} \text{ of } \$12{,}000.$$ ___ ___

7. Special protection other than the standard fire insurance policy is needed to cover the loss by fire of accounts, bills, currency, deeds, evidence of debt, and money and securities. ___ ___

8. If an insured building is vacant or unoccupied for more than 60 consecutive days, coverage is suspended unless you have a special endorsement to your policy canceling this provision. ___ ___

9. If, either before or after a loss, you conceal or misrepresent to the insurer any material fact or circumstance concerning your insurance or the interest of the insured, the policy may be voided. ___ ___

10. If you increase the hazard of fire, the insurance company may suspend your coverage even for losses not originating from the increased hazard. (An example of such a hazard might be renting part of your building to a drycleaning plant.) ___ ___

11. After a loss, you must use all reasonable means to protect the property from further loss or run the risk of having your coverage canceled. ___ ___

12. To recover your loss, you must furnish within 60 days (unless an extension is granted by the insurance company) a complete inventory of the damaged, destroyed, and undamaged property showing in detail quantities, costs, actual cash value, and amount of loss claimed. ___ ___

13. If you and the insurer disagree on the amount of loss, the question may be resolved through special appraisal procedures provided for in the fire insurance policy. ___ ___

14. You may cancel your policy without notice at any time and get part of the premium returned. The insurance company also may cancel at any time with a 5-day written notice to you. ___ ___

15. By accepting a coinsurance clause in your policy, you get a substantial reduction in premiums. A coinsurance clause states that you must carry insurance equal to 80 or 90 percent of the value of the insured property. If you carry less than this, you cannot collect the full amount of your loss, even if the loss is small. What percent of your loss you can collect will depend on what percent of the full value you have insured it for. ___ ___

16. If your loss is caused by someone else's negligence, the insurer has the right to sue this negligent third party for the amount it has paid you under the policy. This is known as the insurer's right of subrogation. However, the insurer will usually waive this right upon request. For example, if you have leased your insured building to someone and have waived your right to recover from the tenant for any insured damages to your property, you should have your agent request the insurer to waive the subrogation clause in the fire policy on your leased building. ___ ___

No action needed | Look into this

17. A building under construction can be insured for fire, lightning, extended coverage, vandalism, and malicious mischief. ___ ___

Liability Insurance

1. Legal liability limits of $1 million are no longer considered high or unreasonable even for a small business. ___ ___

2. Most liability policies require you to notify the insurer immediately after an incident on your property that might cause a future claim. This holds true no matter how unimportant the incident may seem at the time it happens. ___ ___

3. Most liability policies, in addition to *bodily* injuries, may now cover *personal* injuries (libel, slander, and so on) *if* these are specifically insured. ___ ___

4. Under certain conditions, your business may be subject to damage claims even from trespassers. ___ ___

5. You may be legally liable for damages even in cases where you used "reasonable care." ___ ___

6. Even if the suit against you is false or fraudulent, the liability insurer pays court costs, legal fees, and interest on judgments in *addition to* the liability judgments themselves. ___ ___

7. You can be liable for the acts of others under contracts you have signed with them. This liability is insurable. ___ ___

8. In some cases you may be held liable for fire loss to property of others in your care. Yet, this property would normally not be covered by your fire or general liability insurance. This risk can be covered by fire legal liability insurance or through requesting subrogation waivers from insurers of owners of the property. ___ ___

Automobile Insurance

1. When an employee or a subcontractor uses a car on your behalf, you can be legally liable even though you don't own the car or truck. ___ ___

2. Five or more automobiles or motorcycles under one ownership and operated as a fleet for business purposes can generally be insured under a low-cost fleet policy against both material damage to your vehicle and liability to others for property damage or personal injury. ___ ___

3. You can often get deductibles of almost any amount—say $250 or $500—and thereby reduce your premiums. ___ ___

4. Automobile medical-payments insurance pays for medical claims, including your own, arising from automobile accidents regardless of the question of negligence. ___ ___

5. In most States, you must carry liability insurance or be prepared to provide other proof (surety bond) of financial responsibility when you are involved in an accident. ___ ___

6. You can purchase uninsured-motorist protection to cover your own bodily-injury claims from someone who has no insurance. ___ ___

	No action needed	Look into this
7. Personal property stored in an automobile and not attached to it (for example, merchandise being delivered) is not covered under an automobile policy.	___	___

Workers' Compensation

	No action needed	Look into this
1. Federal and common law requires that an employer (1) provide employees a safe place to work, (2) hire competent fellow employees, (3) provide safe tools, and (4) warn employees of an existing danger.	___	___
2. If an employer fails to provide the above, the employer is liable for damage suits brought by an employee and possible fines or prosecution.	___	___
3. State law determines the level or type of benefits payable under workers' compensation policies.	___	___
4. Not all employees are covered by workers' compensation laws. The exceptions are determined by State law and therefore vary from State to State.	___	___
5. In nearly all States, you are now legally *required* to cover your workers under workers' compensation.	___	___
6. You can save money on workers' compensation insurance by seeing that your employees are properly classified.	___	___
7. Rates for workers' compensation insurance vary from 0.1 percent of the payroll for "safe" occupations to about 25 percent or more of the payroll for very hazardous occupations.	___	___
8. Most employees in most States can reduce their workers' compensation premium cost by reducing their accident rates below the average. They do this by using safety and loss-prevention measures.	___	___

Desirable Coverages

Some types of insurance coverage, while not absolutely essential, will add greatly to the security of your business. These coverages include business-interruption insurance, crime insurance, glass insurance, and rent insurance.

Business Interruption Insurance

	No action needed	Look into this
1. You can purchase insurance to cover fixed expenses that would continue if a fire shut down your business—such as salaries to key employees, taxes, interest, depreciation, and utilities—as well as the profits you would lose.	___	___
2. Under properly written contingent business-interruption insurance, you can also collect if fire or other peril closes down the business of a supplier or customer and this interrupts your business.	___	___
3. The business-interruption policy provides payments for amounts you spend to hasten the reopening of your business after a fire or other insured peril.	___	___
4. You can get coverage for the extra expenses you suffer if an insured peril, while not actually closing your business down, seriously disrupts it.	___	___
5. When the policy is properly endorsed, you can get business-interruption insurance to indemnify you if your operations are suspended because of fail-		

	No action needed	Look into this
ure or interruption of the supply of power, light, heat, gas, or water furnished by a public utility company.	___	___
Crime Insurance		
1. Burglary insurance excludes such property as accounts, fur articles in a showcase window, and manuscripts.	___	___
2. Coverage is granted under burglary insurance only if there are visible marks of the burglar's forced entry.	___	___
3. Burglary insurance can be written to cover, in addition to money in a safe, inventoried merchandise and damage incurred in the course of a burglary.	___	___
4. Robbery insurance protects you from loss of property, money, and securities by force, trickery, or threat of violence on *or off* your premises.	___	___
5. A comprehensive crime policy written just for small business owners is available. In addition to burglary and robbery, it covers other types of loss by theft, destruction, and disappearance of money and securities. It also covers thefts by your employees.	___	___
6. If you are in a high-risk area and cannot get insurance through normal channels without paying excessive rates, you may be able to get help through the federal crime insurance plan. Your agent or State Insurance Commissioner can tell you where to get information about these plans.	___	___
Glass Insurance		
1. You can purchase a special glass-insurance policy that covers all risk to plate-glass windows, glass signs, motion-picture screens, glass brick, glass doors, showcases, countertops, and insulated glass panels.	___	___
2. The glass-insurance policy covers not only the glass itself, but also its lettering and ornamentation, if these are specifically insured, and the costs of temporary plates or boarding up when necessary.	___	___
3. After the glass has been replaced, full coverage is continued without any additional premium for the period covered.	___	___
Rent Insurance		
1. You can buy rent insurance that will pay your rent if the property you lease becomes unusable because of fire or other insured perils and your lease calls for continued payments in such a situation.	___	___
2. If you own property and lease it to others, you can insure against loss if the lease is canceled because of fire and you have to rent the property again at a reduced rental.	___	___

Employee Benefit Coverages

Insurance coverages that can be used to provide employee benefits include group life insurance, group health insurance, disability insurance, and retirement income. Key-man insurance protects the company against financial loss caused by the death of a valuable employee or partner.

	No action needed	Look into this
Group Life Insurance		
1. If you pay group-insurance premiums and cover all employees up to $50,000, the cost to you is deductible for Federal income-tax purposes, and yet the value of the benefit is not taxable income to your employees.	___	___
2. Most insurers will provide group coverage at low rates even if there are 10 or fewer employees in your group.	___	___
3. If the employees pay part of the cost of the group insurance, State laws require that 75 percent of them must elect coverage for the plan to qualify as group insurance.	___	___
4. Group plans permit an employee leaving the company to convert group-insurance coverage to a private plan, at the rate for his/her age, without a medical exam, within 30 days after leaving the job.	___	___
Group Health Insurance		
1. Group health insurance costs much less and provides more generous benefits for the worker than individual contracts would.	___	___
2. If you pay the entire cost, individual employees cannot be dropped from a group plan unless the entire group policy is canceled.	___	___
3. Generous programs of employee benefits, such as group health insurance, tend to reduce labor turnover.	___	___
Disability Insurance		
1. Workers' compensation insurance pays an employee only for time lost because of work injuries and work-related sickness—not for time lost because of disabilities incurred off the job. But you can purchase, at a low premium, insurance to replace the lost income of workers who suffer short-term or long-term disability not related to work.	___	___
2. You can get coverage that provides employees with an income for life in case of permanent disability resulting from work-related sickness or accident.	___	___
Retirement Income		
1. If you are self-employed, you can get an income tax deduction for funds used for retirement for you and your employees through plans of insurance or annuities approved for use under the Employees Retirement Income Security Act of 1974 (ERISA).	___	___
2. Annuity contracts may provide for variable payments in the hope of giving the annuitants some protection against the effects of inflation. Whether fixed or variable, an annuity can provide retirement income that is guaranteed for life.	___	___
Key-Man Insurance		
1. One of the most serious setbacks that can come to a small company is the loss of a key employee. But your key employee can be insured with life insurance and disability insurance owned by and payable to your company.	___	___

	No action needed	Look into this
2. Proceeds of a key-man policy are not subject to income tax, but premiums are not a deductible business expense.	___	___
3. The cash value of key-man insurance which accumulates as an asset of the business, can be borrowed against and the interest and dividends are not subject to income tax as long as the policy remains in force.	___	___

Organizing Your Insurance Program

A sound insurance protection plan is just as important to the success of your business as good financing, marketing, personnel management, or any other business function. And like the other functions, good risk and insurance management is not achieved by accident, but by organization and planning. A lifetime of work and dreams can be lost in a few minutes if your insurance program does not include certain elements. To make sure that you are covered, you should take action in four distinct ways:

1. Recognize the various ways you can suffer loss.
2. Follow the guides for buying insurance economically.
3. Organize your insurance-management program.
4. Get professional advice.

Recognize the risks. The first step toward good protection is to recognize the risks you face and make up your mind to do something about them. Wishful thinking or an it-can't-happen-to-me attitude won't lessen or remove the possibility that a ruinous misfortune may strike your business.

Some businesses will need coverage not mentioned in the checklist. For example, if you use costly professional tools or equipment in your business, you may need special insurance covering the loss or damage to the equipment and/or business interruption resulting from not being able to use the equipment.

Study insurance costs. Before you purchase insurance, investigate the methods by which you can reduce the costs of your coverage. Be sure to cover the following points:

1. Decide what perils to insure against and how much loss you might suffer from each.
2. Cover your largest loss exposure first.
3. Use as high a deductible as you can afford.
4. Avoid duplication in insurance.
5. Buy in as large a unit as possible. Many of the "package policies" are very suitable for the types of small businesses they are designed to serve, and often they are the only way a small business can get really adequate protection.
6. Review your insurance program periodically to make sure that your coverage is adequate and your premiums are as low as possible consistent with sound protection.

Have a plan. To manage your insurance program for good coverage at the lowest possible cost, you will need a definite plan that undergirds the objectives of your business. Here are some suggestions for good risk and insurance management:

1. Write down a clear statement of what you expect insurance to do for your firm.
2. Select only one agent to handle your insurance. Having more than one may spread and weaken responsibility.

3. If an employee or partner is going to be responsible for your insurance program, be sure he/she understands the responsibility.
4. Do everything possible to prevent losses and to keep those that do occur as low as possible.
5. Don't withhold from your insurance agent important information about your business and its exposure to loss. Treat your agent as a professional helper.
6. Don't try to save money by underinsuring or by not covering some perils that could cause loss, even though you think the probability of their occurring is very small. If the probability of loss is really small, the premium will also be small.
7. Keep complete records of your insurance policies, premiums paid, losses, and loss recoveries. This information will help you get better coverage at lower costs in the future.
8. Have your property appraised periodically by independent appraisers. This will keep you informed of what your exposures are, and you will be better able to prove what your actual losses are if any occur.

Get professional advice about your insurance. Insurance is a complex and detailed subject. A professionally qualified agent, broker, or consultant can explain the options, recommend the right coverage, and help you avoid financial loss.

Source: U.S. Small Business Administration, Management Aid Number 2.108 (Washington, DC: U.S. Government Printing Office).

CHAPTER 19

Starting Companies and Doing Business in Other Countries

Learning Objectives

After reading this chapter, you will be able to do the following:

- Understand why entrepreneurship in other countries is becoming so important.
- Recognize the relative importance of small businesses in different countries.
- Understand the problems encountered by small businesses.
- Know how government and private groups in foreign countries assist small businesses.
- Determine whether or not exporting is appropriate for American startup entrepreneurs.

Are Americans too parochial? A man asks his friend: What do you call someone who speaks several languages? Answer: Multilingual. What do you call someone who speaks two languages? Answer: Bilingual. What do you call someone who only speaks one language? Answer: An American. This perception is not totally accurate; however, we Americans do tend to ignore much of what happens in the rest of the world. With the continuing internationalization of business, we can no longer afford to be so unaware. Foreign entrepreneurial firms compete internationally with American companies, and American startups can export their products and services to other parts of the world. Knowing something about foreign startups helps American entrepreneurs decide whether or not they should compete or collaborate with them.

This chapter is not designed to make international experts out of budding entrepreneurs. It is, however, designed to make entrepreneurs aware of how businesses are established and nurtured in other countries. We believe that American entrepreneurs might be able to "borrow" some of the startup techniques used by foreign entrepreneurs to make their own venture-creation process more efficient. Why should we continue to reinvent the wheel when someone in another country may already have a perfectly usable one?

It is impossible to adequately cover all aspects of startups in all countries. Therefore, this chapter will cover startup activities primarily in Europe, with special emphasis on Great Britain, but will also include some information on Asian countries. Because of space limitations, we are unable to provide any geographic or demographic data on the countries discussed. So we urge readers to consult other books and periodicals that contain these data before studying this chapter.

Just as we cannot include all countries in this chapter, we cannot hope to cover all startup activities. We have chosen to discuss the following small-business-related areas: the entrepreneurial atmosphere, the importance of small business to local economies, private and government assistance programs, and the desirability of exporting American goods and services. Information on these areas can help American entrepreneurs in at least three ways. First, foreigners may have discovered ways to expedite or simplify the startup process that Americans can use. Second, a knowledge of other countries will help entrepreneurs who plan to start companies that will export their products or services. Third, entrepreneurs planning new ventures that depend on imports should know how the small businesses that supply them with goods and services function in other parts of the world.

ENTREPRENEURSHIP

Entrepreneurship has been considered "fashionable" in Europe and other parts of the world only for the last ten or twenty years. There are a number of reasons why men and women were not encouraged by parents, teachers, or friends to be entrepreneurial and to start new ventures. First, in many foreign countries the most prestigious and powerful jobs were in the public sector. If one did not aspire to a government job, then, at the very least, one was expected to become a member of one of the more respectable professions, such as medicine. Second, becoming a member of a large, well-established corporation was seen as much more prestigious than becoming the owner of a small, struggling business. Third, failure and bankruptcy were shameful. A person whose business failed was stigmatized and castigated rather than encouraged to try again (see The Inside View 19-1). Fourth, education systems did not train young people to become self-employed. Finally, it was extremely difficult to acquire startup capital in most countries.

Encouraging Entrepreneurship

In the 1970s and 1980s, many of the taboos associated with entrepreneurship were mitigated, and the rush to self-employment was on. In Britain, for example, over 2.8 million people (about 12 percent of the working population) are now self-employed. Approximately 75 percent of the self-employed in Britain are males, and nearly two-thirds are in the service industry. Of those people who were self-employed, 17 percent had not been self-employed a year earlier.[1]

19-1 *The Inside View*

STARTUP DIFFICULTIES

The startups around Munich represent a major move by Germany from dying smokestack industries to new technologies and could be the key to the country's future economic vitality. However, establishing a startup in Munich remains a difficult proposition. Risk-taking is still an undervalued commodity; the management and marketing skills of entrepreneurs are limited; and corporate taxes of 65 to 70 percent are a definite disincentive. Moreover, failure is not acceptable: "The person who has the spirit to start a company risks a lot," says Thomas M. Kuchlmayr, head of the Munich Technology Center. "When you fail in Germany, people point and stare, and you'll never get another loan from a bank."[2]

Entrepreneurial Role Models

When we mention entrepreneurs in the United States, names like Fred Smith, Steve Jobs, and Debbie Fields come to mind, but who are the entrepreneurs in the rest of the world? The following are some of the best-known international entrepreneurs:

Germany. Heinz Nixdorf started his one-man computer firm in 1952. A graduate in applied physics from Frankfurt University, Nixdorf built and marketed his electronic gadgetry out of a cramped back room in his parents' small Dusseldorf apartment. Today, Nixdorf Computer AG is one of Europe's largest suppliers of electronic equipment. Revenue has exceeded $1 billion, and the company controls 20 percent of the small and medium-sized computer market.

France. Bernard Tapie, a business consultant specializing in bankruptcy, began his entrepreneurial career in 1978, when he began purchasing dying companies, often for only one franc. Tapie reduced the number of employees and expenses in these companies and made them profitable. Today, his Groupe Bernard Tapie, a broad-based conglomerate, has sales in excess of $650 million and profits of more than $15 million.

Britain. In the late 1960s, Richard Branson sold $20,000 worth of ads from a phone booth at his high school to launch a national magazine. The school dropout then ventured into the record industry and eventually built the $450-million-a-year Virgin Group. One of Branson's latest startups was Virgin Atlantic Airways, a frills-filled airline that flies for no-frills prices from London to New York and Miami. Richard Branson's personal fortune is estimated to be $350 million.[3]

Switzerland. Branco Weiss fled to Switzerland from Zagreb, Yugoslavia, in 1942. A Swiss scholarship enabled him to earn an engineering degree from Zurich's Eidgenossischen Technischen Hochschule. In 1956, Weiss and a Swiss partner founded a company they sold in 1959. With his $43,000 profit, Weiss started Kontron, a company that began manufacturing medical equipment. When he sold Kontron to Swiss chemical giant Hoffmann-La Roche in 1972, Weiss realized a profit of $60 million. He is now chairman of two Swiss technology firms and vice chairman of a third. Weiss is trying to enlarge the venture-capital system in Switzerland, which now spends less than $35 million a year on financing new ventures.[4]

The Value of Small Businesses

The awakening of the entrepreneurial spirit in Europe is, in part, the result of its recognition of the value and importance of small businesses to a healthy economy. It is difficult to determine exactly when this change in the attitudes of foreign governments took place; however, in Britain, the end of 1971 is generally accepted as a turning point. In November of that year, the Committee of Inquiry on Small Firms issued its report to the Queen. Commonly known as the Bolton Report (named after the committee chairman, J. E. Bolton), the document identified the following important economic functions performed by small firms:

1. The small firm provides a productive outlet for the energies of that large group of enterprising and independent people who set great store by economic independence . . . who have much to contribute to the vitality of the economy.
2. In industries where the optimum size of the production unit or the sales outlet is small, often the most efficient form of business organization is a small firm.
3. Small firms add greatly to the variety of products and services offered to the consumer because they can flourish in limited or specialized markets which would not be worthwhile for a large firm to enter.
4. Many small firms act as specialist suppliers to large companies of parts, sub-assemblies or components, produced at lower costs than the large companies could achieve.
5. In an economy in which ever-larger multiproduct firms are emerging, small firms provide competition—both actual and potential—and provide some check on monopoly profits and on the inefficiency which monopoly breeds.
6. Small firms, in spite of relatively low expenditure on research and development by the sector as a whole, are important sources of innovation in products, techniques and services.
7. The small firm sector is the traditional breeding ground for new industries—that is for innovation writ large.
8. Perhaps the most important, small firms provide the means of entry into business for new entrepreneurial talent and the seedbed from which new large companies will grow to challenge and stimulate the established leaders of industry.[5]

IMPORTANCE OF SMALL BUSINESSES

We know that small businesses are a vital part of the American economy; therefore, it should not be surprising to learn that they are also vital to the economies of most other countries. In this section, we will briefly examine the role of small business in a few selected countries.

Denmark

In Denmark's manufacturing industry, 17,872 (92 percent) businesses are small, 1,144 (6 percent) are medium-sized, and only 315 (2 percent) are large. Small and medium-sized businesses employ approximately 310,000 people, or 66 percent of the work force. It is estimated that small businesses generate approximately 20 percent of GNP in Denmark.

France

By the early 1980s, there were approximately 1.6 million firms filing full corporate income tax returns in France. There were 1,608,000 (99 percent) firms with fewer than 50 employees accounting for about 37 percent of sales. There were 23,000 firms (1 percent) employing from 50 to 499 people generating 22 percent of sales. The 2,000 large firms in France employed 4,734,000 people (39 percent) and accounted for 40 percent of the sales.

Germany, Switzerland, and Italy

In the Federal Republic of Germany (West Germany), small and medium-sized firms (SMEs) account for 99.8 percent of all companies, are responsible for 55 percent of all sales, employ 64 percent of all workers, and generate at least 48 percent of the GNP. In neighboring Switzerland, SMEs represent nearly 99 percent of all companies and employ about 77 percent of all workers. In the Italian industrial economy, SMEs represent 90 percent of all firms and employ about 83 percent of all employees.

United Kingdom

England, like its European neighbors, identifies 99 percent of its businesses as small and medium-sized; however, unlike its neighbors, British SMEs employ only 37 percent of the working population. While the percentage of people employed by SMEs seems relatively small, it is likely to increase because SMEs are increasing employment at the rate of about 2 percent per year. In fact, all the net increase in jobs in the industrial sector in the UK from 1975 to 1980 can be attributed to small and medium-sized firms. Since 1979 SMEs have created an estimated 700,000 new jobs.

Malaysia

The manufacturing sector in Malaysia, like that of many other countries, is made up primarily of small firms. In the early 1980s, firms employing less than 50 people accounted for approximately 90 percent of all businesses in Malaysia. These firms employed 29 percent of all paid manufacturing workers and accounted for 17 percent of the total value of fixed assets employed in the manufacturing sector.

There can be no doubt that small businesses are an important part of the economies of most countries. SMEs around the world employ a significant number of workers, account for a substantial percentage of sales, and contribute to GNP. In addition, it is the small and medium-sized businesses around the world that are creating most of the new jobs. Even though SMEs are vital economic factors, they are not without their own particular problems.

SMALL-BUSINESS PROBLEMS

In this section we will discuss some of the more pressing problems affecting small businesses. Since many of these problems are universal, we will identify specific countries only when and if the need arises. Many of the problems experienced by small-business owners are also common to larger businesses; however, the ramifications of these problems are often more severe for the former than the latter. Some of the general problem areas identified by small-business owners are: finance, purchasing, product and production development, personnel, sales, and management. We will discuss some of these problem areas in more detail in this section.

Financing

Capital for small-business expansion is scarce; however, it is even scarcer for startups. The following are some of the reasons why it is so difficult to obtain startup capital in England:

1. Simple ignorance on the part of would-be entrepreneurs about what facilities are available.
2. The banking system in Britain is excessively cautious toward very small firms.
3. Governmental commitment to effective removal of the barriers to small-firm formation remains weak and timid.
4. New small firms lack an effective method of communicating their most pressing concerns to government.[6]

Until recently, European entrepreneurs had to rely almost solely on banks and other lending institutions for startup and expansion capital. However, in the past few years, more venture-capital firms have been created to service the needs of private business (see The Inside View 19-2). Most venture capital goes to operating firms, but some companies are willing to provide seed money to entrepreneurs starting new businesses. The American consulting firm Venture Economics estimates that there are now one hundred twenty-five sources of venture capital and about $5 billion under management in the UK. France and Holland have about $1 billion of venture capital under management.[7] As the number of venture-capital firms increases, it is likely that more startup money will become available.

Lenders and borrowers do not always agree on the cause, scope, or cure of financial problems. Startup entrepreneurs nearly always rank availability of finance as one of their major problems; however, lenders claim that there is sufficient capital for those entrepreneurs with viable startup projects but that borrowers are just not aware of the various lending sources. The Industrial Finance Division of the Bank of England and the City Communication Centre developed a complete list of capital sources available to small businesses (see Figure 19.1).

Location and Facilities

The shortage of suitable locations and premises is one of the most frequently stated problems encountered by startup entrepreneurs in most countries. Locations available to people planning a new venture are usually less than ideal. The best locations are always chosen first, leaving marginal locations for other startup entrepreneurs. Com-

19-2 The Inside View

VENTURE CAPITAL IN EUROPE

Europe is finally warming up to American-style venture-capital investing. Spurred by the European Community's plan to abolish internal trade barriers by 1992, increasing numbers of venture-capital companies and entrepreneurs from Britain to Italy are investing more money than ever. In addition to agriculture, Europe's new venture capitalists are targeting such areas as medical technology, product distribution, and even champagne. The market is so hot that for the first time ever, more venture capital is being amassed in Europe than in the United States. The venture capitalists are focusing on firms that could take off in a more unified and prosperous Europe.[8]

plaints about available facilities include the following: lack of suitability for the type of business being planned, unrealistically high rent or purchase price; reluctance of the building owner to commit to a long-term lease; no room for expansion; and no loading or parking facilities. Startup entrepreneurs who settle for marginal facilities in a less than optimal location stand a good chance of seeing their businesses fail.

Staffing

Startup entrepreneurs around the world complain about the dearth of qualified personnel to staff their new ventures. Complaints about employees voiced by foreign entrepreneurs sound very similar to those often heard in the United States. The complaints of foreign entrepreneurs include the following: potential employees are lazy and not committed to work; employees are poorly educated and lack job training; employees expect too much money; many employees are not honest or reliable; large companies attract the most capable employees; and employees expect to advance too rapidly.

In some countries, such as Japan, employees are often hired for life. Other countries make it very difficult and costly to terminate employees. In some cases, firms that terminate employees must pay for their retraining and assist them in locating other employment. Because of the protection afforded employees, employers must be very careful in deciding whom to employ.

Government Regulation

The last problem we will examine is the one common to small-business owners throughout the world—government regulation and interference. Bureaucracy and red tape appear to exist in every country. Small-business owners and startup entrepreneurs everywhere are burdened by laws, regulations, and reporting requirements. The

FIGURE 19.1
Quick Guide to Sources of Finance

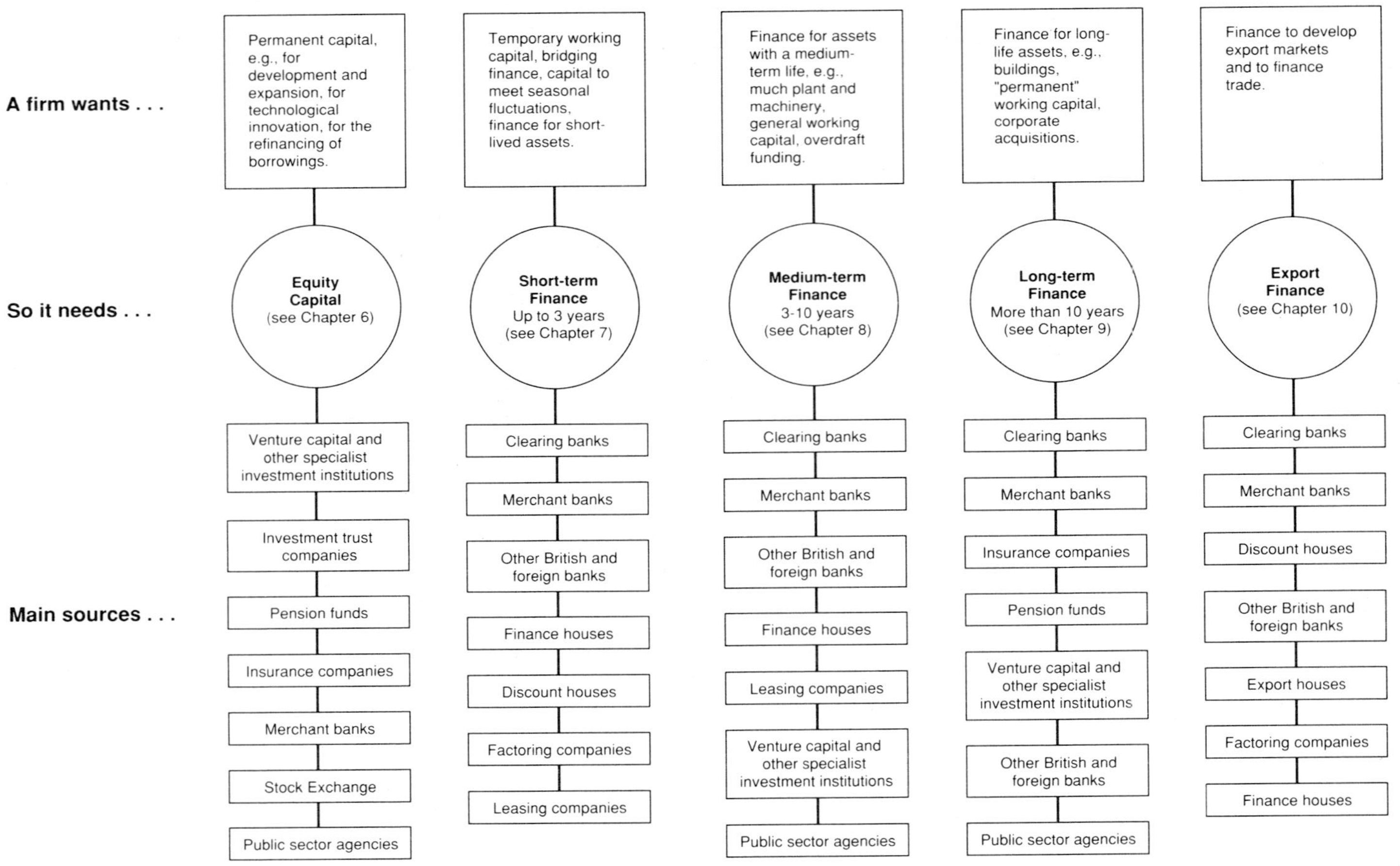

following letter, written in response to a request for information from the Bolton Committee, is representative of the frustration of small-business owners:

> Dear Sirs,
>
> We return herewith your forms SF1 and SF3 uncompleted, and we regret there is not the remotest chance of these being completed within the next six months. We calculate that irrespective of PAYE [Pay as You Earn] and National Insurance, we already spend the equivalent of two months' working time for one man working on Government and semi-Government records, forms and statistics. We regret that these forms can only be completed by the Chief Accountant or myself personally. No member of staff is capable or has access to information to enable them to complete such statistics.
>
> We are driven crazy by all this bureaucracy. You may need the information. We physically cannot give it. These forms will take the equivalent of one full day's work to complete and right now, we wish we could create one full day for ourselves to do the work we have.
>
> Industry is dying under the weight of paper.
>
> Yours faithfully,

Great Britain is not the only foreign country that requires numerous reports from small-business owners. Other countries have equally time-consuming and onerous reporting requirements. However, reporting is not the only government-created small-business problem. In many countries, the requirements for permits, licenses, compliance certificates, and the like appear to be designed to thwart the creation of new businesses (see The Inside View 19-3).

19-3 *The Inside View*

GOVERNMENT REGULATION

While studying English in London, Paolo Vittadini, a twenty-nine-year-old graduate of Milan's prestigious Bocconi University, noticed all the motorcycle messengers roaring through the city streets. Upon his return to Milan, Vittadini and a partner started Pony Express, Italy's first motorbike delivery service. Since Pony Express began, some two hundred similar companies have popped up across Italy. However, Vittadini's biggest problem is not competition; it is regulation. Under Italian law, rapid-delivery services are technically barred from carrying letters, memos, or any other signed communication. The Pony Express cyclists, who pay little attention to the rules, are fined, and the post office is pressing for many more new regulations.[9]

Realizing that small businesses are vital to their economies, many countries are attempting to alleviate the regulatory burden placed on small-business owners. Some countries have experimented with deregulation; some have created agencies to assist small businesses; and some have reduced reporting requirements. In the next section we will examine some of the ways governments are trying to assist small businesses.

GOVERNMENT ENCOURAGEMENT AND ASSISTANCE

In the preceding section we discussed the problems caused by government regulations and reporting requirements. In order to present a balanced picture of the role of government, we must also examine how governments around the world assist small businesses. It would be impossible to discuss all of the assistance programs available to small businesses; however, we will examine some of the major programs in a few countries. In many instances, the programs we examine could very easily be imported to the United States to help our own small businesses.

France

The following are some government programs designed to support small French companies:

- Tax relief to encourage the formation of new enterprises.
- Special loans for exporting firms and for companies in difficulty.
- Subsidies or grants for the creation of jobs for young workers and for the development of new technology.
- Low-interest credit from Agence Nationale pour la Valorisation de la Recherche (ANVAR) for innovation.
- The establishment of institutions to provide equity capital for small businesses.
- Information provided to small-business managers to promote exports.
- Relief from social security payments to encourage recruitment by small firms.
- Advisory services provided by a team of 200 industrial management advisors working from local chambers of commerce and industry.

Italy

The Italian government does very little to encourage or support small businesses. There are no formal financial-assistance programs for small firms, and they receive no support to create new jobs or to engage in research and development. There are no tax incentives for small businesses, and the government has no special programs to encourage them to export their products. What assistance is available to small companies comes from regional and local governments.

Since regional parliaments cannot be directly involved in credit or industrial policies, they must find indirect ways to assist small businesses. Some regional governments establish industrial parks for small businesses and encourage regional agencies to purchase from small firms whenever possible. Other programs such as management training and startup assistance are offered by the chambers of commerce and industry in the different regions.

United Kingdom

Since the assistance programs available to small businesses in Great Britain are so numerous and well documented, we will devote a separate section to them.

ASSISTANCE PROGRAMS IN THE UNITED KINGDOM

The British government has a long history of assisting and encouraging business; however, during the 1950s and 1960s, small-business owners claimed that large companies enjoyed a disproportional amount of that assistance. In response to these claims, the government established the Bolton Committee to study all aspects of small business in Great Britain. In essence, the committee found that there existed some legislation benefitting small businesses but that more was needed.

Between 1946 and 1970, the government passed fifteen laws or formed agencies that provided some form of assistance to small businesses. However, since the Bolton Committee presented its report in 1971, there have been at least thirty-three laws passed or agencies established to assist small firms. The Bolton Report stimulated government to provide more assistance to small firms than it had in the past. In the remainder of this section, we will examine some of the British government's small-business assistance programs.

Investment Assistance

The government is not directly involved in investment programs for small firms; however, it has implemented several plans designed to give tax relief to people willing to invest in small businesses. In some cases, the relief is for startup entrepreneurs, but there are also plans to encourage other investors to provide capital to new businesses. The following are examples of relief plans:

1. ***Relief for certain pretrading expenses.*** Expenditure of a revenue nature that is incurred before trading begins is eligible for relief. Examples of pretrading expenses that are eligible for relief include rent and employees' wages.
2. ***Relief for interest paid on money borrowed for investment.*** In order to qualify for tax relief on money borrowed for investment, individuals must have a material interest in the company (own more than 5 percent of the shares), or they must work for the company.
3. ***The Business Expansion Scheme.*** This plan encourages individuals to invest risk capital in new or existing enterprises based in the UK by allowing tax deductions for losses incurred.
4. ***Relief for costs of raising business-loan finance.*** Expenditure that has been incurred since April 1980 on the incidental costs of either obtaining or repaying qualifying loan finance is allowed as a deduction in computing the trading profits of a business for tax purposes.[10]

Financial Assistance

The British government rarely makes direct loans to small businesses; however, it does guarantee bank loans made to startups and small firms. Under the provisions of the Loan Guarantee Scheme, the government guarantees up to 80 percent of a small-business loan. Loans of up to £75,000 are granted for periods of between two and seven years. Interest rates, determined by participating banks, are usually 2 to 3 percent above the prime rate. The government encourages banks to participate in the Loan Guarantee Scheme, and it encourages them to develop their own small-business lending plans. Several banks have created loan programs especially for new and small businesses. The government also assists small businesses in acquiring venture capital.

The government, through the Bank of England, participates with other large banks in a venture-capital company known as Investors in Industry or 3i. In 1986, 3i invested £67 million in 251 startups and supported 109 management buyout teams with £101 million. In other instances, local governments provide venture capital to startups and small businesses (see The Inside View 19-4).

Enterprise Agencies

Business in the Community (BIC), a private organization, teams up with local and central governments to stimulate the economic prosperity of local communities. BICs sponsor Enterprise Agencies, which respond to the economic, social, and environmental needs of the community by providing various types of assistance. Principal among their activities is the provision of free advice and counseling to support the startup and development of viable small businesses.

Managed Workshops

Managed workshops are similar to American incubators. Their purpose is to provide the types of services that a larger company can organize for itself but that are too expensive for small firms (see The Inside View 19-5). Typically the workshops are run

19-4 *The Inside View*

GOVERNMENT-SPONSORED VENTURE-CAPITAL FIRM

Bexley, on the southeast fringe of London, has taken the unusual step of launching a venture-capital fund to provide risk capital to local businesses. The purpose is to fill the equity gap left by established venture-capital funds and the banks. Bexley Venture Capital, which is the brainchild of the borough council's economic development unit, plans to offer amounts of between £5,000 and £25,000 to local firms. The five-man board of directors of BVC will meet monthly and promises a preliminary decision to applicants within four to five weeks.[11]

19-5 *The Inside View*

MANAGED WORKSHOPS

The North London borough of Hackney charges the seventeen tenants in its managed workshop just £12 per week rent when they start business and may increase it to a maximum of £24 per week after twelve months—levels well below the commercial rate. Another workshop in Islington, North London, charges its twenty-eight tenants just 70 percent of the commercial rate when they start and raises it to the full rate after three years. In addition to subsidized rents, tenants at both workshops benefit from sharing secretaries and receptionists as well as their business experiences and problems.[12]

by a general manager who arranges secretarial services, telephone and telex facilities, and building maintenance and security. There are about five hundred managed workshops in Great Britain, but more will be needed to accommodate new and small businesses.

DOING BUSINESS IN OTHER COUNTRIES

Many startup entrepreneurs ignore foreign markets. Some believe that there is no demand for their product; some feel that they are too small to be international; some believe that there is too much red tape associated with international trade; and some are simply unaware of opportunities in other countries. With a little investigation and assistance, American small businesses can successfully do business in other countries. Today, only 1 percent of American businesses accounts for 80 percent of U.S. exports, but the Department of Commerce estimates that about twenty thousand small U.S. manufacturers and agricultural firms offer goods and services that could be very competitive in foreign markets. Furthermore, according to department statistics, 60 percent of American companies that do export have fewer than one hundred employees.

Becoming Involved

For many startup entrepreneurs and small-business owners, the most difficult aspect of international business is making the decision to participate. However, once they have decided to do business in other countries, entrepreneurs and owners have access to numerous government and private sources of assistance. Entrepreneurs should do some basic planning before they decide to seek assistance. The first order of business is to determine how to become involved in foreign trade. The following are some of the ways to become active in international business:

1. ***Exporting.*** For many new businesses, the most expedient way to become involved in foreign trade is by exporting their products or services to selected markets. While this can be a lucrative way to enter foreign markets, entrepreneurs should do their homework thoroughly before becoming exporters.

2. ***Licensing.*** Entrepreneurs can "license" foreign companies to manufacture their products. In essence, the foreign company pays the domestic company a fee for the right to manufacture and market the latter's product.

3. ***Sales subsidiaries.*** If entrepreneurs want to control their international marketing, they can establish their own subsidiaries in foreign markets to promote and sell their products. This essentially eliminates middlemen.

4. ***Sales representatives.*** If marketing control is not vital, entrepreneurs can contract with individuals or companies to sell their products in foreign markets. The principal drawback to this type of arrangement is that foreign sales agents may handle the products of competing firms.

5. ***Joint ventures.*** Owners of new companies can form joint ventures with foreign firms to manufacture and market the former's products in the latter's markets.

Once startup entrepreneurs have determined how they want to become involved in international trade, they should decide how many and which countries could be attractive partners. There are a number of market-research steps that will help entrepreneurs make their decision. First, obtain export statistics that indicate product exports to various countries. Second, identify five to ten large and fast-growing markets for the firm's products. Third, identify some smaller fast-emerging markets that may have fewer competitors. Fourth, target three to five of the most statistically promising markets for additional assessment and evaluation. Fifth, evaluate the number and strength of competing companies, and ascertain the quality of their products. Sixth, analyze factors such as consumers and channels of distribution affecting marketing and use of the product in each market. Seventh, identify tariff and nontariff import barriers. Now the entrepreneur is ready to choose the countries with which to do business.[13]

Exporting

Many startup entrepreneurs will choose exporting as the most expedient way to become involved in international trade. Exporting eliminates the need for foreign manufacturing facilities and affords new companies immediate international exposure at minimum cost. The first decision new business owners should make is whether to export indirectly or directly.

Indirect Exporting. The major advantage of indirect marketing for smaller American companies is that it allows them to penetrate foreign markets while bypassing the complexities and risks of direct exporting. The following are examples of companies that provide a variety of export services:

1. ***Commission agents.*** These agents find domestic manufacturers who can provide the goods that foreign companies or governments need. Since commission agents are retained by foreign companies, they are paid by that foreign company.

2. ***Export management companies.*** An export management company (EMC) acts as the export department for one or more noncompeting companies. An EMC transacts business in its own name or in the names of the firms it represents. For services rendered, EMCs charge client companies a commission, a salary, or a retainer plus commission.

3. ***Export trading companies.*** Export trading companies (ETCs) are similar to EMCs but generally provide a broader range of services. In reality, there is very little difference between the two organizations.

4. ***Export agents, merchants, or remarketers.*** These people buy the products of domestic manufacturers, who pack and mark them according to the agent's specifications. They then sell the products overseas in their own names.

Direct Exporting. New companies that choose to control the export of their products can bypass the middlemen and deal directly with foreign companies or customers. Direct exporters generally select their target market, determine the most appropriate channels of distribution, and then decide which foreign businesses should handle their products. The channels of distribution that can be used overseas include agents, distributors, retailers, and direct sales to end users.

1. ***Agents or sales representatives.*** Foreign agents who represent U.S. companies in a host country advertise and sell the products of American manufacturers but assume no risk or responsibility for them. The agent receives a commission from the exporting company and may operate on an exclusive or nonexclusive basis.

2. ***Distributors.*** Unlike agents or representatives, distributors purchase products from American companies and resell them in the foreign market. Foreign distributors usually provide the support and service for products that would normally be provided by the manufacturer.

3. ***Foreign retailers.*** Some companies, particularly those that manufacture consumer goods, may choose to deal directly with foreign retailers. Company salespeople can sell directly to foreign retailers, or the selling company may rely on brochures or catalogs.

4. ***Direct sales to end users.*** Smaller businesses can sell directly to foreign end users, who are likely to be governments, hospitals, banks, schools, or other similar institutions. The Department of Commerce maintains an Export Mailing List Service, which interested businesses can use to identify potential foreign buyers.

5. ***Trade fairs.*** A very effective foreign selling technique often overlooked by small firms is attendance at trade fairs. The buyers at trade fairs could be any of the agents, distributors, or other personnel already mentioned. Renting space at fairs is relatively inexpensive, and the payoff can be substantial and immediate (see The Inside View 19-6). Trade fairs are an ideal distribution channel for small companies that cannot afford to pay full-time salespeople or agents.

Mistakes in Exporting

Some entrepreneurs, especially those who do not do their homework, encounter problems and frustrations when they attempt to trade internationally. Problems often arise when American entrepreneurs are not sensitive to foreign cultures and operating methods or when they ignore the basic "rules" of doing business overseas. For example, some business owners translate their product's name, advertising, operating directions, and so forth, into foreign languages without regard for idioms or other language peculiarities. The following are some of the linguistic mistakes that American firms have made:

An American airline in Brazil advertised "rendez-vous lounges" on its jets. In Portuguese, "rendez-vous" means a room hired for lovemaking.
"Body by Fisher" became "corpse by Fisher" in Flemish.
When Pepsi-Cola's slogan "Come alive with Pepsi" was translated in Taiwan, it meant "Pepsi brings your ancestors back from the dead."
When Kentucky Fried Chicken's famous slogan "It's finger-licking good" was translated into Farsi (the language of Iran) it read: "It's so good you will eat your fingers."[14]

In order to avoid such embarrassment, entrepreneurs should familiarize themselves with the cultural, economic, and political systems of foreign countries. It would also be helpful to know something about the history and religion of target countries. However, it is a mistake to believe that all exporting problems are culture or language

19-6 *The Inside View*

SELLING AT TRADE FAIRS

Iris Graphics, Inc., displayed its products at a 1986 West German trade fair billed as "the world's largest printing and paper extravaganza." The company was only two years old and had twenty-four employees producing its color verification equipment for magazines and newspapers. Attendance at the Dusseldorf fair paid off with an order for a $125,000 unit, along with considerable interest from prospective customers and agents: "The response was greater than we had anticipated, both in terms of quality end users and the folks that wished to represent us around the world," says Tad Thompson, an Iris Graphics executive.[15]

based. American exporters make numerous other mistakes. The following are the ten most common mistakes of new exporting firms:

1. Failure to get qualified export advice and to develop an international marketing plan prior to starting an international trade relationship.
2. Insufficient commitment by top management.
3. Poor selection of overseas agents or distributors.
4. Chasing orders from around the world rather than establishing a basis for profitable and orderly growth.
5. Neglect of export business during domestic economic booms.
6. Failure to treat international distributors on an equal basis with their domestic counterparts.
7. Reluctance to modify products to meet preferences or regulations of other countries.
8. Failure to print sales, service, and warranty messages in local language.
9. Failure to consider use of an export management company or other marketing intermediary.
10. Failure to consider licensing or joint-venture agreements.[16]

With a little planning and forethought, exporting mistakes can be avoided. Entrepreneurs who are alert to foreign opportunities and are willing to modify their product to satisfy customer needs should be successful exporters (see The Inside View 19-7).

International Trade Assistance

In an earlier section of this chapter, we discussed how foreign governments and private organizations assist their small businesses. In this section, we will examine some similar assistance available to U.S. small businesses. There are many federal and state agencies as well as private organizations that can help small businesses become

19-7 *The Inside View*

EXPORTING SUCCESSFULLY

Some small U.S. companies have become very successful by customizing products for foreign markets. Adolph Hertrich, the owner of a small lumber mill in Boring, Oregon, switched to metric sizing for his lumber and mastered Japan's complicated grading system. He even stacks his Japan-bound wood to suit the market there—with only vertical grain surfaces exposed. He generates 70 percent of his sales in Japan.[17]

involved in international trade. Sometimes, locating the right source of advice may be an entrepreneur's primary exporting hurdle. We cannot identify all sources of assistance; however, we will briefly examine some of the major helping organizations (see Appendix A at the end of this chapter for other international trade organizations).

U.S. Department of Commerce. The Department of Commerce is the principal government agency providing export assistance (see Figure 19.2 for a listing of the Department's assistance programs). Within the department, the primary organization dealing with U.S. exports is the International Trade Administration (ITA). The services of the ITA are made available at the local level by the U.S. and Foreign Commerical Service (US & FCS), which has forty-eight district offices. A few of the many services offered by the US & FCS are: market research, assistance in promoting U.S. products in overseas markets, computerized trade opportunities, help in locating overseas agents or distributors, trade missions and introductions of U.S. firms to foreign buyers, export seminars and conferences, participation in major international trade fairs, and customer evaluations.

U.S. Export–Import Bank. The Export–Import Bank (Eximbank) is another example of an organization designed specifically to help businesses export. Among the services provided to small businesses by Eximbank are the following: Small Business Advisory Service, export credit insurance, new-to-export insurance policy (Eximbank offers a short-term insurance policy geared to meet the particular credit requirements of smaller, less-experienced exporters), working capital guarantee, and direct and intermediary loans.

Small Business Administration. Through its field offices in cities all over the United States, the Small Business Administration (SBA) provides counseling to potential and current small-business exporters. Services include export counseling, export training, financial assistance, and legal advice.

State Governments. In an effort to encourage small businesses to export their products, many states have created agencies or departments to provide trade assistance. Among the services state agencies offer small businesses are the following: export education, marketing assistance, market development, trade missions, and trade shows (see Figure 19.3 for a list of the services provided by states).

Commercial Banks. Small businesses need capital to finance their exports. Unfortunately, their banks are usually fairly small and do not have the expertise to be involved in international business. It is primarily the large national banks, such as Chase Manhattan, Bank of America, Bank of Boston, and NCNB Corporation, that provide export funds. These large banks, located in major U.S. cities, maintain correspondent relationships throughout the country with smaller banks that can make export services available to small business.

Chambers of Commerce and Trade Associations. Many chambers of commerce and trade associations provide important services to members interested in exporting. Typical services offered include export seminars and workshops, trade promotion, organization of U.S. pavilions in foreign trade shows, contacts with foreign companies

FIGURE 19.2

U.S. Department of Commerce Services

Source: *A Basic Guide to Exporting* (Washington, DC: U.S. Department of Commerce, 1981).

FAST MATCH

A quick, easy way to match your international business requirements to the programs of the Department of Commerce. If you are seeking information or assistance regarding →

USE ↓

	Potential Markets	Market Research	Direct Sales Leads	Agents/Distributors	Licenses	Credit Analysis	Financial Assistance	Risk Insurance	Tax Incentives	Export Counseling/ Education	Export/Import Regulations	Major Overseas Contract Opportunities	Marketing Plans/ Strategies
Foreign Trade Statistics (FT-410)	•	•											
Global Market Surveys	•	•											
Market Share Reports	•	•											
Foreign Economic Trends	•	•											
Commercial Exhibitions	•	•	•	•	•								
Overseas Business Reports (OBR)	•	•											
Overseas Private Investment Corp.		•					•	•					
New Product Information Service			•	•	•								
Trade Opportunites Program (TOP)			•	•	•						•		
Export Contact List Services			•	•	•								
Agent Distributor Service (ADS)				•									
World Traders Data Reports (WTDR)						•							
Export-Import Bank							•	•					
Foreign Credit Insurance Assoc. (FCIA)								•					
Foreign Sales Corp. (FSC)							•		•				
U.S. Commercial Service	•	•								•	•		
ITA Business Counseling	•	•								•	•		
U.S. Foreign Commercial Service	•	•	•	•		•				•	•	•	
International Economic Indicators	•	•											
Country Market Sectoral Surveys	•	•											
Office of Country Marketing	•	•									•	•	•
East-West Trade	•	•									•		•
Office of Export Administration										•	•		
Small Business Administration							•			•			
Private Export Funding Corporation							•						
Major Projects (Overseas)												•	
Webb-Pomerene Association											•		
Product Marketing Service	•	•	•	•									

FIGURE 19.3

State Trade Development Services: *Sources of Assistance by State*

Source: Small Business Success, San Francisco: Pacific Bell Directory in coordination with the U.S. Small Business Administration, 1988, p. 38. Used by permission.

	Seminars/ Conferences	One-on-one counseling	Market studies prepared	Language bank	Referrals to local export services	Newsletter	How-to handbook	Sales leads disseminated	Trade shows	Trade missions	Foriegn offices reps.	Operational financing program
Alabama	•	•			•		•	•	•	•	•	
Alaska									•	•	•	
Arizona	•	•	•			•		•	•	•		
Arkansas	•	•	•	•	•	•		•	•	•	•	
California	•	•		•		• (a)	• (b)	•	•	•		•
Colorado	•	•	•		•			•	•	•		
Connecticut	•	•	•		•	•		•	•		•	
Delaware	•				•			•	•			
Florida	•	•	•					•	•	•	•	
Georgia	•	•	•		•			•	•	•	• (c)	
Hawaii	•	•			•			•	•	•		
Idaho	•							•	•	•		
Illinois	•	•	•		•			•	•	•	•	•
Indiana	•	•		•				•	•	•	•	•
Iowa	•	•	•	•			•	•	•	•	•	
Kansas	•	•			•	•	•	•	•	•		
Kentucky	•	•			•		•	•	•	•	•	
Louisiana (d)												
Maine	•							•		•		
Maryland	•	•				•		•		•	•	
Massachusetts	•	•	•		•				•			
Michigan	•	•	•			•	•	•	•	•	•	
Minnesota	•	•			•	•		•	•	•	•	•
Mississippi	•	•	•			•	•	•	•	•		•
Missouri	•	•	•		•	•	•	•	•	•	•	
Montana	•	•	•		•		•	•	•	•		
Nebraska	•	•		•	•		•	•	•			
Nevada	•			•		•				•		
New Hampshire	•	•			•		•	•				
New Jersey	•	•			•	•		•	•	•		
New Mexico	•	•			•		•	•			•	
New York	•	•			•	•	•	•	•	•	•	
North Carolina	•	•	•	•	•	•		•	•	•	•	
North Dakota	•	•						•	•			
Ohio	•	•	•	•	•	•		•	•	•	•	•
Oklahoma	•	•	•	•	•	•	•	•	•	•		
Oregon	•	•				•	•	•	•			
Pennsylvania	•	•	•		•	•		•	•		•	
Rhode Island	•	•	•		•	•		•	•	•	•	
South Carolina	•	•	•		•			•	•	•	•	
South Dakota	•	•	•	•				•				
Tennessee	•	•	•		•		•	•	•	•		
Texas	•	•					•	•	•		•	
Utah	•	•					•	•	•	•	•	
Vermont	•										•	
Virginia	•	•	•				•		•		•	
Washington	•	•	•	•	•	•	•	•	•	•	•	
West Virginia	•	•								•		
Wisconsin	•	•			•	•	•	•	•	•	•	
Wyoming										•		

(a) California issues a bimonthly column to local chambers and trade groups for publication in their newsletters. (b) California produces a "road map" to low cost and free trade services. (c) Georgia's foreign offices are only active in attracting reverse investment. (d) Louisiana has recently established a new office of International Trade, Finance and Development within the Department of Commerce and Industry. The office is expected to offer a full range of trade promotion services.

and distributors, transportation routings and consolidation of shipments, and hosting of visiting trade missions (see Figure 19.4 for a list of the services provided by different agencies and organizations).

Secondary Sources. Entrepreneurs contemplating exporting may want to read about international business before seeking assistance from the agencies and organizations previously mentioned. A tremendous amount of international trade literature is available, and much of it is provided at no cost to small-business owners. The following is just a sampling of some of the available material:

Market Overseas with U.S. Government Help, a Small Business Administration pamphlet.

International Exhibitors Handbook, published by the International Exhibitors Association (IEA).

FIGURE 19.4
International Trade Assistance

A quick reference for matching international trade business needs with the assistance offered by public and private sector organizations.

USE →
IF YOU WANT ↓

IF YOU WANT ↓ / USE →	U.S. Department of Commerce	U.S. Small Business Administration	Export-Import Bank of the United States	Overseas Private Investment Corporation	U.S. Department of Agriculture	U.S. Department of State	Department of the Treasury	General Agreement on Tariffs and Trades	United Nations	Embassies and Consulates	World Bank	Inter. American Development Bank	Asian Development Bank	State Departments of Commerce	Chambers of Commerce	Port Authorities	Commercial Banks	Export Management Companies (EMC's)	Trade Associations	Export Packers	Freight Forwarders	Custom House Brokers	Consulting Firms	Transportation Carriers	Credit Reporting Firms	Universities
Export/Import Training Programs	•	•	•	•	•									•	•		•				•					•
General Export Information	•	•			•			•	•					•	•	•	•		•		•		•	•	•	•
General Import Information							•			•					•	•	•		•				•	•		
Potential Foreign Markets	•	•		•	•	•		•	•	•				•	•	•	•	•	•				•			•
Trade Statistics	•							•	•									•	•				•			
Foreign Buyers and Representatives	•				•									•	•	•	•	•	•					•		
Foreign Sources of Supply	•									•					•	•	•		•		•		•			
Overseas Projects	•					•					•	•	•		•		•	•								
Overseas Investment Opportunities	•			•					•					•		•		•					•	•		
Foreign Firm Credit/Reliability	•		•							•							•								•	
Corresponding Overseas	•													•	•			•	•				•			
Translation Assistance										•					•		•	•					•			•
Overseas Travel					•					•					•		•	•								
Product Sales Promotion	•				•										•			•	•				•			
Export Financing	•	•	•	•	•	•					•	•	•				•	•					•			
Insurance of Overseas Shipments/Investments			•	•														•			•					
Tax Incentives	•						•																			
Foreign Trade Zones	•						•																			
Collection Documents	•													•	•		•	•			•		•			
Shipping Documents	•																	•			•	•	•			
Packaging and Shipping	•														•	•	•	•	•	•	•	•		•		

Source: Small Business Success, San Francisco: Pacific Bell Directory in coordination with the U.S. Small Business Administration, 1988, p. 39. Used by permission.

A Basic Guide to Exporting, published by the U.S. Government Printing Office.
The Global Edge, written by Sondra Snowdon (New York: Simon and Schuster).
Partners in Export Trade, published by the U.S. Government Printing Office.

Successful International Dealings

We believe that all entrepreneurs with competitive products or services can benefit financially from their involvement in international trade. The most difficult part of the process is making the decision to venture overseas and then following through on the decision. Fortunately, there are numerous government agencies and private organizations that are willing to assist novice exporters. Small-business owners who do their homework should be successful in their dealings with foreign businesses, both large and small. Results of a survey of small businesses that engage in exporting revealed that they were successful and were remarkably flexible in identifying and overcoming external obstacles to international trade.[18]

Summary

Small businesses around the world seem to have more similarities than differences. In every country we have studied, small businesses are a mainstay of the economy. If small businesses are considered to be those with less than five hundred employees, they account for nearly 99 percent of all businesses in most countries. Even if the maximum number of employees is decreased to two hundred, small businesses account for 90 percent or more of all firms in most countries. These small businesses often provide employment for as much as 60 percent of the work force and account for one-third or more of GNP. As vital as these companies are to their country's economy, they are not without natural and government-created problems.

Nearly anyone with a desire to be self-employed can open a business of his or her choosing; however, the problems encountered by those firms often lead to early failure. Most countries do not have accurate failure statistics, but it is believed that their failure rates are comparable to those in the United States. Some of the major problems encountered by small businesses include the following: limited and expensive capital, lack of suitable premises, marketing and competitive problems, shortage of qualified employees, and government regulation and interference. Fortunately, some countries are taking steps to eliminate or reduce bureaucratic regulations and reporting requirements.

Governments are not only reducing regulations, they are also providing direct and indirect assistance to startups and small businesses. Government assistance programs include tax relief, subsidized loans, training programs, partial payment of employee wages, and export assistance. In many countries, government and private-sector groups have formed partnerships to assist startups. Industrial parks, managed workshops, and enterprise agencies are a few of the jointly sponsored programs that assist small businesses. Finally, governments are encouraging banks and other investor groups to make more venture capital available to startups and small businesses.

Small American companies can do business with their counterparts and larger firms in other countries. Owners of small companies with competitive products can become involved in international trade by manufacturing and selling overseas or by exporting their domestically manufactured products. Exporting is probably the most expedient way to get started in foreign trade. There are numerous government agencies and private organizations willing to provide export assistance to small-business owners. If approached correctly, exporting can enhance the profitability of small American businesses.

Assembling the Pieces

At first glance it might appear that Jacki and Carol could operate In Good Taste without much concern for international events or activities; however, that is not true. Jacki and Carol are directly involved in international trade, and they are dependent to a certain extent on the regulations and policies of foreign governments. Most of the items comprising the inventory of In Good Taste are imported. Wines and cheeses come from Europe; coffee beans come from Central and South America, cooking oils come from Spain and Italy; and cooking utensils come from Europe and the Orient.

Carol and Jacki need to be aware of foreign price increases that will be passed on to them and ultimately to their customers. They need to know when government regulations or natural conditions will affect their ability to purchase items such as coffee beans. They even need to be aware of foreign exchange rates and transportation costs because of their effect on the cost of merchandise purchased for In Good Taste.

Jacki and Carol need to be familiar with business conditions and practices in other countries because there might come a time when they decide to become importers. It is conceivable that their business could grow large enough to warrant the establishment of direct relationships with foreign suppliers. Items such as wine or olive oil could be profitably imported by Carol and Jacki for sale through In Good Taste or other retail outlets of their choosing. Knowing how small businesses operate and obtain assistance from their governments could directly benefit Jacki and Carol. ■

Appendix A

ORGANIZATIONS INVOLVED IN INTERNATIONAL TRADE

Agency for International Development (AID). Administers U.S. bilateral development-assistance programs.

Coordinating Committee for Multilateral Export Controls (COCOM). A committee established in 1951 by NATO countries to coordinate policies relating to the restriction of exports of products and technical data of potential strategic value to the Soviet Union and certain other countries.

Customs Cooperation Council (CCC). An intergovernmental organization promoting the simplification, standardization, and conciliation of customs procedures.

European Free Trade Association (EFTA). A group of European countries trying to eliminate trade tariffs for member nations. By 1992 all tariffs in the European Community are to be eliminated.

Foreign Credit Insurance Association (FCIA). An agency established in the United States in 1961 to provide U.S. exporters with insurance facilities in partnership with the Export–Import Bank of the United States.

International Monetary Fund (IMF). An international financial institution that seeks to stabilize the international monetary system as a sound basis for the orderly expansion of international trade.

International Trade Association (ITA). The unit of the U.S Department of Commerce that carries out the government's nonagricultural foreign-trade activities.

United Nations Conference on Trade and Development (UNCTAD). A subsidiary organ of the United Nations General Assembly that seeks to focus international attention on economic measures that might accelerate Third World development.

U.S. International Trade Commission (USITC). An independent fact-finding agency of the U.S. government that studies the effects of tariffs and other restraints to trade on the U.S. economy.

United States Trade Representative (USTR). A cabinet-level official with the rank of Ambassador who is the principal adviser to the U.S. President on international trade policy.

World Bank. An intergovernmental financial institution whose goals are to raise productivity and income and to reduce poverty in developing countries.

World Intellectual Property Organization (WIPO). A specialized agency of the United Nations system that seeks to promote international cooperation in the protection of intellectual property.

Questions for Review and Discussion

1. Explain why entrepreneurship is becoming more prevalent in European countries than it was a few years ago.
2. Are the entrepreneurial traits ascribed to foreign entrepreneurs similar to those attributed to their American counterparts?
3. Why are small firms important to foreign economies?
4. What are the major problems encountered by startups and small firms in foreign countries?
5. Which government-assistance programs do you think are most beneficial to startups and small firms?
6. Do you think American small businesses need more government assistance?
7. Why do so few American businesses, especially small firms, become involved in international trade?
8. Should the U.S. government do more to encourage exporting?

Notes

1. Stephen Creigh, Ceridwen Roberts, Andrea Gorman, and Paul Sawyer, "Self-Employment in Britain," *Employment Gazette,* June 1986, pp. 183–194.
2. Gail Schares, "'Silicon Bavaria': The Continent's High-Tech Hot Spot," *BusinessWeek,* 29 February 1988, pp. 75–76.
3. David Fairlamb, "Europe Rediscovers Entrepreneurs," *Dun's Business Month,* July 1985, pp. 56–59.

4. Richard Morais, "Swiss Risk," *Forbes,* 1 June 1987, p. 49.
5. *Small Firms Report of the Committee of Industry on Small Firms,* Chairman J. E. Bolton (London: Her Majesty's Stationary Office, November 1971), pp. 83–84.
6. Martin Binks and John Coyne, *The Birth of Enterprise* (London: The Institute of Economic Affairs, 1983), p. 72.
7. Richard Morais, "Swiss Risk," *Forbes,* 1 June 1987, p. 49.
8. Richard Melcher, Gail Schares, Frank Comes, and Joyce Heard, "A Continental Spending Spree for Venture Capitalists," *BusinessWeek,* 29 August 1988, pp. 41–42.
9. Richard I. Kirkland, Jr., "Europe's New Entrepreneurs," *Fortune,* 27 April 1987, pp. 253–262.
10. *How to Set Up & Run Your Own Business, 5e* (London: Telegraph Publications, 1986), pp. 148–153.
11. ———, "Venturing Out to Fill a Local Gap," *Financial Times,* 14 July 1987, p. 14.
12. Charles Batchelor, "Managed Workshops: Shortage Is Inhibiting New Start-Ups," *Financial Times,* 17 July 1987, p. 3.
13. ———, "A Step-by-Step Approach to Market Research," *Business America,* 16 March 1987, pp. 10–11.
14. Franklin Root, *Foreign Market Entry Strategies* (New York: AMACOM, 1982), p. 132.
15. Steven Golob, "Sell Overseas at Trade Fairs," *Nation's Business,* March 1988, pp. 57–59.
16. Alice Gray, "Planning an Export Venture," *Business America,* 16 April 1984, pp. 3–9.
17. William Hampton, "The Long Arm of Small Business." *BusinessWeek,* 29 February, 1988, pp. 63–66.
18. Alfred Holden, "Small Businesses Can Market in Europe: Results from a Survey of U.S. Exporters," *Journal of Small Business Management,* January 1986, pp. 22–29.

KNICKERS IN A TWIST

After Peter Barnett left Shiplake College, Henley-on-Thames, Oxon, he became involved in the wine trade. He worked both in his native England and in France, where he visited most of the wine-growing regions. After personality differences with his employer led to his dismissal, Peter was faced with a major career decision. In keeping with a family tradition of self-employment, Peter decided that he, too, should try his hand at being his own boss. However, Peter was not sure what kind of business he should start.

One evening Peter was discussing his dilemma with his father and his father's friend. After Peter had considered several possibilities and was still undecided, his father's friend commented that Peter seemed to have his "knickers in a twist" (an expression meaning that someone is confused or undecided). Peter latched onto this expression and decided that he would start a business called Knickers in a Twist. Now all he had to do was decide what his product would be, who would manufacture it, who would buy it, etc. Peter also had to decide whether his business should be created, or whether he should consider other options.

Peter believed that the name for his proposed company was unique and that it would attract the interest of potential investors, suppliers, and others. However, he knew that any interested parties would also want facts, figures, and projections before they agreed to invest in his company or sell his product. He began his business plan with an introduction explaining his ideas and his business.

INTRODUCTION

Since leaving school in 1979, I have been gaining experience in the workplace and developing an idea that would lead me to bigger and better things. The phrase "Knickers in a Twist" came up in a conversation with a family friend, but the actual idea of putting knickers (ladies underpants) in a twist within a tube is my own. One of my aims is to make buying and giving underwear fun.

With such an enormous market in knickers, it is evident that the consumer is always on the lookout for something new and different. According to my research, there has never been a product called "Knickers in a Twist." Marks and Spencer, the department store, controls a large portion of the underwear market; however, by no means do they dominate the market. This market is more vibrant and fashion-conscious now than ever before. It is my opinion that the market is at a point where it requires a new, interesting, and significantly different marketing idea. I believe K.I.A.T. will fill a gap in the up-scale end of the market.

Consumers are always on the lookout for something new and interesting. I feel, therefore, that I am very much in the right place at the right time with the right product. I believe that I have a product of exciting potential to place in a large and receptive market.

STRENGTHS AND WEAKNESSES OF K.I.A.T.

Peter wanted to provide as much objective information as possible about his proposed business, so he identified what he thought were his company's strengths and weaknesses.

Strengths

The strengths of Knickers in a Twist include the following:

1. The small size of the company allows quick responses to market developments.
2. The nature and presentation of the product will make it possible to change the buying pattern from women buying for women to men buying for women.
3. The company will not be tied to an integrated manufacturer.
4. The customer will receive personal service at all times.
5. The company will be able to develop new products rapidly.
6. It is possible to protect the product by acquiring a trademark for the name *Knickers in a Twist*.

Weaknesses
There did not seem to be many weaknesses associated with the proposed company; however, Peter did identify the following as possible weaknesses:

1. The small size of the company could cause some problems (acquiring capital, interesting retailers in the product, etc.).
2. The company would suffer initially from the lack of resources.
3. Peter acknowledged that his lack of experience might be a problem during the early startup stages.

K.I.A.T.'S ASSOCIATES

Before Knickers in a Twist could begin operations, it was necessary for many suppliers, distributors, attorneys, accountants, and others to agree to provide the company with their products or services. Below is a list of people and companies that Peter selected and the reasons for their selection.

PRODUCTS

The company would initially sell only one product, cotton knickers; however, Peter knew that other products would have to be developed later if his company was to grow.

The Brief
The knicker is designed by Aura, a leading lingerie design firm whose designs fill the shelves of well-known high-street shops. The design is known technically as high-leg

Accountants	Dearden Farrow 1 Serjeants' Inn London EC4	In top-20 listing of accountants.
Solicitors	Prettys Elm House 25 Elm Street Ipswich	Highly reputed firm in East Anglia.
Graphic Designers	First Impression 91A Drayton Gardens London SW10	One of the few firms in London specializing in small-business
Lingerie Design Consultants	Aura St. John's Studios Richmond	Consultants to Berlei, Next, and Undies.
Packaging Materials	AMT Ltd. Amton House Cheltenham	Reliable and recommended.
Designers and Producers of Display	P. M. Crafts Ltd. Hertfordshire	Leader in its field.
Manufacturing	Belfiore Ltd. Malta	Manufacturer for other companies.
Cotton Suppliers	Perido Leicester	Supply Next and Marks & Spencer.
Packagers	Remploy Ltd. 68 Queensland Rd. Islington	Assemble many household goods.
Elastic Suppliers	Charnwood Elastics Leicester	Suppliers to Marks & Spencer.

mini, which is sexier than most types of knickers (see Exhibit 1). While the name Knickers in a Twist provides the company with a marketing edge, the company will not be successful unless the product is different and well-made. In conjunction with Aura, K.I.A.T. has designed a brief that is similar to one currently marketed on the Continent but not widely distributed in England. The knickers will be available in two colors, lemon and aqua, and two other colors, peach and white, will be introduced later.

Additional Products

After the company has achieved a measure of success with its knickers, it might add the following to its product line: silk briefs (a deluxe version of the original cotton brief), men's boxer shorts, men's ordinary underwear, briefs and matching bras, swimwear, bikinis, and hosiery.

PACKAGING AND DISPLAY

The packaging of the briefs should complement the name

EXHIBIT 1

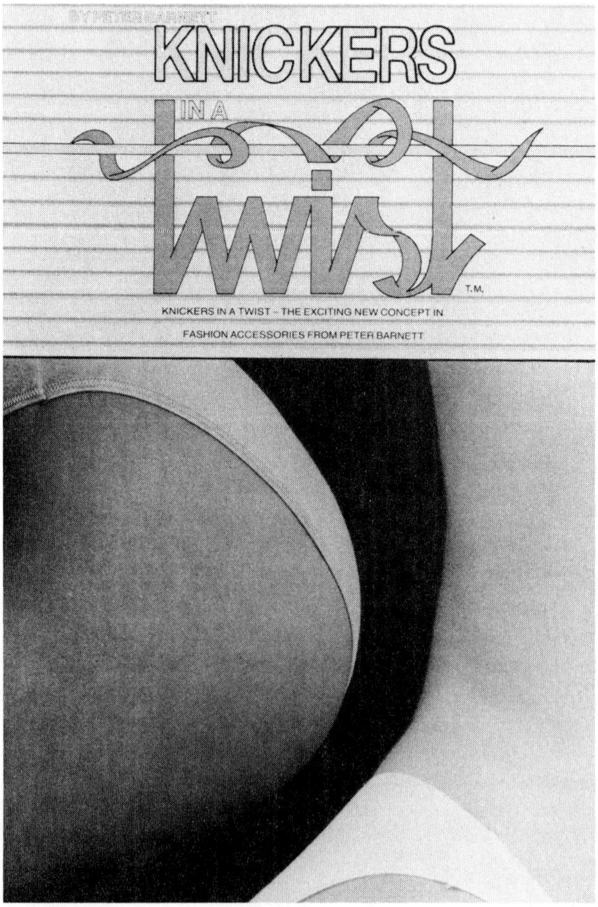
BY PETER BARNETT
KNICKERS
IN A
twist
T.M.
KNICKERS IN A TWIST - THE EXCITING NEW CONCEPT IN
FASHION ACCESSORIES FROM PETER BARNETT

of the product; therefore, Peter decided to twist together two knickers of different colors and package them in a transparent tube measuring 6 inches in length and 2 inches in diameter (see Exhibit 2). A three-color label, using the distinctive Knickers in a Twist logo, would be affixed to each tube. The tubes will be placed in a plastic dispenser (see Exhibit 3) that can hold twenty tubes. The dispenser is designed to convey the same theme as that of the product it dispenses—namely an up-market eye-catching design likely to encourage impulse buying.

PRODUCTION STRATEGY

Initial manufacturing of the briefs will be done in Malta because it is less expensive to have the material shipped to Malta and have the finished product returned to England than it is to manufacture the product in the UK. The production company, Belfiore Ltd., has agreed to manufacture the briefs in lots of 32,000 in colors specified by Peter. The finished briefs will be returned to England, where

EXHIBIT 2

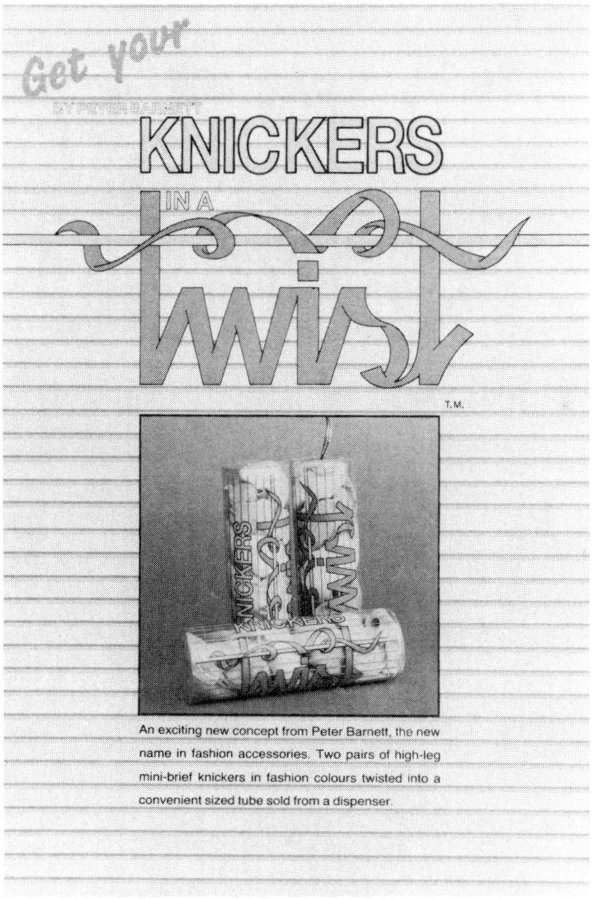

Get your
BY PETER BARNETT
KNICKERS
IN A
twist
T.M.
An exciting new concept from Peter Barnett, the new name in fashion accessories. Two pairs of high-leg mini-brief knickers in fashion colours twisted into a convenient sized tube sold from a dispenser.

EXHIBIT 3

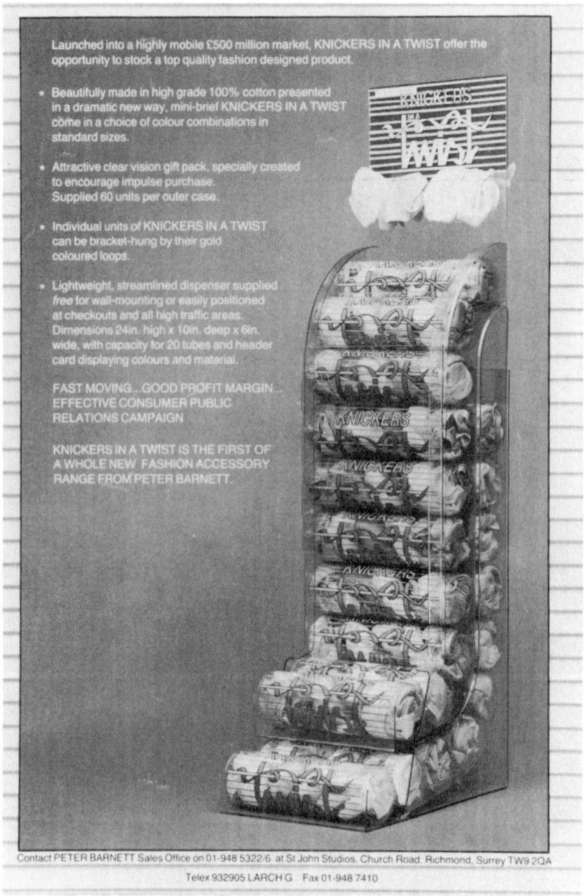

Launched into a highly mobile £500 million market, KNICKERS IN A TWIST offer the opportunity to stock a top quality fashion designed product.
• Beautifully made in high grade 100% cotton presented in a dramatic new way, mini-brief KNICKERS IN A TWIST come in a choice of colour combinations in standard sizes.
• Attractive clear vision gift pack, specially created to encourage impulse purchase. Supplied 60 units per outer case.
• Individual units of KNICKERS IN A TWIST can be bracket-hung by their gold coloured loops.
• Lightweight, streamlined dispenser supplied *free* for wall-mounting or easily positioned at checkouts and all high traffic areas. Dimensions 24in. high x 10in. deep x 6in. wide, with capacity for 20 tubes and header card displaying colours and material.
FAST MOVING...GOOD PROFIT MARGIN... EFFECTIVE CONSUMER PUBLIC RELATIONS CAMPAIGN
KNICKERS IN A TWIST IS THE FIRST OF A WHOLE NEW FASHION ACCESSORY RANGE FROM PETER BARNETT.
Contact PETER BARNETT Sales Office on 01-948 5322/6 at St John Studios, Church Road, Richmond, Surrey TW9 2QA
Telex 932905 LARCH G Fax 01-948 7410

they will be packaged by Remploy, a government-subsidized company that employs the handicapped. Once packaged, the tubes will be shipped to retailers, thereby reducing the need for warehousing finished goods. At some point in the future, Peter hopes to be able to have the briefs manufactured in the United Kingdom.

PRICING

A tube of knickers will have a suggested retail price of £4.95, including Value Added Tax (VAT). Peter knows that the final price charged for his product will be determined to a large extent by the market. Prices charged by other sellers of similar products are listed in the accompanying box.

Marks & Spencer	Pack of 3	£2.99
	Pack of 3	3.50
Sock Shop	Tube of 3	3.99
Selfridges	Single brief	2.99
Richard Shops	Single brief	1.99
Debenhams	Single brief	0.99

Peter believes that the quality and novelty of his product will allow him to charge a price higher than that of his competitors. (See Table 1 for additional price and profit information.)

PROMOTION

Even high-quality, cleverly packaged knickers will not sell themselves. They must be promoted in such a way that customers will choose Knickers in a Twist over comparable products. Peter intends to use the following promotion techniques:

- Attend trade fairs.
- Offer discounts for bulk purchases.
- Obtain free editorials and comments in journals.
- Try to get free publicity in newspapers and on TV.
- Use mail order.
- Have retailers promote the product.

Table 1

Gross Profit at Various Prices

Recommended Retail Price	*Cost per Tube*	*Price to Dealer*	*Gross Profit*
£4.95	£1.20	£1.87	£.67
4.90	1.20	1.85	.65
4.85	1.20	1.83	.63
4.80	1.20	1.81	.61
4.75	1.20	1.79	.59
4.70	1.20	1.77	.57
4.65	1.20	1.75	.55
4.60	1.20	1.73	.53
4.55	1.20	1.71	.51
4.50	1.20	1.69	.49
4.45	1.20	1.67	.47
4.40	1.20	1.65	.45
4.35	1.20	1.63	.43
4.30	1.20	1.61	.41
4.25	1.20	1.59	.39
4.20	1.20	1.57	.37
4.15	1.20	1.55	.35
Cannot sell below this price			

THE MARKET

Peter had done the work required to develop a quality product. Now he had to convince himself and others that there was enough market demand for Knickers in a Twist. Peter knew from secondary sources that about £580 million was spent annually for women's underwear, and he knew from the following chart that briefs were becoming a larger portion of the market. (See Table 2 for additional market data.)

Table 2

Percent of People Who Bought Various Types of Underwear in the Last 12 Months

Item	*All*	Age *15–19*	*20–24*	*25–34*	*35–44*	*45–54*	*55–64*
Brassieres	66%	67%	93%	81%	77%	68%	58%
Corsets/Girdles	19	1	4	6	14	23	38
Nightwear	42	29	52	47	48	51	42
Pants/Knickers	76	69	84	85	89	78	69
Slips							
Full length	19	3	6	11	20	31	31
Half length	27	13	35	34	35	37	25
Suspender Belts	6	8	12	8	7	7	3
None of These	8	13	1	3	2	8	9

PROPORTION OF TOTAL MARKET

Sector	*To April 1985*	*To April 1986*
Bras	28%	29%
Briefs	23	25
Nightdresses	15	14
Slips	12	12
Housecoats	12	10
Corsetry	8	8
Vests	2	2

COMPETITION

Peter is confident that his product will do well in the underwear market; however, he also realizes that he has to overcome several entrenched competitors. Since there is more room for innovation and differentiation at the middle to upper end of the market, competition is fiercest at the lower end of the market. Knickers in a Twist will be positioned at the higher end of the market, thereby eliminating some of the competition. Peter is convinced that good design and high quality with novel packaging and logo will enable K.I.A.T. to compete successfully with other retailers. Advertising and placement of the dispenser near the checkout counter will also give his product a competitive edge.

DISTRIBUTION

Peter had considered a number of different channels of distribution before deciding to sell through retailers. Once Knickers in a Twist becomes a profitable, recognized product, Peter might consider selling by direct mail or using his own sales representatives to distribute the product. Peter has approached the retailers, listed at the bottom of this page, who show some degree of interest in the product.

In addition to the foregoing stores, Peter would also like to do business with the following retailers and mail-order companies:

Undies
House of Fraser
Asda Group
Jenners, Scotland
Sears Stores
Empire Stores
Grattan
International Import & Export Company
Texplant
Great Universal Stores

Debenhams	Very interested, but because of technical reasons and a delivery date that is too late for Christmas, will not purchase this year (1986). They are interested in taking K.I.A.T. in 1987.
Sock Shop	Very interested, but because of heavy commitments in 1986 will not be able to do any business until 1987.
Trust House Forte (retail sales)	Very keen and receptive to the idea; however, they would like to see the finished product before making a buying decision.
Harrod's	Will retail the knickers.
Harvey Nichols	Will retail the knickers.
Underwoods	Same as Trust House Forte
Selfridges	Same as Trust House Forte
Fenwicks	Same as Trust House Forte
Owen & Owen	Same as Trust House Forte
British Home Stores	Same as Trust House Forte

PERSONNEL AND LOCATION

Since all aspects of the business will be subcontracted to other companies, Peter will not need any employees for the first few months. He expects to hire a part-time bookkeeper within the first six months, and he might establish his own sales force if the product sells well. Since Knickers in a Twist will have no employees other than Peter for the first few months, the need for office space is minimal. At present, Peter shares an office with the design consultants, Aura, in Richmond.

FINANCING

Peter did not know exactly how much capital he would need initially to start his business. He knew that the cost of manufacturing two knickers in a tube would be £1.20, and since his initial production run would be 16,000 tubes, he would need at least £19,200. To cover manufacturing costs and other ancillary expenses, Peter estimated that he would need £25,000. With that figure in mind, Peter approached several commercial banks with a request for an essentially unsecured loan. Because he lacked experience and collateral, Peter was unsuccessful in his attempt to borrow £25,000. Peter learned of the government's Small Business Loan Scheme, which guarantees up to 70 percent of a bank loan for new businesses. Using this loan guarantee and his father as a co-signer, Peter was able to secure a £25,000 overdraft.

Knickers in a Twist's lenders wanted to know how many firm orders the company had and when the company would start showing a profit. Peter told the bank that he had firm orders for 5,000 tubes of knickers and that he estimated break-even at 18,417 tubes (see

EXHIBIT 4

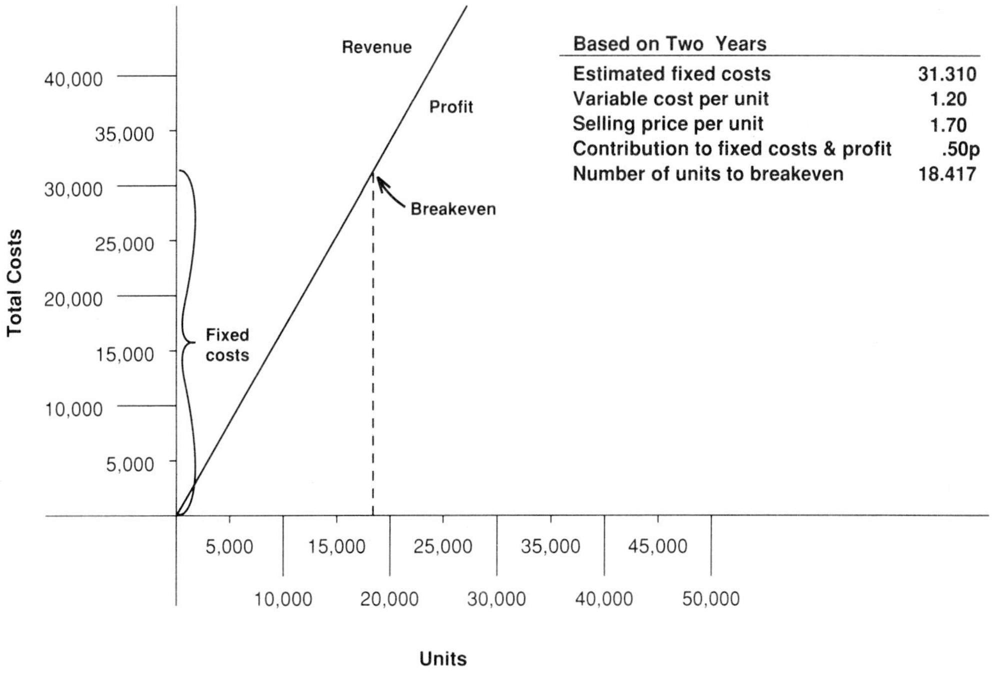

Based on Two Years	
Estimated fixed costs	31.310
Variable cost per unit	1.20
Selling price per unit	1.70
Contribution to fixed costs & profit	.50p
Number of units to breakeven	18.417

Exhibit 4). Peter expected to reach the break-even point in the first full year of business.

THE DECISION

Peter has done all the work necessary to start a new business. He incorporated the business as Knickers in a Twist Ltd., and he has agreements with suppliers and manufacturers. He has a £25,000 overdraft and retailers who have agreed to sell his product. He also has enthusiasm, optimism, and boundless energy. Now Peter Barnett must decide if he should take the plunge and actually start Knickers in a Twist Ltd.

This case was prepared by Robert Anderson, College of Charleston, and John Dunkelberg, Wake Forest University. Used by permission.

QUESTIONS

1. Do you think Peter has entrepreneurial qualities?
2. Did Peter do enough market research?
3. If you were a buyer for a large department store, would you sell Knickers in a Twist? Why, or why not?
4. Will Peter's pricing strategy make his product competitive?
5. If you were Peter Barnett, would you start Knickers in a Twist? Justify your answer.

CHAPTER 20

Starting the Business

Learning Objectives

After reading this chapter, you will be able to do the following:

- Describe how individuals can learn how to start and operate a business.
- Explain prestartup analysis and the planning process.
- Understand what happens after a business becomes operational.
- Know the difference between business theory and business practice.

In the last nineteen chapters, we discussed the prestartup planning and decision making required to open a business. Startup entrepreneurs usually spend several months thinking about and designing their new ventures. They analyze the market, find the best location, plan their financing, staff the business, develop a sound marketing program, and attend to a myriad of other details. Then the day comes when planning, forecasting, and decision making give way to operating the business. For many entrepreneurs, the first day of business—when the first customer arrives or the first product is made and sold—is both exhilarating and terrifying. This day marks the end of long months of preparation and the beginning of the few months it takes to learn if the business is likely to be a success.

To put the startup day and the first few months of operation into perspective, we will begin this chapter with a brief review of the activities that precede them. We will also briefly discuss new-venture management—the doing and evaluating that follows the planning and preparing. To conclude this chapter and the book, we will examine the first few months of operations of several real businesses to import a sense of what "really" happens when a company opens for business. We will see how reality often differs from plans and expectations.

STARTING A BUSINESS

Throughout this book we have maintained that starting a business is hard work. It requires months of dreaming, planning, analyzing, forecasting, and preparing (see the checklist at the end of the chapter). We know that as many as 50 percent of all startups will fail, but we also know that many entrepreneurs who fail the first time often try again—and again if necessary. This fact begs the question of whether it is easier to start the second or third business than the first and of how an inexperienced person can learn to run a business.

Previous Entrepreneurial Experience

Most of us believe that experience is the best teacher. We know, for example, that experienced athletes generally perform better than rookies, experienced actors are more professional than novices, and so on. Therefore it follows that anyone who has successfully started a business should have an easier time doing it again than someone who has never been self-employed. Experienced entrepreneurs should have no trouble writing a new business plan, selecting the best location, hiring the most capable people, acquiring startup capital, and so forth. However, such is not necessarily the case. Startup experience is helpful, but it does not always make the next startup much easier (see The Inside View 20-1).

Although there are entrepreneurs who believe that startup experience does not make the next startup any easier, we should not discount the value of having started and successfully operated a business. There is an entrepreneur in his fourth business who swears that each startup is easier than the last. He knows key people in the financial community; he has made important contacts in other businesses; he knows how to recruit and hire capable employees; he has developed good supplier relationships, and he has become an integral part of several influential networks. In his words, "The most successful entrepreneur is the one with the biggest Rolodex." It is easier to start a business if you know a lot of key people than if you know very few people.

20-1 *The Inside View*

STARTUP EXPERIENCE

In 1975, Buzz Roman and his partners bought the exclusive rights to franchise Wendy's restaurants in San Antonio. By 1984, the sixteen Wendy's in San Antonio were grossing $16 million a year, and franchises were selling for $30,000. Roman and his partners sold their franchise and began a new restaurant, Aunt Julie's Kitchen Inc., which they intended to turn into a multifacility operation. Aunt Julie's features big dining rooms with full kitchens and staffs of 35 or more, and offers menus that run the gamut from soups and vegetable bars to chicken, fish, and beef entrées. After two years, there are still only three outlets, all in San Antonio, and revenues are lagging well behind projections: "We underestimated how totally different a new project would be," Roman says.[1]

Learning to Operate a Business

Startup and operational experience is helpful, but what can novice entrepreneurs do to learn how to start and operate a business? One could start by reading books on the subject and enrolling in college-level business courses, but there are other ways to learn about starting and running a business. Sharon Nelton[2] suggests the following:

1. Agree to serve on another company's board of directors. You will find out how boards are run and how other companies do business.
2. Socialize with people who know things you do not. It is amazing what you can learn during a dinner conversation with an experienced businessperson.
3. Watch television programs that deal with business matters. The Public Broadcasting System, for example, often airs very informative and entertaining business-related programs.
4. Listen to informative business tapes while driving or relaxing at home.
5. Take advantage of all the services offered by the Small Business Administration and other government agencies.
6. Eat lunch in the office with your employees so you can solve problems and learn from each other.
7. Listen to family members who often have good ideas and unorthodox solutions to many problems.
8. Join the chamber of commerce, trade associations, or whatever other groups present opportunities to learn from other businesspeople.
9. Use consultants as both problem solvers and "teachers."
10. Pay attention to customer complaints. Customers will tell you what you are doing wrong and what you are doing right. Correct the mistakes and accentuate the positive.
11. Copy someone else. There is no need to reinvent the wheel. Be sure, however, that you do not copy someone who is only marginally successful.
12. Keep asking questions.

PRESTARTUP ANALYSIS AND PLANNING

A few days before opening for business, startup entrepreneurs should pause to reflect on all the time, energy, and money they have invested in their new venture. It is not possible to review every detail, but it is helpful to go over the major decisions and commitments. Entrepreneurs can use their business plans as a general checklist to ensure that they have not forgotten important items or activities.

Description of the Business

Before opening day, entrepreneurs should review their original description of the business they intended to start. Their business objectives should not have changed significantly between the time the company was first conceived and the actual startup. For example, a company originally designed to sell personal computers but which added software and other peripherals to its product line before startup may have actually become a different company. The goals of the business should remain consistent throughout the planning process.

Other aspects of the business, such as location, financing, and the like, should also not change significantly during the planning process. If a business has been described to lenders as a small manufacturer of aluminum doors and windows, these are the products they expect the company to produce when it begins operations. Lenders might choose to withdraw financing if they learn that the factory will be manufacturing wooden doors and windows instead. Any changes in the business description made during the planning process should be explained and justified.

The Market

Even before deciding to start a business, entrepreneurs should have analyzed their target market to determine if the existing need for their product is great enough to support the company. They should be able to answer the following questions:

How large (geographically) is the market?
How large (number of consumers) is the market?
Who are the customers?
Why will customers choose this product or service?
Will this product be superior to competing products?
Will this product be less expensive than competing products?
What incentive will customers have to try this product?
Will customers become repeat buyers?
How will customer loyalty be established?
Who are the competitors?
Is the market dominated by one or several competitors?
Why will the competition "tolerate" a new entrant?

All relevant market data should be reviewed before opening day to be certain that no significant changes have occurred. It is necessary to make sure that the market is as it was when the planning process began. Entrepreneurs should confirm the number and status of their competitors, the size of their potential market, the incentives they will offer customers to switch from the competition, etc. If the market has changed, entrepreneurs should make any necessary adjustments before opening their doors. For example, if the competition has lowered prices in anticipation of the opening of a new business, the entrepreneur may have to make similar price adjustments.

Marketing

In previous chapters we discussed the importance of an effective marketing program. Startup entrepreneurs should know how they are going to advertise and promote their products and be able to convince lenders, suppliers, and others that their marketing programs are viable. A few weeks before opening day, entrepreneurs should exercise the special advertising and promotion initiatives discussed in Chapter 12. Most new businesses will announce their imminent opening in local newspapers by running advertisements that identify the new business, specify the location, and describe any opening-day festivities, giveaways, or the like.

In addition to advertising the creation of a new business, entrepreneurs will need special promotions to attract customers. Promotions such as two-for-one purchases, discounts, prizes, free vacations, or coupons are some of the devices used to encourage customers to patronize the new business. Special promotions will attract customers to a new business once; however, to keep them coming back requires continuous advertising. For maximum effect, entrepreneurs should develop their ongoing advertising programs before the new firm opens for business.

Entrepreneurs should choose the most appropriate theme for their advertising. For example, will they stress quality, price, service, location, or some other competitive advantage. It is also necessary to select the most appropriate advertising media—newspapers, magazines, radio, television, or some combination of these. Next, ads need to be created, either by the business owner or by advertising professionals, and shown to a few key people for their reactions. Finally, the prepared ads should be readied for presentation to the general public. The frequency of advertising is determined primarily by the amount of money available and the creativity of the advertiser.

Besides creating an ongoing advertising program before opening day, entrepreneurs should develop some techniques to evaluate the success of their programs. It can be financially disastrous to continue allocating scarce money to an advertising campaign that does not contribute to sales and profits. Evaluative techniques can be as simple as using coupons, customer interviews, or sales signals, or can include the use of marketing research firms to determine a campaign's effectiveness (see The Inside View 20-2).

20-2 *The Inside View*

EVALUATING ADVERTISING

IRI began operations about eight years ago and in 1984 was included in the *Inc.* list of the one hundred fastest-growing firms in the country. What IRI does is select a sample of about twenty-five hundred families who have cable television in a client firm's market area and equips each television set in the selected households with an electronic device that monitors the station to which the set is tuned. The information on television watching is transmitted to computers in Chicago that are also connected to electronic scanners (cash registers that read the universal product code) in every large grocery store in the test cities. Test families are provided with a plastic card that is used to activate the scanners whenever they make a purchase in participating stores. All of their purchases are recorded by the Chicago computers so that clients know precisely which of their products are being purchased by the test families. This information helps client companies adjust their advertising to maximize sales.[3]

Staff

Many businesses begin with no employees. The owner is responsible for all aspects of the business, and his or her ability largely determines whether the business will succeed or fail. However, other new businesses start out with a complement of managers and staff. Companies formed as partnerships or corporations usually have a management team and other employees. Managers are selected for their experience and expertise as well as for the contribution they can make to the new venture. In partnerships and corporations, most managers have an equity position in the company and are, therefore, motivated to see the business succeed. The duties, responsibilities, and authority of each manager should be delineated before the company starts business to enable the new company to function smoothly from the opening day and to minimize future conflict.

Like managers, employees are hired for their ability and potential; however, unlike managers, they usually do not own a part of the business. Therefore, employees may need motivation and guidance to perform their jobs to the best of their abilities. Employees should know exactly what is expected of them, and they should be familiar with the rules and policies of the business. Entrepreneurs should develop some basic personnel policies (normal work hours, holidays, causes for termination, etc.) and communicate them to each employee before business commences. Employees who know, understand, and accept a company's rules and policies will function more efficiently and thereby contribute to the success of the new venture.

Finally, business owners should design and implement ongoing training programs that help employees perform successfully and prepare them for more responsible positions. Before the business begins operating, employees will be trained in the basic skills their jobs require; however, after opening day, the wise entrepreneur will expand his or her training to include interpersonal relations, basic supervisory management, and other more advanced skills.

Money

Because finances are so critical to success, entrepreneurs are well advised to carefully review their business plans before opening day. Startup entrepreneurs commonly overestimate revenue and underestimate expenses; so, to avoid potentially disastrous financial crises, entrepreneurs should review their estimates and revise them, if necessary, while they still have the opportunity to do so. Business owners should confirm that the money they have allocated for expenses is sufficient and that their revenue expectations for the first year of business are realistic.

Entrepreneurs should also review the financial commitments they have made prior to opening day. For example, they should know the terms and conditions of any loans they have made, the amount of money they are expected to pay suppliers, and the taxes they will pay in the first year of business. The first few months after a business opens are chaotic and challenging, and the last thing an owner needs is major financial surprises. Diligent financial planning and forecasting can minimize chaos and mistakes.

In addition to operating expenses and revenue, entrepreneurs should review other finance related aspects of their new business such as the break-even point for the new company (at what point will the company become profitable?), the prices charged for different products, and the amount of insurance protection the company will have. Everything relating to money should be reviewed and recalculated to prevent financial disaster.

Miscellaneous

In addition to reviewing their market, promotion strategy, staffing, and finances, there are other aspects of the business that entrepreneurs should review before opening day. First, is the initial inventory on hand and in good condition? Businesses that sell directly to customers can do themselves inestimable damage by running out of their goods on opening day. Customers who have not developed business loyalty are not likely to give a new company a second chance. It is better to be overstocked than understocked when the new company opens for business. Second, is all equipment in place and are the premises neat and attractive? Again, customer-oriented companies need to present an attractive environment to their "new" customers if they hope to make them repeat customers. Third, have security systems been activated? Nearly all businesses have some type of security system to protect them from theft, embezzlement, and other crimes. It is unfortunate that customers, suppliers, and employees cannot always be trusted implicitly; however, for new businesses, it is better to be safe than sorry. Finally, is everything ready to go? A few days from startup, entrepreneurs should check and recheck everything related to their business operations to minimize opening day confusion.

STARTUP AND BEYOND

Finally, planning, forecasting, analyzing, guessing, and anticipating give way to doing. That is opening day or the first day of business for the long-planned new venture. Not that all the planning, forecasting, and other prestartup activities end abruptly, but they do become secondary to the day-to-day activities in the struggle to establish a new company. At this point, marketing, buying, paying debts, and managing are now paramount. For the first year or so, entrepreneurs who cannot manage the basics of business will most likely see their dreams end in failure. We cannot, of course, discuss everything that happens during the first year of business; however, we will examine some of the more important operational activities of new businesses.

Opening Day Emotions

Most entrepreneurs experience many emotions and feelings on their first day of business. There is anxiety, fear, anticipation, exhilaration, doubt, happiness, and terror. Wilson Harrell, an inveterate entrepreneur and frequent contributor to *Inc.* magazine, claims that terror is the one emotion that separates entrepreneurs from the rest of us (see The Inside View 20-3).

Even if terror is common to many entrepreneurs, it does not have to be permanent. Terror and other negative emotions should give way to more positive feelings of anticipation and happiness. Negative emotions will never completely disappear,

20-3 The Inside View

ENTREPRENEURIAL TERROR

Addressing those who have decided to start their own businesses, Harrell says, "By that act, you have joined a very special organization. Admission is automatic; permission is neither needed nor sought; tenure is indefinite. Welcome to the Club of Terror." Entrepreneurial terror is self-inflicted. It occurs when an otherwise normal person makes a conscious decision that carries him or her over the threshold of fear into a private world filled with monsters clawing at every fiber of his or her being. There can be no sleep in this world, just wide-awake nightmares. This terror cannot be discussed with others because they will not be able to empathize, nor should it be taken home because family should not be asked to share this emotion. As Harrell states, "My own belief is that the ability to handle terror, to live with it, is the single most important—and, yes, necessary—ingredient of entrepreneurial success. I also believe that it is the lonely entrepeneur living with his or her personal terror who breathes life and excitement into an otherwise dull and mundane world. From that perspective, the Club of Terror is a very exclusive one."[4]

and they should not because they keep entrepreneurs vigilant and aware of opportunities and threats. Overcoming terror and fear requires positive thinking, which, according to Allan Cox, is "... the lifestyle-wide mental capacity to seek and find workable, beneficial options."[5] He also says, "Life constantly presents us with obstacles and opportunities. Positive thinking is the means for dealing constructively with them."

Managing New Businesses

Once emotions are under control, new business owners need to settle down and concentrate on managing their company. We use the term "managing" in the context of operating the whole business, that is, people management, cash management, marketing management, and so forth. These are all business activities that entrepreneurs need to initiate and oversee if their company is to survive and prosper.

People Management. In Chapter 11 we discussed the prestartup staffing function; therefore, we will not belabor that subject. Instead, we will briefly discuss poststartup personnel management. The following are a few of the more important people-related activities entrepreneurs will engage in:

Motivating. Motivated, enthusiastic employees contribute significantly to the success of new businesses. If they deal directly with customers, apathetic employees can quickly ruin a new business. Owners should determine what motivates each employee and then be sure to supply those motivators. For example, employees who are motivated by money should be shown how they can maximize their earnings, and those who are motivated by praise should be praised whenever possible. To motivate their employees, entrepreneurs can do the following:

- Express your caring.
- Take responsibility for your actions.
- Be tactful with the people who work for you.
- Foster independence in your employees.
- Be enthusiastic and confident.
- Keep lines of communication open.
- Always let employees know where they stand.
- Encourage employee initiative, innovation, and ingenuity.
- Be flexible.[6]

Entrepreneurs who are not familiar with motivation theory and techniques should read one or more of the numerous books that deal with that topic.

Leading. It would be virtually impossible for entrepreneurs not to be leaders. Their nature and instincts mandate that they assume leadership positions, especially in their own businesses. Leading does not necessarily mean that entrepreneurs must be dictatorial or excessively demanding. They can lead by being positive role models and by encouraging their employees to participate in the management of the new business. Many entrepreneurs have found that employees who are encouraged to think independently and creatively make suggestions that enhance the efficiency of a new company. In the long run, entrepreneurs who lead by example rather than by dictate will have productive, loyal employees.

Training. Training does not cease when a new business opens. Employees will need additional training when absenteeism and turnover rates are excessive, employee morale is low, new equipment is purchased, technology changes, the product line is expanded, new jobs are created, or new employees are hired. Entrepreneurs who are unwilling or unable to train employees can pay others to design and conduct training programs. There are, for example, numerous consultants and independent companies that can provide any type of training program needed. These training programs can be either standardized or specialized packages.

Disciplining. Most entrepreneurs hope that the employees they have hired will be enthusiastic, efficient workers who will always treat customers with respect and abide by company rules and policies. Unfortunately, some employees do not live up to their entrepreneurs' expectations and must be disciplined. Disciplining people is one of the most onerous tasks entrepreneurs must face, but if handled properly discipline can have a positive effect on employees. Employees should know what punishment they will receive if they do not abide by prescribed rules and regulations. Punishment should not be extreme, but it should be objective and impersonal.

Facilitating. Current management experts have popularized the word "facilitator" and the act of facilitating. According to these experts, business owners should hire the best people and then create a working environment that encourages them to succeed. This is the basic concept of *participative* or *collaborative management:* The entrepreneur delegates duties, responsibility, and authority to employees, who are encouraged to work to their full potential. The business owner becomes a coach, mentor, cheerleader, advisor, and facilitator.

Facilitators learn to trust their employees and are not constantly checking up on them or trying to second-guess their decisions and actions. A facilitator is more a leader-manager than an authority-manager. The following list illustrates the differences between these two types of leadership:

Authority-Manager	***Leader-Manager***
Authority-based	Influence-based
Position power	Personal power
Tell-oriented	Ask-oriented
Retains authority	Shares authority
Defines limits	Expands limits
Enforces	Reinforces
Restricts creativity	Encourages creativity
One-way communication	Two-way communication
Personal distance	Personal interest
Mandates	Persuades
Dictates	Sells
Task orientation	People orientation
Arbitrates	Negotiates
Demands loyalty	Obtains commitments[7]

It is difficult to say unequivocally which style is most effective because both authority-managers and leader-managers have successfully started and operated new businesses. However, there is growing evidence that leader-managers are more likely than authority-managers to have productive, satisfied employees who contribute to the success of their companies.

Cash Management. Throughout the prestartup planning process, entrepreneurs try to determine how much initial cash they need and who will finance them. They also have to estimate how much money will be coming into their business and how much will be going out (cash flow). Finally, entrepreneurs create cash records and mechanisms for controlling finances. Once the business opens, entrepreneurs spend much of their time implementing their plans and adjusting their forecasts and expectations. Those who do a poor job of managing finances will see their company fail or achieve only marginal success. Following is a brief discussion of the elements of effective cash management.

Cash Flow. The number of new business owners who have said "I have excellent sales, but I can't pay my bills" is legion. Many owners fail to anticipate that their sales are usually on credit and that the money is not collected for thirty days or more. At the same time, their creditors expect to be paid immediately, or they may extend credit for no more than thirty days. The discrepancy between inflow and outflow causes a cash crunch which can be fatal to the business. Therefore, entrepreneurs need to be aggressive in collecting their accounts receivable and pay their debts only when they are due.

Financial Records. On opening day entrepreneurs should begin keeping financial records (see Chapters 15 and 16) by making entries in their cash receipts and disbursements journal and in the general journal and general ledger. Many entrepreneurs, caught up in the excitement of finally starting their business, collect sales receipts, check stubs, invoices, and credit card receipts and store them in the proverbial cigar box. They intend to record this financial information in the appropriate journal or ledger "as soon as they have time"; however, they never seem to have time, and their records are inaccurate or nonexistent. Entrepreneurs who have retained accountants or borrowed money from a bank will be required to keep accurate financial records.

Financial Planning. Owners cannot foresake financial planning just because their business is operational. They should always know approximately how much cash will be coming into the business and how much will be going out for at least one year. These cash forecasts enable owners to plan major purchases and to minimize their expenses. Forecasting cash flow also helps owners prepare more accurate profit plans and cash budgets.

Marketing Management. After startup, owners need to promote their company and persuade customers to patronize their business. Effective advertising campaigns are vital to the lasting success of any new business. Following is a brief discussion of some of the more important startup marketing activities.

Special Promotions. When a company begins operating, its owner will probably use special promotions to attract customers. As discussed in Chapter 12, these promotional activities can include free products, "grand-opening" prizes, coupons, gifts, or reduced prices. Whatever the offer, it must be substantial enough to attract customers to the new business. Once a customer base has been established, owners will most likely phase out the special promotions and rely more on continuous or periodic advertising.

Continuous Advertising. Prior to startup, advertising is mainly informational: telling potential customers that the company is in the works and explaining how they will benefit from patronizing the new business. Poststartup advertising reminds customers that the business exists and announces items such as new products, additional locations, special sales, and the like. Advertising should be informative, interesting, and tasteful, and hopefully achieve its major objective of creating loyal customers. Entrepreneurs should experiment with their advertising to determine what kinds of ads are the most effective and which media provide the best value. Owners who begin to experience a decrease in business should not reduce their advertising in order to save money, because the downturn may be a result of too little advertising. They should spend as much on advertising as possible and hope that customers return and business improves.

Market Research. Just because a business is operational does not mean that its owner can neglect market research. In fact, during the first few months after startup owners can collect data that are more accurate than the data collected prior to startup. For example, customers can complete questionnaires that provide basic demographic data, their reasons for patronizing the business, and other important information. New patrons can become the nucleus of the company's mailing list and can provide the entrepreneur with information on what they like and dislike about his or her business. Owners should also conduct poststartup research to obtain information about competitors, new products, changing customer needs, and changes in the target market.

STARTUP EXPERIENCES

We will end this chapter with a brief examination of what actually happened to some startup entrepreneurs during their first few years of business. We realize that each entrepreneur's experiences may be unique; however, there are some common experiences that might help would-be startup entrepreneurs. The information used in this section was provided by ninety-three men and women who owned and managed their own businesses. Some of the respondents bought their businesses from others, but the majority started their businesses from scratch.

In response to the question "What factor contributed most to your success?" approximately one-third of the small-business owners identified hard work, or some variation thereof as the primary reason for their success. Customer service and previous experience were the next two most frequently cited factors. In response to the question "What was the major difficulty you encountered in your business?" over half of the business owners said that their major problem was hiring competent employees. Other problems, in order of importance, included marketing and acquiring capital. Only one business owner indicated that location was the major problem, and one indicated that competition was the primary difficulty.

Answers to the question "What is the most significant reward you derive from your business?" were very diverse. Over half of the small-business owners said that freedom (independence, being my own boss, ability to "freewheel," etc.) was the primary reward of owning a business. Other responses, in order of importance, included sense of accomplishment, creation of jobs, and customer satisfaction. Only two small-business owners said that money was the primary satisfaction derived from their business. Perhaps the best indicator of the benefits of owning a business was the response to the question "Knowing what you do now, would you do it all over again?" Only two small-business owners said that they would not have started their own businesses if they had known how difficult it was going to be.

A Manufacturer of Handmade Chocolates

Two young men with extensive culinary experience decided to become partners and start a business manufacturing and selling top-quality handmade chocolates. Before opening their business, they sought assistance from a local college, SCORE, and the local chamber of commerce. When the reports from these groups convinced them that there was a demand for their product, they proceeded with their plans to start a business. The business is now successful, but in the process, the partners did encounter some unexpected problems, not least among them being the failure of several businesses (hotels, resorts, specialty shops, etc.) to fulfill their earlier promises of support; the owners' failure to pay themselves for one-and-a-half years (from the opening date), which caused them personal hardship; and their failure to request enough money from the bank.

An Art Gallery

After planning an art gallery for about three years, a young woman with approximately thirteen years of art management experience opened her business at the end of 1987. Because the business has been operational for only six months, it is too early to determine if it will survive; however, it is not too early to examine some of the unforeseen difficulties the owner has already encountered. Among the problems the owner did not expect were: the ill effects of the worst weather in sixteen years; the inability to obtain an awning or sign in front of the business for five months because of Board of Architectural Review procedures and regulations; the inordinate length of time it took to obtain all the permits, licenses, etc., required to open the business; inefficient carpenters, electricians, and other workers; hostile competitors; and the theft of art valued at $600 from a display window on opening day.

A Travel Agency

A husband and wife who were interested in the travel industry wanted to be self-employed. Rather than start their own travel agency, they decided to buy an established business. They talked to travel agency owners in two other cities before finalizing their decision to buy their own agency. Then they thoroughly scrutinized the books, the operations, and the personnel of the company they intended to buy. When asked if they had encountered unexpected problems, they said, "Because of our planning, there were no significant surprises, except for learning that the travel business is very complicated."

A Window Manufacuturing Business

In 1987, one partner of a fairly large window and door manufacturing business decided to leave Charleston, South Carolina. The other partners decided to remain and started a business that manufactures only replacement windows. The new business was operational two weeks after the owner decided to proceed with the venture; so there was not much time for planning or forecasting. The problems that the owner of this new business encountered were not unanticipated; however, they still had to be solved. Among the major problems this new business had to face were: the seasonality of the window business, which makes it difficult to plan production runs; the difficulty of marketing replacement windows with only one full-time salesperson; the reluctance of contractors and other window users to switch from one manufacturer to another; and cash-flow problems.

An Industrial Hygiene Consulting Firm

Two young men with degrees in microbiology and public health started an industrial hygiene consulting firm in 1985. As consultants, their job is to evaluate working conditions (mainly to detect asbestos) in the factories or offices of their clients to ensure that they meet OSHA guidelines. The problems they encountered stem from a condition all new firms crave—too much business. This company has no direct competition, and it does not advertise to attract clients; however, word-of-mouth advertising is so effective that its client base continues to grow. The major problem created by this unanticipated growth is difficulty in hiring enough competent professionals and office staff. Other problems include lack of operating policies and procedures, no formal training programs, and inadequate cash flow.

A Ladies' Clothing Store

A woman started a store that sells casual, comfortable, elegant clothing that can be worn to the beach, on a cruise, or to a nightclub, as well as accessories such as scarfs, jewelry, and belts. Unfortunately the level of sales is much lower than anticipated because of problems with the target market, location, facility layout, and advertising. The owner originally identified young professional women as her primary target market, but she located her business in a tourist area not frequented by the people she wanted as patrons. Her advertising, too, was directed primarily at tourists rather than professional women. To compound matters, the store was cluttered and unattractive. After local consultants brought these problems to her attention, the store owner took steps to correct them.

Summary

We know that not every man and woman is capable of starting and managing a business. However, those who make the decision to create a new venture will need considerable assistance and encouragement from friends, family, consultants, and a host of other professionals. Startup entrepreneurs should not be so self-confident or proud that they ignore the advice and assistance of those who are willing to help. Starting a business is easier if one seeks and accepts the advice of suppliers, government agencies, chambers of commerce, academics, mentors, and other business professionals.

Planning and designing a new venture is exhausting, exhilarating, frustrating, nerve-racking, time-consuming, and exciting; however, once the business is operational, those feelings are often replaced by fear, anxiety, confusion, anticipation, exasperation, satisfaction, and a host of other uncomfortable emotions. Once the business officially starts, entrepreneurs need to learn how to manage people, cash, and operations. Those who cannot successfully make the transition from entrepreneur to manager will have a difficult time nurturing their business.

After opening day, owners of new businesses find that they have to devote significant amounts of time to leading, training, and motivating their employees. Owners will also face the distasteful task of disciplining those employees who do not observe company rules and regulations or do not perform competently. Other activities that will compete for the owner's valuable time include financial management, supplier relations, marketing, customer relations, and all other aspects of day-to-day business operations. Startup entrepreneurs who can cope with the routine of managing a myriad of operating details will most likely see their business grow and prosper.

Assembling the Pieces

After months of planning, Carol and Jacki were ready to open In Good Taste. The first few days after startup were hectic as friends and people who had followed the prestartup advertising came to see what the shop had to offer. Sales were brisk, and Carol and Jacki were sure that their venture was going to be a complete success. Then reality set in, and the co-owners had to learn to live with a few disappointments. Every day was not going to bring hordes of customers who could not wait to spend their money on wine, cheese, coffee, and other gourmet items. In fact, there were going to be days when very few people ventured into the shop, and there would be days when total sales would not even cover the overhead.

Carol and Jacki had underestimated the cost of operating In Good Taste and soon learned that they had seriously miscalculated their utility expenses as well. Refrigerating perishables and keeping the shop cool enough to protect the merchandise was more expensive than they had anticipated. There were also unforeseen problems with the building and surrounding area: Poor construction caused the building to leak during heavy rains; there was too little usable space in the shop; parking was inadequate; and there was no exterior sign identifying In Good Taste. The leaks were eliminated, and Carol and Jacki tried to rearrange their display cases to provide more room. However, they decided that ultimately their original layout was the most efficient and had some walls removed to provide more working space and alleviate customer congestion.

Once the structural and customer-traffic problems had been eliminated, Carol and Jacki had to confront a more long-term dilemma: They realized that if they continued operating the business without other full-time employees, it would always be a "mom-and-pop" operation. If the business were to grow and be successful, Carol and Jacki knew that they would need full-time as well as part-time employees. Hiring employees would enable the owners to plan future growth, look for new opportunities, attend food shows, and spend more of their time conceptualizing rather than dealing with day-to-day activities. After hiring one full-time and two part-time employees, Carol and Jacki were free to spend less time in the shop. Recently they decided to hire only full-time employees because of scheduling and other problems with their part-time employees.

Nearly three years after startup, In Good Taste is successful and profitable. Carol and Jacki have been able to add services such as cooking classes, wine tastings and tours, and food seminars. The mailing list for the newsletter continues to grow as more people "discover" the shop. The original facilities are now too small; however, Carol and Jacki have not yet decided how they should expand: acquire more space where they are or move to a larger building. By closely monitoring inventory, Carol and Jacki have minimized the space needed for their products, and they have been able to eliminate items that do not sell. Sound management policies, fiscal conservatism, and effective planning have paid off—Carol and Jacki are considering the purchase of one of their competitors located in another part of the city. ■

entrepreneur's checklist

STARTING A BUSINESS

Customer Analysis

Have you estimated the market share your company might capture? ____

If you concentrate on a segment, is it large enough to be profitable? ____

Can you foresee changes in the makeup of your company's neighborhood? ____

Are incomes in the community apt to be stable? ____

Have you joined your trade association? ____

Have you subscribed to relevant trade publications? ____

Have you visited market shows and conventions to help anticipate customer wants? ____

The Building

Have you found a suitable building? ____

Will you have enough room when your business gets bigger? ____

Did you fix the building the way you want it without spending too much money? ____

Can people get to it easily from parking spaces, bus stops, or their homes? ____

Did a lawyer check the lease and zoning? ____

Equipment and Supplies

Have you purchased or leased the equipment you need at a reasonable cost? ____

Has the equipment been installed to maximize efficiency? ____

Have you purchased adequate amounts of supplies? ____

Have you established systems to replace your supplies when needed? ____

The Merchandise

Have you decided what products you will make or sell? ____

Have you stocked your business with enough merchandise to see you through the first few weeks of business? ____

Have you found suppliers who will sell you what you need at a reasonable price? ____

Have you compared the prices and credit terms of different suppliers? ____

Do you have a system for reviewing new items coming into the market? ____

Have you considered using a basic stock list and/or model stock plan in your buying? ____

Will you use some type of unit-control plan? ____

Pricing

Have you established pricing policies? ____

Have you determined whether to price below, at, or above the market? ____

Will you set specific markups for each product? ____

Will you use a one-price policy rather than bargain with customers? ____

Will the prices you have established earn planned gross margins? ____

Do you understand the market forces affecting your pricing methods? _____
Do you know the maximum price customers will pay for your products? _____
Are you sure you know all the regulations affecting your business, such as two-for-one sales, etc.? _____

Your Records

Have you planned a system of records that will keep track of your income and expenses? _____
Have you worked out a way to keep track of your inventory so that you will always have enough on hand for your customers but not more than you can sell? _____
Have you determined how to keep your payroll records and take care of tax reports and payments? _____
Do you know what financial statements you should prepare? _____
Have you retained an accountant to help you with your records and financial statements? _____

Your Business and the Law

Have you acquired the licenses and permits you need? _____
Do you know what business laws you need to obey? _____
Have you executed all the contracts required to start your business? _____
Have you retained a lawyer you can go to for advice and for help with legal papers? _____

Protecting Your Business

Have you made plans for protecting your business against thefts of all kinds—shoplifting, robbery, burglary, and employee pilfering? _____
Do you have up-to-date fire coverage on your building, equipment, and inventory? _____
Does your liability insurance cover bodily injuries as well as problems such as libel and slander suits? _____
Are you familiar with your obligations to employees as prescribed by both common law and workers' compensation? _____
Have you looked into other insurance coverage, such as business-interruption insurance or criminal insurance? _____

Advertising

Are you familiar with the strengths and weaknesses of various promotional devices? _____
Have you decided how you will advertise (newspapers, posters, handbills, radio, mail, etc.)? _____
Have you arranged for help with your ads? _____
Have you watched what other stores do to motivate people to buy? _____
Do you know which of your items can be successfully advertised? _____
Do you know which can best be sold by sales representatives? _____
Do you know what can and cannot be said in your ads (truth-in-advertising requirements)? _____

Are cooperative advertising funds available from your suppliers? ____
Will you coordinate your local efforts with your suppliers' national programs? ____
Have you looked for guidelines or ratios to estimate what similar firms are spending on promotion? ____
Have you studied the advertising of other successful firms as well as that of your competitors? ____
Have you some way of measuring the success of the various promotional devices you will use? ____

Customer Credit
Have you decided whether or not to let your customers buy on credit? ____
Do you know the good and bad points about joining a credit-card plan? ____
Can you tell a deadbeat from a responsible customer? ____
Have you discussed credit operations with your local credit bureau? ____
Would a credit program be a good sales tool? ____
Is a credit program of your own desirable? ____
Do you know about the Fair Credit Reporting Act? ____
Are you familiar with the truth-in-lending legislation? ____
Have you discussed your credit program with your accountant and attorney? ____

Management
Have you developed a set of plans for the first year's operations? ____
Do your plans provide methods for dealing with competition? ____
Do they contain creative approaches to solving problems? ____
Are they realistic? ____
Have you written realistic job descriptions? ____
Will your employees know how they will be rated for promotion and pay increases? ____
Will training help your employees perform better? ____
Have you provided good working conditions? ____
Do you have a plan to avoid all forms of discrimination in your employment practices? ____
Do you have a formal program for motivating workers? ____

Source: Most questions came from a checklist developed for the Small Business Administration by George Kress and R. Ted Will in Randy Smith, *Setting Up Shop: The Do's and Don'ts of Starting a Small Business* (New York: McGraw-Hill, 1982) pp. 169–177.

Questions for Review and Discussion

1. Explain how a person can learn how to start and operate a business.
2. How is marketing before startup different from that after startup?
3. What are some of the people-management duties that owners of new ventures must learn?
4. What are the differences between authority-managers and leader-managers?

5. What advice would you give the owner of a new business to avoid cash-flow problems?
6. How much market research should entrepreneurs do after their business becomes operational?
7. Based on everything you have learned, do you think that people are born entrepreneurs or learn to become entrepreneurs?

Notes

1. Curtis Hartman, "Is It Easier Than Ever to Start a Business?" *Inc.,* March 1987, pp. 69–75.
2. Sharon Nelton, "28 Ways to Learn to Run a Business," *Nation'sBusiness,* August 1985, pp. 28–29.
3. Richard Kreisman, "Buy the Numbers," *Inc.,* March 1985, pp. 104–112.
4. Wilson Harrell, "Entrepreneurial Terror," *Inc.,* February 1987, pp. 74–76.
5. Allan Cox, *The Making of the Achiever* (New York: Dodd, Mead & Company, 1985).
6. William Cohen, *The Entrepreneur and Small Business Problem Solver* (New York: John Wiley & Sons, 1983).
7. Douglas Stewart, *The Power of People Skills* (New York: John Wiley & Sons, 1986).

SURVIVAL AIDS, LTD.

Nicholas Steven was born March 20, 1949, in Purley, Surrey, England. In 1960 he moved with his family to Cumbria, where he attended Austin Friars School in Carlisle. There he obtained a GCE 'S' Level in chemistry, 'A' levels in physics and chemistry, and 'O' Levels in eight subjects and represented the school in rugby as well. He also took an active part in the local Army Cadet Force and in 1967 entered Sandhurst, the Royal Military Academy, where he participated in judo, shooting, and other sports.

After receiving a commission in the Royal Signals in 1969, Nick was awarded the Agar Memorial Prize for academic achievement and the Signals Sword for all-around performance while at Sandhurst. In early 1970, he was posted to Germany for a tour as a line troop commander before entering the Royal Military College of Science in October. Nick was awarded a degree in Applied Science in 1973 and went on to command a VHF radio troop in the U.K., a specialist information team with 22 Special Air Services members in Oman, and a signal troop in the Caribbean. He was also an instructor at the School of Signals and served as Adjutant of the 16th Signal Regiment in West Germany.

In 1979, Nick Steven decided to leave the military and begin another career. He considered a number of different options, and finally decided to start his own business. Throughout his military career, Nick had been involved in survival training but had found that good-quality survival equipment was practically unobtainable. His plan, therefore, was to build a company specializing in equipment and training for survival against the elements.

By 1987 Survival Aids, Ltd., was a successful, thriving business. Survival Aids had grown from a business with a single product to one with nearly fourteen hundred different items generating £2.5 million in revenue (turnover) in 1987. Nick was more successful than even he had anticipated, but he now had to decide what to do with his company. He could sell Survival Aids to another larger company; he could acquire one or more of his smaller competitors; he could place more emphasis on retail outlets; he could expand his product line; he could expand into other countries; or he could do nothing and let his company continue its steady growth.

HISTORY

Nick's military career had been very successful. He was told that he would probably have become a major general had he stayed in the service; however, the service had not prepared him to start and operate his own business. In an effort to learn what he could about business, Nick entered his business plan in an Enterprise competition for which he won a free business course at Durham University Business School. Once Nick felt that he was ready to start his business, he and his partner Michael Hunting (whom Nick bought out after the business was formed) took the £5,000 available to them and formed Survival Aids, Ltd.

Initial Product

Survival Aids was a company built around one product—the compact, lightweight Survival Ration Pack, suitable for use by those who indulge in outdoor pursuits. The sealed emergency pack (see Exhibit 1) contained specially selected high-energy foods and drinks as well as solid fuel, matches, instructions, and other ancillaries. The kit contained fourteen different items sealed in an airtight aluminum container that could be used to hold hot food and drinks. The Survival Ration Pack was introduced in August 1979 at a London press reception that featured a wild foods buffet. The pack was originally sold through camping and outdoor leisure shops to both civilians and military personnel.

Location

When Nick began his search for a suitable building to serve as both office and production area for his new company, he established several criteria to

EXHIBIT 1

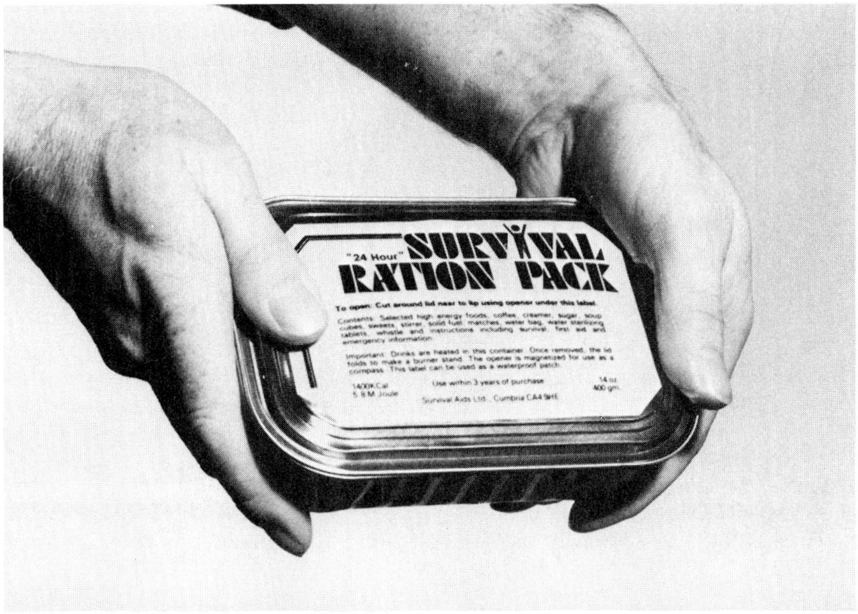

guide him. First, he wanted a location in a rural area to provide jobs for people who might otherwise have difficulty finding work. Second, he believed that his company should be located in an area that offered many outdoor activities. Third, he needed a facility that was inexpensive. As a first step, he selected a building owned by a relative near Carlisle, in Cumbria, but hoped later to find another building large enough for both his current and future needs.

The Lake District location enabled Survival Aids to sell its product to outdoor retailers while Nick continued his search for a more ideal location. Using the same criteria, Nick found a suitable building in Morland, near Penrith, which would suffice for several years since it contained two buildings, one that could be used for offices and a larger building that could be used for production and warehousing.

Product Line and Sales

Although survival ration packs were selling well, Nick realized that his company could not grow with only one product. Therefore, he decided to expand his product line and began selling some ten products by mail order. In 1980, Survival Aids published its first typewritten mail-order catalog, which featured sixty-eight items and contained one black-and-white photograph. In that same year, the company exhibited for the first time at the National Camping and Outdoor Leisure Trade Show at Harrogate. Catalogs, each better-produced than the previous one, were published every six months and distributed to a rapidly growing list of customers.

In January 1983 a quarterly mini-catalog and magazine *Survival News* were launched and distributed free to customers. The catalog was now published annually, with supplemental catalogs published as needed. The thirty-six-page

1985 catalog was produced in full color for the first time, and the forty-eight-page 1986 catalog was distributed to well over one hundred thousand customers. Nick did not want Survival Aids' sales to be totally dependent on mail-order customers, so he began wholesaling to dealers while looking out for new markets.

Nick realized that soldiers were becoming an increasingly important customer group; therefore, in 1983 the company exhibited at the Rhine Army Summer show. Survival Aids was the first company to develop alternative professional equipment soldiers could purchase by mail. In 1984 the Survival Aids Liaison Team conducted a series of survival lectures and equipment briefings around the country that culminated with Nick's presentation to 1,200 survival enthusiasts in Watford Town Hall. Catalog sales and other selling efforts were successful, and Survival Aids enjoyed a turnover in excess of £1 million for the first time in 1985.

COMPANY OPERATIONS

The sales figures for 1985 had not been unanticipated or surprising. Turnover continued to increase, and sales for 1987 reached the £2.5 million mark. Survival Aids, Ltd., was now an established, successful company that was a dominant force in its industry. The company enjoyed a national reputation, and its products were of the highest quality available. Survival Aids would continue to expand its product line and would broaden its selling techniques.

Products and Services

Survival Aids now sells approximately fourteen hundred different products to outdoor enthusiasts. Most products are made by other companies for Survival Aids; however, many are made to the company's specifications, and, in some cases, the company has exclusive rights to other manufacturers' products.

Products. The following products, by major category, are sold by Survival Aids:

- Protection
  - Shell clothing
  - Footwear
  - Outer thermal clothing
  - Inner thermal clothing
  - Immediate care
  - Bivis, bags, blankets
  - Sleeping systems
- Location
  - Navigation, signalling
  - Time
  - Distance
  - Light
- Water
  - Water purification
  - Water carriers
- Food
  - Rations
  - Cooking equipment
- Tools
  - Knives
  - Kits & accessories
  - Pouches & firestarters
- Survival Skills
  - Books and courses
- Military
  - Combat clothing
  - Waterproofs
  - Boots
  - Bergens
  - Webbing
  - Kits & accessories

Product selection. Products that do not sell well are usually dropped from the catalog and new ones added. The following criteria or policy statements were used to select new products included in the 1986 catalog:

1. "No new products are to be offered for sale until they have been thoroughly tested, costed, sourced, sampled, packaged, and stocked."
2. "We want more own/exclusive products in our own packaging but will accept certain high-quality products from companies such as Tekna and Pains Wessex."
3. "New products should have reasonable wholesale margins."
4. "Quality has become a key feature of the company's inventory. Suppliers must

be reliable, and alternative sources must be developed."

5. "No new products may have any assembly requirement. They must be supplied ready for sale."
6. "New products and existing products must have better instructions, labelling, packaging, and documentation in 1986."

Services. In 1982, Nick decided to begin a survival training school that would teach outdoor enthusiasts basic survival skills and would provide some exposure for the company. Initially, Survival Aids would offer twenty courses a year to teach the following skills: expedition training, survival, combat survival, executive development, and civil defense. Nick estimated that the survival school would eventually generate revenue of about £100,000 per year. There were other benefits to be derived from the school. First, Survival Aids employees could be exposed to outdoor activities. Second, the school could provide facilities for research and development. Third, students would be potential customers for the company's products. Finally, the school would be good advertising.

The training programs that were presented to people aged 14 and up were somewhat successful. The programs did meet some of the established goals; however, the survival school was not profitable enough to justify its continuation, and the program was eventually sold to Outward Bound, another organization in the same training business. Other services such as seminars and equipment-demonstration programs were still provided when appropriate.

Organization and Personnel

From a business with no personnel and no structure, Survival Aids has grown into a company with thirty-five people and well-developed organizational structure (see Exhibit 2). Since unemployment in the area is relatively high, it is not difficult to find capable workers; however, because of the company's rural location, it is somewhat more difficult to hire managers with technical skills. Difficulties notwithstanding, Nick assembled a very professional staff capable of managing the company through future growth stages.

The company provides very comfortable working conditions; the management style is participative; and employees are well paid. In addition to above-average wages, all employees participate in a profit-sharing plan. Nick decided to set aside in perpetuity 15 percent of pretax profits for worker incentive. Employees receive a percentage of that lump sum based on their personal performance (very good, satisfactory, or unsatisfactory) and their base salary. Nick has even considered letting his managers buy stock in the

EXHIBIT 2
Organization Chart of Survival Aids, Ltd. 1988

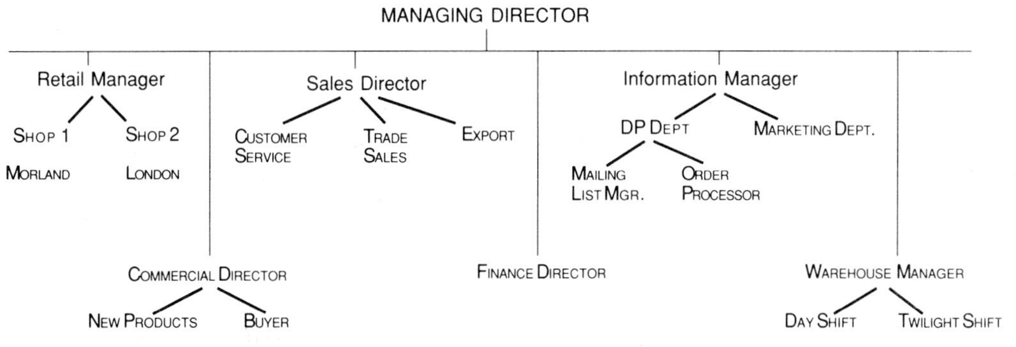
MANAGING DIRECTOR
Retail Manager
Shop 1
Morland
Shop 2
London
Sales Director
Customer Service
Trade Sales
Export
Information Manager
DP Dept
Mailing List Mgr.
Order Processor
Marketing Dept.
Commercial Director
New Products
Buyer
Finance Director
Warehouse Manager
Day Shift
Twilight Shift

company (at present, he owns 100 percent of the company's stock) because he believes that all employees should share in the success of the company.

Marketing and Distribution

Selling survival packs through camping and outdoor leisure shops was satisfactory in the early developmental stages of Survival Aids; however, when the product line expanded, Nick realized that he needed to have more direct control over the selling and distribution of his merchandise. To gain this control, Nick decided that mail-order selling was the most appropriate method.

Selling. The majority of sales of Survival Aids' products comes from mail-order customers. The heaviest selling season is from September to March, when the company averages about one hundred fifty orders per week. Since the quality of merchandise is high and the products are well described in the catalog, very few items are returned. Nick expects mail order to continue to be an important source of sales because he believes that its advantages outweigh the disadvantages. Following is a list of the advantages of mail-order selling for Survival Aids:

- Full price is paid.
- Cash is received in advance.
- Bad debts are few.
- The wide range of customers eliminates dependence on major accounts.
- Lack of stock does not usually lose a sale.
- Cash sales and credit purchases reduce working capital requirements.
- It is the best and sometimes only way to approach military customers.
- Small items are well suited to mail order.
- Location is not a disadvantage.
- Catalogs are an easy and inexpensive way to introduce new products.
- This method affords direct contact with end users.

While mail-order selling seemed to have more advantages than other selling techniques, it also had some disadvantages. Following is a list of some of the disadvantages of relying on mail order selling:

- Small orders may be uneconomic to process, especially if paid for by credit card.
- Returns can be expensive.
- Customers cannot really "examine" products before they purchase them.
- It is necessary to maintain a large and growing mailing list.

Nick realized that Survival Aids would need to utilize more than one selling technique if it were to reach the greatest number of potential customers. In February 1986, the first Survival Shop, a retail outlet for Survival Aids products, was opened in the company's Morland facility. This shop was profitable, especially during the six summer weeks when many tourists visited the Lake District. To further test the profitability of retail outlets, Nick opened a shop in a major London train station in 1987. Early indications that the shop will be profitable have led Nick and his managers to contemplate opening additional shops in London and other parts of the country.

Nick had also tried some other selling techniques with varying degrees of success. The company tried contract sales (selling to the military, government agencies, etc.), but it produced very little continuity. Nick had other difficulties with this method of selling for the following reasons: Survival Aids does not manufacture products, contract business is not repetitive and is time consuming, and one-of-a-kind orders do not fit into the Survival Aids system. While contract selling was continued, it received very little budget support. Survival Aids had been represented at several trade shows, the results of which were greater exposure and advertising value than profitability. The company now sells through mail order, contract sales, and retail shops, and continues to wholesale its products to independent camping shops and the NAAFI (the equivalent of U.S. military post exchanges).

Competition. There are several companies that sell items similar to those offered by Survival Aids, but no single company has a product line as complete as that of Survival Aids. Companies that compete do so on the basis of price rather than quality or service. Nick is aware of a few companies that could expand their product lines to compete with Survival Aids; however, he is confident that good service and high-quality products will keep Survival Aids ahead of its competition.

Advertising. The target market for Survival Aids is primarily military personnel and outdoors enthusiasts (primarily males). To attract this market, Survival Aids relies mainly on its catalogs; however, it does use other advertising media. The company advertises in weekly, monthly, and quarterly magazines such as *Great Outdoors*, *Soldier*, and *Y.H.A. News*. Advertisements are also placed in other local publications. Advertising is important, but effective public relations also sells products. Survival Aids has been the subject of many news and television reports, and company employees have written numerous articles which have appeared in national magazines. Survival seminars have considerable PR value, and Nick and his managers are often asked to speak to local organizations and business schools.

Catalogs. The lifeblood of any mail-order company is its catalog. The catalog offered by Survival Aids in 1987 does not even resemble the first one published in 1980. From a simple, typewritten document listing 68 items, the catalog has grown into a full-color, forty-eight-page annual publication describing more than 1,400 items (most manufactured in the U.K.) purchased from 200 suppliers. In 1987, Survival Aids ordered 200,000 catalogs at a cost of £0.45 each. The mailing list, with approximately 130,000 names, is actively maintained: Customers who have not purchased anything for six months are sent a "last-catalog" notice. Customers who have received such notice are dropped from the mailing list if they do not make a purchase within a reasonable amount of time. People who request their first catalog are sent the latest edition, which includes incentives to recommend Survival Aids to their friends.

Besides being informative, the catalog is also instructive. For example, the 1987 catalog provided information on topics such as how to keep warm in a British winter and what to wear in hot wet climates. The company has also used the catalog to try to expand the target market. The cover of the 1987 catalog featured a woman for the first time in the company's history. The cover caption read as follows: "Front cover picture shows 22-year-old Heather Morris from Chirbury, Shropshire, taking part in 'Operation Raleigh.' Heather was on the Black River Expedition in Honduras, in April 1985." It is too early to judge whether the picture of a woman hiking through the jungle will encourage more females to buy from Survival Aids.

Automation

Processing customer orders, maintaining an extensive mailing list, keeping records, and several other operations eventually became too cumbersome to perform manually; therefore, in 1986 the company purchased and installed a sophisticated mini-computer to provide on-line order processing, stock control, dispatch control, marketing information, office automation, and accounting packages. So many routine functions were computerized that the company soon needed a larger, more powerful machine. Since customer service is so important to the continued growth of Survival Aids, there are manual backup procedures in place should the computer be unavailable.

The introduction of the computer created no problems for Survival Aids. The company was particularly fortunate to have on its staff a person who was interested in computers and whose expertise has grown to keep pace with the company's data-processing needs. Other employees had to be trained to use the computer. Even though the employees were not computer literate, they soon learned enough about the hardware and software to function efficiently. Now most staff have terminals on their desks, and four employees have completed programming courses.

Financial Information

For the last six years Survival Aids has been a profitable company (see Table 1), with turnover nearly doubling each year and profit increasing from £5,000 to nearly £80,000 in 1987. The company's net profit for 1986 (18 months) was £29,200 (see Table 2), and it had tangible assets worth £141,891 (see Table 3). The source and application of funds is shown in Table 4.

Table 1
*Survival Aids, Ltd. Five-Year Summary**

	1983 (12 months)	1984 (12 months)	1985 (12 months)	1986 (18 months)	1987 (12 months)
Profit and Loss					
Turnover	410,648	787,063	1,237,847	2,600,939	2,584,936
Operating Profit	16,726	37,339	42,669	61,570	102,100
Interest	(1,827)	(2,406)	(11,543)	(20,875)	(22,700)
Profit Before Tax	14,899	34,933	31,126	40,695	79,400
Assets Employed					
Fixed Assets	22,039	45,818	50,223	96,104	141,891
Net Current Assets (Liabilities)	2,847	(6,485)	12,524	15,336	37,584
Creditors Due After More Than One Year	(18,576)	—	(1,883)	(19,386)	(45,130)
Deferred Taxation	(1,309)	(9,338)	(9,020)	(11,000)	(11,000)
Shareholders Funds	5,001	29,995	51,854	81,054	123,345

*All figures are in British pounds (£).

Table 2
Survival Aids, Ltd. Profit and Loss Account for the Year Ended 30 September 1987

	Year Ended 30 September 1987	Eighteen Months to 30 September 1986
Turnover	£2,584,936	£2,600,939
Cost of Sales	(1,647,910)	(1,684,201)
Gross Profit	937,026	916,738
Distribution Costs	(86,665)	(131,809)
Administrative Expenses	(748,261)	(723,359)
Operating Profit	102,100	61,570
Interest Payable	(22,700)	(20,875)
Profit on Ordinary Activities Before Taxation	79,400	40,695
Tax on Profit from Ordinary Activities	(22,690)	(11,495)
Profit on Ordinary Activities After Taxation	56,710	29,200
Extraordinary Item	(14,419)	—
Profit for the Financial Period	42,291	29,200
Retained Profit (beginning of period)	55,053	25,853
Retained Profit (end of period)	£ 97,344	£ 55,053

Table 3
Survival Aids, Ltd. Balance Sheet as of 30 September 1987

	1987	1986
Fixed Assets		
Tangible assets	£141,891	£ 96,104
Current Assets		
Stocks	489,500	353,571
Debtors	153,097	113,540
Cash at Bank and in Hand	503	460
	643,100	467,571
Creditors (amounts falling due within one year)	(605,516)	(452,235)
Net Current Assets	37,584	15,336
Total Assets Less Current Liabilities	179,475	111,440
Creditors (amounts falling due after more than one year)	(45,130)	(19,386)
Provisions for Liabilities and Charges	(11,000)	(11,000)
Net Assets	123,345	81,054
Capital Reserves		
Called-up Share Capital	26,001	26,001
Profit and Loss Account	97,344	55,053
Total Capital Employed	£123,345	£ 81,054

Signed on Behalf of the Board,

N. G. Steven)
) Directors
R. W. Farncombe)
12 February 1988

THE FUTURE

Survival Aids, Ltd. has been successful and profitable since its founding. The company's sales have nearly doubled each of the past five years with 1987 sales reaching £2.5 million and 1988 sales expected to be approximately £3.5 million. The products sold by Survival Aids are of the highest quality, management and staff are very capable, and no competitors pose a serious threat to the company. Although the company has been successful in the past, Nick is not sure that it will continue to grow without some changes. There are several options being considered to make Survival Aids even more dominant in its marktet. The following are some of those options:

Retailing. Although the company has been a retailer for just over a year, the indications are that retailing could enable Survival Aids to continue to grow. Expanding retail operations would require several changes in the company's strategies and policies.

Franchising. If retailing proves to be successful, Nick might consider franchising his business. He realizes that this is a fast-growth option and that he might lose some control of his business.

Table 4

Survival Aids, Ltd. Statement of Source and Application of Funds for the Year Ended 30 September 1987

	Year Ended 30 September 1987	*Eighteen Months to 30 September 1986*
Source of Funds		
Profit on Ordinary Activities after Taxation	£ 56,710	£ 29,200
Add (deduct) Items not Involving the Movement of Funds During the Period:		
Depreciation	45,018	25,990
(Profit) Loss on Disposal of Tangible Fixed Assets	(5,518)	1,392
Deferred Taxation Charge	—	1,980
Total Funds from Operations	96,210	58,562
Funds from Other Sources		
Proceeds from Disposal of Tangible Fixed Assets	28,000	1,028
Increase in Long-term Portion of Hire Purchase Creditor	25,744	17,503
Increase in Creditors Falling Due Within One Year	139,242	144,345
	289,196	221,438
Application of Funds		
Extraordinary Item after Taxation	14,419	—
Purchase of Tangible Fixed Assets at Cost	113,287	74,281
Increase in Stocks	135,929	183,447
Increase in Debtors	39,557	5,507
	303,192	263,235
Net Application of Funds	(13,996)	(41,797)
Increase (Decrease) in Net Liquid Funds		
Cash at bank and in hand	43	(28)
Bank overdraft	(14,039)	(41,769)
	£ (13,996)	£ (41,797)

Manufacturing. Survival Aids has always sold products manufactured by other companies; however, it might be possible and profitable for the company to begin manufacturing some of the products it sells.

Expand the product line. It might be advantageous to offer outdoorsmen a larger variety of products. For example, Survival Aids could increase its product line to include guns, boating accessories, mountain climbing equipment, etc. Several customers had requested these types of items in the past, and Nick feels that there would be substantial demand for them in the future.

Acquire other companies. Acquiring complementary companies would provide instant growth and could expand the product line at the same time. For example, there is a relatively small but profitable company that manufactures tents, rucsacs, and climbing hardware. Such a company might be an attractive acquisition candidate.

Sellout. Rather than buying another company, Nick could sell Survival Aids. He had been approached on several occasions by people who expressed an interest in buying his company. Nick could sell Survival Aids to another company and either remain as a key executive or leave and pursue other interests.

Export. Survival Aids catalogs are now distributed in several foreign countries, and orders are received from abroad, but international sales have never amounted to more than 10 percent of total turnover. Nick is particularly interested in exporting to the United States. At one point, the company was represented at a trade show in Chicago, and an advertisement was placed in *Soldier of Fortune* magazine. Sales in the United States were too meager to justify any further selling effort; however, Nick feels that he and Survival Aids may now be ready to make a concerted effort to become established in the United States.

Go public. Since Nick is the sole owner of Survival Aids, he could realize a significant profit and foster company growth by selling Survival Aids stock to the public.

Do nothing. Nick could make no significant changes and simply let things remain the same. Survival Aids would continue its steady growth, and there would be no pressure on the employees to "grow" and accept change.

QUESTIONS

1. Were Nick Steven's location criteria realistic?
2. Is Survival Aids' product line complimentary?
3. Is the product line too large?
4. Was the survival school a good idea?
5. Should Survival Aids continue to rely primarily on catalog sales?
6. Which of the options available to Nick would you suggest he adopt?

This case was prepared by Robert Anderson, College of Charleston, and B. G. Bizzell, Stephen F. Austin State University. Used by permission.

Index